Praise for "The Wiley Blackwell Companion to Patristics"

Ken Parry has led a first class team of experts in producing this excellent *Wiley Blackwell Companion to Patristics*. It advances on the several fine Patrologies already existing to focus critical attention on the issue of how the patristic mindset was received over the ages. Required reading for all serious theologians and historians.

John A McGuckin, *Nielsen Professor of Byzantine Church History*

This is a welcome addition to the field as it is the first time that such a volume has sought to give equal weight to both the Eastern and Western Church traditions. It offers a comprehensive and balanced picture by including material that has long remained obscure because it is primarily known from Arabic, Armenian, Coptic, Ethiopic, Georgian and Syriac sources, rather than privileging the works of more widely known authors utilising Greek and Latin. At a time when many Eastern Christian traditions are increasingly endangered it becomes even more important to bring knowledge of these writings to the forefront of contemporary scholarship.

Emma Loosley, *University of Exeter*

I applaud Ken Parry and his expert collaborators for providing ground-breaking new insights into the lives and writings of a wide representation of Fathers, including those who lived beyond the borders of the Roman and Byzantine Empires. Never have I been so persuasively reminded of the importance and enduring significance of the Fathers for contemporary Christianity. This *Companion* is an indispensable resource for all who truly want to understand and utilize the rich legacy which the Fathers have left us.

William Tabbernee, *Past President, North American Patristics Society*

There is nothing to my knowledge quite like this volume... this is a fascinating and innovative volume. It should certainly be required reading for advanced graduate students, and most professional researchers will gain from considering its challenges to current practices, both in relation to content and methodology.

Frances Young, Zeitschrift für Antikes Christentum,
Journal of Ancient Christianity, 2017; 21(2)

The volume certainly is worth purchasing... It is handy to have now a single volume which holds so many historical keys. Readers may now follow a text through the centuries.

DS Commentary on Historical Books, Fall 2017

The Wiley Blackwell Companions to Religion

The Wiley Blackwell Companions to Religion series presents a collection of the most recent scholarship and knowledge about world religions. Each volume draws together newly commissioned essays by distinguished authors in the field, and is presented in a style which is accessible to undergraduate students, as well as scholars and the interested general reader. These volumes approach the subject in a creative and forward-thinking style, providing a forum in which leading scholars in the field can make their views and research available to a wider audience.

Recently Published

The Wiley Blackwell Companion to Patristics

Edited by

Ken Parry

WILEY Blackwell

This paperback edition first published 2019
© 2015 John Wiley & Sons Ltd

Edition history: John Wiley & Sons Ltd (hardback, 2015)

Registered Office
John Wiley & Sons, Ltd, The Atrium, Southern Gate, Chichester, West Sussex, PO19 8SQ, UK

Editorial Offices
9600 Garsington Road, Oxford, OX4 2DQ, UK
The Atrium, Southern Gate, Chichester, West Sussex, PO19 8SQ, UK

For details of our global editorial offices, for customer services, and for information about how
to apply for permission to reuse the copyright material in this book please see our website at
www.wiley.com/wiley-blackwell.

The right of Ken Parry to be identified as the author of the editorial material in this work has been asserted
in accordance with the UK Copyright, Designs and Patents Act 1988.

Library of Congress Cataloging-in-Publication Data

The Wiley Blackwell companion to patristics / edited by Ken Parry.
   pages   cm
   Includes bibliographical references and index.
   ISBN 978-1-118-43871-8 (cloth : alk. paper); ISBN 978-1-119-51773-3 (Paperback)   1. Fathers of
the church.   I. Parry, Kenneth, 1945– editor.
   BR60.A65W55 2015
   270.1–dc23

                                    2015006384

A catalogue record for this book is available from the British Library.

Cover Design: Wiley
Cover Image: Fresco, Communion of the Apostles, St. George Church, Staro Nargorišane, Macedonia are in
the Public Domain, retrieved from Wikimedia Commons

Set in 10/12.5pt Photina by SPi Global, Pondicherry, India

10 9 8 7 6 5 4 3 2 1

To Mike and Eleni
whose father I am proud to be

Contents

Preface

I should like to thank members of the Patristic Forum at Macquarie University whose participation in discussions over the years has helped shape this *Companion to Patristics*. Two members of the Forum have contributed chapters to it, and I should like to take this opportunity to thank them and the rest of the contributors for agreeing to accept my invitation to participate. It has been a privilege and an honor to work with such a distinguished group of scholars, and I have learned a great deal during the process of reading their chapters and editing this book. It is my wish that our readers will learn as much I have done, and that this *Companion* will be a real friend to those interested in studying the Fathers.

I should also like to thank Rebecca Harkin, publisher, for taking on board my original suggestion for this volume, Peter Lewis, copy editor, Saravanan Purushothaman, project manager, and Annette Musker, indexer, for their work in preparing the manuscript for publication. A good deal of effort from all those involved has gone into getting this volume from conception to publication in a very short time.

Ken Parry
Macquarie University
Sydney, January 2015

Notes on Contributors

Vassilis Adrahtas teaches Ancient Greek Religion and Myth at the University of New South Wales, Sydney. His research interests are in early Christianity, patristics, Byzantine philosophy, and philosophy of religion. His most recent publications are *Rupture: Beyond the Secrets of Stelios Ramfos About the 'Secret of Jesus'* (2012), and *Son of Man: The Resurrection as a Political Hierophany* (2013), both published in Greek.

Alexander Alexakis is Professor of Byzantine Philology, Department of Philology, University of Ioannina, Greece. He has worked extensively on patristic florilegia, and published books and articles on Byzantine ecclesiastical literature, hagiography, and historiography. He is currently working on the critical edition of three eighth-century iconophile texts. Among his recent publications are *The Greek Life of St. Leo Bishop of Catania (BHG 981b)* (2011) and a chapter in *Encyclopedic Trends in Byzantium?* (2011).

Piotr Ashwin-Siejkowski is Visiting Research Fellow at King's College, London. His research is focused on early Christian origins and doctrine, particularly in the Alexandrian milieu. His recent publications include *Clement of Alexandria: A Project of Christian Perfection* (2008), *The Apostles' Creed and its Early Christian Context* (2009), *Clement of Alexandria on Trial: The Evidence of 'Heresy' from Photius' Bibliotheca* (2010), and *SCM Study Guide: Early Christian Doctrine and the Creeds* (2010).

Irena Backus is Professor of Reformation History and Ecclesiastic Latin at the Institut d'histoire de la Réformation at the University of Geneva, Switzerland. Her research and publications focus on the Reformation and the reception of Christian antiquity in the early modern period. She is the editor of *The Reception of the Church Fathers in the West: From the Carolingians to the Maurists*, two vols (1997), and is author of *Life Writing in Reformation Europe: Lives of Reformers by Friends, Disciples and Foes* (2008) and *Calvin and His Influence, 1509–2009* (2011).

Vladimir Baranov is Assistant Professor in the History of Culture, Novosibirsk State University, Russia. His research interests are in Byzantine iconoclasm, Byzantine philosophy, and the theology of images. Among his recent publications are papers in *Origeniana Decima* (2011), *Studia Patristica* 68 (2013), and *Scrinium. Revue de patrologie, d'hagiographie critique et d'historie ecclésiastique* 9 (2013).

Klaas Bentein is Post-Doctoral Research Fellow at the Universities of Ghent and Ann Arbor. He obtained his doctorate with a dissertation on the history of verbal periphrasis in Ancient Greek. In his most recent research he further explores the relationship between language and social context, focusing on morpho-syntax in the Greek documentary papyri. His publications have appeared in journals such as *Classical Philology* (2013), *Novum Testamentum* (2013), and *Classical World* (2015).

George Bevan is Assistant Professor in the Department of Classics, Queen's University, Canada. He has research interests in late antiquity, Syriac, and computational photography. He has recently co-authored with Timothy Barnes *The Funerary Speech for John Chrysostom* (2013) and co-authored a paper in *Archeologia Classica* 63 (2012), as well as contributing a chapter to *Episcopal Elections in Late Antiquity (250–600 AD)* (2011).

Paul Blowers is Dean E. Walker Professor of Church History, Emmanuel Christian Seminary, Johnson City, Tennessee. He has research interests in early Christian hermeneutics, patristic cosmology, and theological anthropology. Among his recent publications are *Drama of the Divine Economy: Creator and Creation in Early Christian Theology and Piety* (2012), translator of *On the Cosmic Mystery of Jesus Christ: Selected Writings from St. Maximus the Confessor* (2003), and co-editor of the *Oxford Handbook of Early Christian Biblical Interpretation* (forthcoming).

John Chryssavgis is Archdeacon of the Ecumenical Patriarchate and serves the Greek Orthodox Archdiocese of America. He studied in Athens and Oxford and has taught theology in Sydney and Boston. Among his recent publications are *The Correspondence of Barsanuphius and John* (2006–2007), *In the Heart of the Desert* (2008), and *Toward an Ecology of Transfiguration* (2013).

Kazuhiko Demura is Professor of Philosophy and History of Ideas in Western Thought at Okayama University, Japan. He is currently President of the Japanese Society of Patristic Studies and one of the organizers of the Asia–Pacific Early Christian Studies Society. Among his recent publications he has authored a monograph on *Augustine's Philosophy of Heart: A Preface* (2011) in Japanese.

Angelo Di Berardino is past president and current Professor of Patrology at the Augustinian Patristic Institute (Augustinianum) in Rome. He is past general secretary and president of the Association Internationale d'Études Patristiques. He is the editor of the three-volume *Encyclopedia of Ancient Christianity* (2014), *Patrology: The Eastern Fathers from the Council of Chacledon (451) to John of Damascus (†750)* (2006), and volume 5 in the series *Ancient Christian Doctrine* (2010).

Mark Edwards has been University Lecturer (now Associate Professor) in early Christian studies for the Faculty of Theology and Religion, Oxford University, since 1993. He is the author of *Origen against Plato* (2002), *Culture and Philosophy in the Age of Plotinus* (2006), *Catholicity and Heresy in the Early Church* (2009), and *Image, Word and God in the Early Christian Centuries* (2012).

Stephanos Efthymiadis is Professor at the Open University of Cyprus. He has published numerous studies on Byzantine hagiography, historiography, and prosopography. He is the editor of the two-volume *Ashgate Research Companion to Byzantine Hagiography* (2011–2014). He co-edited *Niketas Choniates: A Historian and a Writer* (2009), and a volume of his collected articles on Byzantine hagiography appeared in 2011. He is currently working on trends and techniques of rewriting in Byzantium, and on the social history of Hagia Sophia of Constantinople.

James R. Ginther is Professor of Medieval Theology and Chair of the Department of Theological Studies at Saint Louis University, Missouri, and Director of the Centre for Digital Humanities. His research focuses on theological discourse in the medieval schools, traditionally called scholastic theology. He is the author of the *Master of the Sacred Page: A Study of the Theology of Robert Grosseteste* (2004) and *The Westminster Handbook to Medieval Theology* (2009), and is co-editor of *Robert Grosseteste and His Intellectual Milieu: New Editions and Studies* (2013).

David M. Gwynn is Reader in Ancient and Late Antique History at Royal Holloway, University of London. He specializes in the study of religion in late antiquity, with a particular interest in the transformation of Christianity and the Christian controversies of the fourth century. Recent publications include *Athanasius of Alexandria: Bishop, Theologian, Ascetic, Father* (2012) and co-editing *Late Antique Archaeology 6: Religious Diversity in Late Antiquity* (2010). He is also the author of *The Roman Republic: A Very Short Introduction* (2012) and *Christianity in the Later Roman Empire: A Sourcebook* (2014).

H. Ashley Hall is Assistant Professor of Theology at Creighton University in Omaha, Nebraska. His primary research area is the reception of patristic sources. His book *Philip Melanchthon and the Cappadocians: A Reception of Greek Patristic Sources in the Sixteenth Century* was published in 2014.

Kim Haines-Eitzen is Professor of Religion in Late Antiquity in the Departments of Near Eastern Studies and Classics and the Religious Studies Program at Cornell University. She is the author of *Guardians of Letters: Literacy, Power, and the Transmitters of Early Christian Literature* (2000) and *The Gendered Palimpsest: Women, Writing, and Representation in Early Christianity* (2012). She is currently working on a new project on sound and the religious imagination in late-ancient Christianity.

Hans van Loon is Senior Researcher at the Centre for Patristic Research, founded by Tilburg University and VU University, Amsterdam. His research is focused on the mystagogy of the Church Fathers, especially that of Cyril of Alexandria. He is the author of *The Dyophysite Christology of Cyril of Alexandria* (2009) and is co-editor of *Cyprian of Carthage: Studies in His Life, Language and Thought* (2010).

Andrew Louth is Professor Emeritus of Patristic and Byzantine Studies, University of Durham, UK. He has written widely on patristic theology and Byzantine church history and is the author of *St John Damascene: Tradition and Originality in Byzantine Theology* (2002), *Greek East and Latin West: The Church AD 681–1071* (2007), and *Introducing Eastern Orthodox Theology* (2013). His next book will probably be entitled *Modern Orthodox Thinkers, from the Philokalia to the Present* and is scheduled for publication in 2015.

Wendy Mayer is Professor and Associate Dean of Research at Lutheran College, Adelaide. Her research focuses on the life, thought, and works of John Chrysostom, as well as the city of Antioch in late antiquity. Her most recent co-edited books are *Men and Women in the Early Christian Centuries* (2014), *Religious Conflict from Early Christianity to the Rise of Islam* (2013), and *The Churches of Syrian Antioch (300–638 CE)* (2012).

Denis Minns lives in Sydney. He is the author of *Irenaeus: An Introduction* (2010) and co-author of *Justin, Philosopher and Martyr: Apologies* (2009). He has contributed chapters to *The Cambridge History of Christianity: Origins to Constantine* (2006), *The Cambridge History of Philosophy in Late Antiquity* (2010), and *The World's Religions: Continuities and Transformations* (2009).

Bronwen Neil is Professor of Ancient History in the Department of Ancient History at Macquarie University. She is the author of *Seventh-century Popes and Martyrs: The Political Hagiography of Anastasius Bibliothecarius* (2006) and is co-editor of *The Brill Companion to Gregory the Great* (2013), *The Oxford Handbook to Maximus the Confessor* (forthcoming), and *Collecting Early Christian Letters from the Apostle Paul to Late Antiquity* (forthcoming).

Andrew Palmer is a Research Associate at the Institute of Eastern Christian Studies at Nijmegen, Netherlands. His edition of the Syriac Life of Barsawmo (fifth century) is forthcoming in Eastern Christian Texts (2017), and a paper on the reception of this text is forthcoming in a volume in the series The Transformation of the Classical Heritage (2016). A paper about Barsawmo at Ephesus 449 and Chalcedon 451 is to be published in the *Journal of Eastern Christian Studies* (2014), and Mardin Archaeological Museum is publishing his corpus of the Greek and Syriac inscriptions of Dara in Turkish and English (2015).

Ken Parry is Senior Research Fellow in the Department of Ancient History at Macquarie University, Sydney. He researches and publishes in the fields of late antiquity, Byzantine studies, and Eastern Christianity. He is the founding editor of the series Texts and Studies in Eastern Christianity, and editor of *The Blackwell Dictionary of Eastern Christianity* (1999), *The Blackwell Companion to Eastern Christianity* (2007), and co-editor of *Byzantium, Its Neighbours and Its Cultures* (2014).

István Perczel is Professor at the Department of Medieval Studies, Central European University, Budapest. He is a specialist in late antique and Byzantine intellectual history and Eastern Christian studies, especially the history of Indian Christianity, and has published extensively on Pseudo-Dionysius the Areopagite and the late antique tradition of Christian Platonism, and on Byzantine mysticism. He directs an ongoing research project to ditigize and catalogue the manuscripts of the Saint Thomas Christians in India.

Marcus Plested is Associate Professor in the Department of Theology, Marquette University, Wisconsin. He works largely in Greek patristic, Byzantine, and modern Orthodox theology. He is the author of *The Macarian Legacy: The Place of Macarius-Symeon in the Eastern Christian Tradition* (2004), and *Orthodox Readings of Aquinas* (2012).

Richard Price is Professor of the History of Christianity at Heythrop College, University of London. He is producing an English translation and commentary of the volumes in the *Acta Conciliorum Oecumenicorum* series. The volumes on Chalcedon (2005), Constantinople II (2009), and the Lateran Synod of 649 (2014) have already appeared in the Translated Texts for Historians series published by Liverpool University Press.

Abraham Terian is Professor Emeritus of Armenian Theology and Patristics at St Nersess Armenian Seminary, New Rochelle, New York. A recipient of the Fulbright Distinguished Chair in the Humanities award and Fellow of the National Academy of Sciences of the Republic of Armenia, he has extensive publications in the fields of Hellenistic, early Christian, and Armenian religious literature.

Janet Timbie is Adjunct Associate Professor at the Department of Semitic and Egyptian Languages, Catholic University of America, Washington, DC. She researches in the field of Coptic Studies, especially Shenoute of Atripe, and among her recent publications are papers in *Ascetic Culture* (2013), *Christianity in Egypt* (2011), and *Coptica* 13 (2014).

Alexander Treiger is Associate Professor of Religious Studies at Dalhousie University in Halifax, Nova Scotia. His research focuses on the history of Arab Orthodox Christianity, Arabic philosophy, and medieval Islamic theology and mysticism. His recent publications include *Inspired Knowledge in Islamic Thought: Al-Ghazali's Theory of Mystical Cognition and Its Avicennian Foundation* (2012) and a co-edited volume *The Orthodox Church in the Arab World (700–1700): An Anthology of Sources* (2014).

Carolinne White has research interests in patristic and medieval Latin. She has worked on a number of research projects for Oxford University, principally the recently completed Dictionary of Medieval Latin from British Sources. She is the author of several volumes in the Penguin Classics series, namely *Early Christian Lives* (1998), *The Rule of Benedict* (2008), and *Lives of Roman Christian Women* (2010). She has also published a book on Christian friendship in the fourth century

(1992), and translations of a selection of early Christian Latin poetry (2000) and of Gregory of Nazianzus' poems (1996).

Hugh Wybrew is an Associate Member of the Faculty of Theology and Religion in the University of Oxford. His book *The Orthodox Liturgy: the Development of the Eucharist in the Byzantine Rite* (1989) was reissued in 2013. Earlier publications include three books of selected Orthodox liturgical hymns with introduction and commentary; *Orthodox Lent, Holy Week and Easter* (1995), *Feasts of Christ and Mary* (1997), and *Risen with Christ: Eastertide in the Orthodox Church* (2001). He has recently contributed a chapter to *Orthodox Identities in Western Europe* (2014).

Youhanna Nessim Youssef is Associate Professor at St Athanasius Coptic Orthodox College, Melbourne. His research interests are in literary texts relating to Christianity in Egypt, and he is author of several books, including being co-author of *La consécration du Myron par Gabriel IV, 86e patriarche d'Alexandrie (1374)* (2014) and author of *The Life and Works of Severus of Antioch in the Coptic and Copto-Arabic Tradition* (2014).

Part I
Introduction

CHAPTER 1

The Nature and Scope of Patristics

Ken Parry

The *Companion to Patristics* is not another patrology and is not intended to be. There are many excellent and respected patrologies (Chapter 3), as well as monographs devoted to individual Fathers, some of which are referenced within this volume. The *Companion* has a different aim. It focuses on the reception history of a selection of Fathers in order to show how their writings and their reputations were viewed down the centuries. There is a common assumption that the works of the Fathers were always there to be consulted, but the history of their reception tells a different story. By looking at this history we can better understand why some names and texts are more familiar to us than others and the circumstances that have contributed to this. In addition to the reception histories, the *Companion to Patristics* offers a number of studies pertaining to topics that were important to patristic authors and their literary output.

The Patristic Age

There has been something of a resurgence of interest in the writings of the Fathers in the last 30 years or so. While this can be seen as a continuation of movements within the Catholic and Orthodox communities, it has also been due to the promotion of Late Antiquity as a historical period and the contribution made to it by patristic authors. For a long time this period suffered, together with the study of Byzantium, from indifference and neglect, being of no interest to traditional classicists who focused on Greece and Rome. Today, most of that has changed, so that now both Late Antiquity and Byzantium are flourishing fields of research and teaching. The literature written by Christian authors during these periods was composed not only in Latin and Greek, but also in Syriac, Coptic, Armenian, Georgian, Ethiopic, and Arabic. The diversity of languages and cultures embraced by the Fathers was instrumental in the formation of medieval European and Middle Eastern civilization.

The Wiley Blackwell Companion to Patristics, First Edition. Edited by Ken Parry.
© 2015 John Wiley & Sons Ltd. Published 2019 by John Wiley & Sons Ltd.

The language barriers that prevented these oriental Christian texts from being accessible to a western readership are gradually being removed. The situation is improving as new editions and translations into English and other modern languages become more widely available. This is happening along with a revival of interest is learning Syriac, Coptic, and other ancient Christian languages, in addition to Greek and Latin. In the *Companion to Patristics* we have included a Syriac, Coptic, and Armenian Father (Chapters 8, 12, and 19), as well as an assessment of the Fathers in Arabic (Chapter 30), but this hardly does justice to the large body of patristic writings in these languages. There is still some way to go before we have a complete library of patristic literature from these traditions in critical editions and translations.

The old Latin and Greek parameters defining the study of patristics did not allow for this diversity of languages and geographical spread. It was not only the linguistic parameters that defined the patristic age, but also the confessional base that many scholars brought to their study of the Fathers, carrying with them doctrinal positions that determined their perception and acceptance of which Fathers to study. Today, we take a more inclusive approach to the study of church history and who owns that history in line with the ecumenical spirit of our times. This has brought a fresh interest in the transmission of early Christianity to regions beyond the traditional geographical and cultural boundaries (Tabbernee 2014). At the same time, there have been advances in our knowledge of the contribution made by women, as well as the application of a feminist approach to the study of patristics (Levine and Robbins 2008).

Patristics has been defined as the study of the writings of the Fathers of the Church; while this definition may still suffice, we might want to ask which Fathers are meant and which church is being referred to. This is because we are conscious that the early church was fractured and divided along fault lines that are still visible. There is now a clearer understanding of the divisions left behind by the early councils and the subsequent history of Christian communities outside the Rome–Constantinople axis. This, in turn, has led to a less confessional reading of the Fathers and the role they played across the Christological spectrum, irrespective of the process that made some Fathers saints in one church and heretics in another. While the confessional approach has its place, the study of patristics is no longer the prerogative of theological faculties and seminaries.

Certainly, the western definition of the patristic age can be challenged from a variety of viewpoints, especially when looked at from outside a European perspective, where the parameters defining the western time-frame do not apply. The eighth-century terminus traditionally concluded with Venerable Bede in the Latin west and with John of Damascus in the Greek east. The fact that there were Fathers in the Byzantine tradition after John of Damascus, such as Symeon the New Theologian and Gregory Palamas (Chapter 20), as well as in the Oriental Orthodox churches, was seldom mentioned, let alone discussed. This was because the western interpretation of the patristic period was applied to the rest of the Christian world without considering what might have been happening there.

Patristic Literature

Patristic literature covers a wide range of genres, including not only theology, spirituality, and apologetics, but also philosophy, ecclesiology, hagiography (Chapter 25), homiletics, liturgics (Chapter 26), epistolography, hymnography, and poetry. The corpus of writings of an individual Father may embrace only two or three of these, while our interest in them may be from a variety of disciplines and points of view. Generally speaking, patristic literature is retrospective in orientation; that is, it takes its inspiration from the past. However, this does not mean the Fathers were disinterested in the future or indifferent to the present. We know that many of them were personally involved in the political and religious controversies of their times. Some of their writings stem directly from their involvement in such events, for which they suffered persecution and exile, and in some cases imprisonment and torture. Most were canonized by their respective churches as a result of bearing witness to the truth or for their contribution as bishops and church leaders.

It goes without saying that we read patristic literature differently from the way it was read in the past. Many changes have contributed to this. In the age before printing, the writings of the Fathers were known largely through florilegia and collections consisting of thematic excerpts (Chapter 2). Copying manuscripts was time consuming and labor intensive, although the invention of new writing systems, such as the minuscule script, helped to speed things up. Some works owe their existence to the work of stenographers, while others survive as a result of serendipity. Nowadays, the Fathers are benefiting from the digital age, giving us easier access to their writings than previous generations; but whether we are better equipped to understand them is another question. In the case of patristic authors, it may not be what we find as individuals that matters, but what we share with others from earlier generations who also admired them. It is the ability of the Fathers to speak to us across the generations in mainly dead languages that paradoxically keeps them alive.

Many of the writings of the Fathers are highly stylized and rhetorical. They were written at a time when language imitated classical models (Chapters 31 and 32), and in doing so they may appear more focused on eloquence than substance. That being said, patristic literature can convey a dimension beyond the immediate text that obliges us to meditate upon the meaning of what we have read. The words may inspire us to go beyond the literal sense to a level of reflection that is not easy to define, and perhaps impossible to define, given the mystical nature of the message being conveyed. Just as the Fathers contemplated scripture and absorbed it to become living exponents and witnesses to its meaning, so in turn they imbued their own writings with multiple layers of meaning, compelling us to explore more fully the implications of their words. The fact that the Fathers continue to attract our attention shows the power of their message to engage us.

A Major Modern Father

By tracing the reception history of a number of Fathers the *Companion to Patristics* shows the peaks and troughs to which some of them have been subjected. While the names of many Fathers are known to us, just as many have been forgotten or neglected. An example of the latter was the Greek theologian of the seventh century, Maximos the Confessor (Chapter 17). The rediscovery of Maximos' writings in the twentieth and twenty-first centuries has been nothing less than phenomenal. Through translations and studies his work has been brought to a new generation of readers who were barely aware of his existence, let alone the role he played in the ecclesiastical politics of his time. He is now appreciated as a key figure in the Christological disputes of the seventh century and a major theologian in the history of Christian thought (von Balthasar 1961; Thunberg 1965).

In the case of Maximos it was the general neglect of the seventh century that hid his contribution from us. He continued to be known in the Eastern Orthodox world, but due to historical circumstances this knowledge was confined mainly to monastic circles. It was as a result of being given the lion's share of extracts in the *Philokalia* (itself a monastic achievement) in the late eighteenth century that his writings gained a wider audience, but not at that time in the west (Louth 2012). The fact that it took so long for his contribution to be finally recognized might make us think what other Fathers remain to be rediscovered. Now that we are better informed about Maximos' works we recognize him for the outstanding thinker that he was.

In the Greek *Life* of Maximos he is praised for his literary style as well as for his abilities as an expositor of theological problems:

> But no less will someone see the anagogy of Maximus in reading his writings and the scholia composed by him on the compositions of the great Gregory [Nazianzus]; for many of these, as we know, being hard to comprehend and unclear in their wording, especially those which deal with doctrine and Trinitarian theology, he saw the meaning in them and brought it to greater clarity by light of spiritual wisdom, not only by more mystical understanding and contemplation, but also putting the explanation in an excellent style and very beautiful diction (Neil and Allen 2003: 77).

It is through his insights into difficult theological issues that Maximos uncovers the hidden depths in the writings of earlier Fathers. He was able to explicate the theology of Gregory of Nazianzus (Chapter 21) and Dionysius the Areopagite (Chapter 14) for his own generation and subsequently for us as well. In his *Ambigua* he responds to questions raised by various correspondents asking for clarity on certain points in the Theologian's teaching (Constas 2014). In explaining Gregory, Maximos demonstrates the perspicacity of his own thought, and moves us to a greater appreciation of the spiritual world they both inhabited.

The Continuing Tradition

Understanding the place of tradition in the writings of the Fathers is an essential aspect of studying them, although this has not always been acknowledged. Part of the increased interest in patristics in the west has been the need for a more balanced and nuanced response to the role of tradition in shaping early Christianity. The recovery of patristic commentary on the scriptures has led to a revival of interest in the writings of the early Fathers. This has been particularly noticeable among Protestant scholars, who have come to recognize the value of the patristic interpretation of scripture. This has led to the founding of such series as the *Ancient Christian Commentary on Scripture*, which is now set to be translated into a number of European and Asian languages. This, in turn, has given rise to further offshoots, such as *Ancient Christian Doctrine* and *Ancient Christian Texts*.

The value of tradition and the way that it was understood by the Fathers was instrumental in initiating another series, the *Message of the Fathers of the Church*. Each volume in this series took the form of an anthology of primary sources focused on a particular topic, such as biblical interpretation or social thought. It was published in the belief that both scripture and tradition were essential for understanding the formation of the early church, only this understanding needs to be extended beyond the first five centuries. The Reformation notion that the first five centuries represented a kind of golden age meant that theological issues after the Council of Chalcedon in 451 were thought not to be of interest, and belonged to a period that contributed nothing to the advancement of Christian doctrine. Yet, it is interesting to witness the western fascination with icons in recent decades and the need to understand the theology behind the practice of painting and venerating them. This need has initiated a new interest in the topic of Byzantine iconoclasm and the arguments put forward by iconophile Fathers (Chapter 23), such as John of Damascus (Chapter 18) and the bishops at the Second Council of Nicaea in 787 (Pelikan 1990; Parry 1996).

Just as in earlier times, anthologies of the writings of the Fathers have continued into the present century, with such series as the *Early Church Fathers* published by Routledge. This series has attracted new translations of Fathers who have not always been at the forefront of patristic studies. The selections from the works of Theodore of Mopsuestia and Severus of Antioch (Chapter 15) are two that come to mind. Of particular interest has been the *Popular Patristics* series published by St Vladimir's Seminary Press in New York. This series has proved to be successful not only for publishing a range of patristic texts from across the traditions, but also for the high standard of its translations. It has published works from Coptic and Syriac as well as Greek and Latin in paperback editions, making them accessible to a wide readership. Other well-established series continue to flourish, such as *Sources Chrétiennes*, *Ancient Christian Writers*, *Fathers of the Church*, and *Corpus Scriptorum Christianorum Orientalium*. The recently established *Corpus Christianorum in Translation* series is a welcome addition to any patristic collection.

The Authority of the Fathers

While scriptural knowledge is fundamental to patristic thought and authorship, it is far from biblical fundamentalism in the modern sense of the term. This is often missed by commentators not versed in historical theology who imagine that modern biblical fundamentalism can be applied to pre-modern theological thought. The authority of the scriptures was paramount to the Fathers and inseparable from tradition, but it was not their only source of authority. In his discussion on the divinity of the Holy Spirit, Gregory of Nazianzus suggests that doctrine is progressive because divine matters are revealed and understood in stages (*Oration* 31: 26). In the light of this the teachings of the Fathers themselves became authoritative and part of tradition. From the fourth century, the appeal to the Fathers was assimilated into patristic methodology, although not everyone was happy with it, particularly when it appeared to override the authority of scripture (Graumann 2012).

As a scholar of intellectual history, the ninth-century patriarch of Constantinople, Photios, was well acquainted with the historical context in which the Fathers wrote and the controversies they were responding to. Because of this he was able to point out that not everything written by them was binding from a dogmatic point of view. In his second letter to Pope Nicholas of 861 he makes the following remark:

> Everyone should preserve what is defined by common ecumenical decisions, but a particular opinion of a church father or a definition issued by a local synod may be followed by some and ignored by others (*Epistle* 290: 204–208).

This is certainly not an invitation to develop ideas incompatible with the teachings of the church councils, but it does allow for some diversity of thought and opinion. To some extent Photios was following what an earlier patriarch of Constantinople had written in the seventh century. Richard Price in this volume (Chapter 27) has referred to the correspondence between Patriarch Sergius and Pope Honorius on this issue.

The personal opinions (*theologumena*) of the Fathers might not be on a par with the decisions of church councils, but they could still be developed or disregarded as the case may be. The desire to harmonize the teachings of the Fathers in order to arrive at a consensus is understandable in the context of the controversies of the time. The idea that they spoke with one voice had the particular aim of showing that they were witnesses to a shared tradition that was both ancient and orthodox. Yet this was largely achieved by taking their teachings out of their original context and imposing uniformity on disparate material. In the case of the works attributed to Dionysius the Areopagite, the desire to maintain their apostolic authorship meant that ambiguities remained unresolved, even when they were known to be the result of later or non-Christian influences.

The application of non-scriptural terms, however, did not have to mean innovation in doctrine. The Fathers understood perfectly well where they were situated in relation to the cultural environment in which they worked. For example, John of Damascus wrote in the eighth century:

> Where can you find in the Old Testament or in the Gospel explicit use of such terms as "Trinity" or "homoousios" or "one nature of the Godhead" or "three hypostases," or that Christ is "one hypostasis with two natures?" Yet, the meanings of these things are found, expressed in other phrases contained in the scriptures, which the fathers have interpreted for us (*Third Oration on the Holy Images* 11: 1–8).

Searching the scriptures in order to make explicit what was merely implied was standard exegesis among the Fathers (Chapter 24). The patristic commentaries on scripture were a basic resource for authenticating Christian teaching and provided an abundant harvest of scholarship for later generations to reap.

The Ascetic Orientation

It is important to understand the role and function of asceticism in reading the lives and writings of the Fathers. As a result of recent scholarly research, a change has taken place in our understanding of sexual and social renunciation in early Christianity (Brown 1988; Clark 1999). This, in turn, has led to a more nuanced assessment of asceticism and its contribution to Christian culture in the formative period and beyond. It is now accepted that ascetic practice was part of Christianity from the beginning, just as it was for other contemporary philosophical and religions movements (Finn 2009). From the fourth century monasticism became the institutionalized form of Christian asceticism, providing a suitable environment for nurturing literary talent and scholarship. Without the institution of monasticism it is hard to see how patristic literature could have flourished in the way that it did.

The reassessment of asceticism has seen a renewed interest in the writings and spirituality of the desert Fathers and Mothers (Chapter 22). Their attraction for us lies as much in their austere lifestyles as in their sayings, even though most of us will never become desert dwellers. The wisdom of the desert may be remote from us in time, but it has an immediacy and simplicity that makes it accessible to new generations of readers. This wisdom permeates the writings of Isaac of Nineveh, who turned dispassion into compassion for all living things, including demons and those in hell. He writes:

> What is a charitable heart? It is a heart which is burning with charity for the whole of creation, for humans, for birds, for animals, for the demons – for all creatures. He who has such a heart cannot see or call to mind a creature without his eyes becoming filled with tears by reason of the immense compassion which seizes his heart. A heart which is softened and can no longer bear to see or learn from others of any suffering, even the smallest pain, being inflicted upon any creature. This is why such a person never ceases to pray also for the animals, for the enemies of the truth, and for those who do us evil, that they may be preserved and purified. He will pray for the reptiles, moved by the infinite pity which reigns in the hearts of those who are becoming united to God (Hansbury 1989: 12).

Issac's spiritual vision saw divine providence operating in every aspect of our lives in ways that we cannot know or even imagine. Like his contemporary Maximos the Confessor, his writings are just as thought provoking and relevant today as when they were first written. They were soon translated from Syriac into Greek and other languages to become a staple of monastic reading. Some might have thought twice before reading him, however, had they known he was from a church that was dubbed "Nestorian," yet he was acknowledged as a saint across the ecclesiastical divide (Alfeyev 2000).

The modern fascination with the desert Fathers may be traced to 1874 when the French novelist Gustave Flaubert published the final version of his novel *La Tentation de Saint Antoine*. It is written in the form of a play covering one night in the life of Anthony the Great in the desert during which he struggles against a series of demons. It was Athanasius of Alexandria (Chapter 7) who gave us the literary legend on which the novel is based. Flaubert was inspired by a painting he saw of the temptation of St Anthony, and several modern artists have painted the theme of Anthony's temptation, including Paul Cézanne and Salvador Dali. Flaubert's novel deals with the seven deadly sins, originally the eight thoughts of Evagrius of Pontus and modified in the writings of John Cassian. In the music sphere the composers Ottorino Respighi and John Tavener both wrote operas based on the legend of the desert Mother Mary of Egypt.

In 2008 the Egyptian Muslim author and Islamic scholar Yousssef Ziedan published his novel *Azazeel*, which won the International Prize for Arabic Fiction and was recently translated into English (Ziedan 2012). It tells the story of a Coptic monk who travels from Upper Egypt to Alexandria and then to Jerusalem and Syria at the time of Cyril of Alexandria (Chapter 11) and Nestorius of Constantinople (Chapter 13). As well as dealing with historical persons and events, such as the death of Hypatia, it describes the demonic forces that assail the monk, including the demon called Azazeel of the book's title. It is a notable literary acknowledgment of a period that has not been dealt with by modern Egyptian authors.

Conclusion

Thus, the lives and writings of the Fathers, whether of the desert variety or not, continue to find readers from different backgrounds and with different interests. Our reasons for studying them may not be same and may even be at variance, but what is important is that they engage us no less today than they did in the past, and will undoubtedly continue to do so in the future. The *Companion to Patristics* is a tribute to their ability to go on breathing new life into us and our ability to do the same for them.

Bibliography

Primary Sources

Gregory of Nazianzus, *On God and Man: The Five Theological Orations and Two Letters from Cledonius*, Frederick Williams and Lionel Wickham (transl.) (2002). Popular Patristics Series. Crestwood, NY: St Vladimir's Seminary Press.

Isaac of Nineveh, *On Ascetical Life*, Mary Hansbury (transl.) (1989). Crestwood, NY: St Vladimir's Seminary Press.

John of Damascus, *Die Schriften des Johannes von Damaskos III, Contra imaginum caluminatores orationes tres*, P. Bonifatius Kotter (ed.)

(1975). Patristische Texte und Studien, Band 17. Berlin: Walter de Gruyter.

Maximos the Confessor, *On the Difficulties of the Church Fathers: The Ambigua*, Nicholas Constas (ed./transl.) (2014), two vols. Dumbarton Oaks Medieval Library 28 & 29. Cambridge, MA: Harvard University Press.

Maximos the Confessor, *The Life of Maximus the Confessor Recension 3*, Bronwen Neil and Pauline Allen (ed./transl.) (2003). Sydney: St Paul's Publications.

Photios the Great, *Epistulae et Amphilochia*, vol. 3, B. Laourdas and L.G. Westerink (ed.) (1985). Leipzig: Teubner.

Secondary Sources

Alfeyev, Hilarion (2000), *The Spiritual World of Isaac the Syrian*. Kalamazoo, MI: Cistercian Publications.

Brown, Peter (1988), *The Body and Society: Men, Women, and Sexual Renunciation in Early Christianity*. New York: Columbia University Press.

Clark, Elizabeth A. (1999), *Reading Renunciation: Asceticism and Scripture in Early Christianity*. Princeton, NJ: Princeton University Press.

Finn, Richard (2009), *Asceticism in the Graeco-Roman World*. Cambridge: Cambridge University Press.

Graumann, Thomas (2012), "The conduct of theology and the 'Fathers' of the church". In *A Companion to Late Antiquity*, Philip Rousseau (ed.). Oxford: Wiley-Blackwell; 539–555.

Levine, Amy-Jill with Robbins, Maria Mayo (eds) (2008), *A Feminist Companion to Patristic Literature*. London: T&T Clark.

Louth, Andrew (2012), "The influence of the Philokalia in the Orthodox world". In *The Philokalia: A Classic Text of Orthodox Spirituality*, Brock Bingaman and Bradley Nassif (eds). New York: Oxford University Press; 50–60.

Parry, Ken (1996), *Depicting the World: Byzantine Iconophile Thought of the Eighth and Ninth Centuries*. Leiden: Brill.

Pelikan, Jaoslav (1990), *Imago Dei: The Byzantine Apologia for Icons*. Princeton, NJ: Princeton University Press.

Tabbernee, William (ed.) (2014), *Early Christianity in Contexts: An Exploration across Cultures and Continents*. Grand Rapids, MI: Baker Academic.

Thunberg, Lars (1965), *Microcosm and Mediator: The Theological Anthropology of Maximus the Confessor*. Lund: C.W.K. Gleerup & Ejnar Munksgaard.

Von Balthasar, Hans Urs (1961), *Kosmische Liturgie: Das Wiltbeld Maximus' des Bekenners*. Einsiedeln: Johannes Verlag. [English translation: Daley, Brain D. (2003), *Cosmic Liturgy: The Universe According to Maximus the Confessor*. San Francisco, CA: Ignatius Press.]

Ziedan, Youssef (2012), *Azazeel*. London: Atlantic Books.

CHAPTER 2
Byzantine Florilegia

Alexander Alexakis

Introductory Remarks

The practice of putting together collections of extracts from works of various authorities (from Homer to Plutarch or an even later author), under a particular secular or
religious heading (e.g., "on friendship" or "on the beginning of the universe," or "on
God") goes back to ancient Greek times with the genre of "anthology" already appearing from the classical period, and continuing with the addition of Christian authors
after the third century CE (Chadwick 1969: 1131–1142; Searby 1998: 13–22). After
the third century, part of this tradition focused exclusively on Christian authors, while
a second part combined both Christian and pagan authors. These collections were used
for educational, moralizing–spiritual, and argumentative purposes. The general benefit
of this practice is that, for a reader who wishes to absorb the gist of an argument or the
main points of a multipage treatise, the excerption and collection of the crucial in terms
of content passages and their continuous listing under appropriate headings offers the
most convenient shortcut to knowledge and information. As Photius aptly put it in his
evaluation of Stobaeus' *Anthologion*:

> ...for those who have already read the entire works of the ⟨anthologized⟩ authors this book
> is useful as a memory prod, while for those who have not had any glimpse of them ⟨this
> book is also useful⟩ because through continuous study they will soon acquire the knowledge
> of many good and different ideas (although in summary form). Finally, a benefit for both is
> the swift and untroubled detection of what they are looking for, especially whenever they
> decide to move through the chapter-headings to the particular collection ⟨of citations⟩...
> (Photius *Bibliotheca* cod. 167, Henry 1960: 159).

The second benefit is that a number of works both of antiquity and of Christian
times have been preserved, albeit fragmentarily, as a result of their inclusion in

The Wiley Blackwell Companion to Patristics, First Edition. Edited by Ken Parry.
© 2015 John Wiley & Sons Ltd. Published 2019 by John Wiley & Sons Ltd.

florilegia. Given the variety and the breadth of this practice, the term *florilegium* may be narrower than the more generic term *anthology*, usually applied to collections with predominantly secular content. The latter term covers items such as the *Greek Anthology*, an extensive collection of epigrams (Cameron, 1993), or the collection of excerpts by the fifth-century erudite Ioannes Stobaeus entitled *Anthologion* (Chadwick 1969: 1140). However, the Latin term *florilegium* (pl. *florilegia*, (from flores+legere), i.e., collection of flowers) has prevailed in modern patristic terminology, and, as a result of recent efforts at further classifying and defining the categories of these collections, the terminology has developed as follows. In general, florilegium is a collection of excerpts from early patristic authors put together in order to serve an explicit purpose (*ODB*, s.v. "Florilegium"). In his extensive entry in the *DSp*, Richard (1964) has distinguished florilegia into two main categories: (a) dogmatic and (b) spiritual. Furthermore, spiritual florilegia are divided by Richard into (i) Damascenian florilegia (after the *Sacra Parallela* of John of Damascus; Richard 1964: 476–486), (ii) sacro-profane florilegia that were more or less based on the *Loci communes* or *Capita Theologica* attributed to Maximus the Confessor (Richard 1964: 486–499), and the *Anthologion* of Stobaeus, and (iii) monastic florilegia, the content of which focuses on aspects of monastic life both moral–spiritual and practical (Richard 1964: 499–510). On the other hand, dogmatic florilegia are anthologies of excerpts from dogmatic patristic writings and other related texts, compiled for two main reasons: first, doctrinal education and, second, religious controversy (Alexakis, 2011: 45).

One must also note the following particular characteristics of florilegia:

1.   The number of authors anthologized in a florilegium varies from one single author, as is the case of the mid-fourth-century *Philocalia* compiled from texts of Origen by Basil the Great and Gregory of Nazianzus, to dozens of authors, anthologized in the *Doctrina patrum* or the 500 included in Stobaeus' *Anthologion*.

2.   The Damascenian florilegia appear from the eighth century onwards, the sacro-profane ones from the ninth–tenth centuries and the monastic ones from, perhaps, the ninth century (and if we count as florilegia the *apophthegmata patrum* we descend to the fourth–fifth centuries), but they mostly occupy the eleventh and later centuries. Finally, the dogmatic florilegia are the earlier ones starting from the fourth century. The activity of producing Damascenian and monastic florilegia wanes after the fall of Constantinople to the Crusaders in 1204, but it seems that the production of dogmatic florilegia continues unabated until the end of the Byzantine Empire and later.

3.   Terminology is much more varied and complex than already suggested. Some terms are simple synonyms of florilegium, whereas some others denote a genre akin to and in terms of form almost identical with the florilegium. Apart from *anthology* (ἀνθολόγιον), in use are also the following terms, frequently occurring in the titles of florilegia preserved in Byzantine manuscripts: *Loci communes* (κοινοίτόποι), Selection (ἐκλογή), Chapters (*capita*, κεφάλαια), Collection of opinions or sayings, (γνωμολόγιον, *gnomologium*, *sententiae*), Questions and answers (*questiones et responsiones*, ἐρωταποκρίσεις) or simply Questions (*questiones*, ἐρωτήσεις), Treasure/Thesaurus (*thesaurus*, θησαυρός) together

with some other substantives that recall the activity of collecting or of a container of variegated items, such as μέλισσα (bee), λειμών-λειμωνάριον (meadow), πανάριον (basket-container). The particular extracts that make up a florilegium are called excerpts (*excerpta*, from extant works), fragments (*fragmenta*, from lost works) sayings (*dicta, ῥήσεις*), opinions (*sententiae, γνῶμαι*), testimonies (*testimonia, χρήσεις, μαρτυρίαι*), and so on. The activity of compiling a florilegium is described by the verbs ἀπανθίζειν, ἀθροίζειν, ἐρανίζειν, συλλέγειν (all synonyms of "collecting") παρατιθέναι ("to present, to cite"), sometimes combined in the manuscripts with the expression ἐκ πολλῶν ὀλίγα (few out of many); for more on terminology, see also Searby (2007: 1–8).

Exegetical Chains (*Catenae, Σειραί*)

The *exegetical chains* (for which see CPG: vol. 4, 185–259; other earlier terms: ἐξηγητικά, ἐκλογαί, *excerpta* or *collectanea*) are one of the earlier categories of Christian anthologies. Compared with the spiritual and dogmatic florilegia, their distinctive character lies in the fact that the *catenae* form a body of continuous commentary around the text of the Bible and constitute the major instrument of early patristic exegesis on it. A *catena* is an anthology of fragments taken from early patristic works, especially commentaries on the books of the Bible, but also homilies and *scholia* that were written on passages of both the Old and the New Testaments. These commentaries – first compiled in the early sixth century by Procopius of Gaza who imitated in this the ὑπομνήματα or *scholia* to classical texts, (e.g., *scholia* on Homer, or on medical treatises from the Hellenistic period) – are attached/cited next to the continuous text of the Bible. *Catenae* are preserved in numerous catenary manuscripts the contents of which – having to accommodate on the page two different text bodies, the biblical and the commentary – are arranged in the following four formats: (a) Biblical text and corresponding commentary by two or three major Fathers in two or (rarely) three parallel columns. (b) *Marginal catenae*: the biblical text (in semi-uncial or minuscule script) occupies the inner middle of the space provided by the two pages, and the exegetical excerpts (in smaller minuscule or cursive script) are placed around the biblical text on all sides. (c) *Text catena*: in this arrangement the biblical text and the commentary are in one flowing column occupying the entire writing space of the folio and the biblical text is cited verse by verse (in uncial), followed by the relevant excerpts of exegesis (in minuscule or cursive). (d) *Catenae* added in the margin of a biblical manuscript that originally contained the text of the Bible alone. These *catenae* are usually created by later hands that penned the exegeses of the Fathers to obscure passages (Karo and Lietzmann 1902: 331). As of today, the catenaric manuscripts have not been classified in a definitive way. Karo and Lietzmann used the particular groups of authors the *scholia* of which appear in the commentary in order to classify *catenae* in various groups. For example, for the Octateuch they distinguished three group-types of *catenae* (Karo and Lietzmann 1902: 3–17). However, more recent and careful study of the relevant manuscripts by Françoise Petit (1979: 281–286; 1977: xxxi–xxxiii) has reduced the group-types to two. Classification becomes much more complicated with the *catenae* to the Psalms and the Odes, for which Karo and Lietzmann have identified some

26 groups (Karo and Lietzmann 1902: 21–64; *CPG*: vol. 4, 188–207). The same problems of classification are also present in the *catenae* on the Four Gospels or the Pauline epistles. Irrespective of the various group-types of *catenae*, the authors anthologized in them are more or less from among those early Fathers who are also excerpted in other florilegia with a notable exception; as Natalio Fernández aptly put it:

> ...*catenae* have become one of the main sources of information about the thinking of ancient Christianity, a source which for the most part still remains hidden and unknown. Their special value is that they are the only means of rescuing fragments of authors whose works – due to having been condemned or declared suspect by a council – disappeared completely... This affects especially the writers of the school of Antioch who succumbed to the tensions of the Arian disputes and were collected by the catenarists... because they were only interested in the most complete dossier possible of a biblical passage, with no concern for schools. Natalio Fernández (2000: 294).

To witness, F. Petit, in her edition of the *Catena Sinaitica*, next to authorities such as Irenaeus of Lyon, Basil of Caesarea, Gregory of Nyssa, Didymus of Alexandria, Epiphanius of Salamis, John Chrysostom, Cyril of Alexandria, Theodoret of Cyrus, and so on, has also identified fragments from Severus of Antioch (a Miaphysite), and other fragments by Melito of Sardis, Origen, Eusebius of Emesa, Acacius of Caesarea, Diodore of Tarsus, Theodore of Mopsuestia, Severian of Gabala, and Succensus of Diocaesarea, which are uniquely preserved by this *catena* (Petit 1977: xvii–xviii). Severus of Antioch figures prominently in Miaphysite *catenae*.

Historically, the *catenae* originally develop in Palestine where Procopius of Gaza puts together his commentary anthologizing Palestinian patristic authors, but then *catenae* evolve in Constantinople with the appearance of a few models that differ among them. A first model relies heavily on works of John Chrysostom, supplemented by citations from Theodoret of Cyrus. A second model presents the comments of two authors as thoroughly as possible, and in a third one the commentator has inserted fragments from both John Chrysostom and Theodoret without omitting citations from Palestinian authors (Natalio Fernández 2000: 289–290). Compilers of *catenae* known by name are few besides Procopius: a certain Philotheus (*CPG*: vol. 4, 215–216), John Drungarius (*CPG*: vol. 4, 216; *catena* on Isaiah and on other books of the Old Testament), Polychronius Deacon (*CPG*: vol. 4, 223; ninth century), Nicholas Mouzalon (twelfth century), Macarius Chrysocephalus (*CPG*: vol. 4, 241) and a Nicetas of Heracleia, who is also active in the eleventh or twelfth century. His *catena* preserves fragments from the lost commentary on the Psalms by Eusebius. Finally, there are a number of illuminated catenary manuscripts in which the details of the miniatures clarify or interpret the meaning of the text of the passage next to which they are usually placed (Natalio Fernández 2000: 293; also Lowden 2010: 130, 136–139).

The study of *catenae* is one of the rather esoteric fields of Patristic and Byzantine literature; however, the scholarly activity is very vibrant, and the significance of this kind of early florilegia is more than evident, not only on account of the numbers of fragments from otherwise lost patristic writings preserved in them, but also for the richness of the biblical text itself that is used as their primary material and still provides very interesting readings for the biblical translations of Origen's *Hexapla*, exploited in our days by the Göttingen edition of the Bible.

Spiritual Florilegia

In this section I shall follow the categories of florilegia proposed and arranged by M. Richard, under the principle stated by H.-M. Rochais in the first section of the entry "Florilèges Spirituels" of the *DSp*. According to Rochais, spiritual florilegia are "...limited to collections meant to remind, according to the evangelical ideal, the laws of Christian *askesis*, the rules of spiritual combat and the ways of the prayer..." (Rochais 1964: 436). Although they were excluded by Rochais and Richard, I will include in a separate section the dogmatic florilegia. Still, like Richard, I will also omit the liturgical collections, the lectionaries, the *synaxaria* (collections of abridged saints' lives) and the *panegyrika* (collections of sermons for feast days), and the collections of canonical texts (church rules, *nomokanones*).

Damascenian Florilegia: The *Sacra Parallela* and their Descendants

What is presented here as Damascenian florilegia are the ones that begin with the *Sacra Parallela* attributed to John of Damascus and their various recensions preserved in numerous manuscripts and other related florilegia, and not the dogmatic florilegia also compiled by John of Damascus, such as the florilegia on image veneration appended to each one of the three sermons in defense of the holy icons (Kotter 1975, translation into English: Louth 2003). In its original form, not extant today, the *Sacra Parallela* was known under the heading Τἀἱερά (the sacred things) and was divided into three books. The first book was dedicated to the subject of God, the second to mankind, and the third to virtues and their opposing vices (in parallel one-to-one exposition, hence *Sacra Parallela*). In the first two books, the compiler has arranged the citations under a particular chapter title appropriate for the subject matter. The chapter titles are arranged in alphabetical order of their key word (e.g., *PG* 95, 1045: Στοιχεῖον ἄλφα. Α. Περὶ ἀϊδίου θεότητος... (Letter alpha: 1. On eternal Deity...), Β. Περὶ τοῦ ἄφευκτον εἶναι Θεόν... (2. On that God is inescapable...), Γ. Περὶ τοῦ ἀκατάληπτον εἶναι τὸν Θεόν... (3. On that God is incomprehensible...), Δ. Περὶ ἀγάπης καὶ φόβου Θεοῦ... (4. On love and fear of God...), and so on). All the chapters of which the subject starts with the same letter are gathered into sections under the appropriate letter (στοιχεῖον); that is, στοιχεῖονα, στοιχεῖονβ, and so on. Finally, under the particular chapter titles are cited the excerpts starting with biblical citations and continuing with excerpts from works of the early Fathers such as Basil the Great, Gregory of Nazianzus, and John Chrysostom, but also from Philo of Alexandria and Flavius Josephus. No manuscript preserves the original florilegium of the *Sacra Parallela*, and only parts or later recensions of it are transmitted by various manuscripts.

The only extant edition of the work with a Latin translation was done in 1712 by Michel Lequien and is reprinted in *PG* (95 and 96; see Primary sources in the Bibliography). Whatever survives from the first book is transmitted by a single manuscript of the tenth century, the *Parisinus Coislinianus* 276, and consists of 55 chapters, which only reflect part of the original number of chapters. Some of these chapters are also preserved by the *Florilegium Vaticanum*, the *Florilegium Hierosolymitanum*, and the *Florilegium Rupefucaldinum*. The second book has come down to us in two recensions, the appearance of which goes back to the ninth century. The first recension contains 200 chapters, transmitted by codex *Vaticanus graecus* 1553 of the tenth century. The second is not witnessed directly by any single manuscript but can be reconstructed by a number of codices that preserve the florilegia (a) *Rupefucaldinum*, (b) *Thessalonicense*, and (c) *PML*^{b} (=codd. *Parisinus gr.* 923 (ninth century), *Marcianus gr.* 138 (tenth–eleventh centuries), and *Laurentianus plut.* VIII, 22 (fourteenth century)). It is possible that the original Book II of the *Sacra Parallela* comprised more than 200 chapters. The third book is in an even worse state of preservation with only 34 of the 70 *parallela* surviving in the late codex *Athous Iviron* 382 (fifteenth century). Still, this book was amply used in the compilation of sacro-profane florilegia such as those of Pseudo-Maximus and Pseudo-Antonius, so a little more than what is preserved by the Athonite manuscript can be added to it (Richard 1964: 476–480).

Many of the particular Damascenian florilegia have already been mentioned in the treatment of the three books of the *Sacra Parallela*, so here I simply list them.

1. *Florilegium Vaticanum* is the one on which Lequien based his edition, preserved in codex *Vaticanus gr.* 1236 (fifteenth century) a copy of codex *Ottobonianus gr.* 79.
2. *Florilegium Rupefucaldinum*, witnessed by codex *Berolinensis gr.* 46 (Phill. 1450), twelfth century. Segments of it have been published in *PG* 96, 441–544.
3. *Florilegium Thessalonicense*, transmitted by cod. *Thessalonike Mone Vlataion* 9, tenth century.
4. *Florilegium Hierosolymitanum*, preserved in cod. *Hierosolymit. Sancti Sepulchri* 15, tenth century, and should be considered a supplementary witness to the *Florilegium Coislinianum* (see below).

All the above together with the florilegium *PML*^{b} are, in fact, partial witnesses to the *Sacra Parallela* (Richard 1964: 480–484).

The next one, called by Richard *Florilegium Coislinianum secundum alphabeti litteras dispositum*, presents a close affinity to the Damascenian florilegia but is not one of them. It is extant in three recensions transmitted by a total of 10 manuscripts, but the most significant aspect of this florilegium is the inclusion of a number of fragments from works that are rather rare (e.g., belonging to authors such as Amphilochius of Iconium, Anatolius of Laodicea, Cosmas Vestitor, Epiphanius, Eusebius of Caesarea, Eustathius of Antioch, Hesychius of Jerusalem, Hippolytus of Rome, and Nemesius of Emesa) or even unknown from other sources (e.g., fragments of Athanasius of Alexandria and fragments from an otherwise unknown author Leontius of Damascus) (Richard 1964: 484–486; for the edition of letters B and Γ, see now Ilse de Vos *et al.* 2008, 2010).

The Damascenian florilegia are a telling witness to the wealth of the library used by their compiler(s), and chances are that their compilation took place at a time when the compilers still used original works for the extraction of their citations and not pre-existing florilegia (Evangelatou 2008: 116). For this reason their contribution to the critical edition of early patristic works such as, for example, the letters of Basil the Great should not be rejected (Richard 1964: 477). As already mentioned, there are cases in which florilegia have been the only extant sources for a number of lost works. It is also worth mentioning that the *Sacra Parallela* is the major if not the unique source for quite a number of spurious fragments attributed to Philo of Alexandria (Royce, 1991: 26). And, as a final curiosity, it may be noted that the unique illuminated florilegium in the entire corpus of Greek medieval manuscripts is a manuscript containing the *Sacra Parallela*, the cod. *Parisinus graecus* 923 of the tenth century. In its 394 surviving folios are contained some 1658 miniatures, many of which serve as a visual exegesis or plain illumination of the passages of the *Sacra Parallela* that are usually next to them (Evangelatou 2008: 128), or even elaborations on them (Evangelatou 2008: 133, 143ff.) that "...strove to serve the didactic purpose of the florilegium... and emphasize their (i.e. the excerpts') moral message" (Evangelatou 2008: 138 and 150).

The Sacro–profane Florilegia

For this category of florilegia there have been significant scholarly developments since the survey of Richard (1964: 486–499). Not only new editions of the major sacro-profane florilegia have appeared, but some criticism of Richard's work has also developed, especially by P. Odorico. Odorico considers Richard's approach limited. Richard defined as sacro-profane florilegia the *Loci communes* attributed to Maximus the Confessor and its descendants (another nine florilegia). Accordingly, he categorized as sacro-profane the florilegia that in their Christian segment relied heavily on the *Sacra Parallela*, whereas for their pagan–secular section they borrowed mainly from Stobaeus' *Anthologion* and poets who wrote gnomic verses, such as Menander, Moschion, Philistion, Theognis, the seven sages, and the profane collections of *apophthegmata* (Richard 1964: 487). This classification is predominantly based on the way the excerpts are arranged in these particular florilegia (i.e., in chapters), which is more or less an elaboration–expansion of the structure of the *Sacra Parallela*. For example, in chapter 56 of the *Loci communes* of Ps.-Maximus bearing the title "On Self-Knowledge," the citations begin with excerpts from the New and the Old Testaments, then follow the early Fathers (Basil, Gregory of Nazianzus, Didymus the Blind, John Chrysostom, and Clement of Alexandria) and they conclude with the pagan authors (Antiphanes, Demosthenes, Heraclitus, Socrates, Philemon, Thales, Menander, Xenophon, and Chilon). However, as Odorico notes, division in chapters is not the only format under which sacro-profane florilegia may be encountered: some compilers may prefer the purely alphabetical arrangement of the citations (using the first letter of the first sentence of each citation) and avoid clustering the citations under chapters or subject titles (as is the case of John Georgidas' *Gnomologium*); others arrange their material in the form of *Questions and*

Answers, others in mixed forms (Odorico 1986: 4–5). Another topic in which Odorico found fault with Richard is the idea of the French scholar that florilegia, and especially sacro-profane ones, were used exclusively by an audience that was "searching only the solace of faith and the necessary advice for advancement on the road to virtue," whereas for Odorico a *gnomologion* could mix "sacred and mundane/secular wisdom for no purely spiritual purposes" (Odorico 2004: 64). The work of Odorico, combined with recent research by many young scholars, has enormously enriched our knowledge about sacro-profane florilegia, and the widening of the criteria for the classification of them has resulted in a dramatic increase in their number. Consequently, it is impossible to even mention all extant florilegia of this category here, which are many more than the ones described by Richard. Searby lists 25 such florilegia as sources to the *Corpus Parisinum* he edits, and another 11 as occasionally related to it (Searby 2007: 22–46). This list includes a number of *gnomologia*/collections of sayings (see also the extensive list in Gerlach (2008: XXIII–XXIX)). So Richard's basic outline of the sacro-profane florilegia has been further developed by Odorico and Gerlach, who recognize in the florilegium conventionally called *Corpus Parisinum* the intermediary between whatever profane collection existed before it and the appearance of the *Loci communes* of Ps.-Maximus and its successors. Therefore, what we have in this section of spiritual florilegia takes the following shape:

A) Up to the seventh/eighth century – Christian collections (e.g., *Sacra Parallela*, other Damascenian(?) florilegia (Odorico 2004: 75)), χρησμοί (oracles), Plutarch's *homoeomata* (similes) Favorinus, Diogenes Laertius, profane *gnomologia* and collections of sayings, Stobaeus' *Anthologion*, *Gnomologium Byzantinum* (=DEI, sayings by *Democritus, Epictetus, Isocrates*), *ΑΠΜ* (=*Florilegium* ἄριστον καὶ πρῶτον μάθημα), *Apophthegmata Philosophorum*, and so on.

B) Between seventh and ninth centuries – *Corpus Parisinum*.

B₁) Ninth/tenth century – the *Florilegium Marcianum* (=FM) and the *Sententiae a Joanne Georgida monacho collectae* (=JG) (Odorico 2004: 77–81).

C) Ninth/tenth century – Ps.-Maximus, *Loci communes*.

D) Post-tenth century – Ps.-Maximus' descendants: Ps.-Antonius, *Flor. Baroccianum, Flor. Laurentianum, Flor. Rossianum, Gnomica Basileensia*, and so on (Gerlach 2008: 207–208; Odorico 2004: 77).

The most significant or, at least, the better known among them are the following:

1. The *Anthologion* of Ioannes Stobaeus. Since it is the major source of the profane section of sacro-profane florilegia its inclusion in this list is self-evident. The *Anthologion* is the largest collection of excerpts from secular–pagan authors of classical and late Antiquity that has come down to us. It is the work of a certain Ioannes (John) from Stobi (in Macedonia) who lived in the fifth century CE and made this compilation in order to educate his son Septimius. The work was originally divided into two volumes containing two books each. The two volumes became separated in the manuscript tradition, and the first volume was given the title "the *Extracts*" (Ἐκλογαί) and the second volume became known as the

Anthology (*Florilegium*, Ἀνθολόγιον). Modern editions (among which the one by Wachsmuth and Hense (1884–1912) is considered the most accurate) include both volumes under the title *Anthology* (Ἀνθολόγιον). In some 208 or 206 chapters (which Photius had enumerated in his *Bibliotheca* (cod. 197) but not all of them preserved today) the *Anthology* contains extracts from more than 500 writers, especially poets, historians, orators, and philosophers. The subjects covered a range of topics from philosophy, dialectics, ethics, politics, economics, and maxims of practical wisdom. The work preserves fragments of many authors and works, which otherwise might be unknown today. Among others, Stobaeus has excerpted over 500 passages from Euripides, 150 from Sophocles and over 200 from Menander.

2.   The *Corpus Parisinum*, conventionally named so by nineteenth-century scholars, includes some 565 Christian citations and more than 1100 profane ones. It is transmitted by seven manuscripts, but only two are of major importance; that is, the codex *Parisinus graecus* 1168 of the fourteenth century and the *Oxoniensis Bodleianus Digby* 6 of the first half of the sixteenth century. We do not know when the *Corpus Parisinum* was put together, but the presence of excerpts from John of the Ladder (Ioannes Klimakos, †c. 670) among its contents and the existence of a tenth-century manuscript among the witnesses of Ps.-Maximus give the seventh and ninth centuries as *termini post* and *ante quem* for its compilation (Gerlach 2008: 209). Its contents are arranged as follows:

   A.   "Sacred" section
       1.   Christian *sententiae* belonging to 12 Fathers in non-alphabetical order (St Ignatius, Basil the Great, Gregory of Nazianzus, John Chrysostom, Gregory of Nyssa, Nilus of Ancyra, Evagrius of Pontus, Cyril of Alexandria, Clement of Alexandria, Dionysius Areopagite, Didymus the Blind, John of the Ladder and excerpts from the Old and New Testaments and Philo).
       2.   *Pseudepigrapha* oracles of Christian-hermetic nature.
   B.   "Profane" section
       3.   *Sententiae* and *apophthegmata* under the names of pagan authors (in non-alphabetical order)
       4.   Excerpts from Stobaeus' *Anthologion* (books 3 and 4).
       5.   Abridged version of the *Gnomologium Byzantinum* (DEI).
       6.   Second section with Excerpts from Stobaeus' *Anthologion* (book 4).
       7.   Alphabetic collection of sayings with *sententiae* and *apophthegmata* from *AΠM*.
       8.   *Menandri Monostichi* (one-liners), in alphabetical order. For an extensive analysis of this florilegium, see Gerlach (2008: 207–372).

3.   The *Florilegium Marcianum* (=FM) and the *Sententiae a Joanne Georgida monacho collectae* (=JG).

     The first one is preserved by a *codex unicus*, *Marcianus gr.* 23 of the second half of the tenth century. The second, which incorporates many excerpts from the first one, is transmitted by nine manuscripts that are dispersed between the tenth and sixteenth centuries (Odorico 1986: 37). The *FM* seems to be the archetype of an entire family of *gnomologia*, and is the work of a learned person who makes direct use of primary sources. From this collection has also resulted the florilegium of Georgides (Odorico 2004: 77–78). The *FM* contains some 505 citations, arranged in alphabetical order, a small number of which can also be found in the *Sacra Parallela*, the *Corpus Parisinum*, and the *Anthologion* of Stobaeus; 392 exclusively belong to the *FM*. A sizeable part of the citations comes from Choricius of Gaza, followed in quantity by those of Basil the Great, Gregory of Nazianzus, the Old Testament, John of the Ladder, John Crysostom, but also from Isocrates, Plutarch, and Pythagoras. However (and this is really indicative of the significance of florilegia for the preservation of at least snippets of lost texts), out of the 505 citations of the *FM*, Odorico identified some 365; later reviewers (G. Danezis, E.V. Malteze, and I. Vassis, see Odorico (2004: 79 n. 32)) identified another 69 citations. There still remain unidentified another 71 citations, some of which may even belong to lost works. The nature of *FM* and the way its material has been arranged has led Odorico to suggest that this is a florilegium compiled by someone who was interested in his own benefit in terms of wisdom (with a preference in rhetoric) and it simply happened to be attractive for other users as well (Odorico, 2004: 79). Odorico did suggest as a possible compiler the ninth-century Iconoclast Patriarch John VII the Grammarian (Odorico 1986: 17–25).

The *sententiae* of Georgides (*JG*), although related to the *FM*, represents a different stage in the development of sacro-profane florilegia. It is much more extensive, numbering 1233 citations (222 shared with *FM*). There is also a focus shift in terms of content. Whereas *FM* was oriented towards rhetorical sources, in *JG* the citations from the fabulists Aesop and Babrius are more numerous, and Choricius has been almost abandoned. In the religious section preponderance is given to ascetic Fathers such as John of the Ladder (*JG* more than 50 citations, *FM* around ten), John the Monk, John the Faster, Evagrius of Pontus (20 to 1), Nilus of Ancyra, Diadochus of Photike (20 to 2), and certainly a few citations from the New Testament, which is entirely absent from *FM*. Other authors included are Philo of Alexandria, Heliodorus (author of the novel *Aethiopica*), and Lucian, next to the numerous citations from Isocrates, Plutarch, Democritus, and Menander. Another issue with *JG* concerns its sources, because here, contrary to *FM*, one cannot be sure as to how many of the citations are taken directly from primary sources and not from pre-existing florilegia. To be sure, *JG* shares some 219 citations with the *Sacra Parallela*, but Odorico doubts that this anthology is always *JG*'s source. Usually, *JG* offers longer citations than their corresponding ones in the *Sacra Parallela*. The *Corpus Parisinum* and the *Gnomologium Byzantinum* may also have been sources for *JG* (Odorico 2004: 80–81). Since the latest author mentioned in *JG* is Photius (†c. 893) the date proposed for *JG*'s compilation is the beginning of tenth century.

4.   The *Loci communes* attributed to Maximus Confessor but, perhaps, the work of an anonymous compiler, is the next major sacro-profane florilegium containing fragments and sentences by Christian and pagan authors, thematically arranged in 71 chapters. It has been preserved in numerous manuscripts, and

the most recent edition by Sibylle Ihm distinguishes three recensions of the text: (a) a shorter one (MaxI, extant in about 70 manuscripts), (b) a longer one (MaxII in ten manuscripts), and (c) an abridged version of MaxII (=MaxU, in five manuscripts) with a different arrangement of chapters (1–35, 43–71, 36–42). According to Ihm, an original/archetypal compilation of the *Loci communes* (the "Ur-Maximus") could, perhaps, be given the year 650 as a *terminus post quem*, while for MaxI the tenth century seems to be the latest date, MaxII can be placed between the ends of the ninth and tenth centuries, and, finally, MaxU at the end of the tenth century (Ihm 2001: XXII–XXIX). One may gain an idea of the manner in which its contents are arranged by looking at the example in the introductory paragraph of this section. Here, I add the titles of some of its chapters: 1. On Virtuous and Immoral Living; 2. On Prudence; 3. On Purity and Chastity; 8. On Good Deeds and Charity; 9. On Power and Authority; 10. On Accusations and Slander. 19. On Wrath and Temper; 20. On Silence and Secrets; 21. On Over-Anxiety and Calmness; 23. On Filial Piety and Parental Love; 24. On Fear; 25. On Inconstancy and Repentance; 26. On Sin and Confession; 27. On Intemperance and Gluttony. According to Odorico, this is in fact the main florilegium, which, copied, rearranged, abridged or enriched serves as the main gnomological platform until the appearance of printed collections (Odorico 2004: 83). This is a *florilegium florilegiorum* that has more or less borrowed the major part of its preceding collections. Outside the earlier florilegia, the additions of the compiler himself are quite a few, usually from major church Fathers (Gregory of Nazianzus, John Chrysostom, Basil the Great), but also from secular/non-Christian authors such as Libanius, Dion Chrysostom, Menander, and Philo. Whatever innovations are to be spotted in it are lacking in originality (Odorico 2004: 87).

After the *Loci communes* the sacro-profane florilegia enter a phase of unchecked proliferation, in which the rearranging and putting together of sections from the *Sacra Parallela*, the *Loci communes* of Ps.-Maximus, Stobaeus' *Anthologion*, and, perhaps, *FM* and *JG* becomes common practice. MaxU was the main source of the later *Gnomica Basileensia* and the *Florilegium Rossianum*, while MaxII was one of the sources of the *Florilegium Laurentianum*, Ps.-Antonius' *Melissa* (*PG* 136, 765–1244), and the massive *Florilegium Baroccianum* or *Melissa Augustana* or *Flor. Monacense* or (after the edition by Sargologos (1990)), *Flor. Patmiacum*, which contains 3181 citations arranged in 56 chapters.

On the other hand, florilegia not depending on the *Loci communes* are the following ones:

1. The *Florilegium Atheniense*, preserved in cod. *Atheniensis BN* 1070 (fourteenth century fol. 84v–158v).
2. The *Florilegium Mosquense*, witnessed by three manuscripts one of which is *Mosqu. Bibl. Lenin. gr.* 126 (twelfth century fol. 99–107v).
3. The *Florilegium Rossianum*, in cod. *Vat. Rossi* 736 (*gr.* 10) of the eleventh century (Richard 1964: 496–498).

The Monastic Florilegia

Christian monasticism has never been alien to the practice of collecting excerpts from religious writings, starting with some late fourth- to early fifth-century collections of monastic pronouncements and short stories that, under the title *apophthegmata patrum* ("sayings of the fathers") or *historiae animae utiles* ("edifying stories"), practically, belong to the genre of hagiography. Next to them, one might mention the *Pandectes* of Antiochus Strategius, a monk of Mar Sabas (beginning of seventh century), which incorporated in a set of 130 chapters of continuous narrative (a format that, according to Richard (1964: 499), disqualifies *Pandectes* as a florilegium) excerpts from the Bible, the apocrypha, and patristic writings. However, with the exception of the *Questions and Answers* of Anastasius of Sinai, which date towards the end of the seventh century, monastic florilegia proper appear in the eleventh century and later, perhaps, according to A. Rigo, as a reaction to the personal spiritual experience of Symeon the New Theologian (Roelli 2011: 289). They were compiled by monks with a view to moral and ascetic education of their monastic audience (Richard 1964: 499), and they place great emphasis on major aspects of the traditional monastic practice; that is, the liturgical cycle, fasting, and prayer (Roelli 2011: 289–290). The number of extant manuscripts testifies to the wide circulation of very few among them; that is, the following eight:

1. The *Questions and Answers* of Anastasius of Sinai. A compilation of a number of questions on various spiritual and monastic issues (e.g., question 2: "How does a man know that Christ dwelled in him?") the answers to which are usually supported by the citation of short excerpts from the Bible and a number of early Fathers, such as Athanasius of Alexandria, Augustine, Basil of Caesarea, Eusebius, John Chrysostom. No manuscript preserves the original number of the *Questions and Answers*, and the work has come down to us in the form of four partial or augmented collections (Richard and Munitiz, 2006: xviii–xxviii).

2. Paul Evergetinos (†1054), soon after founding the Monastery of Evergetis in Constantinople, compiled a spiritual florilegium for the instruction of his monks. He called it *Synagoge*, but it is generally known as *Evergetinon*. Its influence is evidenced by the 80 or more manuscripts that preserve it. The manuscripts date from the eleventh to the eighteenth centuries, when it was first printed. The *Evergetinon* included a great deal of hagiographic excerpts from the *Menologion* of Symeon Metaphrastes, the *Lausaicon*, the *Pandectes* of Antiochus, the *Dialogues* of Gregory the Great, and a number of monastic authors, Barsanuphius, Diadochus of Photike, Ephraim the Syrian, Maximus the Confessor, and others. Citations are arranged under chapter headings, such as "On death and the future life," and its popularity is still high even today with the existence of at least one major translation into English (Archbishop Chrysostomos *et al.* 2008). Evergetinos died in 1054, but his monastic community continued to thrive.

3. The *Pandectes* of Nicon of the Black Mountain (†c. 1088): a florilegium in 63 chapters, in which are anthologized works of Athanasius of Alexandria, Basil the Great, Barsanuphius, John Chrysostom, John of the Ladder, Ephraim the Syrian, Gregory the Dialogue. It is supplemented by an extensive collection

of canonical and legal texts. As Nicon himself explained in a letter to George, founder and abbot of the Monastery of Koutsovendis in Cyprus, this anthology has nothing to do with dogma and faith as it is exclusively dedicated to the monastic *praxis* (Papacostas *et al.* 2000: 149–156). The *Pandectes* is preserved in at least 32 manuscripts (Richard 1964: 504).

4. The *Florilegium* of John IV Oxeites, patriarch of Antioch (1089–1100) and friend of Nicon. After his retirement to the Monastery of Oxeia on one of the Prince's Islands, John composed two florilegia, the first on the Holy Eucharist and the second under the title *Eclogae asceticae*, which is divided in three chapters, the first on the last judgment, the second on prayer, and the third on the Eucharist. His sources vary: from Abba Ammonas and Ps.-Athanasius to Michael Psellus, Theodorete of Cyrus, and from the *Apostolic constitutions* to Theodore of Stoudios. It is preserved in more than ten manuscripts (Richard 1964: 504–505).

5. The *Florilegium patristicum* in 14 titles, which includes excerpts mostly from John Chrysostom, Basil the Great, Gregory of Nyssa, Gregory of Nazianzus, and many others. At a time when the compilers of florilegia took recourse to using earlier collections, this florilegium copies the fragments directly from the primary sources. This anthology is also witnessed by, at least, 11 manuscripts.

6. The *Florilegia* of Mark the Hieromonch (both contained in codex *Vaticanus Chigi gr.* 27), compiled before 1267, for the spiritual benefit and education of Eulogia, sister of Michael VIII Palaeologus, who became a nun. The first florilegium is an alphabetically ordered work comprising patristic texts on various topics of Christian life. There is a strong possibility that this is the source of the next *Florilegium* (*patristicum* in alphabetical order) (Roelli 2011: 292). The second bears the title "Ascetic treatise for those who renounce the world, men or women, and wish to please God in stillness (*hesychia*)." Mark's sources for this florilegium are other earlier florilegia, such as the *Sacra Parallela* of John of Damascus and the *Loci communes* of Ps.-Maximus.

7. The *Florilegium patristicum* arranged in alphabetical order (extant in three fourteenth-century manuscripts).

8. The *Λειμών* (Meadow) of Nicodemus Rhakendytes, preserved only by a London manuscript (Richard 1964: 505–508).

In the course of the fourteenth century, Hesychasm, as expounded by Gregory Palamas, gave new thrust to the production of monastic florilegia. In the first place, this kind of collections revealed the continuity of the *hesychastic* tradition, tracing it back to authors of monastic spirituality such as Diadochus of Photike, Evagrius of Pontus, and Maximus the Confessor. This is witnessed among many other florilegia, by the Palamite florilegium compiled around the end of fourteenth century and preserved in codex *Atheniensis, Bibl. Nation. gr.* 2583. In fols. 177v–385v, this manuscript contains a monastic florilegium, including excerpts from works of Barsanuphius, John of Damascus, Ephraim the Syrian, Gregory of Nyssa, Gregory of Nazianzus, Maximus the Confessor, and others, next to some anonymous fragments, even from authors of the fourteenth century (description of contents, Van Deun 1987: 140–142).

Second, hesychastic florilegia also carried this tradition over into the post-Byzantine Orthodox world with the enormous success with which the monastic florilegium called the *Philokalia* met since its first publication in Venice in 1782 by Nikodemos and Makarios. In putting together this enormous collection (which in its modern Greek translation counts five volumes, in its English translation four, with the fifth not published yet) the two monks of Mt. Athos (and Saints of the Orthodox Church) used earlier collections. A major source included in the fourth volume of the *Philokalia* (also in PG 147, 638–812) is the *Method and Rule* of the brothers Callistus and Ignatius Xanthopoulos compiled between 1380 and 1395. It was divided in 100 chapters, and the text after the subject title of each chapter was supplemented with supportive citations from the Bible and earlier patristic authorities (Isaac the Syrian, John of the Ladder, John Chrysostom, John of Damascus, etc.). They also included citations from smaller florilegia Gregory Palamas had inserted in his own writings (Rigo 2011: 390–396) and also more recent hesychastic authors such as Nicephorus the Athonite, Gregory of Sinai, and Gregory Palamas himself (Rigo 2011: 397, and for a list of authorities Rigo 2011: 422–429).

Dogmatic Florilegia

The Early Period (Third–Tenth Centuries)

Dogmatic florilegia owe their appearance to dogmatic confrontation. Possibly, the first to introduce this literary genre was Basil the Great in chapter 29 of his *De Spiritu Sanctu* (written in 375, PG 32, 200B–209C; Grillmeier 1986: 52). In order to make clear his ideas on the position of the Holy Spirit within the Trinity, he collected a number of passages from very early Fathers and authors. The list included Dionysius of Alexandria, Clement of Rome, Origen, Julius Sextus Africanus (!), Gregory of Neocaesarea, Firmilianus (of Caesarea, †268), and Meletius of Antioch. Despite some initial objections to this practice (for which see Alexakis (1996: 3 and note 8 for further bibliography)) and as a number of controversies erupted within the early Church, dogmatic florilegia were compiled and used in order to support both heretical and what, usually after a Church Council, became accepted as orthodox Christian dogmatic formulations and beliefs. Owing to this particular dimension of the function of a dogmatic florilegium, their compilation was subject to some stricter rules, which guaranteed their impeccable authority. The following seem to be the most significant ones: (a) acknowledged good standing with orthodoxy of the authors that were anthologized, (b) textual accuracy, and (c) form of presentation that excluded manipulation or even falsification of the text itself (Alexakis 1996: 3–4; Alexakis 2011: 53–54). In this respect, the value of early dogmatic florilegia as trustworthy witnesses to the text of numerous early patristic writings cannot be neglected.

Christological Florilegia

Within the context of the early controversies, which focused on the person of Christ, the florilegia of the period between the fourth and the seventh centuries are predominantly Christological. The long line of these anthologies begins with the florilegia related to the Nestorian controversy and the Council of Ephesus (431). Cyril of Alexandria first, in his *Libri V contra Nestorium* (*ACO* I, 1, 6, 13–106) after anthologizing works and sermons of Nestorius, embarks on an enormous collection of biblical citations against the heresies of the latter. Cyril's example is followed by Theodotus of Ancyra in his *Three books against Nestorius* preserved in Syriac. Then Cyril also included another anti-Nestorian florilegium in his *Oratio ad Arcadiam et Marinam augustas de fide* (*ACO* I, 1, 5, 65–68; Grillmeier 1986: 52–53). Much more significant were the two florilegia presented in the course of the Third Ecumenical Council and used for the condemnation of Nestorius (*ACO* I, 1, 2, 39–45 and *ACO* I, 1, 7, 89–95). The Fathers anthologized in them were few (Gregory of Nyssa and Basil the Great among them), but there were two Apollinarian forgeries among the excerpts (Alexakis 1996: 6–7). Also related to the Nestorian controversy were the later florilegia of Theodoret of Cyrus in his *Pentalogus* (432 AD) and in the *Eranistes* (447/8). This florilegium was presented to the participants of the Fourth Ecumenical Council (Chalcedon, 451) in support of Pope Leo's orthodoxy (*ACO* II, 1, 3, 114–116). After Chalcedon, Pope Leo himself appended a florilegium to his official letter to the Council of Chalcedon (*Tomus*, *ACO* II, 1, 1, 20–25) which was later augmented in his letter 165 to Emperor Leo I (*ACO* II, 4, 119–131, in Latin). The *florilegium Cyrillianum*, a collection compiled in Alexandria, that contains 244 excerpts from 30 works of Cyril of Alexandria originates from the same period. Its purpose was to lend support to the idea that Cyril agreed with the statement "two natures after the union" (in Christ).

The Christological florilegia of the period up to the year 500 consist of either collections of excerpts from a limited number of authors, among which the authority of Gregory of Nazianzus, Gregory of Nyssa, Basil the Great, John Chrysostom, and Cyril of Alexandria gradually increases, or anthologies in which one author is excerpted (Cyril, Nestorius, even Augustine). The citations are still taken from manuscripts containing the original works of the early Fathers, but inclusion of forged or spurious texts is not uncommon (Speyer 1971: 269–276).

From the year 600 onwards the so-called Neo-Chalcedonian florilegia, which are meant to defend the dogmatic resolutions of Chalcedon, become more widespread and in many cases take the form of anonymous patristic collections based on pre-existing florilegia. The term that appropriately describes these florilegia is diphysite or dyophysite florilegia and lay emphasis on fragments that support the two natures in the person of Christ. The most notable compilers of such florilegia were Nephalius of Alexandria (in his *Apologia* against the *Orationes ad Nephalium* of the Miaphysite Severus of Antioch), John of Caesarea (in his *Apologia Concilii Chalcedonensis* and in his *Adversus Aphthartodocetas*), and Eulogius (Melkite Patriarch of Alexandria 580–608). To these must be added Leontius of Jerusalem, whose *Testimonia sanctorum* (*Testimonies of the Saints*) constitute an extensive florilegium with citations arranged under headings such as "What is Christ, whom we are to adore?" or "What kind of union do the Fathers say the union in Christ is?" (Gray 2006: 46–160). The florilegium was compiled in the period 536–538 in an effort to alienate Severus' followers from him (Gray 2006: 40 and 23–25). However, most influential among the compilers of this period is Leontius of Byzantium (c. 485–543?). Dogmatic florilegia have been incorporated in his three works *Contra Nestorianos et Eutychianos*, *Contra Aphthartodocetas*, and *Deprehensio et Triumphus super Nestorianos*, whereas he is also credited with the compilation of an enormous florilegium from works of Apollinarius (*Adversus fraudes Apollinaristarum*). Borrowings from his florilegia can be found in Nephalius, John of Caesarea, and Leontius of Jerusalem, but also in Emperor Justinian's dogmatic works. Leontius has also influenced the patristic documentation of dogmatic arguments in works such as the anonymous *De Sectis* and the *Viae Dux* of Anastasius of Sinai (Grillmeier 1986: 57–61). In all these anthologies the authors excerpted are expectedly few: Athanasius of Alexandria, Gregory of Nazianzus, Gregory of Nyssa, Basil the Great, Cyril of Alexandria, and John Chrysostom. Rarely appear other names, such as Diadochus of Photike or Ps.-Dionysius Areopagite.

Emperor Justinian I (527–565) also compiled florilegia. The following works of his have incorporated florilegia containing citations of rather good textual quality:

1. *Edictum contra Origenem* (text *ACO* III, 189–214, florilegium 197–207 and 208–213 citations from Origen's *Peri Archon*).
2. *Contra Monophysitas* contains a rich florilegium with numerous citations from Cyril of Alexandria, Athanasius, and other early Fathers, followed by two sets of citations from proclaimed heretics such as Paul of Samosata and Nestorius and then Apollinarius, Polemon, Severus of Antioch, Dioscorus of Alexandria, and Timothy Aelurus. Next to them another orthodox florilegium follows with excerpts from Ps.-Athanasius, Gregory of Nyssa, Cyril, and Ambrose of Milan. This is finally complemented with another florilegium of Christological concepts (*physis, ousia, morphe, hypostasis, prosopon*) the first of its kind, with citations from Ps.-Athanasius, John Chrysostom, Basil the Great, Cyril, and both Gregories. The last florilegium in this work displays texts validating the *Trishagion*. In this last florilegium (and to some extent in most of his other florilegia) Justinian sets the example of a hierarchical appeal to textual authority in the following order: Scriptural proof, Church dogmas, traditions of the Fathers, the four Councils, followed by the teaching of the heretics as material for refutation (Grillmeier 1986: 61–62).
3. *Epistula contra tria capitula.*
4. *Rectae fidei confessio* (for the edition of the last three texts see Schwartz (1939: 7–43, 47–69, 72–111 respectively)).

Justinian's hand can also be discerned in the preparation and in the proceedings of the Fifth Ecumenical Council (Constantinople 553); that is: (a) a florilegium containing 71 excerpts from works of Theodore of Mopsuestia, (b) a second one citing 28 quotations mostly from Cyril of Alexandria and to a lesser extent from Gregory of Nyssa and Theodoret of Cyrus, presented in contrast to the first one, and (c) finally, a third collection that offered patristic justification to the possibility of a *post mortem* anathematization of heretics. All these florilegia were well prepared in advance and marked the opening and concluding points of most subjects that filled the agenda of the sessions of this Council (Alexakis 1996: 10–16).

Parallel to the aforementioned florilegia, the same period witnessed the appearance of a number of Miaphysite florilegia compiled mainly by theologians of the eastern part of the empire. In brief, the most significant are the following.

1. The florilegia of Timothy Aelurus (Patriarch of Alexandria 457–460, 475–477):
2. The florilegia against Chalcedon (still extant in Armenian and Syriac).
3. Letters of Timothy with a florilegium against Eutyches.
4. The *Florilegium Edessenum anonymum*, notable for the presence of pre-Nicene Fathers in it (Clement of Rome, Hippolytus, Melito of Sardis, Serapion of Thmuis, etc.).
5. A double anti-Chalcedonian florilegium in codex *Vaticanus gr.* 1431.
6. Two florilegia of Bishop Philoxenus of Mabbog.
7. The patristic florilegia of Severus of Antioch:
8. The florilegia in his *Philalethes*, which reinterpret the citations of the *Florilegium Cyrillianum*.
9. The florilegia in the *Liber contra impium Grammaticum*, which led to the marginalization of other Miaphysite florilegia.
10. *Orationes ad Nephalium eiusdem ac Sergii Grammatici epistulae mutuae*. Both (ii) and (iii) have included the Apollinarian forgeries.
11. The patristic citations in the anti-Julianist works of Severus. Cyril of Alexandria and pre-Nicene Fathers again take the lion's share among the authorities cited.
12. Other *florlilegia* compiled by Severus against the Julianists.
13. Florilegia against the Themistians (Agnoetes).
14. Florilegia related to the Tritheist controversy (mentioned because John Philoponus was also involved in it) (Grillmeier 1986: 63–70).

I might conclude by simply pointing out the existence of a number of Miaphysite florilegia of lesser importance in Coptic, Armenian, Arabic, and Syriac languages (Grillmeier 1986: 70–71) and a number of east Syrian florilegia compiled by post-Chalcedonian Nestorians/Church of the East (Grillmeier 1986: 71–73).

The next controversy about the energies and wills of Christ led to the compilation of some florilegia in defense of "one energy" and "one will," but very little has survived. Lost are also the massive florilegium of Sophronius of Jerusalem and the extensive anthology Maximus the Confessor sent to Stephen of Dora, both in defense of the two energies in Christ. Well preserved are the florilegia of the Lateran Council of 649 and of the Sixth Ecumenical Council (Constantinople III 680/1). In 649 Maximus the Confessor and his disciples drafted the *acts* of a Council in Greek and then translated them into Latin for the Roman bishops to sign (Alexakis 1996: 19, citing earlier bibliography by R. Riedinger). Although the Lateran Council is just a text, its authority has never been contested and the use of florilegia is quite extensive in the course of its purported deliberations. In the third session, a Miathelite florilegium of 11 quotations from the works of Theodore of Pharan was first cited refuted by a small florilegium of six excerpts cited by Pope Martin. After the presentation of two more Miathelite citations of Paul of Constantinople the participants of the Council introduced at the end of the fourth session the orthodox florilegium, which was the most extensive among those used in Church Councils. It counted 123 quotations taken from 58 works of 26 authors. To this, a third Miathelite florilegium of 42 excerpts was added and the Council closed (Alexakis 1996: 16–18). In the Sixth Ecumenical Council the Miathelites represented by Macarius of Antioch submitted three codices with Miathelite florilegia, which, upon close scrutiny, were found to contain abridged citations of earlier Fathers. Taken out of context, these citations were seemingly supporting the one will in Christ. Once the public reading of the Miathelite collections placed in their context revealed their Dyothelite character, the participants of the Council presented the Dyothelite florilegium in the tenth session. The collection of fragments in it (48 citations from 29 works of 14 authors) partly overlaps with that of the Lateran Council. Differences are more pronounced between the Lateran and the Constantinopolitan heretical florilegia: that of Constantinople is much richer (Alexakis 1996: 27–29). Finally, it is worth noting that the orthodox florilegium was brought to Constantinople by the papal delegates, whatever this might mean concerning the availability of patristic books in Rome during the seventh century.

Other Dogmatic Florilegia
A Seventh-Century Florilegium on the Procession of the Holy Spirit
It seems that in the margin of the Christological disputes between Miathelites and Dyothelites the issue of the procession of the Holy Spirit cropped up as an accusation of the Constantinopolitan Miathelites against Pope Theodore (642–649). This is known from the *Epistula ad Marinum Cypri presbyterum* of Maximus the Confessor (PG 91, 133–136, dated to 645). According to this letter, the miathelite Constantinopolitans accused Pope Theodore of inserting the *Filioque* (that is, the expression meaning that the Holy Spirit proceeds from the Father *and* the Son) in his (lost today) Synodal Letter. The Pope and his *curia*, in order to defend themselves against this accusation, put together a florilegium of Latin and Greek patristic authorities (Cyril of Alexandria is explicitly mentioned) that justified the insertion of the *Filioque* (in the Creed?). The Romans, however, made clear that this insertion did not mean to establish a second cause of the Holy Spirit (i.e., the Son), but simply to demonstrate that the Holy Spirit proceeds *through* the Son and that it is *homoousion* with the Father and the Son (Alexakis 2001: 545–547). It so happens that this letter of Maximus the Confessor is preserved, among many manuscripts, by codex *Parisinus graecus* 1115 (of the year 1276, fols. 185v–187) and it is in the beginning of a large florilegium dedicated to the issue of the procession of the Holy Spirit. The florilegium covers fols. 180v–219v of the manuscript and contains some 167 excerpts from 70 works of at least 16 authors; that is, Epiphanius of Salamis, Cyril of Alexandria, Basil the Great, Gregory of Nyssa, Gregory of Nazianzus, Ps.-Dionysius Areopagite, Damasus of Rome, Clement of Rome, snippets from the Acts of Ecumenical Councils, and so on. The presence of a number of textual alterations favoring the *Filioque* or passages that allude to the procession through the Son (that include even a Pseudo-pseudo-Dionysian forgery) leaves no doubt as to the dogmatic character of this collection. It will suffice to say that it was also used a few centuries later in the course of the negotiations between Michael VIII and a papal delegate called Nicholas of Cotrone (Croton) that led to the Council of Lyons (1274) (Alexakis 1996: 75–85 and 283–307 list of excerpts).

The Doctrina Patrum

According to the new editors, the *Doctrina Patrum* is in all probability the work of Anastasius Apocrisiarius, a pupil of Maximus the Confessor, compiled towards the end of the seventh century. In the original edition by Diekamp it contained 977 citations, of which 143 are biblical, 751 patristic, or synodal, and 83 belong to heretic authors. Many of them are also found in works of Maximus and in the Acts of the Lateran and of the Sixth Ecumenical Council. The first 30 chapters inveigh against Miaphysite and Miathelite dogmas, while chapters 31–44 deal with various peripheral issues (chapter 31, for example, is a collection of biblical citations against the Jews). Chapter 45 must be a later addition related to the outbreak of Iconoclasm after 726 (for a thorough analysis of the Christological chapters, see Pelikan (1974: 76–90)).

Other Florilegia of John of Damascus

Apart from the *Sacra Parallela*, John of Damascus compiled a number of florilegia, which bear witness to his great acuity as a compiler and an assessor of what is worth preserving. These are:

1. The florilegium in his *Expositio fidei*, counting more than 600 citations on the Trinity, Christology, the wills and energies in Christ, anthropology, the name of God and the Angels. Authors cited: Ps.-Cyril, Gregory of Nazianzus, Cyril of Alexandria, Maximus Confessor, Nemesius of Emesa, John Chrysostom and Ps.-Dionysius Areopagite (Kotter 1973).
2. The citations inserted in his *Epistola de Hymno Trisagio* (Kotter 1981: 304–332).
3. The florilegium in *Contra Jacobitas*. Most of its 34 citations are also found in the *Doctrina Patrum* (Kotter 1981: 102–103).

Florilegia Related to Iconoclasm (726–842)

Following the pattern established by previous theological confrontations within the Church, once Iconoclasm was proclaimed as the official version of Christian faith by Leo III, a number of florilegia substantiating the theological legitimacy of creation and veneration of images were put into circulation. In terms of content, most of the citations included in these florilegia do not contain any complicated theological arguments or statements. The excerptors were looking in the works of earlier Fathers for simple affirmations of the presence and use of images and sometimes for positive statements about them. Ps.-Dionysius is the most profound author in the subject of the theology of the images, but, although he is included in both Iconoclastic and Iconophile florilegia, his acceptance by the Iconophile Seventh Ecumenical Council (Nicaea II, 787) was not very enthusiastic.

1. The earliest among the Iconophile collections can possibly be chapter 45 of the *Doctrina Patrum*, which contains 18 excerpts from Cyril of Alexandria, Basil the Great, Gregory of Nyssa, Gregory of Nazianzus, John Chrysostom, and Ps.-Dionysius Areopagite (*Doctrina Patrum*, Diekamp 1981: 326–330). This chapter should date before 731 (see immediately below).

2. The outbreak of Iconoclasm was one of the reasons for a Roman Synod that convened in 731 in Rome and condemned this heresy. It also made use of a florilegium with excerpts supporting image veneration, which was reused in another Roman Synod of 769, which again condemned Iconoclasm. A number of citations (in Latin) from this florilegium are preserved or at least alluded to in a letter of the year 793 of Pope Hadrian to Charlemagne, called *Hadrianum*. It is possible that the Latin translation was based on the Greek text provided by the *Doctrina Patrum* and the Iconophile florilegium preserved by codex *Paris. gr.* 1115 (Alexakis 1996: 116–118).

3. The Iconophile florilegia of John of Damascus. The date of the composition of the three Iconophile sermons of John of Damascus, each one of which concluded with a lengthy florilegium, can be placed around the year 731, although the third sermon might be dated later. The florilegia appended to the first two sermons share most of the citations with the exception of seven added by John of Damascus to the second one. Almost every excerpt is followed by a comment (sometimes longer than the citation itself) penned by John of Damascus. The arrangement of the authors in the first florilegium is really interesting because first are anthologized the ones whom John of Damascus considered most authoritative: Ps.-Dionysius Areopagite (unless chronological order is also at play here), Basil the Great, Gregory of Nyssa, and John Chrysostom, and next to them the lesser ones Leontius of Neapolis, Severian of Gabala, and hagiographers. The florilegia count 23 citations in the first, 30 in the second, and almost 100 in the third. At least 20 are common to all three. There is also the possibility that John of Damascus used not only original patristic texts but also chapter 45 of the *Doctrina Patrum* (Alexakis 1996: 125–134).

4. The Iconoclastic florilegia (a) of the *Peuseis* (*enquiries*) of Constantine V (before 754), (b) of the Synod of Hiereia (754), and (c) of the Synod St. Sophia (815). The first one has been partly lost and the exact number of the excerpts included in it is not known; we know of two of its citations presented in the course of the Hiereia Synod and the names of the Fathers anthologized in it. The Patriarch Nicephorus has cited and refuted some of its citations in his works (see 7 (ii) and (iii) in this list). The second only survives because it was included in the Acts of the Seventh Ecumenical Council (sixth session) in order to be refuted. It is a small collection of eight fragments, and the authenticity of two of them has been seriously contested on many occasions (Epiphanius of Salamis, *Testamentum ad cives*, and a fragment assigned to Theodotus of Ancyra with no title). The Iconoclasts of the Synod of Hiereia were also accused of presenting the citations of a second florilegium written on loose sheets of paper (πιττάκια). The story for the compilation of the third florilegium is well known from a contemporary source according to which in the year 814 Emperor Leo V appointed a committee of six headed by John the Grammarian in order to compile an Iconoclastic florilegium. The committee was given quarters in the imperial palace and authority to examine books everywhere. They eventually discovered the dogmatic resolution (*horos*) of Hiereia and borrowed five of its citations for their own. The St. Sophia

florilegium was also enriched with the addition of another 11 quotations, but many of them were of dubious attribution. The work of this committee and the powers it was given by Emperor Leo V has opened the door to wild speculation on the part of some scholars, who have suggested that the search for Iconoclastic citations led to the rediscovery of classical Greek texts (Alexakis 2011: 48 and n. 14).

5. The florilegium of the anonymous author of the *Adversus Iconoclastas* (770 or 774/5). This is the most extensive collection of Iconophile excerpts, and codices *Parisinus gr.* 1115 (fols. 235v–283v), *Venetus Marcianus gr.* 573 (fols. 2–26), and *Mosquensis Hist. Mus.* 265 (fols. 142–241) preserve partly overlapping segments of it. All three manuscripts provide a total of 173 fragments from the authors that are usually represented in other collections. There is no doubt that the compiler of the year 770 used all the florilegia that were available by that time (items 1–3 in this list) and the original of *Parisinus graecus* did include at least the second sermon in defense of the holy icons of John of Damascus and not only his florilegia (Alexakis 1996: 101 and 135, but especially 113). It seems also that the Paris manuscript included as later interpolations a number of citations (most of them short) used by the Seventh Ecumenical Council in 787. Owing to the presence of these later excerpts, the modern editor of the Acts of the Seventh Ecumenical Council (Erich Lamberz) and part of the relevant bibliography consider this florilegium a collection made after 787 (*ACO, Series Secunda*, III.1, xxviii–xxx).

6. The patristic citations of the Seventh Ecumenical Council (787). Owing to the fraudulent practices of the Iconoclasts during the proceedings of the Iconoclast Council of Hiereia (754, see item 4 in this list) the participants in the Seventh Ecumenical Council took particular care to present patristic testimony in the form of books (codices) and not from florilegia. However, the 51 citations presented in the course of the fourth and fifth sessions of this Council are textually very close to what has already been included in the earlier Iconophile florilegia (for detailed study and evaluation, see Erich Lamberz in *ACO, Series Secunda*, III. 2, xv–xxiv and a concordance of all citations from all florilegia in Alexakis (1996: 352–359)).

7. With the temporary lull of Iconoclasm (787–815) dogmatic controversy seemed to have ebbed for a while. Still, the rekindling of this heresy and the renewed dogmatic credence Iconoclasts placed on the St. Sophia florilegium were the reasons behind the creation of the most sophisticated Iconophile theological treatises, which incorporated florilegia. The treatises in question were penned by the Patriarch Nicephorus I of Constantinople and are the following ones:

    i) The *Apologeticus pro sacris imaginibus* (*PG* 100, 533–832), which concludes with a florilegium (*PG* 100, 812–829) from the Bible and some 15 citations from John Chrysostom, Cyril of Alexandria, Basil the Great, Gregory of Nazianzus and of Nyssa, and Ps.-Dionysius. The subject is faith, which constitutes a prerequisite for the acceptance of image veneration. For this reason, none of the quotations in it are to be found in any of the Iconophile florilegia.

ii)   The *Antirrheticus III* is also supplemented with a *florilegium* of 75 quotations on Christ's incarnation, double nature and resurrection in response
to the Iconoclastic question about the scriptural basis for the painting and
veneration of the images of Christ (edition, Pitra 1852: 336–370).

iii) The work entitled by P. Alexander *Contra Eusebium et Epiphanidem* is a
lengthy refutation of Iconoclastic citations contained in the florilegium of
the *Peuseis* of Constantine V and other Iconoclastic anthologies. Particular
emphasis was placed on purportedly iconophobic quotations from
Epiphanius of Salamis (Alexander 1958: 173–178).

iv)   The most significant and the lengthiest of Nicephorus' polemic works is
known by the title *Refutatio et eversio*, and is directed against the dogmatic
resolution (*Horos*) of the Iconoclast Synod of St. Sophia (815). Written
shortly after 820, in its first part it refutes the *Horos* of 815 and in the second criticizes its Iconoclast florilegium. In doing this, Nicephorus either
cites lengthier portions of the purportedly Iconoclastic citations showing,
thus, their genuine tenor (i.e., non-iconophobic), or contests their authenticity, or, finally, juxtaposes to them a number of excerpts from the same
author or from other authors that contradict them. Nicephorus' sources
are the Acts of the Seventh Ecumenical Council (in a very good manuscript), perhaps the florilegium of 770 and even the original works usually
in manuscripts of good textual quality (Featherstone 1998: XXI–XXIII,
3–347; see, however, the reservations of Lamberz in *ACO* III, 2, VIII n. 5; for
a lengthy summary of the treatise see Alexander (1958: 242–262)).

8.   The Iconophile florilegium of Nicetas of Medikion is a very limited Iconophile
anthology composed before 824 for the dogmatic education of the monks of the
monastery of Medikion and preserved in only one manuscript (codex *Vaticanus
gr.* 511) (Alexakis 2011: 48–50). In the manuscript this florilegium is followed
by a short treatise on the obligation of the orthodox not to hold communion
with heretics, which also concludes with a florilegium of excerpts from the
Constitutiones Apostolicae, Leontius of Neapolis, and Ignatius of Antioch.

9.   In the same period, Theodore of Stoudios had access to many Iconophile citations, and a number of his letters have included small florilegia of Iconophile
excerpts; see, for example, his letter 380 to Naukratios (Fatouros 1991: vol. 2,
511–519, especially 518). He follows the same method of documentation of
his Iconophile theses in his *Antirretici I–II* (PG 99, 327–388) citing first biblical passages, followed by the more common patristic excerpts cited by the
Seventh Ecumenical Council and extant in earlier florilegia. The same also
holds true for his other works in defense of the veneration of images (for a list
of authors cited by Theodore, Nicephorus, and John of Damascus, see also
Parry (1996: 153–154)).

With the florilegia of the Second Iconoclasm the early period of dogmatic anthologies comes to its end towards the middle of the ninth century. For some scholars, part
of this period is considered the "golden age of *florilegia*" (Kolbaba 2008: 22). The
remainder of this century and the entire tenth century are "...remarkable for [their]

lack of ethical–philosophical, ascetical, dogmatic, and exegetical anthologies..."
(Magdalino 2011: 143–144). In view of what has already been presented in this entry,
Magdalino's statement proves a little inaccurate, but at least with regard to dogmatic
florilegia he seems to be right. Even Photius, who picked up the issue of the procession
of the Holy Spirit in two of his letters (*Letter 2, Encyclical to the Eastern Patriarchs*
and *291, to the Archbishop of Aquileia*) and in his *Mystagogy* (Kolbaba (2008: 76–100),
who submits a number of doubts concerning authorship and integrity of the text),
avoids entirely the format of florilegium. The same practice is observed in the works of
most polemicists from Photius up to the mid eleventh century, such as Nicetas Byzantius,
Bartholomew of Edessa, and Nicetas Stethatus. Their polemical writings against Latins,
Armenians, and Islam incorporate brief citations from the Bible, and this is all.

The Last Byzantine Centuries (Eleventh–Fifteenth)

In the course of the last four and a half centuries of the Byzantine Empire the first major
domain from which controversy ensued is that of the dogmatic differences between
Rome and Constantinople that led to the Schism (1054). The Byzantines considered as
major errors the use of unleavened bread in the liturgy (performed also by the
Armenians), the addition of the *Filioque* to the Creed, fasting practices, celibacy of
clergy, and so on. A little later (fourteenth century) the second controversial dogmatic
development, Hesychasm, necessitated the compilation not only of monastic florilegia
(as mentioned previously) but also dogmatic ones. The third domain is related to the
various heresies that flourish in that period, including the dualist heresy of the Bogomils.
    Besides these major fields in which the florilegia were again in use, I may mention
in passing a re-emergence of a traditional Iconophile florilegium that was composed
by the Sebastokrator Isaak Comnenus around 1087 in the aftermath of a dispute between the Emperor Alexius I Comnenus, who was forced to finance his wars against
the Normans by confiscating the sacred vessels of the churches (images included),
and ecclesiastics who opposed this policy. The unique manuscript that preserved this
florilegium has been lost, but a list of its contents is preserved and shows that this collection borrows from Iconophile literature of the Second Iconoclasm, especially
excerpts from letters of Theodore the Stoudite and works of Nicephorus I of
Constantinople (Stephanou 1946: 177–199, especially 188–189, where a second
florilegium is also mentioned).

The Dogmatic *Panopliae*
From the eleventh century onwards, a number of authors compiled extensive dogmatic
florilegia against a host of heresies. These florilegia, influenced perhaps by the academic –
encyclopedic spirit of post-ninth century Byzantium, appear to be *partly* dissociated
from direct dogmatic confrontation, although in other parts they are also directly
related to one or another disputed dogmatic issue. The presence of chapters on topics
that arose in the distant past, such as Arianism or Miaphysitism, might be an imprint of
the encyclopedic spirit of the era but also an indication of still extant remnants of
Miaphysites within the Empire. Another explanation could possibly be traced to the

insisting tendency of the Byzantines to see the root of new-fangled heresies in earlier ones (for an example, see Kolbaba (2008: 24)). The most significant florilegia in this category are:

1.   The *Panoplia Dogmatike* (PG 130, 32–1360), the first major florilegium of the middle Byzantine period, written between 1099 and 1114 at the behest of the Emperor Alexius I Comnenus by Euthymius Zygabenus (or Zygadenus). The occasion that led the Emperor to ask for this anthology was the trial and execution of the Bogomil leader Basil the Physician (c. 1099–1100?). It is preserved in approximately 140 manuscripts, among which are the two original ones, which were officially presented to the Emperor Alexius I (codd. *Vatic. gr.* 666 and *Mosquensis Syn. gr.* 387) (Miladinova 2014: 4–5). This lengthy anthology is divided into 28 chapters, of which the first seven deal with Trinitarian and general theological issues by way of presenting an overview of Orthodox dogma. The remaining 21 refute a number of heresies arranged according to their appearance in time: first Judaism (Chapter 8), then Simon, Marcion, Mani, and the Manicheans (Chapter 9), followed by the Sabellians, the Areians, and the Pneumatomachoi (Chapters 10–12). Chapter 13 turns to the issue of the Procession of the Holy Spirit with excerpts from a work of John of Jerusalem attributed to Photius. Other heresies treated in subsequent chapters are the Apollinarians, the Nestorinans, the Miaphysites, the Agnoetes, Origen, the Miathelites Sergius, Pyrrhus, and Paul of Constantinople, and, certainly, the contemporary heresies of Armenians, Paulicians, Messalians, and Bogomils (Chapters 23, 24, 26, and 27 respectively), while Chapter 28 is directed against Muhammad. Despite the fact that the number of authors anthologized in it is relatively small (Athanasius, Gregory of Nyssa, John Chrysostom, Cyril of Alexandria, Leontius of Neapolis, Maximus the Confessor, Photius, and a few more), the importance of this anthology cannot be overstated: among others, it has played a very significant role in the textual transmission of works such as the *Oratio Catechetica* of Gregory of Nyssa, and other works of Maximus the Confessor (Miladinova 2014: 18). It has served as one of the major sources for the history and the dogmatic beliefs of the Bogomils (Miladinova 2014: 26). Finally, the role it played in the theological debates in Europe after its first printed edition in 1710 is the subject of the recent monograph by Miladinova (2014).

2.   Andronicus Camaterus, *Sacred Arsenal* (*Sacrum Armamentarium*, ἹερῆΠ ανοπλία). This is the second anthology commissioned by an emperor (Manuel Comnenus). Transmitted in its entirety by only two manuscripts (*Monacensis gr.* 229 (thirteenth century) and *Venetus Marcianus gr.* 158 (fourteenth century), the work is divided into two parts. The first is a dialogue between the Emperor Manuel and the representatives of the Pope on the topics of the primacy of the Roman Church and on the *Filioque*. The dialogue is followed by a patristic florilegium of 151 excerpts from the Greek Fathers and three Latin ones (Gregory the Great, Augustine, and Jerome) and then a second florilegium on the Procession of the Holy Spirit is added comprising 42 citations from works of Photius, Eustratius of Nicaea, Theophylact of Ochrid, Nicetas of Byzantium,

and Nicholas of Methone. The second part is lengthier and the anthologized works are used for the refutation of Miatheletism, Theopaschism, Docetism, Aphthartodocetism, and the errors of the Armenian Church (Bucossi 2009a: 112–114). It was written, most likely, between 1172 and 1174 (Bucossi 2009a: 130), and its more than 1300 excerpts (Bucossi 2009b: 35–36) served as the treasury for most patristic quotations presented in any subsequent debates between the Byzantines and the Romans on the issues of the primacy of Rome and the *Filioque* (Bucossi 2009a: 113–114). The *Panoplia* and the *Arsenal*, though different in structure and scope, were the result of the Imperial religious policies of Alexius I and Manuel Comnenoi respectively (see Bucossi 2011: 357–358 and 361–366) and reflect, at least in part, the heresies active in that era and the dogmatic priorities of the rulers.

3. Nicetas Choniates, *Thesaurus Orthodoxae Fidei*, edited in part in *PG* 139, 1101–1449 and 140, 9–281. The *Thesaurus* was compiled in exile in Nicaea where the famous historian took refuge after the fall of Constantinople to the Fourth Crusade (1204). In many respects it is similar and covers in its 27 books approximately the same topics one may find in the *Panoplia* of Zygadenos. In fact, with regard to ancient heresies it has been described as "a second revised and extended edition of the [*Panoplia* of Zygadenos]" (Bossina 2009a: 170). Its book 20 is directed against the Hagarenes, while books 21 and 22 deal with the *Filioque* and the unleavened bread (azymes) with a slight but important difference from the *Panoplia* of Zygadenos: whereas the unleavened bread in the communion is treated by Zygadenos as an issue of liturgical practice primarily related to the Armenians, Choniates associates it directly with the Latins (Bossina 2009a: 180). The *Thesaurus* has not been studied in depth by modern scholarship, and a complete edition is still waiting, but the analysis of Bossina in the article referred to here, at least, places it in the context in which most of the subsequent dogmatic florilegia will move: that of the dogmatic disputations between Greeks and Latins. In the work of Choniates, the needs of a dogmatic confrontation with the Western world brings to the fore the renewed necessity to take recourse to the history of the dogmatic development of Christianity in order to confront the divisive issues that separated Rome from Constantinople (Bossina 2009b: 76).

4. The *De Oeconomia Dei*, compiled by Nilus Doxapatres in the middle of the twelfth century, is a much more complex work which reflects more clearly the encyclopedic interests of a segment of Byzantine theologians. However, its composite nature, which only in part enters the field of dogmatic florilegia, entitles it to no more than this brief note (for more, see Neirynck (2011, 258–266)).

Florilegia on the Procession of the Holy Spirit

For the period between the Fourth Crusade and the Second Council of Lyons (1274) it is difficult to speak of florilegia as separate entities because most of what we find in the form of collection of citations as proof texts is incorporated in dogmatic sermons or treatises usually bearing titles such as *Against the Latins* or *On the Procession of the Holy Spirit*. Most of them borrow citations from the earlier *Panopliae* as already mentioned.

The citations against the double Procession of the Holy Spirit are usually excerpted from early Fathers such as Basil the Great, Gregory of Nyssa, Gregory of Nazianzus, John of Damascus, Ps.-Dionysius Areopagite, and especially from Cyril of Alexandria and Maximus the Confessor. Sometimes, later Fathers such as Photius, Nicholas of Methone, and so on are also included. In most cases, the same citations were interpreted in a positive light towards the double Procession simply because the early Fathers had also spoken about the Procession *through* (διά) the Son, and this preposition was used by either side for their own dogmatic purposes.

For this period, I only cite in the following a number of works that include patristic florilegia on the Procession of the Holy Spirit and sometimes on azymes, trying to place them in chronological order. Most of them were compiled in the frame of the negotiations between Rome and Nicaea and, after 1261, Constantinople, with a view to resolving the dogmatic differences that impeded the union of the Churches:

1. The first official meeting between Roman delegates and the theologians of the Empire of Nicaea after 1204 took place in Nicaea and Nymphaeon in 1234. The discussion revolved around the issues of the *Filioque* and, to a lesser extent, the unleavened bread (azymes). Accounts of the proceedings of this Synod are preserved in both Greek and Latin. Therein are also included citations from the New Testament and works of Cyril of Alexandria, Basil the Great, Gregory Thaumaturgus, Gregory of Nyssa, and John Chrysostom, adduced by both sides (for more, see Alexakis (2007: 103–104 and n. 13)).

2. After this synod the Patriarch Germanus II sent the Pope a *memorandum*, summarizing the Greek positions, which in its opening paragraphs briefly cites a number of the patristic citations from works of the Fathers already mentioned above and also discussed in Nymphaeon. The real author, Nicephorus Blemmydes, concluded this section with the following very interesting remark, which, in fact, bears witness to the value even late Byzantines placed on florilegia: "Although we have the luxury of providing many more proof texts on the subject, we leave them aside for the sake of conciseness. This is what we offer as a theological defense relying more on the witness (*testimonia*) of the Fathers than any other proof through syllogisms..." (edition Stavrou 2007: 184–204, citation 192).

3. Nicephorus Blemmydes (1197/8–1269/72), *Two sermons on the Procession of the Holy Spirit*, the first to Iakovos, Archbishop of Bulgaria, the second to the Emperor Theodore Ducas Lascaris (*PG* 142, 533–565, florilegium at 540–557 and *PG* 142, 565–584).

4. Theodore II Lascaris (emperor of Nicaea, 1221/2–1258), *De processione Spiritus Sancti oratio apologetica*, written shortly before his death in 1258 and addressed to Nicholas bishop of Cotrone (Croton). Anti-*Filioque*: the emperor accumulates a *pastiche* of biblical citations followed by patristic excerpts (Alexakis 2007: 107).

5. After the restoration of Constantinople to the Byzantines, the Emperor Michael VIII and Nicholas of Cotrone held dogmatic discussions on Christmas Eve of 1262. The latter produced the archetype of codex *Parisinus gr.* 1115 as a massive collection of proof texts, which not only supported the *Filioque* (with a

number of forged citations among others; see earlier) but also served as another kind of dilapidated *Panoplia* (at least in the state it is preserved today through the Paris manuscript), in order to persuade Michael of the *consensus patrum* on all dogmatic issues that united rather than divided the two Churches (Alexakis 2007: 110).

6. Among the documents that constitute the so-called *Dossier grec de L'Union de Lyon* (1273–1277) (Laurent and Darrouzès 1976) florilegia are included in the following ones:

   i) The *Response* ('Ἀπολογία) of the Patriarch Joseph to the (lost) *Tomus* of 1273 of Michael VIII that promoted the Union of the Churches. Patristic citations oppose communion with the Latins, and the primacy of the Pope (Laurent and Darrouzès 1976: 135–301).

   ii) *The Profession of Faith* of Patriarch Joseph (1275) (Laurent and Darrouzès 1976: 327–331).

   iii) The Testament of the Patriarch Joseph (Laurent and Darrouzès 1976: 511–515).

   iv) Anonymous, *On John Bekkos and Photius* (Laurent and Darrouzès 1976: 529–537).

   v) Meletius the Confessor (*Third Oration*) *against the Italians*. The very interesting characteristic of this brief sermon is that it is all set in iambic 15-syllable verse together with the patristic citations and canons against communion with heretics (Laurent and Darrouzès 1976: 554–564).

   vi) A synoptic florilegium of 48 brief citations from early Fathers and Church canons against the double Procession, the azymes, and other Latin errors (Laurent and Darrouzès 1976: 564–573).

   vii) The *Synodicon against Bekkos* (Laurent and Darrouzès 1976: 574–588).

7. The works of John Bekkos, in which the main argument is that the patristic citations stating or implying that the "Holy Spirit proceeds from the Father *through* (διὰ) the Son" also allow for an understanding of the Holy Spirit proceeding *from* the Son (Papadakis 1983: 20). Bekkos turned from an opponent to a supporter of the *Filioque* after he read the theological works of Blemmydes on the subject, while he was imprisoned in Constantinople (Papadakis 1983: 18–19). However, it might be interesting to check the contents of codex *Parisinus gr.* 1115 against the citations found in Bekkos' florilegia. Bekkos converted to pro-Latin in May 1275 and the codex *Parisinus gr.* 1115 was deposited in the Imperial library in March of 1276. Most of Bekkos' works were written later.

   i) *De Unione Ecclesiarum*, (PG 141, 15–157). In the second half Bekkos refutes anti-*Filioque* excerpts from works of Photius, John of Phourne, Nicholas of Methone, and Theophylact of Bulgaria.

   ii) *De Processione Spiritus Sancti* (PG 141, 157–276).

   iii) *Ad Theodorum Sugdaeae Episcopum lib.* I, II, III (PG 141, 290–309, 309–324, 324–338).

   iv) *Refutationes adversus D. Andronici Camateri* (PG 141, 396–613). In this florilegium Bekkos refutes, one by one, 152 interpretive comments that Andronicus Camaterus appended to citations of his *Sacred Arsenal*.

v)   *Epigraphae* (PG 141, 613–724). This lengthy florilegium was compiled to support Bekkos' belief in the equivalence between ἐκ and διά. Most citations show the common use of the expression διὰ τοῦ υἱοῦ among the early Fathers. The most frequently cited Father is Cyril of Alexandria (123 citations, at least, from a total of around 300), followed by Athanasius of Alexandria and Basil the Great. Most of the citations, at least in the PG edition, are of poor quality. Fourteen Fathers are included in this anthology, together with a few excerpts from conciliar documents.

vi) *Refutatio libri Georgii Cyprii* (PG 141, 864–925).

8. Constantine Meliteniotes, pro-*Filioque*.

i)   *On the Procession of the Holy Spirit, Sermon I and Sermon II* (PG 141, 1032–1140).

ii) *Sermon I Against the Tomus of George Cyprius* (Orphanos 1986: 107–246)

iii) *Sermon II, "that the Holy Spirit exists from the Father and from the Son"* (Orphanos 1986: 247–279).

9. Gregory II of Cyprus (1283–89), *De Processione Spiritus Sancti* (PG 142, 269–300, anti-Latin).

10. Athanasius I of Constantinople (1289–1293 and 1303–1309), compiler of an anti-*Filioque* florilegium proper (Patedakis 2009: 137–142).

Before and after the Council of Blachernae (1285), which repudiated the Union proclaimed at Lyons and officially refuted Bekkos' dogmatic pronouncements, many other treatises included and interpreted patristic citations supporting both the pro- and the anti-*Filioque* positions. All of them shared almost the same citations from the early Fathers. For the sake of brevity, I list here some names of authors that cover the period around that time:

1. George Moschambar (1277–78, anti-Latin).
2. Hierotheos Hieromonk (c. 1281–1284 anti-Latin).
3. George Metochites (1250–1328, pro-Latin).
4. Gregory Palamas (1296–1359, anti-Latin). His *Two Apodeictic sermons on the Procession of the Holy Spirit* (written c. 1335) include numerous citations from patristic sources, almost exclusively from the Cappadocian Fathers; his *Antepigraphae* refute Bekkos' interpretation of the citations in the *Epigraphae*. Later, around the time of the Florence Council, Cardinal Bessarion refuted Palamas' refutation in his *Against Palamas* (all three works printed together in Laemmer (1864: 445–652)).
5. Nilus Cabasilas (1298–1363 anti-Latin).

The middle part of the fourteenth century is covered by the hesychastic controversy and the rich polemic literature together with the numerous florilegia it generated (see the "Hesychast (dogmatic) florilegia" section). The dogmatic issues pertaining to the differences between Rome and Constantinople recede and re-emerge as the dates of the Council of Ferrara–Florence approach (1438–1439). Manuel Calecas (d. 1410) and his *Against the Greeks*, a pro-*Filioque* treatise with numerous patristic citations that was translated into Latin (*PG* 152, 11–258), marks the beginning of this phase. However, by that time the proliferation of florilegia becomes so intense that it is impossible to even give an outline of it. Most of the treatises of this period rely heavily on patristic authority and usually incorporate excerpts from the early Fathers in the flow of their arguments. Also, there are numerous manuscripts from this period that comprise florilegia on all possible dogmatic issues directly or indirectly related to the major topics, which still remain the differences between Greeks and Latins (*filioque*, etc.) and Hesychasm and its primary dogmatic issue, that of the distinction between Divine essence and energies (for an example of this, see the "Hesychast (dogmatic) florilegia" section).

All this activity of compiling patristic florilegia on the Procession of the Holy Spirit eventually boiled down to the relatively few citations presented in the course of the meetings at the Council of Ferrara–Florence. There, textual accuracy again became an issue of paramount importance, and great care was taken to provide the relatively few patristic citations from as many ancient manuscripts as both sides could procure. Apart from the *Letter to Marinus of Cyprus* of Maximus the Confessor, which was discussed but not accepted as a witness, the most significant citation was an excerpt from the third book of the *Adversus Eunomium* of Basil the Great (for a list of the quotations presented by the Latins in the Greek Acts, see Alexakis (2000: 155–156)). Unfortunately, forgeries were not avoided, even of the much-contested passage from the *Adversus Eunomium*. I have suggested that these forgeries are to be traced back to the seventh century and the compilation of the early *Filioque* florilegium by the followers of Maximus the Confessor (Alexakis 2000: 157–165). Here, one might see some kind of tragic irony in this full circle of a citation anthologized by the Byzantines in the seventh century and serving, together with other reasons, as a catalyst for the unsuccessful outcome of the Council of Ferrara–Florence: of all the Byzantine participants, only Mark of Ephesus did not add his signature to the Union of the Churches, opening up the way to its voidance in the East. One of his complaints was that the Latins had tampered with the texts (Alexakis 2000: 165). Still, florilegia on the differences between Greeks and Latins continued to be produced after the Council of Florence, and this is witnessed by the numerous post-1453 florilegia manuscripts that continued to be copied.

Hesychast (Dogmatic) Florilegia

The hesychastic controversy broke out after 1334 in Byzantium, when the major proponent of hesychasm, Gregory Palamas, received an attack from the monk–philosopher Barlaam the Calabrian, who disputed the dogmatic foundations of the hesychastic or Jesus-prayer and the understanding of its results in the light of particular theological distinctions expounded by Palamas in his numerous writings. In these writings Palamas seems to have made ample use of florilegia, and the testimony of the Fathers is constantly invoked in order to lend support to his dogmatic pronouncements on the nature of the light seen on Mount Tabor by Christ's disciples during the Transfiguration (an experience meant for those practicing the hesychastic prayer) and other related issues.

The role florilegia played in this controversy easily becomes evident from the accounts of a disputation that took place in 1355 in the palace between Nicephorus Gregoras and Gregory Palamas in the presence of the Emperor John V Palaeologus. In the beginning of the dialogue, Gregoras, who recorded the entire episode in his own *History*, concludes his initial invective against Palamas with a barrage of testimonies from Athanasius of Alexandria and a citation from Cosmas the Melode, obviously taken from an anti-Palamite florilegium. After his dry statement that he would submit similar quotations in the sequel, he turned to Palamas noting that "Palamas, having not a single scriptural testimony (γραφικὴν μαρτυρίαν) to submit in response, tried his own improvised syllogisms/deductions" (*PG* 149, 241C–243C). However, a pro-Palamite source of the same episode, the *Concise Account of George Phacrases*, presents Palamas' demand for the citation of written excerpts from the Fathers (ἀναγνωσθῆναι... τὰς τῶν ἁγίων πατέρων... ἐγγράφους φωνάς). And there follows the citation of two excerpts from John of Damascus and one from Maximus the Confessor (Candal 1950: 330–334). The discussion continues along the same lines, and it seems that both sides were using florilegia (Candal 1950: 346 ... ὁ φιλόσοφος ἀνοίξας αὐτοῦ τὸ βιβλίον καὶ πολλάκις τὰ φύλλα μετακινήσας, εἶταἀνέγνω... [...the philosopher (Gregoras) opened up his book and leafed through it many times, then he read...] and Candal 1950: 356 ... πάλιν ἀνοίξας τὸ κατεχόμενον ὑπ' αὐτοῦ δελτίον, προήγαγε μαρτυρίαν λέγουσαν... [...and again opening up the book in his possession he adduced a *testimony* that stated...]). Moreover, the use of florilegia is so widespread on both sides that most of the dogmatic treatises are, in fact, accumulations of arguments and syllogisms supported by biblical passages and patristic citations (usually of the early Fathers). Most significant works on both sides of the hesychastic controversy in which we found excerpts from florilegia are the following:

1. Gregory Palamas.
    i) *The Triads, in Defense of the Holy Hesychasts*: nine sermons, distributed in three triads, defending the hesychastic practices and dogma. Two, at least, of them (1.1 and 1.3) conclude with an appended florilegium. Most cited authorities: Ps.-Dionysius Areopagite, Gregory of Nazianzus and Maximus the Confessor (edition Chrestou 1988: 359–694).
    ii) *Antirrhetics to Akindynos* (edition in Chrestou 1970).
All extant works of Palamas with the exception of some prayers (εὐχαί) extensively cite patristic fragments.
2. In the anti-hesychastic camp numerous treatises also display the same use of florilegia, as already mentioned in the case of Gregoras above. Indicative are the following works edited by Polemis in the *Corpus Christianorum* series:
    i) George of Pelagonia, *Adversus Palamam* (Polemis 2012: 2–51).
    ii) Anonymous, *Adversus Canatacuzenum* (Polemis 2012: 55–323).
    iii) Prochorus Cydones, *De lumine Thaborico* (Polemis 2012: 327–379).
These works, and especially the anonymous one, rely not only on patristic florilegia but also on anti-Palamite florilegia exclusively comprising citations from works of Palamas (sometimes with better or even earlier readings from the hand of Palamas himself, before he corrected them in later "edited" versions, Polemis 2012: LXVI–LXX)
3. The field of pro- and anti-Palamite florilegia, and especially of those that are still unedited in various manuscripts, is still in need of much more thorough study. As an example I might mention the existence of a "systematic florilegium of the

Palamite monk, Mark Kyrtos" preserved only in codex *Paris Biblioth. nationale, Coislinianus* 228, which is only mentioned in the bibliography by Sinkewicz (1988: 259–260), and is unrecognized by the editor of the catalogue of the manuscripts of the Coislin collection of the National Library in Paris.

As a second example I may mention the contents of the entire manuscript *Atheniensis gr.* 2583 analyzed in detail by Van Deun and also in part by Patedakis, who further clarified what Van Deun had simply mentioned (Patedakis 2009: 137–140, see earlier). Its first part (fols. 1–79) constitutes a collection of anti-Latin documents and florilegia (Van Deun 1987: 130–132). Its second part (fols. 79v–110v; 115–186) is another collection of pro-hesychastic documents and particular dogmatic florilegia (Van Deun 1987: 133–141).

An interesting trait of the last two categories of florilegia is that there are many manuscripts copied from the fifteenth century onwards in which are included both anti-Latin and pro-hesychastic documents and florilegia (for two of them, see Sinkewicz (1988: 62–65)).

Conclusions

Compared with manuscript collections of theological works, Byzantine florilegia are both narrower and wider: narrower in the sense that they usually include short excerpts from entire works, although it is possible to find among the florilegia contents an integral work; wider because the names and titles included are in many instances more than what is preserved or what we know as works under the name of a particular author. Sometimes we may have the felicitous appearance of an excerpt under the right title and the correct author, whereas the manuscript tradition of the entire work may have misattributed the same work to an unrelated Father. However, this does not preclude the opposite.

Byzantine philologists tend to measure the popularity of a work on the basis of the number of manuscripts that preserve a work or works of a particular author. In the case of florilegia one may go much deeper, but for this good editions of vast numbers of florilegia are needed. Still, the florilegia that have been edited so far may allow the scholarly community, after careful study, to formulate much more nuanced lists of the most influential Fathers of Christianity. The frequency in which a particular work is anthologized in florilegia might become a clear indicator of the "impact factor" of a particular author and work, to use a modern term. Under this criterion, it might not be a surprise if Cyril of Alexandria emerges as the most cited author, followed by the Cappadocians, John Chrysostom, Ps.-Dionysius, Maximus the Confessor, and John of Damascus, but this list is highly speculative. However, it is true that the authority of the early Fathers just mentioned is further corroborated by the fact that in the dogmatic florilegia of the last Byzantine period (anti- and pro-Latin and hesychastic ones) their works are more often excerpted than those of the post-eighth-century Fathers.

And one final point. Judging by the proliferation of the dogmatic florilegia from the fourth century onwards, but especially in the course of the last four centuries of the Byzantine Empire, during which accusation and defense of particular dogmatic positions becomes the call of the day, one might suggest that florilegia become an integral part, in fact, an instrument of the rhetorical nature of all dogmatic confrontations. To become more clear but also as concise as possible, once the Fathers abandoned the deductive processes that could be applied in the context of dialectic (for a failed attempt at abandoning dialectic in dogmatic confrontation in the year 383, see Alexakis (1996: 3 and n. 8)) they were left with the other means of persuasion; that is, rhetoric. According to Aristotle, in rhetoric one of the three means of persuasion is the argument, either inductive or deductive (Aristotle, *Posterior Analytics* I.1 71a5ff.). One of the inductive arguments is the example (*paradeigma*), which moves from one particular to a similar particular if both particulars belong to the same genus (Aristotle, *Rhetoric* I.2., 1357b25ff. ὅμοιον πρὸς ὅμοιον). Now the citations included in the florilegia provide the dogmatic material, which in most of the cases forms the first term in a *paradeigma* (i.e., in an exemplar) to which a dogmatic formulation that is contested in a confrontation must conform. Compared with the Aristotelian presupposition in the construction of an argument, Christianity has the advantage of not using accepted opinions (*endoxa*) but the undisputed authority of the Bible and, in second place, the approved (sometimes through Synodal sanction; Alexakis 1996: 4) patristic authority. Under this light, dogmatic florilegia are an organic part of all dogmatic disputations as repositories of this authority that serves as a yardstick for all contested dogmas in a process of adjudication that has nothing to do with dialectics but is appropriate exclusively to rhetoric. In this way we can understand why Gregoras in the passage mentioned above after having presented his florilegium sneered at Palamas who "... having not a single scriptural testimony (γραφικὴν μαρτυρίαν) to submit in response, tried his own improvised syllogisms/deductions (συλλογίζεσθαι τὰ ἀσυλλόγιστα)."

Bibliography

Abbreviations

ACO   *Acta conciliorum oecumenicorum*, eds E. Schwartz and J. Straub (Berlin, 1914–40), *Series Secunda*, eds R. Riedinger and E. Lamberz

CCSG   Corpus Christianorum, Series Graeca

CPG   *Clavis patrum graecorum*, eds M. Geerard and F. Glorie (Turnhout, 1974–87) (note: 2nd edition underway, with vol. 3 released in 2003)

DOP   *Dumbarton Oaks Papers*

DSp   *Dictionnaire de spiritualité ascétique et mystique*

OCP   *Orientalia christiana periodica*

ODB   *The Oxford Dictionary of Byzantium*, eds A. Kazhdan *et al.* (New York, 1991)

PG   *Patrologiae cursus completus, Series graeca*, ed. J.-P. Migne (Paris, 1857–66)

PTS   Patristische Texte und Studien

RÉB   *Revue des études byzantines*

RSBN   *Rivista di studi bizantini e neoellenici*

Primary Sources

Anastasius Sinaites, *Qvaestiones et responsiones*, eds Richard, Marcel and Munitiz, Joseph (2006), *Anastasii Sinaitae, Qvaestiones et responsiones*. CCSG 59. Turnhout: Leuven.

Catena Sinaitica, ed. Petit, Françoise (1977), *Catenae Grecae in Genesim et Exodum. I. Catena Sinaitica*. CCSG 2. Turnhout: Leuven,

Corpus Parisinum, ed. Searby, Denis (2007), *The Corpus Parisinum: A Critical Edition of the Greek Text with Commentary and English Translation (A Medieval Anthology of Greek Texts from the Pre-Socratics to the Church Fathers, 600 B.C.–700 A.D.)*. Lewiston, NY: E. Mellen Press.

Constantine Meliteniotes, *Sermon I and Sermon II*, ed. by Orphanos, Markos (1986), Κωνσταντίνου Μελιτηνιώτου Λόγοι Ἀντιρρητικοί δύο, Athens.

Doctrina Patrum de Incarnatione Verbi, ed. by Franz Diekamp (2nd edn with corrections by B. Phanourgakis, and Ev. Chrysos) (1981), *Doctrina Patrum de Incarnatione Verbi, Ein griechisches Florilegium des 7. u. 8. Jhs*, Münster.

Florilegium Baroccianum (Florilegium Patmiacum, or Melissa Augustanea), ed. Sargologos, Étienne (1990), *Un traité de vie spirituelle et morale du XIe siècle : le florilège sacro-profane du manuscript 6 de Patmos, Introduction, texte critique, notes et tables*, Thessalonique.

Florilegium Coislinianum B, eds Ilse de Vos, Erika Gielen, Caroline Macè, Peter van Deun (2010), "La lettre B du florilège coislin: Editio princeps". *Byzantion*, 80: 72–120.

Florilegium Coislinianum Γ, eds Ilse de Vos, Erika Gielen, Caroline Macè, Peter van Deun (2008), "L'art de compiler à Byzance: La lettre Γ du florilège coislin". *Byzantion*, 78: 159–223.

Florilegium Marcianum, ed. by Odorico, Paolo (Odorico 1986: 64–118).

Gregory Palamas, *The Triads, in Defense of the Holy Hesychasts*, ed. Panagiotes Chrestou (1988), Γρηγορίου τοῦ Παλαμᾶ Συγγράμματα, vol. 1, Thessalonike; 359–364.

Gregory Palamas, *Two Apodeictic Sermons on the Procession of the Holy Spirit*, ed. in Chrestou (1988: 22–153).

Gregory Palamas, *Antepigraphae*, ed. in Chrestou (1988: 161–175) (florilegia not included).

Gregory Palamas, *Antirrhetics to Akindynos*, ed. in Panagiotes Chrestou (1970), Γρηγορίου τοῦ Παλαμᾶ Συγγράμματα, vol. 3, Thessalonike.

John of Damascus, *Contra imaginum calumniatores orationes tres, Introduction, critical edition* by Bonifatius Kotter (1975), *Die Schriften des Johannes von Damascus III*. PTS 17. Berlin.

John of Damascus, *Three Treatises on the Divine Images, Translation and Introduction* by Andrew Louth. Crestwood, NY: St Vladimir's Seminary Press.

John of Damascus, *Expositio fidei, Introduction, critical edition* by Bonifatius Kotter (1973), *Die Schriften des Johannes von Damascus II.*, PTS 12. Berlin.

John of Damascus, *Liber de haeresibus, Opera polemica, Introduction, critical edition* by Bonifatius Kotter (1981), *Die Schriften des Johannes von Damascus IV*. PTS 22. Berlin.

John of Damascus, *Sacra Parallela*. PG, 95, 1040–1588; PG, 96: 9–442.

John Georgidas, *Gnomologium*, ed. Odorico, Paolo (Odorico 1986: 119–255).

John Stobaeus, *Anthologium*. eds Wachsmuth, Curt and Hense, Otto (1884–1912), *Ioannis Stobaei anthologium*, five vols. Berlin: Weidmann.

Nicephorus I, Patriarch of CP, *Refutatio et Eversio*, ed. Featherstone, Jeffrey-Michael (1998), *Nicephori Patriarchae Constantinopolitani Refutatio et eversio definitionis synodalis anni 815*. CCSG 33. Turnhout: Brepols.

Nicephorus Blemmydes, *Memorandum of Nicaea*, ed. Stavrou, Michel (2007), *Nicéphore Blemmydès, Oeuvres théologiques* I. SC 517. Paris: Éditions du CERF; 184–206.

Palamite Florilegia, see Rigo (2011) and Roelli (2011).

Photius, *Bibliotheca*, ed. Henry, Renè (1960), *Photius. Bibliotèque*, vol. 2. Paris: Les Belles Lettres.

Pseudo-Maximus Confessor, *Loci communes*, ed. Ihm Sibylle (2001), *Pseudo-Maximus*

Confessor. Erste kritische Edition einer Redaktion des sacro-profanen Florilegiums Loci communes nebst einer vollständigen Kollation einer zweiten Redaktion und weiterem Material. Palingenesia 73. Stuttgart.

Philokalia: Palmer, G.E.H., Sherrard, Philip, Ware, Kallistos (1979–1999). *The Philokalia: The Complete Text*, vols 1–4. London: Faber and Faber.

The Evergetinos: A Complete Text, vols. 1–4, ed. and transl. by Chrysostomos Archbishop and Patapios Hieromonk, *et al.*, (2008). Etna, CA: Center for Traditionalist Orthodox Studies.

Theodore Stoudite, *Epistulae*, ed. Fatouros, Georgios (1991), *Theodori Studitae Epistulae*, two vols. Corpus Fontium Historiae Byzantinae, Ser. Berolinensis 30.1–2. Berlin: W. De Gruyter.

Secondary Sources

Alexakis, Alexander (2011), "Some remarks on dogmatic florilegia based mainly on the florilegia of the early ninth century". In Van Deun and Macé (2011: 45–56).

Alexakis, Alexander (2007), "Official and unofficial contacts between Rome and Constantinople before the Second Council of Lyons (1274)". *Annuarium Historiae Conciliorum* 39: 99–124.

Alexakis, Alexander (2001), "The *Epistula ad Marinum Cypri presbyterum* of Maximos the Confessor (CPG 7697.10) revisited. A few remarks on its meaning and history". *Byzantinische Zeitschrift* 94/2: 545–554.

Alexakis, Alexander (2000), "The Greek patristic testimonia presented at the Council of Florence (1439) in support of the *Filioque* reconsidered". *RÉB* 58: 149–165.

Alexakis, Alexander (1996), *Codex Parisinus Graecus 1115 and Its Archetype*. Dumbarton Oaks Studies 34. Washington, DC: Dumbarton Oaks.

Alexander, Paul (1958), *The Patriarch Nicephorus of Constantinople*. Oxford, Clarendon Press.

Bossina, Luciano (2009a), "Niketas Choniates as a theologian". In *Niketas Choniates. A Historian and a Writer*, Alicia Simpson and Efthymiadis, Stephanos (eds). Geneva: La pomme d'or; 165–184.

Bossina, Luciano (2009b), "Qualche nota su Niceta Coniata Storico del Dogma". In Rigo and Ermilov (2009: 71–90).

Bucossi, Alessandra (2011), "Andronico Camatero e la Zizzania: sulla politica Ecclesiastica Bizantina in età Comnena". *RSBN* N.S., 47: 357–371.

Bucossi, Alessandra (2009a), "New historical evidence for the dating of the *Sacred Arsenal* by Andronikos Kamateros". *RÉB*, 67: 111–130.

Bucossi, Alessandra (2009b), "The *Sacred Arsenal* by Andronikos Kamateros, a forgotten treasure". In *Byzantine Theologians. The Systematization of their Own Doctrine and their Perception of Foreign Doctrines*, A. Rigo and P. Ermilov (eds). (2009: 33–50).

Cameron, Alan (1993), *The Greek Anthology, from Melager to Planudes*. Oxford: Clarendon Press.

Candal, Manuel (1950), "Fuentes Palamíticas: Diálogo de Jorge Facrasi sobre el contradictorio de Pálamas con Nicéforo Grégoras". *OCP*, 16: 303–357.

Chadwick, Henry (1969), "Florilegium". In *Reallexikon für Antike und Christentum 7*, cols. 1131–1160.

Evangelatou, Maria (2008), "Word and image in the *Sacra Parallela* (Codex Parisinus Graecus 923), *DOP*, 62: 113–197.

Funghi, Maria Serena (2004), *Aspetti di letteratura gnomica nel mondo antico*, vol. II, Accademia Toscana di Scienze e Lettere "La Colombaria", "Studi" 125. Florence: Leo S. Olschki.

Gerlach, Jens (2008), *Gnomica Democritea. Studien zur gnomologischen Überlieferung der Ethik Demokrits und zum Corpus Parisinum mit einer Edition der Demokritea des Corpus Parisinum*, Serta Graeca 26. Wiesbaden: Dr Ludwig Reichert Verlag.

Gray, Patrick T.R. (2006), *Leontius of Jerusalem. Against the Monophysites: Testimonies of the Saints and Aporiae.* Oxford Early Christian Texts. Oxford: Oxford University Press.

Grillmeier, Aloys (1986), *Christ in Christian Tradition*, vol. 2.1: *From Chalcedon to Justinian*, P. Allen and J. Cawte (transl.). Atlanta, GA: John Knox Press.

Karo, Georgius and Lietzmann, Johannes (1902), "Catenarum Graecarum Catalogus". In *Nachrichten von der Königl. Gesselschaft der Wissenschaften zu Göttingen: Philologisch-historische Klasse*. Göttingen: Dieterich'schen Univ.-Buchdruckerei; 1–66, 299–350, 559–620.

Kolbaba, Tia (2008), *Inventing Latin Heretics. Byzantines and the Filioque in the Ninth Century.* Kalamazoo, MI: Medieval Institute Publications.

Laemmer, Hugo (1864), *Scriptorum Graeciae Orthodoxae Bibliotheca Selecta.* Friburg.

Laurent, Vitalien and Darrouzès, Jean (1976), *Dossier grec de l'Union de Lyon (1273–1277).* Paris: Archives de l'Orient Chrétien 16.

Lowden, John (2010), "Illustrated Octateuch manuscripts: a Byzantine phenomenon". In *The Old Testament in Byzantium*, Paul Magdalino, and Robert Nelson (eds). Washington, DC: Dumbarton Oaks; 107–152.

Magdalino, Paul (2011), "Orthodoxy and history in tenth-century Byzantine 'Encyclopedism'". In Van Deun and Macé (2011: 143–159).

Miladinova, Nadia (2014), *The Panoplia Dogmatike by Euthymios Zygadenos, A Study on the First Edition Published in Greek in 1710.* Texts and Studies in Eastern Christianity IV. Leiden: Brill.

Natalio Fernández, Marcos (2000), *The Septuagint in Context, Introduction to the Greek Version of the Bible*, Wilfred G.E. Watson (transl.). Leiden: Brill.

Neirynck, Stefaan (2011), "The *De Oeconomia Dei* by Nilus Doxapatres: a tentative definition". In Van Deun and Macé (2011: 257–268).

Odorico, Paolo (2004), "Gli gnomologi Greci sacro-profani. Una presentazione". In Funghi (2004: 61–96).

Odorico, Paolo (1986), *Il prato e l'ape. Il sapere sentenzioso del Monaco Giovanni.* Wiener Byzantinistische Studien 17. Vienna: Verlag der Österreichischen Akademie der Wissenchaften.

Polemis, Ioannis (2012), *Theologica Varia Inedita Saeculi XIV.* CCSG 76. Turnhout: Brepols.

Papacostas, Tassos, Mango, Cyril, and Grünbart, Michael (2007), "The history and architecture of the Monastery of Saint John Chrysostomos at Koutsovendis, Cyprus". *DOP*, 61: 25–156.

Papadakis, Aristeides (1983), *Crisis in Byzantium, The Filioque Controversy in the Patriarchate of Gregory II of Cyprus.* New York: Fordham University Press.

Parry, Ken (1996), *Depicting the Word. Byzantine Iconophile Thought of the Eighth and Ninth Centuries,*. The Medieval Mediterranean 12. Leiden: Brill.

Patedakis, Manolis (2009), 'Athanasios' I Patriarch of Constantinople anti-Latin views and related theological writings". In Rigo and Ermilov (2009: 124–142).

Pelikan, Jaroslav (1974), *The Christian Tradition. A History of the Development of Doctrine 2, The Spirit of Eastern Christendom (600–1700).* Chicago, IL: The University of Chicago Press.

Petit, Françoise (1979), "La tradition de Théodoret de Cyr dans les chaines sur la Genèse. Vues nouvelles dans le classement de ces chaines". *Le Muséon* 92: 281–286.

Pitra, Jean Baptiste (1852), *Spicilegium Solesmense I.* Paris.

Rigo, Antonio (2011), "Une *Summa* ou un florilège commenté pour la vie spirituelle? L'oeuvre Μέθοδος καὶ κανὼν de Calliste et Ignace Xanthopouloi". In Van Deun and Macé (2011: 387–437).

Rigo, Antonio and Ermilov, Pavel (eds) (2009), *Byzantine Theologians. The Systematization of their own Doctrine and their Perception of Foreign Doctrines.* Quaderni di Νέα Ῥώμη 3. Rome: Università degli Studi di Roma "Tor Vergata".

Richard, Marcel (1964), "Florilèges spirituels, III *Florilèges* grecs". *DSp* 5, Paris, cols. 475–512.

Rochais, Henri-Marie (1964), "Florilèges spirituels, I *Florilèges latins*". *DSp* 5, Paris, cols.
435–460.

Roelli, Philipp (2011), "Teaching Hesychasm
by means of florilegia: sources of Mark the
Monk's florilegium". In Van Deun and Macé
(2011: 287–296).

Royce, James R. (1991), *The Spurious Texts of
Philo of Alexandria*. Leiden: Brill.

Schwartz, Eduard (1939), *Drei dogmatische
Schriften Iustinians*. Abhandlungen der
Bayerische Akademie der Wissenschaften,
Hist.-Philol. Klasse, N.F. 18. Munich:
Verlag der Bayerischen Akademie der
Wissenschaften.

Searby, Denis (1998), *Aristotle in the Greek
Gnomological Tradition*. Acta Univeristatis
Upsaliensis 10. Uppsala: Uppsala University.

Sinkewicz, Robert (1988), *Gregory Palamas,
The One Hundred and Fifty Chapters*. Studies
and Texts 83. Toronto: Pontifical Institute of
Medieval Studies.

Speyer, Wolfgang (1971), *Die Literarische
Fälschung im heidnischen und Chrislichen
Altertum*. Handbuch der Altertumwissen-
schaft. Einleitende und Hilfsdisziplinen. Band
I, 2. Munich: C.H. Beck.

Stephanou, Pelopidas (1946), "La Doctrine de
Léon de Chalcédoine et de ses adversaries
sur les images". *OCP*, 12: 177–199.

Van Deun, Peter (1987), "Les citations de
Maxime le Confesseur dans le florilège palamite de l'Atheniensis, Bibliothèque nationale 2583". *Byzantion*, 87: 127–157.

Van Deun, Peter, and Macé, Caroline (eds)
(2011), *Encyclopedic Trends in Byzantium?
Proceedings of the International Conference
held in Leuven, 6–8 May 2009.*, Orientalia
Lovaniensia Analecta 212. Leuven:
Peeters.

Part II
Collecting the Fathers

Collecting the Chart here

CHAPTER 3
Modern Patrologies

Angelo Di Berardino

Terminological Questions

The term *patrology* is derived from the Latin *pater* (father) and from the Greek *logos* (discourse, speech). In common language, it has two meanings today that are generally accepted: (a) the study of the Fathers of the Church; (b) a manual or introduction to the study of the ancient Christian writers. A third meaning, that nowadays is obsolete, is a collection of the writings of these authors; for example, the immense series by Migne, or the other collections in different languages, besides Latin and Greek that is (*Patrologia Orientalis*, etc.). I used the expression "Fathers of the Church"; a similar expression to this is that of "ancient Christian writers." The concept of "Father of the Church" is very ancient and makes reference to the teacher, who instructs and generates in the faith by means of the word. Irenaeus had already said that the teacher is a father, while the student is a son (*Adv. haer.* 4.41, 2; Clement Al., *Strom.* I, 1, 2, 1 e I, 1, 1, 3).

The bishop in particular is he who teaches and baptizes; in this way he generates new children for the Church, and in such a manner he is a father. Polycarp of Smyrna (†c. 165) is called the "doctor/teacher of Asia, father of the Christians" (*Martyrdom of Polycarp* 12, 24). Cyprian, the bishop of Carthage, was called pope (*papa*), a diminutive appellation for *pater* (*Ep.* 33; 31; 36). Such a usage is followed by Ambrose and Augustine (Wiest 1795: 530–534).

The bishops who participated in the councils came to be called Fathers, even if they were not writers: those who participated in the council of Nicaea (325), the "318 Fathers" (cf. Basil, *Ep.*, 140, 2; Gregory Naz., *Or.* 35, 15). In our context, on the other hand, one is called a Father only if he was an ancient author who left something written, even if he was not a bishop. The Fathers, in as much as they caused the Christian communities to grow, are to be considered orthodox in their faith. One must not judge their orthodoxy by the criteria of theology that came later. In practice, however, the patrologies include not

The Wiley Blackwell Companion to Patristics, First Edition. Edited by Ken Parry.
© 2015 John Wiley & Sons Ltd. Published 2019 by John Wiley & Sons Ltd.

only orthodox writers, but also all those who were considered Christians. In other words, even the heretics, such as Arius or Nestorius. According to a solidified tradition, *patrologia* studies the "life and the works of the Fathers," but it is added that it also treats their theological thought and the principal themes of each author. And as for the literary aspects, these, too, are not normally ignored.

In fact, the first so-called patrology was written by Jerome (†420) in order to demonstrate that even among the Christians there were men illustrious for the quality of their style and for their teaching. He begins with the Apostle Peter and he finishes with himself, which is notice number 135. As regards the title by which he indicates his work, he writes to Augustine that it can be called by the title *De viris illustribus vel proprie de scriptoribus ecclesiasticis* (*Ep.* 112, 3). There is an apologetic scope to show to the pagans that the Church too has enjoyed her philosophers and teachers, who have grounded, built, edified, and adorned her (*Praef.* 7). The adjective "ecclesiastical" is a reference to the church and, *inter alia* during this period, it indicated a catholic or orthodox Christian, and in this sense it is used by Jerome himself (*Ep.* 62, 1) (cf. Du Cange (1668)). Here, however, he understands all those who have written "regarding the Sacred Scriptures" (*Praef.* 1), and therefore also the schismatics and the heretics, who certainly did not edify and adorn the Church. In a letter to Jerome, Augustine had pointed out that he had also included the heretics, something unbefitting, but at least he should have noted, too, their errors (*Ep.* 40, 6, 9). Some modern authors have followed Jerome, since they include the writings of the New Testament, and everyone today includes the heretical writers. As it was for him, there is an interest in the "literary" aspects in the works of the Fathers. In the *Divinae Institutiones* (at the beginning of Book V) Lactantius expresses judgments of a literary character regarding his Latin predecessors (Tertullian, Minucius Felix, Cyprian). In his *De doctrina christiana* Augustine analyses the style of Paul, Cyprian, and Ambrose (IV, 7, 11ff.; IV, 21, 45ff).

In any case, Jerome's verbal phrasing of "ecclesiastical writers" (*syntagma*) has enjoyed success. His work was continued in the west by other authors: Gennadius of Marseille (467–480), who added another 135 brief biographies; Isidore of Seville (560–636) another 47; and Ildephonsus of Toledo (607–667) 14 names of Iberian writers. For Vincent of Lérins (†c. 450) the Fathers are those "who, after a holy life, a wise teaching, a constant attachment to the faith and to the catholic communion, have merited to die in Christ according to the faith, or to die for Christ according to a blessed lot" (*Comm.* 28). Following this line of thought, the *Decretum Gelasianum*, compiled around the year 550, composed a list "of the Holy Fathers who are to be received in the Catholic Church" and of the works which were not accepted (Di Berardino 2007: 224–246). Hence, it was the doctrinal interest that determined the concept of Father. In the Greek East there were the shorter historical works of the patriarch Nicephorus (758–829) and the *Myriobiblion* (or *Bibliotheca*) of the patriarch Photius from 858, an exposition and review of 279 works, including those written by pagan authors. All of these authors ignore the authors in other oriental languages after the fifth century.

The work by Jerome, who made use of Eusebius of Caesarea, constitutes the premise of that sort of treatise and of studies which, from the seventeenth century, from the impulse by the Lutheran Johannes Gerhard (1582–1637), would come to be called "patrology." The terminological question has its importance, in so much as the modern manuals have different titles: *Patrology*, (History of) *Ancient Christian Literature*, *Ancient Ecclesiastical Literature*, and sometimes even *Patristic Literature* or also *Patristics*.

The Recourse to the Fathers

Gerhard was the author of a *Patrologia sive de primitivae Ecclesiae christianae doctorum vita ac lucubrationibus opusculum posthumum* (Ienae 1653; 1668 and 1773), which begins with the second century (Hermas) and goes to Bellarmine (†1621), his contemporary. He, by means of this title, created the term "patrology," which – to him – embraced "the life and the thought of the doctors of the primitive (early) Christian Church." The concept of "early church" was too vast, in as much as it extended all the way to his own day. In the dedicatory preface he wrote that the Fathers are a divine blessing: *Patrum scripta fidei esse regulam accredendivel Scripturam exponendiunicamvel primariam normam*, on the condition that the word of God which is found in the Holy Scriptures be the *unicumcredendi principium esse et articulorum fidei normam* (p. a2). He cites the sources for every author, he describes the content of the work and he makes numerous critical observations. He very often cited the opinions of Baronius (*Annales ecclesiastici*) and of Bellarmine. Among the first Christian writers he also counts Dionysius the Areopagite and the Pseudo-Clementine works, which he criticized for a lack of accuracy. Bellarmine, with his *De scriptoribus ecclesiasticis*, which included the biblical books and some Jewish authors (Josephus Flavius), wrote an introductory compendium – very schematic – for the reading of the writers up to his time, spread out according to their century. A few years prior to this Simon de Voyon had published his *Catalogue des Docteurs de l'église de dieu*, La Rochelle 1607. Now the work by Bellarmine has had an enormous success, but it was continued by various authors (Ph. Labbe, Casimir Oudin, A. de Saussy) and many have drawn and gleaned from him.

The appeal to the Fathers was common in the polemics between Protestants and Catholics. No less than the study of Christian archaeology served for both a theological and an apologetical interest. Christian antiquities in a broad sense served to construct a confessional identity (Catholics, Lutherans, and Calvinists) (Backus, 2003). The Catholics utilized with great abundance the writings of the Fathers, with the goal of converting the "errant," for they gave great importance to the Tradition. The patristic writings enjoyed an authority in a dogmatic matter together with the conciliar canons. The ascetical writings also served for the renewal of Christian spirituality. The use of the writings of the Fathers created, too, contrarian polemics. In this polemical context there was used the syntagm *theologia patristica*, which was a collection of the Fathers' writings in relation to Christian doctrine.

During the very years of Bellarmine and of Gerhard, the French Huguenot Jean Daillé (1594–1670) wrote a work with a radical critique of the authority of the Fathers and on their "true use." At the beginning he thus gives a summary of his intentions: "The Fathers cannot be the judges of today's controversies which exploded into such as those between the Roman Church and the Protestants, because, if not impossible, it is at least very difficult to know exactly and precisely what their thoughts were" (Daillé 1632: 1). Now, even if we were to know their teaching quite well, it is not infallible; neither is it

immune from errors; nor can it have sufficient authority for its comprehension, especially in matters of religion. The Lutheran Johann Hülsemann (†1661) had given the
title of *Patrologia* (Lipsiae, 1670) to his little known work, thereby contributing to the
diffusion of the term.

Among the Protestants there was a difference in the use of the Fathers. The German
reformers were more "biblical," for they defended the idea of the progressive obscuring
of the comprehension of the Scriptures and therefore of the decrease of the purity of
the faith; the other reformers (Switzerland, Holland, France) gave a greater importance to history and to the patristic argument in their polemics with the Catholics
(Turchetti 1993: 73s).

In the eighteenth century very great and large works were written, which studied
and analyzed the works of the Christian authors. These were not manuals, but rather
immense works, starting with that of L.E. Dupin (or Du Pin) (†1719), who had
tendencies towards Gallicanism. Various parts of this vast work (it extends all the way
to the seventeenth century) have been published with diverse titles, and on account of
some of his opinions he was included in the *Index* of forbidden books in 1757.
He explained the title (*Nouvelle bibliothèque*) as a collection of authors who wrote about
religious matters, according to the ancient tradition and following the model of
Baronius and of the *Centuriatores*, but he wanted his work to be "broader and more
complete than those which had hitherto been published" (Dupin 1686: vol. I, 6). The
work, the first attempt to compose a critical treatise, was approved by the University of
Paris, but it was strongly criticized by the Catholics (M. Petit-Didier, Bossuet; R. Simon)
and greatly esteemed by the Protestants; in fact, it was translated into English by the
Anglicans. He brought together the biography of the authors, an analysis and critiques
on the style of the patristic works, and the theological thought. L.S. le Nain de Tillemont
(1693–1712), in his ample work on ecclesiastical history, in 16 volumes, treats the
Fathers at length. He dedicated the first volume to an introduction and to the personalities or people of the New Testament, with many useful notes. This work reaches unto
the sixth century; it is of great worth and it is still consulted today.

Other authors who have written much concerning the Fathers are: from the
Congregation of Saint Maur, N. le Nourry (†1724), two volumes; Rémi Ceillier (†1761)
23 volumes until 1248; the Benedictines D. Schramm (†1797), *Analysis operum SS.
Patrum*, 18 tomes, Augsburg 1780–1796 (until Epiphanius), and G. Lumper, 13 tomes,
Augsburg 1783–1799 (until the fourth century), a work very valued even by the
Protestants for its rich content and for its critical sense. J.A. Bosius, a classicist,
Schediasma de comparanda notitia Scriptorum Ecclesiasticorum, Jenae 1673. After his
death, it was updated and enlarged by I. G. Walch (*Introductio in notitiam scriptorium
ecclesiasticorum* (Jenae, 1723). It is not of the genre of the scholastic manuals; rather, it
is a collection of biblical and patristic entries (e.g., critical bibliographies). The Jesuit
Carolus Sardagna wrote an *Indiculus patrum ac veterum scriptorium ecclesiasticorum*,
Regensburg 1772, wherein the authors are listed in alphabetical order with 270 entries.

Many of the authors from these centuries, who used the verbal phrase "ecclesiastical
authors," give long annotations and treatments; they even include the Old and New
Testaments and extend their work until the thirteenth century, and sometimes even
beyond that. Moreover, they preface this with broad introductions in order to explain

their method and the works they used. These introductions are quite instructive for understanding the methodology, the theological configuration and their apologetic and counter-controversy ends.

The Protestants, too, of various denominations became interested in the Fathers so as to defend their own teachings. Some of the greatest of the Anglican scholars merit mention, the very same who made use of the doctrinal positions of the Fathers against the Catholics: James Usher (†1656), John Pearson (†1686), Johann E. Grabe (Grabius; †1711), and Henry Dodwell. Of a more general character was the treatise by William Cave (†1713), who wrote a work in two volumes, the content of which was set out according to century; it reaches to the fourteenth century (*Scriptorum ecelesiasticorum Historia a Christo natousque ad saeculum XIV*, London 1688–1698). In 1743 a much enlarged second edition was published by Henry Wharton. Cave published numerous works on Christian antiquities. Casimir Oudin, a Catholic who became a Protestant (†1717), wrote a work in three volumes (*Commentarius de Scriptoribus Antiquis*, Lipsiae 1722), the scope of which was carried to the fifteenth century, and which was published post-humously. In 1668 he had published another work as a supplement to that by Bellarmine and those by other authors, in three volumes. The Lutheran Johann G. Olearius published *Abacus patrologicus* (Jenae, 1673), in alphabetic form (a sort of dictionary until the death of Luther, in one volume) and as the completion to that of Gerhard. For him the Fathers are not *numina*, but only *lumina*. He rewrote the work in another way and in a more ample manner, with the title *Bibliotheca scriptorium ecclesiastiorum* (Jenae, 1710–1717, two volumes).

Johann Albert Fabricius (†1736) published *Bibliotheca latina*, in three volumes (1697), and *Bibliotheca graeca*, 14 volumes (1705–1728), and it also includes pagan authors. The two works report a list of the writings and the editions of the ancient authors. A completion of Fabricius' work, although only for the Christian part, was that by C.Tr.G. Schoenemann, *Bibliotheca historico-literaria Patrum latinorum* (two tomes, Lipsiae, 1792–1794). The two volumes reached the fifth century; he followed this treatment of the Fathers who were cited by adding an index of their works, along with a rich bibliography of the editions, which is still very useful. The work is useful today in order to track down the editions from the fifteenth century and later, and in order to know what was thought of them at that time.

The study of the Fathers, as we have noted above, was used with an eye towards the controversies in theological discussions. The authority of the Fathers was always in discussion. Some authors treated the argument in a detailed manner, as had previously been done by Dallaeus (Jean Daillé; †1670). The following authors were constrained in taking a position in favor of or contrary to that of Daillé. I will mention them here in a schematic way: Philippe Labbe (Labbaeus; †1667); Honoratus a Sancta Maria (1651–1729); Matthæi Scriveneri; Antonius Boucat; Josef W. Eberl; the Anglican J. J. Blunt (†1855). The work by Blunt was a dense critique of the assertions made by Daillé, but also of the work by the Huguenot jurist Jean Barbeyrac, whom he accused of knowing little of the Fathers, and of the insinuations of Edward Gibbon. Bonaventura Argonensis (Noël d'Argonne; †1704) published the *Petit traité de la lecture des Pères de l'Église*, Paris 1688. P. Pelhestre de Rouen updated and completed the work in an abundant way, and it was then translated into Latin and into Italian. It was a work of a methodological character.

The Patrologies

The introductions of the large works cited – they were normally quite vast – explained the method, the sources and the problematics. With the passing of time there were always fewer that were apologetic in nature and more that were critical and scientific. The authors knew the texts very well from a direct reading, for they knew Latin and Greek well. Normally they did not mention the ancient Christian authors who had written in other languages. When the Assemani family published the translations of Syriac works in Latin, then some Syrian authors were also taken into consideration.

Before the nineteenth century, whoever wished to begin study with some knowledge of the Fathers of the Church did not possess smaller manuals; those that existed were very old and inadequate. The progress of the study, a greater attention to philology, the discovery of numerous patristic texts, the interest in Syriac, Armenian and Coptic authors, monographic research on authors and themes, rendered those manuals very insufficient. The Protestants, too, were more interested in Christian antiquity than before. The Catholic clergy did not read the Fathers. They were constrained to study the calendar and how to calculate the date of Easter (an obligatory course) and not to mine the riches of ancient Christian tradition.

Let us begin with the oldest manuals, following the chronological order, whenever possible. All of the manuals were written in Latin; this was a great advantage for their diffusion, in as much as it was not necessary to have translations made. Wilhelm Wilhemus, *Patrologia adusus academicos*, Friburgi Brisgoviae 1775 (up to the fifth century). The long foreword is the history of the publications on the Fathers of the Church. I consider this *excursus* useful for reconstructing the history of the manuals of patrology until the eighteenth century. This is a typical Catholic manual – which treats the authority – of the writings and of the use of the Fathers in the various theological subject matters. Daniel Tobenz (†1819), *Institutiones, usus et doctrina Patrum*, Wien 1777–1779, and *Patrologiae et historiae literar. Theolog. Conspectus*, Wien 1776; Macarius (a Sancto Elia), *Institutiones patrologiae*, Graz 1781, a work that went through numerous editions and translations.

Of the Cistercian Stephan Wiest (†1797), *Institutiones Patrologiae in usum academicum* (Ingolstadii, 1795). In the introduction he explains the concept of Father, their importance and their characteristics. Wiest discussed the concept of *antiquitas*: does it last until Augustine or until Gregory the Great, and so forth. The work was not a manual of patrology in the strict sense; rather, it was a historical, critical, and bibliographical introduction to the principal Christian writers, especially in relation to the various theological subjects. Wiest abounds in citations of patristic texts even in his massive work, the *Institutiones theologicae*, in six volumes.

A.B. Caillau (†1850), *Introductio ad sanctorum partum lectionem*, Parisiis 1825 (two volumes); it is part of a vast work called the *Thesaurus Patrum floresque doctorum*. Franz Wenceslaus Goldwitzer (†1840), *Patrologie Verbunden mit Patristik bearbeitet für Theologen*, two volumes, Nürnberg 1833–1834. Nirschland Rézbányay would do similarly later. Goldwitzer published another very useful work: *Bibliographie der kirchenväter und kirchenlehrer vom ersten bis zum dreyzehnten jahrhunderte*, Landshut 1828.

From around the middle of the nineteenth century the manual of patrology for the use of theologians and of students flourished – not only works made for the library, which are truly introductions to the study of the Fathers. By then in the manuals biblical texts were excluded, since they were not considered ecclesiastical. Today, we are not accustomed to placing and situating the manuals close to their authors' confessional adherence; at that time it was a normal fact in order to indicate the theological positions of the authors, as did E.C. Richardson in his bibliographical supplement to the collection of the *Ante-Nicene Fathers* (Ann Arbor, 1887, pp. 119–123). The greater parts of these manuals were written by German-language scholars and then they were translated into other languages (Italian, French, English). Some manuals were still written in Latin, which permitted a greater circulation. Then, Latin was still very much used and known. Many authors – instead of the terms patrology or patristics – preferred that of "Christian (or ecclesiastical) literature," beginning with Möhler, who considered patrology a "superfluous science" (p. 14, see Möhler below). In this way, the historical and philological aspects were more clearly evidenced, and one could include all of the ancient Christian writers. The Protestants, for the most part, preferred to speak of Christian literature in general.

J.N. Locherer, *Lehrbuch der Patrologie*, Mainz 1837. It was a small manual. Franz Michael Permaneder, *Bibliotheca patristica*. I: *Patrologia generalis*; II: *Patrologia specialis*, Landishuti, 1841–1844. J.P. Charpentier, *Études sur les Pères de l'Église*, Paris 1853, in two volumes. The Anglican J. Donaldson, *A Critical History of Christian Literature and Doctrine from the Death of the Apostles to the Nicene Council*, London, 1864–1866 (three volumes; it covers only the second century). The author insists upon the concept that his work is a critical work on the authors and their thought. J.B.J. Busse, *Grundriss Der Christlichen Literatur von Ihrem Ursprung an bis zur Erfindung der Buchdruckerei*, Münster 1828–1829 (two volumes) (the subtitle says that it is for theologians).

J.A. Möhler (†1838), *Patrologie oder christliche Literärgeschichte*, printed posthumously, with additions and corrections by F.S. Reithmayr, Regensburg 1840. It treats only the first three centuries; a substantial and much appreciated work that was immediately translated both into Italian and into French. J. Fessler, *Institutiones Patrologiae*, Oeniponte, 1850–1851 (in two volumes; later re-edited and reworked by B. Jungmann, 1890–1896); after the death of Jungmann, the work was then under the care of A. Hebbelynk. He brings his treatment up to the time of Gregory the Great. C. Magon, *Handbuch der Patrologie und der kirchlichen Litteraturgeschichte*, Regensburg 1864. J. Alzog (†1878), *Patrologie oder der ältern christlichen Literärgeschichte*, Freiburg 1866; the last edition was updated in 1888.

Bernard Schmid, *Grundlinien der Patrologie*, Freiburg 1879 (many editions; an English translation, Saint Louis, MO, 1899). The introduction and the first part are of great interest so that one may understand the reason for which one should have studied the Fathers of the Church, and to help one understand the environment that reigned in the theological schools of that time. For him, patrology was the preliminary science used in order to acquire a precise knowledge of and familiarity with the Fathers' writings so as to use them well in theology. On the other hand, "patristics as a science" has the aim of a systematic collection from the works of the Fathers, according to quite precise principles, all that which can be related to the faith, morality, and ecclesiastical discipline.

Patrology is different from ancient Christian literature, in so much as the latter deals not only with the works of the Fathers but also with the ancient ecclesiastical writers and it is limited to the literary development. He adds that it lays down the rules and principles whereby one determines the authority of the Fathers, their authenticity, their correct use and the way in which to gather the most fruit in theology from their works. Schmid does not totally exclude those authors who were influential, although they were not Fathers themselves, in Christian life. The ecclesiastical writers (e.g., Clement of Alexandria, Origen, Tertullian, Eusebius) are distinct from those who were "inspired." The elements that are necessary in order for one to be included among the Fathers are: antiquity, ecclesiastical teaching, orthodox doctrine, holiness of life, their approbation by the Church, explicitly (e.g., in a council) or in an implicit or tacit manner. For example, Saint Irenaeus (not withstanding his Millenarianism) and Saint Gregory of Nyssa (despite his Origenist ideas) are enumerated among the Fathers. Between the manuals of patrology, Schmid was the author who dedicated ample space to the definition of the authority of the Fathers of the Church:

> The authority, which was ascribed to those writers, came to be understood as their power and right to claim and require intellectual assent (*auctoritas movens et obligans*). It was a moral power that regarded the mind of the reader, by determining his judgment and by compelling his assent to the words or to the claims of the writer. This authority has a variation of degrees (Schmid 1899: 30ff).

The concept of authority was treated for each one of the Fathers – in dogmatic, moral, and exegetical matters, in pastoral theology and even in the natural sciences.

I have spent some time on these aspects, because all of the authors treat them, even if it is in a more or less concise manner, and they belonged to the traditional way in which treatises handled such issues. In the modern manuals these topics are considered obsolete arguments and no scholars speak of them.

J. Nirschl, *Lehrbuch der Patrologie und Patristik*, Mainz 1881–1885. It is interesting that even in the title we see the words "patrology" and "patristics" used on the part of a Catholic author; this last term was considered to be a Protestant usage even until recent times. J. Rézbányay, *Compendium patrologiae et patristicae*, Quinque ecclesiis [=Fünfkirchen], 1894. This compendium relates, too, some excerpts taken from the Fathers, at the service of theology. A. Retke, *Patrologiae compendium*, Varsaviae 1889.

The Patrologies of the Twentieth Century

In the second half of the nineteenth century and in the first half of the twentieth century there was an increase in new findings of other patristic texts; some of them came from papyrus discoveries; translations of Greek texts into the Oriental languages were recovered. The philological method permitted better critical editions; the authors of some anonymous texts were identified; this enhanced the study of their language and of their style. Not only did this help to investigate the theological thoughts of the Fathers, but also the other aspects of their reflections; this put aside apologetic aims and goals that were too accentuated, and this set apart the lines of demarcation among scholars. Patristics, which had been exclusively at the service of theology, became a science in itself. Theology always kept patristics before its proverbial eyes, but the latter also acquired its own autonomy: one studied the Fathers in their capacity as writers and thinkers, for their works and for their personalities, their sources and their influence. The treatises were focused on the first centuries; the medieval period dropped out of the picture, especially for those who were early. Many scholars would make it to the eighth century, but after the fifth they limited themselves only to naming the great and famous ones.

Before proceeding on to the manuals, truly and properly so called, it is necessary to mention some of the most important works. Ch.Th. Cruttwell, *A Literary History of Early Christianity*, London 1893, reaching Victorinus of Poetovio (today Ptuj, Slovenia). The author acknowledged he is writing an Anglican work that, as he says, defends, against the Lutherans, the possibility of a progressive interpretation of Scripture in relation to its fecundity. Therefore, the Fathers are important for the interpretation of Scripture and for its more comprehensive understanding. In those years A. von Harnack was writing his great work on Pre-Nicene Christian literature: *Geschichte der altchristlichen Literaturbis auf Eusebius*, three volumes, Part I: *Die Uberlieferung und der Bestand*, Leipzig 1893–1904. The same period was also studied by G. Krüger, *Geschichte der altchristlichen Literatur in den ersten drei Jahrhunderten*, Freiburg, 1895, with a later supplement (Krüger 1987). The manual was conceived as a guide for students in order to bring out the literary rather than the theological aspects. That is, it intended to place the Christian authors within the confines of the pagan world of their age and to properly esteem the texts written by the Christians as literary productions and not for their theological or ecclesiological content.

Many authors who studied the literature of the Greek and Latin languages dedicated a part to the Christian authors; for example, A. Ehrhard, M. Schanz, and G. Hosius, Munich 1905–1920. The same von Harnack made himself the champion of "ancient Christian literature," as a means for the historical understanding and knowledge of the evolution of the ancient Church and not as a support for the study of theology.

The list of the new manuals must begin with the work of O. Bardenhewer (†1935), *Patrologie*, Freiburg (Bardenhewer 1894). This was perhaps the first Patrology of a scientific standard in a large volume, which immediately obtained a great prestige among the Catholics and the Protestants and was translated into French, English and Italian (which was prepared by the great A. Mercati). In this edition he radically redid the first part, which was on the subject of the Pre-Nicene authors. In 1910 a third edition appeared, which would be the last. Bardenhewer had complete control of the bibliography, which he knew how to choose, with the conviction that it was not the quantity which counted for quality, but the shrewd choice of that which truly had worth.

We must keep before us some other distinctions and affinities in the titles of the manuals which were occupied with the ancient Christian authors. Bardenhewer (1902–1932) successively composed a great work in more volumes *Geschichte der altkirchlichen Literatur*. The author echoes Jerome by using the term "ecclesiastical" and he wished to differentiate himself from the Protestants. However, both the Catholics (e.g., Funk) and the Protestants (e.g., von Harnack, Krüger) did not accept this terminology, for he included those who were not ecclesiastical authors, such as the Gnostics and the heretics. Bardenhewer considered the term "Christian" ambiguous or neutral; in reality, patrology (or ecclesiastical literature) understood that the ancient church was conscious of its possession of a *deposit um fidei*. The terminology he used was not taken up by others, in so much as the later publications until our day still carry the title of "patrology," "Christian literature," or simply "Fathers of the Church."

In those very years the great von Harnack (1851–1830), among his other numerous works, wrote the work which we have already cited, *Geschichte der altchristlichen Literaturbis auf Eusebius*. He, against the traditional use of the Fathers in theology, preferred the phrase "Christian literature," in order to accentuate the historical aspects of the ancient writings for an understanding of the history of the Christian communities. Both of these authors used the term "literature." Bardenhewer qualified this with the adjective "ecclesiastical," while von Harnack used the adjective "Christian." The specification indicated the difference of approach. The Catholics Möhler and Alzog had already used the adjective "Christian." The intention was that of accentuating the historical aspect and including all of the authors of Christian inspiration, and not only those who were recognized as Fathers, thus even those who were part of different Christian groups, schismatic and even the Gnostics.

The term "literature" had always had a greater diffusion in titles through the influence of historians of literature and philology (De Ghellinck 1947: 150). The Protestant historian of dogma, Friedrich Nitzsch (1865), discussed this problem in favor of the use of the term "ancient Christian literature" (*Geschichtliches und Methodologisches*). Here, we touch upon a delicate and much discussed problem. If for the authors of the patrologies the literary aspects were not interesting, then even the stories of ancient literature neglected them, because as Altaner (1976: 6) wrote, the Christian authors "absolutely did not want to compose literary works in the strict sense. It was their intention to offer and to represent a new conception of life". The very same Altaner acknowledged that some of the Fathers had arrived at high literary pinnacles.

I will also recall here some useful manuals, starting with Jakob Marx, *Abriss der Patrologie*, Trier 1901; Paderborn 1919, translated into Spanish and much used in Spain. A good manual is that by H. Kihn, *Patrologie*, in two volumes, Paderborn 1904–1908. B. Steidle, *Patrologia seu historia antiquae litteraturae ecclesiasticae*, Freiburg im Br. 1937 (later published in a German edition). The manual that had a long history and was used by various generations of students of different nationalities was that written by Rauschen and published for the first time in 1903, *Grundriss der Patrologie*, with the scope of "offering in the first place a book of foundations to serve as a text for the schools, as an aid for those who study by themselves, and as a *commonitorium* for those who have already studied" (from the introduction). The intention was to substitute – in the German-speaking world – the volume by B. Schmid. The complete title explains well the tendencies of the author: "A manual of patrology and of its relation to the history of dogma."

A small manual was really needed, but one that was precise and scientifically reliable, such as the one by Rauschen, for which it immediately had translations into different languages (Spanish 1909; French 1906; Italian 1905; Polish 1904; it was not translated into English. Only the final edition was translated into English). Every successive edition, keeping present the suggestions from various parts of the world, involved an improvement and an expansion. After the death of Rauschen (†1917), Josef Wittig took to editing the editions of 1921 and of 1926. The edition from 1931 was published under the names of G. Rauschen and B. Altaner: there was no longer the title of *Grundriss* (compendium) but that of *Patrologie* (Patrology). In 1938, Altaner oversaw a complete and detailed re-elaboration according to the outline and model of the life, works, and thought – with a rich and precise bibliography – for which reason the volume was published under his name alone. At first it was commonly called: Rauschen–Altaner. On account of this radical makeover the manual carried only the name of Altaner. Of the Oriental authors (Coptic, Syriac, Armenian), not many are mentioned, but there was an ever greater interest in them. The last edition that was personally edited by Altaner was that of 1958, a testimony to the continuity of the great patrologists. The *Patrologie* of Altaner was a true manual that had for its object the life, the writings and the thought of the Fathers with precise bibliographical references. The treatment of authors extends to Gregory the Great. The work enjoyed great success and was translated into many languages, even into Hungarian.

J. Barbel (†1973), *Geschichte der frühchristlichen, griechischen und lateinischen Literatur*, Aschanffenburg 1969, two deft small volumes (256 + 212). H. Kraft, *Einführung in die Patrologie*, Darmstadt 1991. S. Hausammann, *Alte Kirche: zur Geschichte und Theologie in den ersten vier Jahrhunderten*, Neukirchen-Vluyn 2001–2005 in five volumes.

Altaner (†1964), in 1960, had his work edited by Alfred Stuiber; the last edition was in 1978. The last Italian edition had a bibliographical update by A. Di Berardino. The information – brief, packed, informative, and precise concerning every author or anonymous text – makes Altaner (–Stuiber) a text for consultation, in as much as all authors are included, even minor authors. Since it was perceived there was a need for a manual for students, Hubertus R. Drobner published *Lehrbuch der Patrologie* in 1994. The author continues to update it, be it with the original German-language edition or in the translations into many modern languages, even Korean.

The manuals cited were all written by German-language scholars; these were then translated into different languages. There were also other manuals, written in different languages. Let us begin with French. The first that we must cite is from the historian of dogmas, J. Tixeront, *Précis de patrologie*, Paris 1918, a succinct manual for students. It was complementary to the *Histoire des dogmes*. A work that was more extensive and better organized was that by Fulbert Cayré, *Précis de Patrologie*, Paris 1927–1930. Cayré brought forth the novelty of speaking of the moral, ascetical, and mystical doctrines of the Fathers too. In France, numerous works were published under the name of literature. I shall cite the principal works, because some of them were very important. P. Batiffol, *La littérature grecque*, Paris, 1897; Aimé Puech, *Histoire de la littérature grecque chrétienne depuis les origines jusqu'à la fin du IVe siècle*, three volumes, Paris 1928–1930; A. Jeanory and A. Puech, *Littérature latine chrétienne*, Paris 1899; G. Bardy, *Littérature grecque chrétienne*, Paris 1928, and *Littérature latine chrétienne*, Paris 1929; P. Monceaux, *Histoire littéraire de L'Afrique chrétienne depuis les origines jusqu'à l'invasion arabe*, Paris 1901–1923, seven volumes; P. de Labriolle, *Histoire de la littérature latine chrétienne*, Paris 1920; J. Fontaine, *La littérature latine chrétienne*, Paris 1970. In more recent times, Jacques Liebaert and Michel Spanneut published *Les pères de l'Église*, Paris,

Desclée, 1986–1990 (two volumes, until the eighth century). These scholars treat only the principal authors and they added passages from patristic texts. J. Laporte, *Pères de l'Église*, Paris 2001. In addition, the great *Histoire de la litterature grecque chrétienne* is in the course of being published in six volumes under the direction of B. Pouderon and E. Norelli: vol. I, Paris 2008; vol. 2 (*De Paul l'apôtre à Irénée de Lyon*), Paris 2013. The plan is to reach the council of Chalcedon (451). The first volume was an introduction and confronted questions connected with the study of the Fathers; the chapter by Norelli that discusses the problematic of Christian literature is very useful.

In English have been published translations of German and French patrology texts. Of the works originally written in English, I would like to mention: Fr. W. Farrar, *Lives of the Fathers. Sketches of Church History in Biographies*, London 1889. E.J. Goodspeed published *A History of Early Christian Literature*, Chicago 1942. He carries the treatment up to Lactantius and Eusebius of Cesarea. Johannes Quasten (†1987), *Patrology*, three volumes, Utrecht 1950–1960. Four volumes were foreseen, making it to the council of Chalcedon in 451; for health reasons he did not publish the fourth volume; that is, the volume regarding the Latin Fathers. His famous patrology was received with great praise and translated into various languages. The work is characterized by its wealth of information and its bibliographical precision, for its ample and precise treatment, which is also simple and legible, for its exposition of the thought of the Fathers. The elegant presentation and the facility with which one could consult the work contributed to its success among scholars and students, because it is also a work of consultation. Each work of every author is listed, along with their editions, the translations and the recent studies – not those of the previous centuries.

The patrologies written in Latin, in the German-speaking world, were very widespread in Italy, which was an open field of translations. However, there were also numerous manuals written originally in Italian; a group by the name of "literature" and another group with the title of "patrology." From the first group I will only name the most important. U. Moricca, *Storia della letteratura latina cristiana*, Turin 1925–1934, three volumes; A.G. Amatucci, *Storia della letteratura latina cristiana*, Bari 1929; L. Salvatorelli, *Storia della letteratura cristiana dalle origini alla metà del VI secolo*, Milan 1936; M. Pellegrino, *Letteratura greca cristiana*, Rome 1956, and *Letteratura latina cristiana*, Rome 1957; M. Simonetti, *La letteratura cristiana antica greca e latina*, Florence–Milan 1969; C. Moreschini and E. Norelli, *Storia della letteratura cristiana antica greca e latina*, Brescia 1995, three tomes. This work offered detailed and complete information of the Christian writers who were placed in a historical context. M. Simonetti and E. Prinzivalli, *Storia della letteratura cristiana antica*, Casale Monferrato 1999. These two manuals are now the avant-garde for the presentation of the ancient Christian literary production. Both of them were accompanied by large anthologies of texts from the Fathers. The work by Moreschini and Norelli enjoyed a great success, because it was translated into numerous languages (Spanish, Greek, French, English); they also wrote an abridged edition, Brescia 2006.

For the patrologies, those which deserve to be recalled here are the following: E. Ruggeri, *Storia dei santi Padri e dell'antica letteratura della Chiesa*, Rome 1875–1877; U. Mannucci, *Istituzioni di patrologia*, Rome 1914–1915. The fifth (1935) and then the sixth editions were under the care of Antonio Casamassa, Rome, 1948–1950. This last one mentioned was an excellent manual, which presented a detailed analysis of the works, but it does not mention the apocryphal texts. We recall too the manuals of P.G. Franceschini, Milan 1919; G.P. Sinopoli Di Giunta, Turin–Rome 1920–1922; Guido Bosio, Turin 1963–1967 (with brief introductions and an anthology of texts); the work was redone by E. dal Covolo and M. Maritano, Turin 1990–1999.

The great manual by Quasten, with his permission, has been taken up and continued by Angelo Di Berardino, in three large volumes. The fourth volume (III in Italian; Casale Monferrato 1978) treats the Latin Fathers from the time of the council of Nicaea until the council of Chalcedon; this edition also has various translations. Volume IV in Italian comprehends the Latin language literature until the death of Isidore of Seville (Genoa 1996); while Volume V confronts the oriental writers, and not only those who wrote in Greek, but also those of other languages (Coptic, Syriac, Armenian) (Genoa 2000). The volumes that were not edited by Quasten continued to report all the writers, even those who are little known, and even the anonymous texts; the presentation was changed: it did not include translated passages from patristic texts and there is a greater sensibility for other sets of problems, beyond those treating dogma. Since dozens of authors contributed to the work, one can come across divergences of opinion and judgment. They preserved the fundamental schema: all the works of each author are listed by their editions, their translations into modern languages and the most recent studies – not those of past centuries.

Some manuals were published by Spanish scholars, not of great size, but well written and suitable for teaching in the seminaries. We will cite here the following manuals: Miguel Yus, Madrid 1872; Julián Adrián Onrubia, Palencia 1911. E. Monegal y Nogues, Barcelona 1922. In more recent times: E. Contreras and R. Peña, *Introducción al estudio de los Padres*, Azul (Argentina) 1991–1994; R. Trevijano Etcheverría, *Patrología*, Madrid 1994; Alberto Viciano, *Patrología*, Valencia 2001; Juan María de la Torre, *Literatura cristiana antigua, entornos y contenidos*, Zamora 2003–2009, six volumes. B. Sánchez García, *Manual de patrología*, Terrassa 2005. D. Ramos-Lissón, *Patrología*, Pamplona 2005, containing the mature fruit of his long teaching.

The Oriental Patrologies

As I mentioned previously, in the old manuals, the oriental writers who did not write in Greek were completely overlooked. In the more recent patrologies, sometimes only the principal personalities find a place. Today, the *patrology* most widespread is that by H. Drobner. In the first German edition the author passed completely over the oriental writers, some of whom have been added to the successive editions. The only "patrology" that has a specific and thorough treatment of these authors is *Patrology: The Eastern Fathers from the Council of Chalcedon to John of Damascus* (Genoa 2000), edited by A. Di Berardino, which has also been translated into English (Cambridge 2006), with in-depth chapters on Syriac, Coptic, and Armenian literature, with a copious bibliography. We may refer readers to those chapters. Nevertheless, for commodity's sake, I shall add some more bibliographical indications. For the wealth of the bibliographies, one might begin with two very important works. The first is M. Albert *et al.*, *Christianismes orientaux: introduction à l'étude des langues et des littératures*, Paris 1993.

For each of the languages, here is some further information:

1. The Syriac language is still used in the liturgies of some of the Oriental Churches, in the "Assyrian" Church of the East (also known as the "Nestorian" Church) and the Syrian Orthodox Church (known as the "Jacobite" or "Miaphyiste" Church), and sometimes by the Maronite Church. For Syriac literature one must begin with the old work by J.S. Assemani, *Bibliotheca Orientalis*, Rome 1719–1728, in three large volumes: one was dedicated to the "Orthodox" writers, another to the "Miaphysites," and the third to the "Nestorians," The volumes are filled with passages from the writers themselves, translated into Latin. For more recent times we recall here some of the manuals: R. Duval, *La literature syriaque*, Paris 1911. The manual of reference is by A. Baumstark, *Geschichte der syrischen Literatur*, Bonn 1922, an indispensable work still; the author even lists the manuscripts of the works he cites. J.B. Chabot, *Littérature syriaque* Paris 1934, a useful manual. I. Ortiz De Urbina, *Patrologia Syriaca*, Rome 1958, a manual, composed in Latin, that is precise, systematic and complete – until the middle of the eighth century; a text for consultation. In any case, the best synthetic treatment is that made by P. Bettiolo, *Syriac Literature*, in *Patrology: The Eastern Fathers from the Council of Chalcedon to John of Damascus*, ed. A. Di Berardino, Cambridge 2006, pp. 407–490. It is worth mentioning here three "patrologies" that were published by oriental authors: Ignatios Afram (Barsaum) (†1957), *The Book of Unstrung Pearls in the History of Syriac Literature and Sciences*, 1956 (II edn) originally in Arabic; then translated into Syriac (Qamishli, Syria, 1967; and later into English by Matti Moosa, *The Scattered Pearls: a History of Syriac Literature and Sciences*, Piscataway, NJ, 2003. Albert Abuna, *Adab al-lugha al-aramiyya* (=*Aramean Literature*; Beirut 1970). P. Sarmas, *Tash'ita d-siprayutaatoreta* (=*History of Assyrian Literature*), Teheran 1969–70; this work is written in modern Syriac.

2. For Armenian Christian literature, the best manuals are: H. Thorossian, *Histoire de la literature arménienne*, Paris 1951; V. Inglisian, *Die armenische Literatur*, in *Handbuch der Orientalistik*, I, 7, Leiden–Cologne 1963, pp. 157–250; K. Sarkissian, *A Brief Introduction to Armenian Christian Literature*, London 1960; Ch. Renoux, *La littérature arménienne*, in M. Albert *et al.*, *Christianismes orientaux*, o.c., pp. 107–166. S. Voicuhas has written a good synthesis, in *Patrology: The Eastern Fathers*, pp. 571–604. Some patristic texts written in Greek but not preserved in the original language were conserved in Armenian, such as the *Demonstratio apostolica* of Irenaeus for example.

3. Coptic literature begins with the second century CE and is subdivided into different dialects. In antiquity the literary language that was most prevalent was Sahidic. Those who began to write in Coptic were the monks of inland Egypt. The first Coptic Christian literature had a monastic temper. Here are some of the manuals: J. Leipoldt, *Geschichte der koptischen Literatur*, in *Gesch. der christl. Lit. des Orients*, ed. C. Brockelmann, II edn, Leipzig 1909, VII, 2, pp. 131–183; S. Morenz, *Die koptische Literatur*, in *Handbuch der Orientalistik* I, 2, Leiden–Cologne 1970, pp. 239–250; T. Orlandi, *Elementi di lingua e letteratura copta*, Milan 1970.

T. Orlandi, *Patristic texts in Coptic*, in *Patrology: The Eastern Fathers*, ed. A. Di Berardino, pp. 491–470. A. Boud'ors, *The Coptic Tradition*, in *The Oxford Handbook of Late Antiquity*, ed. S. Fitzgerald Johnson, New York 2012, pp. 224–246. This is a brief but well-executed treatment.

Orthodox theologians of the Greek tradition from the beginning of the twentieth century perceived and understood that it was insufficient to cite passages from the Fathers, but that a return to their writings, their thought and their manner of theologizing was necessary (Marinescu 2011). Moreover, ecumenical dialogue, which was then in development, encouraged recourse to the Fathers, which would be favorable to an encounter from among the different Christian confessions. The Orthodox tradition had always been very tied to the Fathers, but now – under Western influence, there was felt the need to make a deeper and more profound study of their texts, their thought and their spirituality. The first "patrology" (*An historical education from the Fathers of the Church*, Saint Petersburg 1859, reprinted 1882) was the one written by Philaret of Chernigov (Chernihiv, Ukraine) (1805–1866), in three volumes, published in Russian and translated into Greek and Romanian (Thessaloniki 1878–1894). Philaret had a great influence in the Orthodox world, creating a school of translators. One last manual, in Russian, was that by Archimandrite Cyprian (Kern) *Patrologiia*, Paris 1963, Moscow 1996. The same author wrote another volume: *The Golden Age of the Writing of the Church Fathers* (in Russian), Paris 1967.

The manuals of patristics in Greece have a long tradition, but focused mainly on the Greek Fathers. The oldest is that of K. Kontogonis (1812–1878) in two volumes, *Filologiki kai Kritiki Istoria*, which deals with the Greek and Latin Fathers until the fifth century (Athens 1851–1853). Up to the fourth century, the three volumes of G. Dervos (1854–1925), *Christianiki grammatology* (Athens 1903–1910). The Dervos volume includes the Latin Fathers, but not those in other oriental languages. For manuals of reduced dimensions there are those of D. Balanos (*Patrologia*, Athens 1930), K. Bonis (*Christianiki grammateia*, Athens 1977), V. Pseftogas (*Stoicheia Ekklisiastikis Grammatologias me anthologio Paterikonergon*, Thessaloniki 1994), D. Tsamis (*Ekklisiastiki Grammatologia*, Thessaloniki 1996), I. Moutsoulas (*Eisagogieis tin Patrology*, Athens 2009). Recently, the study of patristics was promoted in a particular way by Panagiotis K. Chrestou (1917–1995), the author of the *Hellênikê patrologia*, in five volumes. It was an extensive work that took the reader to the fall of Constantinople in 1453 and it was written in an archaic form of Greek (*katharevousa*). The *Patrology* (Πατρολογία) written by the Greek Stylianos Papadopoulos, in three volumes, enjoyed great success (Athens 1977–2010). The first two volumes were reprinted several times and translated into Romanian. The author described the life of those authors studied, and from whom he included lots of texts in order to illustrate the most important themes. The patrology of Papadopoulos is currently the best one written by an Orthodox author. Besides these more significant works, there were also manuals of patrology with a reduced size and with a scholastic character. In general, the works by the Orthodox limited themselves to the Greek Fathers, such as the one of Chrestou for example; while the one by Papadopoulos reaches the fifth century and it also includes a treatment of the Latin Fathers. The Christian writers in other languages (Coptic, Armenian, Syriac, etc.) are excluded.

The Romanians, for linguistic and cultural reasons, have been a bridge between the Byzantine tradition of the east and the western Latin tradition. Their scholars published works in Romanian and in French, and today in Romanian and in English. Furthermore, they translated much from other languages. There are patrologies written in Romanian: I. G. Coman, *Patrologie manual*, Bucharest 1956, only one volume; the same author published a much more comprehensive work, *Patrologie*, Bucharest 1984–1988, in three volumes – the fourth volume is hitherto lacking; the entire work is rather a compilation. I. Bota, *Patrologia*, Cluj-Napoca 1997. Finally, we must mention C. Voicu, *Patrologie*, Bucharest 2009, for students of theology, in three volumes, which was the fruit of the classes he gave at the faculty of Sibiu. The first two carry the treatment until the middle of the fifth century; the third treats the principal authors, especially the Greeks until the Late Middle Ages. The author completely ignored the Coptic and Armenian writers; he names only Ephraem (first) and Aphraates (afterwards).

Bibliography

Altaner, Berthold (1976), *Patrologia*. Casale Monferrato: Marietti.

Backus, Irena (2003), *Historical Method and Confessional Identity in the Era of the Reformation (1378–1615)*. Leiden: Brill.

Bardenhewer, Otto (1894), *Patrologie*. Freiburg: Herder (Paris 1898–1899; II edn 1901 – from which Angelo Mercati composed an Italian translation; 1899, reprod. 1917: St Louis, MO: B. Herder).

Bardenhewer, Otto (1902–1932), *Geschichte der altkirchlichen Literatur*. (The first two volumes came out in 1902–1903 at Freiburg, the third volume in 1912, the fourth in 1924 and the fifth in 1932.)

Bellarminus, Roberto (1613), *De scriptoribus ecclesiasticis liber unus, cum adiunctis indicibus undecim et brevi chronologia ab orbe conditousque ad annum 1612*. Rome: Ex Typographia Bartholomaei Zannetti. (The work was defined by Dupin as a "traité expres.")

Cave, William (1688–1698), *Scriptorum ecelesiasticorum Historia a Christo natousquead saeculum XIV*. London: Typis T.H. and Impensis Richardi Chriswell.

Daillé, Jean (1632), *Traicté de l'employ des Saincts Pères*. Geneva: Pierre Aubert.

De Ghellinck, J. (1947), *Patristique et Moyen Age*. Gembloux: J. Duculot.

Di Berardino, A. (ed.) (2007), *I concili della chiesa antica*, vol. II, *Decretali pontificie e canoni di Serdica*, in collaboration with T. Sardella e C. Dell'Osso. Rome; 224–246.

Du Cange, Charles Dufresne (1668), *Glossarium mediæ et infimæ latinitatis*, vol. 3. Lyon; 227.

Dupin, L.E. (or Du Pin) (1686 ff.), *Nouvelle bibliothèque des auteurs ecclésiastiques*. Paris: André Pralard.

Krüger, Gustav (1897), *History of Early Christian Literature*, Ch.R. Gillett (English transl.). New York: James Westfall Thompson.

Le Nain de Tillemont, L.S. (1693–1712), *Mémoires pour servir à l'histoire ecclésiastique des six premiers siècles,*. Paris: C. Robustel (16 tomes, reprinted often).

Marinescu A. (2011), *Patrology and Related Studies in Orthodoxy in the 20th Century and Early 21st Century*, in: *Orthodoxy Theology in the 20th Century and Early 21st Century. A Romanian Orthodox Perspective*, edn V. Bucharest: Ioniţa; 327–393.

Moreschini, Claudio and Norelli, Enrico (1999), *Antologia della letteratura cristiana antica greca e latina*, vol. I: *Da Paolo all'età costantiniana*; II: *Dal concilio di Nicea agli inizi del medioevo*.

Nitzsch, Friedrich (1865), "Geschichtliches und Methodologisches zur Patristik". *Jahrbucher für deutsche Theologie*, 10: 37–63.

Oudin, Casimir (1722), *Commentarius de Scriptoribus Antiquis*, Lipsiae: Sumptibus Maur. Georg. Weidemanni.

Rauschen, Gerhard (1903), *Grundriß der Patrologie. Mit besonderer Berücksichtigung der Dogmengeschichte*. Freiburg im Breisgau: Herder.

Schmid, Bernard (1899), *Manual of Patrology*. St Louis, MO: B. Herder (German original (1879): *Grundlinien der Patrologie*, Freiburg).

Simon, Richard (1730), *Critique de la bibliothèque des auteurs ecclésiastiques et des prolégomènes de la bible, publiez par M. Elies Du-Pin.*

Avec des eclaircissemens & des supplémens aux endroits où on les a jugé nécessaires. Avec des Remarques (four volumes). Paris: É. Ganneau.

Simonetti, Manlio and Prinzivalli, Emanuela (1999), *Letteratura cristiana antica: antologia di testi*. Casale Monferrato: Piemme (English translation, Baker Academic, 2005).

Turchetti, M. (1993), "Jean Daillé et son Traicté de l'employ des saincts Pères (1632)". In *Les Pères de l'Eglise au XVII s*, E. Bury and B. Meunier (eds). Paris: Cerf; 73s.

Wiest, Stephan (1795), *Institutiones patrologiae ad usum academicum*. Ingolstadt: Kull.

CHAPTER 4
Irenaeus of Lyons

Denis Minns

Introductory Remarks

Irenaeus provides the most comprehensive early exposition we have of mainstream Christian theology. He was probably a native of Asia Minor. In his youth he had known Polycarp, a famous bishop of Smyrna (modern Izmir), who was martyred there around the middle of the second century. By the 170s Irenaeus had settled in Lyons, the principal city of the Roman provinces in Gaul and Germany, with a large and multicultural population. Irenaeus held a position of leadership in the mainly Greek-speaking Christian communities there and is best known for his efforts to overthrow what he regarded as distorting and divisive interpretations of Christian doctrine and practice – heresies – which in modern times have been grouped under the umbrella term "Gnosticism," and to set forth against these the authentic Christian faith handed down in the church from the Apostles.

Writings

In the *Ecclesiastical History* (*EH*) Eusebius of Caesarea mentions two works of Irenaeus that have come down to us. The larger and better known of these is the *Refutation and Overthrow of Knowledge falsely so-called* (*EH* V.7.1). Eusebius also refers to this as *Against the Heresies* (*EH* V.5.9), which is the title by which it is mostly commonly known (here *AH*). Eusebius quotes from all five books of this work in *EH* IV.29 and V.6–9, and presumably had access to the whole of it, as well as to the other works he mentions (Carriker 2003: 217–8). A much smaller work, from which Eusebius does not quote, is the *Demonstration of the Apostolic Preaching*.

The Wiley Blackwell Companion to Patristics, First Edition. Edited by Ken Parry.
© 2015 John Wiley & Sons Ltd. Published 2019 by John Wiley & Sons Ltd.

Eusebius mentions a number of other works, but apart from such fragments as he quotes, these have not survived. They are: a *Letter to Blastus on Schism* mentioned at *EH* V.20.1; a *Letter to Florinus, On Monarchy, or that God is not the Author of Evil*, from which Eusebius quotes a passage in which Irenaeus reminds Florinus that he had heard the teaching of Polycarp who had received it "from the eyewitnesses of the life of the Word" (*EH* V.20.4–8); *On the Ogdoad*, from which Eusebius quotes a short passage at *EH* V.20.2; a *Letter to Victor*, bishop of Rome, concerning the controversy over the proper date for the celebration of Easter, from which Eusebius quotes two passages (*EH* V.24.12–17); *On Gnosis, Against the Greeks*, which Eusebius describes as a "most concise and exceedingly cogent work" (*EH* V.26), though he does not quote from it; a "certain book of various discourses, in which he mentions the Epistle to the Hebrews and the Wisdom of Solomon ... quoting certain passages from them" (*EH* V.26) and an *Answer to Marcion out of his own treatises*. That Irenaeus "promised" to write a work such as this last is inferred by Eusebius at *EH* V.8.9, presumably from remarks of Irenaeus at *AH* I.27.4 and III.12.12. It is possible that Irenaeus may have had a hand in, or even been the author of, the *Letter from the churches of Vienne and Lyons to the Churches of Asia and Phrygia*, from which Eusebius quotes extensive extracts at *EH* V.1.3–2.7.

At III.3.3 Irenaeus names Eleutherus as the current bishop of the church in Rome, which places the time of writing between about 175 and 189. It is clear from Irenaeus' own comments that each of the five books was published separately, and, indeed, that the plan of the whole work evolved in the course of its composition. Irenaeus was still active during the episcopate of Victor (189–198), the successor of Eleutherus. At the end of the *Demonstration of the Apostolic Preaching* Irenaeus mentions that he is the author of the *Refutation and Overthrow of Knowledge falsely so-called*, but it is possible that this refers just to the first two books of *Adversus Haereses* and that the other three were written subsequently to the *Demonstration*.

Early Dissemination

We know that *Adversus Haereses* was being read in Egypt within a few decades of its being written. Papyrus Oxyrhynchus 405 was published in 1903. It contains scraps of the text of III.9.2–3 and is dated to the end of the second century or the beginning of the third. From the way the text is presented, L. Doutreleau proposes that these fragments come from a "rouleau de l'*Adversus Haereses*" rather than from a *florilegium* (SC 210: 128). We have no way of knowing whether the complete work in five rolls once existed in Oxyrhynchus.

The Jena Papyrus originated in Upper Egypt and was first published in 1912. It is dated to the fourth, or possibly the late third century, and is likely originally to have contained the whole of V.1.1–14.4, which constitutes a distinct section, given over to proving the resurrection of the flesh from the Pauline epistles (SC 152, 121–130). Apart from their utility in the reconstruction of Irenaeus' Greek text, these two papyri are important in that they show us that Irenaeus' work was being read many hundreds of miles away from where he wrote, within a decade or two of its publication, and a hundred years later still. Although Irenaeus continued to be read and quoted by Greek-speaking authors, the Greek texts of both *Adversus Haereses* and the *Demonstration* have since been lost. Had the *Demonstration* not been translated into Armenian it would have been known only from its mention by Eusebius, and others dependent on him, such as Jerome (*De viris inlustribus* 35).

Early Notices, Quotations and Influence

Tertullian and Hippolytus are the earliest writers to mention Irenaeus. In the *Refutatio Omnium Haeresium* (VI.55), Hippolytus, according to Photius a disciple of Irenaeus (*Bibliotheca* II.121), says that he has taken over from Irenaeus material about the Valentinians, and this work does incorporate considerable portions of the first book of *AH*. The *Refutatio* was first printed in 1851, since which time editors have been able to make use of it to re-establish the Greek text of those portions. At *Adversus Valentinianos* 5, Tertullian described Irenaeus as "the most painstaking investigator of every teaching" and made extensive use of *AH* I in this work, written in Latin early in the third century.

In the vast repertory he called the *Panarion*, Epiphanius, a fourth-century bishop of Salamis, brought an encyclopedist's range to the work of describing heresies and explaining their interdependence. When he comes to the Valentinians, Epiphanius first presents material he says he has taken from their own books, and then says that he has chosen not to set out the remainder of Valentinus' subtlety himself, as he has found the matter already dealt with previously by the most holy Irenaeus, whom he had earlier described as "a blessed successor of the Apostles" (*Haer.* 24), and he will therefore take the material over more or less from that servant of God (*Haer.* 31). In fact, Epiphanius provides us with the Greek text of two large, continuous sections of the first book and several shorter quotations, more widely dispersed, and mostly following the sequence of *AH*. From these quotations, together with those of Hippolytus, and a few others from elsewhere, it has been possible to recover nearly 75% of the Greek text of *AH* I, far more than for any of the other four books.

In the main, Irenaeus was far more likely to be cited for information about heretics than for the theology he developed in opposition to them, and when he was quoted for his own theological views this was usually done in order to demonstrate continuity between his views and theological views currently under attack as heretical. As Irenaeus expressed his own views in language that was considerably more plastic than that of later generations, he is quoted with approval by advocates on both sides of disputed questions, particularly with regard to Christology and the Eucharist.

At the end of *On the Holy Spirit*, written around 374, Basil the Great cites two short passages from V.8.2 and 9.3. The first of these he identifies as coming from the *book against the heresies* of Irenaeus, "who was near to the Apostles," and the second as coming from elsewhere by the same author. Both passages look as though they have been selected simply because in them Irenaeus describes the Spirit as "divine." These are, in fact, the only passages in the surviving Greek that use this adjective of the Spirit. The Latin translation supplies only one further instance of "divinus Spiritus," at V.8.3, shortly after the first of the passages cited by Basil.

In the florilegia attached to his *Eranistes* (c. 447), Theodoret of Cyr provides 11 short quotations from *AH* III, three from *AH* IV, and two from *AH* V. These are all designed to show that Theodoret's understanding of the incarnation – that Jesus is both fully divine and fully human – is orthodox and traditional. Most of the lemmata for these citations correctly state from which book they are taken. Theodoret also quoted a short passage from I.25.5 in his *Haereticarum Fabularum Compendium* (*Patrologia Graeca* 83, 352C), and says that he has drawn upon Irenaeus in his account of early heresies.

At some time in the eighth or possibly the ninth century, there was put together the work commonly known as the *Sacra Parallela* and commonly attributed to John Damascene (c. 675–c. 754). This is a florilegium of texts from scripture, early Christian writers and some non-Christian writers grouped around theological and ethical themes. It does not exist complete in any one manuscript, as copyists adapted, abbreviated and added to the texts to suit their own needs (Holl 1899, v ff). From these manuscripts a number of fragments of the Greek text can be recovered: 7 from *AH* II, 15 from *AH* IV and 16 from *AH* V, in addition to some small fragments doubtfully or wrongly ascribed to Irenaeus. The passages excerpted bear upon questions about God, the knowledge of God, the Trinity, the creation of humankind in the image and likeness of God, the freedom of the will, the number of the Beast at Revelation 13:18 and the resurrection of the dead. As the lemmata of the fragments generally correctly state from which book they have been taken, it is reasonable to suppose that, at some point in its composition, the whole work, or at least the whole of the books excerpted, was available to a compiler. It is interesting to note, however, that the modern editor of the works of John Damascene can suggest only one place showing a possible, though unacknowledged influence from *AH* (Kotter 1973: 99).

About the middle of the ninth century, Photius, who was to become patriarch of Constantinople, claimed to have read "a *biblion* of Irenaeus, bishop of Lyons, in five *logoi*, the title of which was 'Refutation and Overthrow of Gnosis falsely so-called'; that is, *Against Heresies*" (*Bibliotheca* II. 120). Photius proceeds to give a summary of the five books, and claims that manifold and various writings of Irenaeus are in circulation but notes that in some of these "the exactitude of the truth concerning ecclesiastical dogmas is adulterated by spurious arguments." Given that Photius makes no comment whatever concerning Irenaeus' style, and that his very inadequate summary of *AH* accounts for considerably less than half of his entire notice on Irenaeus, one may wonder how attentively Photius read that work, if he read it at all. In his introductory letter to Tarasius, Photius remarks that it is hard enough to get hold of the gist of just one book and commit it to memory and to paper, and all the harder to do so for many books and after the passage of time. If this explains the inadequacy of his treatment of Irenaeus, one may further wonder whether he found *AH* in a Greek library at Baghdad as is often supposed, or whether he had read it much earlier, in Constantinople. If he found it in Baghdad it may have survived there until the sack of that city in 1258 (Hemmerdinger 1956: 103). In any event, Photius is the last person we know of who claims to have read the text in Greek.

In his far more extensive notice of the sixth-century author Stephen Gobar (*Bibliotheca* V. 232), Photius says that Gobar cites only the witness of Severian of Gabala and that of Irenaeus when discussing whether or not, before the resurrection of the dead, souls remain with their bodies in the tomb (cf. II.34.1; V.5.1; 31.2), and that he did not approve of the opinion of Irenaeus, amongst others, concerning the consumption of material food in the Kingdom (cf. V.33.2–3). Gobar is also credited with claiming that Irenaeus, along with Hippolytus, denied the Pauline authorship of the Letter to the Hebrews.

Notwithstanding Theodoret's drawing on Irenaeus in defense of his own view of the two natures in Christ, Irenaeus was also cited by later Miaphysite writers and compilers. Thus, in the second half of the fifth century, Timothy Aelurus in his *Refutation of the doctrine defined by the Council of Chalcedon*, which survives only in Armenian translation, quoted the creed-like summary at I.10.1 as having been taken from "the blessed Irenaeus, who was an imitator of the Apostles and the bishop of Lyons." Severus of Antioch, a Miaphysite of the early sixth century, quotes from all five books of *AH* in his polemic against John the Grammarian, and from *AH* III in his correspondence with Julian of Halicarnassus. These works of Severus survive only in Syriac translation. Another Syriac fragment (II.34.1), from a collection of testimonies, is described as having been taken "from the second book, and seventy-first section; which is the five hundredth and twenty-seventh of the entire work." This suggests that the original compiler had the whole text of *AH* before him. There is no strong evidence that *AH* was itself translated into Syriac. In the seventh century an Armenian Miaphysite compilation of patristic testimonies entitled the *Seal of the Faith of the Universal Church* included quotations from *AH* I, II, IV and V.

The fact that Irenaeus could be cited as early testimony for contradictory views on the number of natures in Christ suggests one reason for his diminishing influence on the development of theology. For although he had played a major role in the early general shaping of Christian theology, precisely because he stands so early in the theological tradition his views are, in comparison with that later tradition, so inchoate and themselves potentially contradictory that he ceases to be a useful guide on disputed questions.

However, even if, increasingly, mention of and citation from Irenaeus by writers in Greek was to be confined to florilegia, catenae and scriptural commentary, some aspects of his theology do find parallels in later writers. Thus, for example, his soteriology and Christology, and his view that the incarnate Word was the image of God after which humankind was created, find echoes in Marcellus of Ancyra (Parvis 2006: 31–34), and his emphasis on the "convergence of divine transcendence and immanence in the Christian message of salvation" resonates strongly in Athanasius (Anatolios 1998: 4).

The Latin Translation of *Adversus Haereses* and its Manuscripts

In about 421 Augustine of Hippo (*Contra Iulianum* I.3.5; 7.32) quoted two passages from Irenaeus (IV.2.7; V.19.1) among testimonies of the Fathers against Julian of Eclanum, in support of his own doctrine of original sin. It is possible that Irenaeus influenced Augustine at a few other places as well, though it has been considered likely that he did not read him very thoroughly, as, if he had, he might have chosen more apposite proof-texts than those that he did (Altaner 1949). It is plain that Augustine read

Irenaeus in the Latin translation that has come down to us. This translation cannot be shown to have been known to any Latin writer earlier than Augustine (Souter 1923: lxvi), and there is a reasonable case that it was occasioned by the controversy surrounding the Spanish theologian Priscillian (Dodwell 1689: 405; Chadwick 1976: 205–206), and that the translation was made in North Africa between 370 and 420 (Souter 1923: xcvi). Gregory of Tours and the Venerable Bede mention Irenaeus, but what they know of him is likely to have been derived from Rufinus' translation of Eusebius' *Ecclesiastical History*, or from Jerome's *De Viris Inlustribus*. Pope Gregory I (†604) lamented that, though he had long been searching diligently for the deeds or writings of blessed Irenaeus, he had not been able to discover anything of them (*Letters* X. 56: *Patrologia Latina* 77, 1174B). Nevertheless, the Latin translation survives in nine manuscripts, and it must have been copied at least a dozen times between late antiquity and the Renaissance. Given the difficulty and obscurity of at least the first two books, and the fact that Irenaeus made no impact at all upon monastic or scholastic theologians in the West during the medieval period, the interest and industry of these copyists is remarkable.

The modern editors of the text divide the manuscripts into two families, which they call the Irish and the Lyonnais (SC 100: 16–23). The oldest surviving manuscript of the Irish family was copied at the abbey of Corbie in northern France in the ninth century and must derive from an exemplar produced in a scriptorium of Irish monks, either in Ireland itself or one of their monasteries in Britain or on the continent. The other manuscript of this family was made in England from an exemplar in the house of the Carmelite friars in Oxford in 1494 and presented to a house of the Carmelite friars in Paris, where it was copied again in 1510.

The earliest surviving manuscript of the Lyonnais family was copied in Germany, in the second half of the twelfth century, from a manuscript in the abbey of Lorsch in Hessen. A lost ancestor of this manuscript had been copied in Lyons itself in the ninth century, though it is not known where that exemplar came from. Five other surviving manuscripts, mainly humanist productions of the fifteenth or sixteenth centuries, belong to this family, as did the three manuscripts, now lost, that Erasmus relied upon for his *editio princeps*.

The only clue we have for the interest of those who had *AH* copied in the Middle Ages is provided in the prologue written by the Deacon Florus of Lyons in the ninth century, who gives five reasons why the transcription of the work was worth the cost and labor. First, it is very rare, precisely because no one needed to consult it after heresy had been silenced; second, the antiquity of the author and his proximity to the apostles makes him trustworthy; third, his knowledge of heretical doctrine is for the most part first-hand; fourth, no one else is known to have written about the heresies of that time more fully or more clearly; and fifth, heresy is once again beginning to stir, and the armory of the church militant needs to be replenished (Harvey 1857: I. clxxviii). What is conspicuously lacking here is any indication that Irenaeus' own theological outlook was valued for its own sake, or thought likely to enrich monastic spirituality. There is, however, one point at which we are able to see that the reception accorded to Irenaeus by his medieval copyists was not entirely enthusiastic. In all the manuscripts of the Lyonnais family the fifth book comes to an end with chapter 31.2. That is to say, at quite an early point in its transmission, the last six chapters of the work, in which Irenaeus discusses the resurrection of the dead and the thousand-year reign of the just upon the Earth, were deliberately removed. The oldest manuscript of the Irish family breaks off even earlier, in the middle of a scriptural quotation toward the beginning of V.26.1. Though this is undoubtedly due to the loss of the last quires of the volume, showing that this manuscript once contained the whole work (SC 152: 28), the likelihood is strong that these were removed deliberately, for the same reason that transcription was halted, at a slightly later point, in the Lyonnais family. Only the Carmelite manuscript mentioned above continues the work to the end, and even it omits a short section in which Irenaeus' millenarian ideas are given their clearest expression (V.36.3). Fortunately, the translator and scribes of the Armenian version had no scruple about allowing Irenaeus' text to stand here.

Interest in Christian antiquity for its own sake is likely to have been a major motivation for the humanist interest in copying Irenaeus from the fifteenth century onwards, but the transition to print meant that Irenaeus was ready to emerge from the obscurity of centuries into the controversies of the Reformation.

The Armenian Translation of *Adversus Haereses* and the *Demonstration of the Apostolic Preaching*

The Armenian translation of *AH* IV–V and of the *Demonstration of the Apostolic Preaching* was discovered in 1904 in a thirteenth-century manuscript now held in the Matenadaran at Yerevan. The *Demonstration* was first published in 1907, and the two last books of *AH* in 1910. Fragments in Armenian of the first three books of *AH* also survive, and it is plain that they come from the same translation as that which survives complete for books IV and V. The translation itself was made in the sixth century, probably at Constantinople, at a period when many works of philosophy and theology were being translated in a highly artificial, word-for-word manner, possibly designed to ensure that Armenian students could approach an understanding of the Greek original as closely as possible. The translation was utilized in Christological discussions within the Armenian church. Its publication, in addition to supplying the lacuna at V.36.3 in the Latin tradition, provided an invaluable aid to the reconstruction of the original Greek underlying both translations.

Early Printed Editions of *Adversus Haereses,* and the Reception of Irenaeus in the Reformation Period

Erasmus' edition was published in 1526 by the Froben press at Basle. In his dedicatory epistle, addressed to the Bishop of Trent, Erasmus says that he is not yet sure whether Irenaeus wrote in Latin or in Greek, but is inclined to think it was in Latin, even if Irenaeus was more at home with Greek.

Erasmus hoped that the publication of "his" Irenaeus would have a beneficial impact on the troubled church of his own times – for even though Martin Luther had been excommunicated and outlawed only 5 years previously, the troubles now facing the church, he said, were more serious and more widespread than any previously known. Yet Erasmus clearly did not yet appreciate the real gravity of the situation. He contrasts Irenaeus, whose name means peaceable, and who had been active in seeking peaceful resolution to conflicts in the church in Rome, with certain modern equivalents of those Irenaeus opposed "who stir up unfounded accusations of heresy and schism out of insignificant trivialities." Irenaeus' writings, he thought, breathed the original vigor of the Gospel, and Erasmus hoped that more than one new Irenaeus would arise and restore the world to concord in the spirit of the Gospel.

In his short prefaces to books II–V Erasmus draws the attention of readers to discrepancies between Irenaeus' opinions and current theological orthodoxies, some of which might occasion concern, which Erasmus tries to allay, and others of which might point a way out of current conflict. Thus, for example, Irenaeus speaks of the Son of Man being "mixed with," rather than united to the Word of God, and being "adopted" to sonship of God (III.19.1), and has unusual views about the general resurrection. On the other hand, Irenaeus makes no mention of purgatory, and has much to say in support of the freedom of the will – a subject on which Erasmus had written in opposition to Luther 2 years previously. Again, though Erasmus clearly admires what Irenaeus has to say about the Eucharist, he notes that he does not mention transubstantiation expressly, and he approves the greater caution and reserve of early teachers who thus avoid throwing to dogs what is holy. Erasmus' edition was subsequently to be reissued many times, but without ever recapturing the clarity of layout and printing that marked the first edition.

Irenaeus was soon drawn into the confessional debates of the Reformation period. In 1527 Luther quoted him favorably in his *Defensio Verborum Coenae* on the doctrine of the real presence in the Eucharist against Oecolampadius and on the non-propitiatory nature of the Eucharistic sacrifice against Catholics. He was often named and quoted during discussions at the Council of Trent (1546–1563). Most often this was a matter simply of enlisting Irenaeus, often by arguments of no great subtlety and sometimes with no real foundation in what Irenaeus wrote, as a very early and venerable proof-text witness for Catholic positions on a predictable range of topics: scripture and tradition, the canonicity of apocryphal books, episcopal succession, the authority of the Church of Rome (III.3.2 especially), original sin, the sacrifice of the Mass, transubstantiation, communion outside Mass, the use of water in the Eucharistic cup, communion under only one kind, the antiquity of the sacraments of confession and orders, and so on. But there are also a few instances of Irenaeus being read against the prevailing Catholic orthodoxy. In the very first year of the Council, Giovanni Tommaso Sanfelice, bishop of La Cava and one of the papal conciliar commissaries, maintained that Irenaeus and other most sound and ancient authors supported his own view that justification is by faith alone. Towards the end of the Council, Irenaeus' letter to Victor was cited, sadly without success, to support the proposal that communion under both kinds be permitted to those in Bohemia who might be reconciled to Rome if this were to be allowed. The Council's decree accepting the creed of the Catholic faith (1546) paraphrases part of III.3.2: "... the creed that the Roman church uses as the sound and only foundation on which all who profess the faith of Christ, necessarily agree..."

From 1554 the so-called Centuriators of Magdeburg, a group of Lutheran scholars in that town, began publishing their monumental *Ecclesiastica Historia*, which was arranged in volumes by centuries AD. While Irenaeus is judged by the Centuriators to have frequently been negligent and incorrect in his utterance, his statements about the Eucharist at V.2.3 were thought, if properly understood, to contain nothing inappropriate. Similarly, at III.3.2, the context makes it plain that Irenaeus thought every church ought to agree with the church in Rome only in apostolic teaching, though in the index to the second century this place is said to contain Irenaeus' "corrupt opinion about the primacy of the Roman church." It was, however, Irenaeus' understanding of original justice and original sin, of fallen human nature, and of the freedom of the will that really disturbed the Centuriators. Irenaeus' views on these subjects were judged to be in conflict with Scripture, and "very dangerous." The Centuriators acknowledged, however, that, though he did not always clearly distinguish between the Divine Word as substantial reality and as spoken word, Irenaeus openly asserted that Christ's obedience was our righteousness before God.

The attitude of Calvinists to Irenaeus was somewhat different. Calvin approved Irenaeus' understanding of immortality within the context of dependence on God (*Psychopannychia*, 1534), cited him among "all the holy Fathers" for his sound teaching on the presence of Christ in the Eucharist (*Antidotum adversus Articulos Facultatis Theologiae Sorbonicae*, 1542) and thought that his statements about the freedom of the will described the human condition before the sin of Adam, not after it, though if Irenaeus did not in fact distinguish between the two conditions he should not be listened to, as this would be contrary to what is agreed by the unanimous church (*Defensio Doctrinae de Servitute et Liberatione Humani Arbitrii*, 1543, cf. IV.37.1–40.1).

Heinrich Bullinger (*De Origine Erroris*, 1528) and Theodore Beza (*Defensio Sacramentalis Coniunctionis Corporis et Sanguinis Christi cum Sacris Symbolis*, 1578) also approved Irenaeus' understanding of the Eucharistic presence.

In 1560, or a little before, there was published at Geneva a book entitled *Le vray bouclier de la foy chrestienne*, attributed to Barthélémy Causse. This was an answer to a Catholic polemical work by Nicole Grenier called *Le bouclier de la foy*, first published at Paris in 1547 and frequently reissued. Causse shares Calvin's view of the authority of the Fathers in matters of doctrine. He notes that Augustine, whom he much admires, admitted in the *Retractationes* that he had written many things that were worthy of reprehension. All true Christians, he concludes, should adopt this rule and maxim: to accept everything such teachers say that is in accord with the holy faith, and reject everything that is contrary to it (Causse 1560: 175). Causse restricts his attention to Irenaeus' statements that the human race was bound to death by the virgin Eve and released from it by the Virgin Mary, and that Mary was the "advocate" of Eve (V.19.1). The senior interlocutor in Causse's dialogue says that he just does not believe that the martyr Irenaeus had professed such blasphemies against Jesus Christ, and thinks rather that some idolater has inserted this in Irenaeus' works. However, if Irenaeus did in fact write this, he has shown that he did not have a true understanding of the Faith, of the Apostles' Creed, and that he had not read the Scriptures; that he had already become corrupt and fallen far away from the true Apostolic teaching, "under the shadow of good devotion to the virgin Mary" (Causse 1560: 276–279).

When the Calvinist pastor and theologian Nicolas des Gallars (Gallasius) found himself driven out of Orléans in 1568, Theodore Beza suggested to him that instead of lamenting his lot in idleness he should put his hand to something useful, namely an aid to the reading of the "old teachers," which, though known to be useful, is much neglected because of either the obscurity or the impurity of doctrine of those writers. Gallars decided to begin with Irenaeus, considered to be the earliest of the Latin writers, though Gallars was sure that he wrote in Greek, and was able to supply part of the Greek text of *AH* I from Epiphanius. Gallars considered that Irenaeus offered a fine example of how bishops and pastors should protect their flocks from the ravages of heretics (his dedicatory letter was addressed to Edmund Grindal, bishop of London). The heresies described by Irenaeus were no more absurd or revolting than those devised by fanatics of the present day and no less likely to seduce uneducated and simple folk. In this he has Anabaptists particularly in mind, though Irenaeus and other Fathers also serve to puncture the claim of contemporary promoters and patrons of superstitions that, like the heretics of old, they derived their crazy notions from the Apostles. In his preface, Gallars says that he has principally annotated those passages that are used "against us by our adversaries," so that the reader may be protected from certain of their superstitions and know how much weight the authority of ancient teachers ought to have in the church. In the lengthy note he devoted to III.3.2, Gallars took the "potentior principalitas" of Rome to refer not to the city or the see, but to the purity of the word of God that had once flourished within them, but did so no longer. Irenaeus himself treated the church in Rome with the greatest respect so long as it remained pure in doctrine and true in ministry, but opposed Victor with gravity and constancy when he sought to excommunicate other churches during the Quartodeciman controversy. Gallars' edition, the first alternative to Erasmus', appeared in 1570.

A year later Johann Jakob Gryner (Grynaeus), who had moved from Lutheranism to Calvinism, published his edition of Irenaeus at Basle. He grants that the work contains some rough and faulty "lucubrations" about some matters, including free will, but thinks that these have been adequately signposted by Erasmus, and that Irenaeus stands in no need of defense, inasmuch as there is no good person that does not love him, and no evil person is able to harm him by "shadow-boxing" while he rests in Christ. His work, moreover, contains much about the major themes of theology which it will be pleasing and salutary for those of pious mind to know.

The French Franciscan François Feuardent, on the other hand, did think that Irenaeus needed defending from the "impious accusations" of his Protestant critics, and published his edition in 1575 partly to this end. He gives a Latin summary and a rebarbative rebuttal of Causse's critical remarks under the heading "Calvinianorum Maledicta," and of the considerably more detailed "calumnies" of the Lutheran Centuriators. Feuardent's edition was the first to utilize the one manuscript that contained the final chapters of book V.

In 1617 yet another work entitled *Bouclier de la Foy* appeared, this time from the pen of Pierre du Moulin as a defense of the faith of the Reformed Church in France against the objections of a Jesuit named Arnoux. In this Irenaeus is cited against Roman beliefs concerning scripture and tradition, the invocation of angels, purgatory, the veneration of images, and the Eucharist. Du Moulin takes Arnoux particularly to task over his interpretation of III.3.2, which Arnoux has falsified and corrupted, twisting the words from a plain reference to the pre-eminence of Rome as the seat of Empire to the claim that the whole church should agree with and adhere to the church in Rome, in which pre-eminence of principality resides.

The Eighteenth Century to the Present Day

Johannes Ernestus Grabe, a German Lutheran of Catholic inclination who had become an Anglican and settled in Oxford, published his edition there in 1702. Though confessional squabbles inevitably still concerned him – he thought that conflicts between and within the Lutheran and Calvinists camps could be resolved by both of them returning to the doctrine, church order and discipline of the pre-Constantinian church – Grabe's edition is a model of judicious scholarship.

When in 1710 the Benedictine René Massuet published his edition in Paris he described Grabe's as more accurate and more elegant than previous ones, and said that he neither could nor would dissimulate the fact that he had often benefited from Grabe's labors. Nevertheless, Massuet often finds fault with Grabe's text. He thought that just as Gallars had been preoccupied not so much with producing a more careful and more correct edition of the text as with burying it under lengthy notes of a Calvinist hue, so as either to bring the vanquisher of ancient heresies unwillingly over to the side of a new one or else to rail at him abusively, similarly Grabe was more concerned with turning Irenaeus into an unwilling and reluctant Anglican. Massuet considers a new edition to be not only useful, but necessary, so as to provide a more accurate text and one that Catholics could use without risk of being tripped up.

In 1715 Christof Matthaeus Pfaff published four fragments attributed to Irenaeus which he claimed to have found in a manuscript in Turin that had since been lost. Though the genuineness of these was hotly contested, they were printed as genuine by Harvey as fragments 35–38 at the end of the second volume of his edition. They were comprehensively unmasked by A. von Harnack (1900) as concocted for the purpose of supporting Pfaff's efforts for church unity within Protestantism, particularly with respect to the doctrine of the Eucharist.

In 1832 Gregory XVI alluded to IV.6.3 (the Son as the revelation of the Father) in his encyclical against de Lamennais, and in 1864 a letter from the Holy Office of the Roman Inquisition reminded the Catholic bishops of England of the supreme authority and the "potentior principalitas" of the Roman see. The passage from III.3.2 from which these words were taken was to be paraphrased more fully in the Dogmatic Constitution on the Church of the First Vatican Council (1870). This passage had led the eighteenth-century critic Johan Salomo Semler to doubt that *AH* had been written by Irenaeus at all (quoted in Stieren (1853: 356–358)), but its apparently anachronistic elevation of the status of the church in Rome is in fact due simply to the inadequacy of the Latin translation (Abramowski 1977).

Although new editions continued to appear in the nineteenth century, and favorable monographs were devoted to him, by the end of that century Irenaeus had begun to attract the unflattering attention of German critical scholarship. Johannes Werner argued that, for all his citation of the letters of Paul, Irenaeus missed the central religious and theological kernel of Paul's teaching (Werner 1889: 93). In his painstaking, posthumously published study, Friedrich Loofs argued that *AH* was an amalgam of several different sources that had been so poorly absorbed and integrated that Irenaeus emerges as a much less significant theological writer than had previously been assumed (Loofs 1930: 432). Loofs' work was judged to have "exhausted" this problem, and to have discouraged scholarship on Irenaeus for the ensuing 25 years (Benoit 1960: 30). Nevertheless, it was in the twentieth century that Irenaeus was finally allowed his place in the mainstream of theology. The Swedish Lutheran Gustaf Wingren published his enthusiastic and engaging recovery of Irenaeus as a biblical theologian in 1947 (Wingren 1959), and the following year the Methodist John Lawson (1948) entitled his monograph *The Biblical Theology of Saint Irenaeus*. Since then there has been an unabating flood of studies and monographs devoted to Irenaeus by Protestant, Catholic and Orthodox authors in most of the languages of Europe.

The publication of the modern critical edition of Irenaeus, with French translation, began in 1952 with François Sagnard's edition of *AH* III. The series *Sources chrétiennes* in which it was published was itself testimony to the commitment to *ressourcement* that was such a marked feature of Catholic intellectual life in France from the middle of the twentieth century onwards. This edition, including a replacement of Sagnard's *AH* III, and offering a volume of text and a volume of commentary for each book, was finally brought to completion in 1982.

During the debates at the Second Vatican Council (1962–1965), though he continued to be quoted on predictable topics such as tradition, apostolic succession, Roman primacy and the Virgin Mary, Irenaeus emerged as a significant influence. He is quoted or referred to 12 times in the Constitutions and Decrees of the Council, but was appealed to much more frequently during discussions on the floor of the Council, and on a much wider range of subjects, such as the recovery of the universal or "cosmic" character of the liturgy, the celebration of the liturgy in vernacular languages, the collegiality of bishops and their apostolic succession in their own sees, the natural dignity of the human person, and the renewal of the church through the Holy Spirit. Erasmus' rather forlorn hope that Irenaeus would serve as a source of renewal and unity amongst Christians was at last beginning to be realized.

Bibliography

Primary Sources

Eusebius, *The Ecclesiastical History and the Martyrs of Palestine*. Translated with introduction and notes by H.J. Lawlor and J.E.L. Oulton, London: SPCK, 1927.

Irénée de Lyon, *Contre les Hérésies*. Édition critique, Sources chrétiennes (SC) Paris. Livre I (SC 263 & 264, 1979), Livre II (SC 293 & 294, 1982), Livre III (SC 210 & 211, 1974) par Adelin Rousseau et Louis Doutreleau; Livre IV (SC 100, 1965) sous la direction de Adelin Rousseau, avec la collaboration de Bertrand Hemmerdinger, Louis Doutreleau et Charles Mercier; Livre V (SC 152 & 153, 1969) par Adelin Rousseau, Louis Doutreleau et Charles Mercier.

Irenaeus, *Sancti Irenaei Libros quinque Adversus Haereses*, W. Wigan Harvey (ed.). Cambridge: Cambridge University Press, 1857.

Irenaeus, *The Writings of Irenaeus*, A. Roberts and W.H. Rambaut (transl.). Ante-Nicene Christian Library 5. Edinburgh: T&T Clark, 1910.

Irénée de Lyon, Démonstration de la prédication apostolique. Introduction, traduction et notes par Adelin Rousseau. Paris: Éditions du Cerf, 1995.

St Irenaeus of Lyons, *On the Apostolic Preaching*. Translation and introduction by John Behr. Crestwood, NY: St Vladimir's Seminary Press, 1997.

John Damascene, *Die Schriften des Johannes von Damaskos. Herausgegeben vom Byzantinischen Institut der Abtei Scheyern, besorgt von Bonifatius Kotter. II, Expositio Fidei*. Berlin: Walter de Gruyter, 1973.

John Damascene, *Fragmente vornicänischer Kirchenväter aus den Sacra Parallela*. Herausgegeben von Karl Holl. Texte und Untersuchungen zur Geschichte der altchristlichen Literatur 20.2. Leipzig: Hinrichs, 1899.

Secondary Sources

Abramowski, Luise (1977), "Irenaeus Adv. Haer. III.3.2: Ecclesia Romana and Omnis Ecclesia and *ibid.* 3.3. Anacletus of Rome". *Journal of Theological Studies*, 28: 101–104.

Altaner, Bertold (1949), "Augustinus und Irenäus". *Theologische Quartalschrift*, 129: 162–172.

Anatolios, Kahled (1998), *Athanasius. The Coherence of His Thought*. London: Routledge.

Benoit, André (1960), *Saint Irénée. Introduction a l'étude de sa théologie*. Paris: Presses Universitaires de France.

Carriker, Andrew (2003), *The Library of Eusebius of Caesarea*. Supplements to *Vigiliae Christianae* 67. Leiden: Brill.

Causse, Barthélémy (1560), *Le Vray Bouclier de la Foy chrestienne, mis par Dialogues ... reveu et augmenté de nouveau ...* Geneva: Zacharie Durant.

Chadwick, Henry (1976), *Priscillian of Avila. The Occult and the Charismatic in the Early Church*. Oxford: Clarendon Press.

Dodwell, Henry (1689), *Dissertationes in Irenaeum*. Oxoniae: e Theatro Sheldoniano.

Hemmerdinger, C.M. (1956), "Les 'notices et extraits' des bibliothèques grecques de Bagdad par Photius". *Revue des études grecques*, 69: 101–103.

Lawson, John (1948), *The Biblical Theology of Saint Irenaeus*. London: Epworth Press.

Loofs, Freidrich (1930), *Theophilus von Antiochien Adversus Marcionem und die anderen theologischen Quellen bei Irenaeus*. Texte und Untersuchungen zur Geschichte der altchristlichen Literatur 46.2. Leipzig.

Minns, Denis (2010), *Irenaeus. An Introduction*. London: T&T Clark.

Parvis, Sara (2006), *Marcellus of Ancyra and the Lost Years of the Arian Controversy 325–345*. Oxford: Oxford University Press.

Parvis, Sara and Foster, Paul (eds) (2012), *Irenaeus. Life, Scripture, Legacy*. Minneapolis, MN: Fortress Press.

Souter, Alexander (1923), "The date and place of the Latin translator of Irenaeus". In *Novum Testamentum Sancti Irenaei Episcopi Lugdunensis*. Edited from the MSS with introductions apparatus notes and appendices by W. Sanday and C.H. Turner. Oxford: Clarendon Press.

Stieren, Adolf (1853), *Apparatus ad Opera Sancti Irenaei Episcopi Lugdunensis*. Leipzig: Weigel.

Von Harnack, Adolf (1900), "Die Pfaff'schen Irenäus-Fragmente als Fälschungen Pfaffs nachgewiesen". Texte und Untersuchungen zur Geschichte der altchristlichen Literatur 20.3. Leipzig.

Werner, Johannes (1889), *Der Paulinismus des Irenaeus. Eine kirchen- und dogmengeschichtliche Untersuchung über das Verhältnis des Irenaeus zu der Paulinischen Briefsammlung und Theologie*. Texte und Untersuchungen zur Geschichte der altchristlichen Literatur 6. Leipzig.

Wingren, Gustaf (1959), *Man and the Incarnation. A Study in the Biblical Theology of Irenaeus* (translation by Ross MacKenzie of *Människan och Inkarnationen enligt Irenaeus*. Lund: C.W.K. Gleerup, 1947). Edinburgh: Oliver & Boyd.

Part III

Studies in Reception History I: Individual Fathers

CHAPTER 5

Clement of Alexandria

Piotr Ashwin-Siejkowski

Annewies van den Hoek, in her opening paper at *the Colloquium on Clement of Alexandria* which took place in 2010, made the following observation:

> When over thirty years ago my friend and colleague Alan Le Boulluec and I met at the second Origen Conference in Bari, there was only a small minority of specialists on Clement, hardly to be counted on the fingers of one hand: Eric Osborn and André Méhat come to mind as the main protagonists. In those days it was hard to imagine that Clement of Alexandria could merit a conference in his own right, and thus the small group of Clementine specialists was included, perhaps tolerated, as a kind of appendix to the larger contingent of scholars of Origen, Clement's younger Alexandrian contemporary, who was and still is a more prominent and celebrated author (Havrda *et al.* 2012: 3).

This insightful comment from one of the leading scholars on Clement of Alexandria also hints at some difficulties. While presenting a synopsis of Clement's thoughts we ought to mention that modern scholarship and the new generation of scholars represent the whole spectrum of interests in this early Christian polymath. Researchers are not unanimous in discussing Clement's dependence on various philosophical and cultural influences, and they value Clement's contribution to emerging Christian orthopraxis in different ways. In the light of that ongoing discussion I wish to present Clement of Alexandria's thoughts with specific focus on a chosen theme. Primary attention will be given in this contribution to Clement's didactic attempt. I aim to discuss his understanding of Christianity as the ultimate fulfilment of the noblest, philosophical, and sapiential way of life and a genuine encounter with God under the guidance of the divine Logos/Christ. But first, it is helpful to recollect some facts about Clement's life and work.

The Wiley Blackwell Companion to Patristics, First Edition. Edited by Ken Parry.
© 2015 John Wiley & Sons Ltd. Published 2019 by John Wiley & Sons Ltd.

Clement's Life and Works

The date and the place of Clement's birth (*Titus Flavius Clemens*) is still the subject of speculation; however, some scholars argue that he was born around 150 CE and possibly in Athens to a pagan family (Mees 1990: 449). Clement himself, unlike Justin Martyr, does not allude to any events in his life; he does not mention the important event of his conversion. The ubiquitous silence about his personal life remains uninterrupted throughout his works. However, we know from Clement that he was passionate about the philosophical quest, which led him to travel to various places and to listen to a number of teachers and finally to find his favorite tutor in Egypt (*Strom* I.11.1–2). On another occasion, Clement will identify this teacher as Pantaenus (*Ecl* 56.2). André Méhat (1966: 46) reconstructs the date of Clement's arrival in Alexandria on the basis of the testimony of Sextus Julius Africanus, who states that Clement was known in Alexandria under the reign of the Emperor Commodus, which leads us to the period 180–192 CE. There is no doubt that academic, social, and religious life in *Alexandria near Egypt* (*Alexandria ad Aegyptum*) deeply influenced Clement's thought and reflected the aspirations of his audience and disciples. It is correct to assume that all his main works were composed in Alexandria. Finally, short references to Clement's reputation are preserved in Eusebius of Caesarea's account of Alexander's letters. These references suggest that Clement left Alexandria, possibly during the persecution of Septimius Severus (202–203) and went to Cappadocia from where he was sent with a letter from Alexander to the church in Antioch (*H.E.* 6.11.6). Eusebius of Caesarea quotes two letters written by Alexander, Bishop of Jerusalem, which suggest that Clement might have died somewhere between 211 and 215 CE (*H.E.* 6.14.9).

Clement's literary legacy includes a wide range of treatises from various literary genres. Again, Eusebius of Caesarea provides us with a list of then works by (*H.E.* 6.13.1–3). They are: the eight books of *Miscellanies* (*Stromateis*), in which Clement discussed a whole scope of questions related to the Christian way of life and the correct faith, the *Exhortation to the Greeks* (*Protreptikos*) and three books of *The Instructor* (*Paidagogos*). This important 'trilogy' provides us with a unique insight into the richness of Clement's philosophy, theology, and exegesis. Then, Eusebius' list recalls a work entitled as *Outlines* (*Hypotyposes*) and made up of eight books, all lost except for some passages found in later patristic authors; a preserved homily, *Who is the Rich Man that is Saved?*, known under its Latin title *Quis Dives Salvetur*; another work *On the Pascha* (lost, with the exception of a few lines preserved in quotes); and a number of discourses known to us only by their titles: *On Fasting*, *On Slander*, the *Exhortation to Patience or for the newly Baptised* (the last is preserved); and the *Ecclesiastical Canons* or the *Answer to the Judaizers* (again lost). There are also two other treatises, which have been commonly attributed to Clement of Alexandria. The first one is a notebook full of quotations from a lost theological treatise written by Theodotus, a Valentinian theologian and exegete (*Excerpts of Theodotus*). The second, yet again a notebook, offers comments on biblical prophetic writings (*Eclogues of the Prophets*). Maximus the Confessor quotes some sentences from Clement's lost treatise *On Providence*. This list, even if it mentions only the titles, shows Clement's enormous literary efficiency. He was a man of great erudition and intellectual acumen who was in dialogue with other contemporary theologians, philosophers, teachers, exegetes, and school leaders. He considered both Christian and non-Christian ideas, which may have served his project, and he was not afraid of encounter with his theological and philosophical opponents. However, a more detailed encounter with his main trilogy opens to the reader a fascinating, to some extent lost, world of early Christian scholarly dialogue and passionate polemic. This encounter, like a window, gives us a glimpse into the colorful collection of Clement's literary borrowings, and then his very creative composition of these sources (van den Hoek 1990, 1996) into his original model of Christian life dedicated to the quest for wisdom and perfection (Ashwin-Siejkowski 2008). That outlook of Christian spiritual and intellectual maturity developed within the context of the Alexandrian catechetical 'school', which should be acknowledged, at least to some degree.

The Catechetical School and its Significance

The origin and the nature of the catechetical "school" (*didaskaleion*) in Alexandria is the subject of ongoing academic debate (Le Boulluec 1987, 1999; Osborn 2005: 19–24; Pearson 2006: 340–342). The majority of modern historians support one of two views. First, Eusebius of Caesarea mentions "the school of sacred learning" *didaskaleion ton hieron logon* (*H.E.* 5.10.1) in Alexandria, suggesting its official status. However, Eusebius' account has only a vague reference to "the school" of the ecclesiastical organisation in Alexandria. That puzzling note leaves spacious room for modern commentators.

One group of scholars, exemplified by Gustave Bardy's approach, argued that this term describes a method of biblical interpretation taught in an autonomous, small circle. *Didaskaleion* was not an official institution among Alexandrian Christians until the time of Demetrius, Bishop of Alexandria from 189 to 231 CE. During Demetrius' strong leadership, that previous independent group of passionate teachers and students would be incorporated into the ecclesiastical structure, which was growing in importance and provided with teachers, such as Origen, appointed directly by the bishop of the city. According to Bardy, Pantaenus and then Clement were two private tutors offering an advanced exploration of theology, philosophy, and exegesis (Bardy 1935, 1937: 65–90).

The second group of historians, such as André Méhat, assess Eusebius' account critically; however, they acknowledge that the Alexandrian *didaskaleion* fulfilled its educational role within the boundaries of the Church, as was understood by its tutors such as Pantaenus and Clement (Pericoli-Ridolfini 1962; Tuilier 1982; Méhat 1996: 63). Osborn points out that the evidence is ambiguous as, on the one hand, Pantaenus and Clement are called *presbuteroi*, which suggests their age and ecclesiastical status. However, on the other hand, Clement never described his milieu or audience as *didaskaleion* and his oeuvre shows inconsistency by applying other similar terms, such as *schole*, *diatribe*, and *hairesis* (Osborn 2005: 20). It is plausible to see in Eusebius' problematic remark the imposition of an anachronistic construct, which came from his personal understanding of Alexandrian lineage of ecclesiastical orthodoxy. Clement, as earlier his master Pantaenus, was engaged in a specific method of education, which included commenting on the Scriptures and other literary sources, exploring various possibilities found in the material and in some helpful philosophical doctrines. This way of "doing" theology included also polemic with Christian and non-Christian opponents while putting forward their own intellectual stance. That process of education aimed to attract those on the fringes of Christianity, to strengthen the faith of those who have made the first step (baptism) and to further illuminate those who were advanced in knowledge and moral and spiritual life. Was that pedagogical method and educational purpose originally invented by Clement?

There are some strong reasons to believe that Clement, if not Pantaenus earlier, assimilated to his own educational requirements a model known to him and used in an Alexandrian Jewish milieu. Some historians, such as Joseph Mélèze Modrzejewski, highlighted the discontinuity between the original "Judeo-Christianity" in Alexandria and the later (second-century) "Graeco and Egyptian pagano-Christianity" (Mélèze Modrzejewski 1997: 228). However, this opinion found its critique (Le Boulluec 1999: 28–29; Pearson 2007: 100–101). In addition, Roelof van den Broek (1990) convincingly argues that "the school" was based on the Jewish model of teaching by the elders. Within the Jewish community the central place belonged to the institution of the synagogue, where, among other activities, such as the expected acts of worship or offering residence and distributing charity, the same building served as a library and the place for Torah study (Levine 2000: 374–380). Annewies van den Hoek (1997) points out in Clement's exegetical and pedagogical activity the role of Philonic legacy. That heritage will contribute to Clement's own approach to the Scriptures (Osborn 1998), his theological and metaphysical outlook (Berchman 1984: 55–82); it certainly influences some of his notions in his theory of mysticism (Kovacs 1997). Annewies van den Hoek (1997: 71) brings to the surface another very important point that, in Clement's view, as reconstructed from his oeuvre: the opposition between school and church is "nonexistent." For Clement there was no separation between the liturgical public (worship) and private (prayer) way of life and the intellectual inquisitiveness and quest for true knowledge (*gnosis*). On the contrary, he would argue that Christians from the very beginning of their journey in faith should also endorse study of the Scriptures and helpful traditions of philosophy. In brief, the church performed the role of the school, while the achievement of wisdom in a Christian school was only possible if that school was embodied in the true church (Havrda *et al.* 2012: 286–288).

The Main Characteristics of Clement's Theological Pedagogy: The Purpose of Life

Clement's program of leading his disciples to greater maturity and perfection reflected his opinion that Christianity was the noblest philosophical and sapiential way of life. That way of life aspired to the fullness of assimilation to God (Russell 2004: 121–140). First, one crucial assumption has to be highlighted which underpinned Clement's ethics, philosophy, metaphysics, theology, and theory of mysticism. The meaning of human existence and direction of moral progress has been revealed by the teaching of the divine Logos/Christ. This recent revelation has emphasized the crucial role of the attainment of everlasting affinity to God; the decorous ideal already postulated by some philosophers in the past. In Clement's assertion, two, if not three (Philo of Alexandria, cf. Russell 2004: 139), motifs are interwoven: Plato's proposal of aiming for "likeness to God, so that as far as possible a man becomes righteous and holy with wisdom" (*Theatetus* 176 B) and the unique Christian appeal to become disciples and imitators of Christ (e.g., 1 *Cor* 11.1). Two centuries before Clement's time, Plato's proposition had been revised and proclaimed with a new vigor by Middle Platonists such as Eudorus of Alexandria (first century BC). Within that specific philosophical frame, the later Christian encouragement to imitate Christ came to Clement's attention, as also did his exegesis of Hebrew Scripture and Wisdom Literature (here *Ps.* 82:6, *Paid* 1.26.1; *Strom* 2.125.4–5; 4.149.8–4; cf. van den Hoek 1998a). That compilation of various Greek, Jewish, and Christian sources into one coherent and attractive program was one of the most significant features of Clement's pedagogy. His disciples were heartened to believe that, as well as being created in God's image as human beings (*Genesis* 1:26), under the Logos/Christ guidance, they might all achieve "likeness to God." In brief, the ethical, philosophical, and spiritual journey from the stage of "image" to the status of "likeness" was possible, realistic, and well planned by Clement. The long and gradual process of turning from false idols to Christian belief (baptism), then growth in virtue and under-standing (education, ethics, philosophy), culminates in the new status as God's adopted children (cf. *Paed* 1.26.1).

The gradual transformation leads to the greatest affinity with God and participation in God's immortality. This process is possible, in Clement's theory, as it includes God's call and human moral response through freedom. This election is free from any form of determinism (fate), pre-election, or the divine status of human nature itself. On the contrary, at various stages it offers the disciples new opportunity to affirm their choice of growth in knowledge and holiness. Ultimately, the highest level of perfection and maturity can be reached in the current life, in Clement's view; however, its full realization, such as vision of God and communion with God, will take place in the new life after this one.

Further clarifications should be made about the theology of God that is integrated into Clement's pedagogical program. The optimistic assumption about the possibility of reaching "assimilation to God" has to be connected with Clement's strong apophatic tendency (Hägg 2006: 214–215). Clement's metaphysical axiom is that the *Absolute* (particularly in terms of Plato's metaphysics and its more contemporary Middle Platonic reception) is the *Holy One* proclaimed by the Scriptures and the *Father* revealed by the Logos/Christ. Unlike some other contemporary Christians (e.g., Tertullian of Carthage), Clement does not separate philosophy ("Athens") from theology/Scriptures ("Jerusalem"). Unlike Marcion of Synope, who pulled apart the Jewish Scriptures with their idea of God from the Father revealed by Jesus and denied any value of Jewish revelation, Clement clearly emphasized the continuity of revelation of the loving God: the creator of the whole reality, spiritual, and material. Again, Clement brings together various traditions and, in relation to his negative theology, he claims that, although all our human ideas and notions of God are inadequate (cf. Plato, *Timaeus*, 78C), still, by a proper training (purification) of the mind (*nous*) it is possible to gain some knowledge of, as he put it, "not what God is, but what He is not" (*Strom* 5.71.3). That rather speculative ascent towards the divine is strengthened by grace (Havrda 2011) and illuminated by the teaching of the Logos/Christ. Clement's Christology is in the center of his multilevel architecture of what can be depicted as the Christian theory of salvation. Only the Logos/Christ knows the mystery of God and only He can reveal that special insight and certainty (*gnosis*) to those who make progress toward the virtuous life motivated by love (*agape*) which may be expressed by martyrdom or practice in daily life of the highest virtues (van den Hoek 1993: 329). The divine Teacher (*Didaskalos*) in his instruction or, as Clement presents, a "new Orpheus" (Jourdan 2010) attracts by his song all humanity (*Strom* 7.5.6–6.1) to God. In the Logos' school, which for Clement was identified with his own Christian milieu and tradition, the Teacher carefully guides the disciples through stages of intellectual and spiritual development. In the early or elementary stage, the disciple is taught about the value of self-control (ethics), dominion over passions and impulses, and the life according to various classical virtues. At this stage the disciple explores his or her faith as a special relationship with God. The disciple acquires a basic knowledge about the Scriptures and their literal sense. Within that religious framework Clement also allocates some secular, useful "general education" (*enkuklios paideia*) in, for example, geometry, music, and arithmetic. In the higher level the adept enters into a new realm: a more philosophical, theological, and exegetical investigation of the hidden (or spiritual) meaning of the Scriptures. The original faith does not cease to be valuable; it is not replaced by "knowledge," but rather is illuminated by a deeper understanding of God's purpose, expressed by *gnosis*. The complex term *gnosis*, usually translated into English as "knowledge," has a double meaning in Clement's pedagogy. It contains understanding of God's plan of salvation, previously hidden but recently revealed in the Logos, and second, an intimate insight into God's life given to the Christian by the Logos/Christ. The progress from elementary *faith*, *obedience*, and *trust* into the attitude of *insightful knowledge* and *love* is expressed in even greater *piety* (*Strom* 5.5.2). In Clement's comprehensive view, the advance in understanding that characterizes the Christian Gnostic does not marginalize the importance of prayer (worship), daily ethical life (life of virtues), or the serving of others. It does not alienate the individual from the community, but on the contrary inspires that mature Christian to greater service in his or her milieu, in brief, in his or her ecclesiastical community (*Strom* 7.97.4). It is a coherent growth in wisdom, holiness, and righteousness. It is even greater openness to love (*agape*) that now dominates all aspects of involvement of that individual. With this progress may also come mystical experience (e.g., *Strom* 4.155.4).

Clement's portrayal of the mystical ascent and the ultimate state of assimilation to God brings together elements borrowed from Platonic imagery, familiar to Clement's educated audience and some Scriptural motifs originating in both Jewish and Christian literature. While depicting the highest way of life as pure, uninterrupted contemplation (*theoria*) or the mystical vision (*epoptike theoria* – e.g., *Strom* 1.15.2; 5.66.1–4 and *QDS* 37), Clement refers to the "angelic" nature, which represents the spiritual/intelligible (i.e., immaterial) way of existence, liberated from any disturbances of sensual perception, emotions, false precognitions, and vain ambitions. The "angelic" nature facilitates the most important activity of a spiritual being: the continuous contemplation of God, worship, and obedience to God's will (*Ecl* 56.5; Bucur 2009: 32–59). This notion explains the aim of the assimilation, but also in an earlier stage helps to prepare the Christian Gnostic for that marvelous purpose of life as presented by Clement. The

Platonic emphasis on the distinction between visible (sensible) and invisible (intelligible) realms (*Theaetetus* 155 e) and then the appeal to turn towards the intellectual life and the invisible world (e.g., *Republic* 518 c) is reaffirmed by Clement, for example, in the story of the High Priest entering into the Sanctuary (*Lev* 16:4, cf. *Strom* 5.32–40 and van den Hoek 1998b). The figure of the High Priest represents not only the Logos/Christ but also the Christian Gnostic. Equally, the journey recommended by the Platonic tradition towards the intelligible reality is explained by references to Moses' entrance into the darkness on Mount Sinai (*Strom* 2.6.1). Clement, like Philo of Alexandria before him, uses both Platonic metaphysical intuition creatively and allocates it within the frame of various Scriptural narratives. In that harmonious amalgamation of different traditions, Clement develops his mystical discourse in which the assimilation to God is explained as first and foremost the following of the Logos/Christ, and through Him, and only with Him, access to the greatest mysteries (*Strom* 2.134.2).

Through personal and direct relationship with the Logos/Christ, Clement argues, the disciple approaches God and gains a new dignity as "an adopted child." The Pauline motif of "adoption" (e.g., *Gal* 4.5) is included in the colorful mosaic of various literary borrowings in order to depict the richness of Clement's picture. This important term stresses that the new status is not "natural" to the disciple, as human beings do not possess a divine spark in their nature, but it is an outcome of gradual ethical, intellectual, and spiritual transformation. This fascinating outlook is rooted in Clement's pedagogy, in his deep belief about the centrality of the Logos/Christ, his descent and ascent, the first of which brought new knowledge, illumination, and grace to the human community and the second which inspired and empowered all who accepted His teaching to follow their Savior, Guide, and Instructor. Only with the divine Tutor and Mystagogue, Clement persuades his audience, is it possible to ascend to the realm that was seen from afar, both by Moses and then by Plato.

Ambiguous Reception of Clement's Legacy in Late Antiquity

Despite Clement's articulate emphasis on the value of intellectual and spiritual growth within a particular "school" or church community, he did not leave behind a community of disciples. When he moved to Palestine, he probably journeyed on his own, or rather with a collection of his writings and other literary sources, not with a group of followers. He did not entrust his teaching to a specific disciple or even an academic milieu, which would develop his theology and exegesis. The rise of Origen and his career as a theologian soon attracted a great deal of attention, overshadowing some earlier teachers. Origen's immense number of written works (even if only those preserved) do not mention Clement of Alexandria. Still, that lacuna does not suggest that Clement suddenly disappeared from the memory of the Church. Rather, his legacy has been preserved by various ancient authors; however, some element of confusion around the details soon emerged. In the fifth century, Philippus Sidetes, an ecclesiastical historian, introduced confusion as to the origin of the Alexandrian school. He allocated Clement as a successor of Athenagoras and then named Pantaenus as the follower of Clement (Codex Baroccianus 142, fol. 126). Epiphanius of Salamis was not sure about Clement's place of birth; as a result, he suggested either Athens or Alexandria (*Panarion* 30.6). However, these later ambiguities as to the original events did not overshadow earlier admiration. It has been already noted that Alexander of Jerusalem expressed his esteem for Clement, calling him "a holy" (*HE* 6.14.9). Similarly, Eusebius of Caesarea shows a great reverence to one of the "ambassadors" of the orthodoxy of the Church (*HE* 3.23.2). Similar esteem, however, now also including appreciation of Clement's erudition, can be found in Jerome (*Ep* 70.4), while some borrowings may be found in Gregory of Nazianzus (Russell 2004: 222), Basil of Caesarea (Russell 2004: 212), and Gregory of Nyssa (Laird 2004: 66–67). Clement of Alexandria was recognized in Pseud-Dionysius Areopagite as "a philosopher" (*Div. Nom* 5.9). Various passages from his works are spread in later authors, such as Cassiodorus (c. 540), John Moschus (c. 550–619), Pseudo-Oikomenius (sixth–seventh century), St John of Damascus (c. 676–749), Anastasius of Sinai (7th century), Nicephorus of Constantinople (c. 758–829), Nicetas the Bishop of Heraclea (eleventh century), and Anthonius Melissa (c. eleventh century). However, these and other short and vague references to the author without detailed references to his works prove that Clement's reputation as a learned man and orthodox theologian was widespread, while his works were not studied. Visible change comes with Photius of Byzantium, who misjudged Clement's theology and philosophy (Ashwin-Siejkowski 2010). In the latter half of the ninth century the Patriarch not only read Clement's various treatises, which shows that his writings were preserved in some academic centers, but also sharply criticized some errors that he found in Clement's lost work (*Hypotyposes*, cf. *Bibliotheca*, 119–111). During the Medieval period, one of Clement's main works, *Stromateis*, survived in the eleventh-century manuscript (*Laurentianus*), which, like another document (*Parisianus* 451) along with Clement's *Protrepticus*, is believed to have been in the possession of Arethas, the Archbishop of Caesarea (ninth/tenth century), a disciple of Photius.

With the Renaissance, a new interest in Platonism and the Greek Fathers began to flourish in scholars' minds and then appeared in their works now circulating with enormous speed thanks to the invention of the printing press. Fascination with the value of the classical Graeco-Roman civilization and the richness of past culture, literature, and the Greek language led to new interest in early Christian authors, including Clement of Alexandria. In that atmosphere, Cardinal Marcello Cervini degli Spannochi (later Pope Marcellus II, 1555) as a *Bibliothecarius Sanctae Romanae Ecclesiae* requested a comprehensive edition of Clement's works. The man in charge of that enterprise was the Italian philologist Petrus Victorinus, who used the Neapolitan Codex and other sources in his preparation of the new edition of Clement's oeuvre (1550). The next year, Gentian Hervetus published a Latin translation of Victorinus' edition and, in this way, Clement's works became accessible to an even greater audience among the humanists. That publication allowed further development in the reception of Clement's thoughts by three emerging Christian traditions in western Europe: Roman Catholic, Protestant Lutheran, and Anglican, later Methodist. The Orthodox tradition and its various churches, where the Greek Fathers of the Church are the center of admiration and authority, preserved the name of Saint Clement of Alexandria. Clement is depicted as the early Christian apologist and valuable author who advanced the patristic trend in apophatic theology, who was a teacher of asceticism, advocate of equality between men and women, and defender of marriage (Evdokimov 1959).

Clement of Alexandria and Modern Scholarship

In the opening section of this chapter I have mentioned a very encouraging sign of growing interest in Clement's thought and legacy. I wish to highlight some important aspects of that interest in Clement among modern scholars.

First, the scholars are equipped with a new, critical collection of Clement's works. In addition to Otto Stählin's volumes (1905–1936) and later revised by Ludwig Früchtel and Ursula Treu (Osborn 2005: 293), Miroslav Marcovich supplemented his Greek edition of Paedagogus (Marcovich 2002). The French renowned series *Source Chrétiennes* continues to provide academics with a bilingual (Greek and French) publication of Clement's work with apparatus and then insightful commentaries. The most recent volume (2011) offers Clement's exploration of a Scriptural passage (*Mk* 10.17–31) *Quel Riche Sera Sauvé* (Nardi and Descourtieux 2011). A number of Clement's works have been published in the same series: *Le Protreptique* (1942, 2 bis); *Extraits de Théodote* (1948); *Stromate I* (1951); *Stromate II* (1954); *Le Pédagogue I* (1960); *Le Pédagogue II* (1965); *Le Pédagogue III* (1970); *Stromate V* vol. 1 (1981); *Stromate V* vol. 2 (1981); *Stromate VII* (1997); *Stromate VI* (1999); *Stromate IV* (2001). English-speaking readers have access to Henry Chadwick's edition of *Stromateis III and VII* (1954 and 2006), while John Ferguson translated *Stromateis* 1–3 (1991). Some of Clement's works are also now accessible in other languages, such as Italian (Nardi 1995; Rizzi and Pini 2006), Spanish (Díaz revised by Salvá: 2009; Hernández revised by Ramos 1994; Rodriguez 1998–2011), German, Czech, Russian, and Polish (van den Hoek 2012: 14–36). But this revival also reaches a non-European academic milieu, such as, for example, Japanese (O'Leary 2008). That richness of first-hand sources produces an even greater abundance of studies and articles, which discuss the whole spectrum of Clement's thoughts.

Clement's contribution to the emerging Christian pre-Nicene doctrine is well acknowledged by modern scholars (Berchman 1984; Williams 2001; Şchiop 2006; Edwards 2009). Similarly, Clement's Logos-theology and pneumatology are subjects of ongoing research (Bucur 2009). His exegesis and treatment of the Scriptures attracts the attention of commentators (Carabine 1995; Kovacs 1997; Cosaert 2008). Equally, Clement's own cultural background, including borrowings from Philo and Graeco-Roman (esoteric) traditions, stimulates some valuable studies (van den Hoek 1998a; Choufrine 2002; Jakab 2005; Stroumsa 2005: 109–131; Fürst 2007; Gargano 2011). Various approaches to Clement's rhetoric and persuasion are observed by insightful studies offered by female scholars (Gaca 2003; Buell 2008). Finally, Clement's model of Christian life, ethics, and his theory of assimilation to God stimulates various interpretations (Karavites 1999; Russell 2004; Ashwin-Siejkowski 2008; Kovacs 2010). Even this short review shows the amount of recent interest in this second-century author.

Clement of Alexandria remains a subject of controversy. The eclectic character of his thought was not always applauded, as we know from Photius' critique. Although by the ancient Christians he was considered to be "a saint," his position in the Roman Catholic calendar changed under Pope Benedict XIV (1640–1758). While re-editing the *Martyrologium Romanum* in 1749, the Pope found three reasons to remove the name of Clement of Alexandria from the register of Catholic Saints. First, it seemed that the life of Clement was insufficiently known; second, it was hard to find evidence of his veneration in Late Antiquity; and third, Clement's existing works did not always reflect what was supposed to be "orthodoxy" (Ashwin-Siejkowski 2010: 161). Clement's particular style of theology, where he blended together theological statements with numerous quotations from Graeco-Roman philosophy, secular literature, or even with the opinions of his opponents (e.g., *Excerpta ex Theodoto*), often without a proper critique, led some later commentators to raise questions about his orthodoxy. However, these questions reflect more the theological debates of Clement's critics rather than his zealous commitment to orthodoxy and renunciation of "heresy" (Le Boulluec 1985: 391–438).

More recently, Clement's name emerged in a yet again divisive debate around "The Secret Gospel of Mark" (Foster 2008: 171–182; Mayer 2003). Morton Smith claimed that, during his work in the summer of 1958 in the library in the Greek Orthodox Monastery of Mar Saba, he discovered by accident a manuscript in the back of a seventeenth-century edition of the Letters of Ignatius of Antioch, with the opening line: "From the letters of the most holy Clement, the author of the *Stromateis* to Theodore" (Smith 1973: 12). This discovered and photographed letter was written on two sides of the last page of the book. The photographs were published much later (1973). In the letter, Clement seemed to respond to Theodore's question about the followers of Carpocrates, a Christian teacher from the second century. The group or school, according to Clement, practiced a libertine sexual lifestyle. Clement in his letter, as Morton argued, rejected the claim of those Christians that they possessed "The Secret Gospel of Mark," which would justify their way of life. The letter reveals that Clement believed that Mark wrote two kinds of Gospels, the first one written in Rome during Peter's life recollected Peter's memory of events as well as other sources. However, after Peter's death, Mark moved to Alexandria, where he edited the first Gospel and produced another document, more spiritually advanced for the use only by prepared, mature Christians. The second Gospel was seized by the Carpocratians who introduced to the text some events and words which reflected their own immoral theology. It would be, however, unjustified to state that academic interest in Clement's theology, philosophy, ethics, and theory of mysticism are centered on controversy. On the contrary, as I wish to point out, modern scholars explore the whole range of subjects related to Clement's affluent bequest, and this fascination with his thought continues to produce a great number of studies of high academic quality.

Conclusion

Clement of Alexandria, although to some extent overshadowed by Origen's genius and later controversy, remains one of the most important theologians of the second century. His position, in the center of the intellectual crossroads, rather than on its margins, is unquestionable. He not only preserved a great deal of the early Christian assimilation of Jewish Hellenistic thought (Philo of Alexandria) and Graeco-Roman philosophical ideas from various schools (Neopythagorean, Middle Platonic, Stoic, Aristotelian), but he also provided some precious insights into inter-Christian debate about the correct understanding of the nature of salvation (ethics, Christology, the history of salvation). Clement offered his own creative and attractive program for the Christian life, which combined mature piety with intellectual rigorism. It enhanced ethical composure and theological inquisitiveness into the nature of God revealed in the divine Logos/Christ. That was not a theory; it was a program for the Christian life where the life of private prayer comes together with worship in the community, where individual research serves the disciples, where maturity is achieved through ethical practice. His complex thought in many of its aspects escapes from the schemes based on easy categorization. It remains open to new approaches; ultimately it echoes Clement's voice, which was engaged in dialogue and polemic with the most significant theological traditions of his time in Alexandria and beyond.

Bibliography

Primary Sources

Marcovich, M. (ed.) (2002), *Clementis Alexandrini Paedagogus*. Supplements to Vigiliae Christianae 41. Leiden: E.J. Brill.

Marcovich, M. (ed.) (1995), *Clementis Alexandrini Protrepticus*. Supplements to Vigiliae Christianae 34. Leiden: E.J. Brill.

Stählin, O. (ed.) (1970), *Clemens Alexandrinus, Stromata Buch VII und VIII, Excerpta ex Theodoto, Eclogae propheticae, Quis dives salvetur, Fragmente*, L. Früchtel and U. Treu (eds). GCS 17. Berlin: Akademie-Verlag.

Stählin, O. (ed.) (1972), *Clemens Alexandrinus, Protrepticus und Paedagogus*, U. Treu (reed.). GCS 12. Berlin: Akademie-Verlag.

Stählin, O. (ed.) (1985), *Clemens Alexandrinus, Stromata Buch I–VI*, L. Früchtel (ed.). GCS 15. Berlin: Akademie-Verlag.

Recent (since 1990) Translations of Clement's Works
English
Stromateis. Book 1–3 (1991), Ferguson, J., The Fathers of the Church, vol. 85. Washington, DC: The Catholic University of America Press.

French
Les Stromateis: Stromate VII (1997), Introduction, text, translation and notes by A. Le Boulluec. SC 428. Paris: Les Éditions du Cerf.

Les Stromateis: Stromate VI (1999), Introduction, text, translation and notes by P. DesCourtieux. SC 446. Paris: Les Éditions du Cerf.

Les Stromateis: Stromate IV (2001), Introduction, text, by A. van den Hoek, C. Mondésert (transl.). SC 30. Paris: Les Éditions du Cerf.

Clément d'Alexandrie: Quel Riche Sera Sauvé? (2011), C. Nardi and P. Descourtieux. Paris: Les Éditions du Cerf.

Italian
Nardi, C. (1995), *Estratti Profetici*. Bologna: Edizioni Dehoniane.

Rizzi, M. (ed.), Pini M. (transl.) (2006), *Gli Stromati. Note di vera filosofia*. Milan: Paoline Editoriale Libri.

Spanish

Díaz, J.S. revised by Salvá, L.M. (2009), *El Pedagogo*. Madrid: Editorial Ciudad Neuva.

Isart Hernández, M.ªC. revised by Ramos, H. (1994), *Protréptico*. Madrid: Biblioteca Clasica Gredos.

Rodriguez, M.M. (1998–2011), *Stromata 1–8*. Madrid: Editorial Ciudad Neuva.

Secondary Sources

Ashwin-Siejkowski, Piotr (2008), *Clement of Alexandria. A Project of Christian Perfection*. London: T&T Clark.

Ashwin-Siejkowski, Piotr (2010), *Clement of Alexandria on Trial. The Evidence of 'Heresy' from Photius' Bibliotheca*. Supplements to Vigiliae Christianae. Leiden: E.J. Brill.

Ashwin-Siejkowski, Piotr (2012), "The notion of 'heresy' in *Stromateis* VII". In *The Seventh Book of the Stromateis: Proceedings of the Colloquium on Clement of Alexandria (Olomouc, October 21–23, 2010)*, M. Havrda, V. Hušek, and J. Plátová (eds). Leiden: E.J. Brill; esp. 286–288.

Bardy, Gustave (1937), "Aux origines de l'École d'Alexandrie". *RSR*, XXVII: 69–90.

Bardy, Gustave, (1935) *La vie spirituelle d'après les Pères des trois premières siècles*. Paris: Bloud & Gay.

Berchman, Robert M. (1984) *From Philo to Origen. Middle Platonism in Transition*. Chico: Scholars Press.

Le Boulluec, Alain (1985) *La notion d'hérésie dans la littérature grecque IIe–IIe siècles*, vol. II. Paris: Etudes Augustiniennes.

Le Boulluec, Alain (1987) "L'école d'Alexandrie. De quelques aventures d'un concept historiographique", in *Alexandria. Hellénisme, judaïsme et christianisme à Alexandrie. Mélanges offerts à Claude Mondésert, s.j*. Paris: Les Éditions du Cerf, 403–417.

Le Boulluec, Alain (1999) "Aux origines, encore, de l''école' d'Alexandrie", *Adamantius*, 5, 7–36.

Bucur, Bogdan G. (2009) *Angelomorphic Pneumatology. Clement of Alexandria and Other Early Christian Witnesses*, 'Supplements to Vigiliae Christianae'. Leiden: E.J. Brill

Buell, Kimber D. (2008) "Ambiguous legacy: a feminist commentary on Clement of Alexandria's work", in *A Feminist Companion to Patristic Literature*, eds. A.-J. Levine and M.M. Robbins, London: T&T Clark, 26–55.

Carabine, Deirdre (1995) "A dark cloud: Hellenistic influences on the scriptural exegesis of Clement of Alexandria and the Pseudo-Dionysius, 1995", in *Scriptural Interpretation in the Fathers: Letter and Spirit*, eds Th. Finan and V. Twomey. Dublin: Blackrock, 61–74.

Choufrine, Arkadi (2002) *Gnosis, Theophany, Theosis: Studies in Clement of Alexandria's Appropriation of his Background*, 'Patristic Studies' 5. New York: Peter Lang.

Cosaert, Carl P. (2008) *The Text of the Gospels in Clement of Alexandria*. Atlanta, GA: Society for Biblical Literature.

Edwards, Mark J. (2009) *Catholicity and Heresy in the Early Church*. Farnham: Ashgate.

Evdokimov, Paul (1959), *L'Orthodoxie*. Neuchâtel: Delachaux et Nestlé.

Hägg, Henny Fiskå (2006) *Clement of Alexandria and the Beginning of Christian Apophaticism*. Oxford: Oxford University Press.

Foster, Paul (2008) "Secret Mark", in *The Non-Canonical Gospels*, ed. Paul Foster. London: T&T Clark.

Fürst, Alfons, (2007) *Christentum als Intellektuellen-Religion. Die Anfänge des Christentums in Alexandria*. Stuttgart: Verlag Katholisches Biebelwerk.

Gaca, Kathy L. (2003) *The Making of Fornication: Eros, Ethics and Political Reform in Greek Philosophy and Early Christianity*. Berkeley, CA: UCP.

Gargano, Guido I. (2011) *Clemente e Origene nella Chiesa cristiana alessandrina. Estraneità, dialogo o inculturazione?* Milan: San Paulo Edizioni.

Havrda, Matyáš (2011) "Grace and Free Will According to Clement of Alexandria", *JEChS*, 19 (1), 21–48.

Havrda, Matyáš, Hušek, Vít and Plátová, Jana, eds. (2012) *The Seventh Book of the Stromateis: Proceedings of the Colloquium on Clement of Alexandria (Olomouc, October 21–23, 2010)*, 'Supplements to Vigiliae Christianae'. Leiden: E.J. Brill.

Jakab, Attila (2005) *Ecclesia alexandrina. Evolution sociale et institutionelle du christianism alexandrin (II–III siecles)*, 'Christianismes anciens', New York: Peter Lang.

Jourdan, Fabienne (2010) *Orphée et Les Chrétiens. La réception du mythe d'Orphée dans la Littérature Chrétienne Grecque Des Cinque Premiers Siècles*, tom 1. Paris: Les Belles Lettres.

Karavites, Peter (1999) *Evil, Freedom and the Road to Perfection in Clement of Alexandria*, 'Supplements to Vigiliae Christianae'. Leiden: E.J. Brill.

Kovacs, Judith L. (1997) 'Concealment and gnostic exegesis: Clement of Alexandria's interpretation of the tabernacle', *SP*, XXXI, 414–437.

Kovacs, Judith L. (2010) "Becoming the perfect man: Clement of Alexandria on the philosophical life of women," in *Women and Gender in Ancient Religions: Interdisciplinary Approaches*, ed. S. Ahearne-Kroll. Tübingen: Mohr Siebeck, 389–413.

Laird, Martin, (2004) *Gregory of Nyssa and the Grasp of Faith. Union, Knowledge and Divine Presence*. Oxford: Oxford University Press.

Levine, Lee I. (2000) *The Ancient Synagogue. The First Thousand Years*. New Haven, CT: Yale University Press.

Mayer, Marvin (2003) *Secret Gospels. Essays on Thomas and the Secret Gospel of Mark*. London: Continuum, 109–178.

Mees, Michaël (1990) "Clément d'Alexandrie", in *Dictionnaire Encyclopédique du Christianisme Ancien*, vol. 1. Paris: Les Éditions du Cerf.

Méhat, André (1966) *Etudes sur les "Stromates" de Clément d'Alexandrie*, Patristica Sorbonensia, 7. Paris: Le Seuil.

Mélèze Modrzejewski, Joseph (1997) *Jews of Egypt from Ramses II to Emperor Hadrian*, trans. R. Cornman. Princeton, NJ: Princeton University Press.

O'Leary, Joseph S. (2008) "Japanese studies of Philo, Clement and Origen", *Adamantius*, 14, 395–402.

Osborn, Eric (1998) "Philo and Clement: quiet conversion and noetic exegsis", *SPA*, 10, 108–124.

Osborn, Eric (2005) *Clement of Alexandria*. Oxford: Oxford University Press.

Pearson, Birger A. (2006), "Egypt". In *The Cambridge History of Christianity*, vol. 1, M.M. Mitchell and F.M. Young (eds). Cambridge: Cambridge University Press; 330–350.

Pearson, Birger A. (2007) "Earliest Christianity in Egypt: further observations", in *The World of Early Egyptian Christianity. Language, Literature, and Social Context*, eds. J.E. Goehring and J.A. Timbie. Washington, DC: The Catholic University of America Press, 97–112.

Pericoli-Ridolfini, Francesco (1962) "Le origini della Scuola di Aleksandra", *RdSO* 37, 211–230.

Russell, Norman (2004) *The Doctrine of Deification in the Greek Patristic Tradition*. Oxford: Oxford University Press.

Şchiop, Gheorghie (2006) *The Doctrine of the Holy Trinity. Knowledge and Anthropology according to Clement of Alexandria*. Deva: Emia (in Romanian).

Smith, Morton (1973) *The Secret Gospel: The Discovery and Interpretation of the Secret Gospel According to Mark*. New York: Harper and Row.

Stroumsa, Guy G. (2005) "Clement, Origen and Jewish Esoteric Traditions", in his *Hidden Wisdom. Esoteric Traditions and the Roots of Christian Mysticism*, 'Numen Book Series', vol. 70. Leiden: E.J. Brill, 123–142.

Tuilier, André, (1982) "Les évangélistes et les docteurs de la primitive église et les origines de l'Ecole (didaskaleion), d'Alexandrie", *SP* XVII, 2, 738–749.

Williams, Rowan (2001) *Arius*. London: SCM–Canterbury Press

Van den Broek, Roelof (1990) "Juden and Christen in Alexandrien im 2 und 3 Jahrhundert", in *Juden und Christen in der Antike*, eds J. van Oort and J. van Amersfoorts. Kampen: Kok, 181–196.

Van den Hoek, Annewies (1990) 'How Alexandrian was Clement of Alexandria? Reflections on Clement and his Alexandrian background', *HeyJ*, XXXI, 179–194.

Van den Hoek, Annewies (1993) "Clement of Alexandria on martyrdom", *SP*, 26, 324–341.

Van den Hoek, Annewies (1996) "Techniques of quotation in Clement of Alexandria. A view of ancient literary working methods", *VCh*, 50, 223–243.

Van den Hoek, Annewies (1997) "The 'Catechetical' School of early Christian Alexandria and its Philonic heritage", *HRT* 90 (1), 59–87.

Van den Hoek, Annewies (1998a) "'I said you are Gods...' The significance of Psalm 82 for some early Christian authors", in *The Use of the Sacred Books in the Ancient World*, eds Leonard V. Rutgers *et al.* Leuven: Peeters Publishers, 203–219.

Van den Hoek, Annewies (1998b) *Clement of Alexandria and his use of Philo in Stromateis. An Early Christian Reshaping of a Jewish Model*, 'Supplements to Vigiliae Christianae'. Leiden: E.J. Brill, 116–146.

Van den Hoek, Annewies (2012) "*Stromateis* Book VII in the light of recent scholarship: approaches and perspectives (with bibliography), in *The Seventh Book of the Stromateis: Proceedings of the Colloquium on Clement of Alexandria (Olomouc, October 21–23, 2010)*, eds M. Havrda, V. Hušek, and J. Plátová. Leiden: E.J. Brill, 3–36.

CHAPTER 6

Origen of Alexandria

Mark Edwards

Introduction

Origen was born in Alexandria around 185 AD and died in Palestine shortly after the end of the Decian persecution in 252. A disappointed aspirant to martyrdom before the age of 17, he was little older when he began to teach. Although he incurred the displeasure of his bishop, he was ordained in Palestine and was often co-opted by the bishops of his time to take the lead in the public refutation of heresy. Yet, after his death, one catalog of errors after another was drawn up against him, though the contents of these lists were often at variance and sometimes contradictory. The result of his official condemnation in 553 at the Fifth Oecumenical Council was the disappearance of most of his Greek writings, whether by atrophy or by neglect. Much is wholly lost, although a number of important texts, including his *First Principles*, are extant in Latin versions, in which many of the most eccentric doctrines attributed to him are not to be found. It is thus not possible even to give an uncontroversial summary of Origen's thought and then proceed to a history of its reception; for us, it is the interrogation of later witnesses that will define the content of his thought.

It is generally agreed that Origen was the first theologian to state that from all eternity the Trinity has consisted of three hypostases: Father, Son, and Holy Spirit. Whether he held the first to be superior in dignity and power to the other two, and whether he would have characterized the Son and the Spirit as creatures of the Father, are questions still in debate – or, as some would say, what is really in debate is the propriety of asking a theologian of his time to resolve such questions. Again, it is agreed on all sides – in his own time and our own, both by his critics and by his admirers – that Origen was the first Christian theologian who undertook to elicit a higher, or spiritual, sense from every passage of the scriptures. How much of the literal or historical sense he retained (or should have retained), and whether his higher sense is always what we would now

---

The Wiley Blackwell Companion to Patristics, First Edition. Edited by Ken Parry.

call an allegory, are questions on which we cannot even trust the same critic always to entertain the same opinion. Finally, it is admitted that he held, or was willing to entertain, some notion of a pre-existent soul, and that some other notions attributed to him would have been heresies even in his own day; it need hardly be said that no attempt to winnow truth from calumny in these charges has won universal assent.

This chapter is concerned with the explicit reception of Origen, not with his influence, which was all the more pervasive because it was commonly unavowed. Particular attention will be paid to the first assaults on his orthodoxy because the period from Constantine to Justinian was the one in which the greatest number of Origen's works were current, and the one which, by its definition of Origenism, has dictated the shape and substance of almost every book that has since been written about him. The Middle Ages will be passed over lightly because the little that is new in them does not end itself to historical commentary. In the era that follows the Council of Trent, the lion's share of our interest will be claimed by the great lucubration of Pierre-Daniel Huet; because it is impossible to surpass and is almost futile to challenge him in his own vein of writing, the most prominent names in the final section will be those of his countrymen who have taken Origen out of the dock and into the nurseries of modern thought.

The First Assault

What those who were not Origenists thought of Origen we learn from the *Apology* by his Pamphilus, his Caesarean disciple, which Eusebius completed after the death of Pamphilus in 309. The *Apology* commences with a severe reflection on those who will hear no voice but their own on points that scripture leaves undetermined, and who therefore suppose, when Origen seals a charitable armistice between two equally tenable positions, that he has no rule for discerning good from evil. After citing Origen's unexceptionable pronouncements on the transcendence of the Father, the divinity of the Son, and the ubiquity of the Holy Spirit, Pamphilus turns to an inventory of the nine false charges that make up his brief as an apologist, beginning with the most heinous and concluding (as he says) with the most refutable. The first charge is that Origen accorded to the Son all the Father's attributes, including that of being unbegotten. The second answers the question what he might have supposed him to be if not begotten, by imputing to him the doctrine of his infamous predecessor Valentinus, that the Son is an emanation or projection from the substance of the Father. The third – clean contrary to the former two, in the apologist's submission – is that he robbed the incarnate Savior of his Godhead, representing him as a mere man. The fourth, again at odds with its predecessor, is that he slighted the humanity of Christ, reducing all accounts of his work in the flesh to allegory. The contradiction is mitigated by the fifth indictment, that Origen posited two Christs, denying to each the predicates of the other.

After the Nicene council, it was a badge of orthodoxy to maintain the coeternity of the Father and the Son, the consubstantiality of the two, the presence in the incarnate Christ of a human soul, and the union of two distinct and antithetical natures in his person. These catholic resolutions were not the fruit of a single council, and it is a measure of the rigidity that had overtaken Christian speculation in the fourth century that

Origen was not so often commended for his prescient innovations as condemned for his adherence to positions that in his own time it would have seemed perverse to question. As we shall see, he came to be perceived as an apologist for dogmas which he had merely failed to render obsolete.

The last four charges rehearsed by Pamphilus all concern the destiny and constitution of the human agent. It was alleged (6) that he denied the empirical truth of every narrative in the scriptures that purports to be historical; (7) that he treated the resurrection of the body, with its associated penalties and prizes, as an edifying fable; (8) that he entertained false opinions with regard to the soul; and (9) that the most culpable of these was his espousal of the Platonic doctrine of transmigration, according to which the soul, when it quits one corporal tenement, passes not into heaven or hell but into the body of another beast or human. Similar charges were pressed by Bishop Methodius of Olympia in a book on the resurrection, which survives now only in excerpt and epitome (Epiphanius, *Panarion* 64; Photius, *Bibliotheca* 134, 135). On occasion it is difficult to say whether it is he or his annotators who have given the name of Origen to the interlocutor whom he accuses of holding (1) that the coats of skins which God contrived for Adam and Eve are biblical symbols of the flesh which attires the fallen soul; (2) that the man of whom Paul says "I was alive before the law" (*Romans* 7, 9) is the heavenly prototype whom God created before he fashioned his earthly tenement; (3) that while the soul survives death, the body is not renewed; (4) that the bodies of those who rise in glory will be spherical; (5) that after death the soul retains only the incorporeal form or *morphê* of the abandoned body. In his tract *On Things Created* he further accuses Origen of denying the historicity of Adam (Bonwetsch 1917: 499), and the temporal creation of the world.

Nicaea and After

It would appear that the first oecumenical council, convened in 325 by the Emperor Constantine at Nicaea in Asia Minor, borrowed a hitherto contentious term from Origen by proclaiming that the Son is consubstantial (*homoousios*) with the Father (cf. Pamphilus, *Apology* 94). Since it did not expressly proscribe the subordination of the Son to the Father, it can be argued that no tenet held by Origen was pronounced heretical by this assembly. The Nicene champion Athanasius mentions him only to praise his demonstration that the Son is coeternal with Father (*Nicene Decrees* 27). It was a burdensome friend of Athanasius, Marcellus of Ancyra, who took exception to Origen's reading of *Proverbs* 8.22, where Wisdom declares "The Lord created me in the beginning of his ways." To Origen this implied that the Second Person of the Trinity was the inviolable offspring of the Father's will, brought forth before the ages; Athanasius preferred to attach this saying to the formation of Christ's body, while Marcellus, who denied the very existence of a Second Person before the incarnation, urged that the passage is too arcane to serve as the premise of a dogma (Eusebius, *Against Marcellus*: 1.3.13–4.28). Eusebius in reply indicts Marcellus as a Sabellian, who denies the existence of the three divine hypostases before the incarnation; subsequently, Marcellus was anathematized by councils both in the east and in the west.

One vigorous supporter of the Nicene Council, Bishop Eustathius of Antioch, wrote a treatise *On the Pythoness*, upbraiding Origen for his exegesis of the episode at 1 *Samuel* 28 in which the Witch of Endor summons the wraith of the prophet Samuel from Hades (Greer and Mitchell 2007: 62–157). Origen had accepted the literal meaning of the text, whereas Eustathius, with an animadversion on Origen's curious failure to apply his favorite tool of allegory in a case where faith demands it (chapter 21), urges that any apparition of the dead must be a contrivance of the devil (chapter 4). His polemic foreshadows that of Epiphanius the champion of an orthodoxy which recognized no truth before Methodius or later than Nicaea (Dechow 1988; Clark 1992: 43–104). Epiphanius, though he does not revive the charge of teaching the transmigration of souls, was perhaps the first of Origen's critics to scent a heresy in the mere notion of existence before embodiment. According to his report (*Panarion* 64.4), the great heresiarch had declared that souls had been created to dwell eternally with God, but that many have fallen and are now undergoing chastisement in a body. He and other authorities add that the cause of the trespass was satiety or coolness, and that each soul acquires a body of a texture corresponding to the degree of its estrangement (Jerome, *Letters* 51.4, 98.12, 124.9). Humans are those who have fallen further than the angelic powers but not so far as demons. Worse still – since this was an issue on which no latitude was permitted by the church of the late fourth century – Origen had anticipated the "Arian" denial of Christ's divinity by affirming that the Son was merely a creature of the Father. Thus, it was Origen's lot to be attainted first for his failure to uphold and then for his failure to deny the superiority of the Father to the Son.

The most zealous of Origen's partisans, Rufinus of Aquileia, retorted that a man who espoused the term *homoousios* cannot be an Arian (*Adulteration of Origen* 1). Rufinus translated Pamphilus, together with a corpus of works by Origen, few of which have survived in Greek. By his own account he amended any passage on which a reader of the fourth century would be apt to put a heretical construction that would not have been intended in the third. Furthermore, he professed to have detected interpolations which were duly excluded from his Latin versions. He was certainly accused of dissimulation by his embittered friend, the shrewd and acerbic Jerome, who, for reasons which are now not wholly recoverable, had fallen under the spell of men who matched him in neither quality (Clark 1992: 11–42, 159–193). One was Epiphanius, whose letters he translated, and whose cause he espoused against Origen's champion, Bishop John of Jerusalem. The other was Theophilus, patriarch of Alexandria, who taxed Origen not only with lending countenance to astrology and magic but with denying the eternity of Christ's kingdom (Jerome, *Letters* 96.7–17). Tendentiously, he sees an attenuation of God's omnipotence in a text which merely asserted that any actual creation of omnipotence must be finite (Jerome, *Letters* 96.17). A further charge, that Origen forbade prayer to the Son, follows Athanasius rather than Origen in admitting only one species of prayer (Jerome, *Letters* 96.14).

In the west, Jerome was largely content to reproduce the strictures of Epiphanius, though he may have been the first to allege that Origen had posited a second fall from heaven, which would entail a new creation of the material realm as a house of punishment. If we can trust Rufinus in his translation of *First Principles* 3.6.3, Jerome took for Origen's own view what the latter had presented as the absurd result of another's speculations (*Letter to Avitus* 10). Jerome's claim, on the other hand – partly verified by his *Commentary on Ephesians* (*Patrologia Latina* 26: 485–486) – is that, far from augmenting the blemishes in Origen's work, he distilled the best of his exegesis and spared the Greekless reader any knowledge of his doctrinal heresies. He was never less than a scholar, and in contrast to Epiphanius and Theophilus, he knew that it was not the resurrection of the body, but the resurrection of a carnal body (*Letters* 84.5), that Origen had denied.

The strongest proof that Origen was still in high repute was the compilation of the *Philokalia*, an anthology of choice passages from the whole corpus of his writings. The editors plainly thought the *First Principles* a pious work, and did not share the modern aversion to allegory. On the other hand, this publication of excerpts may bespeak a fear that his works were not only too long but too adventurous to be laid in their entirety before the common reader. If the compilation is rightly attributed to Gregory of Nazianzus or Basil of Caesarea, the orthodoxy of its contents is incontestable, but in fact the ascription, like almost every testimony that survives concerning Origen, is now judged insecure (Harl 1983; McLynn 2004).

During the Pelagian controversy, those who urged that we cannot be justly punished for sins unless we have the capacity to be sinless could be represented as Origenists. For the most part they declined the appellation, as they did not wish to be credited with a belief in the pre-existence of the soul (Clark 1992: 223–227). In a letter to Orosius, Augustine laments that some have stumbled into Origen's heresies in escaping those of the Manichees (*Against the Priscilianists and Origenists* 4.4). He does not enter any caveat against the subordination of the Son, and reserves his strictures for three positions. The first is that no punishment will be interminable, even for the devil and his angels (5.5–6.7); the second is that the soul was not created for embodiment, and might have enjoyed eternal felicity in the presence of God had it not fallen into a grosser state as a consequence of satiety or fatigue (8.9–10); the third charge is the attribution of rational souls to the sun and moon.

Oecumenical Condemnation

In 543 the Emperor Justinian, after some years of agitation and counter-agitation in the monasteries (Hombergen 2001), compiled the following list of propositions which had been maintained in error by Origen (Percival 1991: 320):

1. That human souls were once spirits but had been condemned to the body after becoming sated with the vision of God.
2. That the soul of Christ was joined to the Word before the Incarnation
3. That the body of Christ was formed in the womb of Mary and then united to the divine Word and the pre-existing soul.
4. That the Word assumed the form of the angels in order to redeem them.
5. That the resurrection body will be spherical.
6. That celestial bodies and elements are ensouled.
7. That Christ will be crucified also for the demons.

8. That God created only as much as lay within his finite power.
9. That the punishment of demons and men will end, to be followed by the restoration (*apokatastasis*) of all things.

The majority of these charges find some color in Origen's writings, but only after a strange inflection has been imparted to his teaching by embellishment or paraphrase. When the second council of Constantinople met in 553, it added Origen's name to the list of reprobate thinkers, cementing this exhibition of hostility by the promulgation of 15 anathemas, which are clearly based upon the Emperor's strictures. Rather than give a handle to quibblers by attempting to trace the provenance of these errors, the council thought that its work was done if it could punish those who asserted (Percival 1991: 318–319):

10. That our souls were incorporeal before this life and will be so again.
11. That the rational intelligences descended to bodies only when they grew lax in the contemplation of God.
12. That the sun, moon, and stars have been imprisoned in bodies for crimes less heinous than ours.
13. That humans are intelligences whose love of God grew lukewarm, whereas demons are those in whom it has grown cold.
14. That an angel may become a human soul and a human soul an angel or demon.
15. That only the soul of Christ has remained immutable in its love of God.
16. That Christ assumed different bodies to liberate different orders of fallen beings.
17. That the Word and Jesus Christ are not identical.
18. That it was not the Logos but his human intelligence that descended into hell and ascended to heaven.
19. That resurrection bodies will be ethereal and spiritual, as that of Christ already is.
20. That the last judgment will entail the destruction of bodies and matter.
21. That heavenly, earthly, and demonic powers are all united with the intelligence of the Word.
22. That all intelligences will be seated with Christ at the right hand of God.
23. That all reasonable beings will be one.
24. That the end will be the same as the beginning.

It is not known whether these articles were attached to the original proceedings of the council, or whether all of the 15 errors were attributed to Origen. The eighth and ninth appertain to Evagrius, if to anyone (Guillaumont 1962: 156–159), while those that might be laid at Origen's door have not been worded with Justinian's terse exactitude. Theodore of Mopsuestia, Ibas of Edessa, and Theodoret of Cyrrhus were anathematized with Origen, but the Bishop of Rome, Vigilius, refused to lend his name to any posthumous commination. He consented under extreme duress, and was excommunicated by the bishops of Ravenna and Milan. It is still not agreed by all Catholics that the condemnation of Origen has oecumenical force.

Fifteen counts against Origen, not identical with the anathemas of the Fifth Oecumenical Council, were rebutted in a treatise now known only from a synopsis in the *Bibliotheca* of Photius, the ninth-century patriarch of Constantinople, who for all his redoubtable learning does not appear to know either its date or the name of the author (Photius, *Bibliotheca* 117). Although most of the charges are familiar, it is surprising to discover that the belief in fallen angels is now treated as a heresy, and we not possess any previous indictment in which Origen is said to have held that the soul of Adam was also that of Christ. This apologist may have been the first to urge that Origen's refutation of Sabellius ought to count for more, if we have any sense of history, than his failure to pre-empt the Nicene Creed. Writing three centuries later, the superficial polymath Nicetas Choniates was content to reproduce the older caricatures in his catalog of ante-Nicene heresies (*On Heresies* IV.31). Again we hear that Origen denied the Son's equality with and knowledge of the Father; by construing the garden of Eden allegorically, he reduced the whole of scripture to a fable; other blasphemies cannot be rehearsed without offence to the pious ear. Worst of all, to judge by the length and warmth of the invective, is his teaching on the pre-existence of souls, which is said here to have been justified by woefully inadequate citations from the scriptures, not attested in any works that now survive. In the west, an abler theologian had already proved himself a better scholar. John Scotus Eriugena puts Origen at the end of a list of orthodox authorities who (on his tendentious interpretation) have prophesied the salvation of the devil (*Periphyseon* V, Juneau 2003: 100). Thus, it would seem that Origen was no heretic to the Latin church of the ninth century, though in fact the text that Eriugena quotes, in the form most likely to be original, says only that on the last day death will cease to molest the saints (Edwards 2010).

Renaissance and Reformation

It was in the sixteenth century that the Greek remains of Origen became known to the west, in the wake of the revolution that set up Plato as a rival to Aristotle and the original New Testament as a corrective to the Vulgate. Judgment was now being passed on the popes whose forebears had judged Origen; for every controversialist who imputed a heresy to him, there was another who denied that he held it, and yet another who argued that he held it but it was not a heresy. Jacques Merlin, the editor of his Latin remains in 1530, and Gilbert Génébrard, who added the Greek texts to a superior edition in 1574, were Roman Catholics, ready to try any shift to prove that the man on whom they had spent such pains was as orthodox as they were (cf. Westcott 1887: 130). For Erasmus, who completed Merlin's edition, orthodoxy included the vindication of our freedom to accept or reject our calling to salvation. In his controversy with Luther he coupled Origen and Jerome as interpreters who understood the ninth chapter of *Romans* better than Augustine (Rupp 1969: 42, 65). Origen henceforth was a Pelagian, not only in the eyes of Luther and Calvin, but in those of Catholics like Cornelius Jansen, for whom Augustine's teaching remained canonical (Scheck 2008: 211–215). At the same time, the shortcomings in Origen's doctrine of the Trinity were cunningly magnified by Dionysius Petavius to reinforce his argument that the primitive orthodoxy to which some Protestants appealed was a mirage (King 2009: 101). The task of arbitration was undertaken in 1667 by Pierre-Daniel Huet, an inflexible Catholic who was also the leading scholar of the age (Rapetti 2012).

Huet does not find that Origen can be acquitted of every heresy, though he concludes that, when Origen's true thoughts have been rescued from the malice of his detractors and the libels of his friends, we shall often see cause to reverse the less favorable verdicts. In the preface to his review of Origen's doctrines, he notes that his apologists have found three lines of defense: to challenge the integrity of the texts that have come down to us; to urge that any false teaching that Origen entertains is also contradicted in his writings; and to point out that his errors are no graver than those of others who are still deemed orthodox (Huet 1667: II.2, prologue). When Huet applies the first expedient, the result is not always to Origen's advantage; thus, he is apt to discount Theophilus as a prejudiced witness, but regards Jerome as a more scrupulous translator than Rufinus (cf. II.2, *quaestio* 8, xvii–xviii). The second plea, that Origen is not a consistent heretic, is freely admitted, though sometimes as an aggravation of his infidelity. Elsewhere, however, Huet concedes that a dangerous speculation has been rendered innocuous by Origen's rider that it is only a provisional thesis and open to correction (e.g. II.2, *quaestio* 11.xv and xxiii). He convicts some of Origen's recent critics of reading him literally when he was writing allegorically, and in his treatment of Origen's hermeneutical method he repeatedly observes that his allegorical readings of scripture, whether false or true, are more often complementary than inimical to the literal exegesis (*quaestio* 13). The palliative comparison with other Fathers is sparingly employed (e.g., at *quaestio* 2.x and 11.xxv), although Huet is prepared to grant that a doughty rebuttal of Gnosticism may afford a partial excuse for lapsing into Arianism before it had been defined as a heresy (*quaestio* 2.xviii). In his epilogue he maintains that Origen's credit is enhanced by the martyrdom of his disciple Pamphilius, the authenticity of whose *Apology* he upholds against Jerome's mordant skepticism (II.3.xvi).

For all that he says on Origen's behalf, Huet can distinguish 14 points on which he erred, and seems at times to insinuate that he was preserved from greater errors by the virtues of his vices. While he thinks it impossible to identify the Origen of the church with the man of the same name who was a colleague of Plotinus (I.1.vii), he surmises that he imbibed from Platonic teachers not only false doctrines of the afterlife (II.2, *quaestio* 11.xxi), but a limited notion of God's powers as Creator (*quaestio* 1.iv). As a Platonist he is clearly immune to the charge of having made corporeality an attribute of the Godhead (*quaestio* 1.v); his own words, however, manifestly convict him of subordinating the Son to the Father (*quaestio* 2.vii), and, since Huet holds that *ousia* and *hypostasis* are synonyms in Origen's vocabulary, even the affirmation of three hypostases in the Trinity exposes his cloven hoof (*quaestio* 2.iii). Origen's remarks on the peccability of Mary are judged severely (*quaestio* 4), notwithstanding the absence of any ecclesiastical decision on this question in his own day; his opinion that the efficacy of priesthood depends on the worthiness of the incumbent is also stigmatized as an early specimen of Donatism (*quaestio* 14.i). In the long chapter devoted to Origen's teaching on the freedom of the will, Huet takes the opportunity to educate the Lutherans who, in exaggerating Origen's transgressions, have strayed into more heinous errors. While Jansen may not be a heretic, he has wrongly foisted on Origen the Pelagian definition of freedom as unconditioned power to will or not to will in every situation (*quaestio* 8.iii). Origen knew well enough that voluntary acts may be conditioned by our own characters and motions of God within us; if he fell into the

Semipelagian fallacy of supposing that the choice to accept or reject the prompting of God depends only on us (*quaestio* 8.xv–xviii), he did not blaspheme the justice of God, as Protestants do, by denying any agency to the will that God has quickened, or any congruence between works and salvation. Huet, as a loyal son of the church, does not doubt that Augustine is consistent both with himself and with the Council of Trent in his doctrine of salvation, any more than he doubts that the strictures passed on Origen by Aquinas and the Fifth Oecumenical Council were based on knowledge.

For the Anglican divine George Bull, it was equally true that the exculpation of Origen went hand in hand with the vindication of his own theology. As an Anglican, he was bound to resist the argument of Petavius that the church would not have found its way to consensus without a Pontiff. As an Anglican of a certain kind, he maintained that the Nicene Creed had subordinated the Son to the Father, though only insofar as this was implied by the formula "God from God" and not in power or dignity. In undertaking to prove that this was the doctrine of the church before Nicaea, as exemplified in Origen, he draws a sharp dichotomy between Origen's public teaching on behalf of the church and his tentative speculations in letters to friends (Bull 1680). He also, in contrast to Huet, denies all credence to the Latin works, and appears not to be acquainted with all those that survive in Greek. It is thus from the late apology *Against Celsus* that he draws the bulk of his evidence for Origen's belief in the divinity of the Son. This is also his chosen field of battle against Huet, whose criticisms, in Bull's view, always rest either on a misunderstanding of Origen or a misapprehension of the true biblical doctrine. An example of the first is his deduction that, because Origen distinguishes the Son from the universal God, he thinks the Son inferior to the Father; an example of the second is his unwillingness to see that, in enjoining prayer to the Father through the Son but not directly to the Son, Origen simply preaches what the New Testament prescribes. This was a point designed to win allies in the Church of England, which since the Reformation has customarily offered its prayers not to, but through, the Son.

The Modern Age

Origen continued to be handled gently by Anglican divines. Daniel Waterland cites him habitually as a representative of the most ancient traditions, far from "singular" in his opinions (Waterland 1856: 602), albeit he sometimes "led the way" (Waterland, 1856: 41). John Henry Newman, despite his admiration for the Alexandrian fathers, exhibits little knowledge of Origen's writings, but could not believe "that so great a soul was lost" (Newman 1865: 259). Brook Foss Westcott (1887), writing in the *Dictionary of Christian Biography*, provides a useful synopsis of Origen's writings, and pronounces his search for a higher sense in the Bible "right in principle" but marred by the absence of a "historical sense". His doctrine of the Trinity becomes more palatable when we remember that he was speaking of the three persons in their economic, not their essential character. It remains true that he speculated wildly because his Christian philosophy did not take account of the imperfections of the human mankind, which "he himself had pointed out."

Westcott had imbibed something of the critical spirit which had now become active in German scholarship. Isaak August Dorner, in his *History of the Doctrine of the Person of Christ*, maintains that it was the task of all theologians in the early church to hold the balance between the revealed, or Jewish, and the rational, or Hellenistic, strains of Christian thought. Origen's espousal of philosophy is not for him a surrender of the gospel, but an acknowledgment that all human beings share the same cognitive faculties. Origen's depreciation of this world as a transient school of chastisement may have caused him to undervalue Christ's humanity (Dorner 1861: 35–36), but the philosophy which taught him to maintain the immutability of God bore fruit in the salutary assertion of the Son's eternal procession from the Father. The notion that faith can learn from philosophy was less palatable to another Lutheran, Adolf von Harnack, whose *History of Dogma* rained hard words on many early Christian writers. For von Harnack, Origen was a proponent of inward religion, bearing with impatience the yoke of verbal revelation and the supervenient laws of the cultic community. Von Harnack might have applauded his independence but for his enmity to the body, which disposed him to see this world as a prison for souls, who could be rescued only by the condescension of the incorporeal Logos. These assumptions precluded belief in a truly human Savior, and Origen's Christology is belittled by von Harnack as an amalgam of previous heresies (von Harnack 1910: 372–373), held together by exegetical virtuosity rather than theological insight. In his teaching on the relation of the Logos to the Father, Origen follows Philo, his Alexandrian precursor, and falls prey to the same contradictions (von Harnack 1910: 352). His Logos is at once the idea of a world in the mind of God and a distinct hypostasis, marking the first exertion of the divine will and the beginning of a transition from the One to the manifold. While the inferiority of the Logos to the Father is not expressly asserted, the Holy Spirit is evidently a creature in Origen's eyes and is raised to parity with the other two persons only to satisfy the rule of faith (von Harnack 1910: 354–355). The result of these misspent labors was a system that eclipsed its Gnostic progenitors and proved enticing to Greek philosophers even while it justified the hegemony of the church (von Harnack 1910: 378).

A far more detailed study of Origen's debt to Greek philosophy was published by C.H. Bigg (1897); its title, *The Christian Platonists of Alexandria*, exercised more influence than the copious references and annotations which show how carefully Origen strove to maintain the integrity of biblical and ecclesiastical teaching. Protestant theology was thus rendered more receptive to the polar reasoning of Anders Nygren, a Swedish Lutheran, for whom Origen stands close to the head of a chain of Christian trucklers who have confounded eros, the pagan aspiration to be like one's gods, with the sacrificial *agape*, the unconditioned and unacquisitive love of the best for the worst, which was preached and exemplified in Christ (Nygren 1953: 370–373). That Origen's error was grounded in a sophistical reading of the Song of Songs was further evidence that the reformers were right to deplore the abuse of allegory. The Anglican bishop Richard Hanson, having devoted two ponderous monographs to Origen's methods of exegesis, accused him of neglecting the historical character of Christianity (Hanson 1959: 363–364). It is not always clear whether this means that he denied God's action in history or that he failed to anticipate the historico-critical method of the twentieth century; even if the first charge were not false and the second trivial, they could only be brought under one head by an author who believed, as Hanson himself did, that the historico-critical method tends to prove the historicity of the narratives to which it is applied.

It can be argued that the failure of the historico-critical method to underwrite the historicity of the Bible has been the cause of almost every theological revolution in the last century. Among Protestants and Catholics alike, it has become commonplace to maintain that the full revelation lies ahead of us, not behind us, and that until this consummation we must regard all readings of scripture as provisional. To Catholic exponents of the *nouvelle théologie* it appeared that Origen had revealed his awareness of this provisionality in his hermeneutics and in his eschatology – that is, in the very features of his theology that had hitherto been counted among its blemishes. Henri De Lubac found a perfect expression of the catholic temper (though Huet had detected a heresy) in Origen's conjecture that Christ, our great High Priest, will be in pain until the last day puts an end to the travail of sinners (De Lubac 1988: 399–400). Origen's own writing is a seed to be judged by its fruit, and in his response to the pregnant opacity of scripture we see the germ of the fourfold reading that had been the staple of exegesis during the Middle Ages (De Lubac 1959–1964). The spiritual sense of scripture "abuts on the reality of the spiritual life" (De Lubac 1960: 391) and stamps the dogmatic vision with the "individuality of the spirit" (De Lubac 1960: 419). Although Teilhard de Chardin was another visionary for whom De Lubac held a brief, it was left to John Lyons to spell out a comparison between this second Origen and the first (Lyons 1982).

The scholar and cardinal Jean Daniélou argues that for Origen both life and the biblical texts are shadows, one of things to come, the other of truths to be unveiled. A faithful but not a rigid dogmatician, he is happy to grant that this pioneer of speculation predicted an infinite succession of worlds (Daniélou 1955: 269). By contrast, Henri Crouzel, a more conservative believer and a more fastidious scholar, credits Origen with a less equivocal belief in the resurrection of the body (Crouzel 1990). He also observes that Origen's most fanciful theories often arise from readings that we would consider unduly literal, not from the wanton use of allegory (Crouzel 1988: 258). This caveat suggests that Origen's glosses may not always be more perspicuous than the texts on which he is commenting; when she describes his teaching on the fall of souls as a privileged hypothesis, the philologist Marguerite Harl is taking his Platonism seriously enough to read him as Plato himself was read by the later members of his school (Harl 1963: 386–387).

In the last decade, scholars of all traditions have protested that, since Origen's response to Celsus clearly implies that the sobriquet "Christian Platonist" would be an oxymoron, we need subtler locutions to characterize his relation to Plato and other Greek philosophers. The term "anti-Platonist" might have satisfied Origen himself (Tzamalikos 2007: 17, 23–24); the argument that the relation is dialectical, rather than purely antipathetic or dependent (Edwards 2002), acknowledges his readiness to grant Plato an ancillary role in the parsing of obscure texts and elliptical revelations. These matters, together with many nice points of philology, have been in different venues, and by scholars young and old, at 11 "international conferences on Origen studies", each of which has published its own proceedings. An Italian research group also publishes its own journal *Adamantius*, currently maintaining an enviable standard of scholarship under the vigilant eyes of Lorenzo Perrone. It may be said with confidence that few students of Origen now subscribe to Nygren's condemnation of him, and that equally few would urge that we ought not to read him without gilt-edged certificates of his orthodoxy. The emancipation of Origen from confessional debate spares us the trouble of exculpating or condemning him; instead – and with due regard for the dangers of anachronism – he can be held up as a pattern to modern Christians who do not believe that their intellectual probity depends on their being virgins to all philosophy, but are also unwilling to compromise that probity by binding themselves to one intellectual system.

Bibliography

Primary Sources

Athanasius (1935), "De Decretis Synodi Nicaeni". In *Werke* 2.1, H.-G. Opitz (ed.). Berlin: De Gruyter; 1–45.

Epiphanius of Salamis (1915–1933), *Werke*, K. Holl (ed.). Leipzig: Hinrichs.

Eriugena, John Scotus (2003), *Periphyseon Liber Quintus*, E.A. Juneau (ed.). Turnhout: Brepols.

Eusebius of Caesarea (1991), *Gegen Markellos*, E. Klostermann (ed.). Berlin: Akademie Verlag.

Jerome (1996), *Epistulae*, three vols, I. Hilberg (ed.). Vienna: Austrian Academy of Sciences.

Jerome (1846), "In Epistulam ad Ephesios". *Patrologia Latina* 26. Paris: J.-P. Migne.

Methodius of Olympia (1917), *Werke*, N.P. Bonwetsch (ed.). Leipzig: Hinrichs.

Nicetas Choniates, in *Patrologia Graeca* 140.

Origen (1913), *De Principiis*, P. Koetschau (ed.). Leipzig: Hinrichs.

Pamphilus of Caesarea (2005), *Apologia pro Origene*, G. Rowekamp (ed.). Turnhout: Brepols.

Photius, *Bibliothèque*, vol. 2, R. Henry (ed.). Paris: Belles Lettres.

Rufinus of Aquileia (2005), *De Adulteratione Librorum Origenis*, G. Rowekamp (ed.). Turnhout: Brepols.

Secondary Sources

Bigg, C.H. (1897), *The Christian Platonists of Alexandria*. Oxford: Clarendon Press.

Bull, G. (1680), *De Defensione Fidei Nicaeanae*, chapter 9, reprinted 1857 in *Patrologia Graeca* 17. Paris: J.-P. Migne.

Clark, E.A. (1992), *The Origenist Controversy*. Princeton, NJ: Princeton University Press.

Crouzel, H. (1990), *Fins dernières selon Origène*. Aldershot: Ashgate.

Crouzel, H. (1988), "Theological construction and research: Origen on free-will". In *Scripture, Tradition and Reason: A Study in the Criteria of Christian Doctrine*, R. Bauckham and B. Drewery (eds). Edinburgh: T.&T. Clark; 239–265.

Daniélou, J. (1955), *Origen*, W. Mitchell (transl.). London: Sheed and Ward.

Dechow, J.F. (1988), *Dogma and Mysticism in Early Christianity: Epiphanius of Cyprus and the Legacy of Origen*. Macon, GA: Mercer University Press.

De Lubac, H. (1960), *Histoire et Esprit*. Paris: Aubier.

De Lubac, H. (1959–1964), *L'Exégèse Mediévale*, four vols. Paris: Cerf.

De Lubac, H. (1988), *Catholicism*. San Francisco, CA: Ignatius Press.

Dorner, I.A. (1861), *History of the Development of the Doctrine of the Person of Christ*, P. Fairbairn (transl.). Edinburgh: T.&T. Clark.

Edwards, M.J. (2002), *Origen against Plato*. Surrey: Ashgate.

Edwards, M.J. (2010), "The fate of the Devil in Origen". *Ephemerides Theologicae Louvanienses*, 86: 163–170.

Greer, R. and M. Mitchell (eds) (2007), *The Belly-Myther of Endor*. Atlanta, GA: Society of Biblical Literature.

Guillaumont, A. (1962), *Les Kephalaia Gnostica d'Évagre le Pontique*. Paris: Seuil.

Hanson, R.P.C. (1959), *Allegory and Event*. London: SCM.

Harl, M. (1963), "Recherches sur' Origénisme d' Origène". In *Studia Patristica* VIII, F.L. Cross (ed.). Berlin: Akademie Verlag; 373–405.

Harl, M. (1983), *Sur les Écritures: Origène, Philokalie 1–20*. Paris: Cerf.

Hombergen, D. (2001), *The Second Origenist Controversy: A New Perspective on Cyril of Scythopolis*. Rome: Pontificio Ateneo S. Anselmo.

Huet, P.-D. (1667), *Origeniana*. Paris.

King, B. (2009), *Newman and the Alexandrian Fathers*. New York, NY: Oxford University Press.

Lyons, J.A. (1982), *The Cosmic Christ in Origen and Teilhard de Chardin*. Oxford: Clarendon Press.

McLynn, N.B. (2004), "What was the *Philocalia* of Origen?". *Meddelanden från Collegium Patristicum Lundense*, 19: 32–43.

Newman, J.H. (1865), *Apologia pro Vita Sua*. New York, NY: Appleton.

Nygren, A. (1953), *Agape and Eros*, P.S. Watson (transl.). London: Sheed and Ward.

Percival, A. (1991), *The Seven Ecumenical Councils*. Grand Rapids, MI: Eerdmans (often reprinted).

Rapetti, E. (2012), "Res Origenis referre: gli *Origeniana* di Pierre-Daniel Huet e il loro contest storico-culturale". *Adamantius*, 18: 251–282.

Rupp, E.G. (transl.) (1969), *Erasmus and Luther: Free Will and Salvation*. London: SCM.

Scheck, T.P. (2008), *Origen and the History of Justification*. Chicago, IL: University of Notre Dame Press.

Tzamalikos, P. (2007), *Origen: Philosophy of History and Eschatology*. Leiden: Brill.

Von Harnack, A. (1910), *History of Dogma*, vol. 2, N. Buchanan (transl.). London: Williams and Norgate.

Waterland, D. (1856), *A Review of the Doctrine of the Eucharist*, Van Mildert (ed.). Oxford: Clarendon Press.

Westcott, B.F. (1887), "Origenes". In *Dictionary of Christian Biography*, vol. IV, W. Smith (ed.). London: John Murray; 96–142.

CHAPTER 7

Athanasius of Alexandria

David M. Gwynn

Introduction

Across the patristic tradition, few Church Fathers are as renowned or as controversial as Athanasius of Alexandria. His name is forever associated with the Nicene Creed and the doctrine of the Trinity. He is remembered as the champion of orthodoxy against the "Arian" heresy, and for his uncompromising defense of the full divinity of God the Son as the fundamental basis for Christian salvation. Yet, for his contemporaries, Athanasius was a divisive figure who spent long years in exile in the west and among the monks of the Egyptian desert. His authority received universal recognition in the millennium following his death, but his works were little read and pseudonymous texts overshadowed Athanasius' genuine writings. For the medieval centuries and the Reformation, Athanasius was a prestigious yet shadowy figure, and gradually the controversies over his legacy resumed. It is therefore unsurprising that interpretations of Athanasius in modern scholarship still vary widely, although no one would question his significance either within his own times or for subsequent Christian generations.

Life and Writings

Athanasius' life spanned a decisive period in the history of Christianity and the Roman Empire (Barnes 1993; Gemeinhardt 2011; Gwynn 2012). He was born in the closing years of the third century, and was still a child in 303 when the Great Persecution of Diocletian struck the Christians of Egypt. When Constantine became the first Roman emperor to embrace Christianity in 312, Athanasius was nearing adulthood, and his long episcopate from 328 to 373 witnessed the crucial years in which Christianity was transformed into the dominant religion of the Roman world. From Constantine onwards the

The Wiley Blackwell Companion to Patristics, First Edition. Edited by Ken Parry.
© 2015 John Wiley & Sons Ltd. Published 2019 by John Wiley & Sons Ltd.

emperor was a key player in Christian affairs, as Athanasius experienced to his benefit and cost. Converts flocked into the Church, requiring guidance and pastoral care. The rising ascetic movement, in which Athanasius was intimately involved, was in part a response to Christianity's growing prominence and the desire to express a deeper commitment to the faith. Imperial patronage also placed renewed emphasis on doctrinal unity and increased the stakes at issue in internal Christian rivalries. When the presbyter Arius clashed with Athanasius' mentor Alexander of Alexandria in c. 321, the scene was set for the conflict that shaped Athanasius' career and secured his place in patristic tradition.

The theological debates of the fourth century centered around the relationship between the Son and the Father and the need to reconcile belief in the Trinity with Christian monotheism (Hanson 1988; Ayres 2004). Arius defended the unique divinity of God the Father, particularly against the Sabellian Modalism which threatened the individual identities of the Trinity (Williams 2001). He did not deny that the Son, too, was God, but he subordinated the Son to such an extent that Arius could be accused of degrading God's Word and Wisdom. If the Son was so inferior to the Father, could He be our Savior? This was the reaction of bishop Alexander, who circulated his denunciation of Arius across the eastern Church in an *Encyclical Letter* in late 324 or early 325. The emperor Constantine regarded it as his duty to restore Christian harmony, and more than 220 bishops attended the Council of Nicaea in June–July 325. Arius was exiled, and the original Nicene Creed declared Christ to be:

> The Son of God, begotten as only begotten of the Father, that is of the essence (*ousia*) of the Father, God of God, Light of Light, true God of true God, begotten not made, consubstantial (*homoousios*) with the Father.

Nicaea condemned the most extreme ideas associated with Arius, but the Creed raised as many problems as it resolved. *Homoousios* was not a scriptural term, and a number of eastern bishops, including the historian Eusebius of Caesarea and his namesake Eusebius of Nicomedia, shared Arius' fears that such language blurred the distinction between Father and Son and so fell into Sabellianism. Far from ending at Nicaea, the Trinitarian debates were already escalating when Athanasius succeeded Alexander as bishop of Alexandria in 328.

Athanasius himself played a very limited part in the doctrinal exchanges of the 320s. As Alexander's secretary he may have drafted the *Encyclical Letter* which denounced Arius' teachings (Stead 1988), and as a deacon he attended the council in 325. Despite later legends, there is no evidence that he played any public role at Nicaea. But the questions that had divided Alexander and Arius were very much in the air when the new bishop composed his earliest theological work: the double trea- tise *Contra Gentes-De Incarnatione* (c. 328–335). Athanasius would never deviate from the theological principles he laid down in that work, which culminated in the famous words:

> He became human that we might become divine (*theopoiēthōmen*); and He revealed Himself through a body that we might receive an idea of the invisible Father; and He endured insults from human beings that we might inherit incorruption (*De Incarnatione* 54).

"He became human that we might become divine" encapsulated Athanasius' vision of salvation as a process of deification or divinization. For Athanasius, that vision required a Savior who was the eternal Son and Word of the Father. Only if the Son was true God could His Incarnation bridge the ontological divide between God and created humanity (Anatolios 1998). The danger that Athanasius saw in the teachings of Arius lay precisely in the separation of the Son from the Father, to an extent that Athanasius believed made the Son's saving work impossible.

In 335, Athanasius was condemned at the Council of Tyre and exiled to the west by Constantine. This was the first of five periods of exile that Athanasius experienced under four different emperors, spanning in total some 15 years. His critics accused him of violence and conduct unbecoming a bishop. Athanasius maintained that he was the victim of an "Arian" conspiracy, led by Eusebius of Nicomedia and the group Athanasius branded "the Eusebians" (Gwynn 2007a). In the three *Orationes contra Arianos* (c. 339–346) and throughout his polemical writings, Athanasius represented the fourth-century Trinitarian debates as a single "Arian Controversy." He divided the Church into two polarized factions: the "orthodox" (whom he represented) and the "Arians" (everyone he opposed).

> When the blessed Alexander cast out Arius, those who remained with Alexander remained Christians; but those who went out with Arius abandoned the Saviour's Name to us who were with Alexander, and they were henceforth called Arians ... While Arius is dead, and many of his followers have succeeded him, nevertheless those who hold the doctrines of that man, as being known from Arius, are called Arians (*Oratio contra Arianos* I.3).

Against the teachings that he regarded as "Arian," Athanasius emphasized ever more strongly the full divinity of the Son. In the middle decades of the fourth century, however, Athanasius' polemic exerted only limited influence. A wide spectrum of doctrinal positions appeared, from those who taught that the Son was unlike (*anomoios*) the Father by essence to those who believed that He was like (*homoios*) or like in essence (*homoios kat' ousian* or *homoiousios*). Amidst these competing arguments, two influential elements emerged in Athanasius' theology in the 350s. In his *Letters to Serapion on the Holy Spirit* (c. 357–358), Athanasius composed the earliest detailed defense of the Spirit's full divinity and place within the Trinity. And in the *De Decretis Nicaenae Synodi* (c. 350–355), Athanasius for the first time brought the Nicene Creed into the forefront of debate. Nicaea had been consigned to silence for a quarter of a century, and even in Athanasius' writings the term *homoousios* had occurred just once in the three *Orationes contra Arianos* (I.9). But now the Nicene Creed became the essential safeguard against the "Arian" heresy. "One who does not hold the doctrines of Arius necessarily holds and intends the doctrines of the council" (*De Decretis Nicaenae Synodi* 20).

Athanasius' endorsement of the Nicene Creed as the orthodox symbol changed neither his theology nor his construction of "Arianism." He still preached the doctrine of salvation through deification, with *homoousios* now his preferred expression for the ontological unity of Father and Son. Yet Athanasius continued to adapt as the doctrinal debates evolved. In the *De Synodis Arimini et Seleuciae* of 359 and the *Tomus ad Antiochenos* of 362, he expressed a willingness to reconcile with those he had previously regarded as enemies. As late as c. 372, a year before his death, Athanasius' *Letter to Epictetus of Corinth* both reaffirmed his vision of salvation and looked towards the fifth-century controversies over the divine and human natures of Christ.

> What the human body of the Word suffered, this the Word, dwelling in the body, ascribed to Himself, in order that we might be enabled to be partakers of the Godhead of the Word. And truly it is strange that He it was who suffered and yet suffered not (*Letter to Epictetus* 6).

By the standards of later orthodoxy, the teachings of Athanasius left certain crucial questions unresolved. In proclaiming the full divinity of the Son and the Holy Spirit, Athanasius was no less concerned to maintain the individual identities of the Trinity and deny the error of Sabellianism. What Athanasius lacked was the clarity of language to express his conception of the Trinity as three in one. Throughout his writings he preferred to use *ousia* and *hypostasis* as synonyms, although in his later works he accepted those who taught three *hypostases* as orthodox. Athanasius thus never employed the Trinitarian formula of three *hypostases* in one *ousia* developed by the Cappadocian Fathers. A second question regarded the Incarnation. Scholarly accusations that Athanasius taught a "spacesuit" Christology (Hanson 1988: 448), in which the divine Word does not share in His body's human experiences, have been rightly rejected. But while Athanasius emphasized the full humanity and full divinity of the incarnate Christ, he again struggled to define the unity of Christ in one person. He was less adept than his great successor Cyril of Alexandria in the communication of idioms, attributing the properties of each of Christ's two natures to the other. Nor would Athanasius' restricted use of the term *hypostasis* allow him to express the doctrine of the Incarnation adopted at the Council of Chalcedon in 451 as the hypostatic union of two natures in one person.

These were questions of terminology more than of theological principles. Athanasius shared the same fundamental values as the Cappadocian Fathers, whose efforts made possible the Council of Constantinople in 381 which affirmed the triumph of Nicene orthodoxy. His vision of the Incarnation differed little if at all from either the teachings of Cyril or the Chalcedonian Definition. In an age of constantly shifting creeds and definitions, Athanasius held unwaveringly to his conception of the Christian truth against the "Arian" heresy – (for the subsequent history of "Arianism," which inevitably runs parallel to the reception history of Athanasius, see Slusser (1993) and Wiles (1996)). Athanasius' conviction of salvation through the Incarnation of a true divine Son underlay not only his theology but also his promotion of the ascetic movement, most famously through the *Life of Antony*, and the pastoral wisdom that he preached to his congregations. Despite the controversies associated with his name, Athanasius fully deserved the respect in which his memory was held in east and west over the next millennium.

East and West in the First Millennium

His life and habits form an ideal of an episcopate and his teaching the law of orthodoxy (Gregory of Nazianzus, *Oration* 21.37: On the Great Athanasius).

In May 380, 7 years after Athanasius' death, Gregory of Nazianzus gave an oration in his honor in Constantinople (McGuckin 2001: 266–269). Athanasius was cele-brated as a model bishop and the defender of the Trinity. He inspired all in the faith, not only clergy but also monks and laity, and secured the victory of the doctrines that he first preached at Nicaea. Gregory's oration marked the beginning of Athanasius' hagio-graphic tradition, including the oft-repeated legend that Athanasius played a leading role at the Nicene council. While Gregory's admiration was sincere, however, he reveals only limited knowledge of Athanasius' career and rarely refers to Athanasius' own works. This is the pattern that shaped the reception of Athanasius throughout the next millennium. His name demanded respect and many sought to invoke his authority for their own purposes. Yet Athanasius' original voice became increasingly hidden behind legendary stories and pseudonymous or altered writings (see further Gemeinhardt (2011: 390–425) and Gwynn (2012: 159–193)).

Across the Greek east, the historical memory of Athanasius was preserved chiefly through the fifth-century ecclesiastical historians Socrates, Sozomen, and Theodoret. All three upheld the heroic vision of Athanasius presented by Gregory, and derived their narratives of the "Arian Controversy" from Athanasius' polemic. There were still a few dissenting voices, notably the "Neo-Arian" ecclesiastical historian Philostorgius, but his work survives only in fragments. The Athanasius of Greek historiography was the champion of Nicene orthodoxy, persecuted by the "Arians" for his defense of the truth.

The fourth-century Trinitarian debates flowed directly into the Christological controversies that divided the eastern Church from the fifth century onwards (McGuckin 2004; Wessel 2004). Appeals to past Fathers and the collection of patristic florilegia became increasingly influential as these controversies progressed (Graumann 2002), and Athanasius' authority was recognized by all. When Nestorius of Constantinople and Cyril of Alexandria clashed in 428–429 over the title *Theotokos* for the Virgin Mary, both men claimed to follow the teachings of Athanasius and Nicaea. Athanasius' works were cited in the florilegium compiled for the Council of Ephesus (431), and he was invoked on all sides in the debates surrounding the Council of Chalcedon (451). The competing claims of Chalcedonians and Miaphysites to Athanasius' legacy further encouraged the translation of his writings into other east-ern languages. The Coptic, Syriac, and Armenian collections of Athanasiana have proved extremely valuable for modern editors, although the works prized by these oriental traditions were not primarily Athanasius' polemical or doctrinal treatises but his pastoral and ascetic writings.

Unfortunately for eastern Christianity, appeal to Athanasius' authority – like appeal to Scripture – could not resolve the Christological questions under dispute. Athanasius certainly emphasized the humanity and divinity of Christ and their role in our salvation. But by later standards his Christological language was too impre-cise and his anti-"Arian" writings of limited relevance. The circulation of edited and pseudonymous works in Athanasius' name added further complications. Notoriously, Cyril derived his expression "one nature (*mia phusis*) of the Word incarnate" from a work that he believed to be by Athanasius, the Apollinarian *De Incarnatione Dei Verbi*. The genuine Athanasian *Letter to Epictetus*, perhaps Athanasius' most influential statement on the Incarnation, already circulated in multiple versions by the 430s (Cyril, *Letters* 39 and 45). One later Armenian text of this letter rewrote Athanasius' teaching that "the body that the Word indwelt was not co-essential with the Godhead but truly born of Mary" to read that "the Word was indissolubly united to His body which He took from the Virgin; and the uniting shows the indissolubility and unity of the natures" (*Letter to Epictetus* 8, see Thomson (1965)).

Over the following centuries, Athanasius' prestige in the east never diminished. He was hailed repeatedly as one of "the holy fathers and doctors of the holy church of God" by Justinian's Council of Constantinople in 553, and in the conflict over Iconoclasm his works were cited by Iconoclasts and Iconophiles alike (Alexakis 1996; Gwynn 2007b). Not all those works were authentic, however, and the volume of Athanasian citations is far less than for the Cappadocian Fathers or for Cyril of Alexandria. Athanasius' writings had little to add to these ongoing debates, and the increasing use of florilegia focused attention on isolated passages rather than the original texts. Athanasius remained the champion of Nicene orthodoxy, but knowledge of his teachings did not rival the fame of his reputation.

Athanasius was one of the rare Greek Fathers to attract a following in the Latin west within his own lifetime. His periods of exile in Gaul and Italy during the 330s and 340s laid strong roots, and in the 350s the western defense of Athanasius became inseparable from defense of the Nicene Creed. The Alexandrian was also remembered for his role in promoting the westward expansion of the ascetic movement. Yet to an even greater degree than in the east, the western memory of Athanasius increasingly separated itself from the bishop's genuine writings and historical context. With the exception of the *Life of Antony*, few of Athanasius' Greek works were widely read or translated into Latin in the centuries after his death. Although so-called "Germanic Arianism" survived longer in the west than in the east (Wiles 1996: 27–51), Athanasius' apologetic and doctrinal treatises received little or no attention, and by far the most influential western "Athanasian" work was a creed that he did not write.

Already in 356, Hilary of Poitiers (sometimes known as the "Athanasius of the west") hailed his older contemporary as the champion of Nicaea and the innocent victim of "Arian" persecution (Hilary, *Against Valens and Ursacius* I.IX.6). But there is scarce sign of Athanasian influence upon Hilary's theology, while Athanasius makes no reference to Hilary anywhere in his extant writings. Ambrose of Milan, whose knowledge of Greek exceeded most of his fellow westerners, certainly had studied several Athanasian works. He drew heavily on Athanasius' treatises on virginity (Duval 1974), and echoes Athanasius' anti-"Arian" polemic in his own *De fide* (Williams 1995: 128–153). Nevertheless, Ambrose does not acknowledge such a debt, and rarely names Athanasius at all. The only detailed account of Athanasius' career in any early western author is found in Rufinus of Aquileia's continuation of Eusebius of

Caesarea's *Ecclesiastical History*. Athanasius is the hero of much of the first book of Rufinus' continuation, which recounts his sufferings for the true faith. As the Greek historian Socrates (II.1) observed, Rufinus repeatedly misdates key events from Athanasius' career and relies on legendary tales rather than Athanasius' writings. It is striking that so inaccurate a narrative could be composed less than a generation after Athanasius' death by a serious scholar who had lived in Alexandria. Rufinus' erroneous chronology and exaggerated stories contributed significantly to the western separation of the hagiographical Athanasius from the historical bishop.

Perhaps the strongest barometer to assess Athanasius' reception in the late-antique west is provided by the two most renowned Latin fathers of the age: Jerome and Augustine. The entry for Athanasius in Jerome's *De Viris Illustribus* 87 praised his resistance to the "Arians" and listed several writings alongside "other works too numerous to mention." But the sole Athanasian text of which Jerome reveals detailed knowledge is unsurprisingly the *Life of Antony*. Jerome recommended Athanasius' ascetic writings to the women of his circle (*Letter* 107.12), and even sought to outdo Athanasius and Antony in his *Life of Paul the First Hermit*. Augustine shared Jerome's admiration for the Alexandrian, but his understanding of Athanasius' thought and writings was no more extensive. The *Life of Antony* was again the great exception, and the role it played in Augustine's conversion to an ascetic Christian life in 386 is remembered vividly in his *Confessions* (8.6). By contrast, Athanasius plays almost no role in Augustine's numerous theological and exegetical works. He is not even mentioned in the *De Trinitate*, written during Augustine's anti-"Arian" campaign in the later years of his episcopate, nor does Athanasius appear in Augustine's *magnum opus*, the *City of God*.

For all these western churchmen, the memory of Athanasius inspired admiration. But deep and sincere respect did not require close study of Athanasius' ecclesiastical career or theology. A major contribution to western knowledge of the historical Athanasius was made in the sixth century with the Latin *Historia ecclesiastica tripartita*. Prepared in the Italian community of Cassiodorus, this work was a compilation and translation of passages from the Greek ecclesiastical histories of Socrates, Sozomen, and Theodoret, and preserved a far more accurate account of Athanasius' life than that by Rufinus. Still more important for Athanasius' standing in the west was his inclusion in another sixth-century text: the pseudonymous *Decretum Gelasiani*, falsely attributed to Gelasius I of Rome (492–496). Under the heading *de libris recipiendis et non recipiendis*, the works of Athanasius were listed among the books that the faithful should read. In the eyes of the Middle Ages, Athanasius thus received papal recognition as one of the approved fathers of the Church.

The single greatest influence upon Athanasius' reception in the Latin west, however, lay in the most famous pseudonymous work to bear his name (Kelly 1964; Drecoll 2007). The so-called Athanasian Creed (also known as the Quicunque from its opening word) is first explicitly attested by Caesarius of Arles (bishop 502–542). Probably composed in southern Gaul in the late fifth or early sixth century, the creed's theology is post-Athanasian (particularly in Christology) and western in the double procession of the Spirit. For over 1000 years, this was the work that the majority of Latin Christianity associated most strongly with Athanasius. The Second Council of Autun in Burgundy in c. 670 required that all clergy should be able to recite "the Faith of the holy primate Athanasius" without error (canon 1). In the Carolingian age the creed became firmly established in educational and liturgical use, and it was not least through the creed that Athanasius remained a prominent figure in the early centuries of the second Christian millennium.

From Scholasticism to the Reformation

The period between 1100 and 1600 poses a particular challenge for the study of Athanasius' legacy (reflected in the relative paucity of Athanasian references in the extensive articles on patristic reception edited by Backus (1997a)). Athanasius' authority as a Church Father was acknowledged by all, and his name remained a byword for the defense of the orthodox faith. Yet quotations from his writings are rare, with citations dominated by the *Life of Antony* and the pseudonymous creed. Nevertheless, we should not be too quick to disregard Athanasius' enduring influence upon medieval Christianity. Direct citation is not in itself an adequate measure of his legacy, and from Thomas Aquinas to Martin Luther and John Calvin we can still trace Athanasius' teachings underlying the fundamental doctrines of the Trinity, Christology, and salvation.

With the rise of the Scholastic movement, the patristic tradition in the west entered a new era. The early scholastics admired Athanasius' reputation, but any knowledge of his writings is difficult to discern behind their universal respect for the Athanasian Creed. Peter Abelard was required to recite that creed to confirm his orthodoxy at the Council of Soissons (1121), and Bernard of Clairvaux again invoked the creed in accusing Abelard of "Arian" teachings at the Council of Sens (1140). The two greatest twelfth-century scholastic collections, the *Decree* (c. 1140) of Gratian and Peter Lombard's *Sentences* (c. 1150), each identify Athanasius as one of the approved fathers (drawing on the *Decretum Gelasiani*) but prefer to quote from the Athanasian Creed not Athanasius' own works. We can therefore understand why Adilbert of Augsburg near the end of the twelfth century felt moved by the prevailing ignorance to write a *Life of Athanasius*. This *Vita* was drawn chiefly from the *Historia tripartita* and confirms that at least some westerners were interested in Athanasius' career, if not his writings.

When we turn to assess the place of Athanasius in the supreme monument of the scholastic age, the *Summa Theologiae* (1265–1274) of Thomas Aquinas, a similar picture unfolds. Aquinas had no hesitation in naming Athanasius as one of the *sancti doctores* of the Church. But his rare citations derive almost exclusively from the Athanasian Creed.

> Athanasius drew up a declaration of faith, not under the form of a symbol, but rather by way of an exposition of doctrine, as appears from his way of speaking. But since it contained briefly the whole truth of faith, it was accepted by the authority of the Sovereign Pontiff, so as to be considered as a rule of faith (Thomas Aquinas, *Summa Theologiae* 2-2, Question 1, Article 10).

For Aquinas, the Athanasian Creed was particularly valued as an "eastern" statement of the *Filioque* doctrine for the procession of the Holy Spirit. Elsewhere in the *Summa*

Theologiae, Aquinas shows almost no awareness of Athanasius' original teachings. Even when he refutes "Arian" errors on the Trinity and the Incarnation, Aquinas' preferred authority is always Augustine. Aquinas reveals slightly greater knowledge of Athanasius' works in his other writings, notably the *Catena on Luke* and the *Contra Errores Graecorum* (the latter including Athanasius' *Letters to Serapion on the Holy Spirit* and the *Letter to Epictetus*). No early Christian writer comes close to challenging the dominance of Augustine in Aquinas' thought, however, and among the eastern fathers Aquinas was far more acquainted with Origen, John Chrysostom, and John Damascus than with Athanasius (Elders 1997).

The emphasis that Aquinas and other western theologians placed upon the Athanasian Creed in support of the *Filioque* brought Athanasius into the dialogue of reunion between east and west. The Athanasian Creed was little known in the east and was only translated into Greek in the twelfth or thirteenth century. At the Council of Lyon (1274) the creed was cited alongside the genuine Athanasian *Letters to Serapion*. More significant for Athanasius' legacy were the debates that surrounded the second unsuccessful council of reunion, held in Ferrara and Florence in 1438–1439 (Brennecke 2011). The authenticity of patristic witnesses was a major focus for discussion; and while the Athanasian Creed remained largely uncontested, increasing attention was now paid to the manuscripts of Athanasius' writings. New copies of the Greek texts were made and Latin translations flourished. The Italian humanist Ambrogio Traversari had already translated the *Contra Gentes-De Incarnatione* in the 1420s, and attended the Council of Ferrara–Florence to offer guidance on controversial texts. The decades following the council saw a new Latin *Life of Athanasius* drawn from the Greek hagiographic tradition of Symeon Metaphrastes. Gregory of Nazianzus' oration in honor of Athanasius was translated into Latin, and in 1492 Angelo Poliziano likewise translated much of Athanasius' *Letter to Marcellinus on the Interpretation of the Psalms* for inclusion in his own *Opusculum in psalmos*. By this stage the first printed edition of Latin translations of Athanasius had appeared in Vicenza in 1482. The reception of Athanasius thus reached new heights in the west just at the dawn of the sixteenth century and the Reformation.

Our chief witness, who played his own part in promoting knowledge of Athanasius, is Erasmus of Rotterdam. Erasmus' contribution to preserving the patristic tradition is well known, although he devoted his energy above all to Jerome, Origen, and John Chrysostom (den Boeft 1997). His only edition of Athanasian writings appeared as an annex to the *Chrysostomi lucubrationes*, published in Basel in March 1527. In the dedicatory letter that accompanied his *Athanasii lucubrationes aliquot*, addressed to bishop John Longland of Lincoln, Erasmus was fully aware of the danger of false attribution ("works were attributed to Athanasius that one would scarcely believe had come from a sane man"). Yet Athanasius' true works made the labor worthwhile:

> He speaks plainly, he is intelligent, sensible, and conscientious, in a word he is ideally qualified to be a teacher. He has none of the heaviness that offends in Tertullian; there is nothing flashy as in Jerome; nothing laboured as in Hilary, nothing redundant as

there is in Augustine and even in Chrysostom, nothing that smacks of the cadences of Isocrates or the studied artistry of Lysias such as one finds in Gregory of Nazianzus. Instead he concentrates wholly on making his meaning clear (Erasmus, *Letter* 1790, March 3, 1527).

Despite the enthusiasm of Erasmus, we must not exaggerate Athanasius' prominence at this turning point in western Christian history. Few of the leaders of the early Reformation show any real acquaintance with Athanasius and his works. Martin Luther himself seldom referred to Athanasius, even when Luther entered contemporary debates over "Arianism" (Lohse 1993). The Athanasian works he does identify are largely pseudonymous, with the Athanasian Creed now important less for the *Filioque* clause than as a statement of the two natures of Christ. Philip Melanchthon came from a more humanist background than Luther, and drew material from the *De Incarnatione* and the *Letters to Serapion on the Holy Spirit* (Meijering 1983). But he, too, cites Athanasius rarely. For Ulrich Zwingli, the only "Athanasian" writings to exert any influence are the creed and the pseudo-Athanasius *Commentaries on the Pauline Epistles* (Backus 1997b, 630–631). The *Commentaries* were the sole text that Zwingli annotated in his manuscript of Athanasius' *Opera*, still extant in Zurich Library, although their correct attribution to Theophylact of Ochrid was noted by Erasmus in his letter to John Longland. And there is no conclusive evidence that John Calvin ever read a single one of Athanasius' works (Lane 1999). In 1537 Calvin memorably declared against Caroli that "we swear in the faith of the one God, not of Athanasius whose creed no legitimate church has ever approved" (*CO* 10b: 83–84). Nevertheless, Calvin upheld the authenticity of the Athanasian Creed, and regarded Athanasius as a champion of true doctrine whom Calvin wrongly believed had presided at Nicaea (*Institutes* IV.7.1.5).

The Greek fathers, in general, played little role in the debates surrounding the Reformation, and Athanasius was thus no exception (see also Goudriaan (2010)). The competing claims of Protestants and Catholics, however, placed new emphasis on the patristic past. The two great ecclesiastical histories of the sixteenth century, the Magdeburg *Centuries* and the *Annales Ecclesiastici* of Baronius, both derived their knowledge of the fourth century from Rufinus and the *Historia tripartita*. Each then interpreted Athanasius' career according to their own principles. The Athanasius of the *Centuries* was an opponent of Roman primacy, and that of Baronius acknowledged the authority of Rome during Athanasius' western exile. For Protestants and Catholics alike, Athanasius represented a key stage in Christian history and doctrine. His name was tied to the Nicene Creed, and his defense of the unscriptural term *homoousios* was a potential point of conflict with the Protestant principle of *sola scriptura*. Debates over Christology brought renewed attention to Athanasius' vision of salvation through deification. More significantly for Athanasius' legacy, the rising tide of anti-Trinitarianism which began in the sixteenth century led to the first concerted attacks upon Athanasius for almost a millennium, attacks that inspired a more critical understanding of his life and writings.

From the Reformation to the Modern Age

In 1642, the Dutch humanist Gerhard Jan Voss published his *De tribus symbolis*, conclusively demonstrating the impossibility of Athanasius being the author of the Athanasian Creed. Voss was by no means alone in questioning the creed's authenticity, but his arguments were compelling and swiftly gained near-universal acceptance. Attention could now focus more closely on Athanasius' original theology, for his fundamental doctrine of the equal divinity of Father and Son had come under threat. The anti-Trinitarian teachings of Michael Servetus and Faustus Socinus in the sixteenth century gained support among the seventeenth-century Unitarians, and led to the revival of views that could be condemned as "Arian." Athanasius was an obvious target for those who subordinated or denied the Son's divinity, an attitude particularly obvious in the writings of the two most famous figures of "British Arianism": Isaac Newton and William Whiston.

Newton undertook detailed theological study in the 1670s, and during those years came to reject the prevailing doctrine of the Trinity. He regarded that doctrine as neither scriptural nor logical, and concluded that in the fourth century the Christian message had become corrupted into idolatry. The man whom Newton held most responsible for that corruption was Athanasius, his "personal nemesis" (Westfall 1980: 318). Newton condemned the adoption of the term *homoousios*, and summarized Athanasius' errors in the unpublished work entitled *Paradoxical Questions Concerning the Morals & Actions of Athanasius & his Followers*. Whiston succeeded Newton, with the latter's approval, as Lucasian Professor of Mathematics at Cambridge in 1703. Unlike Newton, Whiston refused to keep his theological views secret, and in 1710 was dismissed from his Chair as an "Arian" (Force 1985). He continued to maintain that the Son was not co-eternal or co-essential with the Father, and accused Athanasius of forging the Nicene anathema against teaching that the Son was "created" (W. Whiston, *Athanasius Convicted of Forgery. In a Letter to Mr. Thirlby of Jesus College in Cambridge* (London 1712), an argument restated by Wiles (1993)). As Whiston recalled, Newton had shared the same convictions:

> Sir I. N. was one who had thoroughly examined the state of the Church in its most critical Juncture, the fourth Century. He had early and thoroughly discovered that the Old Christian Faith, concerning the Trinity in particular, was then changed; that what has been long called Arianism is no other than Old uncorrupt Christianity; and that Athanasius was the grand and very wicked Instrument of that Change (W. Whiston, *A Collection of Authentick Records Belonging to the Old and New Testaments* (London 1728) 2: 1077).

The hostility that Newton and Whiston expressed towards Athanasius remained very much a minority view in England and the continent. Indeed, the opposition that such anti-Trinitarian arguments generated reinforced admiration for Athanasius (Muslow and Rohl 2005; Brennecke 2010). In 1698 the Benedictine monk Bernard de Montfaucon published the first true critical edition of Athanasius' writings, while at the same time Lenain de Tillemont was preparing his ecclesiastical history. This highly influential work, published in a second edition in 1704–1707 shortly after the author's death, returned to the traditional heroic narrative of Athanasius' career drawn from Tillemont's fifth-century predecessors. When Edward Gibbon began his *Decline and Fall* some 70 years later, it was Tillemont's account of Athanasius that he followed. Rarely moved to offer praise of Christianity or Christian bishops, Gibbon conceded that:

> Although his mind was tainted by the contagion of fanaticism, Athanasius displayed a superiority of character and abilities which would have qualified him, far better than the degenerate sons of Constantine, for the government of a great monarchy (Edward Gibbon, *The History of the Decline and Fall of the Roman Empire* (1776–88) chapter 21).

At the beginning of the nineteenth century, Athanasius' reputation thus stood high in continental and British Christianity. Yet relatively few studies appeared concerning the Alexandrian bishop and his writings. In response to that neglect, Johann Adam Möhler published his *Athanasius der Grosse und die Kirche seiner Zeit, besonders im Kampfe mit dem Arianismus* (1827). Möhler's biography, which at times crossed the border into hagiography, sought to promote Athanasius' reception by underlining his status as the central figure of the formative fourth-century Church (van Wilgenburg 2010). A rather different approach was adopted by Joseph von Görres, whose *Athanasius* (1838) was actually a reaction to the arrest of the Catholic archbishop of Cologne by the Prussian authorities in 1837. Athanasius was invoked as a model of Church resistance to state pressure (one man upon whom von Görres' *Athanasius* had an immediate impact was the Danish philosopher Kierkegaard; Puchniak 2008). Both works succeeded to some degree in drawing attention to Athanasius. But the developments that laid the foundation for modern Athanasian studies came in the decades either side of the turn of the twentieth century.

For British scholarship, these were the years in which Athanasius arguably reached the pinnacle of his prestige. The negative voices had been largely silenced, and the prevailing tone had been set by John Henry Newman's depiction of Athanasius in *The Arians of the Fourth Century*, which first appeared in 1833. This panegyrical vision was reflected in the entry for Athanasius contributed by William Bright to the *Dictionary of Christian Biography* (1877), and the introduction of Archibald Robertson to the *Nicene and Post-Nicene Fathers* translation (1892) which brought Athanasius' works to a wider English-speaking audience than ever before.

A more analytical approach, and one that would exert a powerful influence throughout the twentieth century, was emerging in Germany. Adolf von Harnack admired Athanasius no less than his British counterparts (Meijering 2010). He compared Athanasius to Luther, and his words are often repeated that "If we measure him by the standard of his time we can discover nothing ignoble or mean about him" (von Harnack, *Lehrbuch der Dogmengeschichte* (third edition 1894–1898), translated into English as *History of Dogma* IV.62). But while von Harnack praised Athanasius' doctrine of salvation through the Incarnation of the divine Son, he also highlighted what he regarded as the chief weakness of Athanasius' theology:

> Nothing can more clearly illustrate the perverse state of the problem in the Arian-Athanasian controversy than the notorious fact that the man who saved the character of

Christianity as a religion of living fellowship with God, was the man from whose Christology almost every trait which recalls the historical Jesus of Nazareth was erased (von Harnack, *Lehrbuch der Dogmengeschichte* (third edition 1894–1898), translated into English as *History of Dogma* IV.45).

The concern that Athanasius downplayed the humanity of the incarnate Jesus has influenced many modern assessments (see in particular Grillmeier (1975)). Nevertheless, von Harnack's appraisal of Athanasius' theology and character was fundamentally positive. Von Harnack's contemporary Eduard Schwartz took a very different stance. In his portrayal of Athanasius as a power-hungry politician and polemicist (*Zur Geschichte des Athanasius*, 1904–1911), Schwartz for the first time placed a negative interpretation of Athanasius on a scholarly footing. Although many of his conclusions have since been questioned, Schwartz's studies left an enduring mark. He also inspired one of his pupils, Hans-George Opitz, to begin the ongoing *Athanasius Werke* project that has produced the essential critical editions of Athanasius' writings and the key texts of the early "Arian Controversy."

Athanasius in the Twenty-First Century

The last 50 years have witnessed a resurgence of interest in Athanasius, with two generations of scholars standing on the shoulders of the giants of previous centuries. Athanasius has been restored to a central role in modern debates over the Trinity and Christology, not only in academic circles but also through popular websites and Christian discussion groups that have made his writings accessible to far broader audiences. Yet respect for Athanasius' theological achievement has been balanced by an increasing awareness that his doctrinal polemic may have distorted our understanding of the fourth-century Trinitarian controversies.

To an extraordinary degree the faith of Athanasius has become the faith of the Church, and to criticize him must look as if we wished to shatter the rock from which we were hewn. Nevertheless I have come to think that the methods used by Athanasius in defending his faith will not serve to commend eternal truths to the present age; and it is for the Church's ultimate good that we seek to show where their weakness lies (Stead 1976: 136–137).

It is this tension that has fueled many of the advances of recent decades, which have placed Athanasian studies on a stronger and more diverse platform. The depth of Athanasius' theology has received greater appreciation, which in turn has required a reassessment of the influence that he exerted on the evolution of Christian doctrine (Anatolios 1998; Morales 2006; Weinandy 2007). Patristic theology, however, must never be studied in a vacuum. The need to place Athanasius within his own historical context has been clearly recognized (Barnes 1993), and the ascetic and pastoral teachings of Athanasius have taken their rightful place alongside his ecclesiastical and doctrinal legacy (Brakke 1995; Ng 2001). The survival of so much of the ascetic and pastoral Athanasiana in Coptic and Syriac rather than Greek and Latin has helped to generate awareness of the immense value that these eastern traditions have to offer to patristic scholarship and the very different vision of figures like Athanasius that those traditions depict. With the editing of his works still proceeding and recent syntheses drawing together the current status quo (Gemeinhardt 2011; Gwynn 2012), the stage has been set to begin a new chapter in Athanasius' enduring contribution to the life and history of Christianity.

Bibliography

Alexakis, Alexander (1996), *Codex Parisinus Graecus 1115 and its Archetype*. Washington, DC: Dumbarton Oaks.

Anatolios, Khaled (1998), *Athanasius: The Coherence of His Thought*. London: Routledge.

Ayres, Lewis (2004), *Nicaea and its Legacy: An Approach to Fourth-Century Trinitarian Theology*. Oxford: Oxford University Press.

Backus, Irena, ed. (1997a), *The Reception of the Church Fathers in the West: From the Carolingians to the Maurists*, two volumes. Leiden: Brill.

Backus, Irena (1997b), "Ulrich Zwingli, Martin Bucer and the Church Fathers". In Backus (1997a: 627–660).

Barnes, Timothy D. (1993), *Athanasius and Constantius: Theology and Politics in the Constantinian Empire*. Cambridge, MA: Harvard University Press.

Brakke, David (1995), *Athanasius and the Politics of Asceticism*. Oxford: Clarendon Press.

Brennecke, Hanns Christof (2010), "Athanasius von Alexandrien in der abendländischen Rezeption bis zur Frühen Neuzeit". In *Patristic Tradition and Intellectual Paradigms in the 17th Century*, Silke-Petra Bergjan and Karla Pollmann (eds). Tübingen: Mohr Siebeck; 137–157.

Brennecke, Hanns Christof (2011), "Die Filioque-Kontroverse auf dem Konzil von Florenz". In Gemeinhardt (2011: 425–428).

Den Boeft, Jan (1997), "Erasmus and the church Fathers". In Backus (1997a: 537–572).

Drecoll, Volker Henning (2007) "Das Symbolum Quicumque als Kompilation augustinischer Tradition". *ZAC*, 11: 30–65.

Duval, Yves-Marie (1974), "L'originalité du 'De virginibus' dans le mouvement ascetique

occidental: Ambroise, Cyprien, Athanase". In *Ambroise de Milan: Dix Etudes*, Yves-Marie Duval (ed.). Paris: Études Augustiniennes; 9–66.

Elders, Leo J. (1997), "Thomas Aquinas and the Fathers of the Church". In Backus (1997a: 337–366).

Force, James E. (1985), *William Whiston: Honest Newtonian*. Cambridge: Cambridge University Press.

Gemeinhardt, Peter (ed.) (2011), *Athanasius Handbuch*. Tübingen: Mohr Siebeck.

Goudriaan, Aza (2010), "Athanasius in reformed Protestantism: some aspects of reception history (1527–1607)". *Church History and Religious Culture*, 90 (2–3): 257–276.

Graumann, Thomas (2002), *Die Kirche der Väter: Vätertheologie und Väterbeweis in den Kirchen des Ostens bis zum Konzil von Ephesus (431)*. Tübingen: Mohr Siebeck.

Grillmeier, Aloys (1975), *Christ in Christian Tradition*, Volume One: *From the Apostolic Age to Chalcedon (451)*, 2nd revised edn, J. Bowden (transl.). London: Mowbray.

Gwynn, David M. (2007a), *The Eusebians: The Polemic of Athanasius of Alexandria and the Construction of the 'Arian Controversy'*. Oxford: Oxford University Press.

Gwynn, David M. (2007b), "From Iconoclasm to Arianism: the construction of Christian tradition in the Iconoclast Controversy". *GRBS*, 47: 226–251.

Gwynn, David M. (2012), *Athanasius of Alexandria: Bishop, Theologian, Ascetic, Father*. Oxford: Oxford University Press.

Hanson, Richard Patrick Crosland (1988), *The Search for the Christian Doctrine of God: The*

Arian Controversy 318–381. Edinburgh: T&T Clark.

Kelly, John Norman Davidson (1964), *The Athanasian Creed*. London: A&C Black.

Lane, Anthony N.S. (1999), *John Calvin: Student of the Church Fathers*. Edinburgh: T&T Clark.

Lohse, Bernhard (1993), "Luther und Athanasius". In *Auctoritas Patrum: Zur Rezeption der Kirchenväter im 15. und 16. Jahrhundert*, Leif Grane, Alfred Schindler, and Markus Wriedt (eds). Mainz: Verlag Philipp von Zabern; 95–115.

McGuckin, John A. (2001), *Saint Gregory of Nazianzus: An Intellectual Biography*. Crestwood, NY: St Vladimir's Seminary Press.

McGuckin, John A. (2004), *Saint Cyril of Alexandria and the Christological Controversy*. Crestwood, NY: St Vladimir's Seminary Press.

Meijering, E.P. (1983), *Melanchthon and Patristic Thought: The Doctrines of Christ and Grace, the Trinity and the Creation*. Leiden: Brill.

Meijering, E.P. (2010), "The judgement on Athanasius in the historiography of Christian dogma (Mosheim–Baur–Harnack)". *Church History and Religious Culture*, 90 (2–3): 277–286.

Morales, Xavier (2006), *La Théologie Trinitaire d'Athanase d'Alexandrie*. Paris: Études Augustiniennes.

Muslow, Martin, and Jan Rohl (eds) (2005), *Socinianism and Arminianism: Antitrinitarians, Calvinists and Cultural Exchange in Seventeenth-Century Europe*. Leiden: Brill.

Ng, Nathan Kwok-kit (2001), *The Spirituality of Athanasius: A Key for Proper Understanding of This Important Church Father*. Bern: Peter Lang.

Puchniak, Robert (2008), "Athanasius: Kierkegaard's curious comment". In *Kierkegaard and the Patristic and Medieval Traditions*, Jon Stewart (ed.). Aldershot: Ashgate; 3–7.

Slusser, Michael (1993), "Traditional views of late Arianism". In *Arianism after Arius: Essays in the Development of the Fourth Century Trinitarian Conflicts*, Michel R. Barnes and Daniel H. Williams (eds). Edinburgh: T&T Clark; 3–30.

Stead, G. Christopher (1976), "Rhetorical method in Athanasius". *VC*, 30: 121–137.

Stead, G. Christopher (1988), "Athanasius' earliest written work". *JThS*, NS, 39: 76–91.

Thomson, Robert W. (1965), "The transformation of Athanasius in Armenian theology (a tendentious version of the *Epistula ad Epictetum*)". *Le Muséon*, 78: 47–69.

Van Wilgenburg, Arwin (2010), "The reception of Athanasius within contemporary Roman Catholic theology". *Church History and Religious Culture*, 90 (2–3): 311–337.

Weinandy, Thomas G. (2007), *Athanasius: A Theological Introduction*. Aldershot: Ashgate.

Wessel, Susan (2004), *Cyril of Alexandria and the Nestorian Controversy: The Making of a Saint and of a Heretic*. Oxford: Oxford University Press.

Westfall, Richard S. (1980), *Never at Rest: A Biography of Isaac Newton*. Cambridge: Cambridge University Press.

Wiles, Maurice (1993), "A textual variant in the creed of the Council of Nicaea". *StP*, 26: 428–433.

Wiles, Maurice (1996), *Archetypal Heresy: Arianism through the Centuries*. Oxford: Clarendon Press.

Williams, Daniel H. (1995), *Ambrose of Milan and the End of the Nicene–Arian Conflicts*. Oxford: Clarendon Press.

Williams, Rowan D. (2001), *Arius: Heresy and Tradition*, 2nd impression. London: SCM Press.

CHAPTER 8
Ephrem of Nisibis

Andrew Palmer

Introduction

This chapter is divided into two parts: one on the reception of Ephrem (†373) in the Syriac and modern western worlds, the other on his reception in the medieval world of Christendom. The first part is subdivided into three sections on the *person* of Ephrem, his *poems* and his *prose*. In the first, we shall ask how contemporaries and later generations reacted to the Syrian sage; this section includes a glance at the reception of his philosophy. In the second, we shall trace through the centuries the reception of his numerous *madrâshê* ("doctrinal hymns") and less numerous *mêmrê* ("metrical homilies"); this includes the theological vision they express. In the third, it is only the reception of Ephrem's unique *Commentary on Genesis* (*GenCom*) that will be discussed in any detail. The second part deals with the Greek Fathers of the fourth and fifth centuries, with the sixth-century Romanos, with liturgical drama and with the pseudepigraphic corpus called "the Greek Ephrem."

Part 1. The Syriac and Modern Western Worlds

The Person

Ephrem was brought up as a Christian in Nisibis, where he was appointed one of the bishop's assistants, a position he retained when he moved to Edessa about 364 (*Heresies* 26:10, 56:10, with which cf. *Nisibis* 17:4). Jacob of Serûgh (†521), who attended around 470 the School of the Persians (i.e., of the Eastern Syrians resettled at Edessa) calls him "Ephrem, the head/and master of/the teaching art." Barḥadbeshabbâ (c. 600) passes on the traditions that Jacob, the first real bishop of Nisibis, appointed Ephrem

The Wiley Blackwell Companion to Patristics, First Edition. Edited by Ken Parry.
© 2015 John Wiley & Sons Ltd. Published 2019 by John Wiley & Sons Ltd.

"exegete" and that, as late as the mid-fifth century, his successors at Edessa (generalizing from the case of Qyôrâ) based their exegesis on "the traditions of Mâr Ephrem, which, it is said, were handed down from the Apostle Addai" (*Foundation of the schools* 377, 382f.). A school with formal debates and a broad curriculum can be inferred from Ephrem's *Metrical Homilies on Faith* (Beck 1953: 59–63; Palmer 1998: 134–142). There had once been a rabbinic academy at Nisibis and the art of the midrash continued to be taught there. The invective aimed by Ephrem at the Jews looks more culpable in retrospect than in context. Ephrem's community was just one of many competing religious groups in society. His midrashic approach implies respect for living rabbis. Ephrem knew more of Greek philosophy than his disapproval of a rationalist approach in theology might suggest (Possekel 1999).

Ephrem's *madrâshê* were written for performance from a platform in the middle of the nave, with congregational responses led by a choir.

In the middle of the church/stood a platform, like a source:
thirsty ears would flock around,/drinking life that never ends.
Men received instruction there;/in return, they brought a gift:
scripture was explained for ears;/mouths repaid the debt with praise (*Mêmrê on Nicomedia* 8: 619–626, imitating Ephrem's meter).

Ephrem seems to have belonged to a group composed of celibate people of both sexes whose lives were dedicated to God, though not in remote monasteries. They lived near the cathedral, where they received communion daily. These "covenanters" led the Nicene congregation, whom others in the city called the "Palutians" (*Heresies* 22:5), in their responses at big services. In this circle, to judge from the preface to *GenCom*, his writings were valued.

[...] but under the pressure of the love of friends, I write briefly here, after all, that which I have (already) written at length in my *mêmrê* and *madrâshê*.

By a treaty of the year 363 Nisibis was ceded to Iran. Its Christian population, including Ephrem, was housed, with other new settlers, at Amida, which had lain in ruins since 359, for the siege of that year is described in the *Mêmrê on faith* (Palmer 1998: 119f., n. 1, overlooked by Lange [2005]). Lines 355f. of the sixth of these suggest that he found this city, too, unreceptive: "Is any city big enough for us to write there about our quarrels?" At this time he took up an "anarchic" stance as a critic of official religious policy.

If your teacher goes astray,/go, read scripture for yourself! (*Mêmrê on faith* 6: 167f.)

Faith was composed at Edessa, where Ephrem spent the remainder of his life. The form of these *madrâshê* may have been intended to remind Ephrem's fellow didactic poets that God reveals himself to those who pray, not to those who pry. Perhaps Ephrem was chief exegete at the Edessa seminary, for the teachers had to listen to his *madrâshê*, even if they did not agree with them.

> Cause no loss, then, to the people by your songs!
> Part no more united brothers by debate!
> Bring between the clear-eyed faithful not that blade, which is the urge to probe! (*Faith* 23:10; cf. 12.2)

Some of these *madrâshê* contain an indirect warning to the emperor to respect the boundary between Church and State (Palmer 1999a); but Valens, if he ever received this message, only interfered in the province of the sacred all the more. In September 373 the Arians expelled the "Paluṭians" from the cathedral of Edessa. "Mâr Ephrem of the crafted compositions" had died on 9 June of that same year (*Chronicle of Edessa*).

Ephrem invites his readers to help him collect the "figures" (of the divine in scripture and nature), because there are too many of these for him to delineate them alone; he asks younger poets to share their insights with him, as he shares his with them (*Faith* 25:18). As if in answer to this call, extra stanzas by various unknown hands were jotted in the margins of Ephrem's *madrâshê* and in the spaces he left blank. These secondary stanzas are direct evidence of the ways in which Ephrem's work was understood (Palmer 2009).

Soon after Ephrem's death, Trinitarianism was restored and a codicil on the third person of the Trinity added to the Creed. Research may have been done to discover the consensus of the Fathers on the Holy Spirit, for a Greek translation of Ephrem on this subject was read by Jerome, Ch. 115 of whose book on *Famous men* (released in 392) is on "the deacon of Edessa." Ephrem wrote no book on the Spirit, so the papyrus role with this title was either spurious, or – more probably, considering its merit in Jerome's ever-critical eyes – a *florilegium* of relevant quotations from the genuine Ephrem.

The history of Ephrem's school, for which the *Gospel commentary* is a source, has begun to be written (Lange 2005). The *Chronicle of Edessa* tells us that Ephrem's sister had a son called 'Absamya, who after an invasion of the Huns in 358 wrote "*madrâshê* and *mêmrê*" about it (c. 404). An *Excerpt* from the work of Ephrem's disciple Abâ has been preserved; "Abbas" is one of several disciples named by Sozomen (*Church history* 3.16). Isaac of Amida, according to *Letter* 14 of Jacob of Edessa, studied under Ephrem. A fifth-century *mêmrâ on Abel and Cain* builds on Ephrem's treatment of this subject (Glenthøj 1997). Gennadius includes some of Ephrem's followers in his continuation of Jerome's *Famous men*. Jacob of Serûgh (†521) wrote a *Mêmrâ on Ephrem*, already quoted, in which he calls him "the Moses of/the female sex" and "the crown/ of Aram" (Palmer 2007). Ephrem, he says, gave women a voice in the Church. He portrays him – "an eagle perched/among the doves" – justifying the fact that the women sang unveiled.

> Remove your shame/and, bare-faced, sing/in praise of Him! (Jacob, *Mêmrâ on Ephrem*, Couplet 113)

More than once, alive, Ephrem had experienced rejection; dead, he commanded universal lip-service. A rare example of a true disciple is the Syrian Orthodox patriarch John Bar Shûshan (†1073). This man continued, as patriarch, to embrace the virtues Ephrem praises in the first three bishops of Nisibis (though not in Abraham, his successful rival for the throne): asceticism, poverty, and humility. Death prevented John from completing his collection of "the teachings of Mâr Ephrem and Mâr Isaac [of Antioch]," expressing his gratitude, it seems, to those who had formed him (*Chronicle of Michael* Book 15, Ch. 3). Barhebraeus' *Chronicon ecclesiasticum* (I: 447) specifies that this book contained *mêmrê*; since Michael was his source, this means Barhebraeus knew Bar Shûshan's compilation.

The bibliography of the twentieth and twenty-first centuries includes many titles (Den Biesen 2011: §292, §294) which show that "the Syrian sage" has recently been consulted again, not only on celibacy, asceticism, and monasticism at the heart of Christian society, but also on reading the Bible – with special sympathy for biblical women (cf. Botha 1997), on symbolic thought (e.g., Den Biesen 2006), on responsiveness, on repentance, on attaining holiness, on the prayer of the heart, on taking communion with love and fear, on purifying the spiritual eye, on wonder, on harmony with nature, on God's feminine side, on paradox, and on serious comedy (e.g., Koonammakkal 2006). An example of his use of humor in instruction is the comparison between the anthropomorphic names for God in scripture and a bird's reflection in a mirror (*Faith* 31: 6f.).

The Poems

Rome and the Syriac Churches

Ephrem's poetry is didactic, and what he taught was theology. It is impossible to separate the reception of his poems from that of his theology; both were chiefly received in the Syriac churches. It is necessary, therefore, first to recall the relationship of these churches to one another. In the century after Ephrem's death the political separation of the Church of the East (sometimes called "Nestorian") led to schism from the Church in the Roman Empire. In the following century a dissension that had begun in 451 led to a further separation, from which was born the Syrian Orthodox Church (sometimes called "Jacobite"). In the seventh century one wing of *this* church was reunited with the imperial Church, only to become isolated in the eighth as the Maronite Church (in the time of the Crusades, it would be embraced by Rome). In the sixteenth century a faction of the Church of the East split off to form the Chaldean Catholic Church; in the eighteenth, the Syrian Catholic Church came into being when five Syrian Orthodox bishops were received as Catholics.

Half a century earlier, in 1732–1746, there had appeared in Rome a comprehensive edition of Ephrem which presented the Greek Ephrem and the Syrian as one and the same person and argued that "his" works were Catholic, so that, in submitting to Rome, eastern and oriental Christians would be returning to their roots after centuries of isolation (Palmer 1999b). Rome thus used Ephrem with apparent success to gain a reception for its own authority in the east. Since the eastern and oriental Catholics were allowed to keep much of their liturgical heritage, this proselytism favored the reception of Ephrem's *madrâshê*. In 1920 Rome declared Ephrem "a Doctor of the Universal Church"; this has recommended him to western Christians, so that he is now more widely read than ever before. The widest circulation was achieved by his *madrâshê*, by which, incidentally, Ephrem had earlier influenced the Anglo-Catholic Oxford Movement through E.B. Pusey and J.B. Morris (Rowell 1999). Beck and others have now edited Ephrem critically (Den Biesen 2011: §8f.).

Armenia and Syria

Each of the Syriac Churches sings Ephrem's *madrâshê* to its own traditional melodies. If these have something in common, a fourth-century original might be inferred; but most of Ephrem's modes are lost: only their moods remain. The Armenians produced accurate translations, both of *madrâshê* and of *mêmrê*, as a comparison of the extant fragments of the *Mêmrê on Nicomedia* with the Armenian version shows. Fifty-one Armenian *madrâshê* are ascribed to Ephrem; No. 48f., written to be sung while communion was received, is probably authentic. The imitation of Ephrem's meters suggests that the translations were chanted by Armenians to something like the original Syrian melodies. In the Syriac-speaking world, Ephrem was used and abused from the beginning. His liturgical work had "a public service character" and was adapted, added to, and pruned at need (Griffith 1998).

Narsai and Jacob of Serûgh

The East Syrian Narsai (†502/3) and the West Syrian Jacob of Serûgh cast their exegetical *mêmrê* in a new metrical mold: dodecasyllabic couplets of 4 + 4 + 4 syllables. *Mêmrê* and *madrâshê* were easier to learn by heart, ensuring their faithful transmission by word of mouth in musical performances accessible to the illiterate majority. The "150 psalms" of Bar Dayşân (†222) were still to be heard in the streets of tuneful Edessa when Ephrem arrived there. With glorious song, Ephrem silenced Bar Dayşân, as he stuck the pages of that philosopher's heretical book together in the legend. Narsai, Qyôrâ's successor, used song to disseminate the ideas of Theodore of Mopsuestia (†428), whose sober approach thereby became, to Ephrem's cost, the East-Syrian yardstick. Jacob of Serûgh was one of those who followed the "one-nature" teaching; *he* remained true to the Ephremic tradition of the school. Among Jacob's sources, Ephrem, much of whose work he surely knew by heart, is second only to the Bible. Where Greek cosmological notions (e.g., of creation and anthropology) conflict with Ephrem's, the latter's influence prevails (Bou Mansour 1993: 308), though Jacob is more inclined, with the Alexandrians, to allegory. Like Ephrem, Jacob sees impatient "probing" as the antithesis of faith, which is constant trusting love; but in his judgment on the mendacious "wisdom" of the world, as opposed to religious cognition, Jacob has more frequent recourse to Saint Paul (Bou Mansour 2000: 465f.). For most of his life Jacob, while he defended the external boundaries of the Church, obeyed Ephrem's injunction not to "part united brothers by debate" (*Faith* 23:10). Evidently, though, "Nestorians" did not count, for him, as brothers.

Philoxenus of Mabbûgh

Unlike Jacob, Philoxenus of Mabbûgh (†523) did not take refuge in silence at a time when the unity of Christ's Church was threatened by a nonscriptural controversy about who Christ may have been. Philoxenus taught that Chalcedonians place themselves outside the Church, a step towards schism that Jacob resisted until that schism seemed a reality. In refuting a certain Ḥabbîb c. 483, Philoxenus cited Ephrem first on almost every dogma and by far more often than any Greek. Unable to say how "the Word became flesh" (John 1:14), he cited Ephrem's advice not to go beyond the written revelation.

> Following his master, Saint Ephrem, in his reaction against Eunomian 'rationalism', he [Philoxenus] insisted on the inaccessible mystery of the divine nature to the point of only recognizing, as legitimate in principle, a 'negative theology' (De Halleux 1963: 428f.).

Philoxenus was indebted to Ephrem (whom he calls, with ethnic pride, "our Syrian teacher") for aspects of his Trinitarian doctrine (Beck 1962) and for much else. But he criticized his master for saying that the Word "put on a body," pointing out that the Syriac version of *Hebrews* 5:7, which opens with the words "When he was clothed in flesh," is a free translation of the Greek: "*In the days* of his flesh." The expressions "clothed in flesh" and "put on a body," which Jacob accepted as both idiomatic and scriptural, were open, Philoxenus feared, to a "two-nature" interpretation. Indeed, in quoting one passage where Ephrem says "the Word put on a body," he prefers a variant reading that replaces "put on" with "became."

He also finds fault with the idea that divinity is *mingled* with humanity in Christ, saying Ephrem must have meant "united," not "mingled" like water with wine. Philoxenus writes *To the monks of Senoun* in 521 that they "have many of Ephrem's books and are in the habit of reading in them frequently" (De Halleux 1963: 49). For that reason alone, perhaps, he refers to him still in this late letter, though by now the Greek-speaking Cyril has become his main authority. Dismissively, he tells those monks to search Ephrem themselves "since it befits you, rather than us, to remember the formulations of this saint" (De Halleux 1963: 49).

Since Ephrem did not, in fact, anticipate the debate about the definition of Christ in two natures, Philoxenus was obliged to look for passages that could be *interpreted* as anti-Chalcedonian. Chalcedonians, for their part, cited other passages which seemed to them to imply that Ephrem would have supported *their* doctrine.

There was probably nothing in the genuine Ephrem to support explicitly the use of the phrase "two natures" in describing Christ, for the Chalcedonians resorted to forgery. A passage (Ch. 34) was interpolated in Ephrem's *Homily on our Lord* and a Greek text about the pearl was circulated under Ephrem's name; both speak of "two natures" in Christ. The latter was probably used by John of Caesarea in his *florilegium*, for at the beginning of *Against the Grammarian*, Ch. 39, Severus (†538) writes that he had searched everywhere in the east for a Syriac text by Ephrem entitled "On the pearl" and that no such text had been found. It is true that the Greek text to which John must have appealed (D §224) is no translation of the Ephrem sub-cycle of five *madrâshê* on the pearl (*Faith* 81–85). The fact that both sides appealed to Ephrem is proof that he belonged to neither.

The Relative Decline in the Reception of Ephrem

Athanasius and Cyril gained ground in Syria during the fifth century, where the opponents of Chalcedon made common cause with the Alexandrians. Philoxenus is not the only one to reflect this trend. Cyril, not Ephrem, is quoted repeatedly in Elijah's Syriac

Biography of John of Tella (542); Athanasius, the Cappadocians, and Cyril, not Ephrem, are quoted in a mid-sixth-century collection of "one-nature" writings in Syriac; none of the Syrian Orthodox writings of the mid to late sixth century refers to Ephrem (Van Rompay 2007: 101). The *Sinai index of melodies* informs us that nine whole volumes containing a total of about 600 *madrâshê* were known, well over half of which have come down to us in codices written in or about the sixth century. These were saved by the climate of Egypt and by the abbot Moses, who collected them there in the tenth century. The completeness of the works in these manuscripts is evidence that Ephrem's *madrâshê* continued to be faithfully transmitted down to about the year 600; later they would be excerpted for liturgical use.

The Cave of Treasures

The Syriac *Cave of Treasures* is a popular retelling of sacred history from the creation to Pentecost. While it incorporates some elements that may go back before Ephrem, the Eastern recension of the *Cave* was written in Iran c. 600 and may be regarded as one of the books that have popularized certain of his ideas. This may be why the manuscripts attribute it to Ephrem. It constitutes an exception to the usual avoidance of typology and allegory in the Church of the East; but Ḥᵉnânâ of Adiabene, at exactly this time, provoked a major controversy at the School of Nisibis by his openness to methods *other* than that of Theodore. In the *Cave*, Adam is depicted as a priest in paradise, an idea that is first found in Ephrem's *Paradise* 3:16f. (Toepel 2006: 243). The strong continuity between the Old Testament and the New, the importance of Adam's being clothed in glory until the Fall, and the idea of a second world after *Genesis* 9:17 are just a few of the features that seem to derive from Ephrem's *GenCom* (on which more later). The remorse of Adam and Eve is one of several Jewish traditions that have perhaps found their way into the *Cave* from Ephrem.

Isaac of Nineveh

Despite the general isolation of the Church of the East, to which he belonged, Isaac of Nineveh (late seventh century) is widely read by the Eastern Orthodox and was one of only two Syriac sages known to the west in the Middle Ages (Brock 2003). The magnanimity of his *Ascetical homilies* makes them attractive beyond the monastic circles for which they were written. In his ninth *mêmrâ* (11.24) Isaac explains, in Ephremic terms, who he believes Jesus to have been: his humanity was "the garment of his divinity." The East Syrians defined Jesus as a compound of two unlike natures; they did not speak of him as a "mixed" being. But Isaac *is* comfortable with the Ephremic metaphor of "mingling" when describing God's immanence in his creation. Another of Ephrem's graphic metaphors – that of intoxication – is used by Isaac to describe an ecstatic experience of the love of God (10.35). Ephrem was first to develop this theme in Syriac.

Jacob of Edessa

Jacob of Edessa (†708) is one of the earliest explicit witnesses to a conscious perception of "Syriac literature" as having at its core such authors as Ephrem, Jacob of Serûgh, and Philoxenus of Mabbûgh (Van Rompay 2000: 79). In *Letter 12* he identifies the "woman" who was enthroned on the *bêma* in the Sabbath-observers' church

(*Heresies* 2:6) with Qamṣô (*Heresies* 24:19), a cross-dressing bishop. Jacob consulted Ephrem as a "qualified teacher" and "one of the authors through whom the Spirit speaks." In *Letters* 4 and 5 Jacob interprets passages in *Nativity* 25 (our *Nativity* 21) and *Faith* 44.

The Islamic Period
In the Islamic period the general level of Syriac education declined. The average cleric did not have the staying power or the comprehension to take in the architectural structures of a song-cycle, such as the *Madrâshê on paradise*, or even the unity of one whole poem. None of the 10 liturgical manuscripts of the eighth to thirteenth centuries contains one of his *madrâshê* in its entirety. Individual stanzas, like the pearls of a necklace, are recycled to make new sequences which alter their order and their context (Brock 1997: 502). But each "pearl" is complete in itself and does not lose that completeness when "unstrung."

The Prose

Ephrem also left rhythmic, patterned prose-poems (cf. Palmer 1999b: 103–105) and works in plain prose. In 823 the *Prose refutations*, sophisticated treatises displaying familiarity with Greek philosophy, were expunged and overwritten (Palmer 1999b: 97), so this work of Ephrem's was by then unwanted. His commentaries, on the other hand, gathered no dust on the library shelves. The texts of *GenCom* and of his *Exodus Commentary* appear to have been left unaltered, but the *Gospel commentary*, while much of it reflects the lectures Ephrem must have given on the subject, was added to by the anonymous who published it from his lecture-notes and brought up to date again later; for example, by the addition of the Syriac equivalent of the term "consubstantial" (Lange 2005). Commentaries, possibly genuine, on other parts of the New Testament are preserved in Armenian.

GenCom
Together with Aphrahaṭ, Ephrem established *Genesis* in the Syriac Church as *the* decisive document of revelation for the interpretation of the cosmos and the role of humanity in the world. Against Bar Dayṣân, Mani, and Marcion, Ephrem argues that no creator ever was the cause of evil, which comes, instead, from human choices (Kremer 2012: 493f.). The Jewish origins of the "Paluṭian" community (cf. "the traditions of Addai," above) are reflected in the "midrashic" exegesis practiced there (Lange 2005: 17).

Narsai
The early reception of *GenCom* was mainly in *mêmrê* by Narsai and by Jacob of Serûgh. Theodore had denied that the dogmas of Christianity were anticipated in the Old Testament; accordingly, Narsai resists the charms of Ephrem's typological theories. Yet, according to Kremer (2012: 210f., 471), the debt of Narsai's *Homilies on creation* to Ephrem's uniquely Syrian interpretation has been underestimated;

indeed, this new insight confirms what is said in the *Foundation of the schools* (383) about Narsai's reception, not only of Theodore, but also of "the tradition of the (Nisibene) School."

Jacob of Serûgh and the Sixth Century

In his own *Mêmrê on creation* Jacob of Serûgh produced the first Syriac treatise on the "Hexaemeron" (God's six-day creation). He does not imitate *GenCom* slavishly and has other sources, including even Theodore; but much that is distinctively Ephremic is found in Jacob's work. Literal quotations, such as that of *GenCom* II 1.1 in Jacob's second *Mêmrâ on creation* (63), prove he was using Ephrem's text. Most important is the shared emphasis on human freedom and responsibility. Like Narsai, he follows Ephrem in speaking of God's justice and mercy in connection with Noah's Flood. The *Life of Abel* (c. 500) attributed to Symmachus borrows directly from *GenCom* (Anon. *Life of Abel*: 468, 489–491). As we have seen, the *Cave of Treasures* (c. 600) does so, too.

West Syrian Reception in the Islamic Period

Jacob of Edessa, as we have seen, read at least some *madrâshê* by Ephrem; but he may not even have known *GenCom*, since his *Hexaemeron* reflects it not at all. Most of the Syriac bible-commentaries are rag-bags of earlier traditions from which *GenCom* is never absent; Ephrem is the main authority in the *Commentary* by Severus (dated to 861), Jacob of Serûgh his elucidator. Moses bar Kêfâ (†903) cites *GenCom* among other commentaries, but his allegorical approach puts Ephrem a little in the shade. Dionysius bar Ṣalîbî (†1171), who mainly follows Bar Kêfâ, also independently cites *GenCom* (Kremer 2012: 479). Of the modern Indian, Middle Eastern, and diasporic Syrian reception of Ephrem, Koonammakkal (2006), Bou Mansour (1988), and Shemunkasho (2002) are examples.

East Syrian Reception in the Same Period

The East Syrians were more faithful to the principle, honored by Ephrem, that a commentary should begin with a close literal reading of the text; and although, unlike Ephrem, most of them stand in the Antiochene tradition, they do not reject the "Syriac interpretation," of which Ephrem is "the portal figure" (Hidal 1974: 140), nor its distinctive midrashic wisdom. In the judgment of its editor, the eighth-century *Diyarbakır commentary*, for example, uses *GenCom* without always acknowledging Ephrem by name, though it refers to his positions implicitly as part of "the tradition of the School" (cf. *Foundation* 383). Accordingly, the *Anonymous commentary*, edited by Levene, f. 1a (pp. 68, 71) refers first to Theodore and after that to "the traditions of the Syrians," of whom the first-named is Ephrem. These traditions constituted "a common heritage, more or less impersonal, of which anyone can make use, [...] adapting it to his own ideas" (p. xxxiv). Theodore bar Kônî, whose *Book of scholia* was written in 791, went back to the Greek Fathers; of the Syrians, he includes only Ephrem. Îshôʿdâd of Merv (†c. 859), the most comprehensive commentator and the main source for most of his successors, cites *GenCom* more often than any other commentary.

Part 2. The Medieval World of Christendom

The Greek Fathers

Basil (†379) twice mentions anonymous Syrian sources, one of whom has been identified as Eusebius of Emesa. Admittedly, this contemporary of Ephrem's from Edessa
wrote in Greek; yet his influence shows that Basil did not despise the Syrians. Gregory of
Nyssa (†394) may have agreed, though the *Encomium*, which calls Ephrem "the
Euphrates of the Church" (p. 824A), is not by him. Like Ephrem, Pseudo-Macarius
(late fourth century) used the myth of "the robe of glory"; and the theology of divine
names ascribed to Dionysius the Areopagite (from fifth-century Syria) may owe a debt
to Ephrem (Taylor 1998).

Already c. 375 (*Panarion* 51.22.7) Epiphanius of Salamis had quoted *Nativity* 5:13
(or a parallel statement). The Georgian *Homilies* by Meletius (†381), if correctly ascribed
(Van Esbroeck 1975: 308f.), show that *Virginity* 2:19 and the *Gospel commentary* §20
were read in Antioch soon after they were written. Epiphanius cites Ephrem's typological observation that Jesus was born on the thirteenth day from the winter solstice in
order to symbolize himself and his 12 disciples, while Meletius accepts Ephrem's
psychological hunch that Gabriel appeared to the young Mary as an old man, lest,
seeing a youth, "her expression cloud over." Chrysostom (†407) has striking agreements
with Ephrem, who, according to Kremer (2012: 487), was also a source of inspiration
for Severianus of Gabala. The bilingual Theodoret (†c. 460) has a threefold scriptural
hermeneutic, like Ephrem and Chrysostom, though each has his own emphasis; in his
Church history, 4.30.1f., Theodoret devotes such a positive note to Ephrem that it seems
likely he had read him.

Romanos

Of all those who wrote Greek, Romanos learned the most from Ephrem. This liturgical poet began as a Jew in Aramaic-speaking Ḥomṣ and moved on to Beirut and
Constantinople. The *poetic* form in which he cast all his Greek compositions had
been developed from the *madrâshâ* perfected by Ephrem. The *literary* form – a dialogue with a dramaturgical prologue and moralizing asides – was developed from
the Syriac *mêmrâ*, which was perfected by Jacob of Serûgh. The number of the
motifs in Romanos' work which have been traced, directly or indirectly, to Ephrem
has grown steadily over the last 30 years (Petersen 1984). The following example
proves at least indirect influence.

Ch. 22 of *Genesis* tells how Abraham took his only son, Isaac, up a mountain, in
order to sacrifice him. Did Abraham tell Sarah, Isaac's mother, that their son had to die?
If he had told her, what would she have said? Here is the answer given by Ephrem:

> The reason why Abraham did not tell Sarah is that he had not been commanded to do so.
> Had he done so, she would have begged him to let her come and share in his sacrifice, as he
> had shared with her the promise of Isaac's birth (*GenCom* §20).

An anonymous poet subsequently worked out this theme in a *mêmrâ* entitled *On the binding of Isaac*, adding a distinctive touch from Jewish rabbinic tradition: Isaac, too, wanted to share in his father's sacrifice and asked him to bind him tightly, so that he would not spoil it by some involuntary movement. In Greek literature these two traditions were both received in the *Kontakion on Abraham* by Romanos. The Byzantine cantor must have known the Syriac *mêmrâ* and, through it, Ephrem (cf. Brock 1989).

Sozomen (*Church history* 3.16, before 450) attests the translation of Ephrem's poems into Greek. There is, nevertheless, an undercurrent of chauvinism in this notice, which claims that Syriac music and meter were acquired early in the third century from the Greeks. In fact, not only Armenians and Greeks, but even Latin speakers, such as Ambrose (†397), followed the lead of the Syrians in casting doctrine in the form of hymns. The only extant Greek text that is translated from an authentic work of Ephrem's is the *Metrical Homily on Nineveh and Jonah*, which imitates the Syriac meter. This was a step toward the metrical revolution that took place in Greek during the fifth century and prepared the way for Romanos.

Pseudo-Ephrem

Intermediaries, often called "Ephrem" in the manuscripts, transmitted his ideas, usually adding something of their own. Greek translations of these compositions – Ephræm Græcus – sprang up in the bilingual culture of late antique Syria. "Few if any" of these (Lash 1999) are by Ephrem; but there are traces of the authentic Ephrem in the *Ascetical homily* (ed. Phrantzolas; Suh 2000), of which medieval Arabic, Armenian, Coptic, Ethiopic, Georgian, Greek, Latin, and Slavonic versions are extant. Some of the Greek Ephrem also exists in Melkite, or Palestinian, Aramaic.

Conclusion

"Ephrem's symbolic theology [...] profoundly shaped the liturgy, spirituality, and poetry of Syriac Christianity" (Possekel 2015). He is sometimes called "the prophet of the Syrians" (e.g., by the fourteenth-century 'Abdîshô' bar Brîkhâ). The genuine Ephrem was hardly received in Greek, except by the bilingual poet Romanos, who was influenced by him in approach, themes, form, and metrical devices. Ephrem was the first to enliven Christian teaching with the dialogue-poem, a legacy of ancient Mesopotamia; through him and his school this innovation reached Romanos, who passed it on to Europe. Ephrem's poetic work was interpreted sympathetically by Jacob of Serûgh. For reasons of Christology, Philoxenus at last distanced himself from Ephrem, whom he had once cited frequently, proudly calling him "our Syrian teacher." After the seventh century the *madrâshê* ceased to be read in their entirety and instead were excerpted for liturgical purposes, though the *mêmrê* may have continued to be read entire. Alone of all Ephrem's prose-works, *GenCom* was always consulted.

Bibliography

Abbreviations

CSCO   Corpus Scriptorum Christianorum Orientalium. Louvain.
Beck   Beck. *Des heiligen Ephraem des Syrers [...]*.
FC   Fathers of the Church. Catholic University of America.
GenCom   Ephrem. *Genesis Commentary*.
OC   *Oriens Christianus*.
PO   Patrologia Orientalis.
ROC   *Revue de l'Orient Chrétien*.
SC   Sources Chrétiennes.
SP   *Studia Patristica*. Ed. E.A. Livingstone.

Primary Sources

N.B. For more translations of Ephrem's works, see Den Biesen (2011).

Abâ. *Excerpt*. Ed./tr. E. Beck. *Nachträge zu Ephräm Syrus*. [The last text.] CSCO 363f., 1975.

Anon. *Ascetical homily*. Ed./tr. K.G. Phrantzolas. ([The Greek] *Ephrem. Works*.) Thessaloniki, 1988–1998. [Greek.] Cf. Ephrem. *Mêmrâ of reproof*. Ed./tr. E. Beck. *Sermones I*. CSCO 305f., 1970 (No. 1).

Anon. *Cave of Treasures*. Ed./tr. S.-M. Ri. *La Caverne des Trésors. Les deux recensions syriaques*. CSCO 486f., 1987.

Anon. *Chronicle of Edessa*. Ed./tr. I. Guidi. *Chronica minora*. Vol. 1. CSCO 1f., 1903 (No. 1).

Anon. *Diyarbakır commentary*. Ed./tr. L. van Rompay. *Le commentaire sur Genèse-Exode 9,32 du ms. (olim) Diyarbakır 22*. CSCO 483f., 1986.

Anon. *Gospel commentary*. Ed./tr. L. Leloir. *S. Éphrem. Commentaire de l'Évangile concordant*. Dublin 1963. *Id.*, [Same title.] *Folios additionnels*. Louvain, 1990.

Anon. *Life of Abel*. Ed./tr. S.P. Brock. "A Syriac life of Abel". *Muséon*, 87 (1974): 467–492.

Anon. *Mêmrâ on the binding of Isaac*. Ed./tr. S.P. Brock. "Two Syriac verse-homilies on the binding of Isaac". *Muséon*, 99 (1986): 61–129 (No. 2).

Anon. *Sinai index of melodies*. Ed. A. de Halleux. "Une clé pour les hymnes d'Éphrem dans le ms. Sinaï Syr. 10". *Muséon*, 85 (1972): 171–199.

Barḥadbeshabbâ. *Foundation of the schools*. Ed./tr. A. Scher. *Mar Barḥadbeshabba 'Arbaya. Cause de la fondation des écoles*. PO 4/4. Paris, 1907.

Dionysius bar Ṣalîbî, *Genesis commentary*. Unpublished. MSS include Paris Syr. 9, ff. 355–361 (13th century).

Elijah. *Biography of John of Tella*. Ed./tr. E.W. Brooks. *Vitae virorum apud monophysitas celeberrimorum*. CSCO 7f., 1907. (The last text.)

Ephrem. *Armenian madrâshê*. Ed./tr. L. Mariès/C. Mercier. *Hymnes de S. Éphrem conservées en version arménienne*. PO 30/1. Paris, 1961.

Ephrem. *Faith (Madrâshê on)*. Ed./tr. E. Beck. *Hymnen de fide*. CSCO 154f. 1955. Tr. J. Wickes. FC, 2015.

Ephrem. *GenCom*. Ed./tr. R.-M. Tonneau. *S. Ephraem Syri commentarii in Genesim etc.* CSCO 152f., 1955.

Ephrem. *Heresies (Madrâshê against)*. Ed./tr. E. Beck. *Hymnen contra haereses*. CSCO 169f., 1957.

Ephrem. *Homily on our Lord*. Ed./tr. E. Beck. *Sermo de domino nostro*. CSCO 270f., 1966.

Ephrem. *Mêmrâ on Nineveh and Jonah*. Ed./tr. E. Beck. *Sermones II*. (No. 1.) CSCO 311f., 1970.

Ephrem. *Mêmrê on faith.* Ed./tr. E. Beck. *Sermones de fide.* CSCO 212f., 1961.

Ephrem. *Mêmrê on Nicomedia.* Ed./tr. C. Renoux. *Éphrem de Nisibe. Memre sur Nicomédie.* PO 37/2f. Turnhout, 1975.

Ephrem. *Nativity (Madrâshê on).* Ed./tr. E. Beck. *Hymnen de Nativitate.* CSCO 186f. 1959. Tr. McVey, 1989: 61–217.

Ephrem. *Nisibis (Madrâshê on).* Ed./tr. E. Beck. *Carmina Nisibena.* Part 1. CSCO 218f., 1961.

Ephrem. *Paradise (Madrâshê on).* Ed./tr. E. Beck. *Hymnen de Paradiso etc.* CSCO 175f., 1957.

Ephrem. *Prose refutations.* Ed./tr. C.W. Mitchell. *St Ephraim's prose refutations.* Vol. 1. London 1912.

Ephrem. *Virginity (Madrâshê on).* Ed./tr. E. Beck. *Hymnen de Virginitate.* CSCO 223f., 1962.

Epiphanius. *Panarion.* Ed. K. Holl. *Epiphanius.* GCS 37. Leipzig 1933. Tr. F. Williams. *The Panarion of Epiphanius of Salamis. Books II and III. De Fide.* 2nd ed. Nag Hammadi and Manichaean Studies 79, 2013.

Gregorius Barhebraeus. *Chronicon ecclesiasticum.* Ed./tr. J.B. Abbeloos/T.J. Lamy. Louvain, 1872.

Gregory of Nyssa [Pseudo-]. *Encomium on Ephrem.* Ed./tr. G. Voss. *Patrologia Graeca,* 46: 819–850.

Isaac (of Antioch?). *Mêmrâ on Abel and Cain.* Unpublished. Vatican Syr. 120, ff. 172b–185a.

Isaac of Nineveh. *Ascetical homilies.* Ch. 4–41. Ed./tr. S.P. Brock. *Isaac of Nineveh. "The second part".* CSCO 554f., 1995.

Îshô'dâd of Merv, *Commentary on Genesis.* Ed./tr. J.-M. Vosté/C. van den Eynde. *Commentaire d'Išo'dad de Merv sur l'ancien testament. I. Genèse.* CSCO 126/156, 1950/1955.

Jacob of Edessa. *Hexaemeron.* Ed./tr. J.-B. Chabot/A. Vaschalde. *Iacobi Edesseni Hexaemeron seu in opus creationis libri septem.* CSCO 92/97, 1928/1932.

Jacob of Edessa. *Letters.* (a) *Letter 4.* Ed./tr. F. Nau. *ROC,* 6 (1901): 115–131. (b) and (c) *Letters 5* and *14.* Unpublished. Br. Libr., Add. MS 12,172, ff. 85a–87b, 121b–126b; cf. Nau (1909: 437–440), Wright (1872: 603). (d) *Letter 12.* Ed. W. Wright, "Two epistles of Mār Jacob, Bishop of Edessa".

Journal of Sacred Literature and Biblical Record, 10 (1867): 430–460. Tr. F. Nau, *ROC,* 10 (1905): 277–282.

Jacob of Serûgh. *Mêmrâ on Ephrem.* Ed./tr. J.P. Amar. *A metrical homily on holy Mar Ephrem by Mar Jacob of Serugh.* Tr. Palmer, 2007.

Jacob of Serûgh. *Mêmrê on creation.* Ed./tr. K. Alwan. *Jacques de Saroug. Quatre homélies sur la création.* CSCO 508f., 1989.

Jerome/Gennadius. *Famous men.* Ed. E.C. Richardson/O.L. von Gebhardt. *Hieronymus/Gennadius. Liber de viris inlustribus.* Texte und Untersuchungen 14. Leipzig, 1896. Tr. T.P. Halton. *St Jerome. On illustrious men.* FC 100. Washington, DC, 1999.

Meletius. *Homilies* (Georgian). Unpublished. For the MSS, see M. van Esbroeck 1975: 59 (P5); 84 (A31); 86/150 (A36/U35).

Michael. *Chronicle.* Ed./tr. J.-B. Chabot. *La chronique de Michel le Syrien, patriarche jacobite 1166–1199,* four vols. Paris, 1899–1910.

Moses bar Kêfâ, *Hexaemeron.* Ed./tr. L. Schlimme. *Der Hexaemeronkommentar des Mose bar Kepha.* Wiesbaden, 1977.

Narsai. *Mêmrê on creation.* Ed./tr. P. Gignoux. *Homélies de Narsaï sur la création.* PO 34/3-4. Turnhout, 1968.

Philoxenus. *Letter to the monks of Senoun.* Ed./tr. A. de Halleux. *Philoxène de Mabbog. Lettre aux moines de Senoun.* CSCO 231f. 1963.

Romanos. *Kontakion on Abraham.* Ed. P. Maas/K.A. Trypanis. *S. Romani Melodi cantica.* Vol. 1 (No. 41). London 1963. Ed./tr. J. Grosdidier de Matons. *Romanos le Mélode. Hymnes.* Vol. 1 (No. 3). SC 99. Paris, 1964.

Severus of Antioch. *Against the Grammarian.* Ed./tr. J. Lebon. *Severi Antiocheni liber contra impium grammaticum.* 3.2. CSCO 101f., 1952.

Severus of Edessa. *Commentary on Genesis.* Ed./tr. P. Benedictus, *S. patris nostri Ephraem Syri opera omnia.* Vol. 1 of the Syriac–Latin trilogy. Rome, 1737: 116–193.

Sozomen. *Church history.* Ed. J. Bidez/G.C. Hansen. *Sozomenus. Kirchengeschichte.* GCS 50. Berlin 1960. Tr. A.-J. Festugière. *Sozomène. Histoire ecclésiastique. Livres I–II.* SC 306. Paris, 1983.

Theodore bar Kônî. *Book of scholia.* Ed. A. Scher. *Theodorus bar Kōnī. Liber scholiorum.* [Siirt recension.] Two vols. CSCO 55/69, 1910/1912. Tr. R. Hespel/R. Draguet. *Théodore bar Koni. Livre des scolies.* CSCO 431f., 1981/1982. Ed./tr. R. Hespel. [Same title.] *(Recension d'Urmiah).* CSCO 447f., 1983. [Same title.] *Les collections annexées par Sylvain de Qardu.* CSCO 465f., 1984.

Theodoret. *Church history.* Ed./tr. L. Parmentier/G.C. Hansen. *Théodoret de Cyr. Histoire ecclésiastique.* Vol. 2. Books 3–4. SC 530. Paris, 2009.

Secondary Sources

Beck, E. (1953), *Ephraems Reden über den Glauben.* Studia Anselmiana 33. Rome: Herder.

Beck, E. (1962), "Philoxenos und Ephräm". *OC,* 46: 61–76.

Botha, P. (1997), "Original sin and sexism: St Ephrem's attitude towards Eve". *SP,* 33: 483–489.

Bou Mansour, T. (1988), *La pensée symbolique de Saint Éphrem le syrien.* Kaslik, Lebanon: Université Saint-Esprit.

Bou Mansour, T. (1993), *La théologie de Jacques de Saroug,* vol. 1. Kaslik, Lebanon: Université Saint-Esprit.

Bou Mansour, T. (2000), *La théologie de Jacques de Saroug,* vol. 2. Kaslik, Lebanon: Université Saint-Esprit.

Brock, S. (1989), "From Ephrem to Romanos". *SP,* 20: 139–151.

Brock, S. (1997), "The transmission of Ephrem's *madrashe*". *SP,* 33: 490–505.

Brock, S. (2003), "The changing faces of St Ephrem as read in the West". In *Abba: The Tradition of Orthodoxy in the West,* J. Behr, A. Louth, and D. Conomos (eds). Crestwood, NY: St Vladimir's Seminary Press; 65–80.

De Halleux, A. (1963), *Philoxène de Mabbog. Sa Vie, Ses Écrits, Sa Théologie.* Louvain: Imprimerie Orientaliste.

Den Biesen, K. (2006), *Simple and Bold: Ephrem's Art of Symbolic Thought.* Piscataway, NJ: Gorgias Press.

Den Biesen, K. (2011), *Annotated Bibliography of Ephrem the Syrian,* 2nd edition. Lulu.

Glenthøj, J. (1997), *Cain and Abel in Syriac and Greek Writers (4th–6th Centuries).* Louvain: Peeters.

Griffith, S. (1998), "A spiritual father for the whole Church: the universal appeal of St Ephraem the Syrian". *Hugoye,* 1.2: 197–220.

Kremer, T. (2012), *Mundus primus. Die Geschichte der Welt und des Menschen im Genesiskommentar Ephräms des Syrers.* Louvain: Peeters.

Koonammakkal, T. (2006), "Ephrem's theology of humor". *SP,* 41: 51–56.

Hidal, S. (1974), *Interpretatio syriaca. Die Kommentare Ephräm zu Genesis und Exodus.* Lund: Gleerup.

Lange, C. (2005), *The Portrayal of Christ in the Syriac Commentary on the Diatessaron.* Louvain: Peeters.

Lash, E. (1999), "Ephrem, Greek". *The Blackwell Dictionary of Eastern Christianity,* K. Parry *et al.* (eds). Oxford: Blackwell; 180.

Nau, F. (1909), "Cinq lettres de Jacques d'Édesse". *ROC,* 14: 427–440.

Palmer, A. (1998), "A single human being divided in himself". *Hugoye,* 1.2: 117–163.

Palmer, A. (1999a), "The prophet and the king: Mâr Ephrem's message to the Eastern Roman emperor". In *After Bardaisan,* G. Reinink and A. Klugkist (eds). Louvain: Peeters; 213–236.

Palmer, A. (1999b), "The influence of Ephraim the Syrian". *Hugoye,* 2.1: 83–109.

Palmer, A. 2007. "What Jacob actually wrote about Ephraim". In *Jewish and Christian Liturgy and Worship,* A. Gerhards and C. Leonhard (eds). Leiden: Brill; 145–165.

Palmer, A. (2009), "Interpolated stanzas in Ephraim's *Madroshe* III–VII on faith". *OC,* 93: 1–27.

Petersen, W. (1984), *The Diatessaron and Ephrem Syrus as Sources of Romanos the Melodist.* Louvain: Peeters.

Possekel, U. (1999), *Evidence of Greek Philosophical Concepts in the Writings of Ephrem the Syrian*. Louvain: Peeters.

Possekel, U. (2015), "Syriac theology". In *The Oxford Handbook of the Reception of Christian Theology*, Sarah Coakley and Richard Cross (eds). Oxford: Oxford University Press (in press).

Rowell, G. (1999), "'Making the Church of England poetical': Ephraim and the Oxford Movement". *Hugoye*, 2.1: 111–129.

Shemunkasho, A. (2002), *Healing in the Theology of St Ephrem*. Piscataway, NJ: Gorgias Press.

Suh, W. (2000), *From the Syriac Ephrem to the Greek Ephrem*. Dissertation, Princeton Theological Seminary. [*Non vidi.*]

Taylor, D. (1998), "St Ephraim's influence on the Greeks". *Hugoye*, 1.2: 185–196.

Toepel, A. (2006), *Die Adam- und Seth-Legenden im syrischen Buch der Schatzhöhle*. Louvain: Peeters.

Van Esbroeck, M. (1975), *Les plus anciens homéliaires géorgiens*. Louvain: Peeters.

Van Rompay, L. (2000), "Past and present perceptions of Syriac literary tradition". *Hugoye*, 3.1: 71–103.

Van Rompay, L. (2007), "*Mallpânâ dilan Suryâyâ*. Ephrem in the works of Philoxenus of Mabbug". *Hugoye*, 7.1: 83–105.

Van Rompay, L. (2010), "Sin in paradise: Ephrem, Jacob of Serug and Narsai in conversation". In *Jacob of Sarug and His Times*, G.A. Kiraz (ed.). Piscataway, NJ: Gorgias Press; 211–230.

Wright, W. (1872), *Catalogue of Syriac manuscripts in the British Museum*. London.

CHAPTER 9
John Chrysostom

Wendy Mayer

Introduction: The Popularity of John Chrysostom

John Chrysostom holds a special place today within the eastern Christian traditions, where his works have been received since the fifth century. He has also via his theology and preaching had a lasting, if smaller, influence upon western Christianity. It was in the West in the mid-sixth century that the epithet "golden mouth" (*os aureum/ chrysostomos*) is first found applied to him. A number of the early Protestant theologians drew upon his teachings on grace, the freedom of the will, and divine adaptability in the course of the Reformation. These same teachings had been embraced by Pelagian theologians in Italy during the second decade of the fifth century. During the Reformation, Chrysostom was also claimed as an authority within Roman Catholicism. The Counter-Reformation provided the impetus for the production in England of the first edition of his complete works in Greek, which Catholic interests had, since the advent of the printing press, collated and published in Europe in Latin translation. This activity led in subsequent centuries to the translation of his works into a variety of modern European languages. Today, his works are generating renewed interest within Evangelical circles, while John himself continues to be venerated as a saint in the Roman Catholic and Orthodox calendars and is revered as one of the three hierarchs within Orthodox Christianity. In Greek Orthodox Christianity, a liturgy, still in use today, is attributed to him (Taft 1975–2008).

As witness to the extent of his reception, just over 1000 authentic works (Geerard 1974: 491–540) survive to the present day, to which can be added a larger number ("mehr als 1000", Voicu 1997: 503) that erroneously bear his name. Genres can be fluid, but the authentic works essentially comprise some 13 treatises, 239 letters, and more than 800 homilies and scriptural commentaries. Prior to the advent of the printing press, through translation many of these works, authentic and inauthentic,

---

The Wiley Blackwell Companion to Patristics, First Edition. Edited by Ken Parry.

spread well beyond his original spheres of influence – north-west Syria and the eastern imperial capital, Constantinople – into the far corners of the Mediterranean world. These developments resulted in the survival today of more than 5000 manuscripts that contain works attributed to Chrysostom transmitted in Greek (Bady 2012: 67), not counting papyri and the hundreds, perhaps even thousand or more, manuscripts that preserve Chrysostomian works in other languages.

Chrysostom's enduring popularity is remarkable, given the modern tendency to dismiss his contribution to theology by comparison with his contemporary, Augustine, in the West, and in the East the other theologians of the so-called Antiochene school, the Cappadocians, and subsequent mystical theologians like ps-Dionysius the Areopagite and Maximus the Confessor. His popularity can be ascribed to his preaching style, which was forthright, entertaining, and accessible, and to his emphasis in his preaching on the timeless subject of personal morality. Even as his treatises on asceticism became dated, the link he drew between pursuit of the moral Christian life and the call to a life of simplicity (moderate asceticism) contributed to an interest in his works over the centuries within monastic circles. His emphasis on care for the poor via almsgiving continues to attract attention. His extensive exegesis of scripture, particularly Genesis, the Gospels of Matthew and John, Acts, and all of the "Pauline" epistles, has long been respected.

His prominent place in history, resulting from his personal charisma and the events of the early fifth century in which he became embroiled, boosted the popularity of his works. Consecrated bishop of Constantinople in 398, John inherited a see whose power base was still being developed, but which by virtue of its access to the imperial court and the secular powerbrokers of the East was viewed as strategic (Tiersch 2002). When he fell foul of competing interests in 403 and again in 404, John's popular and ecclesiastical support base was significant. The resulting schism between his supporters (Johannites) and enemies (anti-Johannites), which was only finally resolved in the 430s, drew in the two reigning emperors, the elite of Constantinople, Antioch, and Rome, and many of the bishops of Italy, in addition to those of the eastern provinces and Egypt. More importantly, the propaganda generated by both sides of the conflict and the eventual success of the Johannite authors, which led to their version of events being adopted as authoritative, laid the foundation for the promotion of John as a martyr, saint, and champion of orthodoxy, securing his fame for all time (Mayer 2008; Wallraff 2008). This foundation was strengthened within little more than a decade, when the events that led to the Council of Chalcedon (451) in combination with John's rehabilitated status and uncontroversial theological teachings led to his adoption by subsequent generations on a variety of sides as a standard of orthodoxy. It is these factors in particular that made it common from the fifth to seventh centuries to attribute the original works of others to him, which attached to those products his celebrated status and thus improved their chances of survival.

As we proceed to outline his reception in greater detail, we use "John" to refer to the historical person, "Chrysostom" to refer to the constantly shifting perception of the man and his works.

The Ps-Chrysostomica

The ps-Chrysostomica, labeled thus to distinguish them from authentic Chrysostom works, are an important witness to the rapidity with which John's fame spread within the early centuries following his death and are important to understanding his reception. From the very beginning the view of John and his works that we have received was strongly influenced by his supporters. So the earliest ps-Chrysostomica, generated between 403 and 438 CE, originate from within the Johannite–anti-Johannite schism. Of the two categories – "mosaic" works originally authored by John, intentionally altered by others, and circulated in that form; and works originally authored by another and circulated under John's name – there survive one letter and six sermons in the first instance, and one letter and forty-seven sermons in the second (Mayer 2013, with extensive reference to the work of Voicu). The success of the first category is such that opinion has wavered up to the present as to the authenticity of the sermons. In the case of the second, a number of the sermons had by 420 been translated into Latin and received as genuine by Augustine, among others (Bady 2008: 306–309). Thus, from the beginning, what fellow clergy within the wider Mediterranean world thought were the genuine writings and teachings of John Chrysostom and with which they engaged had been manipulated. The homilies of two of John's enemies, Severian of Gabala and Atticus of Constantinople, were in the majority of manuscripts transmitted under John's name, introducing a third category of relevance to the fifth to seventh centuries, where the attribution was intended not to present John in a particular light, but to ensure those works' survival (Voicu 2008: 66).

By 438, when John's remains were brought back in triumph to Constantinople and the account of events circulated by his supporters had begun to dominate, this last strategy took on broader application. So there exist some 60 sermons attributed to him that originated not within the conflict that surrounded John's deposition but in a local dispute in which Augustine became engaged in North Africa (Shaw 2011: esp. Appendix H). These Latin sermons were preserved in Spain by the dissenters or their supporters. The momentum surrounding John's fame and orthodox status at this point was such that the ps-Chrysostomica could now include works penned originally in a language dissociated from the authentic corpus. These were not the only reasons that corpora original to other authors came to be transmitted under John's name. So, in the case of the sixth-century presbyter Leontius of Constantinople, of 11 homilies that can be traced back to him four are predominantly assigned to John Chrysostom in the manuscripts, while a shortened version of a fifth homily is transmitted solely under the latter's name (Datema and Allen 1987: 55 n. 85). The attribution here and in similar cases is more likely due to the fact that the sermons are lively examples of the genre in Greek and to the scribes copying these manuscripts John was the best-known exponent of Greek preaching from earlier centuries. As the ps-Chrysostom corpus expanded, so ps-Chrysostom works of earlier origin continued to circulate side by side with these new categories, as evidenced by a sixth-century papyrus from Egypt that contains a now fragmentary copy of the sermon *In decollationem s. Ioannem* (Papathomas 2001), famously cited as genuine by the mid-fifth-century church historian Socrates (*HE* 6.18).

A different category of ps-Chrysostomica is represented by the 48 or more Greek "eclogues" (Geerard 1974: 594–595; Voicu 2008: 65), which constitute collages constructed of thematic material extracted almost entirely from genuine Chrysostomic works, pieced together to suit the needs of the time. Thirty-three of these were assembled in the mid-tenth century by Theodore Daphnopates, who interestingly included only a tiny amount of material from among the ps-Chrysostomica (de Aldama 1965: 20–21). Theodore's collection did not dictate how these newly formed works were subsequently used, however. Individual eclogues are found located together in a variety of numbers and ways in Greek manuscripts from the eleventh century onwards, indicating that whatever need prompted their creation continued to exert influence. Nor was this development unique to the Greek-speaking world. The same process was occurring during the first quarter of the tenth century in Bulgaria, where, as an example, the production of a collection of Chrysostom's homilies in Old Slavonic (the *Chrysorrhoas* or *Zlatostruy*) prompted the creation of a homily *De tormento* ascribed to him, which constitutes a mosaic of 11 smaller or larger extracts from his genuine works (Miltenov 2012). Similar moral works constructed from genuine exegetical homilies are found in the Bohairic Coptic tradition, witnessing to this same practice in Egypt (Voicu 2013: 43).

The ps-Chrysostomica continued to influence the reception of Chrysostom's works into the late medieval and early modern periods. European writings that on the basis of Latin editions cite him as an authority, such as the *Malleus maleficarum* (1490), attribute to him without discrimination citations from both genuine and inauthentic works, since these were considered in the prevailing Latin collections to be authentic. In at least one instance the transmission of John's works has led to a distinct bias at this time toward ps-Chrysostomica. This appears to be the case in Ethiopia, where translations into Ethiopic were made on the basis of Arabic versions (themselves late), which were in turn often based on Syriac, Coptic, or Christian Aramaic versions, resulting in a new crop of ps-Chrysostomica in Arabic and a preference in Ethiopia for works that are inauthentic (Witakowski 2008; Voicu 2013). The emergence of new ps-Chrysostomica in this instance occurred side by side with an expansion of the Ephraemic corpus as works that were originally anonymous were, as a result of the fame of both authors, assigned to one or the other by the translators. The definition of the authentic corpus continues to be the subject of debate, and it is still the case today that some works, such as the treatise *Comparatio regis et monachi*, and particularly some of the mosaic early ps-Chrysostom homilies that contain material of mixed authenticity (e.g., *In s. Phocam*; see Voicu [2008: 64]) and the four homilies associated with John's exile (Geerard 1974: 512–513; Bonfiglio 2011), are as often as not treated by those studying his thought as fully authentic.

The Early Translations

The translation of Chrysostom's works into other languages has played a pivotal role in their dissemination and their use by later polemicists and theologians. It has likewise influenced the way that John himself has been perceived by subsequent generations. Perhaps inevitably, owing to John's support base in Syria, to his episcopate in

Constantinople, and the constantly changing ecclesiastical alliances in the later fourth and early fifth centuries between the major sees of Italy and North Africa in the West and those of Constantinople, Alexandria, and Antioch in the East, and to his exile in Armenia (404–407), where he was warmly received, the earliest translations of his works are found in Latin, Armenian, and Syriac. The translation of his works into Latin, while extremely early, is mixed as a result of his status at that time in the West, where, by individuals allied with the Paulinian Nicene faction in Antioch and with Alexandria, such as Jerome, he was viewed as an Origenist sympathizer and the disciple of a schismatic (Bady 2008: 310). Jerome indicates awareness of possibly two of John's authentic works – the treatise *De sacerdotio* and homily *In illud: In faciem ei restiti* – which he would have read in Greek, but is otherwise unenthusiastic. It is not until after 414 that we find clear evidence of the circulation of Chrysostom writings in Latin, but in limited numbers and within a limited circle. Both Julian of Eclanum and the 18 Pelagian bishops who were signatories to a *Libellus fidei* in 418 utilized the third in the collection of eight baptismal catecheses (Geerard 1974: 535). Augustine, in his *Contra Julianum*, was able to compare the text cited with other available Latin versions, including one revised on the basis of the Greek, while invoking a range of other Chrysostom texts, not all of which were genuine (Bady 2008: 311). The texts he cites witness to the early date and circulation of a collection of 38 homilies in Latin attributed to Chrysostom. As Bady (2008: 311–312) points out, not only does this indicate the translation into Latin before 420 of works of diverse genre – catecheses, letters, homilies from exegetical series – but also shows that by this early date not just original Greek works, but those of Latin authors (both Augustine and the collection attribute to him a homily in Latin by Potamius of Lisbon) had come under his authority. Both witnesses further demonstrate that John's notoriety obscured a poor knowledge of his oeuvre in the West, since there is also attributed to him a homily by Basil of Caesarea.

At this same time (419–420) a Pelagian, Annianus of Celeda, translated into Latin the first 25 homilies *In Matthaeum* and in 421 the seven panegyrics on St Paul. Although collections of Chrysostom's works in Greek of some kind were clearly available in Constantinople by 431, since Cassian in his *De incarnatione* encourages Nestorius to read them (Plested 2007: 4), Bady (2008: 312–13) takes a pessimistic view of the number of texts in Latin translation available in the West into the seventh century. This is despite Isidore of Seville's claim that these were numerous, which encouraged earlier more optimistic estimates (e.g., Bouhot 1989, Plested 2007). Bady's conclusion regarding the limited dissemination of Chrysostom's works in early medieval Europe is supported by the evidence from Anglo-Saxon witnesses, where, along with an early ps-Chrysostom commentary composed in Latin, the *Opus imperfectum in Matthaeum*, only the Collection of 38 homilies and an equally restricted corpus transmitted in the eighth-century homiliary of Paul the Deacon were utilized (Hall forthcoming).

In at least one instance, that of the authentic *ep.* 112 to Theodore, Latin translation preserves information that was expunged for church–political reasons in the East. So c. 547 Facundus of Hermiane in his *Pro defensione trium capitulorum* cites the letter as evidence of the esteem in which John held Theodore of Mopsuestia, preserving its title as *Mopsuesteno Theodoro*. The Greek manuscripts uniformly neutralize both the title ("to Theodore the bishop") and a geographically specific reference within the letter to

Cilicia, which both Facundus and a tenth-century Latin manuscript retain (Bady 2008: 315–316). Facundus, who describes Chrysostom as "revered" (*Pro def. trium cap.* 6.5.15), further witnesses to the position he was accorded in Facundus' circles at the time, by defending his Christology against that of Theophilus of Alexandria (that is, situating Chrysostom as an authority for the pro-Chalcedonian position).

The importance of the early Syriac translations cannot be overstated. Since the majority were produced as early as the fifth and before the end of the eighth centuries and many of the surviving manuscripts are old (some dating to the sixth and seventh centuries), the translations often witness to a much earlier version of a work than survives in Greek (Childers 2013), where the majority of manuscripts date from the tenth century onwards. In some cases they preserve the sole surviving fragment or text of an authentic work (Voicu 2013). They point equally to the plasticity of Chrysostom in terms of his reception and to his subsequent influence upon Syriac literature by virtue of his adoption into that language. As Childers (2013: 326) states:

> As an instance of cross-cultural reception and recontextualization, the Syriac [translations put] the voice of Chrysostom into an oriental idiom, effectively naturalizing him as a participant in conversations that were fundamental to the development of the Syriac Christian heritage. It is not surprising that Chrysostom would find a ready welcome in the Syriac community, who are naturally attracted to his practical moralism, ascetic bent, and affinities with the Antiochene exegetical tradition. Furthermore, his tendency to focus on pragmatics rather than finely nuanced theological discussion ensures for him a place across the theological spectrum – miaphysite, diaphysite, and Chalcedonian.

These perceptions could apply equally to the adoption of Chrysostom into the other pre-modern languages. In regard to the last point, just as Facundus could in the sixth century claim him as a champion for the Chalcedonian position, Philoxenus of Mabbug (c. 484) could readily adduce citations from the Syriac version of Chrysostom's homilies *In Johannem* as a patristic witness that supported his own Miaphysite Christology. That same florilegium indicates that the homilies *In Matthaeum* had by that time been translated in all or part into Syriac (Childers 1997: 510–511, who distinguishes two separate translations, both early). Probably by the mid-sixth century translations of the majority of Chrysostom's homilies on the "Pauline" epistles were available, although those on Hebrews may not have been translated in full and nothing survives of the homilies on 1 and 2 Timothy (Childers 1997: 511–512). For the translation of the homilies *In Johannem*, Childers (1997: 513) arrives at a date at the very beginning of the sixth century.

Interest in Chrysostom's scriptural exegesis is only one way, however, in which he was received in Syria. Homilies or extracts thereof were translated and gathered into collections of various kinds, including topical anthologies, books on canon law, homiliaries, catenae, and florilegia (Childers 1997: 510). Even more interesting is a case in which a sixth- or seventh-century Syriac copy of the Gospel of John that includes *hermeneiai* for the purposes of divination that do not match anything in the Chrysostom corpus is subscribed as having been commented on by John, bishop of Constantinople, called Chrysostom (Childers 2013: 327–332). Here, the connection would appear to have nothing to do with a direct link between "John," the homonymous Gospel and the *sortilegia*, but rather with the status in Syria of Chrysostom and his Johannine commentary. Childers points to the practice of referring to Athanasius on the Psalms in West Syrian Psalters as support for the ad hoc mention in biblical codices of an influential interpreter on the book in question as a form of admiration. The attribution of this phenomenon to West Syria is noteworthy. The history of Christianity in Syria after the Council of Chalcedon led to the formulation by the sixth century of a different picture of Chrysostom in East Syrian tradition. There, other fathers of the Antiochene school, most notably Theodore of Mopsuestia, were privileged over Chrysostom, while in the seventh century in some rare instances citations of his exegetical works subtly Nestorianized them (Pinggéra 2008). Only in the seventh century do his works slowly begin to influence the East Syrian exegetical tradition, although by the tenth century his status had improved to the point that he is now viewed as one of the heroes of Christian orthodoxy, opposed by Cyril's uncle, just as Nestorius was opposed by Cyril, and honored together with Theodore and Nestorius.

Armenian translations, which are even less well studied than those in Syriac, date to as early as the first half of the fifth century and are equally significant (Smelova 2013; Voicu 2013). Like the translations into Syriac, Armenian versions provide an important witness to earlier Greek recensions of both authentic and inauthentic works and can preserve authentic works that have failed to survive elsewhere. The former is the case with the ps-Chrysostom homily *Cum iret in exsilium* (Bonfiglio 2011), where both Syriac and Armenian translations of the homily witness to a different Greek text, as well as permitting correction of the Greek version that does survive and which had become corrupted. The latter is the case with the commentary *In Isaiam*, which in the Greek manuscripts cuts off in the middle of chapter 8, but in an Armenian translation believed to date from the fifth century continues to chapter 66 (Smelova 2013: 209–301). If speculation is correct, then John may have taken up continuation of this commentary in exile in Armenia, where it was adopted and translated into Armenian by his local admirers, accounting for the failure of survival of that portion in Greek or Syriac. The full text was well known to Armenian writers of the twelfth to thirteenth centuries, who cited it in catenae and used it substantially in their own commentaries (Smelova 2013: 301).

Translations into Coptic are also significant, if equally poorly studied, and witness to Chrysostom's early reception in Egypt. More than 17 texts were translated into Sahidic in the fifth century, in regard to three of which the Greek original appears not to have survived, while one of these witnesses to a substantially different text (Voicu 2013). Translation of some further 46 pieces into Bohairic is dated to the very end of the seventh or beginning of the eighth century, again preserving one text that has no surviving Greek counterpart. Voicu notes further that the translation process produced a corpus of ps-Chrysostom works original to both Sahidic and Bohairic.

The Influence of the Lives

A survey of the early reception of Chrysostom would not be complete without discussion of the role played by his biographers. The earliest accounts of his life, the *Dialogue* by Palladius (Meyer 1985) and *Funeral Oration* by ps-Martyrius (Barnes and Bevan 2013), the latter produced in late 407, the former between 408 and 419, played a major role in the success of the Johannite perception of John and his episcopate in the fifth century, but had surprisingly little direct influence afterwards. Aside from a brief reappearance as a source utilized by an anonymous tenth-century life of Chrysostom (van Ommeslaeghe 1976), the account by ps-Martyrius, employed as a source by the mid-fifth-century church historian Sozomen, disappeared from view after that point and regained prominence only in the early twenty-first century (e.g., Tiersch 2002). The *Dialogue*, although drawn upon in the second half of the seventh century by Theodore of Trimethus, who produced a lengthy homily in Greek concerning Chrysostom's life (Halkin 1977: 8–44), and by the author of a lengthy Greek hagiography produced in the late seventh or early eighth century attributed to George of Alexandria (Halkin 1977: 70–285), itself appears to have gone out of fashion within a few centuries, perhaps because of the change in Byzantine literary tastes that occurred in the eighth century. Very few manuscripts of the *Dialogue* survive. Only in the eighteenth to twentieth centuries was Palladius' account rehabilitated as a source in its own right, subsequently shaping the picture of Chrysostom that appears in modern biographies (e.g., Baur 1929–1930; Kelly 1995; Brändle 1999). The life that dominated the perception of Chrysostom in the intervening centuries, that came to be copied, translated, and imitated, is the rhetorically elaborate hagiography by ps-George. Through the incorporation of a large amount of fanciful new material, the author in his own words presents Chrysostom as:

> The blessed preacher and exegete and driver of the apostolic and orthodox faith, who taught fasting, proclaimed asceticism, rejected arrogance, praised humility, persuaded people to abandon the theatres and Olympic games and rush to the churches, and to forget lewd and dissolute songs in favour of learning by heart psalms and hymns and God's word (*V.Joh.* 74).

In the Byzantine world in an age that valued rhetorically elaborate literary productions, ps-George's account marks the beginning of a florescence of homilies and lives in Greek over the next three centuries by authors such as Cosmas Vestitor, John of Damascus, Emperor Leo VI, and Nicetas the Paphlagonian, all of them highly encomiastic and in turn influencing the production of fresh anonymous lives (Halkin 1977; Antonopoulou 1997: 123–124 re Leo VI). Characteristic of these productions, a homily by John of Damascus delivered on the feast day of John Chrysostom is unashamedly triumphalist and frames John as the champion of orthodoxy and as an ideal priest and monk (Brottier 2004: 66–94). The influence of ps-George's *Vita* spread via translation into Old Slavonic towards the end of the ninth century by the school of John the Exarch in Bulgaria (Dimitrova 2012) and via translation into Ethiopic in the medieval period (perhaps via Arabic) where it spawned the production of an anonymous Ethiopic life that attracted considerable popularity and was itself frequently copied (Witakowski 2008).

It is at this same time that the first evidence of churches dedicated to John Chrysostom appears in the Byzantine world, indicating that the emergence at this period of homilies on his feast day and translation was part of a growing development of his cult as a saint.

Photius (*Bibl.* 8.106–111) preserves summaries of five panegyrics on John Chrysostom produced in the first half of the fifth century by the Johannite Theodoret of Cyrrhus, and Proclus, the bishop of Constantinople who presided over the translation of John's remains to the city in 438 and their burial there in the Church of the Apostles, preached an encomium on him (Leroy 1967: 134–135) at the time, but there is no evidence of homiletic activity in Greek celebrating him in Constantinople or elsewhere prior to the late seventh century. It is noteworthy that, perhaps in connection with these developments, Proclus' encomium was itself translated into Armenian and Old Slavonic. A church dedicated to Chrysostom was built in Constantinople in the ninth century, as witnessed by a distich composed by Theodore the Studite (Janin 1969: 271–272), while at Antioch in the tenth century under the Byzantine reconquest of that city a church dedicated to him is said to be one of two new buildings constructed there (Zayat 1952: 336–337), although it should be noted that it receives no mention in other sources on Antioch in the tenth to thirteenth centuries. The same source, the Arabic life of the Melkite patriarch of Antioch, Christophoros, mentions a staff of John Chrysostom that, along with relics such as Christ's lance, lay at that time among the treasures of the cathedral church of St Peter (Zayat 1952: 360–361). In the West in Rome in the eighth century, under the cross-influence of a local Greek community, there appears on the left nave wall of the church of Santa Maria Antiqua an image of John standing directly at Christ's right hand, positioned first in a procession of eastern saints. Standing to Christ's left is a procession of western saints in which some eighth-century Roman popes are incorporated (Lucey 2007). It is at roughly this same period, usually after the second iconoclast controversy (814–842) had been resolved, that the surviving portraits of John Chrysostom begin to appear in Byzantine churches, such as the famous late-ninth-century mosaic in a north tympanum of Hagia Sophia in Constantinople.

The Modern Editing and Publication of his Works and the Reformation and Counter-Reformation

Over the centuries the very act of translating, collecting, or editing Chrysostom's works has both been shaped by and had a marked influence on his reception. This emerges very clearly in the European activity that surrounded the Reformation. Baur (1907) catalogues the flurry of editions of individual and collected works that were printed in both Latin and Greek from the early 1500s onwards, and Quantin (2008: 341–346) those in Latin for the critical period between 1525 and 1624. Appeals to the church Fathers as authorities on all sides of the Reformation provided the impetus for the production of new scientific collections of the works of authoritative Fathers of the church, side by side with the long-standing practice of collecting their wisdom in extracted form in catenae and florilegia. As an author of the first four centuries, a period now looked back on as one of church unity and thus a foundation common to both eastern and western Christianity, Chrysostom's works were swept up in this endeavor. The fall of Constantinople in 1453 and consequent influx of Greek scholars into the West may also have been instrumental (Plested 2007). Although Plested argues for the translation into Latin of several Chrysostom commentaries (John, Matthew, Genesis) in the twelfth century, with subsequent influence on Thomas Aquinas and Bonaventure, it is in the sixteenth century that Chrysostom's reception in the West takes on momentum.

That reception was varied. Here, distinction needs to be drawn between apologetic citation of a variety of Fathers to support one's own theology, which was common, and the attentive reading of complete Chrysostomic works, leading to direct influence. As an example of the first, apologetic appeal to Chrysostom in polemics of this period on both sides of the divide survives in pamphlets such as Vrancx's *Malleus Calvinistarum* (Antwerp 1590) and those produced in the 1680s during a local dispute between Johan Friedrich Mayer and two Jesuit preachers in Germany in which Chrysostom's theology was claimed respectively as Lutheran and Catholic (Baur 1907: 280–281). As Quantin (2008) documents, publication of the Greek Fathers in Latin in the sixteenth century was itself explicitly located within a larger Catholic strategy of reconquest directed towards the Protestants and the separated Christians in the East. That strategy, which multiplied the Latin editions of Chrysostom's works, undermined the production of an edition in Greek, explaining why this was undertaken privately by the English nobleman Henry Savile (1612–1613), rather than in Europe.

Concerning the second category of reception, Huijgen (2011) and Moore (2013) persuasively argue that both directly and indirectly (via Erasmus) Chrysostom influenced Calvin's theology of divine accommodation, the will, and human anthropology, as well as his mode of preaching. Although never completed, Calvin had intended to produce what would have been the earliest French translation of Chrysostom's homilies, of which there survives a Latin Preface (Hazlett 1991). By contrast, estimates of the influence of patristic works, including those of Chrysostom, on John Wesley have been exaggerated. It is now clear that his access to these was limited and largely mediated (Heitzenrater 2002). Ritter (2012: 155–182) reconstructs a more optimistic view of the access to and reception of Chrysostom within German Lutheran pietism from the sixteenth to eighteenth centuries, concluding with Bengel's publication in 1725 of an edition, translation, and commentary on the treatise *De sacerdotio*. A different reception is witnessed within the English Reformation. Thomas Cranmer, whose interest in Chrysostom was scanty and only for his usefulness for apologetic purposes, in 1544 adopted in English translation the third antiphon of the Liturgy of St John Chrysostom as a prayer within the first Anglican liturgy. From there it made its way into the *Book of Common Prayer* (1662), securing its continual use into the present day (Plested 2007).

Modern Reception of Chrysostom and His Works

The production of the de Montfaucon (1718–1738) edition and the decision by Jacques Paul Migne to incorporate it virtually intact within the Patrologia Graeca (vols 47–63), ensuring its widespread availability, have dominated reception of Chrysostom in the modern era, continuing to exert influence today. In the de Montfaucon text the editorial process begun at the time of the Reformation ended with the corpus being arranged in a distinctly new shape. As illustrative examples, in editing the letters to diverse correspondents from exile he followed an earlier edition in which they were arranged ad hoc, matching neither their chronological order nor that of the majority of the manuscripts

(Mayer 2015); the series of three homilies *De diabolo tentatore* is his own, incorporating as *hom.* 1 a sermon originally associated with *De osbcuritate hom.* 1–2 (Peleanu 2011); and, similarly, he brought together as a single series six homilies *In illud: Vidi dominum* that never constituted an original series, but were earlier grouped together in a variety of ways (Smelova 2013). Also influential on Chrysostom biographies of this period has been the reintroduction of the *Dialogue* of Palladius, whose legal defense of John, now treated as a trustworthy historical account, better suited modern tastes. Influential in the West was the development in the nineteenth century of the discipline of systematic theology, which led simultaneously to a decline in Protestant circles in interest in Chrysostom as a theologian, since his approach to theology did not fit its criteria, and to the division of study of his theology in Catholic circles into systematic categories (pneumatology, ecclesiology, soteriology, eucharistic thought, etc.). The reception of Chrysostom's theology in Greek and Romanian Orthodox circles continued largely unaffected (Popa 2002; Dragas 2008). Throughout the modern era the apologetic use of Chrysostom for denominational purposes continued, stimulating the production of translations of his works into a variety of languages (Plested 2007 on this development in England), as well as the production of edifying biographies (Baur 1907: 231–245).

A perhaps new development is the influence on the reception of Chrysostom of two nonreligious movements of the twentieth century. The rise of both Marxist and socialist economic theory in the first half of the century is reflected in interest in Chrysostom's teachings on wealth distribution, social justice, and class, particularly in countries where those theories dominated (e.g., Carillo de Albornoz 1936; Kurbatov 1958; González Blanco 1980). In a similar fashion, the feminist movement of the 1970s sparked a wave of interest in his teachings on and personal relations with women, especially the ascetic deaconess Olympias (e.g., Clark 1979; Militello 1985). Noteworthy from a religious perspective has been the influence of Vatican II on the reading of Chrysostom's thought in Catholic circles in the decades following, and the apologetic appeal to Chrysostom's teachings on women resulting from debate concerning the role of women within the Greek Orthodox Church in North America in the 1980s and 1990s. Hand in hand with all of these developments has been the emergence within the modern period of a drive to recover the original words of Chrysostom and the original historical person. The first emerged as part of the modern discipline of text editing and led to the distinction for the first time between authentic and inauthentic, and the second has been accelerated by the emergence of the discipline of Late Antique Studies in the 1970s, with its emphasis on transformation of the classical world and on the role played in that transformation by Christianity, locating John Chrysostom in the spotlight. Both drives have prompted the geographic expansion of the reception of Chrysostom into new countries, including South Africa and Australia.

The Gaps and Future Directions

The reception of Chrysostom has been traced here in broad strokes. Given the present state of scholarship, gaining a complete overview and balanced understanding of his reception throughout the Mediterranean world and beyond those confines into the late medieval and then modern periods is impossible. Huge gaps remain, influenced by the language limitations of scholars and a western bias. The early and medieval translation of the corpus, authentic and inauthentic, into all of the known languages has barely been studied. The ps-Chrysostomica, which provide important evidence of how different cultures received Chrysostom, as well as their own piety (as reflected in the production of new spuria), require focused attention on their own. Systematic study of the cult of John Chrysostom in different regions throughout the centuries, including how he was depicted in the visual arts up to the present, is entirely lacking. The study of the editing of Chrysostom's works from the Reformation to the late nineteenth century by Baur (1907) is now outdated and in any case ignores activity that took place beyond the borders of western Europe. The popular reception of John Chrysostom, which prompted developments such as the naming of a steamship after him in pre-Communist Russia and a township in early nineteenth-century francophone Canada (Saint-Jean-Chrysostome, Quebec), remains virtually unstudied.

Bibliography

Antonopoulou, Theodora (1997), *The Homilies of the Emperor Leo VI*. Leiden: Brill.

Bady, Guillaume (2008), "Les traductions latines anciennes de Jean Chrysostome: motifs et paradoxes". In *Formation et transmission des collections textuelles de l'Antiquité tardive au Moyen Âge central (IVe – début XIIIe siècle)*, Stéphane Gioanni and Benoît Grévin (eds). Rome: L'École Française de Rome; 303–316.

Bady, Guillaume (2012), "Les manuscrits grecs des œuvres de Jean Chrysostome d'après la base de données *Pinakes* et les *Codices Chrysostomici Graeci VII: Codicum Parisinorum pars prior.*" *Eruditio antiqua*, 4: 65–82.

Barnes, Timothy D. and George Bevan (transl.) (2013), *Funerary Speech for John Chrysostom*. Liverpool: Liverpool University Press.

Baur, Chrysostomus (1907), *S. Jean Chrysostome et ses œuvres dans l'histoire littéraire*. Louvain/Paris: Bureaux du Recuei/ Albert Fontemoing.

Baur, Chrysostomus (1929–1930), *Johannes Chrysostomus und seine Zeit*, two vols. Munich: Hueber.

Bonfiglio, Emilio (2011), "John Chrysostom's discourses on his first exile. Prolegomena to a critical edition of the *Sermo antequam iret in exsilium* and of the *Sermo cum iret in exsilium*". Dissertation, University of Oxford.

Bouhot, Jean-Paul (1989), "Les traductions latines de Jean Chrysostome du V\u1d49 au XVI\u1d49 siècle". In *Traduction et traducteurs au moyen âge*, Geneviève Condamine (ed.). Paris: Éditions du CNRS; 31–39.

Brändle, Rudolf (1999), *Johannes Chrysostomus. Bischof-Reformer-Märtyrer*. Stuttgart: Verlag W. Kohlhammer.

Brottier, Laurence (2004), *Figures de l'évêque idéal. Jean Chrysostome, Panégyrique de Saint Mélèce; Jean Damascène, Panégyrique de Saint Jean Chrysostome*. Paris: Belles Lettres.

Carillo de Albornoz, A. (1936), "Mas sobre el comunismo de san Juan Crisóstomo". *Razón y Fé*, 110: 80–98.

Childers, Jeffrey W. (1997), "Chrysostom's exegetical homilies on the New Testament in Syriac translation". *Studia Patristica*, 33: 509–516.

Childers, Jeffrey W. (2013), "Chrysostom in Syriac dress". Studia Patristica, 67: 323–332.

Clark, Elizabeth A. (1979), *Jerome, Chrysostom and Friends. Essays and Translations*. New York, NY: The Edwin Mellen Press.

Datema, Cornelis and Allen, Pauline (eds) (1987), *Leontii presbyteri Constantinopolitani homiliae*. Turnhout: Brepols.

De Aldama, J.A. (1965), *Repertorium Pseudochrysostomicum*. Paris: Éditions du CNRS.

De Montfaucon, Bernard (1718–1738), *Sancti Patris Nostri Ioannis Chrysostomi archiepiscopi Constantinopolitani opera omnia quæ exstant, uel quæ eius nomine circumferentur*. 13 vols. Paris.

Dimitrova, Aneta (2012), "Zwei chrysostomische Predigten (CPG 4396, 4399) in der Vita des Johannes Chrysostomus (BHG 873)". In *Diachrone Aspekte slavischer Sprachen. Für Ernst Hansack zum 65. Geburtstag*, Björn Hansen (ed.). Munich: Verlag Otto Sagner; 129–137.

Dragas, George D. (2008), "Perceptions of Chrysostom in contemporary Greek Orthodoxy". In Wallraff and Brändle (2008: 373–409).

Geerard, Maurits (1974), *Clavis Patrum Graecorum: Ab Athanasio ad Chrysostomum*, vol. 2. Turnhout: Brepols.

González Blanco, Antonino (1980), *Economia y sociedad en el bajo imperio segun San Juan Crisostomo*. Madrid: Fundaçíon Universitaria Española.

Halkin, François (1977), *Douze récits byzantines sur Saint Jean Chrysostome*. Bruxelles: Société des Bollandistes.

Hall, Thomas N. (Forthcoming), "John Chrysostom". In *Sources of Anglo-Saxon Literary Culture. Volume 5: Julius Caesar to Pseudo-Cyril of Alexandria*, Thomas N. Hall (ed.). Kalamazoo, MI: Medieval Institute Publications. Accessed November 10, 2013. www.bede.net/saslc/samples/c/chrysostom.pdf.

Hazlett, Ian P. (1991), "Calvin's Latin preface to his proposed French edition of Chrysostom's homilies: translation and commentary". In *Humanism and Reform: The Church in Europe, England and Scotland, 1400–1643*, James Kirk (ed.). Oxford: Blackwell; 129–150.

Heitzenrater, Richard P. (2002), "John Wesley's reading of and reference to the early church Fathers". In *Orthodox and Wesleyan Spirituality*, S.T. Kimbrough (ed.). Crestwood, NY: St Vladimir's Seminary Press; 25–32.

Huijgen, Arnold (2011), *Divine Accommodation in John Calvin's Theology: Analysis and Assessment*. Göttingen: Vandenhoeck & Ruprecht.

Janin, Raymond (1969), *La géographie ecclésiastique de l'empire byzantin. III. Les églises et les monastères*. Paris: Institut français d'études byzantines.

Kelly, John Norman Davidson (1995), *Golden Mouth. The Story of John Chrysostom – Ascetic, Preacher, Bishop*. London: Gerald Duckworth.

Kurbatov, George L. (1958), "Klassovaja suscnost ucenija Ioanna Zlatausta". *Ezegodnik muzeja istorii i religii i ateiznoz*, 2: 80–106.

Leroy, François J. (1967), *L'homilétique de Proclus de Constantinople. Tradition manuscrite, inédits, études connexes*. Vatican City: Biblioteca apostolica vaticana.

Lucey, Stephen J. (2007), "Art and sociocultural identity in early medieval Rome: the patrons of Santa Maria Antiqua". In *Roma Felix – Formations and Reflections of Medieval Rome*, Éamonn Ó. Carragain and Carol Neuman de Vegvar (eds). Aldershot: Ashgate; 139–158.

Mayer, Wendy (2008), "The making of a saint. John Chrysostom in early historiography". In Wallraff and Brändle (2008: 39–59).

Mayer, Wendy (2013), "Media manipulation as a tool in religious conflict: controlling the narrative surrounding the deposition of John Chrysostom". In *Religious Conflict from Early Christianity to the Rise of Islam*, Wendy Mayer and Bronwen Neil (eds). Berlin: De Gruyter; 151–168.

Mayer, Wendy (2015), "The ins and outs of the Chrysostom letter-collection: new ways of looking at a limited corpus". In *Collecting Early Christian Letters: From the Apostle Paul to Late Antiquity*, Pauline Allen and Bronwen Neil (eds). Cambridge: Cambridge University Press; 234–275.

Meyer, Robert T. (transl.) (1985), *Palladius. Dialogue on the Life of St. John Chrysostom*. New York, NY: Newman Press.

Militello, Concetta (1985), *Donna e chiesa. La testimonanza di Giovanni Crisostomo*. Palermo: Edi-Oftes.

Miltenov, Ivor (2012), "Пъзел с единадесет елемента. Източници, текстология и значение на старобългарската компилация Слово о моукахъ, приписвана на Йоан Златоуст". *Palaeoslavica*, 20: 291–303.

Moore, Peter (2013), "Gold without dross: an assessment of the debt to John Chrysostom in John Calvin's oratory". Dissertation, Macquarie University.

Papathomas, Amphilochios (2001), "'Keine Bestie auf der Welt gleicht der schlechten Frau': frauenfeindliche Polemik aus der ps.-chrysostomischen Homilie *In decollationem Praecursoris* in einem Berliner literarischen Papyrus." *Museum Helveticum*, 58: 47–53.

Peleanu, Adina (2011), "Deux séries chrysostomiennes: *Sur l'impuissance du diable* et *Sur l'obscurité des prophéties*". *Revue d'études augustiniennes et patristiques*, 57: 89–108.

Pinggéra, Karl (2008), "Das Bild des Johannes Chrysostomos in der ostsyrischen Kirche". In Wallraff and Brändle (2008: 193–211).

Plested, Marcus (2007), "The influence of St John Chrysostom in the West". Paper delivered at Symposium in honour of the 1600th anniversary of St John Chrysostom held under the aegis of the Ecumenical Patriarchate, Constantinople, 13–18 September. Accessed November 6, 2013. www.iocs.cam.ac.uk/resources/texts/st_john_chrysostom_in_the_west.pdf.

Popa, Daniel (2002), *Opera Bibliographia Sfântului Ioan Gura de Aur/Of Saint John Chrysostom*. Cluj-Napoca: Editura Renasterea.

Quantin, Jean-Louis. 2008. "Du Chrysostome latin au Chrysostome grec. Une histoire européenne (1588–1613)". In Wallraff and Brändle (2008: 267–346).

Ritter, Adolf Martin (2012), *Studia Chrysostomica. Aufsätze zu Weg, Werk und Wirkung des Johannes Chrysostomos (ca. 349–407)*. Tübingen: Mohr Siebeck.

Savile, Henry (1612–1613), *Τοῦ ἐν ἁγίοις πατρὸς ἡμῶν Ἰωάννου τοῦ Χρυσοστόμου τῶν εὑρισκομενων Τόμος (1–8)*, eight vols. Etonae: John Norton.

Shaw, Brent D. (2011), *Sacred Violence: African Christians and Sectarian Hatred in the Age of Augustine*. Cambridge: Cambridge University Press.

Smelova, Natalia (2013), "St John Chrysostom's exegesis on the prophet *Isaiah*: the oriental translations and their manuscripts". *Studia Patristica*, 67: 295–310.

Tiersch, Claudia (2002), *Johannes Chrysostomus in Konstantinopel (398–404). Weltsicht und Wirken eines Bischofs in der Hauptstadt des Oströmischen Reiches*. Tübingen: Mohr Siebeck.

Taft, Robert F. (1975–2008), *A History of the Liturgy of St. John Chrysostom*, four vols. Rome: Pontificio Istituto Orientale.

Van Ommeslaeghe, Florent (1976), "Une vie acéphale de saint Jean Chrysostome dans le Batopedinus 73". *Analecta Bollandiana*, 94: 317–356.

Voicu, Sever J. (1997), "Johannes Chrysostomus II (Pseudo-Chrysostomica)". *Reallexikon für Antike und Christentum*, 18: 503–515.

Voicu, Sever J. (2008), "L'immagine di Crisostomo negli spuri". In Wallraff and Brändle (2008: 61–96).

Voicu, Sever J. (2013), "John Chrysostom in the oriental languages". *Comparative Oriental Languages Studies Newsletter*, 5: 41–46.

Wallraff, Martin (2008), "Tod im Exil. Reaktionen auf die Todesnachricht des Johannes Chrysostomos und Konstituierung einer 'johannitischen' Opposition". In Wallraff and Brändle (2008: 23–37).

Wallraff, Martin, and Brändle, Rudolf (eds) (2008), *Chrysostomosbilder in 1600 Jahren: Facetten der Wirkungsgeschichte eines Kirchenvaters*. Berlin: De Gruyter.

Witakowski, Witold (2008), "The Ethiopic Life of John Chrysostom". In Wallraff and Brändle (2008: 223–231).

Zayat, Habib (1952), "La vie du patriarche melkite d'Antioche Christophore (†967) par le protospathaire Ibrahim v. Yuhanna. Document inédit du Xe siècle. *Proche Orient Chrétien*, 2: 11–38, 333–366.

CHAPTER 10

Augustine of Hippo

Kazuhiko Demura

The Starting Point of Augustine's Reception: Augustine's Original Figure

Among the most influential Church Fathers in the West, such as Ambrose, Jerome, and Gregory the Great, Augustine of Hippo (354–430) is quite particular. Not only because of the unrivalled quality and voluminous diversity of his writings that have had such a lasting and persistent influence on later readers and theologians, and came to shape a strong tradition of so-called Augustinianism, but also because of the unique fact that nearly all of his books, letters, and sermons that were preserved in his library at Hippo during his lifetime were carefully edited by Augustine himself. His library narrowly escaped damage during the Vandal siege. It was taken to the Pontifical Library in Rome or to other libraries in Italy in the middle of the fifth century just after his death. The existence of the complete collected works edited by the author himself is a unique case among patristic writers. O'Donnell rightly observes:

> His office, his holiness, and his orthodoxy were all factors in claiming his place: but had he not written, had he not written so much, and had his works not survived so consistently ... he would never have become the authority figure that he did become. He was the right man in the right place at the right time (O'Donnell 1991: 22).

We might say that the Augustine who has been received is the Augustine he himself would have liked to have received. In 427, at the age of 73, he wrote a book listing all his books and treatises with a critical comment. He said in the prologue to this book, the *Revisions* (*Retractationes*): 'My task is to reconsider my works from an uncompromisingly critical perspective, whether they be books or letters or sermons, and in these pages to single out for censure what I disapprove of' (trans. by Ramsey 2010: 21). It is not certain

The Wiley Blackwell Companion to Patristics, First Edition. Edited by Ken Parry.
© 2015 John Wiley & Sons Ltd. Published 2019 by John Wiley & Sons Ltd.

which passages he deleted and what words and phrases he inserted from the critical viewpoint of the older Augustine. It appears that Augustine's editorial measures were to leave the published texts untouched and only to add some critical comments in these revisions. The *Revisions* is a collection of his nervous comments and a list of the opening words (*incipits*) of his books. It includes 94 books in order of the dates written, volume 1: from the works after his conversion to Christianity (386) till his ordination as bishop (395/396); volume 2: the works during his bishopric (Madec 1996: 159–165). This means that the author himself guaranteed the authenticity of these titles. This fact has had a unique influence on the reception of Augustine (O'Donnell 1991).

And further, Augustine and his colleagues started to edit the collection of his letters and sermons, but their compilation was not completed. He added the titles to some letters during his revisions of them. For example, thanks to the title "On the coercion against the Heresies [=Donatists]," Epistle 93, one of his longest letters has attracted special attention. To his Epistles 145, 186, 194, and 217 were added titles such as "On Grace," giving an overview of the focus points of the Pelagian controversy, and to some extent they may have been sorted into chronological order. Generally speaking, the preservation of letters depends upon circumstances and which letters should be preserved and which removed, and is solely under the control of the intentions of the preservers or editors of the letter collections. In Augustine's case, his letter collections preserved in his library had been tagged to his books and included as treatises. So we are naturally prompted to read them with reference to Augustine's *Revisions* and Possidius' *Indiculum* (the appendix to Possidius' *Life of Saint Augustine*), but all the other letters he might have written and received have vanished (Allen Neil and Mayer 2009: 122–124).

Concerning Augustine's sermons, scholars have been confronted with the extreme difficulty of their dating (Brown 2000: 447–449; Hombert 2000). Despite these difficulties, F. Dolbeau (1996) effectively used the list of sermons in Possidius' *Indiculum* to specify the genuineness and written order of his newly discovered sermons. In order to build Augustine's original image his close colleague for some 40 years and his biographer Possidius played a crucial role.

Possidius reported: "He made no will, because as a poor man of God he had nothing from which to make it. He repeatedly ordered that the library of the church and all the books should be carefully preserved for future generations" (Possidius, *Life of Saint Augustine* (*Vita Sancti Augustinii*) chap. 31, trans. by H.T. Weiskotten 1918). He reported that Augustine's strong intention was to preserve in his library what he wrote:

> He left ... the library and books containing treatises of his own and of other holy men. By the
> help of God, one may find therein how great he was in the Church and therein the faithful
> may always find them living ... And so many things were dictated and published by him and
> so many things were discussed in the Church, written down and amended, whether against
> various heretics or expounded from the canonical books for the edification of the holy sons
> of the Church, that scarcely any student should be able to read and know them all.

The establishment of Augustine's library must have occurred in the earlier years, when the need to reply to requests from colleagues, friends, and acquaintances who would like to read his books and treatises increased. The library kept the master copy of Augustine's works. The oldest extant manuscript (St. Petersburg Q.v.I.13), with

Augustine's autograph signature at the end, contains four titles: *Ad Simplicianum, Contra epistolam Manichaei quam vocant fundamenti, De agone Chrisiano,* and *De doctrina Christiana* (Weidman 2012: 434). The order of these titles perfectly follows the order listed in the *Revisions* Book II from chapters 1 to 4. It is interesting to note that *De doctrine Christiana* in this manuscript has only the first two books without the latter ones. Augustine completed this part in 426. We can safely conjecture that the master copies of Augustine's books in his library at Hippo were already sorted out before he wrote the *Revisions.*

Possidius was a long-term cooperator in the management of Augustine's library, and he contributed by compiling a catalogue of Augustine's works. He reported:

> However, lest we seem in any way to deprive those who are very eager for the truth of his word, I have determined with the aid of God, to add also an Indiculus [=Indiculum] of these books, homilies and epistles at the end of this little work. When those who love the truth of God more than temporal riches have read this, each may choose for himself what he wishes to read. And in order to copy them let him seek them either from the library of the church of Hippo, where the more perfect copies can probably be found, or search wherever else he can, and when he had found them let him copy and preserve them and also lend them willingly to anyone who wishes to make copies (chap. 18).

The *Indiculus* (*indiculum*) of Possidius enumerated Augustine's books, letters and sermons into the 10 chapters as follows:

[I.] In Answer to The Pagans (23 items); Letters In Answer To The Aforementioned (9 items); Sermons Against The Aforementioned (10 items); [II.] In Answer To The Mathematicians (2 items); [III.] In Answer To The Jews (4 items); [IV.] In Answer To The Manicheans (28 items); Sermons Against The Aforementioned (4 items); [V.] In Answer To The Priscillianists (2 items); [VI.] Against The Donatists (19 items); Letters In Answer To The Aforementioned (18 items); Sermons In Answer To The Donatists (7 items); [VII.] In Answer To The Pelagians (10 items); Letters (2 items); and others (4 items); [VIII.] Against The Arians (6 items); Letters (4 items); Various Sermons Against The Aforementioned Who Contend That The Son Is Unequal To The Father (6 items); [IX.] Against Apollinarians (1 item); [X.] Again, Various Books And Sermons And Letters Composed For The Benefit Of All Those Who Desire To Learn (12 items); [X/2.] (45 items); [X/3.] (30 items); [X/4.] (5 items); [X/5.] Letters (180 items); [X/6.] Various Sermons (202 Items).

And at the end of this catalogue of all the works of Augustine, Possidius concluded:

> Holy bishop Augustine produced books, sermons and letters to the number of one thousand and thirty, apart from those that cannot be numbered because he himself did not give them a number.

All of Augustine's writings are classified according to the order of dates of his writing and topics dealt with in the *Revisions* and *Indiculum.* They have functioned as the completed picture of the jigsaw puzzle whenever we try to construct or reconstruct Augustine's original figure.

Augustine's Reception in the Late Antique and Middle Ages

Beneath the oldest fresco portrait of Augustine from the late sixth century in the Lateran Library, the phrase is added "this father told everything of the Christian mystery in the Roman language" (*Divers idiversa patres s[ed hic] omnia dixit/Romano eloquio mysticas sensatonans*) (Leyser 2012: 451). It appears that Augustine became the Father among Fathers, the outstanding teacher in the Latin West: *Augustinus Magister*. We can possibly assume that the whole corpus of Augustine had been accepted as authoritative in the Roman Pontifical office in the fifth and sixth centuries. But the establishment of his fame as the Father of the Church is one thing; the certainty of what he really read and accepted is another. His voluminous complete works were not always referred to from their original perspective. Rather, they were used from the perspective of the recipients. For example, the Emperor Charlemagne's biographer reports that the emperor's favorite reading was the *City of God*, but it is not certain whether he accepted Augustine's view of history and the notion of the two cities and their destination in the future. As Kent (2012: 227) pointed out: "Most medieval theologians read *City of God* selectively, if at all, Aquinas was no exception." In this respect, as Saak (2012b: 12) has said: "The reception of Augustine, the influence of Augustine, and Augustinianism are three distinct phenomena, even if there are overlaps."

Augustine's works were, first of all, transmitted through the various collections of excerpts (florilegia). Eugippius' collection *Excepta ex operibus s. Augustini* was one of the first and most influential. Eugippius (c. 455–c. 535) has subdivided his florilegia into 348 chapters (CSEL 9/1) or into 352 chapters (PL 62). His extractions from Augustine's writings were spread over some 39 books, 17 letters, and 7 sermons. Eugippius, therefore, would not be able to compile his florilegia without knowing the complete works of Augustine in the Library in Italy. His excerpts are very substantial; sometimes they consist of several continuing pages from the original text with some introductory words, but his choice of passages was highly selective. For example, he cited from the *Confessions* these passages: 1, 1–6 (ch. 8); 10, 8–10 (ch. 5); 10, 35–53 (ch. 5); 10, 66–69 (ch. 6); 11, 29–31; 34–41 (ch. 9); 12, 34–35 (ch 25); 12, 37–43 (ch. 26). He does not include Augustine's autobiographical narratives from Book 1 to Book 9 in the *Confessions*.

He edited them not in accordance with the order in the *Revisions* or the *Indiculum*, but edited them by his own principle. He did so in response to the needs of readers who had difficulty in obtaining the complete works. He also edited a selection of the monastic rules. The rules (CSEL 87) include *Regula Augustini* (*reg.* 1–29: *Ordo monasterii* 30–154, *Praeceptum*) together with excerpts from *Regula magistri* and others (Basil, Pachomius, Cassian, and Jerome). As Fürst pointed out:

> Both Eugippius' genres and the contents of his works were in tune with the general trend of his time. Hardly any original theological schemes were produced: instead, it was the theology of the heyday of the ancient Church that was taken up and passed on, mostly in simplified form and in excerpts (Fürst 2013: 958).

However, the project of making excerpts might have been in accord with Possidius' and Augustine's expectations. Just after he wrote the *Revisions*, Augustine himself edited a book called *Speculum*, which Possidius reported together with the *Revisions*. It is a selection of passages from the Old and New Testaments that concerns the Lord's proscriptions and prohibitions in order to know how one should live.

With regard to the life of Augustine as a monk, Possidius vividly depicted it in his biography of the saint. It is true that Augustine's Monastic Rules were characteristic of the Western tradition, but its outstanding influence only emerged in the thirteenth century, when it was used by the mendicant orders. The Augustinian Order (Ordo Eremitarum Sancti Augustini (O.E.S.A.)) has Augustine as the founder of its spirituality, and other mendicant orders made their rules based upon his. Although they were already present in Eugippius's writings, while Caesarius of Arles (468/470–542) uniquely used them for his sister's monastery in the sixth century, the mainstream of monasticism in the late antique and early medieval West was Benedictine, founded by Benedict of Nursia (480–547). It was highly symbolic that Pope Gregory the Great (590–604), although he was deeply influenced by Augustine in many respects (Markus 1997: 40), sent the Benedictine monk Augustine of Canterbury and his entourage on the mission to England. As Markus points out:

> "Gregory's world had become a Christian world in a manner Augustine could not have imagined. In Augustine's world the question that haunted Christians was 'what is a Christian?', "what is it that distinguished him from his non-Christian fellows?" The society of Augustine's North Africa still contained a complex fabric of intellectual and religious traditions of great diversity. Gregory lived in what was intellectually a far more homogeneous world. Everyone, for practical purposes, was a Christian (Markus 1997: 40).

To be aware of this difference between Augustine's world and Gregory's is extremely important in order for us to understand Augustine's reception and its influence.

Concerning the problem of how to deal with the assets of the church and the private possessions of each clergy and monk, Augustine's sermons 355 and 356 of 426 had a special importance. The old Augustine at the age of 72 requested each of his colleagues who lived with him in his monastery at Hippo to declare their own private property, and if someone kept something secretly he would be solemnly asked to leave the community and renounce his clerical status.

The Semi-Pelagian controversy contributed to another characteristic stream of Augustine's reception. The controversy emerged in the latter days of Augustine's life, and he himself was involved in it. He wrote letters and treatises on the subject in his last years and these writings were read intensively. This is the starting point for establishing Augustine's authority as the "doctor of grace." Prosper of Aquitaine (390–455) took over Augustine's position against the so-called Semi-Pelagian tendency. The controversy continued for a century after Augustine's death till the decision of the Council of Orange in 529 when the victory of the Augustinian position was finally settled. Caesarius of Arles took an important role in it, and he was famous for simplifying the sermons of Augustine. Among his 238 sermons (CCSL 103, 104) about 30 were titled under the name of Augustine and some others were more or less based upon his sermons. He shortened, simplified and adapted them for his own pastoral purposes. Throughout the Semi-Pelagian controversy, Augustine's claim for the absolute priority of divine grace shaped so-called Augustinianism and seemed to be received with unshakable authority. But Benedict, the founder of Western monasticism, who had been strongly influenced by John Cassian, was the mentor to the anti-Augustine side in this controversy. The final decision of the Council of Orange (*Conclusio*, DS 136–137), at which Caesarius presided, clearly rejected the doctrine of predestination and advocated that of human cooperation. It is paradoxical that the victory of Augustine's position had come to be preserved beyond his expectation. So-called "Augustinianism" is a useful but vague term of labeling, and as Pollmann has pointed out, Augustine's authority is "protean authority" (Otten 2012: 204; Pollmann 2013a).

A fuller investigation of Augustine's reception in Peter Lombard (c. 1096–1164) deserves to be made. His four books of *Sententiae* was a common textbook at theological faculties in medieval universities, and lecturers were expected to make a commentary. Thousands of these commentaries were produced, with Thomas Aquinas, Bonaventure, Duns Scotus, and Martin Luther being no exception. According to Bourgerol, among the 680 passages quoted by Lombard from Augustine, he knows only four works directly: *De doctrina Christiana* (63 times), *Enchiridion* (117 times), *De diversis quaestionibus LXXXIII* (30 times), and *Retractationes* (32 times). Lombard mentions many passages in *De Genesi ad litteram* (129 times) and *De trinitate* (310 times), but they were taken from either the *Glossa ordinaria* or *Expositio* of Florus of Lyons (ninth century) (Bourgerol 1997: 115). It is to be noted that the basic structure of his four books of *Sententiae* is composed of the first division (Bk. 1–3) on the "thing" (*res*), and the second division (Bk. 4) on the "sign" (*signum*) – that is, following the structure of *De Docrina Christiana* – and he uses the framework of Augustine's "using" (*uti*) and "enjoying" (*frui*). However, it is not certain whether Lombard had a systematic understanding of his thought based upon a comprehensive reading of Augustine's texts in their original contexts. Most of the theologians of the Middle Ages who made commentaries on Lombard's *Sententiae* did not try to consult Augustine's original texts.

In this respect Possidius' prediction that one will scarcely be able to read all of Augustine's works was right. Augustine was received on demand in the life and thought of later generations. The Augustinian tradition in monasticism and its development in the middle and late medieval periods is one of the outstanding receptions of Augustine in response to the urgent demand of medieval Europe.

Reception of Augustine in the Modern Period

The situation of Augustine's reception changed dramatically in the late medieval and early modern period. It is needless to say that Augustine's influence on Luther and Calvin was considerable. The revolution of printing after Gutenberg's Bible appeared prompted the Protestant Reformation and the spread of classical and patristic literature. The theologians in this period came to have the printed *Opera omnia Sancti Augustini* in their hands and possibly read through it, since the first printed *opera omnia* published by Amerbach in 1506. This new dimension to Augustine's reception occurred in this period.

At the same time, a keen interest in listening to Augustine's individual inner voice emerged and developed. It is no coincidence that the interest in the autobiographical parts of the *Confessions* now became one of the characteristic features of Augustine's reception. It is notable that Petrarch (1304–1374) read Augustine's *Soliloquy* and the *Confessions* and wrote in the same genre of literature (Lee 2012). It was the beginning of a new era, with the Renaissance itself being in a sense the renaissance of Augustine. We may say that it was not necessarily the influence of Augustine himself, but more a discovery or invention of Augustine. His reception spread beyond the limits of universities and religious orders to the spirituality of lay people. People liked to read Augustine's books selectively with their own interests in mind and to depict their own image of him. It was a very modern tendency.

Apart from paying attention to the activities and contributions of the Augustinian order (Saak 2012b), one of the most remarkable phenomena of the time was the cultivation and emphasis on lay spirituality. The *Devotio moderna* was just one aspect among various types of devotion that emerged. A central image of this spirituality was the iconography of the heart. As the emblem of the Augustinian order symbolically shows, an iconography of Augustine with the flaming heart pierced with an arrow became popular. This trend was reinforced in the seventeenth century with the emergence of the devotion to the sacred heart of Jesus. Ted Campbell has characterized the spirituality of this age as "religion of the heart" (Campbell 2000). It became an attribute of Augustine (Madec 1998: 1), and was closely related to his narrative in the *Confessions* 9.2.3, "Thou hadst pierced our hearts with Thy charity, and we carried Thy words as it were fixed in our entrails"; and 10.6.8, "Thou hast stricken my heart with Thy word, and I loved Thee."

The seventeen century is called "the age of Augustine." The case of Cornelius Jansen (1585–1638), who claimed that he had read the whole of Augustine's works through about 10 times and his anti-Pelagain treatises more than 40 times, is significant. How to understand Augustine became the focus of the modern debate on the nature of divine grace and human free will. Turning to the subject of patristics, historians and scholars showed a renewed interest in studying Augustine in his historical context.

When Louis Sebastien Le Nain De Tillemont (1637–1698) wrote a close historical study of Augustine's life (Van Fleteren 2012), Augustine's own description of his life and works in the *Confessions* and *Revisions*, and Possidius' *Vita St. Augustini* and his *Indiculum*, became all the more important. He divided his life of Augustine into three parts: (1) Anti-Manichean period (354–396), (2) Anti-Donatist period (396–411), and (3) Anti-Pelagian period (411–430). In viewing Augustine's work in chronological order, modern and contemporary Augustinian students have investigated his life and thought by dividing it into three or more of his life stages: (1) early years before conversion (386) and baptism (387) (the so-called young Augustine); (2) between baptism and ordination to presbyter (391) and to bishop (395/396); (3) the earlier part of his bishopric (396–411), and the later part (411–430). It is no coincidence that these divisions are almost the same as the chapters in Possidius' *Indiculum*. Naturally,

Possidius' claim that "scarcely any student should be able to read and know them all" was still true. Assuming that people were already familiar with Augustine's *Confessions*, Adolf von Harnack (1922) compiled a book of excerpts under the title of *Augustin Reflexionen und Maximen* with a view to understanding him systematically, and Erich Przywara (1936) edited another collection of excerpts *An Augustine Synthesis*. They were in response to the need of popular readers and students of theology at that time. Such a reception of Augustine might have some remote resonance with Euggipius and Peter Lombard.

While some scholars have tried to show how the precise image of Augustine changes alongside his response to the circumstances of his age (Brown 2000; Lancel 2000), others have tried to discuss his thought in terms of continuity (Harrison 2006; Martin and Fitzgerald 2010). Despite the various tendencies in the reception history of Augustine down the ages, concentrated efforts to understand him in the context of his life and writings have been made. It is difficult to discern whether or not this is owing to the special tendency of the modern mind based upon the historical–critical method. It might be an invitation that Augustine himself made when he left his library. Anyway, it was Possidius who claimed "Augustine is still alive in his writings." Trying to approach an unwritten "real" Augustine seems impossible and beyond the scope of patristics at least.

Augustine's Reception in China: The Case of Matteo Ricci's Mission

The Italian Jesuit Matteo Ricci (1552–1610) was assigned to the China mission in the late Ming period in 1582 by Alessandro Valignano (1539–1606), who was to direct the affairs of the Society of Jesus in India, Japan, and China.

The encounter of Christianity with the traditional religious cultures of East Asia (China, Korea, and Japan) in the sixteenth and seventeenth centuries and its development offers some interesting material regarding the reception of Augustine and the Fathers in general. It is noticeable that Augustine was introduced to the Japanese through translations of the highly intellectual and spiritual writings of European Christians of the time: Luis de Granada's *La Guía de Pecatores* (*The Guide for Sinners*) and Thomas à Kempis' *Contemptus Mundi* (*De Imitatione Christi*) were the most popular and representative. They were translated with the cooperation of European and Japanese Jesuits and laymen.

So the initial reception of Augustine in Japanese reveals strong connections with the contemporary reception of Augustine in Europe: the interest in Augustine's life story from sinner to saint and his philosophical search for the wisdom of God. These points are also clearly seen in Matteo Ricci's *The True Meaning of the Lord of Heaven* (*T'ien-chu Shih-i*). This book is written in the form of a dialogue between a Western scholar and a Chinese scholar in order to show the impossibility of knowing the true essence of God. Ricci (Ri Ma-dou) begins his narrative as follows:

> Formerly there was also a sage of the West called Augustine who wanted to understand completely the truth about the Lord of Heaven so that he could write a book about it.

One day he went for a walk beside the sea, and was just searching in his mind for this truth when he suddenly saw a child digging the ground to make a small pool and using a shell to scoop up sea water to fill his pool (Ch. 1: 90–93).

This episode of Augustine and the boy on the shore is found not in Augustine's works or Possidius' *Vita*, but in the *Golden Legend* by Jacobus de Voragine (d. 1298) from the late thirteenth century. Ricci cited this episode not in order to relinquish intellectual enquiry concerning the existence of the Lord of Heaven, but to emphasize that his supreme greatness lay beyond human understanding and that this had attracted Western intellectuals. In another passage, where Ricci apparently has in mind the opening passage of Augustine's *Confessions* (1.1.1.) but without referring to him by name, he writes:

> The Western sage of ancient times [Augustine], understood this truth and, therefore, looking up to Heaven he sighed and said: "Supreme Ruler of all men, you have produced us men for yourself, and only you can satisfy our minds. When man does not turn to you, his mind cannot be at peace and be satisfied!" (Ch. 3: 159, 165)

This allusion to the *Confessions* represents the intention of the book and functions as a leitmotiv which is reinforced throughout the work. For example, at Part 1, 19 the Chinese philosopher agrees: "As I listened to you I saw the great Way for the first time and returned to the Supreme Source of all phenomena"; and at Part 2, 33, he comes to confess: "I am ashamed that we Confucian scholars have not been able to see clearly the important matters in life. We have investigated other things in detail, and have been unaware of the learning which leads us to return to the Supreme Source" (不知帰元之学). He says to the Western philosopher, "People who do not accept the musings of the Buddhists and Taoists drift through this world like sheep without a shepherd ... I now know that human beings have a real home, and I should like to learn of the path which leads to that home" (Part 6, 51). Finally, at the end of the whole volume, he says:

> As I silently think things over I find myself experiencing both great joy and a deep feeling of sorrow. ... I hope I can hear everything about this true doctrine concerning man's return to his source! ... so that every person will chant them, and so that everyone will cultivate goodness and cease to do evil. The contribution this would make to the general welfare of mankind would be so great as to be beyond calculation!

The dialogue form of *The True Meaning of the Lord of Heaven* has the Western philosopher refuting the Buddhist claim for the voidness of the universe and the migration of the soul, and the Taoist claim for the generation of the world from original chaos. With his religious background, the Chinese philosopher had a theory of the principles such as理 (Li) "intrinsic order" and 気 (Qi) "vital energy," and was able to explain the universe and human life metaphysically as well. The Western philosopher (Ricci himself) had to persuade the Chinese philosopher to admit the existence of the Creator (the Lord of Heaven), the immortality of soul and the Last Judgment. The dialogue is to some extent written in the form of a catechism. However, it does not deal with the whole creed of the Council of Trent, but is based more on the assumptions of monotheist religion. Ricci's arguments have a background not only in Aristotelian–Thomistic philosophy and theology, but also in the Italian humanism of the sixteenth century. The Western philosopher discovered in the Chinese philosopher, and in the Asian religious traditions, the spontaneous search for the original source and the whole-hearted wish to return to it. Of course, this Chinese philosopher was an imaginary or ideal figure that Ricci invented for his catechetical dialogue. In reality, such an argument was not necessarily accepted by Chinese intellectuals at that time or later on. Yet it became the focus of public attention and generated a fierce debate. Copies of *The True Meaning of the Lord of Heaven* were imported into Korea and Japan and widely read (Shibata 2004: 330–337). The earliest evidence for its impact was recorded in a debate between a Japanese Neo-Confucian philosopher and a Jesuit immediately after the publication in 1604.

We can conclude that Augustine's philosophical way of thinking in the search for the fundamental and transcendent source had a great influence on the spread of Christianity in East Asia. It is not clear that it was part of the preparation for evangelization that Valignano and others had in mind, but it was surely in accord with the Jesuit policy of making useful adaptations. Ricci himself found the moral and intellectual principles of Chinese Confucianism were not so remote from his own background in Renaissance Neo-Platonism. In this context, Augustine was a very fitting figure.

Augustine's Reception in Japan

The importance of Augustine's approach towards God can be found in the Jesuit missionary experience in Japan just prior to Ricci's mission to China. About a half century passed before Francis Xavier (1506–1552), one of the founding members of the Society of Jesus, first came to Japan carrying the message of Christianity. It was Valignano (1539–1606), as the successor to Xavier, who was responsible for the mission to East Asia, and who noticed the strong intellectual interest the Japanese people had and observed that the Japanese will "form the conviction through reason (convencidos de la razón) and be led by their own free will to convert to Christianity" (Orii 2010: 102). A detailed description of the first century of Christianity in Japan (1549–1650) must be left for another occasion, but for now we will concentrate on what the Jesuit missionaries considered was the central message of Christianity and how it would be possible to teach it to people from very different cultural backgrounds. I will argue that Augustine emerged as a leading figure in this enterprise.

Looking at these years in Japan we can see an increase in Christian converts that is quite remarkable. From 1590, when a printing press was brought from Europe to Japan and installed in a Jesuit seminary, until the final banishment in 1614, when Japanese Christians and European missionaries were expelled by a strict governmental decree, various kinds of books were being published in succession. Before the publishing of Christian books was abruptly and totally prohibited, about 100 titles were printed in this period and 45 of them at the most are extant. For European priests and monks, translating Christian books into Japanese had been the backbone of their mission.

This was true not only in relation to educating Japanese priests, but also in response to requests from congregations and general readers. One remarkable fact was that the moral asceticism of the *devotion moderna* expressed in Thomas à Kempis' *De imitatione Christi* attracted a great following in Japan. The *De imitatione Christi* was translated and published not only by the Jesuit seminary, but also by a Japanese publisher in Kyoto, and the texts were copied by hand many times. So we can see a kind of globalization in the fact that this kind of spirituality was flourishing across cultures and continents.

The Jesuits' plans for publishing were carefully considered and highly selective. For their purposes, Luis de Granada's books of catechetical introduction and Christian ethics were singled out to be published as a priority.

As mentioned already, Luis was one of the most popular and influential theologians and preachers advocating ascetic discipline at the time. His books were widely read, with St Theresa of Avila (1515–1582) being one of his admirers. His theological position embodied the spirit of the generation of the Council of Trent (1545–1563). His thought has sometimes been evaluated as syncretic, but his vast volume of writings and his active engagement with the world show that he was a representative figure of the sixteenth century (Huerga 1988; Orii 2010: 20).

Among the many volumes of Luis' publications, *The Book of Prayer and Meditation* (1554) and *The Guide for Sinners* (second edition 1567) were widely read and spread beyond Europe to Brazil, India, the Philippines, and Japan. *The Guide* was translated into Japanese and published in 1599. As its title suggests, this book was written with the thoughtful intention of leading people to virtue. In the original text, Augustine has the most citations from patristic literature, with Dionysius the Areopagite and Gregory the Great in second and third places. Augustine was cited 38 times, and one-third of them were from the *Confessions* (*Conf.* 10.6.8 (*Guide* vol. 1.Part. 1.Chap. 1); 10.6.9 (1.1.2); 1.20.31 (1.1.5); 10.27.38 (1.2.4); 8.5.10 (1.2.7); 8.5.12 (2.1.1); 13.31.46 (2.1.4); 8.11.25-27 (2.1.4); 1.1.1. (2.1.5); 1.1.1. (2.1.5). Sometimes he introduces actual passages from Augustine's writings: "St. Augustine by his own *Confessions*, had sufficient experience of this, for he says..."; or "St. Augustine tells us, it was thus he answered God before his conversion ..." All such passages from Augustine's *Confessions* were carefully translated into Japanese, and they were able to convey his original nuanced understanding for readers from quite different cultural backgrounds. For example, the passages from Augustine's *Confessions* Book 8 (8.11, 25–27) were amply cited: "St. Augustine in the eighth book of his *Confessions*, tells us, that ..." These depicted his inner struggle between the spirit and the flesh just before his conversion, which in Japanese translation conveyed his reflections on the merit of human effort and the acceptance of absolute grace. The translation focused on the contrast between "the salvation by his own efforts (*ji-riki*)" and "salvation by the absolute power of the Other (*ta-riki*)" (Orii 2010: 138–148).

It is important to note that the detailed arguments for divine grace and human free will and Augustine's theory of predestination that introduced Luis' book (*Guide* 1.1.6) were carefully omitted in the Japanese translation. It was no coincidence that the theological debate between the Jesuit Luis de Molina (1535–1600) and the Dominican Domingo Bañes (1528–1604) had just started in 1581. Valignano carefully avoided getting involved in the delicate issues of this debate (Orii 2010: 142). As a result,

Augustine as the "doctor of grace" was not the main focus of his reception; rather, the image of the inner searcher for God was promoted all the more strongly. *The Guide* mentioned Augustine's episode with the child on the shore and concluded:

> If there are so many reasons, so many examples, and so many experiments, to prove that the happiness and safety we look for in the world, is to be found nowhere but in God: why do we not seek for it in him? It is what St. Augustine advised in these words; "Compare the sea and earth, and go where you please; but assure yourself, that wheresoever you go, you will be miserable, if you do no go to God." (*Guide* 1.1.5)

These citations found in Luis's book must have been read by many Japanese, but we have no evidence of a Japanese translation of Augustine's complete *Confessions*, nor of any Japanese essay focusing on his thought at that time. His direct influence on Japanese Christians has not been investigated. However, a newly discovered Japanese translation of Luis de Granada's *Introduction to the Symbol of the Faith Part I* named *Fides no kyo* (1611) has a special modified passage that was added to the original chapter 34 by an anonymous Japanese (?) translator (Orii 2011). This passage, divided into eight articles, explained more philosophically in detail the intellectual soul and its functions than the original version. Based upon Aristotelian explanations of the various functions of the human soul, it paid special attention to the activity of the will as the intellectual appetite, specially citing Augustine's famous phrase in the *Confessions*, "*amor meus pondus meum, illo fereo quo cumque feror*" ("My love is my weight: wherever I am carried with the love, I am carried") (13.9.10). Here, we can infer that the translator was familiar with Augustine's thought and had used his own initiative in presenting the argument.

We find interesting evidence that a passage from the *Confessions* 1.1.1 played a leading role: "When man does not turn to you, his mind cannot be at peace and be satisfied!" In the Jesuit seminary a new compendium of lectures was introduced for the Japanese novices to understand the European view of human beings and the universe based upon Aristotle's philosophy. The original texts were written in Latin (1593) by a Spanish Jesuit Pedro Gomez (1535–1600) and were translated into Japanese (1595). When we compare these two versions, the Japanese version added a special chapter demonstrating the immortality of the rational soul (Ohara 1997: 210–234). Generally speaking, the arguments were based upon Aristotelian–Scholastic philosophy, but they demonstrated the immortality of the soul by showing repeatedly that the soul's desire to know the truth will not be satisfied until we see God in the future, just like the ultimate beatitude we all wish to attain. And referring to Augustine's phrase *varitas immortalis est* ("the truth is nothing but the immortal truth," *Expositions of the Psalms* 123.2) (Ohara 1997: 219), the arguments emphasized that the ultimate human wish is to know this truth and love the supreme goodness. It concludes by saying that if the rational soul is restless when it is in the sensible world then its ultimate rest lies in another world. I do not think any of these arguments would have come to the mind of the author had he not known Augustine's *Confessions*.

In conclusion, we may say that Augustine was viewed by Japanese intellectuals as someone who had a keen spiritual concern for the individual self and for true peace. Etienne Gilson claimed that Augustine was a true philosopher and that: "There is no Augustinism without the fundamental postulate that true philosophy implies an act of adherence to the supernatural order which frees the will from the flesh through grace and the mind from scepticism through revelation" (Gilson 1959: 235). If this is so, then the Japanese and Chinese reception of Augustine is a reflection of this sentiment.

One great difficulty in dealing with the reception and influence of Christianity in early modern Japan lies in the historical fact that government suppression was extraordinary harsh and cruel after 1636. The translations of Augustine's original texts are now being realized after an interruption of 400 years. The 30 volumes of the Japanese translation of the complete works of Augustine are being published (Toda, forthcoming), and the complete books of the *Confessions* have been published more than five times. The secret of such contemporary interest in and affinity with Augustine can already be discerned in the Japanese reception of him in the early modern period.

Conclusion

It remains true that Augustine of Hippo teaches "everything" of Christianity and that his reception and influence has been and still is extremely great in the West. A well-balanced and comprehensive encyclopedia devoted solely to Augustine was published in English recently (Fitzgerald, 1999), and this was followed in 2013 by a pioneering three-volume work on the historical reception of Augustine (Pollmann 2013b). It is no exaggeration to say that almost everything that can be said about Augustine has been said at one time or another, but the reception and effectiveness of Augustine in the multicultural environment of East Asia has not always been recognized. Perhaps by acknowledging this gap in the reception history of Augustine there is room for a future study on this neglected topic.

Bibliography

Abbreviations

CSEL Knöll, P. (ed.) (1885), *Eugippii Excerpta ex operibus s. Augustini*, Corpus Scriptorum Ecclesasticorum Latinorum 9/1. Vienna: F. Tempsky.

VillegasF. and de Vogue, A. (eds) (1976), *Eugippii Regula*, Corpus Scriptorum Ecclesasticorum Latinorum 87. Vienna: Verlag der Österreichischen Akademie der Wissenschaften.

CCSL Morin, D. Germani (ed.) (1953), *Sermones Sancti Caesarii Arelatensis*, Corpus Christianorum Series Latina, 103, 104. Turnhout: Brepols.

DS H.J. Denzinger and A. Schönmetzer, (ed.) (1976), *Enchiridion Symbolorum et Definitionum*, 36th Ed. Barcelona: Herder.

PL Migne J. P. (ed.) (1863), *Eugyppii Abbatis Africani Thesaurus ex S. Augustini operibus*, Patrologia: Latina 62.

Primary Sources

Luis de Granada (1995[1567]), Guia de
Pecadores, in *Obras Completas* VI. Madrid:
Domicos de Andalucia.
Luis de Granada (1996[1584]), Introducción
del Simbolo de la Fe I, in *Obras Completas* IX.
Madrid: Domicos de Andalucia.
Matteo Ricci (Ri Ma-dou) (1983), *The True
Meaning of the Lord of Heaven*, translated,
with Introduction and Notes by Douglas
Lancashire and Peter Hu Kuo-chen,
S.J. Varétés Sinologiques N.S. 72. Taipei:
Kuangchi Press.
Ramsey, B. (transl.) (2010), *Augustine, Revisions,
The Works of Saint Augustine: A Translation
for the 21st Century*. Hyde Park: New City
Press.

Secondary Sources

Allen, P., Neil, B., and Mayer, W. (eds) (2009),
*Preaching Poverty in Late Antiquity: Perceptions
and Realities.* Leipzig: Evangeische Verlaganstalt.
Bachus, I. (ed.) (1997), *The Reception of the
Church Fathers in the West*. Brill: Leiden.
Bougerol, J.-G. (1997), "The Church Fathers
and the Sententiae of Peter Lombard". In
Bachus (1997: 113–164).
Brown, P. (2000), *Augustine of Hippo: A
Biography*, revised edition. London: Faber &
Faber.
Campbell, T. (2000), *The Religion of the Heart: A
Study of European Religious Life in the
Seventeenth and Eighteenth Centuries*. Eugene,
OR: Wipf and Stock Publishers.
Dolbeau, F. (ed.) (1996), *Augustin d'Hippone
Vingt-six Sermons au Peupled 'Afrique*. Paris:
Institut d'Études Augustinniennes.
Fitzgerald, A. (ed.) (1999), *Augustine through
the Ages: An Encyclopedia*. Michigan: W.B.
Eerdmans Publishing.
Fürst, A. (2013), "Eugippius". In Pollmann
(2013b: 954–959).
Gilson, E. (1959), *The Christian Philosophy of
Saint Augustine*. New York: Random House.
Harrison, C. (2006), *Rethinking Augustine's
Early Theology: An Argument for Continuity*.
Oxford: Oxford University Press.
Hombert, P.-M. (2000), *Nouvelles Recherches de
Chronologie Augustinienne*. Paris: Institut
d'Études Augustinniennes.
Huerga, A. (1988), *Fray Luis de Granada: Una
Vida al Servicio de la Iglesia*. Madrid: Editorial
Catolica.

Kent, B. (2012), "Reinventing Augustine's ethics:
the afterlife of *City of God*". In Wetzel (2012).
Lancel, S. (2002), *Saint Augustine*, A. Nevill
(transl.). London: SCM Press.
Lee, A. (2012), *Petrarch and St. Augustine:
Classical Scholarship, Christian Theology and
the Origins of the Renaissance in Italy*. Leiden:
Brill
Leyser, C. (2012), "Augustine in the Latin
West, 430–ca.900". In Vessey (2012:
450–464).
Madec, G. (1996), *Introduction aux Révisions et
à la lecture des oeuvres de Saint Augustin*. Paris:
Institut d'Études Augustinniennes.
Madec, G. (1998), "Cor". In *Augustinus Lexikon*,
Cornelius Mayer (ed.). Basel: Schwabe.
Markus, R.A. (1997), *Gregory the Great and his
World*. Cambridge: Cambridge University
Press.
Martin, T.F., and Fitzgerald, A.D. (2010),
*Augustine of Hippo: Faithful Servant, Spiritual
Leader.* Upper Saddle River, NJ: Prentice Hall.
O'Donnell, J.J. (1991), "The Authority of
Augustine". *Aug Stu*, 22: 7–35.
Ohara, S. (ed.) (1997), *The Compendium of the
Jesuit College in Japan I*. Tokyo: Kyo bun kwan.
Orii, Y. (2010), *A Comparative Studies in Japanese
and European Culture in the Ki-ri-shi-tan
Literature: Luis de Granada and Japan*. Tokyo:
Kyo bun kwan (in Japanese).
Orii, Y. (ed.) (2011), *Fides no Kyo*, with notes.
Tokyo: Kyo bun kwan.
Otten, W. (2012), "Between praise and
appraisal: medieval guidelines for the

assessment of Augustine's intellectual legacy". *Aug Stu*, 43.1/2: 201–218

Pollmann, K. (2013a), "The proteanism of authority: the reception of Augustine in cultural history from his death to the present". In Pollmann (2013b: 3–16).

Pollmann, K. (ed.) (2013b), *The Oxford Guide to the Historical Reception of Augustine.* Oxford: Oxford University Press.

Przywara, E. (1936), *An Augustine Synthesis/ Arranged by Erich Przywara*; introduction by C.C. Martindale. London: Sheed & Ward.

Saak, E.L. (2012a), "Augustine in the Western Middle Ages to the Reformation". In Vessey (2012: 465–477).

Saak, E.L. (2012b), *Creating Augustine: Interpreting Augustine and Augustinanism in the Later Middle Ages.* Oxford: Oxford University Press.

Shibata, A. (2004), *Tenshu Jitsugi (The Complete Translation of T'ien-chu Shih-I with the Introduction and Notes)*. Tokyo: Hei-bon-sha.

Toda, S. (forthcoming), "Patristic studies in Japan". *Patristic Studies in the Twenty-first Century*, Proceedings of an International Conference to Mark the 50th Anniversary of AIEP/IAPS, Turnhout: Brepols.

Van Fleteren, F. (transl.) (2012), Le Nain De Tillemont, Louis Sébastien, *The Life of Augustine of Hippo. Part Two: The Donatist Controversy (396–411)*. Mémoire ecclésiastique, volume XIII. New York: Peter Lang.

Von Harnack, A. (1922), *Augustin: Reflexionen und Maximen/ausseinen Werkengesammelt und übersetzt von Adolf von Harnack.* Tübingen: J.C.B. Mohr (Paul Siebeck).

Vessey, M. (2012), *A Companion of Augustine.* Oxford: Wiley–Blackwell.

Weidmann, C. (2012), "Augustine's works in circulation". In Vessey (2012: 431–449).

Wetzel, J. (ed.) (2012), *Augustine's City of God: A Critical Guide.* Cambridge: Cambridge University Press; 225–244.

CHAPTER 11

Cyril of Alexandria

Hans van Loon

Introduction

Cyril of Alexandria (c. 378–444) succeeded his uncle Theophilus as archbishop of Alexandria in 412, and he occupied this see till his death. According to the church historian Socrates, the first 3 years of his episcopate were volatile. The archdeacon Timothy was also a candidate for the bishopric, and Cyril was elected in a riotous atmosphere. The relationships with the Jews were tense, and 2 years after his consecration the Jews lured Christians into an ambush and murdered a number of them, after which Cyril expelled the majority of the Jews out of Alexandria. And in 415 the pagan philosopher Hypatia was brutally murdered by a mob of Christians. After that, it was quiet until the Nestorian controversy broke out.

Cyril is especially known because of the Christological conflict with Nestorius. When we view his literary output, however, he was first and foremost a biblical commentator. In Migne's *Patrologia Graeca*, 10 volumes are devoted to Cyril of Alexandria (vols 68–77), seven of which contain commentaries, four on Old Testament books and three on New Testament writings. Moreover, from a number of his commentaries we only have fragments, so that Cyril's original output in this genre was even larger. One volume contains letters, festal letters, and homilies, while Christological and Trinitarian writings fill up the two remaining volumes.

Christological Controversies

Soon after Nestorius had been consecrated archbishop of Constantinople in 428, he took sides with those who rejected the title θεοτόκος ("Mother of God") for Mary, the mother of Jesus, and he started to disseminate sermons and other writings on the subject.

The Wiley Blackwell Companion to Patristics, First Edition. Edited by Ken Parry.
© 2015 John Wiley & Sons Ltd. Published 2019 by John Wiley & Sons Ltd.

When these reached the monks of Egypt, Cyril responded to what in his eyes was a heretical Christology, according to which Christ was divided into two sons, the divine Word and the man Jesus. When both church leaders corresponded with other bishops about the controversy and unrest spread, the emperor Theodosius II (408–450) convened a council, to be held in Ephesus in 431. Celestine, archbishop of Rome (422–432), gave Cyril a mandate to act on his behalf.

When John of Antioch (429–441) and the oriental bishops, many of whom were favorable towards Nestorius, were 2 weeks late in arriving due to difficult traveling conditions, Cyril opened the council in their absence. Nestorius's teaching was condemned and Cyril's *Second Letter to Nestorius* canonized. When John of Antioch arrived and learnt that the council had already come to a decision without him, he set up his own council ("conciliabulum") and excommunicated Cyril. The emperor tried to settle the matter and summoned a delegation from each party to Chalcedon, but without the desired result. Cyril and John returned to their cities, whereas Nestorius was sent into exile.

Theodosius II continued to urge the church leaders to come to a settlement. In the course of the negotiations Cyril sent "presents" to the emperor's entourage, which have added to his reputation of being a power-hungry individual. Although bribery was quite common at the time, the scale of Cyril's donations was extraordinary. It is likely, however, that his zeal for the orthodox faith and his concern for the faithful were as much, if not more, responsible for such questionable actions than hunger for power. In 433, John of Antioch and Cyril of Alexandria came to an agreement on Christology, known as the Formula of Reunion.

After Cyril's death, the Christological debate flared up once more, when the aged monk Eutyches (c. 378–454) stressed the unity of Christ to such an extent that he appeared to deny the remaining difference between Christ's divine and human natures. To settle this dispute, the new imperial couple, Marcian and Pulcheria, summoned the bishops to attend a council at Chalcedon in 451. The council condemned both Nestorius and Eutyches, and declared in its "definition" that Christ is "known in two natures," which "come together in one person and one hypostasis."

Older historians of theology, like von Harnack and Seeberg, have interpreted the council of Chalcedon as a victory of pope Leo of Rome and the Antiochenes over Cyril and the Alexandrians. Newer research, since the 1500th anniversary of the council in 1951, however, has shown that the definition is fundamentally a declaration of faith from a Cyrillian perspective, to which a few clauses have been added to satisfy the wish of the Roman delegates and the imperial commissioners that Leo's *Tomus*, his letter to Flavian of Constantinople, should be taken into account (de Halleux 1976). And even one of these added clauses is an almost verbatim quotation from Cyril's *Second Letter to Nestorius*. Since the definition of Chalcedon has officially been accepted by the Roman Catholic Church, the Eastern Orthodox Church, and the major Protestant churches, through this definition Cyril of Alexandria has influenced the Christology of the majority of Christendom through the ages.

It is a long-standing myth that Cyril would have favored the μία φύσις formula, "one incarnate nature of the Word of God," over two-nature language. In fact, he rarely used the formula before the reunion with John of Antioch in 433, and when he did, the main reason for using it was that he had found the formula in a letter which he thought had been written by his revered predecessor Athanasius. One-nature language can mainly be found in a number of letters that Cyril wrote in the period 433–435, because others who favored the formula had accused him of giving in to the Antiochenes when he accepted the Formula of Reunion (van Loon 2009: 518–530). In his Christological writings before the reunion, two-nature language abounds.

The Reception of Chalcedon

In the reception of the council of Chalcedon, Cyril of Alexandria played a major role. Among those who accepted the council's definition, a distinction into "strict Chalcedonians" and "neo-Chalcedonians" was introduced by historical theologians in the twentieth century. The definition of these groups and even the validity of the distinction has been hotly debated (Helmer 1962). In general, one may say that the strict Chalcedonians adhered to the definition without taking into account further Christological notions from Cyril's writings, whereas the neo-Chalcedonians combined the definition with the broader framework of Cyril's Christology.

Probably the most important Cyrillian notion that was added is what has been called his "intuition." The definition of Chalcedon is rather symmetric, in the sense that the divinity and the humanity of Christ are placed side by side as if they are of equal stature. And the one hypostasis is only mentioned as the result of the union of both natures. There is in the definition no reference to the hypostasis of the Son of God which, according to Trinitarian theology, he had before the incarnation. G. Jouassard (1953) wrote an influential article in which he spoke of Cyril's "fundamental intuition" that Christ's divinity is primordial, while his humanity is added. The result is a more asymmetrical understanding of the relationship between the two natures of Christ. It also does more justice to the narrative form of the Gospels: Christ is not just described in the static terms of a relationship between natures, but as the movement of the incarnation. It is this intuition and asymmetry that neo-Chalcedonians, basing themselves on Cyril, added to the Christology of Chalcedon.

Of course, there were also those who rejected the two-nature language of the council of Chalcedon and who championed the μία φύσις formula. The traditional epithet "Monophysites" for this group was originally a polemical title introduced by their opponents. They themselves never accepted the name, because μόνη φύσις could suggest a Eutychian understanding, in which Christ's humanity was as it were swallowed up by his divinity. Their "one nature" was, however, a synthesis of humanity and divinity. Therefore, the name Miaphysites is to be preferred. The Miaphysites saw themselves as the rightful heirs of Cyril of Alexandria.

Since both the neo-Chalcedonians and the Miaphysites based themselves on Cyril, a struggle over the right interpretation of his writings ensued. During the controversy, the patristic argument in general, in which earlier Church Fathers were cited as authorities, gained in importance. Florilegia with quotations from various Fathers, including Cyril, were used as instruments for underpinning one's position. In the second half of the fifth century, a special *Florilegium Cyrillianum* was compiled in Alexandria, to which various people at different times contributed (Hespel 1955). It contains 244 passages from about 30 of Cyril's writings, and it intended to show that the archbishop of Alexandria, like the council of Chalcedon, taught that there are two natures in Christ after the union of the Word with his flesh. This florilegium found its way to Constantinople, where the Miaphysite theologian Severus, later patriarch of Antioch, encountered it during his stay in the imperial city from 508 till 511. In response, Severus wrote a work, called the *Philaletes*, in which he wanted to refute the claim that Cyril spoke of two natures after the union. There are indications that there existed a second Cyrillian florilegium in the first half of the sixth century.

It was also at that time that neo-Chalcedonian theology combined Cyril's intuition with Chalcedon's "in two natures" and "into one person and one hypostasis." A key player in this was Leontius of Jerusalem (*fl.* c. 540), who equated the hypostasis of the definition of Chalcedon with that of the Son of God in Trinitarian theology, and who used the notion of enhypostasia for the relationship between Christ's human nature and his hypostasis. Before the incarnation the Word had his own hypostasis, which contained his divine nature. When the Word became man, the human nature was added, so that the divine hypostasis of the Word now contains two natures, the divine and the human natures of Christ. In general, one can say that every nature needs to be in a hypostasis if it is to exist in reality. In ordinary human beings each individual has his human nature in his own (human) hypostasis. Christ's human nature, however, does not have its own (human) hypostasis, but it exists in the divine hypostasis of the Word. It is "enhypostasized" in the hypostasis of the Word. In this way the neo-Chalcedonian Leontius worked out Cyril's intuition into a metaphysical conception. In doing so, he changed the meaning of the word "hypostasis" and of the expression "union according to hypostasis" (ἕνωσις καθ' ὑπόστασιν). In Cyril's writings, "hypostasis" denotes real existence and usually also separate existence, so that "union according to hypostasis" meant to him that the result of the incarnation was one reality, not two. For Cyril, this expression did not indicate that the preexisting, divine hypostasis was the unifying entity, as it did for Leontius. Of course, Cyril taught that it was the divine Word who unified himself to the flesh – that precisely was his "intuition" – but he did not use the technical term "hypostasis" to express the initiative of the Logos (van Loon 2009: 507–509).

The canons of the fifth ecumenical council, held in Constantinople in 553, speak repeatedly of a union "according to hypostasis." That in itself is a revival of an expression which Cyril had used many times, but he had dropped it after Theodoret of Cyrus had criticized its use, and it is absent from his writings during and after the council of Ephesus (except for a quotation of the second anathema in his *Explanation of the Twelve Chapters*). In the canons, just as in Cyril's writings, the expression is especially used to stress that the result of the union is one hypostasis or one person, not two. It does not have the neo-Chalcedonian meaning, for it is not explicitly stated that the hypostasis after the union is the same as that of the divine Word before the union, to which the human nature has been added. Canon 5 comes closest to this, when it says that there was no addition of person or hypostasis to the holy Trinity, when one of the Trinity became flesh. This suggests that there is continuity between the hypostasis of the Son of God before and after the incarnation, but it does not declare that the divine hypostasis is the unifying entity. Thus, the conclusion should be that the council adopted Cyril's terminology rather than Leontius's. Another neo-Chalcedonian expression we do find in the canons: several times "union according to composition" (ἕνωσις κατὰ σύνθεσιν) is juxtaposed to "union according to hypostasis." Cyril himself also used the term "composition" for the union of the divinity and the humanity in Christ. But this way of speaking does not highlight Cyril's intuition of the Word's initiative.

In other respects, however, the fifth ecumenical council did go beyond Chalcedon and gave space to other aspects of Cyril's teaching. The councils of Chalcedon (451) and Ephesus (431) had not adopted Cyril's "twelve chapters," the anathemas which he had appended to his *Third Letter to Nestorius*. It was these anathemas in particular which in Cyril's time had roused the indignation of the Orientals. In 553, however, Cyril and his anathemas were defended, while the Oriental "Three Chapters" were condemned; that is, the person and writings of Theodore of Mopsuestia, certain writings of Theodoret of Cyrus, and Ibas of Edessa's letter to Mari. Canon 13 deals with some of the writings of Theodoret, and it states that all those who have written "against holy Cyril and his twelve chapters" are to be anathematized. And in canon 14, Ibas of Edessa's letter to Mari is rejected because, among other things, it "condemns holy Cyril as a heretic" and it "calls the twelve chapters of holy Cyril impious and opposed to the right faith." Moreover, canon 10 seems inspired by Cyril's twelfth anathema: "If anyone does not confess that our Lord Jesus Christ, who is crucified in the flesh, is true God and the Lord of glory [1 *Corinthians* 2:8] and one of the holy Trinity, let someone like that be anathema." It also reminds one of the theopaschite formula of the (neo-Chalcedonian) Scythians monks, "one of the Trinity was crucified." We may add that according to canon 8 the μία φύσις formula is permitted, if it is interpreted correctly: there is no confusion of divinity and humanity in Christ, but after the union each nature remains what it was.

For the Eastern Orthodox Church the second council of Constantinople (553) is the fifth of the seven ecumenical councils, and as such its teachings are regarded as authoritative. From the very start the attitude of the Western Church towards this council has been more ambiguous. Pope Vigilius (537–555) refused to attend the council, but in the end he agreed with its condemnation of the "Three Chapters." It seems that the objections were more ecclesiological than Christological: decisions made at the council of Chalcedon (regarding the Oriental theologians) could not be reversed, and someone who had died (Theodore of Mopsuestia) could not be condemned. In later Western theology we do find a more asymmetrical Christology, which is in line with Cyril's intuition and with neo-Chalcedonianism.

Texts and Translations

Cyril of Alexandria wrote in **Greek**, and of the vast majority of his writings that are still extant we have Greek texts. This applies first of all to his Christological works and letters, many of which have been preserved as part of collections of writings pertaining to the councils of Ephesus and Chalcedon. We also have Greek texts of his commentaries on the Pentateuch (both *De adoratione* and the *Glaphyra*), on Isaiah, the Twelve Prophets, and the Gospel of John. Cyril must have written commentaries on many other biblical books, both from the Old and the New Testaments, but only fragments of them have survived, mainly through the catenae. Three other larger works have been preserved in the language in which they were written: the *Thesaurus* and the *Dialogues on the Trinity* (both anti-Arian), and *Against Julian* (the Apostate; partly lost). And finally, we still have in Greek a number of letters and homilies – mainly those held during the council of Ephesus – and 29 festal letters, those for the years 414–442.

Cyril's homilies on the Gospel of Luke have largely survived in Syriac, whereas only fragments remain in Greek. Of the *Scholia on the Incarnation* only a small part is extant in Greek; the remainder has survived in a Latin translation. Also, about a dozen of Cyril's letters are only available in Latin, and several other letters and homilies only in Coptic, Syriac, Armenian, Arabic, or Ethiopic.

Surprisingly, only few of Cyril's writings have survived in **Coptic**, although it is assumed that a Coptic version often was an intermediary between original Greek texts and Arabic translations, which suggests that a number of Coptic translations have disappeared over time. For example, for at least fragments of the *Thesaurus* there are indications that such a Coptic text once existed. On the other hand, several letters and homilies are only extant in Coptic. The Coptic acts of the council of Ephesus (431), from which large parts are still available, are a translation from the Greek acts, adapted to glorify a certain Egyptian monk, archimandrite Victor, by ascribing to him an (unhistorically) important role. These acts contain several of Cyril's letters.

The first **Latin** translations of Cyril's writings were produced during his lifetime. In 430, Cyril sent his deacon Posidonius to archbishop Celestine of Rome, not only with a dossier of sermons by Nestorius, but also with a patristic florilegium and his own *First* and *Second Letters to Nestorius*, all translated into Latin. And he probably sent a Latin translation of the *Scholia on the Incarnation* to Celestine's successor, Sixtus III, in 432 or 433, and sometime later his *Letter to John of Antioch*, containing the Formula of Reunion. Around the same time, Marius Mercator also translated Cyril's first two letters to Nestorius into Latin, as well as his letter to the clergy in Constantinople. A Latin version of the *Third Letter to Nestorius* with the 12 anathemas in the *Collectio Palatina* was not produced by Marius Mercator, as was once assumed, but it stems from the sixth century.

In 453, pope Leo I asked his legate John of Cos for a full translation of the acts of the council of Chalcedon, which would have included more of Cyril's writings, but there is no evidence that his request was ever fulfilled. At that time, Arnobius the Younger wrote his *Conflictus cum Serapione*, a (probably fictitious) dialogue with a Miaphysite, from which we learn that there existed a dossier of Cyril's letters in Latin. The *Conflictus* contains a translation of Cyril's seventeenth festal letter, written for the year 429, regarded as Cyril's first work in the Nestorian controversy.

In 518, the Scythian monks entered Constantinople with their theopaschite formula. During the debate that ensued with pope Hormisdas (514–523), Dionysius Exiguus, himself a Scythian, translated several of Cyril's writings into Latin in support of his compatriots. Among them were Cyril's *Third Letter to Nestorius* with the 12 anathemas, his two *Letters to Succensus* and parts of his *Letter to Acacius of Melitene*. In the last three letters Cyril had to defend himself for his reunion with the Antiochenes, and he discusses the μία φύσις formula. Grillmeier (1953) calls this debate over theopaschism one of the "waves" by which neo-Chalcedonian Christology came to the West.

A second wave was the Three Chapters controversy, somewhat later in the sixth century, which gave rise to translations of the acts of the councils of Ephesus and Chalcedon into Latin and of works that were relevant to the discussions, including a number of works by Cyril of Alexandria, among which were *Against the Orientals* and *Against Theodoret*. So far, it was mainly writings that were related to the Christological controversies that had been translated. In the (Latin) defense of the Three Chapters by Facundus of Hermiane (*fl.* c. 550), however, we find texts from several of Cyril's biblical commentaries, which otherwise remained rare in the West until the time of Thomas Aquinas. In the following century, at the Lateran council of 649, a Latin florilegium was used, which contained passages from Cyril's commentary on John and from the *Thesaurus*. And during the Adoptionist controversy in Spain (end of the eighth century), Alcuin quoted from a number of Cyril's Christological writings. After that, Cyril is mentioned relatively rarely and seemed almost forgotten in the West until Thomas Aquinas (c. 1225–1274) turned his attention to the Greek Fathers. Even Peter Lombard's *Sentences* contains only one quotation from Cyril's oeuvre (Haring 1950).

In Christological passages of his writings, Thomas Aquinas refers to and quotes from the acts of the councils of Ephesus (431), Chalcedon (451), and Constantinople (553), as well as writings of Cyril of Alexandria that are related to the Christological controversies. In his *Catena Aurea* we find many passages from Cyril's commentaries, especially in the catena on the Gospel of Luke. Part of them Thomas borrowed from the catenae by Nicetas of Heraclea, but in the dedication of the catena on the Gospel of Mark he writes that certain passages (*expositiones*) from the Greek doctors had been translated into Latin at his request (Backus 1997a: 344–351).

Integral translations of Cyril's non-Christological writings had to await the Humanist endeavor to render Greek works from Antiquity into Latin. In the middle of the fifteenth century, George of Trebizond translated Cyril's *Thesaurus* and Books 1–4 and 9–12 from his *Commentary on John* (Books 5 and 6 and fragments from Books 7 and 8 were found later). In the beginning of the sixteenth century, Johannes Oecolampadius added to Cyril's works available in Latin: Book I of *De adoratione*, the *Dialogues on the Trinity*, *Against Julian*, *Oratio ad Theodosium*, *Oratio ad augustas*, and *Oratio ad dominas*. Origen's commentary on Leviticus, also published at that time, was erroneously attributed to Cyril. Later that century, more writings were translated into Latin, including Cyril's commentaries on Isaiah and on the Twelve Prophets. And then in 1638 Jean Aubert published the works of Cyril of Alexandria in a bilingual edition, Greek and Latin, in six volumes, through which the vast majority of Cyril's extant writings had finally become available to Western Christianity.

Just as into Latin, translation of Cyril's work into **Syriac** started during his lifetime. A Syriac rendering of *Oratio ad Theodosium*, produced by Rabbula of Edessa, is still extant. Other Christological writings by Cyril were also translated into Syriac in the middle of the fifth century, but it is unclear whether Rabbula is responsible for them. To these belong the twelve anathemas, *Against Nestorius*, *Against the Orientals*, *Against Theodoret*, the *Explanation of the Twelve Chapters*, the *Scholia on the Incarnation*, and *That the Christ is One*. From the Syriac translation of the acts of the council of Ephesus (431), only fragments have been preserved. Since for the Miaphysites Cyril of Alexandria was the authority *par excellence*, they translated many of his works. In the middle of the sixth century, Moses of Aggel rendered the *Glaphyra* into Syriac. At that time, or even before it, other Cyrillian works became available in Syriac, too: the *Thesaurus*, the *Commentary on Isaiah*, *Against Julian* (of these three works only fragments have survived), *De adoratione* (large parts are preserved), and the homilies on Luke (almost entirely preserved, while only three of these homilies are extant in Greek).

The Miaphysites also produced translations of Cyril's works into Armenian, Arabic, and Ethiopic. Besides many Christological works also several commentaries and the *Thesaurus* were rendered into **Armenian**. The same applies to **Arabic**, although the number of Cyril's writings in this language seems to be smaller than that in Armenian. In **Ethiopic** the collection *Qerellos* is important, since it contains documents pertaining to the Christological controversy from before the council of Chalcedon (451), which were translated directly from the Greek as early as the beginning of the sixth century. They include Cyril's *Oratio ad Theodosium*, *Oratio ad dominas*, *That the Christ is One*, six homilies, and his *Letter to John of Antioch* (*ep.* 39). Other works of Cyril were translated into Ethiopic from Arabic at a much later date.

A **Georgian** translation of the *Thesaurus* must have existed in the eighth century, but is no longer extant. Several of Cyril's letters pertaining to Nestorius's condemnation were available in the eleventh century, but have also been lost. From the same time stem *Explanation of the Twelve Chapters*, a homily on Mary, and passages from Cyril's commentary on the Psalms, while parts of his other commentaries were translated in the twelfth or thirteenth centuries. A larger portion of Cyril's oeuvre was rendered into Georgian from Armenian at the time of Catholicos Anton I in the eighteenth century.

Middle Ages and Reformation

Since the Chalcedonians in the East fully accepted the council of Constantinople (553) as the fifth ecumenical council and its decisions as normative, Cyril of Alexandria's Christology has been most influential among them up to the present day. Anastasius of Sinai (seventh century) called Cyril "the seal of the Fathers." Maximus Confessor (c. 580–662), who refers regularly to Cyril, embedded his dyotheletism in a neo-Chalcedonian Christology, and his understanding of the two wills in Christ was canonized by the sixth ecumenical council of Constantinople (680–681). In the eighth century, John of Damascus (c. 675–749) wrote his compendium of Greek theology, *De fide orthodoxa*, in the neo-Chalcedonian tradition, which became a theological textbook for the following generations.

As mentioned, the reception of the council of 553 was not as straightforward in the West. During the Monothelite controversy, however, Maximus Confessor and other Greek monks were highly influential at the Western Lateran council (649), presided over by pope Martin I (649-655), which implied a new influx of neo-Chalcedonian Christology into the West. At the council, Cyril was explicitly quoted in a Latin florilegium. Cyril's authority was also invoked during the Adoptionist controversy (end of the eighth century), especially by Alcuin. But after that, knowledge of Cyril and his writings waned for several centuries (Haring 1950). Although after the schism between the Western and the Eastern Churches Cyril occurs in Latin florilegia supporting the *Filioque*, he is little mentioned in this controversy before the eleventh century. And even John Scotus Eriugena (c. 810–877), who was highly interested in Greek theology, hardly refers to Cyril, although he was familiar with several of Maximus Confessor's writings and stresses the unity of Christ.

During the discussions concerning the three Christological theories that Peter Lombard had presented in his *Sentences*, however, Cyrillian theology gradually gained influence (Backes 1953). According to the *habitus* theory, the Logos put on body and soul like pieces of clothing. It came to be rejected, because it did not do full justice to Christ's humanity. For some time, the *assumptus* theory, which taught that the Logos assumed a complete man, was regarded as a better alternative. But soon it was criticized for insufficiently safeguarding the unity of Christ: the full man seemed to be a separate person besides the Word of God. Finally, the subsistence theory gained the upper hand, according to which body and soul were simultaneously assumed by the Logos and Christ's human nature only subsists because of its union with the Word.

One of the arguments during the debate was that the human nature was added to the divine person of the Son of God, which already existed before the incarnation. This is Cyril's "intuition," which had come down to the scholastic theologians through Boethius, but even more so through John of Damascus. In the middle of the twelfth century, pope Eugenius III had John's *De fide orthodoxa* translated into Latin by Burgundio of Pisa, and from then on we see references to this work occurring regularly.

But it is with Thomas Aquinas that Cyril's influence on Western Christology has become enduring. As mentioned above, Thomas had access to the acts of the ecumenical councils of 431, 451, and 553, as well as to part of Cyril's writings. It was he, more than anyone else, who incorporated neo-Chalcedonian thinking into Western Christology, and who made sure that Cyril's heritage had a lasting effect on Roman Catholic theology.

But also in Trinitarian theology, Cyril was called on as an authority. At the time of the reunion council of Lyons (1274), John Beccus (patriarch John XI of Constantinople from 1275 till 1282) compiled a florilegium of patristic texts, the *Epigraphae*, to show that the Greek Fathers had the same understanding of the procession of the Holy Spirit as the Latin Fathers. The *Epigraphae* contains many quotations from Cyril's writings. When the Eastern and the Western Churches met again at the council of Ferrera–Florence (1438–1439), the *Epigraphae* once more played a role, while also new passages from Cyril's writings, especially from the *Thesaurus*, were adduced.

Despite the fact that in these debates on Trinitarian theology Cyril was hailed as a witness to the *Filioque* among the Greek Fathers, it seems that the Swiss Reformer Huldrych Zwingli (1484–1531) was critical of Cyril for defending the doctrine of single procession (Backus 1997b: 663f.). Zwingli had a copy of the Latin translation of Cyril's commentary on the Gospel of John by George of Trebizond, to which he added negative comments in the margin. His associate at Basel, Johannes Oecolampadius (1482–1531), who himself translated several of Cyril's writings, was more positive about the Alexandrian Church Father. In the preface to his translations, he calls Cyril an outstanding witness to the faith in Christ. And he appeals to Cyril's writings in support of his own views, although he is critical of allegorization, which he also finds in Cyril.

Martin Luther (1483–1546) emphasized in general that Scripture was the norm for theology, and he criticized the Church Fathers if according to his interpretation they missed the mark, but he used their support if he was in agreement with them. Although allegory could not be dismissed altogether, one should be committed to the plain sense of Scripture, he maintained. In this area the main culprits were Origen and Jerome, whereas Hilary of Poitiers, Augustine, and Cyril of Alexandria are praised for their commentaries on the Gospel of John. To Luther, justification through faith in Christ was the center of the biblical message, and in his view the teaching of all the Fathers fell short on this essential issue, but he mentions Cyril together with Hilary, Ambrose, and Augustine as men in whose writings he does find it, although it does not get the emphasis it should receive (Backus 1997b: 610f.). And in support of his understanding of the Lord's Supper, he points to Cyril's teaching about the *communicatio idiomatum*.

Luther stood in the neo-Chalcedonian tradition and defended theopaschite language like "God has suffered," although he preferred biblical over patristic arguments for it. But early Lutheranism placed four of Cyril's anathemas – including the twelfth anathema, which contains theopaschite language – at the beginning of the *Catalogus Testimoniorum*, attached to the *Formula of Concord* (1577), and presented them as canons of the council of Ephesus (431).

As for Luther, so for John Calvin (1509–1564), Scripture was the highest authority, but he supported his argumentation by references to the Fathers, especially in polemical contexts. At other times he could be critical of their views. Whereas Augustine was by far his favorite, John Chrysostom was praised as the best interpreter of Scripture among the Greek Fathers, and Cyril of Alexandria came second after Chrysostom (Backus 1997b: 693). Cyril was influential on the development of Calvin's Trinitarian theology, while he is also appreciatively referred to in relation to the doctrines of the person of Christ and the Lord's Supper. Calvin agreed with Cyril's teaching on the *communicatio idiomatum*, but he insisted that Luther's application of the exchange of properties to the Lord's Supper was incorrect.

In their polemics with the Reformers, Roman Catholic theologians obviously appealed to the Church Fathers as well. Cyril of Alexandria was particularly invoked on the issue of the Real Presence in the Eucharist (Backus 1997b: 733f.).

The Modern Period

Whereas during the Middle Ages and at the time of the Reformation Cyril was referred to for theological reasons, in modernity we also find a more historical and psychological approach to the events in Cyril's time. But the presentation more than once contains polemical elements.

John Toland (1670–1722) set the tone in an essay about Hypatia, in which he contends that the majority of those whom the Church calls "Saints" have been canonized for dubious reasons. And Cyril is no exception, as the full title of his essay makes clear:

"Hypatia: or, the History of a Most Beautiful, Most Vertuous, Most Learned, and Every Way Accomplish'd Lady; Who Was Torn to Pieces by the Clergy of Alexandria, to Gratify the Pride, Emulation, and Cruelty of their Archbishop, Commonly but Undeservedly stil'd St. Cyril." Socrates, the most reliable source on the event, does not involve Cyril directly in the murder. The neo-Platonic philosopher Damascius wrote about a century after the event, and Toland (1720: c. 13) states: "I frankly confess, that I more than suspect many of the things he reports." Nevertheless, he calls him "the other contemporary witness of her murder" (c. 20), besides Socrates, and adopts Damascius's interpretation that it was Cyril's, rather than the Christian people's, envy that was the occasion for Hypatia's murder.

Toland's view has often been repeated, in early modernity and up to the present day. Voltaire (1694–1778) made use of it in his attacks on the Catholic Church. And the historian Edward Gibbon (1737–1794) painted Cyril as "the Catholic tyrant of Alexandria" in his *The Decline and Fall of the Roman Empire* (c. 47). Cyril and Hypatia also featured in several novels, of which *Hypatia* by Charles Kingsley (1853) is the most well known. Here, Cyril is depicted not as the one who plotted the murder, but as one who refused to hand over the perpetrators of the crime to the authorities.

In the nineteenth century, theological interest in the Church Fathers, including Cyril of Alexandria, grew once again. Under the auspices of the Oxford Movement, P.E. Pusey published critical editions of many of Cyril's writings, while also English translations of part of his work appeared. As already mentioned, Cyril's oeuvre makes up 10 volumes of J.-P. Migne's *Patrologia Graeca*. In the series *Nicene and Post-Nicene Fathers*, however, none of Cyril's works can be found, apart from three letters and the 12 anathemas, which were published in the volume on the seven ecumenical councils. The standard critical edition of Cyril's writings that relate to the Christological controversy can be found in Ed. Schwartz's *Acta Conciliorum Oecumenicorum*, Book I, published in the first half of the twentieth century. In the meantime, Cyril had been declared a Doctor of the Church by pope Leo XIII, in 1882.

Whereas the church historians of the first half of the twentieth century downplayed the role of Alexandrian theology in general, and Cyril in particular, at the council of Chalcedon, newer research since 1951 acknowledges that Cyril's Christology was the norm at the council of 451. This has contributed to renewed interest in Cyril's writings, which has resulted in a number of monographs on his theology. And not only have critical editions with French translations been published in the series *Sources chrétiennes*, but also a growing number of translations into English are appearing.

In addition, theologians from the Eastern Orthodox Church and from the Oriental Orthodox Churches – the latter being the heirs of the Miaphysites, who started their own hierarchy in the sixth century – began ecumenical consultations in the 1960s to overcome their long-standing separation. They saw in Cyril of Alexandria their common Church Father, and they referred to his Christology in their agreed statements.

At the same time, Cyril continues to be depicted as a potentate with a lust for power, in the tradition of John Toland. In 2009, the film *Agora* from director Alejandro Amenábar was released, in which Hypatia is portrayed as a saintly scientist who perishes due to the machinations of archbishop Cyril. In the same year, Youssef Ziedan's novel *Azazeel* appeared in Arabic (the English translation in 2012), in which a monk, born in Upper

Egypt, travels to Alexandria, where he witnesses the murder of Hypatia, after which he baptizes himself and takes on the name Hypa, the first part of the philosopher's name. He then moves on to Jerusalem, where he becomes friends with Nestorius. While living in a monastery near Aleppo, he is acutely aware of the growing Christological controversy, and even meets Nestorius, now archbishop of Constantinople, in Antioch. The colophon states that "this novel is entirely a work of fiction," but the translator of the book is struck by Ziedan's "meticulous commitment to the original sources" (Ziedan 2012: 311). This mixture of historical fact and ingenious fiction aroused a storm of indignation among the Copts because of its portrayal of Cyril. Highly suggestive are passages like the description of a church service, held just before Hypatia is killed: Cyril shouts in his sermon: "So, children of the Lord, free your land from the defilement of the pagans, cut out the tongues of those who speak evil" (Ziedan 2012: 122).

And so, Cyril of Alexandria will continue to be remembered as a dual character. On the one hand, as the "seal of the Fathers," the "Pillar of Faith" (in the Coptic Orthodox Church), a Doctor of the Church, as the one who dug the bed through which the stream of dogmatic developments has subsequently passed, so deeply that, generally speaking, it has never left it since (Hans von Campenhausen). On the other hand, as a church leader whose episcopate started with 3 years of violence, who expelled the Jews from Alexandria, who was associated with the murder of the neo-Platonic philosopher Hypatia, and who did not shun intimidation and bribery. A Saint who sinned.

Bibliography

Primary Sources

S.P.N. Cyrilli Alexandriae Archiepiscopi Opera. Patrologiae Cursus Completus: Series Graeca 68–77, edited by J.-P. Migne. Paris, 1859–1864.

Sancti Patris nostri Cyrilli archiepiscopi Alexandrini [opera], seven vols, Philippus Eduardus Pusey (ed.). Oxford: Clarendon Press/James Parker, 1868–1877. (Reprint: Brussels: Culture et Civilisation, 1965.)

Cyril of Alexandria [various titles in English translation], Philippus Eduardus Pusey/Thomas Randall (eds). Library of Fathers of the Church 43, 46–48. Oxford: James Parker, 1874–1885.

Acta Conciliorum Oecumenicorum, Book I, *Concilium Universale Ephesenum*, five vols, Eduardus Schwartz (ed.). Berlin: W. de Gruyter, 1927–1930.

Matthäus-/Johannes-/Lukas-Kommentare aus der griechischen Kirche: aus Katenenhandschriften-gesammelt, Joseph Reuss (ed.). Texte und Untersuchungen zur Geschichte der altchristlichen Literatur 61, 89, 130. Berlin: Akademie-Verlag, 1957–1984.

Cyrille d'Alexandrie [various titles, Greek text and French translation], G.M. de Durand *et al.* (eds). Sources chrétiennes 97, 231, 237, 246, 322, 372, 392, 434. Paris: Éditions du Cerf, 1964–1998.

Qērellos, five vols, Bernd Manuel Weischer (ed.). Vol. I: Afrikanistische Forschungen 7. Glückstadt: Augustin, 1973. Vols. II/1, III, IV/1, IV/3: Äthiopische Forschungen 31, 2, 4, 7. Wiesbaden: Steiner, 1977–1993.

Cyril of Alexandria [various titles in English translation], John I. McEnerney, Robert C. Hill, and Philip R. Amidon (eds). The Fathers of the Church 76–77, 115–116, 118. Washington, DC: The Catholic University of America Press, 1987–2009.

Cyril of Alexandria, *Commentary on Isaiah*, Robert Charles Hill (ed.), three vols. Brookline, MA: Holy Cross Orthodox Press, 2008.

Secondary Sources

Backes, Ignaz (1953), "Die christologische Problematik der Hochscholastik und ihre Beziehung zu Chalkedon." In *Das Konzil von Chalkedon: Geschichte und Gegenwart*, vol. 2, Aloys Grillmeier and Heinrich Bacht (eds). Würzburg: Echter Verlag; 923–939.

Backus, Irena (ed.) (1997a), *The Reception of the Church Fathers in the West: From the Carolingians to the Maurists*, vol. 1. Leiden: Brill.

Backus, Irena (ed.) (1997b), *The Reception of the Church Fathers in the West: From the Carolingians to the Maurists*, vol. 2. Leiden: Brill.

Boulnois, Marie-Odile (1994), *Le paradoxe trinitaire chez Cyrille d'Alexandrie: Herméneutique, analyses philosophiques et argumentation théologique.* Collection des Études Augustiniennes, Série Antiquité 143. Paris: Institut d'Études Augustiniennes.

De Halleux, André (1976), "La définition christologique à Chalcédoine". *Revue théologique de Louvain*, 7: 3–23, 155–170.

Grillmeier, Aloys (1953), "Vorbereitung des Mittelalters: Eine Studie über das Verhältnis von Chalkedonismus und Neu-Chalkedonismus in der lateinischen Theologie von Boethius bis zu Gregor dem Grossen". In *Das Konzil von Chalkedon: Geschichte und Gegenwart*, vol. 2, Aloys Grillmeier and Heinrich Bacht (eds). Würzburg: Echter Verlag; 791–839.

Haring, N.M. (1950), "The character and range of the influence of St. Cyril of Alexandria on Latin theology (430–1260)". *Mediaeval Studies*, 12: 1–19.

Helmer, Siegfried (1962), *Der Neuchalkedonismus: Geschichte, Berechtigung und Bedeutung eines dogmengeschichtlichen Begriffes*. Bonn.

Hespel, Robert (1955), *Le florilège cyrillien réfuté par Sévère d'Antioche: Étude et édition critique.* Bibliothèque du Muséon 37. Louvain: Publications Universitaires.

Jouassard, G. (1953), "Une intuition fondamentale de saint Cyrille d'Alexandrie en christologie dans les premières années de son épiscopat". *Revue des étudesbyzantines*, 11: 175–186.

Keating, Daniel A. (2004), *The Appropriation of Divine Life in Cyril of Alexandria*. Oxford Theological Monographs. Oxford: Oxford University Press.

Kerrigan, Alexander (1951), *St. Cyril of Alexandria: Interpreter of the Old Testament.* Analecta Biblica 2. Rome: Pontificio Istituto Biblico.

Kingsley, Charles (1853), *Hypatia: or, New Foes with an Old Face*. London: Parker.

McGuckin, John A. (1994), *St. Cyril of Alexandria: The Christological Controversy: Its History, Theology and Texts.* Supplements to Vigiliae Christianae 23. Leiden: Brill. (Reprint: Crestwood, NY: SVS Press, 2004.)

Meunier, Bernard (1997), *Le Christ de Cyrille d'Alexandrie: L'humanité, le salut et la question monophysite*. Théologie historique 104. Paris: Beauchesne.

Münch-Labacher, Gudrun (1996), *Naturhaftes und geschichtliches Denken bei Cyrill von Alexandrien: Die verschiedenen Betrachtungsweisen der Heilsverwirklichung in seinem Johannes-Kommentar.* Hereditas: Studien zur Alten Kirchengeschichte 10. Bonn: Borengässer.

Norris, R.A. (1975), "Christological models in Cyril of Alexandria". Studia Patristica, 13: 255–268.

Romanides, John S., Paul Verghese, and Nick A. Nissiotis (eds) (1964–1965). *Unofficial Consultation between Theologians of Eastern Orthodox and Oriental Orthodox Churches, August 11–15, 1964: Papers and Minutes.*

Thematic Issue of The Greek Orthodox Theological Review 10/2. Brookline, MA: Holy Cross Orthodox Press.

Toland, John (1720), "Hypatia." In idem, *Tetradymus*. London: Brotherton. Reprint: *Atheism in Britain* 2, Bristol: Thoemmes, 1996: 101–136.

Van Loon, Hans (2009), *The Dyophysite Christology of Cyril of Alexandria*. Supplements to Vigiliae Christianae 96. Leiden: Brill.

Wilken, Robert L. (1971), *Judaism and the Early Christian Mind: A Study of Cyril of Alexandria's Exegesis and Theology*. Yale Publications in Religion 15. New Haven, CT: Yale University Press.

Ziedan, Youssef (2012). *Azazeel*. London: Atlantic Books.

CHAPTER 12

Shenoute of Atripe

Janet Timbie

Introduction

As the third leader of the White Monastery Federation in Upper Egypt, across the
Nile from Panopolis, Shenoute of Atripe (d. 465) had an in-house audience for his
work when he addressed the men and women of his monastic community in letters
and sermons. He also preached regularly in the White Monastery church to a mixed
audience of Christian clergy and laity. In addition, he tried to curb the activities of
local pagans through the "open letter" and through attacks on pagan shrines. But it
is difficult to determine the extent of his influence in his own lifetime. Early references to his genuine works are rare. The replacement of Coptic by Arabic in Egypt
simply added to the problems of access to the work of Shenoute. The rediscovery of
Shenoute by Western scholarship began with the collection of Coptic manuscripts
and their preservation in European libraries. But the first substantial publications of
the works of Shenoute were based on partial texts, and judgments of his place in
Egyptian Christian history seem to be slanted in the direction of the early editors'
interests. Recent growth in Coptology, stimulated by manuscript discoveries and
linguistic studies, has made it possible to base the study of Shenoute on more
complete texts that are read with better understanding. Thus, the judgment pronounced by Johannes Leipoldt in his foundational monograph, *Schenute von Atripe
und die Entstehung des national ägyptischen Christentums*, that Shenoute meant
nothing in world history, but everything to the Copts (Leipoldt 1903: 191) can now
be reevaluated and perhaps modified.

The Wiley Blackwell Companion to Patristics, First Edition. Edited by Ken Parry.
© 2015 John Wiley & Sons Ltd. Published 2019 by John Wiley & Sons Ltd.

Shenoute in Late Antiquity: Coptic and Greek

In order to assess the influence of Shenoute during his lifetime, and for the period immediately following, establishing his chronology is an early challenge. This is a difficult
problem because some evidence seems to suggest that he was born c. 350 and
died 464/465 (Emmel 2004: 6–12), giving an age at death of approximately 115 years!
Some recent scholarship has tried to revise this picture and correct his chronology,
either by changing the date of death to 450/451 (Luisier 2009: 275) or by changing
the birth date to the 380s (López 2013: 133). Neither of these revised chronologies has
found much support, but they have stimulated discussion of the impact of Shenoute's
written work and direct action in his lifetime. Was he an important monastic leader,
anti-pagan agitator, defender of the poor, and ally of the patriarchs in Alexandria?
Or was he a marginal figure in his own time? Does reliance on Shenoute's own writings
in the attempt to answer these questions prejudice the analysis? Perhaps, but there is
little other evidence to bring to the discussion for the early period.

Letters written by Shenoute to several archbishops of Alexandria survive, but
their addressees are not always named. One reconstruction (Emmel 2004: 7–8)
identifies Timothy I (d. 385), Theophilus (d. 412), and Timothy Aelurus (in office
457–477) as the recipients of short, formal letters from Shenoute (Leipoldt 1906–
1913: vol. 42, 13–15). Shenoute appeals to the power of Cyril of Alexandria (d.
444) in threatening statements to an opponent and probably joined the monastic
entourage that accompanied Cyril to the First Council of Ephesus in 431. When
Shenoute says "we returned from Ephesus" in a sermon (*I Have Been Reading the Holy
Gospels*, Moussa 2010: 117), and refers to theological matters from the Council in
other works, there is no strong reason to doubt that he was present, even though the
evidence comes from his own writings.

There is very little evidence outside of Shenoute's own work for his activities and
influence in the late fourth and fifth centuries. An exception is a letter from the archbishop Dioscorus to Shenoute (Thompson 1922), asking him to take action against an
Origenist priest in Upper Egypt. Otherwise, where some mention might be expected,
there is nothing. The Coptic *Acts of the Council of Ephesus* (Kraatz 1904) make Victor of
Pbow the principal Coptic monastic actor, not Shenoute. Neither Shenoute nor the
White Monastery is mentioned by any of the Greek monastic surveys of the period, such
as the *Lausiac History* or the *Historia Monachorum*. Though Shenoute wrote many Coptic
letters and sermons for monastic and lay audiences, nothing seems to have circulated in
a Greek version that could be read by Palladius or others. Where the Pachomian
movement had Jerome as translator and publicist (Boon 1932), no one did the same for
Shenoute and the White Monastery.

After his death (c. 465) Shenoute is mentioned by his successor, Besa (Kuhn 1956),
in ways that show awareness of authentic writings and historical events of the
fifth century. The written style of Shenoute, which combines aggressive language with
extensive allusion to, and quotation of, scripture, is imitated in an unskillful manner
by John the Archimandrite, who followed Besa as head of the White Monastery
(Emmel 2007: 94), and also by a writer known as Pseudo-Shenoute (Kuhn 1960).
While this suggests that his works were read in the monastery, there is no real

engagement with his teaching in the areas of monastic ideology, Christology, and guidance for Christian laypeople. Stories attributed to Benjamin I, patriarch from 626 to 665, mention Shenoute several times in accounts of travel through Egypt to escape from imperial forces seeking to enforce Chalcedonian doctrine. But in these stories Shenoute is a saintly figure from the past who appears miraculously to support this Pseudo-Benjamin in his trials by identifying a sinful priest so that he can be expelled: "We knew that the monk we saw was the holy priest Apa Shenoute, and the two soldiers (with him) were authorities from God" (Müller 1968: 134–142). Ps.-Benjamin refers to the "monastery of Apa Shenoute" several times, but does not use his writings. The same transformation from leader and writer to saint and prophet who intervenes to support later leaders is found in the *Life of Moses of Abydos*, and similar texts (Moussa 2003: 78). On his deathbed, Shenoute predicts that Moses of Abydos – still a child in 465 – will eventually end the pagan practices there: "He prophesied to those who were gathered around him, 'A man shall rise from that village and ... abolish the sacrifices of the pagans and overturn their temples'."

The *Life of Shenoute*, which survives in Sahidic fragments and in complete Bohairic, Arabic, and Ethiopic versions, depicts a similar saintly, miracle-working leader. Evidence suggests that the *Life of Shenoute* developed from encomia delivered on his feast day, which were preserved in the monastery library and then supplemented with material known from other oral and written sources (Lubomierski 2007). The *Life* was attributed to Besa at a later stage and so gained increased authority as the work of an eyewitness to the career of Shenoute.

Shenoute in Medieval Egypt: Coptic and Arabic

Following the Arab Conquest of Egypt in 642, the story of Shenoute is one of limited and declining use of his Coptic work, along with the translation of hagiographic works about him into Arabic. New sermons appeared in Arabic under the name of Shenoute, but only a very small portion of his genuine work was translated into Arabic. As Coptic was gradually replaced by Arabic as the language of daily life, the writings of Shenoute became inaccessible to most readers. He continued to be an important saint in the Coptic Orthodox Church, but lost many of his distinctive features.

The White Monastery survived for a time as an important institution, and the manuscripts of Shenoute were copied and recopied there into the twelfth century. Lectionaries were produced for liturgical use in the monastery and drew on the works of Shenoute. Liturgical *typika* combine the expected references to the Bible with references to Shenoute in the following form: attribution to Shenoute, opening words of lection, or incipit of work in which the lection is found (Emmel 2004: 75). The White Monastery lectionaries contain excerpts from Shenoute's *Discourses* (sermonic material addressed to monastic and nonmonastic audiences), but not from the *Canons* (advice to monastics, including rules). A twelfth-century manuscript of a Holy Week lectionary contains nine readings from Shenoute, mostly in Bohairic, which proves that he was read outside the White Monastery (Burmester 1932).

The steady Arabicization of Egypt eventually affected the transmission and understanding of the works of Shenoute. To date, only one genuine work of Shenoute is found with a complete Arabic translation. *Good is the Time for Launching a Boat to Sail* is known from an incipit list and survives in Coptic and Arabic in BN 68, a fifteenth–sixteenth-century paper manuscript that records the itinerary of a pilgrimage rite near the White Monastery celebrating the feast of Apa Shenoute (Timbie 1998). The entire manuscript has portions in Coptic (both Sahidic and Bohairic), Greek, and Arabic. The pilgrimage rite probably ceased by the twelfth century and the White Monastery was in ruins by 1450, yet the manuscript was recopied and offered some access to authentic Shenoute in Arabic. The sermon outlines appropriate ascetic practices for laypeople and for monks: "Some are meant to be virgins, others to keep their beds pure. Some are meant to take up their cross and follow the Lord, others to be charitable when they have means, without wealth. Some are meant for prayer and asceticism, others for every sort of good work" (Leipoldt 1906–1913: vol. 73, 178, my translation). The Arabic translation found in the manuscript is generally accurate. Yet the fact that so little of Shenoute was translated suggests that understanding of literary Coptic (especially Sahidic) was in decline.

As a substitute, the memory of Shenoute was preserved through new compositions, first in simple, awkward Bohairic, then in Arabic. Hymns to Shenoute (Leipoldt 1908: vol. 42, 226–242) praise him and offer prayers to God: "forgive us our sins because of Shenoute" (Leipoldt 1908: vol. 42, 232, my translation). "Our God, scatter our enemies, O Christ, and trample on them, O man of God, Shenoute" (Leipoldt 1908: vol. 42, 240, my translation). Some hymns refer to his feast day: "Let all of us gather, O Orthodox, and keep the feast in the name of the man of God, Shenoute" (Leipoldt 1908: vol. 42, 240, my translation). By the early medieval period, Shenoute is considered to be a powerful saint who can offer all sorts of heavenly aid.

Sermons were also written in Arabic and attributed to Shenoute in medieval manuscripts. While Arabic sources state that the White Monastery is in ruins in the fifteenth century and only the church still functions, a seventeenth-century manuscript (BN ar. 4761), with an undated dedication to the monastery, contains nine homilies that are attributed to Shenoute (Swanson 2005: 29). Their style of Arabic and some of the issues addressed in the homilies exclude the possibility that they are translations from Shenoute's Coptic. Homily 3 begins, "Glory be to God – the Eternal without **beginning**, the everlasting without **end**, one **in essence**, threefold **in attributes**; 'speaking' through his **eternal**, essential Word, 'living' through his **life-giving**, holy Spirit" (Swanson 2005: 33). The homilies include passages of rhymed prose (indicated in bold type is Swanson's translation), common in Arabic, and use theological language (e.g., the Trinity of attributes) developed in conversation with Muslims in the ninth century (Swanson 2005: 35). Stories from the Greek Alexander romance, sayings attributed to Luqman the Wise (see Qur'an surah 31), and references to the encounter between Barlaam and Prince Yuwasaf are worked into the homilies, demonstrating that they are steeped in an Arabic wisdom tradition shared by Muslims and Christians in Egypt in the medieval period.

The more mundane themes of these homilies also have features that are quite different from authentic Shenoute. Fasting, prayer, and almsgiving are recommended in light of the Last Judgment, as in authentic Shenoute, but there is also a special concern for the conduct of women: they should not chat in church and, in general, should follow the biblical example of "silent" women such as Sarah and Hannah (Swanson 2005: 31–32). The same biblical matriarchs are used by the Coptic Shenoute in a discourse known as *Abraham Our Father* to inspire nuns to care for their monastic companions with the same energy shown by Sarah and Hannah when they prayed for offspring (Leipoldt 1913: 26–37). Silence and shy, retiring behavior are not part of his argument. It is unclear exactly when the White Monastery ceased to function as a monastery (Coquin and Martin 1991). Similarly, it is hard to know when knowledge of literary Coptic had declined to the point that authentic Shenoute could not be read and translated in Egypt.

Shenoute Rediscovered in Europe in the Early Modern Period (Seventeenth to Nineteenth Centuries): Studies in Latin and Modern Languages

The foundation for a rediscovery of Shenoute was laid in the Ottoman Period but came to partial fulfillment much later, mainly in the nineteenth century. Many factors were involved on the European side: Catholic missionary efforts aimed at both conversion of individual members of the Coptic Orthodox Church and union of the Coptic Church with Rome; interest in deciphering hieroglyphics led to interest in Coptic language and manuscripts; European military actions in Egypt, particularly those of Napoleon, also promoted scientific exploration.

The sixteenth century presented a series of challenges to the Coptic Christian community in Egypt. Incidents of violence against Christians and forced conversion to Islam occurred in the early Ottoman period. At the same time, representatives of various French and Venetian interests increased their activities within the Ottoman Empire, and this included Roman Catholic missionary activity among Coptic Orthodox Christians (Armanios 2011: 42–45). Several Coptic patriarchs came close to union with the Catholics – Ghubriyal VII (1525–1568), Yu'annis XIV (1571–1585), Ghubriyal VIII (1586–1601) – at least partly due to a belief that the Christian community in Egypt would be safer with a Roman connection. But the cost in terms of changes in long-standing belief and practice, as well as in the risk of seeming disloyal to Ottoman rulers, stood in the way. As the prospect of union faded, missionaries still sought to convert individual Copts to Catholicism, resulting in some progress in the study of Coptic language and manuscripts in Europe.

Raphael Tuki (1703–1787), born in Girga in Upper Egypt (not far from the White Monastery), met the Jesuit missionary Claude Sicard and converted to Catholicism in 1719. Eventually he was sent to Rome to study as part of a plan to train converts and then return them to their homelands as effective missionaries. Tuki worked in Egypt from 1737 to 1739 to build up the Coptic Catholic Church, then returned to Rome due to illness. In Rome he trained the small number of Coptic converts but mainly edited and translated Coptic and Arabic texts. Tuki's Coptic grammar, *Rudimenta linguae Coptae sive Aegyptiacae*, which included both Bohairic and Sahidic examples with Arabic and

Latin translation, was an improvement over some earlier attempts to write a grammar, and he also started work on a Bohairic–Arabic dictionary (Hamilton 2006: 234–242). These works later played a role in the effort to decipher hieroglyphics that was successful in the nineteenth century. But Tuki is also associated with criticism of the removal of Christian manuscripts from Egypt (mainly by members of the Assemani family) in order to add to the Vatican collection (Hamilton 2006: 97). Yet the Coptic manuscript collections in European libraries, which included works of Shenoute taken from the decaying White Monastery, eventually made it possible to recover authentic Shenoute and incorporate him into the history of Christianity in Egypt.

Roman Catholic missionary activity in Egypt sought both union of the churches and individual converts; early missions by the German Lutheran Church had similar goals but, like the Catholic Church, achieved more in the areas of manuscript collection and language study. The travels of Johann Michael Wansleben (1635–1679) to Egypt in the seventeenth century originated in German Lutheran interest in making contact with the Church of Ethiopia, but the lasting result of his work came from his reports on Coptic monasteries and acquisition of manuscripts. In 1673, Wansleben visited the White Monastery, which was associated with "S. Sennode," whom he correctly identified as a contemporary of Cyril of Alexandria. During his travels, Wansleben acquired Coptic and Copto-Arabic manuscripts that eventually entered Paris collections. Other European scholars provided bits and pieces of information about Shenoute as they began to read and study the manuscripts in their libraries, leading to a correct, summary statement by Étienne Quatremère in 1811, who located Shenoute in time and place and identified him as the author of *Good Is The Time for Launching the Boat* preserved in BN 68, a liturgical manuscript (Emmel 2004: 16–18).

Throughout the eighteenth and into the early nineteenth centuries, fragments of Sahidic manuscripts were finding their way into European collections. Only at the end of the nineteenth century did it become clear that they came from the storeroom of the White Monastery, which was described by Gaston Maspero in 1892, shortly before it was emptied and the manuscripts completely dispersed (Maspero 1892: 1). Much of the material went to the Bibliothèque Nationale in Paris, with the remainder scattered in major libraries and private collections (Emmel 2004: 23).

European military activity in Egypt also played a part in the rediscovery of the Egyptian language, leading to better understanding of the work of Shenoute. Napoleon's invasion of Egypt in 1798 and the discovery of the Rosetta Stone in 1799, with its parallel texts in Greek, Demotic, and hieroglyphics, gave proper direction to the study of Egyptian hieroglyphics. But the scholars who contributed to the decipherment of the hieroglyphics, including Johan Åkerblad and Jean-François Champollion, had also studied Coptic and believed in its value for understanding the earlier form of the language (Hamilton 2006: 249). Champollion recognized the diversity of Coptic dialects and also corrected the view that Bohairic was standard and Sahidic a later development. Thus, into the nineteenth century, European collection of Coptic manuscripts in Egypt, including many from Shenoute's White Monastery, led to better understanding of all phases of the Egyptian language. This was going on before there was much interest in the history of Coptic monasticism or awareness of the career of Shenoute. Later on and up to the present, studies of the Egyptian language have generated interest in the works of Shenoute since they constitute the largest surviving corpus of original Coptic literature. Gradually, during the nineteenth century, more scholars became aware of Shenoute as the author of works in the White Monastery codices; as a result, fragments were published from the Borgia collection and correctly attributed to him by Georg Zoega (1810). This made it possible for scholars such as Leipoldt and Amélineau to assemble and publish editions of Shenoute in the early twentieth century.

Shenoute in the Modern World, from the Beginning of the Twentieth Century to the Present: Modern Languages

Émile Amélineau was the first to publish a lengthy collection of the works of Shenoute, with French translation, that was assembled from different manuscripts (Amélineau 1907–1914). This edition has many mistaken transcriptions, grammatical mistakes, and misidentification of biblical quotations and allusions, yet it is still valuable because some of the texts have not been republished and because it has a modern language translation. Amélineau had previously published (with translation) a set of Coptic and Arabic texts related to Shenoute, but without analysis of the issues of authorship, historical accuracy, and so on (Amélineau 1888–1895). Johannes Leipoldt produced an edition of the works of Shenoute at approximately the same time as Amélineau, but with much greater accuracy (Leipoldt 1906–1913). Leipoldt published many texts from the Borgia and Paris collections, correcting some defective readings while footnoting the text as it appears in the manuscript. This was very useful at an early stage in the study of literary Coptic and Coptic codicology. But only a Latin translation was published, and at a later date (Wiesmann 1931–1936), which may have slowed the modern study of Shenoute.

Leipoldt's edition was unusual in the fact that it followed his publication of a monograph on Shenoute: *Schenute von Atripe und die Entstehung des national ägyptischen Christentums* (Leipoldt 1903). The opposite is often the case: text critical work followed by monograph. *Schenute von Atripe* was the first full-length study of Shenoute, and it remains the only study to deal with all aspects of his activity, from enforcer of monastic rules to anti-pagan organizer to Bible-based preacher on Christian life. Eugène Revillout had analyzed the work of Shenoute somewhat earlier (Revillout 1883) in long articles, emphasizing the anti-pagan side without trying to offer a complete picture. But it was Leipoldt's view of Shenoute that had lasting influence on scholarship. According to Leipoldt, Shenoute was important as the advocate of an Egyptian ethnic consciousness that supported the anti-Chalcedonian schism and led to the separation of the Coptic Orthodox Church. This view was taken up and repeated in some influential work (for example, in W.H.C. Frend, *Rise of the Monophysite Movement*), spreading a one-sided view of Shenoute that was based on Leipoldt rather than the works of Shenoute. Leipoldt also offered a concise summary of the theology of Shenoute that was influential, even though based on partial sources. Leipoldt argued that Shenoute taught a "Christless piety" (Leipoldt 1903: 82), emphasizing sin, judgment, and punishment both inside and outside of the monastery. Later work on Christianity in Egypt repeated this view, "Christ, for Shenoute, was little more than a suffering figure whose example can provide us with comfort in our own affliction, or a final judge who will come at the end to call us to account" (Bell 1983: 19), and circulated it to an audience without much access to the works of Shenoute, either in Coptic or in a good modern language translation. And the monasticism of the White Monastery was unfavorably compared to that of the Pachomian Federation in early studies: "Pjol, Shenoute's uncle, had simply adopted the rule of the Pachomian monasteries, modifying it ... in the direction of greater austerity. Shenoute accentuated still more that tendency to exaggeration. With that, we are very far from real Pachomian spirituality" (Veilleux 1983: x).

Several different factors led to more study of Shenoute, and this eventually produced more-nuanced views. The discovery of the Nag Hammadi library in the 1940s drew many scholars to the study of Coptic, and some of them later redirected their attention to original Coptic literature. The slightly earlier discovery of Manichaean texts at Medinet Madi led to publications by H.J. Polotsky and others, who also made breakthroughs in the study of Coptic grammar by analyzing the works of Shenoute. Students of Polotsky have continued to produce grammatical works that both draw much of their evidence from Shenoute and enable others to read and translate his work with greater accuracy (Shisha-Halevy 1986; Layton 2011). As manuscripts continue to emerge from Egypt – the Kellis texts produced by a fourth-century Manichaean community and the *Gospel of Judas* to mention just a few – more attention is paid to Shenoute because of his stature as an original Coptic writer and monastic leader. Defining "Late Antiquity" as a significant period and focusing on the "holy man" within that period under the influence of the work of Peter Brown (as in *The Making of Late Antiquity* and *The Body and Society*) had the same result: more interest in the work of Shenoute.

Meanwhile, from the mid-twentieth century, scholars with experience in Coptic studies began to publish single works by Shenoute in fairly complete versions with modern language translations (Lefort 1955; Barns 1964; Orlandi 1985; Young 1993). Barns' translation of *Not Because a Fox Barks* (in which Shenoute attacks a local landowner for abusive labor practices) included historical background and commentary, which was very important since it introduced an authentic Shenoute to the wider world of papyrology and Late Antique studies. Barns noted that Christian leaders could gain power by supporting the laboring population in conflicts with landowners: "His account of the pagan landlord is doubtless exaggerated, but it seems unlikely that the details of his oppression are invented" (Barns 1964: 155). Barns recognized that the works of Shenoute could be major sources of evidence for the social and economic history of Egypt in Late Antiquity. The translations by Lefort (*And It Happened One Day*) and Orlandi (the earliest study of *I Am Amazed*, also known as *Contra Origenistas*; Orlandi 1985, updated Cristea 2011) began to bring the theological position of Shenoute into better focus and place him in the Christological conflicts of the fifth century.

A major turning point for Western scholarship on Shenoute came with the two-volume work published by Stephen Emmel, *Shenoute's Literary Corpus* (Emmel 2004). This was a revision of his 1993 Yale doctoral dissertation. Drawing on principles of codicology, and some key pieces of manuscript evidence, Emmel was able to reconstruct the plan of the White Monastery codices that contained the *Canons* and *Discourses* of Shenoute from the remnants that are now scattered among many libraries. *Canons* is a label derived from the manuscripts, and *Discourses* is a neutral term covering various designations in the manuscripts; for example, *logos*. The *Canons* contain works for monastic guidance, while the *Discourses* have a broader audience.

The Vienna incipit list (ms. AT-NB K 9634), whose first 26 titles are lost, numbers and gives the opening line of sermons by Shenoute, from *The Lord Thundered* (#27) to *Now It Is Established from the Beginning* (#91). These are known as the *Discourses*, and they were collected in eight volumes in the White Monastery library (Emmel 2004: 235–292). Using the incipit list, the order of works in volumes 4–8 can be established. Meanwhile, other works survive that cannot be clearly assigned to a *Discourse* volume or come from a library other than the White Monastery. And a group of letters written to and from Shenoute fill up some *Discourse* volumes. Emmel used a *florilegium* of Shenoute's works – a series of passages excerpted in sequence from the nine-volume set of *Canons* (Emmel 2004: 112) – to reconstruct the *Canon* part of the corpus.

By using Emmel's work, first as a dissertation and later in the two CSCO volumes, scholars had much better tools in hand for the study of Shenoute. Texts could be reassembled from a variety of published (Leipoldt, Amélineau) and nonpublished (manuscript collections) sources with Emmel providing the road map. The complete works of Shenoute, including Coptic text and modern language translation, are being prepared for publication by an international team of scholars, but many have not waited for this publication. Translations of single texts have appeared in articles and dissertations (Brakke 1989; Behlmer 1996; Foat 1996; Moussa 2010) , and a few monographs have offered thematic studies of Shenoute. Leipoldt finally has scholarly successors, and his view of Shenoute is being challenged on several fronts.

Leipoldt's 1903 monograph emphasized a few points about Shenoute: (1) he was a representative of an emerging Egyptian national consciousness, (2) his works made literary Coptic a medium for Coptic self-expression, and (3) he used the resources of the monastery to alleviate poverty in his area (Leipoldt 1903: 191). His final assessment was that "Shenoute means nothing in world history, (but) everything for the Copts" (Leipoldt 1903: 191). The modern reception of Shenoute is inspired, in part, by the desire to refine or revise each of these points. Taking the language question first, it is clear that improved understanding of the Coptic language has enabled us to better appreciate Shenoute and "his way of mixing formal rhetoric and biblical quotations and reminiscences with what seem to be everyday colloquialisms and lower-register formality" (Emmel 2007: 91). The challenge for translators of Shenoute is to capture this mix of registers; a recent translation of Shenoute's *Let Our Eyes* (Emmel 2008) illustrates how this could be done. The poverty question came up in Barns' article, which included the translation of *Not Because A Fox Barks*, as he called attention to the way Shenoute criticized a local, possibly crypto-pagan landowner for the exploitation of workers on his estates (Barns 1964). As more work has been done on the rural economy of Egypt in Late Antiquity, utilizing documentary papyri, some have turned to monastic sources to see if the evidence that they provide fits into the documentary picture (Wipszycka 2011). Ariel López, in *Shenoute of Atripe and the Uses of Poverty*, has published the only full-length study of this aspect of Shenoute's work. López argues that Shenoute needed to justify his public role, which seemed to conflict with his monastic identity, and did so by portraying himself as the champion of the poor (López 2013: 128). As large monasteries became wealthy through donations (both imperial and private), they naturally took over charitable activities, especially in rural areas. Therefore, Shenoute simply fits an established pattern, and we should not overestimate his importance simply because he left so many letters and sermons on this subject. Yet his many writings fill an important gap by offering economic evidence specific to the fifth century (López 2013: 129–130).

The first point, which was most significant for Leipoldt, focused on Shenoute as a representative of Egyptian national consciousness. Ewa Wipszycka (1992) published a direct refutation of the argument. But most recent scholarship has worked on the margins of the question, to shape a picture of a multi-ethnic, multilingual Egypt in the time of Shenoute, who was literate in both Greek and Coptic (Emmel 2007: 90–91). The striking centralization of the Egyptian Church, with a Greek-speaking archbishop in Alexandria and local bishops but no metropolitans throughout the country, did not derive from Egyptian consciousness. Caroline T. Schroeder begins her monograph on Shenoute, *Monastic Bodies: Discipline and Salvation in Shenoute of Atripe*, with a review of previous scholarship that includes a critique of Leipoldt's Egyptian argument (Schroeder 2007: 7), but soon moves on to the study of Shenoute's monastic ideology in which the individual bodies of monks, the corporate monastic body of the community, and the body of Christ (i.e., the Church) all strive for purity in order to gain salvation. Rebecca Krawiec, in *Shenoute and the Women of the White Monastery*, briefly mentions Leipoldt's criticism of the leadership practices of Shenoute and counters the criticism (Krawiec 2002: 21–22). Modern study of Shenoute asks different questions; nationalism does not have the same interest that it had for Leipoldt. Three monographs have joined Leipoldt's work on the shelf devoted to Shenoute, and each has a different focus: Krawiec on gender issues, Schroeder on theories of the body, and López on the holy man as actor in the economy of Late Antiquity.

However, the broader judgment that Leipoldt pronounced on Shenoute, that he means nothing in world history, (but) means everything to the Copts, remains at the center of some of the work being done on Shenoute. The Coptic Orthodox community, both in Egypt and outside of Egypt, has worked to increase awareness of the authentic Shenoute. Samuel Moawad published the first volume of a monograph in Arabic on Shenoute, *Apa Shenoute the Archimandrite: His Life, His Discourses, and His Canons* (Moawad 2009). In the United States, both the St. Mark Foundation and the St. Shenouda the Archimandrite Coptic Society support educational activities for the Coptic Orthodox community in order to increase understanding of Coptic language, literature, and history. Some conferences (including one at the White Monastery in 2006) and publications have specifically focused on Shenoute, which fits with the growth of monasteries in Egypt (Guirgis and van Doorn-Harder 2011: 173–174) under the leadership of Pope Cyril VI (1959–1971) and his successor, Pope Shenoudah III (1971–2012). Monastic renewal is understood to be supported by study of the significant Coptic monastic leaders of the past (Takla 1983). The Coptic heritage is bigger than Shenoute, but recovery of authentic Shenoute is valued and supported by the Coptic Orthodox community.

Finally, whether Shenoute "means nothing in world history" is the issue in some scholarly debates. Much is at stake in establishing the chronology of Shenoute, as noted above. If he did not attend Ephesus I (López 2013: 131–133) or died in 450/451 (Luisier 2009: 275) before the Council of Chalcedon, perhaps he was a minor monastic leader on a level below Victor of Pbow. If Shenoute attended Ephesus I as an important ally of Cyril of Alexandria, and also visited the imperial court in Constantinople, he is more important as a historical figure even though his authentic writings were lost for centuries. However, apart from the chronology question, the 500 or so rules that can be extracted from his monastic writings provide significant evidence for patterns of communal life, even though it takes place in isolation from the Western tradition of the Rule of Benedict. As Bentley Layton stated, "They are our most extensive, detailed, first-hand evidence for how a Christian monastery actually worked in the early centuries" (Layton 2007: 46). Layton has recently published the Coptic text, with English translation, of the 500 rules, which should facilitate comparison (Layton 2014). Also, the critical edition of *Canons*, Book 8, has appeared, with French translation and complete indices (Boud'hors 2013). A better assessment of Shenoute's place in world history and in the history of the Copts may result from the publication of critical editions and translations of all his works.

Bibliography

Primary Sources

Besa, *Letters and Sermons*, K.H. Kuhn (ed./transl.) (1956), Corpus Scriptorum Christianorum Orientalium 157, 158. Louvain: L. Durbecq.

Fragments de la version thébaine de l'Ancien Testament, Gaston Maspero (ed.) (1892), Mémoires publiés par les membres de la mission archéologique française au Caire 6. Paris: Ernest Leroux.

Hymns to Shenoute, Johannes Leipoldt (ed.) (1913), Corpus Scriptorum Christianorum Orientalium 73. Paris: Imprimerie nationale.

Koptische Akten zum Ephesinischen Konzil vom Jahre 431. Wilhem Kraatz (ed.) (1904), Texte und Untersuchungen 26/2. Leipzig: J.C. Hinrichs.

Monuments pour servir à l'histoire de la Égypte chrétienne, Émile Amélineau (ed./transl.) (1888–1895), Mémoires publiés par les membres de la mission archéologique française au Caire 4. Paris: Ernest Leroux.

Pachomiana Latina, Amand Boon (ed.) (1932). Louvain: Bureaux de la Revue.

Ps.-Benjamin I, *Homily on the Wedding at Cana*, C.D.G. Müller (ed.) (1968), *Die Hömilie uuber die Hochzeit zu Kana und weitere Schriften des Patriarchen Benjamin I von Alexandrien*. Heidelberg: Carl Winter.

Ps.-Besa, *The Life of Shenoute* (1983), "Preface" by Armand Veilleux. Introduction and translation by David Bell. Cistercian Studies. Kalamazoo, MI: Cistercian Publications.

Ps.-Shenoute, *On Christian Behavior*, K.H. Kuhn (ed./transl.) (1960), Corpus Scriptorum Christianorum Orientalium 206, 207. Louvain: Secrétariat du Corpus SCO.

Shenoute of Atripe: Collected Texts

Le Canon 8 de Chénouté, Anne Boud'hors (ed./ transl.) (2013), Bibliothèque d'études coptes 21.1, 21.2. Cairo: Institut français d'archéologie orientale.

Coptic Manuscripts from the White Monastery, Dwight W. Young (ed./transl.) (1993), Mitteilungen aus der Papyrussammlung der Österreichischen Nationalbibliothek 22. Vienna: Verlag Brüder Hollinek.

Oeuvres de Schenoudi, Émile Amélineau (ed./transl.) (1907–1914). Paris: Ernest Leroux.

Sinuthii Archimandritae Vita et Opera Omnia, Johannes Leipoldt (ed.) (1906–1913), Corpus Scriptorum Christianorum Orientalium 41, 42, 73. Paris: Imprimerie nationale. Latin translation by H. Wiesmann (1931–1936), Corpus Scriptorum Christianorum Orientalium 96, 108. Paris: Imprimerie nationale.

Zoega, Georg (1810) *Catalogus Codicum Copticorum Manu Scriptorum Qui in Museo Borgiano Velitris Adservantur*. Rome: Sacra Congregatio de Propaganda Fide.

Single Texts (Listed in Alphabetical Order According to Incipit Title (Emmel 2004) or Title in Modern Publication)

And It Happened One Day, L.-Th. Lefort (ed./ transl.) (1955), "Catéchèse christologique de Chenoute". *Zeitschrift für ägyptische Sprache und Altertumskunde*, 80: 40–45.

Contra Origenistas, H.J. Cristea (ed./transl.) (2011), Studien und Texte zu antike und Christentum 60. Tübingen: Mohr Siebeck.

Contra Origenistas, Tito Orlandi (ed./transl.) (1985), *Shenute Contra Origenistas*. Rome: C.I.M.

God Is Blessed, David Brakke (transl.) (1989), "Shenute: on cleaving to profitable things". *Orientalia Lovaniensia Periodica*, 20: 115–141.

De Iudicio, Heike Behlmer (ed./transl.) (1996), Catalogo del Museo Egizio di Torino, 1st ser., Monumenti e Testi 8. Turin: Ministero per I Beni Culturali e Ambientali.

I Have Been Reading the Holy Gospels, Mark Moussa (ed./transl.), (2010), Ph.D. dissertation. Catholic University of America.

I Myself Have Seen, Michael Foat (ed./transl.) (1996), Ph.D. dissertation. Brown University.

Let Our Eyes, Stephen Emmel (ed./transl.) (2008), "Shenoute of Atripe and the Christian destruction of temples in Egypt: rhetoric and reality". In *From Temple to Church*, Johannes Hahn, Stephen Emmel, and Ulrich Gotter (eds). Religions in the Graeco-Roman World 163. Leiden: Brill; 161–201.

The Lord Thundered, Janet Timbie and Jason Zaborowski (transl.) (2006), "Shenoute's sermon *The Lord Thundered*: an introduction and translation". *Oriens Christianus*, 90: 93–125.

Not Because a Fox Barks, John W.B. Barns (transl.) (1964), "Shenute as a historical source". In *Actes du Xe congrès international du papyrologues*, Jozef Wolski (ed.). Wroclaw: Zaklad Narodowy Imienia Ossolinskich Wydawnictwo Polskiej Akadmii Nauk; 151–159.

Secondary Sources

Armanios, Febe (2011), *Coptic Christianity in the Ottoman Egypt*. New York: Oxford University Press.

Burmester, O.H.E. (1932), "Two services of the Coptic church attributed to Peter, Bishop of Behnesa." *Muséon*, 45: 21–70.

Coquin, R.G. and Maurice Martin (1991), "Dayr Anba Shinudah". In *Coptic Encyclopedia*, vol. 3. New York: Macmillan; 761–766.

Emmel, Stephen (2004), *Shenoute's Literary Corpus*. Corpus Scriptorum Christianorum Orientalium 599, 600. Leuven: Peeters.

Emmel, Stephen (2007), "Coptic literature in the Byzantine and early Islamic world". In *Egypt in the Byzantine World 300–700*, Roger S. Bagnall (ed.). Cambridge: Cambridge University Press; 83–102.

Guirgis, Magdi and Nelly van Doorn-Harder (2011), *The Emergence of the Modern Coptic Papacy*. Cairo: American University in Cairo Press.

Hamilton, Alastair (2006), *The Copts and The West, 1439–1822: The European Discovery of the Egyptian Church*. Oxford: Oxford University Press.

Krawiec, Rebecca (2002), *Shenoute and the Women of the White Monastery: Egyptian Monasticism in Late Antiquity*. Oxford: Oxford University Press.

Layton, Bentley (2007), "Rules, patterns, and the exercise of power in Shenoute's monastery: the problem of world replacement and identity maintenance". *Journal of Early Christian Studies*, 15/1: 25–55.

Layton, Bentley (2011), *A Coptic Grammar* 3rd ed., rev. Wiesbaden: Harrassowitz.

Layton, Bentley (2014), *The Canons of Our Fathers: Monastic Rules of Shenoute*. Oxford: Oxford University Press.

Leipoldt, Johannes (1903), *Schenute von Atripe und die Entstehung des national ägyptischen Christentums*. Texte und Untersuchungen 25.1. Leipzig: J.C. Hinrichs'sche Buchhandlung.

López, Ariel (2013), *Shenoute of Atripe and the Uses of Poverty*. Berkeley, CA: University of California Press.

Lubomierski, Nina (2007), *Die Vita Sinuthii*. Studien und Texte zu Antike und Christentum 45. Tübingen: Mohr Siebeck.

Luisier, Philippe (2009), "Chénoute, Victor, Jean de Lycopolis et Nestorius. Quand l'archimandrite d'Atripé en Haute-Égypte est-il mort?" *Orientalia*, 78: 258–281.

Moawad, Samuel (2009), *Apa Shenoute the Archimandrite: His Life, His Discourses, and His Canons*, vol. 1. Cairo: Panarion (in Arabic).

Moussa, Mark (2003), "The Coptic literary dossier of Abba Moses of Abydos". *Coptic Church Review*, 24/3: 67–90.

Revillout, Eugène (1883), "Les origins du schism égyptien, premier recit: le précurseur et inspirateur, Sénuti le prophète". *Revue de l'histoire des religions*, 8: 401–467, 545–581.

Schroeder, Caroline (2007), *Monastic Bodies: Discipline and Salvation in Shenoute of Atripe*. Philadelphia, PA: University of Pennsylvania Press.

Shisha-Halevy, Ariel (1986), *Coptic Grammatical Categories: Structural Studies in the Syntax of Shenoutean Sahidic*. Analecta Orientalia 53. Rome: Potificio Istituto Biblico.

Swanson, Mark (2005), "St. Shenoute in 17th century dress: Arabic Christian preaching in Paris, BN ar 4761". *Coptica*, 4: 27–42.

Takla, Hany N. (1983), *St. Shenouda the Archimandrite*. Part 1, *The Ecclesiastical Position of St Shenouda in the Coptic Church*. Los Angeles: St Shenouda Coptic Society.

Thompson, Herbert (1922), "Dioscorus and Shenoute". *Recueil d'études égyptologiques. Bibliothèques de l'École des hautes etudes. Sciences historiques et philologiques*, 243: 367–376.

Timbie, Janet (1998), "A liturgical procession in the desert of Apa Shenoute". In *Pilgrimage and Holy Space in Late Antique Egypt*, David Frankfurter (ed.). Leiden: Brill; 415–441.

Wipszycka, Ewa (1992), "Le nationalisme a-t-il existé dans l'Égypte byzantine?" *Journal of Juristic Papyrology*, 22: 83–128.

Wipszycka, Ewa (2011), "Resources and economic activities of the Egyptian monastic communities (4th–8th century)". *Journal of Juristic Papyrology*, 41: 159–263.

CHAPTER 13

Nestorius of Constantinople

George Bevan

Nestorius and "Nestorianism"

In approaching the reception of the bishop Nestorius of Constantinople one must carefully distinguish Nestorius the man, bishop of Constantinople from 428 to 431, from
"Nestorianism," a fluid and sometimes pejorative term that usually refers to, at best, a
caricature of the teachings of Nestorius as modern scholarship understands them.
Indeed, if an eponymous founder were needed for the Church of the East, as Macomber
suggested many years ago, the so-called "Nestorian" church would be more aptly
termed "Theodorean" after Theodore of Mopsuestia, the Antiochene teacher who had
vastly greater influence than Nestorius over the Dyophysite Christology that thrived
beyond Rome's Eastern frontier (Macomber 1958). Indeed, the history of the later
"Nestorian" Church that flourished in Persia, India, and China could be written without
a detailed account of the career of Nestorius, or an account of what modern scholarship has determined about his teaching on Mary and the incarnation to be, so little lasting influence did his writings have on their intellectual formation. As Sebastian Brock
argued in an oft-cited paper, the very term "Nestorian" is a "lamentable misnomer," one
based on centuries of misunderstanding of the theological foundations of the Church
that would bear its name (Brock 1992; 1996). We would, it seems, be better to replace
the term entirely, much in the same way "Monophysite" seems to have been supplanted
by the neologism "Miaphysite," one without philological or historical precedent, in contemporary scholarship (Winkler 1997; Millar 2013: 50–51).

Yet should "Nestorianism" be so easily purged from discourse of church history for
more anodyne alternatives, and the man Nestorius confined to his role only in the
events between 428 and 451? While the Nestorius of history may have had significantly less direct influence than Theodore of Mopesuestia, religious identity rests as
much on a shared history as it does on the abstruse principles of Christology – whether

The Wiley Blackwell Companion to Patristics, First Edition. Edited by Ken Parry.
© 2015 John Wiley & Sons Ltd. Published 2019 by John Wiley & Sons Ltd.

one professes one or two natures, or one or two *hypostases*. For a time, at least, the Church of the East taught works of Nestorius, incorporated Nestorius among the Antiochene Church Fathers, and even came to self-identify as "Nestorians." For the opponents of the Council of Chalcedon, the name of Nestorius came to be associated, indelibly, with the dyophysitism of that council. Both sides, for their own reasons, preserved accounts of his episcope and downfall for centuries, and modern scholarship has wrestled fervently with whether or not Nestorius was a heretic, even as the very category began to lose its sting in the increasingly secular twentieth-century West. The understanding of how Nestorius' career and teachings were received reveals much about how Christian orthodoxy was created in the conciliar epoch, how the names of individual "Fathers" came, very imperfectly, to denominate theological positions, and how even debates about the natures of Christ still resonate today.

Career of Nestorius, 428–c. 451

Prior to surveying how Nestorius was received in various later traditions, it is of central importance to understand how he was received by his contemporaries, for unlike many other church Fathers, his life was enveloped in controversy. Nestorius became bishop of Constantinople on 10 April 428, selected, according to Socrates *scholasticus*, a contemporary observer, at the instigation of the emperor as an outside candidate to cut through the vicious ecclesiastical rivalries besetting the Eastern capital. Known in his home of Antioch as a formidable public speaker he must have recalled in the minds of many John Chrysostom who had been brought to Constantinople from Antioch 30 years prior. Perhaps in recognition of this obvious parallel, under Nestorius the first liturgical commemoration of John in Constantinople was celebrated later that same year. Surprisingly, this parallel, obvious to us in hindsight, was emphasized neither by Nestorius' supporters nor by his opponents. The sixth-century Syriac historian Barhadbeshebba (see "The Church of the East" section) is almost unique in making the comparison. His apparent similarities with John were insufficient to outweigh his serious missteps in the capital; unlike John's, his downfall was the result not of clashing personality and politics, but of core doctrine. Even as ardent a follower of John as Philip of Side, a competitor for the See of Constantinople in 428 and a historian of the church, became an early opponent of Nestorius.

Although, again according to Socrates *scholasticus*, Nestorius acted arrogantly as bishop, proclaiming in his first public sermon that if the emperor Theodosius were to give him an empire free of heretics, he would give to the emperor Persia in return, it was a debate over the epithet *theotokos*, "bearer of god," for the Virgin Mary that began a crisis that would lead to the deposition of Nestorius at the Council of Ephesus in 431, and began centuries of intractable dispute over the natures of Christ. Eduard Schwartz, in an enormously influential account of the outbreak of the controversy, argued that the controversy was formented by Cyril of Alexandria who was hoping to distract attention away from accusations then being made against him by the Egyptian Monk Victor (Schwartz 1928). This account brought the story of Nestorius' fall even more closely in line with that of John Chrysostom, who earned enmity of Theophilus of

Alexandria when he sheltered the so-called "Tall Brothers," monks on the run from the tyrannical authority of the bishop in Egypt. This account also fitted well with the one Nestorius himself gave of his unfair persecution by Cyril and his "Egyptians" in his own *Liber Heraclidis*. Schwartz's authority on these issues since cast a very long shadow over the interpretation of Nestorius' career. A reexamination of the documents, however, shows that the controversy began first in Constantinople, as early as August of 428, and only later reached the attention of Cyril in 429 (Redies 1998). Similarly, the West responded to the work of Nestorius independently of Cyril in early 429, and the abbot John Cassian, who had a good command of Greek from his time in Egypt, was commissioned to write a treatise against Nestorius, the *De Incarnatione*, armed only with the most slender of selections of his sermons. So infelicitous was Cassian's work, at least judged by later standards of orthodoxy such as Cyril's *Twelve Anathemas*, that it would never reappear again in the debate. Instead, Pope Celestine relied on Cyril of Alexandria to guide his response to the disputes in the East.

Despite what his opponents claimed, Nestorius did not reject the term *theotokos* outright. Instead, he expressed reservations about it – that the unwary could be led into believing that Mary was herself a goddess and that Christ was born into the world on the model of a pagan god – and proposed one of two solutions. First, one could use the term *anthropotokos* alongside *theotokos* to make clear that only the human nature of Christ was created in Mary's womb not the divinity, which could not be said to have been created. Alternatively, one could adopt a neologism that seems to originate with Nestorius himself, *christotokos*, "bearer of Christ." In the Antiochene exegetical tradition in which he was formed, "Christ" stood for both the human and divine natures, an entity that Mary could indeed be said to have brought forth into the world without letting users fall into the error of believing that Mary could give birth to the divinity on its own. Unsurprisingly, Nestorius' academic reservations about *theotokos* did not win over the growing number of faithful who already in 428 prayed for the intercession of Mary *Theotokos*. On the contrary, they heard in Nestorius' quibbles the *denial* of Christ's divinity and that he taught that Christ was a "mere man" like the notorious heretic Paul of Samosata, a connection that Nestorius could not shake. Even Nestorius' colleagues in the East, like John of Antioch, believed that he was going too far in insisting that *theotokos* not be accepted at face value (Fairbairn 2007). If the objections to *theotokos* were carried too far, then their deeper, shared beliefs about the two natures would have to be aired publicly and the subtleties of Theodore's thought lost as the debate devolved into competing slogans. As it turned out, Nestorius was deposed only for his failure to accept Mary as *theotokos*, not for the rigorous dyophysitism his name would soon be associated with.

Much has been made of Nestorius' distinctive Christological beliefs at this time, yet a perusal of the works of Theodore of Mopsuestia, the leading light of the so-called Antiochene School, who died the year Nestorius became bishop, shows that the careful distinction between the human and divine natures was already well established some time before. According to Theodore, one could, and should, distinguish in scripture between those things done by Christ that required the human nature and those that required the divine. Since the divine nature was, by definition, impassible, it was only through the human nature that Christ could be said to be tired or feel pain. Similarly, the miracles of Christ could be accomplished only through the divine nature. The danger in such a rigorous distinction, however, was that, at the end of the day, one was left with the uneasy feeling the Christ was two individuals, not one. Moreover, important scriptural passages like *John* 1:14 ("And the Word became flesh") could no longer be read literally and required the mediation of nonscriptural philosophical terms like "nature" to be understood properly. Theodore never provided a theoretical framework to explain how the two natures, the actions of which could be distinguished in scripture, came together in a single individual with a single will, other than to say that the divine nature dwelt in the human nature "by good pleasure." This problem Theodore left to his followers. Nestorius' solution to the problem made use of *prosopon*, a semi-technical term that ranged in meaning from an actor's mask to something approximating the sense of "individual."

The controversy in Constantinople spread with remarkable speed. Although the epithet *theotokos* was not yet part of the official teachings of the church, it had by the early fifth century been widely adopted in Egypt. To deny *theotokos* was to call the believers in Egypt heretics. Cyril, bishop of Alexandria, wrote two letters to Nestorius asking for clarification on what he meant. Despite the later narrative, due in no small part to Schwartz, Cyril was patient and avoided making direct accusations. His first answer met with silence, and his second with a brusque dismissal by the bishop of Constantinople. In the west, where the finer points of *theotokos* and the natures of Christ were less obviously contentious and talk of two *naturae* was hardly earth shattering, Nestorius' acceptance of Pelagian exiles in Constantinople must have aggravated western authorities. Finally, within Constantinople itself, Nestorius created a hostile climate by vigorously pursuing his opponents who spoke out. In fact, Nestorius seems to have used one of the Pelagian exiles then resident in Constantinople to run the synod in 429 that pursued his opponents (Bevan 2010).

The First Council of Ephesus was called to meet in 431 to resolve the controversy that had arisen in Constantinople. Although Schwartz argued that the Council was pushed for by Cyril of Alexandria and that it was rigged to condemn Nestorius from the very beginning, there is every indication that the emperor, Theodosius II, was the author of the decision to convene the council and hoped thereby to bring clarity to the issue of *theotokos* and thereby exonerate Nestorius. What actually transpired in Ephesus is well known. The bishops from the diocese of *Oriens*, with John of Antioch at their head, were weeks late for the scheduled opening of the council. Cyril and Memnon of Ephesus then took control of the proceedings and tricked the Roman representative into opening the council. When Nestorius refused to present himself, he was deposed. On his arrival, John of Antioch convened a counter council, but Nestorius never attended. His surprising absence would be explained later in October when the emperor accepted his offer to enter into retirement. It was clear from the letter accepting the offer that Nestorius had been petitioning to retire throughout the summer. Nestorius failed to attend a single session of the council on either side, and retired before the council had even closed. Both these facts his opponents took as a tacit acknowledgment of his guilt, and made continuing support of his cause by any but his most committed followers impossible. More importantly, the Council of Ephesus never examined Nestorius' underlying belief in "the two natures" and only affirmed the orthodoxy of *theotokos*. Whether

Nestorius thought that after the incarnation Christ had one or two *hypostases*, a term introduced into the debate by Cyril of Alexandria without any technical definition, was in 431 of uncertain importance; only with Chalcedon was the "one *hypostasis*" made and pronounced orthodox. With no definition of Nestorius' heresy concluded at Ephesus, just what constituted "Nestorianism" remained nebulous. He was widely thought to have denied the divinity of Christ by rejecting *theotokos*, but the underlying reasons why he had done so were not yet understood by his opponents.

Outside of the documents in the *Acta Conciliorum Oecumenicorum* and his own writings, Socrates *scholasticus* is alone among the troika of ecclesiastical historians – Socrates, Sozomen, and Theodoret – contemporary to treat Nestorius. His chief indictment of Nestorius was that he was arrogant and intemperate in character, and incendiary in his pursuit of heretics. The controversy in the capital, Socrates claims, was due to Nestorius' support for the extreme condemnation of *theotokos* by presbyter Anastasius, who was numbered among the bishop's associates. That Nestorius could be led so easily to support this extreme view, Socrates goes on to say, was due to his ignorance of the teaching of earlier Church Fathers like Origen and Eusebius of Pamphilia on the subject. It is remarkable that in this earliest historical account of Nestorius' episcopate, one written well before the Council of Chalcedon, Socrates could claim to have himself read the writings of Nestorius to have judged from them that the deposed bishop was hardly a denier of Christ's divinity in the manner of Paul of Samosata. Whether Socrates read Nestorius' work before or after the imperial order to destroy them in 436, an order to correspond with the deposed bishop's exile to Petra, is not known – as later evidence shows, many of Nestorius' writings were preserved in Constantinople well into the sixth century – but even by the end of the 430s or even the 440s an educated Christian could vindicate Nestorius' from the most extreme accusations hurled at him. Nestorius' reputation had not yet solidified as an irredeemable arch-heretic.

Nestorius was exiled by imperial order first to Petra, then later to Egypt, where by all accounts he died (Parry 2013). Why should there have been so long a gap between his deposition at the Council of Ephesus and his exile, events normally co-incident? As Nestorius himself would write, the emperor had been a "friend" to him and was perhaps reluctant to take the step of issuing an order for his arrest and exile. While Nestorius lived a free man, however, there remained the possibility that he could recant his views on *theotokos* if his friends could convince him and the proper venue showed itself. The view Socrates espoused – that Nestorius' error was principally one of ignorance – was perhaps shared more widely than later sources suggest. Events following Ephesus suggest, in fact, that Nestorius was not far from the ecclesiastical "mainstream," once his apparent criticism of *theotokos* was put aside. In 433, Cyril of Alexandria's letter *Laetentur Caeli* ("Let the heavens rejoice") reported a series of doctrinal points shared between Antioch and Alexander, commonly referred to in modern scholarship as the "Formulary of Reunion." The text is striking in that it permits the faithful to interpret passages of scriptures as referring either to the human or divine natures, a concession that more or less permitted the Dyophysite tradition of Theodore of Mopsuestia, from which the core of Nestorius' Christological thought derived, to continue unmolested.

Even from his exile Nestorius kept abreast of developments in ecclesiastical politics. He knew of the (failed) attempts by Cyril of Alexandria to have the writings of Diodore of Tarsus and Theodore of Mopsuestia condemned by the Eastern bishops under the leadership of John of Antioch at the end of the 430s, and he had a reasonably good idea of the events surrounding the Second Council of Ephesus in 449. He claimed to have read Pope Leo's *Tomus ad Flavianum*, a text sent to him by his supporters, and approved its contents as a belated vindication of his Dyophysite position. The available evidence points to the uncomfortable possibility, one almost entirely suppressed within pro-Chalcedonian sources, that the emperor Marcian summoned Nestorius from exile in Egypt to attend the Council of Chalcedon. In any case, the anathema against Nestorius was renewed at Chalcedon and he came in the propaganda of the council to be part of an Aristotelian triad that placed the "two natures in one person" formula of 451 between the two extremes of Nestorius and Eutyches, who had parroted Cyril's "one incarnate nature" at a synod in 448 (Shin 2006). Eutyches denied the humanity of Christ, Nestorius denied the divinity, but Chalcedon took the *via media*. This was the artificial role cast for Nestorius in 451, one often accepted without question into the modern era.

Anti-Chalcedonian Polemic

For the opponents of Chalcedon, of which there were many in the Roman East, the rumors that Nestorius had been summoned to attend Chalcedon only confirmed the "Nestorian" character of the council. It was for this reason – to condemn Chalcedon – that the heresy, exile, and recall of Nestorius became relevant for those who supported Cyril's post-434 formulation in his *Second Letter to Succensus* of "the one incarnate nature" (Ibrahim 1998; Kosinski 2007). These stories about Nestorius, surely in circulation even in 451, survive in Syriac from later authors. Zachariah of Mytilene, writing at the end of the fifth century, used a lost history written by Timothy Ailurus, the anti-Chalcedonian bishop of Alexandria, to describe the circumstances of Nestorius' recall from exile by the emperor Marcian. Similarly, John Rufus' *Plerophories*, written at the beginning of the sixth century, relates accounts, said to be from eyewitnesses like Peter the Iberian, from Nestorius' episcopate in Constantinople. Like Zachariah, John uses Timothy Ailurus to provide the details of Nestorius' last days in exile in Panopolis in Egypt, and his recall to Chalcedon by the emperor Marcian. Both accounts relate that Nestorius died on the road, his tongue consumed by disease, a fitting punishment for an eloquent heresiarch. This story of Nestorius' end would be reiterated by Michael the Syrian in his *Chronicle* in the twelfth century, along with quotations from John Rufus.

The anti-Chalcedonian sources show, unsurprisingly, no particularly nuanced understanding of Nestorius' work, although Severus of Antioch at least cited him and preserved fragments not known from elsewhere. Philoxenus of Mabbug also offered apparent details of Nestorius' early life not otherwise preserved, although they should probably be seen as legend. In general, Nestorius was referenced in the anti-Chalcedonian tradition only to demonstrate that the Council of Chalcedon was "Nestorian" in its tenor, even though Nestorius had died before he could attend. The anti-Chalcedonian criticism of Nestorius would have a definite impact on their opponents, both inside and outside the empire. Their insistence that Nestorius carried on the tradition of Theodore of Mopsuestia would be addressed by Justinian's proposed condemnation of the "Three Chapters", and the Church of the East would be driven to look more closely at Nestorius and his work in order to refashion their identity in the face of encroachment by anti-Chalcedonian missionaries. Ironically, the story of Nestorius' recall from exile would later prove as equally appealing to "Nestorian" Christians as it had to their fiercest doctrinal opponents.

Chalcedonian Sources

The Chalcedonian sources had little or no reason to dwell on the details of Nestorius' case. The condemnation of Nestorius in 451 did not, however, define just what he was being condemned for. Chalcedonians still needed to define Nestorius as an extreme of dyophysitism that was fundamentally different than the definition of orthodoxy proclaimed at Chalcedon. If this distinction were not maintained, Chalcedon would be dismissed as "Nestorian", just as the anti-Chalcedonians argued. The most committed defenders of Leo's *Tome* and the dyophysitism of Chalcedon were in the west. There, the name of Nestorius had become a byword for heresy early on in the debate, although precious little of his work was available in Latin. Marius Mercator supplied new Latin translations of Nestorius' most incriminating sermons, which John Cassian had earlier deployed in his polemic, but Nestorius was hardly the subject of serious research.

The notable exception was Boethius, the western consul for 510 and celebrated as the author of the *Consolation of Philosophy*. In late 512 or early 513 he wrote a treatise *Contra Eutychen et Nestorium*, a mostly ignored text filed among his *Opuscula sacra*. Written in response to a letter of Eastern monks to Pope Symmachus, Boethius brought to the Christological problems of the first half of the mid-fifth century an unparalleled level of philosophical acumen, even by the standards of the east where the controversies had arisen. A close reader of Aristotle, Boethius offered careful, philosophically informed, definitions of the terms of the debate: *prosopon*, *hypostasis*, *ousia*, and *physis*. While his goal was to provide a philosophical support for the Council of Chalcedon's "in two natures" formulation, Boethius did not present Nestorius' position in any great detail. He condemned Nestorius only for teaching that Christ was two persons. He showed no awareness, for instance, of Nestorius' "*prosopon* of the union," the mechanism by which he joined the two "natural *prosopa*" together in dynamic reciprocity (Bradshaw 2009).

The serious defense of Chalcedon began in the east only in the sixth century. Although Nestorius was not one of the "Three Chapters," the condemnation of whose writings the emperor Justinian saw as a solution to the impasse over Chalcedon in the sixth century, he was, of course, perceived as entangled with Theodore, Theodoret, and Ibas of Edessa. There was no need to include Nestorius in their number for he had already been explicitly condemned at Chalcedon. But, to the Miaphysites, Justinian's proposals did not go far enough; Leo's *Tomus ad Flavianum* was just as offensive as Ibas' letter *Ad Marim*. While Justinian's proposal failed to win over the Miaphysites, the suggestion that men who had died in the peace of the Church, as all three unquestionably had, ought to be condemned rankled with many supporters of Chalcedon. The deacon Rusticus, nephew of Pope Vigilius and a monk in the monastery of the *Akoimetai* or "Sleepless Monks" in Constantinople, undertook to create his *Synodicon*, a text transmitted to us in the *Collectio Casinensis*. Beyond translating into Latin and correcting the acts both of the First Council of Ephesus and the Council of Chalcedon, texts still largely inaccessible to those in the Latin west, he translated a large number of letters between bishops from supporters of Nestorius, most of which are now lost in the Greek, and supplied commentary on them from the *Tragoedia* of Irenaeus of Tyre, a close supporter of Nestorius who had been exiled with him in the same imperial order. This extraordinary undertaking was intended to demonstrate not the orthodoxy of Nestorius, as we might expect from Rusticus' use of the highly partisan *Tragoedia*, but to demonstrate that Theodoret was no supporter of Nestorius, and to cleave him away from the so-called "Irreconcilables" in the diocese of *Oriens* who continue to protest Nestorius' deposition at Ephesus and renounced John of Antioch's overtures towards Cyril of Alexandria. Apart from vindicating Theodoret, Rusticus attempted to show that the Antiochene Dyophysite position, was, on the surface at least, very similar to the Chalcedonian definition, but rooted in the work of Theodore of Mopsuestia could be saved from the excesses of Nestorius, particularly his apparent condemnation of *theotokos*. Few letters of Nestorius were preserved in the *Synodicon*, and one must suspect that Rusticus suppressed those that showed him willing to compromise. Similarly, Rusticus must have selected from among the letters to Nestorius by his allies that showed their cooling relationship even before the Council of Ephesus. The *Synodicon*, while hardly successful as a defense of Theodoret, bequeathed to scholarship precious sources for the ecclesiastical politics of *Oriens* that would not have otherwise survived.

With the exception of Socrates *scholasticus*, little is known of how the Nestorian controversy was treated by the ecclesiastical historians, or even a secular historian like Priscus, who were outside of the Miaphysite tradition. Theodoret ends his *Ecclesiastical History* in 428, even though he lived into the 450s, and thereby neatly sidesteps potentially embarrassing events to which he himself was a party. Theodoret's letter to John of Aegea gives us a glimpse of the contortions that Theodoret, who had been forced to condemn Nestorius at Chalcedon, had to go through after the council to win a supporter of Nestorius over to the council (Gray 1984). So little has survived of Theodore Lector, who worked in the first half of the sixth century, that we cannot judge well how he treated Nestorius. But citing Theodore, Theophanes in the ninth century repeated the claim common in the anti-Chalcedonian sources that Nestorius' tongue rotted before his death.

Quite a different approach to Nestorius' career was taken by Evagrius *scholasticus*, who completed his *Ecclesiastical History* by 593. Evagrius chose to begin his history, decidedly pro-Chalcedonian in tenor, not in 451, but in 431, the year of Nestorius' deposition, a starting point that foregrounded Nestorius in the narrative of the travails that beset the Church following the Council of Chalcedon. The prominence of Nestorius is surely a response to the work of the Miaphysite Zachariah of Mytilene, whom Evagrius refers to as a source of misinformation. Evagrius had available to him a letter of Nestorius that had remarkably survived into the late sixth century and that is found in no other source today. What is more, he had available to him a historical account of his travails that Nestorius' wrote, a work that has not survived. These documents he first used to paint a picture of the miserable life of Nestorius in exile in Egypt, a time about which the surviving *Liber Heraclidis* is silent. Most importantly, however, Evagrius challenges the Miaphysite claim that Nestorius was summoned by Marcian to attend Chalcedon. Evagrius quotes a letter by Eustathius of Berytus that claimed some bishops at Chalcedon clamored for the return of Nestorius' bones to the council. It is strange that Eustathius has the partisans of Nestorius refer to him as a "Saint," a title he did not bear even in the Church of the East at the height of his popularity. Stranger still is Evagrius' logic in adducing Eustathius' letter to refute Zachariah's claim that Nestorius was recalled to Chalcedon. The letter shows only that Nestorius died before he could reach the council, not that he was not recalled. Indeed, the shouts Eustathius' reports at the council suggest partisans of Nestorius had been promised his return by the emperor.

The Church of the East

The Christians of Persia were absent from the deliberations at Ephesus and Chalcedon. In 424, at the Synod of Dadisho, they had separated themselves from the ecclesiastical hierarchy of the Roman Church, a move perhaps calculated to remove themselves from the suspicion of the Persian king as covert agents of Roman political will inside his territory. Nestorius and his writings in Greek played no role, as far as we can tell, in their development until the end of the fifth century, when a Syriac metrical homily of Narsai of Nisibis on the "Three Greek Doctors" places Nestorius alongside Diodore of Tarsus and Theodore of Mopsuestia. Narsai would have had access to the exegetical work of Theodore at the School of Nisibis, but the same was not the case for Nestorius' work. Narsai's inclusion of Nestorius was based on reputation alone, it seems, not for the details of his account of Christ's incarnation. Nestorius was included among the spiritual founders of the Persian Church only because had been deposed by the Roman ecclesiastical establishment for his unyielding defense of Theodore (Kavvadas 2012).

The wide circulation of Narsai's homily reflected an increased interest, particularly at the School of Nisibis, in just what Nestorius had taught. By 540, some of Nestorius' writings, still remarkably preserved in Constantinople in the monastery of the *Akoimetai*, were brought east and translated into Syriac by the catholicos Mar Aba. Once translated, Nestorius' *apologia pro vita sua* soon became a core text for the Church of the East. According to the *History of Rabban Bar 'Idta* (c. 509–612), the Nestorian curriculum required students to memorize the *Liber Heraclidis*, surely an arduous task given its length and, at times, tortured syntax. The new availability of Nestorius' work in Syriac translation also provided the basis for a new historiographic tradition (Wood 2013). Barhadbeshebba Arabaia composed an *Ecclesiastical History* at the end of the sixth century or the beginning of the seventh. Less a chronological history than a series of short biographies of figures important to the Church of the East such as Diodore of Tarsus, John Chrysostom, and Theodore of Mopsuestia, Barhadbeshebba styles Nestorius a "Christian martyr," not simply a "Greek doctor," and places him as a student of Theodore. Much like the stories propagated about

John Chrysostom by his partisans that his downfall was due in large part of the "New Jezebel" Eudocia, wife of the emperor Arcadius, Theodosius II's sister, Pulcheria, is given a significant role in the deposition of Nestorius. What is more, Barhadbeshebba relates the story of Nestorius' recall by Marcian to Chalcedon, though his death is not described in as gruesome terms as in the anti-Chalcedonian sources. The Syriac *Letter to Cosmas* is likely part of the same intellectual milieu in the sixth century. Though it purports to be an authentic text written not long after the Council of Chalcedon, it is decidedly hagiographic in tone. The letter moves from a description of Nestorius' zealous defense of orthodoxy against heretics as bishop of Constantinople and his struggles against Pulcheria, to miracles he performed while in exile in Egypt, as well as miracles after his death, including a Lazarus-like resurrection of a dead man, a story repeated centuries later in the Chronicle of Seert. Shahdost (Eustathius) of Tarihan in the eighth century could call Nestorius the "righteous martyr and *christophoros*" (Abramowski and Goodman 1972: 19). Notwithstanding the growing importance of Nestorius in the sixth and seventh centuries, Nestorius was not yet part of the official identity of the Church of the East; Nestorius was not even named in any of the eight synods, preserved for us in the *Synodicon Orientale*, held by the Church between 486 and 612 (Baum and Winkler 2003: 30).

By the eighth century Nestorius came to be viewed not only as a revered teacher, and perhaps even a saint-like figure in some quarters, but to be the spiritual founder of an eponymous "Nestorian" Church (Reinink 2009; Seleznyov 2010). While church writers were quite aware that Nestorius was not the exclusive author of the Dyophysite and two-*hypostasis* (referred to as *qnome* in Syriac) Christology that by the seventh century had become the orthodoxy of the Church of the East, the new status of Nestorius was due to a confrontation with Miaphysite propaganda. Under the influence of the debates in the west in the sixth and seventh centuries that followed from the Fifth Ecumenical Council in 553, the School of Nisibis under the leadership Henana of Adiabene became a venue of considerable debate between the proponents of one-*qnoma* and two-*qnome*. The intervention of Miaphysite outsiders on behalf of the one-*qnoma* may have radicalized the followers of two-*qnome* by elevating Nestorius to the status of their founder, a figure they staked out a position for that made any form of compromise with the Miaphysites impossible. While Theodore was still recognized as a teacher of unparalleled importance in their tradition, Nestorius was then perceived, by Miaphysites and the Church of the East alike, as giving the work of Theodore a decisively two-*qnome* interpretation. Bar Hebraeus, a bishop and historian of the West Syrian Church in the thirteenth century, records that in the eighth century Nestorians attempted to recover the bones of Nestorius from Egypt and bring them back to Iraq, an anecdote surely indicative of the growing reputation of Nestorius.

This "Nestorian" Church, through its vigorous missionary efforts, would spread to India and China, but there is no evidence that the work of Nestorius was central to its belief. The *Liber Heraclidis* was a long and unwieldy text that was unsuitable to wide dissemination, and probably dropped out of the core curriculum of even the Christians of Persia. The works of Nestorius were not discarded, however. The patriarchal library of Ebed-Jesu, the metropolitan of Nisibis from 1290 to 1318, is recorded as holding not only copies of Nestorius' *Liber Heraclidis* and *Letter to Cosmas* (texts that have survived), but also to his *Tragedy*, a *Book of Letters*, and the *Book of Homilies and Sermons*, three works now lost. The person of Nestorius continued to be widely known and venerated, even if the details of his teaching were no longer taught. The rediscovery of these "Nestorian" Churches by the west, as well as works Nestorius lost to the west, would again problematize the role of Nestorius in their teaching and raise the thorny question of whether Nestorius was a "Nestorian", and whether these eastern churches were tainted with his ancient heresy.

Modern Reception

The modern, western reception of Nestorius begins with Martin Luther's work on Nestorius and Eutyches, which, surprisingly, upheld the traditional case against him and criticizes his failure to appreciate the so-called *communicatio idiomatum*, as did most other reformers of his era (Grillmeier 1961). A notable exception is the Calvinist J. Bruguier of Lille, who published a work anonymously in 1645 that argued that Nestorius was orthodox, and Cyril a heretic, an anticipation of a common view three centuries later. The evidence Bruguier and Luther had to work with was minimal, however. The great conciliar collections of Giovanni Domenico Mansi would appear more than a century later. The reception of Nestorius in the modern era showed a dramatic change in the early twentieth century when new evidence became available.

First, the Protestant scholar Friedrich Loofs collected all the fragments of Nestorius known up until his time in a single volume, the *Nestoriana*, in 1905. Most of these fragments were culled from the conciliar collections and were preserved as evidence of Nestorius' heresy. Second, even before Loofs set to work, Anglican missionaries had discovered a mutilated Syriac manuscript in the library of the Nestorian patriarch at Kotchanes in Turkish Kurdistan in 1889. It took until 1910 before the Lazarist priest Paul Bedjan published and edited the Syriac text, and the French scholar Francois Nau produced a careful French translation in the same year. Another less felicitous translation, in English, was made by Hodgson and Driver in 1925. According to the manuscript, this was the *Liber Heraclidis* of Nestorius, the discovery of which then seemed to give scholars the chance to appreciate the full scope of his thought; in the twentieth century, the prospect of recovering the "historical Nestorius" was at hand in a moment of *ex oriente lux*.

Reactions to the *Liber* were mixed, but all conceded that his terminology was unclear, particularly his use of *prosopon* (Braaten 1963). Martin Jugie, a Catholic scholar of considerable authority, reacted swiftly in 1912 and argued that *Liber* only proved that Nestorius was indeed guilty of teaching that Christ was two distinct persons; Nestorius' "*prosopon* of the union" was an illusory ground for the single personhood of Christ. Yet many other scholars in the Anglican and Protestant traditions published accounts of Nestorius that either exonerated him of the ancient accusations against him or at least presented sympathetic accounts. Perhaps the culmination of these attempts was Milton Anastos' provocatively titled paper "Nestorius was Orthodox" (Anastos 1962).

Debate soon shifted to questions about the *Liber* itself, ones that had been put to one side in the rush to present and assess what seemed to be Nestorius' unadulterated thought. Luise Abramowski, in her 1963 monograph on the *Liber*, not only argued against the *Liber* being a single work, but that there were extensive inauthentic interpolations in the transmitted text. Both Scipioni (1974) and Chesnut (1978) have since argued persuasively for Nestorius' authorship, and that the full text of the *Liber* could be used to reconstruct Nestorius' thought. Abramowski and Goodman (1972) also brought to light some new fragments of Nestorius that can be added to the corpus, but no profound revelations about Nestorius' teaching or biography have since resulted.

The expanded corpus of Nestorius' writings available to western scholarship in the twentieth century provided the grounds for a rapprochement with the Church of the East (Brock 2004). This encounter culminated in 1994 when Pope John Paul II and Patriarch Dinkha IV of the Church of the East signed a common Christological Declaration where the signatories agreed to accept their differences over the term *theotokos*. While sensitive and expert assessments of Nestorius' place in history by Abramowski (1995) and de Halleux (1993) were contributed as part of an effort undertaken by *Pro Oriente* to reconcile the churches, the question of whether Nestorius could be rehabilitated was not officially decided. That the same Patriarch Dinkha had explicitly rejected the epithet "Nestorian" for his church on his elevation in 1976, despite the call of some Western scholars for Nestorius' rehabilitation on the appearance of the *Liber Heraclidis*, suggests that it is unlikely that Nestorius and his work will ever enjoy the same status in the Church of the East as they did in the sixth to ninth centuries. However, new discoveries in the future may change that.

Bibliography

Primary Sources

Barhadbeshebba Arabaia, *Historia patrum sanctorum persecutionem passorum propter vertitatem*. F. Nau (ed. and French transl.) (1913–1932). PO 9 pp. 503–631; PO 23 pp. 183–342. Paris.

John Cassian, *De incarnatione contra Nestorium Libri VII*, M. Petschenig (ed.) (1888), CSEL, 17, 233–391, Vienna (also PL 50 cols. 9–270). M.-A. Vannier (French transl.) (1999), *Traité de l'Incarnation*. Paris.

Cyril of Alexandria, *Select Letters*, Lionel R. Wickham (ed. and Eng. transl.) (1983). Oxford.

Evagrius *scholasticus*, *Historia Ecclesiastica*, J. Bidez and L. Parmentier (eds) (1898). London (reprinted, Amsterdam, 1964). Michael Whitby (Engl. transl.) (2000), *The Ecclesiastical History of Evagrius Scholasticus*. Translated Texts for Historians 33. Liverpool.

Letter to Cosmas, M. Oscar Braun (ed. and German transl.), *Zeitschrift der Deutschen Morgenländischen Gesellschaft* 54 (1900) 378–395; F. Nau (ed. and French trans.). PO 13 (1919), pp. 271–286 (French transl. repr. in Nestorius, *Liber*, transl. Nau, pp. 362–366).

Nestorius, *Liber Heraclidis*, P. Bedjan (ed.) (1910), Leipzig and Paris. *Le Livre d'Héraclide de Damas*. F. Nau (French transl.) (1910). Paris. *The Bazaar of Heraclides*. G.R. Driver and L. Hodgson (Engl. transl.) (1925). Oxford.

Rabban Bar 'Idta. *The Histories of Rabban Hormizd the Persian and Rabban bar 'Idta*, E.A. Wallis Budge (ed. and English transl.) (1902), two volumes. London.

John Rufus, *Plérophories*. F. Nau (ed. and transl.). PO 8 (1911), 5–208.

Socrates *scholasticus*, Socrates Scholasticus, *Historia Ecclesiastica*, G.C. Hansen and M. Sirinjan (eds) (1995), *Sokrates Kirchengeschichte*. GCS NF 1. Berlin.

Zachariah of Mitylene, *Historia Ecclesiastica*. E.W. Brooks (ed. and Latin transl.) (1919–1921, 1924). CSCO Scr. Syr. 38–39 and 41–42. Louvain. G. Greatrex, R. Phenix, and C.B. Horn (2011), *The Chronicle of Pseudo-Zachariah Rhetor: Church and War in Late Antiquity* (Engl. transl. with commentary). Liverpool.

Secondary Sources

Abramowski, L. (1995), "Histoire de la recherche sur Nestorius et le nestorianisme". *Istina*, 40: 44–55.

Abramowski, L. (1963), *Untersuchungen zum Liber Heraclidis des Nestorius*, CSCO 242, Subsidia 22. Louvain: Secrétariat du Corpus SCO.

Abramowski, L., and A.E. Goodman (1972), *A Nestorian Collection of Christological Texts, Cambridge University Library Ms. Oriental 1319*. Vol. 1: *Syriac Text*, Vol. 2: *Introduction, Translation and Indexes*. Cambridge: Cambridge University Press.

Anastos, M.V. (1962), "Nestorius was orthodox". *Dumbarton Oaks Papers*, 16: 117–140.

Baum, W. and Winkler, D.W. (2003), *The Church of the East: A Concise History*. London: Routledge.

Bevan, G. (2010), Augustine and the Western dimension of the Nestorian controversy. *Studia Patristica*, 49: 347–352.

Braaten, C.E. (1963), "Modern interpretations of Nestorius". *Church History: Studies in Christianity and Culture* 32(03): 251–267.

Bradshaw, David (2009), "The *Opuscula sacra*: Boethius and theology". In *The Cambridge Companion to Boethius*, John Marenbom (ed.). Cambridge: Cambridge University Press; 105–128.

Brock, S. (1992), "The Christology of the Church of the East in the Synods of the fifth to early seventh centuries: preliminary considerations and materials". In *Studies in Syriac Christianity*, S. Brock (ed.). London: Variorum; 125–142.

Brock, S.P. (1996), "The 'Nestorian' Church: a lamentable misnomer". *Bulletin of the Joyn Rylands University Library of Manchester*, 78: 23–36.

Brock, S. (2004), "The Syriac churches and dialogue with the Catholic church". *The Heythrop Journal*, 45(4): 466–476.

Chesnut, R.C. (1978), "The two prosopa in Nestorius' *Bazaar of Heraclidis*". *The Journal of Theological Studies*, 29(2): 392–409.

De Halleux, A. (1993), "Nestorius, histoire et doctrine". *Irénikon*, 66: 38–51.

Fairbairn, D. (2007), "Allies or merely friends? John of Antioch and Nestorius in the Christological controversy". *JEH*, 58.3: 383–399.

Gray, P.T.R. (1984), "Theodoret on the 'one hypostasis.' An Antiochene reading of Chalcedon". *Studia Patristica*, 15: 301–304.

Grillmeier, A. (1961), "Das *Scandalum oecumenicum* des Nestorius in kirchlich-domatischer und theologiegeschichtlicher Sicht". *Scholastik*, 36: 321–356 (translated in Grillmeier (1975)).

Grillmeier, A. (1975), *Christ in Christian Tradition. From the Apostolic Age to Chalcedon (451)*, Vol. 1, 2nd ed., John Bowden (Engl. transl.). Atlanta: John Knox Press.

Ibrahim, G.Y. (1998), "Nestorius dans la tradition syrienne orthodoxe". *Istina*, 43: 166–178.

Kavvadas, N. (2012), "Narsais Homilie 'Über die Väter, die Lehrer Diodor von Tarsos, Theodor von Mopsuestia und Nestorios'". *Sacris Erudiri*, 51(1): 215–232.

Kosinski, R. (2007), "The life of Nestorius as seen in Greek and Oriental sources". In *Continuity and Change. Studies in the Late Antique Historiography*, D. Brodka and M. Stachura (eds). Electrum Studies in

Ancient History, Vol. 14. Warsaw: Jagiellonian University Press; 155–170.

Macomber. W. (1958), "The Christology of the Synod of Seleucia–Ctesiphon A.D. 486". *Orientalia Christiana Periodica*, 24: 142–154.

Millar, F. (2013), "The evolution of the Syrian Orthodox Church in the pre-Islamic period: from Greek to Syriac?" *Journal of Early Christian Studies*, 21(1): 43–92.

Parry, K. (2013), "'Rejoice for Me, O Desert': fresh light on the remains of Nestorius in Egypt". *Studia Patristica*, 68: 41–50.

Redies, M. (1998), "Kyrill und Nestorius: Eine Neuinterpretation des Theotokos-Streits". *Klio*, 80: 195–208.

Reinink, Gerrit J. (2009), "Tradition and the formation of the 'Nestorian' identity in sixth- to seventh-century Iraq". *CHRC*, 89(1–3): 217–250.

Schwartz, E. (1928), "Cyril und der Mönch Viktor". *Sitzungsberichte der Akademie der Wissenschaften in Wien, philosophisch-historische Klasse*, 208.4: 1–51.

Scipioni, L.I. (1974), *Nestorio e il concilio di Efeso. Storia dogma critica*. Milan: Università Cattolica del Sacro Cuore.

Seleznyov, N. (2010), "Nestorius of Constantinople: condemnation, suppression, veneration". *Journal of Eastern Christian Studies*, 62.3–4: 165–190.

Shin, A.K. (2006), "The images of Nestorius and the factionalism after Chalcedon". *Studia Patristica*, 39: 125–130.

Winkler, D.W. (1997), "Miaphysitism: a new term for use in the history of dogma and in ecumenical theology". *The Harp*, 10(3): 33–40.

Wood, P. (2013) "The *Chronicle of Seert* and Roman ecclesiastical history in the Sasanian world". In *History and Identity in the Late Antique Near East, 500–1000*, Philip Wood (ed.). Oxford: Oxford University Press; 43–60.

CHAPTER 14

Dionysius the Areopagite

István Perczel

Introduction

This study treats the Dionysian Corpus as a late antique "literary fiction" consisting of a core collection normally regarded as being the Corpus itself, a set of missing writings playing a structural role in the fiction, several layers of the textual transmission, early commentaries appended to the original core collection, and a series of legends that, from an early date, surrounded the fiction. Also, it presents the fictitious setting and its implication for the structure of the Corpus, briefly treats the questions of the date of appearance, of the early manuscript tradition, and of the first commentaries before, finally, giving a brief sketch of the scholarly debates on the problem of the possible aims of the fiction and its milieu of provenance.

These considerations are based on the author's personal research and do not intend to present any received wisdom about the Corpus. Rather, the author's conviction is that such received wisdom could possibly not exist, as the Corpus has been the object, throughout the ages, of the most contradictory interpretations. Presenting the Dionysian Corpus as a literary fiction (while avoiding the ill-sounding expression of "fraud") partly explains why all these divergent interpretations were possible: because this is a purposefully underdetermined text that does not yield its secret easily.

This framework does not permit a detailed discussion either of the individual parts of the Corpus, or of its long and adventurous reception history. For a detailed modern commentary on the contents, the interested reader might turn to Rorem (1993). For a good overview of the reception history of the Corpus one might recommend Rorem (1993) and Coakley and Stang (2009).

The Wiley Blackwell Companion to Patristics, First Edition. Edited by Ken Parry.
© 2015 John Wiley & Sons Ltd. Published 2019 by John Wiley & Sons Ltd.

The Dionysian Corpus: A Late Antique Literary Fiction

The Dionysian Corpus could be most conveniently characterized as a late antique literary fiction consisting of a core collection of pseudonymous writings attributed to Dionysius the Areopagite, the disciple of Saint Paul, mentioned in chapter 17 of the Acts of the Apostles. This collection the fiction declares incomplete; accordingly, it constitutes only a small part of the pretended literary oeuvre of the author. The fate of this fiction was such that the original text is inseparable from the later sediments created during its reception history. If the intention of the author of the Corpus was to create an inextricable puzzle for posterity, then he was very successful, as the roughly 15 centuries that have elapsed since the composition of the Corpus were not enough for solving this puzzle.

The Core Collection

According to the story of the Acts, Saint Paul was preaching to the Athenians and, particularly, to the Epicurean and Stoic philosophers at the Areopagus, north-west of the Acropolis, where the Athenian city court of appeal, still functioning in Roman times, was gathering. During this sermon a certain man called Dionysius the Areopagite – presumably a judge in the court – and a woman called Damaris converted (Acts 17:22–34). It is notable that in this sermon Paul referred to an altar that the Athenians erected "to the unknown God," so that the Apostle claimed that he had come to preach this God whom the Athenians venerated without knowing, namely Jesus Christ. Ever since the studies of Eduard Norden, we know that this altar really existed but was in fact dedicated "to the unknown gods," in plural (Norden 1913: 41–45). We also know from Norden that Paul, speaking to the Epicurean and Stoic philosophers, constructed his Christian preaching entirely from the philosophical tropes and expressions of these two schools (Norden 1913: 13ff). Later tradition held it that Dionysius, converted at that occasion, had become the first bishop of Athens (Eusebius, Ecclesiastical History, III. 4, 10).

Sometime at the end of the fifth to the the beginning of the sixth century there appeared a collection of writings attributed to this Dionysius the Areopagite. Their language was that of the philosophy of the times. Namely, they imitated, going even as far as a kind of "plagiarism," the great Neoplatonist philosopher and Athenian Diadochus of Plato, Proclus (412–485), whose figure dominated the pagan intellectual landscape of almost the entire fifth century (Stiglmayr 1895; Koch 1900). However, these writings had a Christian content, cited the Bible throughout their text, and pretended to have been composed by a Christian bishop and a disciple of the Apostles. In this way these compositions, if their pretended authorship was to be believed, had to be taken as the first corpus of systematic theology, composed in Apostolic times. Moreover, they displayed a structure analogous to that of the New Testament. They consisted of four treatises: three of them, On the Divine Names (DN), On the Celestial Hierarchy (CH), and the On the Ecclesiastic Hierarchy (EH), tell the same story from three different angles – that of the descent of the divine Light in the world and the manner in which it imparts on the world a sacred structure. These treatises

seem to be analogous to the three synoptic gospels, while the fourth, very short, treatise, *On the Mystical* (or *Secret*) *Theology* (MT), describes the road of the ascension of
the human soul toward God, speaking rather in terms of transcendent darkness than
in those of immanent light, rather in negative (*apophatic*), than in positive (*cataphatic*)
language. In the fourfold structure of the Dionysian treatises this latter corresponds
to the gospel according to Saint John. There is no writing corresponding to the Acts of
the Apostles but there are letters, ten in number, addressed to persons known from
the Apostolic age, out of which the first nine apparently correspond to the nine
hypotheses of the Platonic dialogue that the Neoplatonists considered as the par excellence theological treatise of Plato, namely the *Parmenides* (Hathaway 1969: 80ff).
Finally, the tenth letter, fictitiously addressed to Saint John the Evangelist during his
exile at the island of Patmos, stands apart, and seems to contain a cryptic reference to
contemporary history (Perczel 2012: 79–81).

The 'Lost' Works: An Incomplete Structure of the Pseudo-Dionysian Theology

To the structure of the Pseudo-Dionysian literary fiction there contribute a number of
treatises that are mentioned in the Corpus and to which cross-references are made, but
which are not included in it and, so, make up for a named absence of a part of the
Corpus. The two most important are: *The Outlines of Theology* (OT: mentioned eight
times in MT and DN), in which the author would have developed his positive Trinitarian
theology, his "theology of the Spirit," and his theology of the Incarnation (reference in
MT III, p. 146, 1–9; Luibheid and Rorem (L-R): 138–139); and *On the Symbolic Theology*
(ST: mentioned nine times in MT, DN, and CH), which treatise would have contained the
author's interpretation of the various corporeal symbols that the Scriptures attribute to
God (reference in MT III, p. 146, 11–147, 3; L-R: 139). Other works mentioned but not
contained in the Dionysian canon are: *On the Angelic Properties and Orders* (APO: con-
cisely described in DN IV. 2, p. 145, 1–3; L-R: 72–73), *On the Soul* (*De anima*, DA: DN IV.
2, p. 145, 10–17; L-R: 73), *On Justice and the Divine Tribunal* (JDT: concisely described in
DN IV. 35, p. 179, 14–22; L-R: 96), *On the Divine Hymns* (DH: concisely described in CH
VII. 4, p. 31, 16–32, 12; L-R: 166) and *On the Intelligible and the Sensible Things* (IS: concisely described in EH I.2, pp. 8–19; L-R: 197; and II. Contemplation, 2, p. 74, 7–11;
L-R: 204–205) (Mazzucchi 2006: 305–306; Perczel 2012: 5–6). From a hint of the
author, according to which ST in itself is longer than DN and OT taken together (MT III,
p. 147, 4–14; L-R: 139), we may understand that what is unreadable from the Corpus
is much more than what is readable. The entire setting is there to suggest that the most
part of the Corpus is missing and that, consequently, what we have in our hands is just
a fragment of what had been sometime Christianity's first and most fundamental
theological exposition.

Scholars' opinions are divided as to the real role of the "lost" treatises. Some consider
them as entirely fictitious (Louth 1989: 120; Mazzucchi 2006, 305); others think that
they were written but indeed lost (Von Balthasar 1984: 154), while recently I suggested
that the author of the Corpus was practicing pseudonymous writing under different

pseudonyms and that, most probably, some of the "lost" treatises are extant under different, mostly fourth-century, pseudonyms. This hypothesis was triggered by the unexpected discovery that one of the "lost" works, namely the *Outlines of Theology*, can be identified with the extant *De trinitate*, earlier attributed to Didymus the Blind. The latter work, although obviously written in the second half of the fifth century, pretends to be a fourth-century composition and had been considered as such even by those scholars who rejected its attribution to Didymus (Stang 2012: 25–26; Perczel 2013). The basis for this identification is, first, the literary method of transcribing Proclus used by the author of the *De trinitate*, which he shares with the Dionysian Corpus – otherwise unique in Patristic literature; second, the references to the OT in the Corpus referring to the whole, or to specific passages, of the *De trinitate*; and third, a shared vocabulary and a number of close parallel passages.

The Pseudonym and the Pseudo-Dionysian Writing Technique

It was not in vain that the author of the Corpus had chosen the pseudonym "Dionysius the Areopagite." Among others, the name seems to point toward the method adopted in the literary fiction, consisting in rearranging the contemporary philosophical teachings and expressions, mostly those of Proclus, so that they might express a Christian doctrine (Schäfer 2006: 163ff; Stang 2012). Also, most probably, the author knew the source of Paul's word play, by which the Apostle transformed the many unknown gods venerated by the Athenians into the one unknown God (Stang 2009; 2012: 144ff). In fact, any time that Proclus speaks about the gods of late antique pagan polytheism, Pseudo-Dionysius, in his paraphrase, transforms the multiple subjects into a unique one, generally the "divine Ray," meaning an emanation simultaneously one and multiple of the divinity. Proclus, whose highest god was the absolute One of Platonist metaphysics, identified the many gods of Greek religion to the highest metaphysical principles, the *henads*, or "unities," being a kind of super-ideas, a multiplicity in complete oneness, mediating between the transcendent One and the immanence of Being. In Proclus' metaphysics, these unities are commanded by the immediate double offspring of the One, Limit and Infinity. Correspondingly, in Pseudo-Dionysius, the divine Ray is, following a traditional patristic metaphor, the Son born from the Father, represented in this light-metaphor by the solar disc, while the glamour of the Light transmitted and dispersed by the unique Ray corresponds to the Holy Spirit, from whom all the divine "gifts," playing in Pseudo-Dionysius the structural role of the Proclian divine unities, are spreading upon the rational beings. Thus, Proclus' *henadic* theory has become in the hands of Pseudo-Dionysius the metaphysical explanation of his Trinitarian theology and his theory of salvation or divinization (Perczel 2000).

For operating this transfer, Pseudo-Dionysius elaborated a literary method as simple as it is elusive: he created a broken paraphrase of one particular work of Proclus, the *Platonic Theology* (PT), which was the Athenian philosopher's most important and extensive compendium of pagan metaphysical theology, as the warp of the texture of his texts, in which he was interweaving as the weft all the other allusions, references, and paraphrases, either Christian or pagan, either theological or philosophical. The meaning of the new, "Dionysian," text is given through the way the threads of the warp intersect with those of the weft. Thus, an analysis of the sources of the Dionysian texts and, most importantly, of the way the author used the PT are a necessary precondition to understand their hidden meaning (Perczel 2000; Lankila 2011).

The recognition of the importance of this particular Proclian work raises many problems concerning both the respective chronologies of the PT and the CD and the authorship of the CD, as the PT is believed to be one of the last works of Proclus and one that, for some time after the death of Proclus, was not circulating outside the inner circles of the Athenian school (Lankila 2011). For sure, the hypothesis that the author had belonged to Proclus' close circle stands to reason (Dodds 1963; Lankila 2011: 33).

The Hierarchies: Another Incomplete Structure

While there are many modern studies dedicated to Pseudo-Dionysius' theological writings, namely the DN and the MT, much less attention has been paid to the two treatises on the *Hierarchies*. The most important are a classical study by René Roques (1954) and two successive monographs of Alexander Golitzin, who inaugurated a new era in Dionysian studies by setting the Corpus, with a commanding array of erudition, in the framework of the Orthodox Christian tradition and who claims that the ET is at the core of the Dionysian Corpus (Golitzin 1994; 2013). Dominic O'Meara has given a thought-inspiring comparison of Pseudo-Dionysius' and Proclus' hierarchies in the framework of late antique Platonist political philosophy (O'Meara 2003: 159–171). Yet, the *Hierarchies* would merit more attention as they exerted no less influence on the Church tradition in the east and west than the Dionysian positive and negative theologies and also as their text tradition is far from being sufficiently clarified.

If the *Divine Names* describes generally the manifestation of the divine Light through the gifts given to the universe, the two *Hierarchies* are treating the descent of the same Light through the structured order of the rational beings, constructed upon the model of the Neoplatonist metaphysics. Also, if to the downward motion expressed in the *Divine Names* corresponds to the ascent described in the *Mystical Theology*, the *Hierarchies* are built upon the two motions simultaneously. It is everywhere stated that their *raison d'être* is the union of all the rational creatures to God (CH I, pp. 7–9; L-R: 145–147; III, pp. 17–20; L-R: 153–155; EH I, pp. 63–68; L-R:, 195–200). Their construction is described according to the standard Neoplatonist triadic motion of remaining, procession, and return. The highest order of the celestial hierarchy is the one which remains in the immediate proximity of the Light – called the Principle-of-divinity; that is, Principle-of-divinization (*thearchia*) – while the other orders are proceeding to a greater distance from the starting point, which is God. So, in the measure of their procession, they need a return that is operated through the descent of the Light – also called "the Ray that is Principle-of-divinity" – through the variegated orders of the hierarchy. The return is operated through a threefold motion, consisting of purification, illumination, and perfection. Thus, in every triadic order there is a purifying, an illuminating, and a perfecting rank, corresponding to the orders that are purified, illuminated, and perfected. Also, this triple motion pervades the entire hierarchy of the rational beings, beginning with the highest – that is, the Seraphim, Cherubim, and Thrones – and ending up with the lowest, constituted by those humans who have no access to the sacraments (Roques 1954: 68ff; Golitzin 1994: 139–141).

The entire triadic system of the hierarchical order is outlined only on one occasion at the beginning of Chapter V in the EH (pp. 104–110; L-R: 233–239; see Roques (1954: 68ff)). It is an eminently incomplete structure completed only through what has never been written by Pseudo-Dionysius. According to this description (EH V. 1, p. 104, 13–15; L-R: 233 gives a different translation):

> ...every hierarchical treatment (*pragmateia*) is to be divided into [those parts referring to] the most holy initiations (*teletai*), to their inspired connoisseurs and initiates, and to those who are saintly initiated by them.

This means the following triadic structure for the celestial orders (EH V. 2, p. 104, 15–105.2; L-R: 233–34):

> For the most holy hierarchy of the supra-celestial substances the initiation is the most immaterial intellection proper to God and the things divine according to their power as well as the perfect possession of the image of God, imitating God as much as this is possible, while the illuminators and guides into this perfection are the first substances around God [...] The orders inferior to the first substances, which are holily led up by them to the illumination, operated by God, of the Principle-of-divinity, are and are truly called the initiated order.

While it has been argued that this gives a ninefold structure of the celestial hierarchy in contradistinction to a sixfold structure of the ecclesiastic hierarchy (Roques 1954: 69–70; O'Meara 2003: 162), this is an oversimplified and misleading view. It should be corrected taking into consideration the ever-present incomplete structure of Pseudo-Dionysius' thought as well as his insistence on our ignorance concerning these matters. In fact, he has not proposed any rigid number or structure but a manifold division arranged in innumerable triads, whose order he himself relativizes saying that it is known only to God (CH VI.1, p. 26, 1–3; L-R: 160). Yet, conveniently, the celestial hierarchy is divided into a twelvefold structure at the first instance: first, there is a triple gnosis, that of the Trinity, which is the initiation itself; the rank of the initiators filled by the substances next to God is also triple, consisting of the Seraphim, Cherubim, and Thrones, while the subordinate ranks are sixfold, consisting of the Powers, Dominations, and Authorities being the middle triad, and of the Principalities, Archangels, and Angels being the last one (CH VI, pp. 26–27; L-R: 160–161). Yet, every rank within the ninefold angelic hierarchy consists of three positions repeating the initiation–initiator–initiated paradigm (this gives at least 27) and every mind itself, be it angelic or human, has threefold subordinate powers (giving at least 81, but in fact this number is multiplied by three indefinitely: CH X. 2–3, pp. 40–41; L-R: 173–174). However, Pseudo-Dionysius, in his usual way, breaks even this open-ended system when he claims that the first celestial order receives its initiation from the "highest substances" (CH VII.1, p. 27, 8–12; L-R: 161 is misleading here). What these latter are is never defined in the Corpus, but this indicates that there are also other substances above the Seraphim.

At the other extremity of the hierarchy is the legal hierarchy of the Old Testament, not treated in any separate treatise by Pseudo-Dionysius, which is entirely engulfed in corporeal symbols. Here, the initiation is "the uplifting to the spiritual worship," the instructors are the priestly orders, the Cohanites and the Levites, who had been initiated to the temple worship by Moses, while the initiated are the people of Israel, "who are led up analogically by the legal symbols toward the more perfect initiation" of the gospels (EH V. 2, p. 105, 3–16; L-R: 234). Thus, this hierarchy also has three fundamental ranks. Yet a further multiplication by three can be inferred, as Moses is the initiator of the priests (EH V. 2, p. 105, 10–12) and as there is the rank of the Levites prefiguring that of the deacons in the Church, while the tribes of Israel are in the number of 12. However, these multiplications are not explicated but only insinuated here.

In between the two extremes is placed the ecclesiastic hierarchy, which communicates to the celestial one through its intelligible contemplations and to the legal one through its use of corporeal symbols. Here, the initiations are the three fundamental sacraments, being the embodiments of Christ: baptism operating the purification, the Eucharist performing illumination, and the holy unction perfecting the faithful. In the initiatory rank there are the bishops, priests, and deacons, while, among those initiated, the highest, on the way to perfection, are the monks, the middle position is filled by those lay people having access to the sacraments, and the last rank, needing purification, are those unbaptized or for some sin or possession excluded from communion (EH V. 2–3, p. 105, 17–106, 16; L-R: 234–235 see Golitzin 2013: 210–213). As within all these ranks there are subordinate positions and as every human mind also has a threefold structure, here as well the triadic structures are multiplied *ad libitum*.

This concept of the ecclesiastic hierarchy is entirely centered on the spiritual and excludes worldly concerns. As the emperor has no role in this hierarchy and as all the bishops are equal and are subordinated to the sacraments that they are administering (O'Meara 2003: 170–171), the latter being the embodiment of Christ, this theory could very well serve a dissident community but was not apt to serve as mainstream theory in the Church. This has triggered a series of changes in history, through which the original theory was adapted.

The first is palpable already in the transmission of the original text. I have proposed that the first Syriac translation of the Corpus by Sergius of Reshaina (d. 536) goes back to a lost Greek version that was, in many respects, more original than the Greek text that we have in later manuscripts (Perczel 2000; 2009). Emiliano Fiori is of the opposite view, thinking that whatever significant difference there is between our Greek text and Sergius' Syriac is due to the changes Sergius introduced into the text during the translation (Fiori 2011; 2014: vol. 1, xxx–xxxviii). Yet, it seems that this debate becomes immaterial concerning the text of the *Ecclesiastic Hierarchy*. Here, the entire chapter structure is different in the Syriac. While the presently known Greek version contains seven chapters, the Syriac has 18 chapters corresponding to a more linear and less complicated structure, where the chapter endings often do not correspond to any subdivision in the Greek EH (Perczel 2009: 32). Moreover, some of the chapter titles, inexistent in the Greek, are clearly derived from chapter titles in the *Platonic Theology* of Proclus (Perczel 2000: 498–499), so that it is unreasonable to suppose that they would have been added by Sergius. Also, the Syriac text is more complete, symmetrical, and coherent, containing elements that later, long after the death of Sergius, were condemned by the anti-Origenist councils of 543 and 553. Thus, the Greek text that we have seems to constitute the first revision of the *Ecclesiastic Hierarchy*.

A second revision of the theory, not any more the text, can be dated to the time of Justinian. It is the reuse of Pseudo-Dionysian theory and terminology in an anonymous dialogue *On Political Science*, of which only fragments were transmitted. In this dialogue, which uses distinct Pseudo-Dionysian language, the head of the Church hierarchy becomes the emperor (O'Meara 2003: 171ff). The third is the revision of the fundamental theory of Dionysius by Nicetas Stethatus in the eleventh century, for whom the highest order in the hierarchy is no longer constituted by the sacraments representing the corporeal presence of Christ, but by the patriarchs, metropolitans, and archbishops (Nicetas, *On Hierarchy* III, 21–23, pp. 326–328). Thus, what, for Pseudo-Dionysius, had been a direct rulership over the Church by Christ in his corporeal presence through the sacraments was gradually replaced by the medieval theocratic idea of a rulership by the secular and spiritual heads of the community, namely the emperor and the patriarchs. Yet, the original concept continued to animate alternative views on the Church.

An Anomaly in the Fiction: The Divine Hierotheus

The literary fiction is further complicated by the anomalies introduced into it. The most disharmonious element is that Pseudo-Dionysius did not respect the very setting that he had invented. While he presents himself as the Athenian convert of Saint Paul, whom tradition considered, until his writings, as the first bishop of Athens, he inserts between Saint Paul and himself another figure, without any trace in the Apostolic writings, the "divine Hierotheus," this name apparently meaning "divine priest." Pseudo-Dionysius makes this Hierotheus a direct disciple of Saint Paul and the teacher of himself, while attributing to him a work entitled *Elements of Theology*, consisting of "concise definitions," this title and genre coinciding almost verbally with those of a work by Proclus (DN III.2, 139.17–140.8; L-R: 69 is misleading here). Moreover, he introduces this Hierotheus as being present at an event that, in a very cryptic way, he calls "the contemplation of the body that is principle-of-life and the receptacle-of-God," at which event "James the brother-of-God and Peter the highest and most venerable summit of the theologians" were also present (DN III.2, 141.5–8). From this contradictory data, subsequent tradition developed the idea of Hierotheus being the first bishop of Athens, Dionysius being only the second, as well as the legend that both Hierotheus and Dionysius were present at what came to be called "the Dormition of the Mother of God," thus understanding "the body that is principle-of-life and the receptacle-of-God" as meaning her body. I suggested a different interpretation for this scene: that the Apostles Peter and James are pseudonyms for holders of apostolic sees; that "the body that is principle-of-life and the receptacle-of-God" is not the body of the Virgin but of Christ; and that the event described is not the Dormition but a council where questions of the Incarnation were discussed, namely Chalcedon (held in 451); and that Hierotheus is an anagram for the name of Pseudo-Dionysius' real teacher, Theodoret of Cyrus (Perczel 2012). Yet, all these issues will continue to be discussed for a while.

All this legendary detail entered the Church tradition. So, in the liturgical practice of the Byzantino-Slavic Orthodox Churches, Dionysius the Areopagite is celebrated on the 3 October, while Hierotheus on the 4 October, his brief Life, read during the morning service, being entirely based on chapter III of the DN, while the canon of the Dormition of the Mother of God, read on 15 August, is equally saturated with the expressions of the same text.

This newly invented Hierotheus has triggered the imagination of the posterity. Hierotheus became a standard Byzantine and, later, Greek name. Among others, several bishops, such as the first Byzantine bishop of Hungary, were named Hierotheus. There are also several alchemists who were bearing the name Hierotheus. Most importantly, not long after the appearance of the Corpus and, probably, shortly after its Syriac translation was made, another pseudonymous writing appeared, attributed to the holy Hierotheus. Its author is probably Stephen Bar Sudhaili, a famous Origenist monk who was the representative of a monist mysticism (Marsh 1927: 227–232). The work teaches the final confusion of everything into the unique divine Substance, and certainly the image suggested by it does not correspond to Dionysius' hierarchical universe. Yet, it is conspicuous that the *Book of the Holy Hierotheus* uses the same language as that of Sergius' Syriac translation of the Corpus and that, as it is roughly contemporary to that translation, apparently both are emanating from the same milieu. It is even possible that Stephen Bar Sudhaili is identical with that Stephen whom Sergius acknowledges as his co-translator of the Corpus (Perczel 2009: 33–34).

Date of Appearance, Layers of the Text, and Commentaries

The question of the date of the Dionysian Corpus was magisterially treated by Paul Rorem and John Lamoreaux (1998: 9–22). Although earlier scholarship established a triple time barrier as *terminus post quem*, namely (1) the introduction of the Nicaea–Constantinopolitan Creed to the Syrian–Antiochian liturgy by Peter the Fuller, Miaphysite Patriarch of Antioch, in 476, (2) the promulgation of the *Henoticon* edict of emperor Zeno in 482, and (3) the death of Proclus in 485, Rorem and Lamoreaux have rightly pointed to the conjectural character of these dates. Only the *terminus ante quem* is certain, which is furnished by the fact that Severus of Antioch (465–538), the greatest theologian of the Miaphysite party in the sixth century, at three instances cited the authority of Dionysius the Areopagite as a witness to the Miaphysite doctrines. We cannot date these works precisely, but we know that they were translated into Syriac in the year 528 (Rorem and Lamoreaux 1998: 11–15).

The earliest of our Greek manuscripts dates probably to the eighth century. It is Paris Bibliothèque Nationale, Cod. Gr. 1330, a palimpsest whose undertext contains at least 89 folios of the Corpus and its earliest commentary by John of Scythopolis (Faraggiana di Sarzana 2009). This manuscript was not used for the recent critical edition (B.R. Suchla lists it among the lost manuscripts: Suchla 1990: 33; Faraggiana di Sarzana 2009: 206–207). The second oldest is Paris, Bibliothèque Nationale, Cod. Gr. 437, dated 827, a famous gift of the Byzantine Iconoclast emperor Michael II the Amorian to the Frankish king Louis the Pious (Pa in B.R. Suchla's list: Suchla 1990: 31), which contains the text without the scholia. Yet, the oldest extant manuscript of the Corpus is that of its first Syriac translation by Sergius of Reshaina, contained in Sinai, Saint Catherine's Monastery, Cod. Syr. 52, and in a number of scattered fragments of the same manuscript on Mount Sinai, Paris, and Milan (Géhin 2006, 37–38; 2007: 21). This manuscript probably dates to the seventh century.

According to B.R. Suchla (1995: 18–19), all the Greek manuscripts come from the edition made in the circles of John of Scythopolis, the first commentator of the Corpus, so that we have got no Greek text independent of the editorial work and commentaries of John. If this were true, then Paris Cod. Gr. 437 containing only the text of the Corpus would be an exception. According to Suchla (1984: 186–187), it was copied in haste in order to complete the imperial gift, so that the glosses were left out. However, I find this scenario highly improbable. Moreover, a personal reading of Paris Gr. 437 has convinced me that it is a unique witness to an independent, Constantinopolitan, version, used by the Iconoclasts and replaced everywhere, after the victory of the Iconophiles, by the Palestinian version. Yet, all this notwithstanding, the fact that the Armenian translation of Stephen of Siunik and David the Consul, made on the Constantinopolitan version in the early eighth century, also contains the scholia of John speaks in favor of Suchla's hypothesis (Thomson 1987: vii–xii). Be this as it may, Sergius of Reshaina translated an earlier version of the text, in many respects different from the extant Greek versions, both the Palestinian and the Constantinopolitan ones, and his text is independent from the one formed in the circles of John of Scythopolis (Perczel 2009, criticized by Fiori 2011).

Given that the versions of Sinai Cod. Syr. 52 and of Paris Cod. Gr. 437 are unique and that all the rest of the manuscripts go back to the annotated version, so, properly speaking, we should consider this first layer of glosses, as well as the introductions transmitted with the Greek text, as part of the Corpus. It is significant that in the oldest Greek manuscript, Par. Graec. 1330, John of Scythopolis' glosses are intercalated in the text, just as in the oldest Syriac manuscripts containing the second Syriac translation, that of Phocas Bar Sargis, made in 684/686 (Faraggiana di Sarzana 2009: 212) and in some of the oldest Armenian manuscripts (Thomson 1987: x–xii). In fact, it is to this version that we owe the Dionysian legend as it was spreading in Late Antiquity and the Middle Ages as well as the authoritative interpretation of the Corpus.

To this, further layers were added through the additional glosses of Saint Maximus Confessor and of Patriarch Germanus of Constantinople, as well as through the identification of Dionysius the Areopagite with Saint Denys, the first martyr-bishop of Paris, by Abbot Hilduin of Saint-Denis after the reception of the imperial gift Paris Cod. Gr. 437 in 827.

The Possible Aims of the Fiction and its Milieu of Provenance

Innumerable are the speculations about the possible aims of the Corpus and its authorship. I am not entering here the thorny question of the individual author of the Corpus, but only that of its milieu of provenance.

Because of the earliest mention of the Corpus by Severus of Antioch, Josef Stiglmayr, one of the pioneers of modern Dionysian studies and also one of the two scholars who demonstrated Pseudo-Dionysius' dependence on Proclus (Stiglmayr 1895; Koch 1900), thought that the Corpus comes from Severan Miaphysite circles – he even thought that Severus himself was the author (Stiglmayr 1928). While the attribution to Severus has been refuted, the idea of a Miaphysite affiliation strongly holds itself in scholarly circles. This idea, including the identification by Shalva Nutsubidze, Ernest Honigmann, Michel Van Esbroeck, and Basile Lourié of Pseudo-Dionysius with Peter the Iberian, Miaphysite bishop of Maiuma in Palestine (c. 411–491), is to a large extent based on the acceptance of the scene of the "contemplation of the body that is principle-of-life and the receptacle-of-God" as being that of the Dormition of the Holy Virgin (Van Esbroeck 1993).

Yet, according to Rorem and Lamoreaux (1998: 11–15), there are all the indications that Severus only wanted to snatch away this Apostolic authority from his Chalcedonian opponents who were using it before him. Also, I believe to have demonstrated that all the important tenets of miaphysitism, even Cyrillian Chalcedonism or Neochalcedonism, are missing from the Corpus, whose Christology rather testifies to an Antiochian interpretation of Chalcedon. The only exception would be the "Dormition of the Virgin scene," so-called, but this seems to speak about something else, namely the council of Chalcedon (Perczel 2012).

Thus, the idea that the cause for the author's pseudonymity would be his belonging to a group deemed heretical and thus persecuted in the time of writing the Corpus was for only too long connected to his alleged "monophysitism." Yet, the Miaphysites were a strong political force rather than a persecuted minority and had the ear of the emperors, not only those leaning to their side, such as Zeno (474–491) and Anastasius (491–518), but also of the Chalcedonian Justinian (527–565), who needed their cooperation for being able to govern the eastern provinces. I believe that the lead for discovering Pseudo-Dionysius' real aims was given by a little-read study of David B. Evans (1980). Evans discovered in the Christological writings of Leontius of Byzantium – one of the leaders of the Isochrist Origenist monks in Palestine – a polemic with Pseudo-Dionysius, who was used as an authority by a rival faction of monks whom Leontius calls "Nestorians" and whom Evans identified as being the so-called Protoctist faction of the Palestinian Origenists. I followed Evans' lead in a number of publications, where I claim that the Dionysian Corpus was written as a kind of esotericist encoded writing for members of a specific community, professing both Origenist metaphysics and Antiochian Christology, whose intellectual legacy was followed by the Palestinian Protoctist monks.

This view provoked criticism on the part of scholars, the most thoroughgoing being those by Karl Pinggéra (2008) and Emiliano Fiori (2010; 2011); also Golitzin (2013: xxix–xxxi). One must admit that the suggestion gives rise to misunderstanding as long as what this alleged "Origenism" means is not clarified sufficiently. Presently, I think that "Origenism" is a misnomer for a Christian Platonist school, in constant dialogue with the pagan Platonists ever since the time of Origen and Plotinus, using the same tools of Platonic philosophy as their pagan counterparts, including that of the Platonist philosophical myth. Thus, it was an intellectual movement allowing for serious differences of philosophical opinion, which gradually came under pressure due to the ever-hardening anti-heretical legislation but survived in a new form even the ecumenical condemnations of the year 553. Understood so, "Origenism" is as much of a philosophical school as it is theological, and thus Pseudo-Dionysius is not an oddity of Christian intellectual history but rather one of the representatives of a continuous philosophical tradition, who was active in a time of lack of intellectual freedom.

Another idea, based on the dependence of the author on Proclus is that of a "crypto-pagan project." This was first proposed by E.R. Dodds (1963: xxvi ff). After Dodds, an impressive number of historians of philosophy cherished and still cherish the idea that the Corpus is the work of one of the pagan members of the Athenian Neoplatonist school, who wanted to smuggle in Neoplatonism into Christianity. So Ronald Hathaway (1969: 28–30) thought that the author might have been a member of Damascius' circle. Recently, Carlo Maria Mazzucchi proposed Damascius in person as the author. Moreover, he identified the Paul of the Corpus with Proclus, and Hierotheus with Isidore, while "the contemplation of the body that is principle-of-life and the receptacle-of-God" is, in Mazzucchi's interpretation, a pseudo-story about the funerals of the wife of the philosopher Hermeias, Aedesia, the mother of Ammonius (Mazzucchi 2006). Mazzucchi claims such a certitude that, according to him, after his demonstration the burden of proof falls on those who want to claim that Pseudo-Dionysius *is not* Damascius (Mazzucchi 2006: 328). He thinks that Damascius, facing persecution, intended to transform Christianity from the inside by "selling" surreptitiously pagan Neoplatonism to the Christians. Tuomo Lankila rejects this thesis and proposes that the Corpus was written by some undefinable member in Damascius' environment in the face of imminent persecution on the part of Christian authorities. Thus, the project would be to hide the doctrine for a time of persecution when overt representation of philosophical thought would become impossible. According to Lankila, I am right in claiming the Corpus' esoteric intention but wrong in indicating that this would stem from a position deemed a Christian heresy (Origenism or Antiochian Dyophysitism) rather than from a pagan one (Lankila 2011: 39).

Yet, the idea of a "crypto-pagan project" is normally based on an excellent knowledge of the Corpus' Neoplatonic philosophical background and a very deficient knowledge of its patristic background, let alone the intellectual history of the Christian Church. So both Mazzucchi and Lankila claim that a superficial layer of scriptural and Christian theological thought was enough for the author to clothe his philosophical thought in Christian garb. This stance ignores the degree to which the Dionysian text is saturated with the presence of the Bible, both the Old and the New Testaments, and with that of Christian theological allusions and references. It is true that representatives of a "Christian interpretation" are also responsible for such misunderstandings. An exhaustive study of Pseudo-Dionysius' patristic sources is yet a desideratum, as the representatives of the mainstream Christian interpretation often content themselves with drawing parallels, or referring to the main theological authorities, such as the Cappadocian Fathers, whose thought is naturally present in any theological writing claiming to be a Christian doctrine, be it fictitiously written in the Apostolic age. Attempts at finding "pious" reasons for the Corpus' pseudonymity, such as the author's self-effacement or humility, also remain unconvincing for those who insist that, after all, this literary fiction is a fraud, perhaps the most successful one in Christian intellectual history.

Thus, such an exhaustive study of the Christian texts used by the author, which would show how the Christian threads of the "weft" intersect with the Proclian "warp" of the texture of the Corpus, would greatly contribute to the clarification of the vexed questions. Also, the discovery of the *Outlines of Theology* being the Pseudo-Didymian *De trinitate* (Perczel 2013) should be further exploited. If this hypothesis were to be definitively proven, then the dogmatic content of the author's thought – that is, his positive Christian theology – could be much more clearly seen.

Bibliography

Primary Sources

Critical Edition of the Greek Text of Dionysian Corpus

Heil, Günter and Adolf Martin Ritter (eds) (1991), *Corpus Dionysiacum II: Pseudo-Dionysius Areopagita De coelesti hierarchia, De ecclesiastica hierarchia, De mystica theologia, Epistulae. Patristische Texte und Studien 36.* Berlin: De Gruyter.

Suchla, Beate Regina (ed.) (1990), *Corpus Dionysiacum I: Pseudo-Dionysius Areopagita De divinis nominibus. Patristische Texte und Studien 33.* Berlin: De Gruyter.

Suchla, Beate Regina (ed.) (2011), *Corpus Dionysiacum IV/1: Ioannis Scythopolitani Prologus et Scholia in Dionysii Areopagitae librum De divinis nominibus cum additamentis interpretum aliorum.* Patristische Texte und Studien 62. Berlin: De Gruyter.

Critical Edition, Italian Translation and Study of Sergius of Reshaina's Syriac Translation of the Divine Names, the Mystical Theology and the Epistles

Fiori, Emiliano (ed.) (2014), *Dionigi Areopagita, Nomi divini, Teologia mistica, Epistole: La versione siriaca di Sergio di Rēšʿayna (VI secolo).* *CSCO vol. 656, Sriptores Syri, tomus 252* (text). CSCO vol. 657, Sriptores Syri, tomus 253 (translation). Leuven: Peeters.

English Translation with Notes, and Introductions

Luibheid, Colm and Paul Rorem (translators), René Roques, Jaroslav Pelikan, Jean Leclercq, and Karlfried Froehlich (introductions) (1987), *Pseudo-Dionysius: The Complete Works.* London: SPCK.

Nicetas Stethatus, On Hierarchy

Darrouzès, Jean (ed./transl.) (1961), Nicétas Stéthatos, *Opuscules et lettres.* Sources Chrétiennes n°81. Paris: Cerf; 292–365.

The Book of the Holy Hierotheus

Marsh, Fred Shipley (ed./transl.) (1927), *The Book of the Holy Hierotheos, Ascribed to Stephen Bar-Sudhaile (c500 A.D.), with Extracts from the Prolegomena and Commentary of Theodosios* of Antioch and from the "Book of Excerpts" and Other Works of Gregory Bar-Hebraeus. London: Text and Translation Society. (Reprint 1979. Amsterdam: Apa-Philo Press.)

Secondary Sources

Coakley, Sarah and Stang, Charles (eds) (2009), *Re-thinking Dionysius*. Oxford: Wiley–Blackwell.

Dodds, Eric R. (1963), "Introduction". In *Proclus, The Elements of Theology*, 2nd edition, E.R. Dodds, (ed.). Oxford: Clarendon Press; ix–xlvi.

Evans, David Beecher (1980), "Leontius of Byzantium and Dionysius the Areopagite". *Byzantine Studies/Etudes byzantines*, 7: 1–34.

Faraggiana di Sarzana, Chiara (2009), "Il *Nomocanon Par. Gr.* 1330, «horride rescriptus» su pergamene in maiuscola contenenti un antico commentario ad Aristotele, il *Corpus Dionysiacum* e testi patristici". *Nea Rhome*, 6: 192–225.

Fiori, Emiliano (2010), "The impossibility of the apocatastasis in Dionysius the Areopagite". In *Origeniana Decima: Origen as Writer: Papers of the 10th International Origen Congress, University School of Philosophy and Education Ignatianum, Kraków, Poland, 31 August–4 September 2009*, Sylwia Kaczmarek and Henryk Pietras (eds). Leuven: Peeters; 831–843.

Fiori, Emiliano (2011), "Sergius of Reshaina and Pseudo-Dionysius: a dialectical fidelity". In *Interpreting the Bible and Aristotle: The Alexandrian Commentary Tradition between Rome and Baghdad*, Joseph Lössl and John W. Watt (eds). Aldershot: Ashgate; 179–194.

Géhin, Paul (2006), "Manuscrits sinaïtiques dispersés I". *Oriens Christianus*, 90: 23–43.

Géhin, Paul (2007), "Manuscrits sinaïtiques dispersés II". *Oriens Christianus*, 91: 1–24.

Golitzin, Hm. Alexander (1994), *Et Introibo ad Altare Dei: The Mystagogy of Dionysius Areopagita, with Special Reference to Its Predecessors in the Eastern Christian Tradition*. Thessalonike: Patriarchikon Idryma Paterikon Meleton.

Golitzin, Hm. Alexander (2013), *Mystagogy: A Monastic Reading of Dionysius Areopagita*, Bogdan G. Bucur (ed.). Collegeville, MN: Cistercian Publications.

Hathaway, Ronald (1969), *Hierarchy and the Definition of Order in the Letters of Pseudo-Dionysius: A Study in the Form and meaning of the Pseudo-Dionysian Writings*. The Hague: Nijhoff.

Koch, Hugo (1900), *Pseudo-Dionysius Areopagita in seinen Beziehungen zum Neuplatonismus und Mysterienweisen. Eine litteraturhistorische Untersuchung*. Mainz: Verlag von Franz Kirchheim.

Lankila, Tuomo (2011), "The Corpus Areopagiticum as a crypto-pagan project". *The Journal for Late Antique Religion and Culture*, 5: 14–40.

Louth, Andrew (1989), *Denys the Areopagite*. London: G. Chapman.

Mazzucchi, Carlo Maria (2006), "Damascio, autore del Corpus Dionysiacum, e il dialogo Περὶ πολιτικῆς ἐπιστήμης". *Aevum*, 80/2: 299–334.

Norden, Eduard (1913), *Agnostos Theos: Untersuchungen zur Formengeschichte religiöser Rede*. Leipzig: Teubner.

O'Meara, Dominic J. (2003), *Platonopolis: Platonic Political Philosophy in Late Antiquity*. Oxford: Clarendon Press.

Perczel, István (2000), "Pseudo-Dionysius and the Platonic theology". In *Proclus et la Théologie Platonicienne. Actes du colloque international de Louvain (13–16 mai 1998) en l'honneur de H. D. Saffrey et L. G. Westerink*, Alain Ph. Segonds and Carlos Steel (eds). Leuven/Paris: Leuven University Press/Les Belles Lettres; 491–532.

Perczel, István (2009), "The earliest Syriac reception of Dionysius". In *Re-thinking Dionysius*, Sarah Coakley and Charles Stang (eds). Oxford: Wiley–Blackwell; 27–42.

Perczel, István (2012), "Pseudo-Dionysius the Areopagite and the Pseudo-Dormition of the Holy Virgin". *Le Muséon*, 125/1–2: 55–97.

Perczel, István (2013), "The Pseudo-Didymian *De trinitate* and Pseudo-Dionysius the Areopagite: a preliminary study". In *Studia Patristica 58/6: Neoplatonism and Patristics*,

Markus Vinzent (ed.). Leuven: Peeters; 83–108.

Pinggéra, Karl (2008), "Die Bildwelt im „Buch des heiligen Hierotheos" – Ein philosophischer Mythos?" In *Mystik – Metapher – Bild: Beiträge des VII. Makarios-Symposiums, Göttingen 2007*, Martin Tamcke (ed.). Göttingen: Universitätsverlag; 29–41.

Roques, René (1954), *L'univers dionysien. Structure hiérarchique du monde selon le pseudo-Denys*. Paris: Aubier.

Rorem, Paul (1993), *Pseudo-Dionysius: A Commentary on the Texts and an Introduction to Their Influence*. Oxford: Oxford University Press.

Rorem, Paul, and Lamoreaux, John C. (1998), *John of Scythopolis and the Dionysian Corpus: Annotating the Areopagite*. Oxford: Clarendon Press.

Schäfer, Christian (2006), *Philosophy of Dionysius the Areopagite: An Introduction to the Structure and the Content of the Treatise On the Divine Names*. Leiden: Brill.

Stang, Charles (2009), "Dionysius, Paul and the significance of the pseudonym". In *Rethinking Dionysius*, Sarah Coakley and Charles Stang (eds). Oxford: Wiley–Blackwell; 11–25.

Stang, Charles (2012), *Apophasis and Pseudonymity in Dionysius the Areopagite: "No Longer I"*. Oxford: Oxford University Press.

Stiglmayr, Joseph (1895), "Der Neuplatoniker Proclus als Vorlage des sogenannten Dionysius Areopagita in der Lehre vom Übel". *Historisches Jahrbuch*, 16: 253–273, 721–748.

Stiglmayr, Joseph (1928), "Der sogennante Dionysius Areopagita und Severus von Antiochien". *Scholastik*, 3: 1–27, 161–189.

Suchla, Beate Regina (1984), "Die Überlieferung des Prologs des Johannes von Skythopolis zum griechischen *Corpus Dionysiacum Areopagiticum*. Ein weiterer Beitrag zur Überlieferungsgeschichte des CD". *Nachrichten der Akademie der Wissenschaften in Göttingen, phil.-hist. Klasse*, 1984/4: 177–188.

Suchla, Beate Regina (1995) "Verteidigung eines platonischen Denkmodells einer christlichen Welt". *Nachrichten der Akademie der Wissenschaften in Göttingen, phil.-hist. Klasse*, 1995/1: 1–28.

Thomson, Robert (1987), "The Armenian version of Pseudo-Dionysius: introduction". In *The Armenian Version of the Works Attributed to Dionysius the Areopagite*, Robert W. Thomson (ed.). Leuven: Peeters; vii–xv.

Van Esbroeck, Michel (1993), "Peter the Iberian and Dionysius the Areopagite: Honigmann's thesis revisited". *Orientalia Christiana Periodica*, 59: 217–227.

Von Balthasar, Hans Urs (1984), "Denys". In *The Glory of the Lord: A Theological Aesthetics*, vol. 2, Edinburgh: T&T Clark; 144–210.

CHAPTER 15

Severus of Antioch

Youhanna Nessim Youssef

Introduction

As the patriarch of the great cosmopolitan city of Antioch (r. 512–518), Severus had an in-house audience for his work when he addressed the men, women, clergy, and monks of his diocese. For 6 years he delivered 125 homilies covering many topics, and in addition he wrote letters to clergy, laymen, and officials. Unfortunately, most of his works, written originally in Greek, were destroyed so that only translations in Syriac, Coptic, and other languages of Oriental Christianity survive. At a Home Synod in Constantinople in 536 during the reign of the Emperor Justinian (r. 527–565) Severus and his writings were condemned. An imperial edict banned him and his supporters from the capital and copies of his books were ordered to be burned (Frend 1972: 273). Perhaps it is somewhat surprising that even in the Chalcedonian churches, after his condemnation in 536, the biblical exegetical interpretations of Severus were included in Greek catenae (Cramer 1840–1848).

The rediscovery of Severus by western scholarship began with the collecting of Syriac manuscripts, especially from the monastery of the Syrians – Dayr al-Suryān – in Egypt, by European libraries such as those of the Vatican and the British Museum. However, the first substantial publications of the works of Severus were based on judgments of his place in the theological debates of the sixth century (Lebon 1978[1909]: 419–580).

Severus in Late Antiquity

In order to assess the influence of Severus during his lifetime, and for the immediate period following, we should give an historical overview of his chronology. Severus was born around 465 at Sozopolis in Pisidia in Asia Minor. His father was a member

The Wiley Blackwell Companion to Patristics, First Edition. Edited by Ken Parry.
© 2015 John Wiley & Sons Ltd. Published 2019 by John Wiley & Sons Ltd.

SEVERUS OF ANTIOCH   227

of the local council, and according to Athanasius of Antioch (d. 631) in his *Conflict of Severus*, his grandfather was a bishop who attended the Council of Ephesus in 431 (Goodspeed 1909: 592 [24]; Youssef 2004b: 384–385 [20]–[21]). However, despite this latter assertion of Athanasius and that of his friend and biographer Zachariah Scholasticus (Brock and Fitzgerald 2013: 1), Severus' own words confirm that his family was pagan (Allen and Hayward 2004: 5). Yet the tradition of him having a bishop as a grandfather is recurrent in the liturgical hymns in both Coptic and Syriac. His family was wealthy and Severus received an excellent education along with his two brothers, who went overseas with their servants to study. Later, when Severus converted to Christianity, he used his wealth to build his own monastery. He went to Constantinople and was later ordained as the patriarch of Antioch. After the death of the Emperor Anastasius (r. 491–518) he fled to Egypt, where he died in exile in 538.

Sources of His Life

We have first-hand information about the life of Severus as expressed in the surviving corpus of his letters. The Coptic version of his homily on the Martyr Leontius of Antioch contains an autobiographical section (Garitte 1966: 335–386). We also possess several sources relating to the life of Severus. The first was written by his friend Zachariah Scholasticus and it narrates his life from his beginnings up to his ordination as patriarch of Antioch (Kugener 1904a; Brock and Fitzgerald 2013). This biography aimed to defend Severus as a good Christian even though he was not baptized until the age of 30. It emphasized that Severus did not participate in any pagan practices and that he encouraged the Christian zealots at Alexandria. This biography survives only in Syriac translation, and we may suspect that it was originally written in Greek. The second biography was written by, or at least attributed to, another contemporary of Severus, John abbot of the monastery of Beth Aphtonia (Kugener 1904b; Brock and Fitzgerald 2013). The writer of this biography began from the start of Severus' life through till his death and it survived in Syriac together with a Coptic fragment.

The third complete biography was written by the anti-Chalcedonian patriarch of Antioch, Athanasius (the "Camel Driver") in the seventh century (Youssef 2004a). This is not strictly a *vita* but an encomium praising the virtues of Severus and highlighting his theology in two lengthy quotations in a speech against the Patriarch Macedonius (r. 495–511) of Constantinople and in a letter to the Emperor Justinian. The original language is not known but was probably Greek, and there are some fragments in Coptic Sahidic (the dialect of Upper Egypt) (Orlandi 1968), and a fragment in Coptic Bohairic (the dialect of Lower Egypt), there are also complete texts in Arabic (Youssef 2004b), which were translated into Ethiopic (Goodspeed 1909).

These biographies served as a basis for George bishop of the Arabs (d. 724), who wrote a verse homily (*memra*) on Severus based mainly on the biography of John of Beth Aphtonia. This text survives in Syriac, and we may suspect that it was written essentially in Syriac (McVey 1993). There is another unpublished biography of Severus of Antioch by Patriarch Cyriacus of Tagrit (r. 793–817) and this text is also in Syriac (Vööbus 1975–1976). In the fifteenth century a bishop of Assiut used the biography of Athanasius of Antioch and added some data taken from other liturgical and local traditions to compose a homily on Severus. The important part of this homily is the section relating to the translation of his relics from the monastery of Enaton (named after the ninth milestone, west of Alexandria) to the monastery of Assiut (320 km south of Cairo) (Youssef 2006a). The Coptic liturgical texts contain some episodes from the life of Severus which are not known from elsewhere (Youssef 2004c).

The Life and Times of Severus

Severus studied first at Alexandria for nearly 2 years, of which his friend Zacharias gave a detailed description (see earlier). He studied the classical curriculum, but he was not directly involved in any Christian activity, such as undertaken by the "*Philoponoi*" or zealots, who destroyed pagan sanctuaries. It was while in Alexandria that he began to discover the writings of Basil the Great and Gregory of Nazianzus. Their writings so impressed him that he devoted a homily in praise of them each year of his patriarchate. After his studies in grammar and philosophy at Alexandria he moved to Beirut, where he spent several years studying law. In addition to his law studies, he read the writings of Athanasius, Cyril of Alexandria, John Chrysostom, and other Fathers of the Church. He began to practice Christian asceticism, such as prayer, fasting, chastity, and avoiding bodily care by not going to the public baths. While at Beirut he went to Tripoli on a pilgrimage to the sanctuary of St Leontius, where he was baptized. He finished his studies and was prepared to become a lawyer and return to Sozopolis, but instead he longed to attain spiritual perfection and so entered the monastic life.

He went to the monastery of Peter the Iberian (d. 497) near Maiouma in Gaza. This monastery had the reputation as a center of resistance to the Council of Chalcedon and Severus stayed several years in the monastery under the guidance of Peter's successor Theodore of Ascalon. Here he practiced asceticism and spent some time as a hermit until around the year 500, when he founded his own monastery and became its abbot. He was ordained priest by Epiphanius bishop of Magydos in Pamphilia. Severus spent his time at the monastery studying patristic literature, especially Cyril of Alexandria, and mastered all the theological works he was to use in his own writings. However, owing to the machinations of Nephalius, an anti-Chalcedonian turned ardent Chalcedonian, he was expelled from his own monastery in 508 and was forced to go to Constantinople to plead his case in front of Emperor Anastasius, who was sympathetic to the anti-Chalcedonian cause. The emperor was impressed by Severus and directed that his property be restored to him, but he remained in Constantinople as a theological advisor to the emperor.

During his stay in Constantinople he wrote his *Orationes ad Nephalium*, in which he demonstrated how the Nestorian heresy made dangerous use of Dyophysite expressions, and hence the need for caution in reading patristic quotations (Moeller 1944–1945). It was also at this time that he wrote, between 510 and 512, his most important book, the *Philalethes* or *The Lover of Truth*, in answer to the Chalcedonian faith. This book survived in Syriac (Hespel 1952; 1955) and also in Arabic translated from a Coptic original (Youssef 2001a; 2009). After composing the *Philalethes*, John the Grammarian of Caesarea wrote a book against Severus using a florilegium of Cyrillian (Dyophysite) extracts. John pretended to attack the Eutychians (the extremist Miaphysites) but in reality his main target was the *Philalethes*. In this work Severus discusses the quotations of Cyril in a critical way and cites 230 quotations from his writings.

After Justin became emperor in 518, Severus fled to Egypt, where he was to spend 20 years traveling from one monastery to another (Youssef 2006b). While in exile he composed a work against John the Grammarian of Caesarea which was greatly appreciated by readers at different theological levels. The book survived in Syriac. Meanwhile, during this polemical period, Sergius the Grammarian, a Eutychian, appeared on the scene and exchanged a series of three letters with Severus (Torrance 2012[1988]). The correspondence began during Severus' patriarchate and continued during his exile after 518. It was Sergius' contention that the Council of Tyre of 515, which was presided over by Severus, had made a serious and unintelligible concession to the Chalcedonians. The first letter from Sergius was addressed originally not to Severus, but to Antoninus, the Bishop of Aleppo, who seems to have asked Severus to reply to it.

The last of Severus' polemical engagements was with Julian of Halicarnassus and his teaching on the incorruptibility of Christ's body, known as Aphthartodocetism, a position the Emperor Justinian is said to have endorsed later in his life. This polemic had started in Constantinople in 510 and entered a new phase after both were exiled to Egypt in 518. Julian supported the idea that the body of Christ before the crucifixion and resurrection was incorruptible. However, Severus refuted this position in a long treatise using both biblical and patristic quotations. In response, Julian wrote another tome, to which Severus responded with a further refutation. The debate did not end until 527. The writings of Julian survived mostly in Syriac (Hespel 1964; 1968; 1969).

In addition to his theological works, Severus delivered the 125 homilies mentioned earlier. This corpus survived entirely in Syriac, with a few extracts in Greek through catena as well as in Coptic catena and homilies, and was published by several scholars in the collection *Patrologia Orientalis*. These homilies deal with many diverse subjects, one of which, Homily 77, treats the sequence of the resurrection as found in the four Gospels. This homily was considered so important that even the Chalcedonians accepted it, but changed its attribution to either Gregory of Nyssa or Hesychius of Jerusalem. This unique homily survives in its Greek original in addition to Syriac and Coptic translations.

In addition to the theological, homiletic, and epistolographic works cited above, Severus, as an heir of John Chrysostom, was also a liturgist who authored a liturgy that survives in Syriac and Coptic and a rite of Baptism that is used in the Coptic, Syriac, and Byzantine churches.

Reception in Late Antiquity and the Middle Ages

The fame of Severus was not limited to Egypt and Syria but spread throughout most of the Christian Orient. Paul of Callinicus, a Miaphysite bishop of the sixth century, was deposed in 518 and banished to Edessa, where he dedicated his life to literary activity by translating the polemic works and the homilies of Severus (Brière 1960). Jacob of Edessa was born in En Deba near Antioch in about 630; he studied first in the Monastery of Qenneshrin and then in Alexandria, before his ordination as a Miaphysite bishop of Edessa around 684. After a conflict with his clergy over canon law, he left his ministry to live in the monastery at Kaisoum. The monks of the Monastery of Eusebona then invited him to teach the scriptures in Greek, which he did for 11 years. After that he went to the Monastery of Tell Ada, where for 9 years he revised the Syriac translation of the Bible. Finally, in 708, he returned to his bishopric at Edessa, where he died shortly after. His revised translation of the 125 homilies of Severus was completed in 701.

Paul of Edessa was a bishop of Edessa during the Persian invasion of Mesopotamia in 619. He left for Cyprus, where he translated the 295 hymns attributed to Severus in the period 619–629. These were later revised by Jacob of Edessa in 675 (Brooks 1902; 1904; 1910; 1911; 1916; 1920). A translation of the letters of Severus was completed by patriarch Athanasius II of Balad in 669.

Although the original language of the works of Severus was Greek, owing to the edict of Justinian in 536 only a few fragments in Greek have survived in exegetical catenae, or under pseudonyms, such as Homily 77, which came down to us under the name of Gregory of Nyssa (Kugener and Triffaux, 1924), as well as some other fragments (Carrara 1985; 1988).

In Egypt, during his exile, Severus was fleeing from the Chalcedonian authorities from one monastery to another. In his correspondence with his followers he explained theological issues as well as giving advice on pastoral problems. In one of his letters he evokes a local tradition related to the martyrs of Scetis killed by the barbarians (Youssef 2006b). The Coptic translations of his writings remain anonymous. Most of his works were read during liturgical ceremonies, but very few theological texts survived in catenae (de Lagarde 1886) and florilegia. Some of these texts were translated into Arabic (Caubet Iturbe 1969–1970) and later into Ethiopic. We find homilies of Severus for different occasions, such as reading during Lent or for Holy Week. For example, the letter of Severus to Anastasia the Deaconess is read on the feast of Zacharia (Chaîne 1913; Youssef 2001b).

In addition to the texts of Severus, medieval authors quoted many citations from his works. The first of these is Severus ibn al-Muqaffa', or Severus bishop of Ashmunein (d. 987) in Upper Egypt, who is known as the author of the *History of the Patriarchs of the Coptic Church of Alexandria*. He was followed by others, such as the anonymous author of the book of the *Confessions of the Fathers* (Youssef 2003a). This author quoted also from the synodical letters exchanged between the patriarchs of Alexandria and the patriarchs of Antioch, where the texts of Severus enjoyed the lion's share.

Severus is commemorated in the Coptic calendar four times a year: once for his coming to Egypt, another for his repose, and two for the translation of his relics, first to the monastery of Enaton and then to the monastery at Assiut. His name is mentioned after Saint Mark, the traditional founder of the Alexandrian Church.

The Protestant reformers did not pay much attention to Severus because at that time Syriac manuscripts containing his works were virtually unknown in the West. The first scholar to collect his manuscripts was Joseph Simeonis Assemani (1687–1768), who was of Maronite origin (hence his mastering of the Syriac language) and who graduated from the Maronite College of Rome. He became an active collector of manuscripts on behalf of the Vatican, especially those in Syriac, Coptic, and Arabic from Middle Eastern locations, notably the Coptic monasteries of Wadi al-Natrun. He was sent to Egypt by Pope Clement XI in 1715 and 1735 for this purpose. He was the first to give an idea of Severus' writings in his *Bibliotheca Orientalis* printed in four volumes in Rome in 1719–1728. It is worth mentioning that most of the Syriac Severian corpus that reached Europe came originally from the monastery of Wadi al-Natrun. However, Severus' important work the *Pilalethes* was translated into Arabic and survived in two manuscripts copied in the fourteenth and nineteenth centuries (Youssef 2001a; 2009).

Reception in the Modern Period

It was not until the modern period that western scholars began to rediscover Severus' writings and to study his theological contribution. Joseph Lebon in his book *Le monophysisme sévérien: Étude historique, littéraire et théologique de la résistance monophysite au concile de Chalcédoine jusqu'à la constitution de l'Eglise jacobite* (Louvain 1909, rpt. New York 1978), stated the difference between the "official Monophysites" ("Miaphysite" is meant here) – that is, the Egyptian patriarchs and later Severus of Antioch – and those who adopted the heresy of Eutyches. In order to study the doctrinal points, which was his primary aim, he studied the historical context and then the literary works, which were at that time still unpublished. His method was to start with the history, followed by the literature and then the theological study.

The main obstacle to understanding Severus was the fact that most of the sources were in Syriac, and until the eighteenth century were hidden in unexplored libraries. By the end of the nineteenth century, however, many Syriac texts had been published, and several collections in Europe started to establish their catalogues, which were beneficial for Lebon's historical study.

In the second part of his book, Lebon studied what is known about the works of Dioscorus of Alexandria, Timothy Aelurus, Philoxenus of Mabboug, and Severus, where he distinguished the different phases of his polemic against Chalcedonians, Eutychians, and Julianists. In the theological section of his study, he analyzed all the literary material, especially the terminology of the theological vocabulary, such as *physis, hypostasis, prosopon*. He concluded that the Miaphysite doctrine of the incarnation in its Severian form is exactly the Cyrillian Christology. He further stated that it is improper to call the followers of Severus "Monophysites" as they never referred to themselves by this name but called themselves "Orthodox." For Lebon, the schism after Chalcedon was largely a verbal schism, and in the final part of his study he published some texts of Severus. The work of Lebon was the forerunner to the ecumenical dialogue between the Chalcedonian (Eastern Orthodox) and the non-Chalcedonian Churches (Oriental Orthodox).

Despite the importance of the writings of Severus of Antioch, however, the great collections of patristic texts, such as the *Nicene and Post-Nicene Fathers* and *Sources Chrétiennes*, did not include them in their publications. Only the series dedicated to the Oriental texts such as *Patrologia Orientalis* and *Corpus Scriptorum Christianorum Orientalium* published his texts. It is also worth noting that the collection of the *Traditio Exegetica Graeca* has published the fragments of Severus on Exodus (Petit and Van Rompay 1999).

After World War II, important changes took place that led the Roman Catholic Church to be more open to dialogue with other churches, especially as a result of Vatican II in 1965. In the east a new generation of Church leaders entered into contact with their western counterparts; thus, the future Bishop Samuel represented the Copts at the World Council of Churches meeting in the USA in 1954. The Coptic Pope Shenouda visited Rome in 1973, where he and the Roman Pope Paul VI issued a joint statement on Christology. This statement was mainly inspired by the Severian terminology that was explained in detail in the work of Lebon. The Syrian Orthodox Patriarch Mar Ignatius Yacob III met with Pope Paul VI in 1971, and both agreed that the differences between the two churches were mainly verbal. The Oriental Orthodox and Eastern Orthodox churches also engaged in a dialogue and reached an agreement (Chaillot and Belopoposky 1998).

Following the work of Lebon, the *Patrologia Orientalis* launched the publication of the *Cathedral Homilies* with a French translation; this project started in 1906 with the publication of homilies 52–57 by Duval. The project was completed by several scholars, such as Guidi, Kugener, and Triffaux. The name of Maurice Brière (1911–1948) should be mentioned, as he translated most of the homilies of Severus (*Patrologia Orientalis*); however, he did not live to see the end of the project, and some of his colleagues, F. Graffin, C. Lash, and J.M. Sauget, completed his work in 1976.

Severus' homilies are a mine of information on the occupation of a bishop in the sixth century. They show not only his spiritual duties but also his responsibilities towards the emperor and the governing authorities. In addition to the Chalcedonians or Dyophysites who were present in his diocese, Severus had to combat local customs and superstitions, such as attending the spectacles and races, as well as the use of amulets and magic: pagan practices were still prevalent in some places. It was his duty to prepare catechumens to receive baptism at Easter and to make pastoral visits to the countryside and to the monasteries. He participated in the cults of local saints or martyrs and explained passages from the scriptures and tackled theological subjects.

A name associated with the first English translation of Severus is that of E.W. Brooks (Brooks 1902; 1904). He was the first scholar to publish the *Sixth Book of the Select Letters of Severus of Antioch*, as well as two volumes in the *Patrologia Orientalis* series containing the collection of letters of Severus from numerous Syriac manuscripts (Brooks 1916; 1920). In addition to these, Brooks also published *The Hymns of Severus and Others in the Syriac Version of James of Edessa* in the series *Patrologia Orientalis* in the years 1910–1911. More recently, a selection of Severus' writings in English translation has appeared in the Early Church Fathers series published by Routledge (Allen and Hayward 2004).

It is important to say that every contemporary scholar of Severus has his or her own approach. For example, the studies of Aloys Grillmeier concentrate mainly on Severus' perception of Christ as part of his opus magnum *Christ in Christian Tradition*.

This theological approach helps those interested in Christian intellectual history to evaluate objectively the orthodoxy of Severus. And Syriac specialists such as Rifaat Ebied, Sebastian Brock, and Kathleen McVey offer readers excellent translations of the original works of Severus that allows the nonspecialist to appreciate the quality of his teaching. These works are complemented by recent scholars such as René Roux (2002), who analyze the writings of Severus in order to extract their deeper meaning. Pauline Allen, as a scholar of patristics, places Severus' works in their historical context by comparing his role as a bishop in late antiquity and evaluating his thought along with that of other church Fathers such as John Chrysostom and the Cappadocian Fathers.

Despite these recent studies and the publication of the corpus of Severus, we are still at the beginning of appreciating his contribution to the patristic tradition and understanding his place within it. For example, we look forward to the publication of the biography of Severus by Cyriacus of Tagrit (Vööbus 1975–1976), and the Copto-Arabic version of the book of *Philalethes* (Youssef 2001a), as well as some letters of Severus announced by Brock (1975). There are also many other texts that have yet to be identified and published in the various languages that kept his work alive.

Severus' Liturgical Contribution

An example of Severus' hymnography is the following troparion:

> O Only Begotten Son and the Word of God the immortal and everlasting, accepting everything for our salvation, the Incarnated from the Theotokos ever-Virgin Saint Mary, without change, Christ God becoming Man, crucified, trampling down death by death, one of the Holy Trinity to whom is glorification with the Father and the Holy Spirit, save us.

This monostrophic troparion is used in the Byzantine and Syriac Liturgies of St Mark and St James. It is sung in the Coptic Church on three occasions; namely, at the Consecration of Bishops, the Consecration of the Holy Chrism, and the canonical hour of Sext on Good Friday. It is used also in the Armenian and Georgian church traditions. It contains one long sentence with one finite verb, which is found in the last phrase "save us." It is true that the writer of this *troparion* has selected almost all of his vocabulary from different sources, and has combined them to form a pattern that had become traditional from the earliest times. Yet this is no random selection and combination, but one in which a fine balance of phrases and sentences is created, and in which a definite pattern of verbal repetition is cleverly constructed. This hymn is a compilation of the faith of the councils of Nicea–Constantinople and Chalcedon that could be accepted by both Chalcedonians and non-Chalcedonians. In the Byzantine Rite it is ascribed to the Emperor Justinian and in the Syriac Rite to Severus of Antioch, and was composed around 535–536.

We have from Severus a collection of 295 hymns relating to the feasts of the year. Such hymns are for the Nativity, Lent, the feast of Hosannas (Palm Sunday), the Passion week (on Judas the traitor, the wife of Pilate, the robber, the Holy Cross), the Resurrection, Holy Mid-Pentecost, the Ascension, the Genuflexion and the Holy Pentecost, as well as for John the Baptist, the Apostles, Sergius and Bacchus, Thecla, and so on. As the book bears the title *Hymns of Severus and Others*, it is not an easy task to determine what belongs to Severus and what belongs to others, but we may assume that he composed hymns for each subject treated in his homilies. We have a similar situation in the Ethiopic *Synaxarion*, where after each saint or event commemorated we find a hymn called the "*Salam*" or "Praise."

Table 15.1 compares the topics treated in the hymns and the homilies. We give the number of each homily and hymn (see References, especially the edition of Brooks for the hymns and Brière for the homilies).

Table 15.1   Comparison of the topics treated in the hymns and homilies.

Subject	Homily	Hymn
Nativity	7, 36, 63, 101, 115	1–14/228
Epiphany	10, 38, 66, 85, 103, 117	15–25/211/255
Lent	15/16, 39, 68, 87, 105, 120	26–34
On the preparation to enter to the Baptistery	40, 69, 88, 106, 121	90, 91
Palm Sunday	22	51–57
On the robber	20	65
On persons baptized	21, 42, 70, 90, 109, 123	92–101/229
On the Holy mid-Pentecost	46, 92	102
On the Ascension of our Lord	24, 47, 71	103–107/230
On the Genuflexion/the Pentecost	25, 48; 74, 92	108–114
On the holy God Bearer	14, 67	117–122/217/231
On John the Baptist	32, 61	123–126
On the holy Stephen the martyr	7	127, 128
The Apostles		129
On the Apostle Thomas	28	134
Sergius and Bacchus	57	143, 144/145
On Saint Thecla the Martyr	97	160
Thalleliaos	110	
Leontius the Martyr	27, 50	138
On St Babylas the Martyr	11	141, 142
Simon the Stylite	30	147
St Antony the Great	12, 86	148
On the holy Maccabee martyrs	52	149, 150
On the XL martyrs	18, 41	155–159
On Saint Drosis the martyr	5, 100, 114	161, 162
On Saint Athanasius	91	183
On SS Basil and Gregory	9, 37, 65, 84, 102, 116	182, 184
On Drought	19	252–254/256
On Earthquake	31	257–262
On Vitalian the Tyrant	34	263
When he returned from visitation of monasteries	61	272
Of admonition and on theaters and dancing	26	274–293

To the authentic works are many other works ascribed to Severus, such as the encomium of Claudius of Antioch in Coptic (Godron 1970), Philotheus of Antioch in Arabic (Youssef 2002), and the Archangel Michael (Youssef 2003b) in Coptic.

Finally, Severus has been considered by some scholars and critics to have been a heretic; however, his writings are the expression of Cyrillian theology, which is the basis of most of the ecumenical dialogues of the late twentieth and early twenty-first centuries (Chaillot and Belopoposky 1998: 60). His liturgical texts are used in Chalcedonian and non-Chalcedonian churches, and his interpretations of the Bible became standard for all exegetes of all times (Roux 2002).

Bibliography

Primary Sources

Brière, M. (1911–1948), *Sévère d'Antioche Les Homiliea Cathedrales traduction Syriaque de Jacques d'Edesse. PO.*

Brière, M. (1960), *Sévère d'Antioche Les Homiliea Cathedrales traduction Syriaque de Jacques d'Edesse – Introduction générale à toutes les homélies, Homélies CXX–CXXV. PO* 1 No. 138.

Brock, S. (1975), "Some new letters of the patriarch Severus", *Studia Patristica* 12: 17–24.

Brock, S. and Fitzgerald, B. (2013), *Two Early Lives of Severos, Patriarch of Antioch.* TTH 59. Liverpool: Liverpool University Press.

Brooks, E.W. (1902), *The Sixth Book of the Select Letters of Severus of Antioch in the Syriac Version of Athanasius of Nisibis.* London: Williams & Norgate.

Brooks, E.W. (1904), *The Sixth Book of the Select Letters of Severus of Antioch,* Vol. II, part II. London: Williams & Norgate.

Brooks, E.W. (1910), *The Hymns of Severus and Others in the Syriac Version of James of Edessa as Revised by James of Edessa. PO* 6.1 No. 26.

Brooks, E.W. (1911), *The Hymns of Severus and Others in the Syriac Version of Paul of Edessa as Revised by James of Edessa. PO* 7.3 No. 35.

Brooks, E.W. (1916), *A Collection of Letters of Severus of Antioch from Numerous Syriac Manuscripts I. PO* 12.2 No. 58.

Brooks, E.W. (1920), *A Collection of Letters of Severus of Antioch from Numerous Syriac Manuscripts II. PO* 14.1 No. 67.

Caubet Iturbe, F.J. (1969–1970), *La Cadena Arabe del Evangelio de San Mateo.* Studi e Testi 254–255. Vatican City: Biblioteca Apostolica Vaticana.

Cramer, J.A. (1840–1848), *Catenae graecorum in Novum Testamentum,* eight vols. Oxford: Oxford University Press.

Garitte, G. (1966), "Textes Hagiographiques Orientaux relatifs à Saint Léonce de Tripoli II, L'homélie de Sévère d'Antioche", *Le Muséon,* 79: 335–386.

Godron, G. (1970), *Textes Coptes relatifs à Saint Claude d'Antioche. PO* 35. 4 No. 166.

Goodspeed, E.J. (1909), *The Conflict of Severus, Patriarch of Antioch, by Athanasius. PO* fasc. 6 No. 20.

Hespel, R. (1952), *Sévère d'Antioche, Le Philalèthe.* CSCO 133–134. Louvain: Secrétariat du Corpus SCO.

Hespel, R. (1955), *Le florilège cyrillien réfuté par Sévère d'Antioche: étude et édition critique.* Bibliothèque du Muséon 37. Louvain: Institut Orientaliste.

Hespel, R. (1964), *La polémique antijulianitste, I: les trois échanges de lettres; la critique du Tome; Refutation des propositions hérétiques.* CSCO 245–246. Louvain: Secrétariat du Corpus SCO.

Hespel, R. (1968), *Sévère d'Antioche la polémique antijulianiste contra additiones Iuliani.* CSCO 295–296. Louvain: Secrétariat du Corpus SCO.

Hespel, R. (1969), *L'Adverus Apologiam Iulianini.* CSCO 301–302. Louvain: Secrétariat du Corpus SCO.

Kugener, M.-A. (1904a), *Textes Syriaques relatifs à la vie de Sévère, patriarche d'Antioche, Première partie. Vie de Sévère par Zacharie le Scholastique.* PO 2.1 No. 6.

Kugener, M.-A. (1904b), *Textes Syriaques relatifs à la vie de Sévère, patriarche d'Antioche, Deuxième partie. Vie de Sévère par Jean de Beith Aphtonia.* PO 2.3 No. 8.

Kugener, M.-A. and Triffaux, E. (1924), *Sévère d'Antioche Les Homiliea Cathedrales traduction Syriaque de Jacques d'Edesse Homélies LVII.* PO 15.5 No. 81.

De Lagarde, P. (1886), *Catenae in Evangeli a Aegyptiaca quae supersunt.* Gooteingae: Prostant in Aedibus Dieterichianis.

McVey, K.E. (1993), *George, Bishop of the Arabs: A Homily on Blessed Mar Severus Patriarch of Antioch.* CSCO 531, Syr 217. Leuven: Secrétariat du Corpus SCO.

Moeller, C. (1944–1945), "Un représentant de la Christologie néochalcédonienne au début du sixième siécle en Orient: Nephalius d'Alexandrie", *Revue d'Histoire ecclesiastique,* 40: 73–140.

Petit, F. and Van Rompay, L. (1999), *La Chaîne sur l'Exode, I. Fragments de Sévère d'Antioche.* Texte grec établi et traduit par Françoise Petit. Glossaire Syriaque par Lucas Van Rompay. Traditio Exegetica Graeca, 9. Leuven: Peeters.

Youssef, Y.N. (2004b), *The Arabic life of Severus of Antioch attributed to Athanasius.* PO 49.4 No. 220.

Youssef, Y.N. (2006a), *A Homily on Severus of Antioch by a bishop of Assiut.* PO 50.1 No. 222.

Secondary Sources

Allen, P. and Hayward, C.T.R. (2004), *Severus of Antioch.* The Early Church Fathers. London: Routledge.

Carrara, P. (1985), "I frammenti greci del 'contra additiones Iuliani' di Severo di Antiochia". *Prometheus,* 11: 82–92.

Carrara, P. (1988), "Severo di Antiochia nelle catene esegetiche alla Genesi". *Sileno,* 14: 171–178.

Chaillot, C. and Belopopsky, A. (1998), *Towards Unity: The Theological Dialogue between the Orthodox Church and the Oriental Orthodox Churches.* Geneva: Inter-Orthodox Dialogue.

Chaîne, M. (1913), Une lettre de Sévère d'Antioche à la diaconesse Anastasie. *Oriens Christianus,* 3: 32–58.

Frend, W.H.C. (1972), *The Rise of Monophysite Movement.* Cambridge: Cambridge University Press.

Lebon, J. (1978[1909]), *Le monophysisme sévérien. Étude historique, littéraire et théologique de la résistance monophysite au concile de Chalcédoine jusqu'à la constitution de l'Eglise jacobite.* Louvain: Université Catholique; repr. New York: AMS.

Orlandi, T. (1968), "Un Codice Copto del 'Monastero Bianco' Economii de Severo di Antiochia, Marco Evangelista, Atanasio di Alessandria". *Le Muséon,* 81: 351–405.

Roux, R. (2002), *L'exégèse biblique dans les Homélies Cathédrales de Sévère d'Antioche.* Studia Ephemeridis Augustinianum. Rome: Institutum Patristicum Augustinianum.

Torrance, I.R. (2012[1988]), *Christology after Chalcedon: Severus of Antioch and Sergius the Monophysite.* Norwich: The Canterbury Press.

Vööbus, A. (1975–1976), "Discovery of the biography of Severus of Antioch by Qyriagos of Tagrit". *Rivista di studi bizantini e neoellenici* n.s., 12–13: 117–124.

Youssef, Y.N. (2001a), "Arabic manuscripts of the Philalethes of Severus of Antioch". *Proche Orient Chrétien,* 51: 261–266.

Youssef, Y.N. (2001b), "Letter of Severus of Antioch to Anastasia the Deaconess". *Bulletin de la Société d'Archéologie Copte,* 40: 126–136.

Youssef, Y.N. (2002), "The Encomium of St. Philotheus ascribed to Severus of Antioch". *Coptica*, 1: 169–221.

Youssef, Y.N. (2003a), "The quotations of Severus of Antioch in the Book of the *Confessions of the Fathers*". *Ancient Near Eastern Studies*, 40: 178–229.

Youssef, Y.N. (2003b), "The homily on the Archangel Michael attributed to Severus of Antioch revisited". *Bulletin de la Société d'Archéologie Copte*, 42: 103–117.

Youssef, Y.N. (2004a), "A new fragment of a life of Severus of Antioch?". *Oriens Christianus*, 88, 109–114.

Youssef, Y.N. (2004c), "A contribution to the Coptic biography of Severus of Antioch". In *Coptic Studies on the Threshold of a New Millenium: Proceedings of the Seventh International Congress of Coptic Studies – Leiden, August 27–September 2, 2000*, M. Emmerzeel and J. Van der Vliet (eds). Orientalia Lovensiensa Analecta 133. Leuven: Peeters; 413–426.

Youssef, Y.N. (2006b), "Severus of Antioch in Scetis. *Ancient Near Eastern Studies*, 43: 141–162.

Youssef, Y.N. (2009), "Some preliminary remarks on the Copto-Arabic version of the *Philalethes*". *Bulletin de la Société d'Archéologie Copte*, 48: 85–92.

CHAPTER 16

Gregory the Great

Bronwen Neil

Introduction: Gregory the Great and his Contemporaries

Gregory the Great came from one of the leading families of Rome, one that had already produced two popes, Felix III (483–492) and Agapetus (535–536) (Moorhead 2006). It may surprise the modern reader, however, to learn that the official record of the bishops of Rome and their achievements, known as the *Book of Pontiffs (Liber Pontificalis)*, had very little to say about Gregory's pontificate, even though it was updated in Gregory's own day. The *Liber Pontificalis* entry for Gregory I is no longer than average, even though his rule lasted almost 15 years, and its tone strikingly neutral. While some of his major works are listed there (e.g., *Homilies on Ezekiel*, *Moralia*, *Pastoral Rule*, and *Dialogues*), his many letters go unmentioned. The defeat of the Lombards in northern Italy was attributed in *Liber Pontificalis* not to Gregory, who negotiated a settlement with the Lombards in the absence of aid from the Byzantine Empire, but to the exarch of Ravenna. Although Gregory's mission to the English is praised, his major liturgical contribution is reported to have been the addition of some words to the recital of the Canon. In fact, Gregory was responsible for the singing of the *Alleluia* and *Kyrie eleison*, and the diaconal service, which he made the subject of a renewed discipline in the Roman synod of 595 (Baroffio 2011: 145). Gregory is said to have given donations of purple cloth, gold, and silver to the shrines of Rome's protectors, saints Peter and Paul, so that mass could be celebrated above their tombs. He returned to orthodox usage a church owned by the Arian Goths in the Subura, and established his own house as a monastery. He performed two ordinations of 39 priests and five deacons in Rome, and ordained an enormous number of bishops, some 62, for "various places." Apart from notice of his death and burial in St Peter's Basilica, following the custom of the four preceding popes (Pelagius I, John III, Benedict I, and Pelagius II), this is the sum

The Wiley Blackwell Companion to Patristics, First Edition. Edited by Ken Parry.
© 2015 John Wiley & Sons Ltd. Published 2019 by John Wiley & Sons Ltd.

total of information given about Gregory's pontificate in *Liber Pontificalis*. Only his written works, and the mission to England, serve to distinguish this bishop's contribution from that of any of his predecessors. Gregory's reputation for greatness seems to have got off to a slow start.

Gregory's influence was recognized in his own lifetime, however, by the bishop of Ravenna. Agnellus, author of the ninth-century chronicle *Liber Pontificalis of Ravenna* claims that Gregory's *Pastoral Rule* was written expressly for his friend Marinian, bishop of Ravenna (595–606), who, like Gregory, had been reluctant to take up the episcopal office (Deliyannis 2006: 268). Deliyannis suggests that Agnellus must have seen a manuscript inscription addressed to Marinian. Other manuscripts say that the *Pastoral Rule* was dedicated to Marinian's predecessor John II. Whatever the case, the close relationship between the sees of Ravenna and Rome was improved by Gregory's pontificate. Gregory's namesake, the bishop of Tours – the great ecclesiastical center in Gaul – also played his part in building the pope's reputation by describing his accession in Rome, an event he claims to have witnessed (*History of the Franks* 10.1; Krusch 1942: 477–481). Gregory of Tours relates that Gregory the Great left with reluctance his sequestered life in the monastery of St Andrew's that he founded as a young man in his family home on the Coelian Hill to take up the burdens of the leadership of the Roman church in September 590. He praised Gregory's actions in helping the people of Rome recover from the devastating flooding of the Tiber in 589 – the plague that followed the floods carried off his predecessor Pelagius II (579–590). Gregory continued the tradition of Rome acting as a court of appeal for bishops and priests from Antioch, Alexandria, and Constantinople. It was one of these exiled priests, Athanasius of Antioch, who translated Gregory's *Pastoral Rule* into Greek in 602. The translation of this work into Anglo-Saxon by King Alfred the Great in the ninth century is also a mark of the early recognition of this work's utility for managing the nascent church of Britain.

Gregory I's pontificate shows the continuation of a trend that was first obvious in the time of Gelasius: from the end of the fifth century there was a profound shift in the production, function, and preservation of papal letters. Such a shift is evident from this fact alone, that 854 of his letters were preserved in one *Registry* in his own lifetime. Gregory's letters demonstrate his fulfillment of all the normal duties of an elite patron, making many bequests of money, food, grain, and wine to the needy, many of whom were impoverished elites, or their widows and children. He was also highly involved in the election of bishops to key sees in Sicily, where the administration of papal estates was crucial for the Roman food supply. He petitioned on behalf of Sardinian landowners who were unable to bear the increasing burden of imperial taxes. After the flooding of the Tiber River in 589 he petitioned the governor of Sicily for grain supplies, desperately needed by the people of Rome who had suffered waves of plague and famine after the floods. Gregory's many letters are rich in material pertaining to his dual roles as pastoral carer and administrator of Rome and the wider church. Not for nothing was he buried in St Peter's under the epitaph "Consul of God." His epitaph may also be an indirect reference to his office as praetor of the city before taking up the monastic life in the monastery of St Andrew's on the Coelian Hill.

Gregory's Impact on Seventh-Century Italy and Beyond

Richards (1979: 54) singles Gregory out from other bishops of Rome as one whose exercise of charity extended far beyond the city itself, and to people of all backgrounds and conditions. In his letters we find Gregory helping the formerly wealthy as often as he helped the perennially poor: gentlewomen of Campania (*Letter* 1.39), a governor who had fled his office in Samnium (*Letter* 2.28), a lawyer from Naples (*Letter* 9.136), the blind son of a farmer–soldier (*Letter* 3.55), a debt-ridden Syrian whose sons had been sold into slavery (*Letter* 4.43), and the children of a Jewish convert (*Letters* 1.39; 2.38; 3.55; 4.28; 4.31; 4.43; 9.136).

Gregory's energies as bishop of Rome were focused in two domains: the spiritual leadership of the church of Italy and the wider church; and administration, both of the dioceses of Italy and the wider church. Gregory's first concern was the preservation of the social order in order to facilitate the salvation of souls. The tension between the twin demands of pastoral care and administration plagued Gregory, who maintained that he felt torn between the demands of the job and his personal desire to devote himself to his monastic vocation, as he relates in the preface to the *Moralia*, a commentary on the book of Job (*Letter* 5.53a.1) (Markus 1997: 9–11). *Letters* 1.7 and 1.24 also bemoan the burdens of pastoral care. This tension was typical of bishops in late antiquity, when they were called upon to shoulder more burdens for civic administration than previously, due to the breakdown of municipal government, the demise of the Roman senate, and, from 476 until 536, the lack of an imperial presence in the Western empire. Gregory's struggle to resolve this tension is a major theme of early hagiographers of his life and works.

Some commentators attribute the reticence of the Roman records to the operation of two opposing factions: those who embraced monasticism and believed it important to balance the active and contemplative lives, such as Gregory, and those who championed the clergy and its interests. Gregory's successor Sabinian (604–606) was part of the opposing clerical faction, and perhaps had a hand in suppressing the memory of his predecessor. Sabinian himself sank to new levels of unpopularity after he attempted to sell papal grain stores to the starving people of Rome at exorbitant rates. His funeral procession through the streets of Rome in 606 was interrupted by a rioting mob. After Sabinian, a monastic disciple of Gregory was elected to the papal throne, Boniface IV, who converted his house in Rome into a monastery. Boniface held a synod in 610 to promote discipline within the monastic life. He was replaced by a member of the clerical faction, Deusdedit, who gave the first recorded papal bequest to his clergy, the equivalent of a year's salary (McBrien 2000: 100). Another clerical support followed, in the election of Boniface V (619–625). Thus, it can be seen that Gregory's influence on the activities of the papacy in the first quarter of the seventh century was limited in its scope.

Gregory's impact in the seventh century beyond Italy can be seen in the many letters he exchanged with the Byzantine imperial family, other bishops, and significant lay persons during his pontificate. These letters reflect his talents as an administrator, petitioner, and negotiator. The reception of so many of Gregory's letters into medieval canon law is testimony to his spiritual authority, particularly in the West, but also in the eastern churches of Byzantium. Both these areas of his influence will be discussed below.

Apart from his literary works, the other cause of Gregory's spreading influence was his far-sighted sponsoring of missions to the Lombards, recently arrived in Italy, the Anglo-Saxons in Britain, and the peoples of Gaul (modern France and Germany). The *Pastoral Rule* was among the Latin books taken to Kent in 597, as noted in the preface to Alfred's Anglo-Saxon translation of the work, one of the earliest books written in that language. In his preface, Alfred states his intention that every bishop in the kingdom should have access to the work for the benefit of less-educated clergy. The *Pastoral Rule* went on to become the most copied Latin book in the Middle Ages. A very early manuscript copy survives from France (Troyes, *Bibliothèque Municipale MS* 504, c. 600). The work was prescribed as recommended reading for Charlemagne's bishops at a series of Gallic councils held in 813, at Rheims, Tours, Mayence, and Châlon-sur-Seine. Hincmar, archbishop of Rheims (845–882), notes in a letter that a copy of it, together with the *Book of Canons*, was given into the hands of bishops before the altar at their consecration, and they were "admonished to frame their lives accordingly" (Barmby 1886: xxxii).

The Early *Lives* of Gregory

The earliest *Vita* of Gregory was written by a monk of Whitby c. 713, and was used by Bede as a source for Book 2 of his *Ecclesiastical History*. The *Life* presents a sympathetic picture of "our Gregory," who was celebrated as the founder of the English church. Interestingly, the author's sympathy did not extend to Gregory's successor Sabinian. The Whitby monk gives a surprisingly violent account of Gregory's appearance in a dream to his successor Sabinian. While Gregory reproached him for his jealousy and greed, Sabinian remained obdurate and unrepentant, so Gregory kicked him in the head, causing his death. The author relays some more factual information – such as the name of Gregory's mother, Silvia, independently of the *Book of Pontiffs*, Book 2 of Bede's *Ecclesiastical History* (composed by 731), or the brief *Life of Gregory* by Paul the Deacon, composed between 770 and 780. Paul is better known for his *History of the Lombards*, which also contains an account of Gregory's pontificate. For the sake of completeness we should also mention two seventh-century Spanish sources: Isidore of Seville's *On Famous Men* 40 and Ildefonsus of Toledo's *On the Writings of Famous Men* 1 (Fontaine 1973: 171).

In the late ninth century, court historiographer John the Deacon composed the first Roman life of Gregory, dubbing him "the Great." John the Deacon's preface notes the request of Pope John VIII (872–882) for a *Life of Gregory*, since the English and Lombards had one, but not the Roman church (Patrologia Latina (PL) 75: 61). John's *Life* records Gregory's aid to the nameless poor, through distributions of food – grain, wine, cheese, vegetables, meat, fish, and oil – and sending out from the Lateran palace a "meals on wheels" service for the sick. According to John, the pope also shared his own table with refugees, almost certainly members of the upper class who had been displaced by the Lombard invasions (*Life of Gregory*, 2.24–30; PL 75: 96D–98A). Gregory's concern to provide for the *declassé* rich came to be construed in the ninth century as a concern for the poor (Brown 2002: 60). Gregory's annual subsidy of 80 pounds of gold for 3000 Roman nuns (*Life of Gregory* 2.27; PL 75: 97B–C) could be seen as contributing to the welfare of the church in the same way as his financial support for clerics. In other words, Gregory's commitment to the "poor" was part of a larger commitment to the preservation of the social order.

Gregory in Byzantium

Rather than considering Gregory the first medieval pope, we might better consider him a Byzantine patriarch (Llewellyn 1993: 141, 316). Gregory had successfully negotiated the right for the see of Rome to be considered an independent jurisdiction, the first to do so after the Byzantine "restoration" of Italy. The Gothic wars had freed the bishop of Rome from being a pawn of the Gothic kings. However, it took another 150 years after Gregory's pontificate for Rome's ties with Byzantium to wear thin to breaking point, when Stephen II turned to the Merovingian king Pepin for help in defending Rome against the Lombards.

While still a deacon, Gregory had been employed for about 6 years as papal *apocrisiarius* for Pelagius II in the imperial capital, a formative experience with implications for a continued intellectual exchange between Rome and Constantinople during his pontificate. Gregory's allegiances were influenced by his own contact with eastern monasticism (Ekonomou 2007: 24). The question of how well he knew Greek, if it all, has been the subject of mixed scholarly opinion, but most studies conclude that he knew at least a little, as would have been required by his post as *apocrisiarius* for some 6 or 7 years from 579. It was during this posting that he began his enduring friendship with the patriarch of Antioch, Anastasius, with whom he was to correspond throughout his pontificate. Like popes Vigilius and Martin (649–653), Gregory reserved the right to make his own judgments on matters of orthodoxy, rather than blindly following Constantinople's lead. This was already obvious when, as *apocrisiarius* for Pelagius II, he engaged in a heated exchange with the patriarch of Constantinople over the nature of the resurrection body.

Gregory may have been responding to the doctrine of Julian of Halicarnassus on the incorruptibility of Christ's body (*aphtharsia*), a teaching introduced to Byzantium between 510 and 518, thus causing a major crisis in both the Chalcedonian and anti-Chalcedonian parties that lasted at least until the death of Justinian in 565. Emperor Justinian himself seems briefly to have adhered to the heretical doctrine known as Aphthartodocetism – the idea that Christ, the new Adam, was not subject to the limitations of human flesh but voluntarily underwent suffering and death. "Julianism," as it became known, spread through monastic circles in Egypt and Armenia, causing a serious schism among anti-Chalcedonians, and even in Chalcedonian circles.

More drastic than Julian's teaching on the incorruptible body of Christ was that of the Alexandrian philosopher John Philoponus (c. 490–c. 570), who argued that the resurrection of the body was not physical. John's tract *Diatetes seu arbiter* survives only in Syriac and some Greek fragments in John of Damascus' *De haeresibus* 83 (Patrologia Graeca (PG) 94: 744–755). Eutychius, patriarch of Constantinople (552–582), took the same line. The future Pope Gregory I, resident in Constantinople as *apocrisiarius*, defended the physical resurrection of Christ against Eutychius in a public debate in the Constantinopolitan court. If we compare Gregory's arguments with a contemporary compendium of opposing sentences preserved in Greek fragments by Stephen Gobar

(Bardy 1947), we find that Gregory's position was itself part of the contemporary Greek debate, as Matthew dal Santo affirms, and not a debased form of it (Dal Santo 2013). Four of Stephen Gobar's orthodox responses to heretical statements concern the resurrection of believers (Henry 2003[1967]: 67–69; transl. von Harnack 1923: 207). From Stephen's responses we can see that the same issues were troubling him as Gregory: the material substance of the resurrection body; its incorruptibility; the form it would take; whether people would be recognizable to each other in the afterlife. Whether or not he knew of Stephen's *Florilegium*, Gregory's arguments in favor of physical resurrection were found persuasive by Emperor Tiberius, and Eutychius' tract was destroyed in a public burning. The "subtlety of the Greeks" was no match for western theological reasoning on this occasion.

Also, like Pope Martin, and later Hadrian I, he resisted the claims of Constantinople's bishop to the title "ecumenical patriarch" (Demacopoulos 2009). It is implicit in Gregory's letters and actions that he respected the "two swords" theory, emphasizing the strict separation between the secular power of the emperor and the spiritual power of the church. This separation of powers had been promoted by Pope Gelasius (492–496). Gregory represented the temporal interests of Rome when it became obvious that these were being neglected by the exarch of Ravenna, Romanus, who refused to negotiate a truce with the Lombards on behalf of Rome. Gregory's works were some of the few Latin patristic writings to be translated into Greek before the thirteenth century, as Louth (2013) notes. In fact, Anastasius, patriarch of Antioch, had the *Pastoral Rule* translated into Greek as early as 602, a translation that unfortunately does not survive (*Letter* 12.6).

There is evidence from Gregory's preface to the second book of the *Pastoral Rule* that the author was indebted to Gregory Nazianzen's second oration, composed c. 362. This oration, known as his *Apology*, was written in an effort "to excuse the writer's reluctance to accept the episcopate, and to set forth the responsibilities of the office" (Barmby 1886: xxxii). The parallels with Gregory the Great's *Pastoral Rule* are obvious. In the mid-eighth century, Pope Zacharias (741–752), a Greek by birth, made a translation of his *Dialogues* into Greek (PL 77: 147–432), Gregory's most popular work among Byzantine readers and mentioned in the *Liber Pontificalis* as one of Zacharias' greatest achievements (Duchesne 1955: vol. 1, 435; see Lizzi (1991)). It was so popular that Gregory became known in the East as "the Dialogist." In the second half of the ninth century, Photius in his *Bibliotheca* comments that Zacharias translated "other valuable works" by Gregory, but these do not survive; Photius also gives notice of a Greek *Life* of Gregory. The *Dialogues* were an important source for Paul Evergetinos' *Synagôgê*, a florilegium of extracts from various fathers on the monastic life (Louth 2013). Paul, founder of the monastery of the "Beneficent Mother of God" (*Theotokos Evergetis*) near Constantinople, completed this massive work there before his death in 1054.

Gregory in the Middle Ages

A number of vernacular translations made of Gregory's writings in the Middle Ages have been surveyed in the recently published *Brill Companion to Gregory the Great* (Mews and Renkin, 2013). These include Old English versions of Gregory's *Dialogues* (Hecht

1965[1900]) and *Pastoral Care* (Sweet 1958[1871–1872]); an Old German paraphrase in rhyming verse of the *Moralia* in the eleventh century (Murdoch 2001); an Old French version of the *Dialogues* in the twelfth century (Foerster 1965[1876]); a Norse–Icelandic version of the *Homilies on the Gospels* by 1150 (Wolf 2001); a Middle French version of the *Pastoral Rule* (Pagan 2007); and a Middle Dutch version of the *Dialogues* (Claassens 2001). Other French productions included the *Dialogues* in rhyming couplets (S. Sandqvist 1989) and a poem on the *Life of Gregory*, both products of Normandy in the fourteenth century (O. Sandqvist 1989).

In the twelfth century, a curious legend circulated in an Old French *Life* (Bastiaan 1977) that Gregory was the offspring of twins. Gaunt (1995) suggests that the author's intention was to highlight two key theological issues: the notion of sin without intent and the elevation of the clerical life over the chivalric. According to the Old French *Life*, Gregory's incestuous origins caused him to be set adrift by his mother, and after growing up under the protection of a monk he chose to become a knight. Eventually ending up in his home country, he unwittingly married his mother. This unconscious but sinful act compelled him to endure a harsh penance, stranded on a rock in the ocean for 17 years. At that time he was released when a giant fish turned up with the key to his chains in its stomach. Almost immediately he was chosen as bishop of Rome. This was apparently a popular narrative in the twelfth and thirteenth centuries, with numerous manuscripts of the Old French version in circulation, and translations into Middle High German and Middle English (Gaunt 1995: 201). Perhaps this legend was partially a response to Gregory's definition of incest as extending to the fourth degree of consanguinity – that is, marriage between first cousins, which until then had been acceptable to the church. Gregory also developed the church's teaching on the practice of penance, which influenced the Middle Ages by the inclusion of several of his decretals in the canon law collection of the jurist Gratian, known as the *Decretum* (c. 1050).

Gratian attributes four decretals on public penance to Gregory (Mansi 1960–1961: vol. 10, 439). The first (no. 4) forbids the ordination of anyone who has undergone public penance for mortal sins. The second (no. 9) concerns bishops and those who exercised public judgments, that they should never pronounce sentences either in levity or rage. The third decree (no. 12) allows priests and monks who "hold the place of the apostles" to impose penance and absolve sins. The last (no. 19) concerns the sanctity of the confessional. Gregory adjures priests who have heard private confessions never to repeat what they have heard, either to intimates or strangers. Any priest who breaks this confidentiality is to be deposed and condemned to ignominious wandering for the rest of his days. This last decree is the most interesting, in that it acknowledges the possibility of private confession, the first reference to such a practice in the Roman church, although it may have been going on since the time of Augustine (Saint-Roch 1991: 49–51). Certainly, the "mortal sins" of adultery, murder, and apostasy, which required a lifetime of public penance, were always confessed in public, but those who committed lesser sins could make private confessions. In the latter case, the secrecy of the confessional was sacrosanct. In the era of scholasticism, Gregory's works were transmitted in fragments by Thomas Aquinas (d. 1274), who cited him 374 times in Part 2 of the *Summa theologiae* (McBrien 2000: 98).

Gregory in the Renaissance (Late Fourteenth to Sixteenth Centuries)

The Renaissance saw the flowering of Gregory's reputation as a man of learning, with the first printing of his works in Latin. Ann Kuzdale (2013) has produced an admirable survey of his printed works in this period, including a list of incunabula and early printed Latin books of Gregory the Great from c. 1460–1619. The earliest known printed work was, not surprisingly, the *Pastoral Rule*, printed at Mainz in 1460. Gregory's *Commentary on the Song of Songs* was printed at Cologne in 1465 to 1473. The same publisher produced a copy of the *Dialogues* in 1470. Kuzdale notes that one of the earliest vernacular printed works was a Middle German version of the *Dialogues*, produced at the monastery of saints Ulrich and Afra in Augsberg in 1473, by Abbot Melchior, within a year of his acquisition of a printing press. This was calculated to increase the revenue of the monastery. Others were quick to follow suit. The second book of the *Dialogues*, with its *Life* of Benedict of Nursia, was one of the first works to be printed, in Venice in 1505. In 1515 the first translation of the *Dialogues* in Spanish appeared in Toledo. Cornagliotti (1992: 356) concludes that those Spanish monks who translated the *Rule of Benedict* from the *Dialogues* wanted to make a translation that would develop the discourse in the Spanish language, and so they did not follow or stick to the structure of the original text. The words of Benedict were thereby confirmed again, and restated in the vulgar tongue. The wide dissemination of most of Gregory's works followed, although the first translation of his work into early modern English appeared only in 1608.

The Dutch humanist Erasmus (1466–1536) championed Gregory, and early patristic theology generally, as an alternative to scholasticism, and as representative of a purer form of Christianity (Kuzdale 2013). However, Erasmus disparaged the *Dialogues* as being symptomatic of Rome's false attachment to the cult of the saints.

Gregory in the Reformation

Gregory's reception in the centuries of the Reformation generally hit a trough, but some peaks can be observed. Even before the Protestant reformer Martin Luther posted his 95 theses on the door of Wittenberg in 1517, Gregory's name was frequently mentioned during debates over papal primacy, with the English theologian John Fisher (1459–1535) being staunchly pro-Gregory even during Henry VIII's separation from Rome and dissolution of the monasteries of England. Thomas More (1478–1535) also quoted Gregory in his repudiation of Henry's right to break with Rome. For many Protestant reformers the Fathers, including Gregory, were seen as a fundamental part of all that was wrong with Catholicism.

With the Council of Trent, held between 1545 and 1563, the Roman church undertook its own internal reforms. The Catholic reformation made good use of Gregory as part of its long tradition. Pope Gregory XIII (1572–1585), a supporter of the Tridentine reforms, had a strong devotion to the saint whose name he adopted at his election to the pontifical throne. Gregory XIII would cite Gregory I as his model for rebuilding and reforming the papacy and the Roman church according to the Tridentine recommendations.

Contemporary perceptions

Gregorian studies received a boost in the 1980s to 1990s, with the fourteenth centennial of the pope's accession. No less than three compiled volumes were produced in quick succession, from symposia held in France (Fontaine *et al.* 1986), Italy (*Gregorio Magno e il suo tempo* 1991), and the United States (Cavadini 1995). Joseph Campbell (2008: 277–278) cited Gregory as an archetypal hero who endured a difficult childhood and a period of exile and return, like two other heroes of the church, Charlemagne and Abraham.

In the modern era of the Catholic and Orthodox churches, Gregory's popularity has endured. On the thirteenth centenary of his death, Pius X delivered a panegyric on the Feast of Gregory, in which he cited part of John the Deacon's epitaph: "He lives eternal in every place by his innumerable good works" (*Life of Gregory*, 4.68; PL 75: 221C). Gregory's name, according to Pius X, was synonymous with the triumph of the Roman church over adversity (*Jucunda sane* 2, 1904). With the *resourcement* of patristic writers since the Second Vatican Council in 1962–65, the Roman church has also found a valuable resource in Gregory's writings. He is still regularly cited in papal encyclicals.

Gregory's psychological subtlety is one reason for his enduring appeal, even to modern readers, in the view of Moorhead (2005). Gregory's rich portrayal of the conflicted inner life of the Old Testament figure Job in the *Moralia* is evidence of such subtlety.

In the current era, Gregory is regularly dubbed "the first medieval pope." In his history of the papacy, McBrien (2000: 432) avers that Gregory was one of only two "outstanding popes" in history, the other one being John XXIII (1958–1963). Gregory deserves this accolade, according to McBrien (2000: 433), because he was a "genuinely pastoral pope, with a profound concern for the poor," and the first to use the expression "servant of the servants of God" for the papacy, an expression that has continued in use to the present day. Alfred's translation of the *Pastoral Rule* was recently inscribed in UNESCO's *UK Memory of the World Register* of May 2011.

Although it could indeed be said that, by the time of Gregory, Rome had seen the end of ancient Christianity, it is no less true that we need to make a distinction between how Gregory was perceived in his own day and how he was constructed in later ages, as Durliat reminds us:

> In the eyes of his contemporaries, Gregory appeared to be the model of the western Byzantine patriarch, faithful to the emperor while at the same time being spokesman for populations placed under his religious and administrative authority, in discussion with the Germanic kings only if their relations with the sovereign from Constantinople were good or nonexistent. After his death, he was increasingly presented as the staunch manager of papal patrimonies that represented the earliest foundations of the Papal States ... (Durliat 2002: 641)

In the end, whatever one makes of Gregory's attempts to manage the patrimonies of Rome, it seems from the volume and quality of his works, and their wide dissemination in Latin, Greek, and vernacular languages, even to the present day, that Gregory deserved his reputation for greatness, even if this was only recognized posthumously.

Bibliography

Primary Sources

Dialogues, Adalbert de Vogüé and Paul Antin (eds) (1978–1980), SC 251, 260, 265. Paris: Editions du Cerf.

Homilies on Ezekiel, Marcus Adriaen (ed.) (1971), CCSL 142. Turnhout: Brepols.

Homilies on the Gospels, Raymond Étaix (ed.) (1999), CCSL 141. Turnhout: Brepols.

Letters, Dag Norberg (ed.) (1972), *Sancti Gregorii Magni registrum epistularum libri I–XIV*, CCSL 140 and 140a. Turnhout:

Brepols. John R.C. Martyn (transl.) (2004), *The Letters of Gregory the Great*, Mediaeval Sources in Translation, three vols. Toronto: Pontifical Institute for Medieval Studies.

Pastoral Rule, James Barmby (transl.) (1886), *The Book of Pastoral Rule and Selected Epistles*: preface and translation, Philip Schaff (ed.), *Nicene and Post-Nicene Fathers*, ser. 2, vol. 12, Oxford: Parker.

Early Translations of Gregory's Works

Pastoral Rule

Alfred, *King Alfred's West-Saxon Version of Gregory's Pastoral Care*, Henry Sweet (ed.) (1958[1871–1872]), two vols. Early English Texts Society, 45, 50, London: Oxford University Press for the Early English Text Society. Reprint, Oxford: Oxford University Press.

Le Pastoralet. Traduction médiévale française de la Regula Pastoralis; édition critique du manuscrit 868 de la Bibliothèque municipale de Lyon, Martine Pagan (ed.) (2007). Paris: H. Champion.

Dialogues

Bishop Waerferth of Worcester, *Bischof Waerferth von Worcester Übersetzung der Dialoge Gregors des Grossen*, H. Hecht (ed.) (1965[1900]), two vols. Leipzig–Hamburg, 1900. Reprint, Darmstadt: Wissenschaftliche Buchgesellschaft.

Le Dyalogue Saint Gregore: les Dialogues de saint Grégoire le Grand traduits en vers français à rimes léonines par un Normand anonyme du XIVe siècle, Sven Sandqvist (ed.). Lund: Lund University Press, 1989a.

Li dialoge Gregoire lo Pape: altfranzosische Übersetzung des XII. Jahrhunderts der Dialogen des Papstes Gregor, Wendelin Foerster (ed.) (1965[1876]). Halle–Paris: Niemeyer. Reprint, Amsterdam: Rodopi.

Padre Fray Gonzalo de Ocanna, (transl.) (1514), *Los Diálogos del bienaventurado papa sant Gregorio sacados del latin en Romance.* Toledo.

Dialogues, Book 2

Secundus dyalogorum liber beati Gregorij pape de vita ac miraculis beatissimi Benedicti, Venice, 1505.

Other Ancient Works

Agnellus of Ravenna, *Liber Pontificalis Ecclesiae Ravennatis*, Deborah Mauskopf Deliyannis (ed.)

(2006). Corpus Christianorum Continuatio Medievalis 199. Turnhout: Brepols.

Anonymous of Whitby, *Liber beati et laudabili viri Gregorii papae urbis Romae de vita atque eius virtutibus*, Bertram Colgrave (ed./transl.) (1968), *The Earliest Life of Gregory the Great by an Anonymous Monk of Whitby*. Cambridge: Cambridge University Press.

Greek fragments in John of Damascus, *De haeresibus* 83, PG 94, 744–755.

Gregory of Tours, *Historia Francorum*, Bruno Krusch (ed.) (1942), *Gregorius Turonensis, Historia Francorum*. Monumenta Germaniae Historica, Scriptores rerum merovingicarum 1. Hannover: Hahn.

John Philoponus, Diatetes seu arbiter

John the Deacon, Vita Gregorii, PL 75: 61–242.

La vie de Saint Gregor: poème normand du XIVe siecle, publié avec introduction, notes et glossaire, Olle Sandqvist (ed.) (1989). Lund: Lund University Press.

La vie du pape saint Grégoire le Grand. Huit versions françaises médiévales de la légende du Bon Pécheur, Hendrik Bastiaan (ed.) (1977). Amsterdam: Rodopi.

Liber Pontificalis, Louis Duchesne and Cyril Vogel (eds) (1955–1957), *Le Liber Pontificalis*, 2nd edn, three vols. Paris: De Boccard. Raymond Davis (transl.) (2000), *The Book of Pontiffs (Liber Pontificalis)*, 2nd edn. Translated Texts for Historians 6. Liverpool: Liverpool University Press.

Paul the Deacon, Vita Gregori, PL 75: 41–62.

Photius, *Bibliotheca*, René Henry (ed.) (2003[1967]), *Photius Bibliothèque*, vol. 5: *Bibliotheca Codex* 232. Paris: Société d'Édition les Belles Lettres.

Pius X, *Jucunda sane*, 12 March 1904, Vatican City. English translation at http://www.papalencyclicals.net/Pius10/p10greg.htm. Accessed January 28, 2015.

Sacrorum conciliorum nova et amplissima collectio, Giovanni Domenico Mansi (ed.) (1960–1961), 53 vols. Florence, 1759–1798. Reprint, Graz: Akademische Druck- und Verlaganstalt.

Stephen Gobar, *Florilegium*, Gustav Bardy (ed.) (1947), "Le florilège d'Étienne Gobar". *Revue des études byzantines*, 5: 5–30. Transl.: Adolf von Harnack (1923), "The 'Sic et Non' of Stephanus Gobarus". *The Harvard Theological Review*, 16: 205–234.

Secondary Sources

Baroffio, Giacomo (2011), "Liturgie e culture tra l'éta di Gregorio Magno (590–604) e il pontificato di Leone III (795–816): le tradizioni musicali". In *Liturgie e culture tra l'éta di Gregorio Magno e il pontificato di Leone III. Aspetti rituali, ecclesiologici e istituzionali*, Renata Salvarani (ed.). Rome: Edizioni del Galluzzo; 141–159.

Bremmer Jr, Rolf, Dekker, Kees, and Johnson, David F. (eds) (2001), *Rome and the North: The Early Reception of Gregory the Great in Germanic Europe*. Mediaevalia Groningana n.s. 4. Paris: Peeters.

Brown, Peter R.L. (2002), *Poverty and Leadership in the Later Roman Empire*. The Menahem Stern Jerusalem Lectures. Hannover, NH: University of New England Press.

Campbell, Joseph (2008), *The Hero with a Thousand Faces*. Bollingen Series 17, 3rd edn. Novato, CA: New World Library.

Cavadini, John C. (ed.) (1995), *Gregory the Great: A Symposium*. Notre Dame Studies in Theology 2. Notre Dame, IN: University of Notre Dame Press.

Claassens, Geert H.M. (2001), "Gregory's *Dialogi* in Middle Dutch literature". In Bremmer *et al.* (2001: 207–238).

Cornagliotti, Anna (1992), "Gregorio Magno e la *Regula* di san Benedetto". In *Lo Spazio letterario del medioevo, vol. 2: Il medioevo volgare. 3. La recezione del testo*, Piero Boitani, Mario Mancini, and Alberto Vàrvaro (eds). Rome: Salverno Editrice; 331–356.

Dal Santo, Matthew (2013), "Gregory, the empire and the emperor". In Neil and Dal Santo (2013: 57–81).

Demacopoulos, George (2009), "Gregory the Great and the sixth-century dispute over the ecumenical title". *Theological Studies*, 70: 600–621.

Durliat, Jean (2002), "Gregory I". In *The Papacy: An Encyclopedia*, vol. 2, Phillippe Levillain (ed.), London: Routledge; 639–642 (transl. from French.).

Ekonomou, Andrew J. (2007), *Byzantine Rome and the Greek Popes: Eastern Influences on Rome and the Papacy from Gregory the Great to Zacharias, 590–752 A.D.* Lanham, MD: Lexington Books.

Fontaine, Jacques (1973), "Chronique de Littérature wisigothique (1970–1972)". *Revue d'Études augustiniennes*, 19: 163–176.

Fontaine, Jacques, Gillet, Robert, and Pellistrandi, Stan (eds.) (1986), *Grégoire le grand.* Chantilly, Centre culturel, Les Fontaines, 15–19 septembre 1982. Paris: Editions du CNRS.

Gaunt, Simon (1995), *Gender and Genre in Medieval French Literature.* Cambridge Studies in French. Cambridge: Cambridge University Press.

Gregorio Magno e il suo tempo (1991), XIX *Incontro di studiosi dell'antichità cristiana in collaborazione con l'Ecole Française de Rome, Roma, 9–12 maggio 1990.* Studia Ephemeridis Augustinianum 33–34. Rome: Institutum Patristicum Augustinianum.

Kuzdale, Ann (2013), "The Reception of Gregory in the Renaissance and Reformation". In Neil and Dal Santo (2013: 359–386).

Lizzi, Rita (1991), "La traduzione greca delle opere di Gregorio Magno dalla *Regula Pastoralis ai Dialogi*". In *Gregorio Magno e il suo tempo* (1991: vol. 2, 41–57).

Llewellyn, Peter (1993), *Rome in the Dark Ages*, 2nd edn. London: Constable and Robinson.

Louth, Andrew (2013), "Gregory in the Byzantine Tradition". In Neil and Dal Santo (2013: 343–358).

Markus, Robert A. (1997), *Gregory the Great and his World.* Cambridge: Cambridge University Press.

McBrien, Richard P. (2000), *Lives of the Popes. The Pontiffs from St Peter to Benedict XVI.* New York: HarperCollins.

Mews, Constant J. and Renkin, Claire (2013), "Gregory the Great and the Latin West". In Neil and Dal Santo (2013: 315–342).

Moorhead, John (2005), *Gregory the Great.* The Early Church Fathers. London: Routledge.

Moorhead, John (2006), "On becoming pope in late antiquity". *Journal of Religious History*, 30.3, 279–293.

Murdoch, Brian (2001), "Using the *Moralia*: Gregory the Great in Early Medieval German". In Bremmer *et al.* (2001: 189–206).

Neil, Bronwen and Dal Santo, Matthew (eds) (2013), *A Companion to Gregory the Great.* Leiden: Brill.

Richards, Jeffrey (1979), *The Popes and the Papacy in the Early Middle Ages 476–752.* London: Routledge & Kegan Paul.

Saint-Roch, Patrick (1991), *La Penitence dans les Conciles et les lettres des papes des origines à la mort de Gregoire le Grand.* Studi di antichità cristiana. Vatican City: Pontificio istituto di archeologia cristiana.

Wolf, Kirsten (2001), "Gregory's influence on old Norse–Icelandic religious literature". In Bremmer *et al.* (2001: 255–274).

CHAPTER 17

Maximos the Confessor

Andrew Louth

Introduction

A brief outline of the life of St Maximos the Confessor will be necessary to place him in his historical context. He was born, most likely in Constantinople, in 580, and when he was 30, with the accession of the Emperor Herakleios in 610, became head of the Imperial Chancellery (the contemporary Syriac *Life*, discovered 40 years ago, has him born in Palestine, but this part of the *Life* is probably not to be trusted; see Brock (1973)). After a few years, he retired and became a monk, initially at Chrysopolis (modern Scutari) across the Bosphorus from Constantinople, and later at the Monastery of St George at Kyzikos (now Erdek, on the south coast of the Sea of Marmara). He retained, probably for many years, his contacts with the court in Constantinople. After a short time at St George's, the monks there fled as the great Persian army advanced on Constantinople for the siege of 626. Maximos ended up in North Africa at the Eukratas Monastery, where Sophronios, the future patriarch of Jerusalem, was abbot. On his way there he spent time in both Crete and Cyprus. In 633 the Christological controversy, in which Maximos was to play a major role, began with Sophronios' protest against the *Nine Chapters* of Patriarch Kyrrhos of Alexandria, which had been the basis of reconciliation between the Orthodox and the Monophysites (the "Theodosians") of Egypt. Kyrrhos had proposed agreement based on acceptance of the Chalcedonian Definition, but with the clarification that there was only one theandric (or "divine-human") activity (Greek: *energeia*) in Christ. This, Sophronios condemned as monenergism. Patriarch Sergios of Constantinople responded with his *Psephos*, which forbad any discussion of the number of activities in Christ. Elected Patriarch of Jerusalem in 634, Sophronios, in his *Synodical Letter*, keeps to the letter of the *Psephos*, but argued against monenergism, maintaining that it entailed monophysitism. At this stage, Maximos seems to have held his counsel.

The Wiley Blackwell Companion to Patristics, First Edition. Edited by Ken Parry.
© 2015 John Wiley & Sons Ltd. Published 2019 by John Wiley & Sons Ltd.

In 638, a refinement of monenergism, Monotheletism, which maintained that in Christ there was only one (divine) will, was promulgated by an imperial edict, the *Ekthesis*. Maximos now became involved in the struggle for what he regarded as Orthodoxy. Various treatises were written, upholding Chalcedon and condemning Monotheletism (and monenergism). In 645, a public debate was held in Carthage under the auspices of the exarch, Gregory, between Maximos and the deposed Patriarch of Jerusalem, Pyrrhos, with whose authority the *Ekthesis* had been issued, but who had fallen from favor in the court struggle following the death of Herakleios in 640. Pyrrhos was defeated in the debate and departed to Rome to be reconciled with the Church by Pope Theodore (the reconciliation was not to last). In 648, the Emperor Constans II issued the *Typos*, which forbade "any discussion of one will or one energy, two wills or two energies." By this time Maximos had made his way to Rome, and the new pope, Martin, doubtless encouraged by Maximos, refused to accept the *Typos*, and declined to seek confirmation of his election, either from the emperor or from his exarch in Ravenna.

In 649, Martin called a synod at the Lateran, which condemned the Christological heresies, and the churchmen who had promulgated them. The Latin *acta* of the synod are a translation of the Greek original, which suggests that Maximos and other Greek churchmen in Rome were behind the decision of the synod, regarded in some circles in the next few decades as the "sixth" Œcumenical Synod. The convening of the synod was regarded in imperial circles as an act of sedition; Pope Martin was soon arrested, tried for sedition, and exiled to the Crimea, where he died in 655. Maximos' turn came next: it proved impossible to make a charge of sedition stick, and after repeated attempts to break his will, Maximos was condemned with his two companions, both called Anastasius, one his long-standing disciple from 618, the other a papal *apocrisiarius* to the emperor, who had thrown in his lot with Maximos. Exiled to Lazica in Georgia, Maximos soon died, on 13 August 662, his disciples not long surviving him. A cult of St Maximos began almost immediately; recently, what appear to be the relics of the three saints have been discovered in Georgia, in confirmation of a long tradition that Maximos' relics were never translated to Constantinople as Greek tradition maintains, but remained in Georgia at the Monastery of St Maximos in Tsageri (Khoperia 2009: 44–6, written before the rediscovery of the relics).

During Maximos' lifetime, the Mediterranean saw political changes that altered the political and cultural landscape forever. Maximos was born in the Byzantine Empire that had, a few decades earlier, under Emperor Justinian, regained something of its unity as a Mediterranean empire; when he died, the Eastern provinces of the Empire (Syria, Palestine, and Egypt) had fallen to Islam, and were part of the Umayyad Empire, while the North African provinces would become part of the Islamic Empire by the end of the century, with much of Spain (Al-Andalus) falling to Islam by 711. The world in which Maximos had begun his life was something recognizable as the Roman Empire; in the last decades of his life this began to fragment. The world in which Maximos would be received was one made up of increasingly distinct, if not antagonistic, political regions.

The public account of Maximos' life is dominated by his struggle for Orthodoxy against the imperial Christological nostrums, intended to heal the divisions in the Church, caused by the Synod of Chalcedon in 451, that weakened the Roman Empire in the face of emergent Islam. What is mostly reflected in his writings is rather the inner life of the monk that characterized most of his adult years. Certainly, there are several works directed against Christological heresy, but the bulk of his works are monastic, representing the summation of the Greek intellectual and ascetic tradition, firmly rejecting Origenism, but finding his own answers to the metaphysical questions Origen and those inspired by him had grappled with, and thus drawing together the several threads of the Greek patristic tradition – ascetic, philosophical, doctrinal, liturgical – into a synthesis with cosmic entailments and insights for the personal life of prayer and asceticism, as well as for the life of the Church.

Maximos made his physical presence felt in many areas of the Mediterranean – in Constantinople, the islands of Crete and Cyprus, North Africa, Rome, Palestine (if not directly, as the Syriac *Life* claims, then through Sophronios, and the monasteries of the Judaean Desert, which had become "the very hearth of Chalcedonianism," in Flusin's phrase; Flusin 1992: ii.59) and Georgia. They all felt his intellectual presence, too.

Early Reception in the East

Let us start, nearest the source, as it were, with Georgia and Palestine. Maximos died in Georgia, and Anastasius the Apocrisiarius records in a letter that there appeared a miracle of "three shining lamps illuminat[ing] the holy tomb of that holy martyr Maximus" (Allen and Neil 2002: 136–137). Maximos continued to be venerated in Georgia, many of his works were translated into Georgian, legends and folkloric customs grew up around the Saint, his influence can be detected on the great Georgian poet Shota Rustaveli, and there is a long-standing iconographical tradition of the saint (see Mgaloblishvili and Khoperia (2009)).

Maximos (and Martin) were vindicated at the Sixth Ecumenical Synod held in Constantinople in 680–681; nonetheless, no mention was made of them at the synod, their opposition to the churchmen and theologians of the reigning city may have been too raw a memory, not to mention sparing the reputation of the imperial family. Barely a decade earlier, during the pontificate of Adeodatus II, the *Hypomnesticon*, one of a dossier of works detailing the trials and last days of the Confessor, found its way to Rome, stimulating a revival of interest in the witness to Orthodoxy of the martyrs Martin and Maximos (Kelly 1986: 76).

The real beginnings of Maximos' theological reception are to be found in Palestine, where the commitment of the conciliar Orthodoxy of the Roman Empire was deeply rooted, as we have seen. St John of Damascus betrays the influence of Maximos in several ways. It is most obvious in his Christology, where he follows Maximos closely and perhaps even develops his response to Monotheletism (Louth 2002: 157–172). There is further evidence of the influence of the Confessor: Maximos seems to have been the first Father to value the work of Nemesios of Emesa, whose ideas, especially on providence, he borrows; John of Damascus is indebted to precisely the same passages, though he seems to have taken them from Nemesius' text itself, rather than from the Confessor. The Damascene also shares Maximos' interest in the cosmos; he does not, however, take up his doctrine of the *logoi*, the structural principles, of creation. Under Islam, forms of Christianity that did not conform to imperial Orthodoxy continued to flourish, no longer threatened by the political powers (anti-Chalcedonians, the Monotheletism of the Maronites, especially; the extent to which these nonconformists identified conciliar Orthodoxy with the teaching of Maximos is manifest in their dubbing them "Maximians" (Palmer 1993: 26)).

Early Reception in the West

It is in the ninth century that we are first able to gauge something of the reception of Maximos the Confessor (outside Georgia): in the West, with Eriugena, who became a luminary in the Carolingian court circles, and Anastasius the Librarian in Rome, and in the East, with Photios, Patriarch of Constantinople (857–67, 877–886). Eriugena and Anastasius were in touch with each other over the question of translating Maximos (Simonopetrites 2013: 25–36), but their reception of the Confessor was very different. Anastasius' interest seems to have been very practical (Neil 2006). Restored to favor under Pope Nicholas I after an earlier checkered career, Anastasius was concerned to find support for the claims being made by Popes Nicholas and Hadrian (who gave him the title of Librarian of the Roman Church in 867) for the universal authority of the Roman see. Maximos' veneration of the Roman see, the fate he shared with Pope Martin after the Lateran Synod, and his apparent attempts to defend Latin theologians against Greek attacks (over the *Filioque*, for example) evidently attracted Anastasius' attention, and he translated some of Maximos' works, as well as the dossier about his trials and condemnation, into Latin, thus preserving some parts of Maximos now lost in Greek (there have been doubts about the authenticity of some of these texts, not, in my view, adequately grounded). Anastasius himself asserts that his translations were done "for the recognition and power of the Apostolic See against those who are bent on violently extorting something from it" (cited Simonopetrites 2013: 35).

Anastasius had acquired his knowledge of Greek presumably from some of the many Greek monks then resident in Rome, and maybe improved it by his acquaintance with Cyril and Methodios, who were there in the later 860s. In contrast, Eriugena must have acquired his knowledge of Greek in Ireland, along with his contemporaries, Sedulius Scottus and Martin the Irishman; but from whom remains a mystery. Whereas Anastasius' interest in Maximos was practical and tangential, Eriugena's interest was fundamental and central. Nevertheless, as well as the works already mentioned, Anastasius had translated a set of *scholia* to the works of Dionysios, discovered while on a diplomatic mission to Constantinople. These *scholia* had been written by John of Scythopolis (the editor of the *Corpus Areopagiticum*) and supplemented by Maximos the Confessor; Anastasius says he had marked Maximos' *scholia* with a cross, but these marks were not retained by later copyists, and the distinction was lost. Eriugena found these *scholia* invaluable, remarking that, without them, he would never have been able to "enter into such dense darkness" as he found in the writings of the Areopagite (cf. Simonpetrites 2013: 27–28). It was in the 860s, by which time Eriugena had arrived at the court of Charles the Bald, that he, at the request of his sovereign, translated the works ascribed to Dionysios the Areopagite (revising the older translation of Hilduin), and then turned to Gregory of Nyssa's *De hominis opificio*, and finally Maximos' *Quaestiones ad Thalassium* and his *Ambigua ad Ioannem*. Although Anastasius may have had better Greek than Eriugena (Simonopetrites 2013: 28), Eriugena's lengthy engagement with the Greek of these Fathers, especially Maximos, took him into the heart of Byzantine theology.

Alongside his work of translation, Eriugena was also engaged in writing his *magnum opus*, *Periphyseon*, "On the division of nature" (to translate the Latin title). From this we can get a sense of the nature and depth of his engagement with Maximos. It is striking that Eriugena translated the most difficult and demanding works of the Confessor, rather than the *Centuries* or the *Liber Asceticus*; his engagement with the metaphysical heart of Maximos' theological vision is manifest in *Periphyseon*. In origin it seems to have been an essay on dialectic, drawing exclusively on Latin authors, and it may well be that this original core belongs to an earlier stage in Eriugena's life. This early essay introduces the fourfold division of nature, multiplying, as it were, two fundamental divisions – that between uncreated and created, and that between creating and not creating – to give a fourfold division between uncreated and creating, created and creating, created and not creating, uncreated and not creating, and moves on to a discussion of the categories. However, in the version as we have it now, it has become part of a much larger whole, which is not at all Latin in its inspiration and its sources. This larger whole seems to make of a primarily logical division of nature something much more metaphysical, and does this by linking it to a notion of the division of nature derived from St Maximos' *Amb.* 41 (and behind that from Gregory of Nyssa), and rehearsed at the beginning of Book II of *Periphyseon*.

Maximos' division starts from the division between uncreated and created, then divides the created into invisible and visible, the visible into heaven and Earth, Earth into paradise and the inhabited world, and within the inhabited world finds a final division between male and female. In the *Ambiguum*, Maximos sees this sequence of divisions as a movement of procession, terminating in the Fall, which turns the divisions of nature into cosmic fault-lines. Originally the divisions should have terminated in the human, as microcosm and bond of creation, in which the extremities of the divisions are held together. As a result of the Fall, however, the only remedy is the Incarnation of the Word of God, which recapitulates the divisions of nature, and reestablishes the cosmos. Eriugena's division of nature is now made to incorporate Maximos' division, and produce a cosmic cycle. The four categories now are seen to be more than merely logical categories; rather, they set out a metaphysical understanding of the cosmos, the four categories corresponding to God the creator, the primordial causes (more or less equivalent to the Platonic forms), the material world, and then God as the final cause, at rest, uncreated and uncreating. The categories move, then, through a cycle, from rest, out through procession and back through return to God as rest. This is the familiar Neoplatonic triad: rest, procession, return. Furthermore, procession is understood in terms of theophany, divine manifestation, the principal theme of Book I before it moves on to a discussion of the categories. To theophany corresponds contemplation, which accomplishes the movement of return.

What we find in Eriugena is something remarkable: he draws a central element of Maximos' vision (repeated also in the *Mystagogia*) into a much more explicitly

Neoplatonist context, one influenced by Augustine, with whom Eriugena was deeply imbued. What in Maximos is primarily ontological becomes something to do with the movement of the intellect: the metaphysical is interiorized, a process that seems to me not uncommon in Latin appropriations of Greek theology.

Further reception of Maximos in the West would take place mostly through the influence of Eriugena and his vision in *Periphyseon*, though in the twelfth century a Latin translation of the *Four Centuries on Love* was made in Hungary (Beck 1959: 440). This fact became, in the event, a hindrance; *Periphyseon* was criticized as pantheistic and several times condemned, finally in 1225. The fate of *Maximus philosophus* became entangled with that of Eriugena (Lévy's (2006) remarkable book, though detecting affinities between Maximos and Aquinas, does not alter the question of the historical reception of Maximos).

Further Reception in the Byzantine Period

Parallel to the engagement with Maximos in the West, we find the first comprehensive knowledge of the Confessor in the Byzantine Empire in the learned Patriarch of Constantinople, Photios. In his *Myriobiblion* ("thousand books"), or *Bibliotheca* ("library"), Photios reviews several works of Maximos: *Questions to Thalassius* (cod. 192A); a collection of 27 letters, a somewhat different collection from the 45 letters edited by Combefis (1648) and found in Migne (Patrologia Graeca (PG) 91: 364–649) (cod. 192B); the *Ascetic Life* and the *Four Centuries on Love* (cod. 193); a letter to George the Prefect, which may be Combefis' *ep.* 1, *Two Centuries on Theology and Oikonomia*, letters 13, 15, and 19 (in Combefis' enumeration), and two letters to Thomas, the first of which consists of *Ambigua* 1–5 (*Ambigua ad Thomam*, or the later *Ambigua*), the second being another letter (the "second"), unknown to Combefis (cod. 194); a letter to Marianus (which seems to be the same as *Opusculum* 1) and the *Disputation with Pyrrhos* (cod. 195). The only major omissions from this list are the earlier *Ambigua ad Ioannem* and most of the *opuscula theologica et polemica*, and a few smaller works, such as the *Exposition of Ps. 59*, *Exposition of the Lord's Prayer*, and his *Mystagogia*. It is striking that while Eriugena knew only the *Ambigua ad Ioannem*, Photios knew only the *Ambigua ad Thomam*, even though Maximos himself seems to have known an edition of the *Ambigua*, which combines the later *ad Thomam* and the earlier *ad Ioannem* (cf. *opusc.* 1:33A10, which refers to *Amb. ad Ioan.* 2 as *Amb.* 7); as late as the tenth/eleventh century, Euthymios the Georgian seems to have known only the *Ambgiua ad Ioannem* (Khoperia 2009: 28). Photios complains about Maximos' style, finding it repetitive, ill-constructed, and obscure, though "his piety and the purity and sincerity of his longing for Christ shines forth" (Henry 1962: 80–1).

Photios then knew a great deal of the Maximian *corpus*. How much did it influence his own theological reflection? We can see this influence in two ways, both in the way he practices theology and in the way he formulates it. The most important of Maximos' works take the form of responses to questions about difficult passages (hence the title *Ambigua*, which deals with difficulties found, mostly in the works of St Gregory the Theologian; the *Questions to Thalassius* are concerned with difficulties in the scriptures).

This became a popular *genre* in Byzantine theology, producing a meditative, ruminative approach to theology, something that could feed the life of the monk. Photios' *Amphilochia* stand in this tradition (though more scholarly than monastic). In questions of Christology, Photios shows a firm grasp of the intricacies of Maximos' arguments over nature, person, and will (for more detail, see Louth (2006)).

Photios seems to have known Maximos' works in several discrete volumes; it is not until the tenth century that the so-called Constantinopolitan edition of his works was assembled, which is the basis of all subsequent manuscripts of the works of the Confessor; this edition is directly related to the endeavors of Euthymios, of the Georgian monastery of Iveron on Mt Athos, which included the first translation of many of the Confessor's works into Georgian (Khoperia 2009: 27–30). The Constantinopolitan edition led to the diffusion of Maximos' works in the form of excerpts, thus making the difficult treatises of the Confessor more accessible. The most important of these collections of excerpts is the anthology of 500 chapters, beginning with a genuine treatise of 15 chapters, but drawn mostly (414 chapters) from the *Quaestiones ad Thalassium* (with some excerpts from *Ambigua ad Ioannem*, *Letters*, and the *Scholia* to the *Corpus Areapgiticum*), called *Five Centuries of Various Chapters on Theology, the Divine Economy, and virtue and vice* (PG 90: 1177–1392) – "centuries" being a long-established monastic *genre*, of which the Confessor himself had made use (for excerpts from *ad Thalassium* incorporated in the centuries, see Laga and Steel (1980: lxxvi–lxxix; 1990: xlv–xlvii). There are also over 200 excerpts from Maximos included in the *Synagogi*, compiled by Paul, the eleventh-century founder of the Evergetinos Monastery.

Alongside this popular dissemination of Maximos in predominantly monastic circles, Maximos was read and appreciated in court circles, famously by the Empress Irene Doukaina, as related by her daughter Anna Comnena in the *Alexiad* (Sewter 1969: 178–179). This interest in court circles (which included, too, Isaac Sebastocrator), as well as in wealthy monastic circles, accounts for some of the *de luxe* manuscripts of the Confessor from this period. Maximos was also read in lay circles, where the tradition of reflective theology more or less inaugurated by Maximos and found, as we have seen, in Photios continued. Maximos features frequently in the theological works of Michael Psellos, who draws, as one might expect, on *ad Thalassium* and the *Ambigua*, but seems also to have been fond of Maximos' brief exposition of Psalm 59. He typically refers to Maximos as *philosophos*, which reveals where his true interests lie, for in Psellos' works we find the rediscovery in Byzantine thought of the whole philosophical tradition of pagan Greece, especially revolving around late Neoplatonists such as Proklos.

It has been argued that we can see two divergent ways of receiving the Confessor in the eleventh century – traditions represented by Psellos and by the Emperor Alexios I's older brother, Isaac Sebastocrator – one of which led to the condemnation of Psellos' disciple, John Italos, at a trial presided over by Isaac Sebastocrator. Psellos drew on Maximos, in whom one finds a serious reception of Neoplatonic ideas, but followed rather the source of Maximos' ideas rather than the way Maximos incorporated these ideas into a genuinely Christian metaphysic; Isaac, on the other hand, followed Maximos more closely, using his doctrine of the principles, or *logoi*, of creation to Christianize Proklos' universe. The condemnation of Italos, and the addition of anathemas to the *Synodikon of Orthodoxy*, had the net effect of preventing the flourishing of even Isaac's own Maximian brand of Neoplatonism (Simonopetrites 2013: 36–44; on Psellos, also Duffy (1995; 2002)).

We can be sure, from the existence of the *Five Centuries* and the *Evergetinos*, that Maximos continued to be read in monastic circles throughout the Byzantine Middle Ages. This, however, makes it very difficult to be clear about how much Maximos himself was read; for example, in the writings of St Symeon the New Theologian (949–1022), there are many parallels with the theology of the Confessor, but it is not possible to be clear how much Symeon was indebted to Maximos directly. Nevertheless, it is not surprising that Maximos emerges in the controversies of the fourteenth century concerning Hesychasm, which was at least as much a controversy among the monks of Mount Athos as a clash between monastic piety and (secular) humanism, as it is often interpreted. He is quoted very generally, on both sides: St Gregory Palamas, in his *Triads*, quotes largely from *Ambigua ad Ioannem*, but also from *ad Thalassium*, *Capita theologica et economica*, with a few citations from elsewhere (of the 25 clear citations from *Ambigua*, 15 are from *Amb*. 10, perhaps not surprisingly as much of it is a meditation of the Transfiguration, a central issue of the Hesychast controversy); one of his principal opponents, Gregory Akindynos (probably himself an Athonite monk: Nadal Cañellas 2006: 28–103) cites Maximos very frequently, more than any other Father save Gregory the Theologian and Dionysios the Areopagite, drawing mostly on Maximos' various *Centuries*, the *Ambigua* (almost all from *Amb*. 10), and *Quaestiones ad Thalassium*.

As is the case with polemical literature, Maximos can hardly be said to shape the argument; rather, he is drawn on as remarks of his seem to support, or cause embarrassment to, the warring antagonists. A good deal is made of his remark in *Amb*. 10 (1165D) that in the Transfiguration he accepted "out of his immeasurable love for mankind to become the type and symbol of Himself,... and through the manifestation of Himself to lead to Himself in His complete and secret hiddenness the whole creation." For the opponents of the Hesychasts the word "symbol" was held to indicate that the light of the Transfiguration was merely created light, symbolic of the godhead; to which the Orthodox responded that being a "symbol of Himself" implied a closer relationship between symbol and the one symbolized such that the light was itself uncreated was, indeed, a "natural symbol," sharing the nature of what it symbolized. This debate continued over the rest of the century, being treated most fully by Gregory's thoroughly Aristotelian supporter, Theophanes III of Nicaea (see Simonopetrites (2013: 48–51)). Maximos is also cited by the Hesychasts in defense of a realistic doctrine of *theosis*, or deification, especially his remark in *ad Thal*. 22 (repeated in *Amb*. 41: 1308B) that "the one divinized by grace will be everything that God is, apart from identity of substance" (e.g., cited *Capita CL*, 111). It is surprising (or maybe not, given the nature of polemic) that Maximos' doctrine of the *logoi* of creation is rarely encountered.

Reception in Seventeenth to Twentieth Centuries

Maximos seems not to have been much known in the period of the Renaissance and the Reformation/Counter Reformation that ensued. The first edition of his works did not appear until 1675 in an incomplete edition by Francis Combefis (a third volume that would have completed the edition was ready by the time he died in 1679, but never published); the missing texts, most importantly the *Ambigua*, were only published by F. Oehler in 1867.

In the Greek East, now under the Ottoman yoke, Maximos continued to be read in monastic circles, something confirmed by his being the writer most fully represented in the Athonite anthology of ascetic texts, the *Philokalia*, compiled by St Makarios of Corinth and St Nikodimos the Athonite (Venice, 1782). Included are the four *Centuries on Love*, the two *Centuries on Theology and the Oikonomia*, and the five *Centuries on Diverse Texts*, presented as a continuation of the *Two Centuries*, with, finally, the *Exposition of the Lord's Prayer*. The selection leans strongly towards the ascetic side of the Confessor's teaching, though there are many demanding chapters in the *Centuries* on theology. The *Philokalia* was destined to have a profound influence on Orthodox theology and spirituality, which contributed to a wider reception of the theology of St Maximos (though this influence is mitigated by the fact that the Slavonic translation omitted Maximos' treatises altogether, while the Russian translation included only a selection (Conticello and Conticello 2002: 1006–1007). In the nineteenth century, Maximos benefited from the extensive program of translation of patristic texts, fostered by Metropolitan Philaret of Moscow; by the end of the century, Russian theologians had easy access to a vast range of patristic texts in Russian translation, including those of the Confessor.

Modern scholarship on Maximos the Confessor began in the Slav world with S.L. Epifanovič's *Prepobodnyi Maksim Ispovedik i vizantiskoe bogoslove* ("St Maximos the Confessor and Byzantine theology": Kiev, 1915) and *Materialy k izučeniju žizni I tvorenij prep. Maksima Ispovednika* ("Materials for the study of the life and works of St Maximos the Confessor": Kiev, 1917). This latter published 37 texts hitherto unknown, or known only partially (not all of which have turned out to be genuine). Maximos was, however, by no means unknown to Russian theologians: Vladimir Solov'ev had read him; Pavel Florensky (1997: 312) cites him several times in his monumental *Pillar and Ground of the Truth*, at one point making him a key witness to his controversial ideas on friendship; Sergei Bulgakov finds in Maximos' doctrine of the *logoi* the essentials of his sophiology (Bulgakov 2008: 126 n.) and draws on him for his middle way between Filioquism and Monopatrism in the doctrine of the procession of the Holy Spirit (Bulgakov 2004: 91–92); in the lectures that he gave at the newly established Institut St-Serge in Paris, Georges Florovsky (1987: 208–253) gives a well-rounded account of the theology of the Confessor. However, by this time, the loadstar of Orthodox theology was increasing becoming St Gregory Palamas.

Epifanovič's work was soon to be followed by studies of the Confessor among Western scholars (mostly Roman Catholic), some of which concentrated on his role in the history of dogma, notably the immensely learned Martin Jugie in his *Theologia dogmatica Christianorum Orientalium ab Ecclesia Catholica dissendentium*, which appeared in five volumes from 1926 to 1935, who draws on the whole range of Maximos' dogmatic theology, and V. Grumel and Robert Devreesse, who published articles clarifying aspects of the Confessor's life and his role in the Monothelete controversy (Devreesse publishing in 1937 the lost conclusion of a letter protesting to the Emperor Herakleios about the forced baptism of Jews in 632 – a letter already published by Epifanovič).

Attention began to be paid to Maximos' teaching on the spiritual life, with an important (though reductive) article by M. Viller (1930) on Evagrios as the source of Maximos' spirituality. More important were the articles by the Russian émigrée, living in Paris, Myrrha Lot-Borodine: a series on deification in the Greek Fathers (Lot-Borodine 1932–1933), which drew heavily on Maximos, and her French translation of his *Mystagogia* (Lot-Borodine 1936–1938); these articles introduced the spirit of Greek theology, especially that of Maximos, to the West, and made a strong impression on scholars, such as the future Cardinal, Jean Daniélou (Lot-Borodine 1970: 9–18).

Through the Twentieth to the Twenty-First Century

The real beginnings of attention to Maximos as a theologian of towering stature is to be found in the early works – a couple of articles and a book – by the then Jesuit theologian Hans Urs von Balthasar. His great work, *Kosmische Liturgie, Maximus der Bekenner. Höhe und Krise des griechischen Weltbild* (Freiburg im Breisgau, 1941), presented Maximos as a theologian who drew together all the strands of Greek theology – ascetic, doctrinal, metaphysical, and liturgical – into an imposing synthesis; it was, however, in Balthasar's view, unstable, with little posterity in the East, Maximos' heritage really being found in the theology of the West. Maximos is presented as a figure belonging to both Eastern and Western Christianity. Soon figures who are going to swell the ranks of Maximian scholars begin to emerge: people such as I.H. Dalmais and Irénée Hausherr (some of whose articles on Maximos appear under the pseudonym of I. Lemaître), whose most important early treatments of the Confessor are Dalmais' (1952) short but important article on the doctrine of the *logoi* and Hausherr's (1952) account of Maximos' doctrine of love. Maximos figured prominently in Vasilios Tatakis' (1949) remarkable but somewhat neglected *La philosophie byzantine*. The next major figure in the realm of Maximian scholarship was to be the Benedictine monk Polycarp Sherwood, whose two volumes provided a still not-superseded attempt to date the works of the Confessor (Sherwood 1952) and a major study of the *Ambigua ad Ioannem* (Sherwood 1955), which overthrew Balthasar's theory that Maximos himself had been an Origenist and reacted against it, and maintained that in the earlier *Ambigua* we find "a refutation of Origenism... with a full understanding and will to retain what is good in the Alexandrian's doctrine – a refutation perhaps unique in Greek patristic literature" (Sherwood 1952: 3). Another important article of the 1950s explored the Aristotelian roots of Maximos' analysis of the human will (Gauthier 1954).

The 1960s saw an enormous expansion of works on or about the Confessor; it is, however, dominated by three major works: the second edition of von Balthasar's (1961) *Kosmische Liturgie*; Lars Thunberg's (1965) monumental work, *Microcosm and Mediator*; and Walther Völker's (1965) major study of Maximos' spiritual theology. Von Balthasar's book is a complete revision of the original; his theory about Maximos' Origenist stage is abandoned and the Confessor presented not just as embracing both Eastern and Western Christendom, but rather as one who spans East and West in a global sense (Louth 1997). The book by the Swedish Lutheran Thunberg complements von Balthasar's work and demonstrates in immense detail the way in which the Confessor sees the human person as standing at the center of the cosmos, intended to hold together the oppositions of a world that partakes of multiplicity. Maximos is discerned as a theologian with much to say to a world that is experiencing fragmentation and ecological disaster. Völker's work was one a series of major studies of the spirituality of the spiritual giants of the Greek Church, from Clement of Alexandria to Nicolas Kavasilas; in it he explored in depth the Confessor's understanding of the spiritual life.

By the mid-1960s, scholarship of Maximos was becoming something of an industry. The reception of Maximos had shifted from the Confessor, the witness to Chalcedonian Christology, to the monk, the spiritual theologian who, in the line of "Origenism," set his ascetical theology against a metaphysical and cosmic background, his metaphysics being informed by what a number of scholars came to call his "Chalcedonian logic."

In the 1970s and 1980s there appeared a series of works, published in the series Théologie Historique, by a group of French-speaking scholar, all with an introduction by M.J. Le Guillou, their mentor, that presented Maximos very much as a precursor of Thomas Aquinas (Le Guillou and most of his disciples were Dominicans), and finding in him an approach to theology that could bring about union between the Orthodox East and the Catholic West (Riou 1973; Garrigues 1976a; Léthel 1979; Piret 1983 – belonging to the same group was Christoph von Schönborn (1972) with a book on Maximos' mentor Sophronios of Jerusalem). Articles by Garrigues explored the Confessor's mediating position on the *Filioque* (Garrigues 1975) and on the Roman primacy (Garrigues 1976b). Pope John Paul II's conciliatory allocution on the *Filioque*, delivered in Rome in the presence of the Ecumenical Patriarch on June 29, 1995, "The Greek and Latin Traditions concerning the Procession of the Holy Spirit," adopted some of Garrigues' arguments.

By the 1980s, the fruits of a long-term research project aimed at producing critical texts of the works of the Confessor began to appear, and this was heralded by a symposium held in Fribourg in 1980, at which most of those involved in the editions, and many other Maximian scholars, contributed (Heinzer and Schönborn 1982).

Hitherto, virtually all scholarship in the West on Maximos had been by Western scholars, mostly Catholic. However, from the 1940s, in Romania, Dumitru Stăniloae had been translating virtually the whole of the Maximian corpus, partly for his Romanian *Philokalia*, but also independently (the *Ambigua*, for instance). This work of engagement with the thought of the Confessor is manifest in his own works of theology, notably his *Orthodox Dogmatic Theology*, where the theological insights of the Confessor powerfully inform his own dogmatic theology (Stăniloae 1996–1997). Since the 1990s, Orthodox scholarship has begun to catch up, notably with the work of Jean-Claude Larchet (1996, and many other works), Loudovikos (1992), Bathrellos (2004), Törönen (2007), and Tollefsen (2008). What is striking about these Orthodox contributions to Maximian scholarship is that, without any detriment to their scholarly rigor, these treatises are also works of engaged theology.

Maximos' vision of a world integrated through the *logoi* of creation in the *Logos* through human kind seems increasingly relevant to the fate of the world in which we live (see, from many examples, Ware (1997)).

Bibliography

Primary Sources

Maximos' works can be found in PG 90–91. A critical edition is steadily appearing in CCSG: *Quaestiones ad Thalassium*, with the Latin translation of Eriugena, Carl Laga and Carlos Steel (eds) (1980, 1990). CCSG 7, 22.

Quaestiones et dubia, José H. Declerck (ed.) (1982), CCSG 10.

Ambigua at Johannem, Eriugena's Latin translation only, Eduardus Jeanneau (ed.) (1988). CCSG 18.

Opuscula exegetica duo (Expositio in Ps. LIX, Expositio Orationis Dominicae), Peter Van Deun (ed.) (1991). CCSG 23.

Scripta Saeculi VII vitam Maximi Confessoris illustrantia, with the Latin translation of Anastasius the Librarian, Pauline Allen and Bronwen Nei (eds) (1999). CCSG 39; with English translation and notes: *Maximus the Confessor and his Companions. Documents from Exile*, Pauline Allen and Bronwen Neil (eds) (2002). Oxford: Oxford University Press.

Liber Asceticus, adiectis tribus interpretationibus latinis sat antiquis, Peter Van Deun (and Steven Gysens) (ed.) (2000). CCSG 40.

Ambigua ad Thomam una cum Epistula Secunda ad eundem, Bart Janssens (ed.) (2002). CCSG 48.

Mystagogia, Christian Boudignon (ed.) (2011). CCSG 69.

Also

Massimo Confessore, *Capitoli sulla Carità*, Aldo Ceresa-Gastaldo (ed./Italian transl.) (1963). Verba Seniorum, NS 3. Rome: Editrice Studium.

Disputatio cum Pyrrho, critical ed. with Russian translation and other material in: *Disput s Pirrom. Prp. Maksim Ispovednik I khristo-logicheskie spory VII ctoletiya*. Moscow: Khram Cofii Premydrosti Bozhiey, 2004.

Brock, Sebastian (1973), "An early Syriac life of Maximus the Confessor". *Analecta Bollandiana*, XCI, 299–346 (=Sebastian Brock, *Syriac Perspectives on Late Antiquity*. London: Variorum Reprints, 1984, item XII).

Other

Anna Comnena, *The Alexiad*, E.R.W. Sewter (transl.) (1969). Harmondsworth: Penguin Books.

Palmer, Andrew (1993), *The Seventh Century in West-Syrian Chronicles*, translated with an introduction. TTH 15. Liverpool University Press.

Photius, *Bibliothèque*, III, René Henry (ed.) (1962). Paris: Les Belles Lettres.

Secondary Sources

Bathrellos, Demetrios (2004), *The Byzantine Christ. Person, Nature, and Will in the Christology of St Maximus the Confessor.* Oxford University Press.

Beck, Hans Georg (1959), *Kirche und Theologische Literatur im Byzantinischen Reich.* Munich: C.H. Beck'sche Verlagsbuchhandlung.

Bulgakov, Sergii (2004), *The Comforter*, Boris Jakim (transl.). Grand Rapids, MI: William B. Eerdmans (first published: Paris, 1936).

Bulgakov, Sergii (2008), *The Lamb of God*, Boris Jakim (transl.). Grand Rapids, MI: William B. Eerdmans (first published: Paris, 1933).

Conticello, Carmelo Giuseppe and Conticello, Vassa (eds) (2002), *La Théologie byzantine et sa tradition*, II. Turnhout: Brepols.

Dalmais, I.H. (1952), "La théorie des «logoi» des creatures chez S. Maxime le Confesseur". *Revue des sciences philosophiques et théologiques*, 36: 244–249.

Duffy, John (1995), "Reactions of two Byzantine intellectuals to the theory and practice of magic: Michael Psellos and Michael Italikos". In *Byzantine Magic*, Henry Maguire (ed.). Washington, DC: Dumbarton Oaks Research Library and Collection; 83–95.

Duffy, John (2002), "Hellenic philosophy in Byzantium and the lonely mission of Michael Psellos". In *Byzantine Philosophy and its Ancient Sources*. Oxford: Clarendon Press; 139–156.

Florensky, Pavel (1997), *The Pillar and Ground of the Truth*, Boris Jakim (transl.). Princeton University Press (first published: Moscow, 1914).

Florovsky, Georges (1987), *The Byzantine Fathers of the Sixth to Eighth Centuries*, Raymond Miller, Anne-Marie Döllinger-Labriolle, and Helmut Wilhelm Schmiedel (transl.). Vaduz: Büchervertreibanstalt (first published: Paris, 1933).

Flusin, Bernard (1992), *Saint Anastase de Perse et l'histoire de la Palestine au début du VIIᵉ siècle*, two vols. Paris: Éditions du Centre National de la Recherche Scientifique.

Garrigues, Juan Miguel (1975), "Procession et ekporèse du saint Esprit. Discernement de la tradition et reception œcuménique". *Istina*, 20: 345–366.

Garrigues, Juan Miguel (1976a), *Maxime le Confesseur. La charité avernir divin de l'homme*. Théologie Historique 38. Paris: Beauchesne.

Garrigues, Juan Miguel (1976b), "Les sens de la primauté romaine chez saint Maxime le Confesseur". *Istina*, 21: 6–24.

Gauthier, R.A. (1954), "Saint Maxime le Confesseur et la psychologie de l'acte humaine". *Recherches de Théologie ancienne et médiévale*, 21: 51–100.

Hausherr, Irénée (1952), *Philautie. De la tendresse pour soi à la charité selon Maxime le Confesseur*. Orientalia Christiana Analecta 137. Rome: Pontificium Institutum Orientalium Studiorum.

Heinzer, F. and Schönborn, C. (eds) (1982), *Maximus Confessor. Actes du Symposium sur Maxime de Confesseur, Fribourg, 2–5 septembre 1980*. Paradosis 27. Fribourg: Éditions Universitaires.

Kelly, J.N.D. (1986), *The Oxford Dictionary of Popes*. Oxford University Press.

Khoperia, Lela (2009), "Maximus the Confessor: life and works in the Georgian tradition". In Mgaloblishvili and Khoperia (2009: 25–48).

Larchet, Jean-Claude (1996), *La divinisation de l'homme selon saint Maxime le Confesseur*. Paris: Le Cerf.

Léthel, François-Marie (1979), *Théologie de l'agonie du Christ*. Théologie Historique 52. Paris: Beauchesne.

Lévy, Antoine (2006), *Le Créé et l'incréé. Maxime le confesseur et Thomas d'Aquin*. Bibliothèque Thomiste LVIX (sic). Paris: J. Vrin.

Lot-Borodine, Myrrha (1932–1933), "La doctrine de la deification dans l'Église grecque jusqu'au XIᵉ siècle". *Revue de l'histoire des religions*, 53: 5–43, 525–574; 54: 8–55.

Lot-Borodine, Myrrha (1936–1938), "Mystagogie de Saint Maxime". *Irénikon*, 13: 466–472, 595–597, 717–720; 14: 66–69, 182–185, 282–284, 444–448; 15: 71–74, 185–186, 276–278, 390–391, 488–492.

Lot-Borodine, Myrrha (1970), *Le Déification de l'homme selon la doctrine des pères grecs*, with an introduction by Jean Cardinal Daniélou. Paris: Le Cerf (reprinting Lot-Borodine 1932–1933, with some other articles).

Loudovikos, Nikolaos (1992), *I Eukharistiki Ontologia*. Athens: Ekdosis Domos. (English translation by Elizabeth Theokritoff (2010), with additional material: *A Eucharistic Ontology*. Brookline, MA: Holy Cross Orthodox Press).

Louth, Andrew (1997), "St Maximos the Confessor between East and West". *Studia Patristica*, 32: 332–345.

Louth, Andrew (2002), *St John Damascene. Tradition and Originality in Byzantine Theology*. Oxford: Oxford University Press.

Louth, Andrew (2006), "Photios as theologian". In *Byzantine Style, Religion and Civilization: In Honour of St Steven Runciman*, Elizabeth M. Jeffreys (ed.). Cambridge University Press, 206–223.

Mgaloblishvili, Tamila, and Khoperia, Lela (2009), *Maximus the Confessor and Georgia, Iberica Caucasica 3*. London: Bennet and Bloom.

Nadal Cañellas, Juan (2006), *La Résistance d'Akindynos à Grégoire Palamas. Enquête historique, avec traduction et commentaire de quatre traits édités récemment*, two vols. Spicilegium Sacrum Lovaniense 50–51. Leuven: Peeters.

Neil, Bronwen (2006), *Seventh-Century Popes and Martyrs. The Political Hagiography of Anastasius Bibliotecarius*. Studia Antiqua Australiensia 2. Turnhout: Brepols.

Piret, Pierre (1983), *Le Christ et la Trinité selon Maxime le Confesseur*. Théologie Historique 69. Paris: Beauchesne.

Riou, Alain (1973), *Le Monde et l'Église selon Maxime le Confesseur*. Théologie Historique 22. Paris: Beauchesne.

Sherwood, Polycarp (1952), *An Annotated Date-List of the works of Maximus the Confessor*. Studia Anselmiana 30. Rome: Herder.

Sherwood, Polycarp (1955), *The Earlier Ambigua of Saint Maximus the Confessor and His Refutation of Origenism*. Studia Anselmiana 36. Rome: Pontificiae Universitatis Gregorianae.

Simonopetrites, Fr Maximos (Nicholas Constas) (2013), "St Maximus the Confessor: the reception of his thought in east and west". In *Knowing the Purpose of Creation through the Resurrection. Proceedings of the Symposium of St Maximus the Confessor, Belgrade, October 18–21, 2012*, Bishop Maxim (Vasiljević) (ed.). Alhambra, CA/Belgrade: Sebastian Press Publishing House/The Faculty of Orthodox Theology of the University of Belgrade; 25–53.

Stăniloae, Dumitru (1996–1997), *Teologia Dogmatică Ortodoxă*, three vols. Bucharest: Editura Institutului Biblic şi de Misiune sl Bisericii Ortodoxe Române (English transl.: *The Experience of God*, vols. 1–6. Brookline, MA: Holy Cross Orthodox Press, 1994–2013).

Tatakis, B. (1949), *La philosophie byzantine*. Fascicule supplémentaire IIᵉ to É. Bréhier, *Histoire de la philosophie*. Paris: Presses Universitaires de France.

Thunberg, Lars (1965), *Microcosm and Mediator: The Theological Anthropology of Maximus the Confessor*. Lund: Gleerup. (Second revised edition, Chicago, IL: Open Court, 1995.)

Tollefsen, Torstein Theodor (2008), *The Christocentric Cosmology of St Maximus the Confessor*. Oxford University Press.

Törönen, Melchisedec (2007), *Union and Distinction in the Thought of St Maximus the Confessor*. Oxford University Press.

Von Balthasar, Hans Urs (1961) *Kosmische Liturgie: Das Weltbild Maximus' Des Bekenners*, 2nd edn. Einsiedeln: Johannes Verlag.

Von Schönborn, Christoph (1972), *Sophrone de Jérusalem, Vie monastique et confession dogmatique*. Théologie Historique 20. Paris: Beauchesne.

Viller, M. (1930), "Aux sources de la spiritualité de S. Maxime. Les œuvres d'Évagre le Pontique". *Revue d'Ascétique et de Mystique*, 11: 156–184, 239–268, 331–336.

[Ware], Bishop Kallistos of Diokleia (1997), *Through the Creation to the Creator*. London: Friends of the Centre.

CHAPTER 18

John of Damascus

Vassilis Adrahtas

Introduction: The Bearing of John Damascene's Œuvre

The issues involved in John Damascene's *œuvre* (i.e., authenticity, genres, chronology) can be approached in a manner that elucidates its reception. Although a stringent chronology is not possible, a general outline of John's theological development is indeed plausible. In particular, as a well-educated Christian and high-rank official, the Damascene would most likely have been involved in the theological debates of his time early on. Thus, one could argue for a Damascus period (c. late 680s–early 710s) and a Jerusalem period (c. early 710s—early 740s), the former being shorter and formative and the latter longer and productive. Furthermore, owing to John's administrative position, the Damascus period must have predisposed him to reflect on Islam, Manichaeism, and diverse Christian traditions, and also elaborate on the logical/philosophical component of his education for the sake of argumentation. Therefore, it is justified to suppose that works such as *Dialogue against the Manicheans*, *On Heresies*, *Elementary Introduction*, *Dialectica* (in its incipient form), or even material that eventually was incorporated into the dubious *Dispute between a Saracen and a Christian*, date from the Damascus period or first phase of the Damascene's literary production. This could explain why most of them did not form a basis for any substantial tradition of reception.

On the other hand, the Jerusalem period was conditioned by John's becoming a monk and entering the priesthood. It could be divided into two sub-periods: the first being the middle phase (c. early 710–late 720s) and the second the last phase (c. late 720s–early 740s) of John's theological development. In this perspective, the least refined of his homilies (e.g., *Homily on the Nativity of the Lord*), perhaps his compilation-like biblical material (the *Hiera/Sacra Parallela* in its lost original form), and most of his specifically targeted dogmatic–polemical writings (*On Right Thinking*; *On the Composite Nature, against the Acephali*; *On the Faith, against the Nestorians*; *Against the Nestorians*; *Against the Jacobites*;

The Wiley Blackwell Companion to Patristics, First Edition. Edited by Ken Parry.
© 2015 John Wiley & Sons Ltd. Published 2019 by John Wiley & Sons Ltd.

Letter on the Thrice-Holy Hymn; *On the Two Wills in Christ*) would seem to fit into the middle phase. According to this approach, the last phase of John's literary production would have to be reserved for his most refined homilies (e.g., *Homily on the Transfiguration of the Lord*), his *Three Treatises against Those Who Attack the Holy Icons*, *On the Orthodox Faith* (in its final form), *Dialectica* (in its *recensio fusior* form), and finally the considerable volume of his liturgical poetry. Thus, the Jerusalem period was John Damascene's proper theological period, which gave rise to two substantial traditions of reception: a dogmatic–polemical one and a poetic–liturgical one. This was most likely due to the authority that *On the Orthodox Faith* eventually acquired, on the one hand, and the dominance that the genre of the liturgical Canon gradually achieved, on the other hand.

John Damascene is one of those cases in which the issue of reception presents itself in quite an intriguing way owing to the fact that his authority was co-opted by a substantial number of dubious or spurious works (Geerard and Noret 2003): at least 25 major titles in total, not to mention the amount of liturgical poetry that bears his name (for the latter, Louth 2002: 252–253). To identify these works and then disregard them altogether is uncritical, since some of them can indeed be utilized as important indicators of the Damascene's reception. A survey of these works demonstrates that roughly 56% of the titles refer to dogmatic–polemical material, 16% to biblical–exegetical, 12% to sermonic–homiletic, 8% to ascetical, 4% to liturgical (poetry excluded), and another 4% to hagiographical material. These figures indicate that the co-option of John Damascene's authority by subsequent literature was predominantly part of a tradition of reception that understood the Damascene as a dogmatic–polemical theologian. On the other hand, these figures have to be treated with caution, for in the combined 20% of the biblical–exegetical and hagiographical material one is confronted with the disproportionate volume of two works: the *Hiera/Sacra Parallela* (in its surviving manuscript form) and the *Vita Barlaam et Joasaph*. Although the latter does not really challenge the dogmatic–polemical reception of John Damascene, the former actually does, since strictly speaking it is concerned with ethics (cf. Holl 1897: 392). This peculiarity becomes all the more significant if one takes into account the spurious ascetical material attributed to the Damascene, which in itself also conveys a particular interest in morals. To phrase it differently, there seems to have been another tradition of reception: namely, an ethical–ascetical one, which in general was at odds with the genres of John Damascene's authentic *œuvre*. Whatever the explanation of this tradition of reception – for example, a need to counterbalance an otherwise excessively dogmatic–polemical Damascene – in effect it did affirm one and the same Damascene: the theologian who recapitulated patristic tradition, either dogmatic or ethical, in the most definitive systematic way.

The Medieval Reception of John Damascene's *Œuvre*

The Byzantine Reception

The Byzantine trajectory of the reception of John Damascene's *œuvre* was the strongest throughout the "Middle Ages" and probably the earliest. However, it started in a rather reserved and reluctant manner (as evidenced in the *Acta* of Nicaea II in 787), and it took more than 100 years to really build up. However, before we trace the main land-marks in the Byzantine reception of the Damascene, it would be useful to bear in mind that this reception was realized through four different modes: (a) an implicit eidetic mode (as can be detected in a series of derivative expositions of the Eastern Orthodox faith during the middle and late Byzantine periods), which used conventionally the content and formal qualities of John's work; (b) an explicit eidetic mode (as witnessed, for example, in the embellishment of liturgical collections attributed time and again to John), which relied mostly on the authority of John; (c) an explicit noematic mode (seen in the adoption of various *loci* taken overtly from the Damascene), which utilized selectively the thought of John; and finally (d) an implicit noematic mode (traceable in the use of Damascenian *loci* without any reference to John), which reflected creatively on the thought of the Damascene. In light of this schema, the Byzantine reception of John Damascene would have to be viewed as a quite extensive and diverse network of traditions.

The vehement condemnation of John Damascene at the Synod of Hiereia (754) suggests that it can be seen as a negative indication of a certain reception of his icon theology. More specifically, in less than a decade after John's death he was regarded by his opponents as the "iconophile" who advanced a new and most compelling argument in favor of icons, namely their justification on the basis of the doctrine of the Incarnation. Thus, we would argue that it is no coincidence that the Synod of Hiereia responded to this challenge with a *Definition* that reflected the Incarnation-oriented *Peuseis* of Constantine V (for the latter, see Hannephof (1969: 140–187)). At the end of the first "iconoclastic controversy" the Damascene was celebrated – in a more or less sketchy manner – by the Synod of Nicaea II. However, the generality of the Synod's commemo-ration would seem to suggest not so much a lack of knowledge of his actual work, but rather a deliberation not to make specific references to his theological argument – most likely out of political expediency with regard to the Isaurian Dynasty. Nonetheless, the second "iconoclastic controversy" focused on the Christology of icons, supplementing thus the general theological framework of Nicaea II and actually addressing the challenge of the "iconoclasts" of the previous period. Regardless of whether the Byzantines had first-hand and detailed knowledge of the Damascene's icon theology or not, it seems that his focus on the Incarnation did set the backdrop for the heated theological discussions in the first 100 years after his death.

"Question 80" in the *Amphilochia* of Photius (c. 870) seems to draw upon chapter 36 (and probably chapters 58 and 59) of *On the Orthodox Faith*, as well as on John's *On the Two Wills in Christ* (for "Question 80" of the *Amphilochia*, see Westerink (1986)). Thus, one could assume first-hand knowledge of these works by Photius; and such knowledge seems to be even more the case when one considers the sophisticated manner in which Photius elaborates on the two wills in Christ, suggesting that there is a way to speak of one gnomic will in Christ, something that John Damascene was the first to have pro-posed. Although Photius does not mention the Damascene, this occurrence in the *Amphilochia* – most likely of the implicit noematic mode of reception – suggests a certain authoritative status of the Damascene in Byzantine theological circles, especially given the delicate dogmatic character of the issues involved. A century after Photius the entry of *Suda* on the Damascene testifies to his dogmatic, exegetical, and liturgical reception;

moreover, it is in light of the last that the Damascene is deemed insuperable (for the relevant entry, see Adler (1928–1930)).

During the same period, *On the Orthodox Faith* must have been regarded as very authoritative, given the fact that it was translated into Slavonic, whereas Symeon the New Theologian seems to be also a case of the implicit noematic mode in John Damascene's Byzantine reception (especially when he touches upon Triadology or considers the issue of deification). Besides, according to the manuscript tradition of *The Fountain Head of Knowledge*, it seems that from the tenth century onwards this work by the Damascene became the dogmatic handbook of Byzantine theologians.

Around the turn of the millennium the Greek *Vita* of John Damascene would start to circulate more and more, testifying and at the same time consolidating his authority. In the eleventh century, Peter Damascene became the first case of the explicit noematic mode of the Damascene's reception since he quotes John several times in his works that have survived in the *Philokalia* (Palmer *et al.* 1984: vol. 3, 74–281). Furthermore, this was the period that witnessed the popularity of the *Vita Barlaam and Joasaph* in Byzantium. The unmistakably Damascenian flavor of the dogmatic sections of this work renders it a prime example of the explicit eidetic mode of reception, since it was believed to be of Damascenian provenance. During the twelfth century a number of synods convened by Manuel Comnenos rendered the by then authoritative status of *On the Orthodox Faith* into an official one, and it is in this context that one should approach the explicit eidetic mode of Damascene's reception in works such as Michael Glykas' *On the Obscure Passages of the Holy Scriptures*, Euthymios Zygabenos' *Dogmatic Panoply*, or Andronikos Kamateros' *Holy Arsenal* (Arambatzis 2010: 459–461). Finally, it is worth noting that Michael Glykas is a potent witness of the already highly esteemed biblical–exegetical reception of John Damascene – all the more so, since it was the whole spectrum of John's works that he utilized exegetically.

The thirteenth century theological debates in Byzantium would focus on *Filioque* polemics, and the *œuvre* of John Damascene would be evoked accordingly – especially in the writings of Nikephoros Blemmydes and John Bekkos, wherein the Damascene was treated as having the same authority as Nicaea II (Arambatzis 2010: 459–461). In this type of polemic theology the reception of the Damascene seems to have oscillated between the explicit eidetic and the explicit noematic modes. In the work of Gregory of Cyprus, which would anticipate the basic issues of the so-called "Hesychast controversy," the Damascene remains of paramount importance. It is noteworthy that both sides of this controversy relied on the authority of John: the "anti-Hesychasts" more in the explicit noematic mode and to varying degrees – for example, Barlaam of Calabria quite extensively, whereas Akindynos rather reservedly – while the "pro-Hesychasts" more in the implicit noematic mode and with considerable consistency – for example, Gregory Palamas in his appreciation of the Damascene as the recapitulation of patristic tradition, and Neilos Cabasilas in his defense of the Damascene's authority against Thomist objections (Kislas 2001: 389–394, 410–414). Lastly, in the fifteenth century, Mark of Ephesos and Gennadios Scholarios were the most characteristic cases of John Damascene's reception: the former of the explicit eidetic mode (i.e., of adherence to John's formulations; Karmiris 1952: 354), and the latter of the explicit noematic mode (i.e., of the importance of John's methodology; Jugie *et al.* 1929: 114, 247, 343).

It is worth mentioning Constantinos Akropolitis' *Oration on Saint John Damascene* (Migne PG 140 1865) as perhaps the text that sums up the reverence with which the Byzantines came to receive the *œuvre* of the Damascene.

The Latin Reception

Although the reception of John Damascene in the West exhibits a belated commencement compared with his reception in the East, it was from the very beginning a quite potent one, and it developed throughout the "Middle Ages" into a very seminal influence on Scholastic Theology. Nevertheless, one should bear in mind that the Latin reception of John – in distinction to his more extensive and diverse Byzantine reception – consisted exclusively of two reception modes: (a) an explicit eidetic mode (as witnessed in a substantial number of translations produced of the Damascene's works), which reflects the authority of John; and (b) an explicit noematic mode (seen in citations from John within the works of the Scholastics), which utilizes critically the thought of the Damascene. Furthermore, in light of these remarks, it could be maintained that the modes at work in the Latin reception of John correspond partly and at the same time distinctively with those at work in the Byzantine reception; and more importantly, the distinctiveness of the Latin reception can be conceptualized as a less traditionalist and more personal engagement with certain ideas found in the Damascene's *œuvre*.

Starting at the middle of the twelfth century with the translation of *On the Orthodox Faith* by Burgundio de Pisa (1153/1154), and continuing right through to the fourteenth century, the explicit eidetic mode of John's reception yielded a number of translations, which in turn formed a substantial manuscript tradition in their own right. Regardless of how much Burgundio's translation was subsequently ignored or not (Callari 1941), it seems that it inaugurated a certain way of reading the magnum opus of the Damascene: *On the Orthodox Faith* was divided into four "books" (theology, cosmology, Christology, miscellanea), and in this way it was modeled upon the Scholastic way of systematizing the content of the Christian faith. In the thirteenth century, further translations of this work appeared (e.g., the *translatio Lincolniensis*), as well as translations of other works of the Damascene, most notably the *Dialectica* by Robert Grosseteste (Holland 1983). Moreover, it seems that the manuscript tradition of these translations took on the character of a subtle editorial commenting/hermeneutics on the Damascene's thinking according to the interests and intentions of the theologians that found his *œuvre* appealing.

Although the entrance of John Damascene's theological views into the Western history of religious ideas coincides with the translation enterprise of the twelfth century (de Ghellinck 1948), he was not unknown in the more general theological sense. Nevertheless, as soon as Western theologians became familiar with his specific views, they never stopped drawing upon them up until the fourteenth century. The most significant cases of the Damascene's influence seem to be on Candulphe de Bologne, Albert the Great, Thomas Aquinas, Bonaventura, Gerhoh of Reichersberg (Buytaert 1950), and William of Occam. It is interesting to note that this influence was quite variegated, and it could range from controversial topics such as astrology in the work of

Albert the Great (Zambelli 1982) to pure philosophical questions, such as the interface between language and knowledge in the *Summa logica* of William of Occam (Siclari 1980). That notwithstanding, the *œuvre* of John Damascene was more often than not drawn upon for the sake of theological contemplation – with Thomas Aquinas being perhaps the most typical example of this kind of reflection. The latter was always critical, and this aspect is what defines best the Latin explicit noematic mode of the Damascene's reception. Critical reflection enabled Thomas Aquinas to talk about Jesus as God's salvific instrument (Schoof 1974), God's salvific plan in terms of predestination (Arfeuil 1974), or the necessary distinction between antecedent and consequent Divine will (Antoniotti 1965) by utilizing time and again certain Damascenian *loci*. However, it was the same critical reflection that allowed him – as well as Bonaventura – to express reservations about John's Triadology or Christology, and ascribe to him a "Nestorian"-type of Pneumatology (Grégoire 1969).

On the one hand, this attitude of the Latin explicit noematic mode of reception was conducive to much more creativity in dealing with John Damascene's thought than in the East; but on the other hand, it was prone to go beyond the real (i.e., historically-conditioned) intentionality of his views. The Latin reception of the Damascene attests to the fact that Western theologians found here and there in his *œuvre* points of interest vis-à-vis the specific questions they were dealing with, rather than points of reference that affirmed their historical continuity with the past. Thus, for instance, the Damascene's "psychological" anthropology of action was to be deemed expedient for the conceptual articulation of the individualization process taking place in the West during the twelfth and thirteenth centuries (Lottin 1949). Finally, two last remarks are worth considering: (a) the explicit eidetic mode of the Damascene's reception in the West was more pronounced than in the East as far as his polemic against Islam was concerned; and (b) the Latin explicit noematic mode of John's reception was caught up in the *Filioque* controversy due to the fact that it was the Byzantines that basically regarded him as an authority on this topic.

The Slavonic, Armenian, and Georgian Reception

The remainder of John Damascene's medieval reception is most strongly witnessed in the Slavonic, Armenian, and Georgian cases. In the first of these it dates back to the middle of the tenth century when parts of John's *œuvre* started being translated. Throughout the "Middle Ages," though, a number of translations – with more or less editorial reworking – would come to dominate the reception of the Damascene by theologians writing within the Slavonic, Armenian, and Georgian traditions. One should specifically note the Slavonic translations of *Dialectica* (Weiher 1969), and *On the Orthodox Faith* by John Exarch of Bulgaria in the ninth century (Kopreeva 1983); the Armenian translation of *Dialectica* by Simeon of Plinžahank in the thirteenth century (Akinian 1947); and the Georgian translations of both *On the Orthodox Faith* and *Dialectica* by Ephrem Mzire in the eleventh century and Arsen Iqaltoeli around 1100 (Rapava 1976). Furthermore, there seems to have been a continuous interest in the Damascene's homiletic and hymnographic works: the former being the case more in the Armenian tradition of reception, and the latter quite extensive in the more Byzantine-conditioned Slavonic tradition of John's reception.

Although the reception of John Damascene via translations would seem to represent a kind of explicit eidetic mode, the most interesting feature in all these cases is the role that John's work played with regard to the reception of Greek philosophical terminology in the respective languages. For example, terms such as "ousia," "physis," or "hypostasis" were rendered into Slavonic in close connection with *On the Orthodox Faith* (Podskalsky 1970), whereas John Damascene occupied a significant place in the dogmatic current in Georgian philosophy throughout the eleventh and twelfth centuries (Khidašeli 1977). Here, we do have an explicit reference to John that exceeds mere eidetic reproductions, and in that respect one could justifiably speak of a noematic mode of reception. The distinctiveness of the latter was not about the consolidation of a continuity with the past (as in Byzantium), or its expediency in dealing with pressing questions of the present (as in the West), but more pointedly about the foundation of a new conceptual world-view. In his Slavonic, Armenian, and Georgian reception the Damascene was treated as the starting point of a language that could serve conceptually either Christianization (in the case of the Slavs) or Christian revitalization (in the case of the Armenians and Georgians).

Two additional remarks are needed in order to conclude the medieval reception of John we are discussing. First, the *Vita* of the Damascene (i.e., a text that testifies to his prevalent authority) circulated widely through repeated translations in all languages involved. Second, the Georgian reception in particular deserves closer attention, for – regardless of other apparent literary backgrounds (e.g., Manichean, Arabic) – it was most likely responsible for the production and acceptance of the *Vita Barlaam and Joasaph* as one of the works of John Damascene. There were numerous recensions, shorter and larger, of this work in Slavonic, Armenian, and Georgian, and thus one can assert that what this work achieved in Byzantium as to the Damascene's esteem was repeated throughout the northern Balkans, eastern Europe, and the Caucasus region.

The Arabic Reception

The Arabic reception of John Damascene during the "Middle Ages" presents a number of very interesting features of its own. First, it set forth the image of the Damascene as a model for theologizing, as one can attest in the case of the work of his "disciple" Theodore Abū Qurrah, "Melkite" bishop of Harran (d. c. 820). Second, by 1100 it had already introduced the liturgical cult of John, at least in Palestine (Wilkinson *et al.* 1988: 140). Third, this reception of the Damascene involves a substantial manuscript tradition of versions of John's works in Arabic that is little known, but presumably became formative of Palestinian and more generally Arabic Eastern Orthodoxy (Griffith 2006). Fourth, it allows us to get a glimpse into how the argumentation of the Damascene's type of systematic theology may have interacted with early Islamic *kalam* and *falsafa*. And last but not least, one should keep in mind that it was the Arabic *Vita* of John Damascene – originating possibly from the tenth century – that became the basis for his acclaim as an unsurpassed hymnographer and model theologian.

The Arabic reception of the Damascene differs from the aforementioned medieval traditions of his reception insofar as it is more focused on the very person and life of John. This is totally expected, since John was embedded within his contemporary Arabic milieu, and at the same time emerged as a potent symbol of Arab Eastern Orthodox identity. Thus, one could schematically conceptualize the Arabic reception of the Damascene as a set of co-centric circles, starting with the cult around John's person and popular devoutness with regard to his *Vita*, expanding towards the Damascenian literature in Arabic, and ending with the impact of the "Damascene-phenomenon" on early Islamic intellectual developments. The latter circle would stand for the only case of the Damascene's reception taking place beyond the confines of Christianity. This, undoubtedly, would have to be regarded as an indirect reception that nonetheless constituted an alternative implicit noematic mode giving rise to an inter-religious preoccupation with issues such as will, freedom, evil, and rationality.

The Modern Reception of John Damascene's *Œuvre*

The Historical Development of the Modern Reception of the Damascene

Around 1500 the reception of John Damascene entered into what could be called its modern phase. Although multiple translations and editions of the Damascenian *œuvre*, as well as theological works centered upon John's ideas, continued to be produced more or less in the fashion of the medieval period – establishing, thus, a continuity with past reception – at the same time the modern reception of the Damascene has been marked by a discontinuity with the past in the sense that it has progressively treated John with a much more critical attitude (especially in circles of a Protestant background) than the one traditional thinkers had. More specifically, modern secularization and Enlightenment have eventually rendered the Damascenian *œuvre* a stronghold of tradition that, nonetheless, has to be thoroughly examined in order to assess the role it played in paving the way for the emergence of modern Christianity and/or Europe itself.

During the last five centuries the reception of the Damascene could be said to conform roughly to the following developmental sequence: (a) basically and primarily John Damascene was received in modernity – and has consistently been read – as a systematic theologian; (b) John has likewise been studied throughout the modern period as the (alleged) author of the *Vita Barlaam and Ioasaph*; (c) the Damascene has received considerable attention as a hymnographer, and a poet in general; (d) John has time and again been utilized and examined as one of the earliest Christian adversaries of Islam; and lastly (e) the Damascene has been brought forward as a thinker of philosophical importance in his own right. Furthermore, it is worth noting that, interestingly enough, some of these ways of dealing with John Damascene have occupied more certain periods of the modern era than others. For instance, John as a hymnographer was particularly a focus of interest from the middle of the eighteenth century to the middle of the nineteenth century, whereas the Damascene as a philosophically inclined theologian has basically been a twentieth-century concern. However, it seems that all the types of reception of the Damascene during modern times somehow have reflected and responded to certain sensitivities and dispositions operative in the West.

Another point that should be considered is a rather paradoxical – but not unexplainable – coexistence of two oppositional modes in the Damascene's reception throughout the modern era. Although several very important works on the theology of the Damascene have been published (mainly after the middle of the nineteenth century), the approach to his *œuvre* has disproportionately been philological and historiographical. More specifically, it is noteworthy that this kind of approach originated in its early stages (i.e., in the sixteenth and seventeenth centuries) from a humanistic interest in the writings of John, but as time went on it ended up being a thorough and critical inquiry into the sources and influences upon which his work actually was or might have been dependent. On the other hand, especially within the circles of Protestant scholasticism and up until the end of the eighteenth century, there has consistently been a strikingly different approach in the reception of the Damascene, an approach that strangely enough has built upon the traditional legacy of John's medieval reception – although in a freer and more critical manner.

The *œuvre* of John Damascene entered modernity and has remained thereafter a point of repeated interest basically due to its systematic/rational aspects and thanks to the successive humanistic, Enlightenment, and historicist agendas of the Western intellectual world. From the sixteenth century up to the middle of the seventeenth century the Damascenian *œuvre* appealed particularly to moderate Roman Catholic humanism, as exemplified in cases such as those of Jacobus Faber Stapulensis and Leo Allatius. Subsequently, and until the beginning of the nineteenth century, it was looked upon as a logically defensible Christianity by moderate Enlightenment circles throughout Europe. And finally, in the following period until the end of the twentieth century, the rationally constructed edifice of his *œuvre* has attracted the counter-rationality of historicist analysis. Nevertheless, all along, the Damascene has intrigued scholars through the *Vita Barlaam and Ioasaph*: at the beginning presumably because this *roman*-like work reflected an experience that was rather close to modern Western individualism, then due to the luring exoticism that the work exerted on the Enlightened European consciousness, and lastly thanks to the possibilities that this work presented regarding inter-religious contact.

On the other hand, when the Damascene started being appraised as a hymnographer, it was basically out of traditional regional interests (Greek and Slavic), and only in the twentieth century did a nonreligious appreciation of him as a poet really take root. John Damascene as an adversary of Islam should be expected to have been rhetorically useful to a Europe that for more than half of modernity confronted the Ottoman Empire, while in the twentieth century his anti-Islamic polemic, based as it was on first-hand knowledge, would come to be utilized otherwise in light of Ecumenism and Christian–Islamic dialogue. Finally, the modern philosophical interest in John Damascene was a direct consequence of the rational quality of his *œuvre*. However, the latter has been treated with much ambivalence from the Western rationalistic point of view.

The "Schools of Thought" in the Modern Reception of the Damascene

The above outline of the historical development of John Damascene's modern reception takes into account more western and central European circumstances, and so it should be complemented with a typological presentation that considers other regional traits as well. What is quite interesting with regard to the modern reception of the Damascene's *œuvre* is that the researcher is able to follow up some more or less discernible and distinct from one another strands of thinking, which we would dare characterize as regional interpretative "schools of thought." Moreover, each of these "schools of thought" stands for a history of hermeneutics in its own right, exemplifying, as it were, a certain *Tendenz*. The latter in some of the cases to be discussed (the Roman, the Greek, and the Russian) continues or reflects partly medieval preoccupations, but apart from that it does contribute something new to the reception of John. Finally, in the remaining cases (the German, the English, and the Romanian) the reception of the Damascene seems to be totally new.

In general, the Roman "school of thought" concerning the Damascene has tended to treat John's *œuvre* as a justification either for later Roman Catholic developments in belief and practice or against Protestant challenges to traditional Roman Catholic piety. The latter has been the case with the Counter-Reform defense of religious images, a number of ecclesiastical services, monasticism, and the cult of saints, as well as with the persistent reminder of the direness of heresy, while the former has perhaps been most recognizable in the promotion of Mariology. In more recent times, though, there has been a Roman *Tendenz* to review John's theology by holding a critical distance in light of what has been regarded as John's systematic or exactitude shortcomings. On the other hand, the Russian "school of thought" has taken on the exact opposite stance and employed the Damascene in a very stark anti-Catholic polemic. To an extent, this has been a continuation of the later Byzantine reception of John; and not without a reason, since some of the most typical exponents of the Russian "school of thought" in its early phase were Greeks (e.g., Mogila 1763). However, the dominant reason behind the anti-Catholic polemic of this "school" seems to have been the confessional need to circumscribe Russian Orthodox identity in the face of Roman Catholic missionary activities. Moreover, in more recent times it was this "school" that inaugurated the systematic study of John Damascene's *œuvre* by producing monographs on various aspects of his theology.

What for purposes of convenience could be dubbed the Germanic "school of thought" in the modern reception of the Damascene is one of those "schools" that has developed into a proper hermeneutics in the study of the Damascene's *œuvre*. What is particularly interesting about this "school" is its twofold nature: one part of it goes back to the beginnings of Protestant scholasticism and has been traditionalist in its approach to John, although at the same time allowing for independent inspiration as evidenced, for example, in Schleiermacher (cf. Louth 2002: 3), whereas the other part of it dates back to the start of the eighteenth century and has been the most critical "school" regarding John's work in light of his historical setting and intellectual sources. However, it is this latter part of the Germanic "school" that has yielded some of the best works of historicist scholarship in the study of the Damascene. The Russian trend in the production of monographs has been superseded herein, and more sophisticated studies on virtually all aspects of the "Damascene-phenomenon" have come forth. However, more often than not, the phenomenon itself has been lost under the excessive exercise of analysis.

In a particular kind of dialogue with the Germanic "school" – since the nineteenth century – has been the Greek "school of thought" on John Damascene, a "school" that is perhaps the most expanded in time and consistent in outlook. Actually, during the first centuries of the modern era it emerged as a kind of natural extension of the Byzantine reception of the Damascene, for it perpetuated mainly the explicit eidetic mode of reception and continued the copying of John's works. Throughout the sixteenth to eighteenth centuries the dogmatic formulations of the Damascene became the hallmark of Greek Orthodox confessional statements, to the extent that one could talk about a certain reverential imitation. Nonetheless, since the founding of the Modern Greek State – with its Bavarian connections to the German academic establishment – the Greek approach to the Damascene, without overlooking historical and/or literary conditions (according to the German model), has espoused in general a highly creative if not an original Damascene. Throughout the twentieth century the Greek "school" has become more distinct in acquiring a kind of phenomenological perspective and in affirming the Damascene's *œuvre* as a genuine continuation of the Greek philosophical tradition (Matsoukas 1969; Siasos 1989).

There are two more regional "schools" in Damascenian studies; namely, the English and the Romanian. The first is the most recent of all "schools of thought" we are discussing, dating basically from the end of the nineteenth century (Lupton 1884). However, during the twentieth century it has built up into the most moderate and balanced one, combing both scholarly standards and a sense of reverence toward John Damascene as a great patristic figure (Parry 1996; Louth 2002). The basic characteristics of the English approach form an integral agenda of social and cultural priorities – as a deeper historical texture; and on the basis of this, a distinctively "Middle-Eastern" Damascene has emerged as part and parcel of the more general contours of the Palestinian Christianity of his time and age (Sahas 1972). Lastly, the Romanian "school of thought," although it set off at around the beginning of the nineteenth century, has only yielded a consistent production of works during the twentieth century. Most of the Romanian researchers have followed in the steps of the overall European research agenda on John Damascene – with some notable, though, and insightful studies on Christology and the Virgin Mary (Pintea 1980); but what really makes this "school" characteristic is its understanding of the Damascene as part of the cultural capital that has given rise to a distinctively Romanian national/ethnic identity (especially through hymnography, hagiography and folklore). Finally, this "school" could be said to reflect and at the same time supplement the more general project/movement of promoting an exclusively Romanian way of thinking (Romanianism).

The above typological presentation of the regional "schools of thought" at work in the modern reception of John Damascene is not intended in any way to be exclusive or exhaustive. Presumably, there has been substantial overlapping and cross-fertilization between the "schools of thought" discussed here, and these two situations seem to be particularly the case as one comes to consider more recent Damascenian scholarship. At the same time, there have been studies that do not fit easily or at all into categories, even when the scholars involved come from within specific interpretation traditions. Nevertheless, we think that a typology like the aforementioned is useful insofar as it positions this or that reception of the Damascene into broader intellectual agendas.

The Current Dominant Perspectives in the Study of the Damascene

The appeal of philosophical movements such as existentialism on post modern/modern mentalities or the pervasiveness of neo-mystic spiritual orientations in the global market of ideas have generally contributed to the fascination with more emotionally inclined and mystical Christian thinkers than the proto-"Scholastic" Damascene. However, during the last two decades or so there has been a shift in interests resulting in a fresh re-evaluation of the possibilities offered by the content of the Damascene's œuvre beyond its logically rigid structuring. More specifically, the issues that seem to be gradually dominating the research agenda on John Damascene are associated with the question of his originality, both as a theologian and as a philosophically minded thinker in general. In this respect, John's work (a) is being reevaluated as to what exactly it constitutes as a recapitulation of patristic tradition; (b) it is appreciated as a cardinal point of transition from Ancient to Medieval philosophy; (c) it is seen as offering some interesting insights from a Philosophy of Religion point of view; and (iv) in more than one way, it becomes implicated in the much debated postmodern obsessions on aesthetics, symbolism, and the iconic/virtual.

Bibliography

Primary Sources

Constantinos Akropolitis, *Λόγος εἰς τὸν ἅγιον Ἰωάννην τὸν Δαμασκηνόν* [*Oration on St John Damascene*], Jean-Paul Migne (ed.) (1865). Patrologiae Cursus Completus Series Graeca, 140. Paris.

Die Schriften des Johannes von Damaskos, Bonifatius Kotter (ed.) (1969–1988). Patristische Texte und Studien 7, 12, 17, 22, 29. Berlin: Walter de Gruyter.

Gennadios Scholarios, *Περὶ τῆς ἐκπορεύσεως τοῦ Ἁγίου Πνεύματος* [*On the Procession of the Holy Spirit*], M. Jugie, L. Petit, and X.A. Siderides (eds) (1929). Oeuvres complètes de Georges (Gennadios) Scholarios. Paris: Maison de la Bonne Presse.

Markos of Ephesos, *Ἐγκύκλιος Ἐπιστολὴ κατὰ Λατίνων* [*Encyclical Epistle against the Latins*]. Ioannis Karmiris (ed.) (1952). *Τὰ δογματικά*

καὶ συμβολικὰ μνημεία τῆς Ὀρθοδόξου Καθολικῆς Ἐκκλησίας [*The Dogmatic and Symbolic Monuments of the Orthodox Catholic Church*]. Athens.

Neilos Kavasilas, *Sur le Saint-Esprit*. Theophile Kislas (ed./transl.) (2001). Paris: Le Cerf.

Peter Damascene, "A treasury of divine knowledge" and "Twenty-four discourses". *The Philokalia: The Complete Text Compiled by St Nikodimos of the Holy Mountain and St Makarios of Corinth*. G.E.H. Palmer, Philip Sherrard, and Kallistos Ware (transl./eds) (1984). London: Faber and Faber.

Peter Mogila, *Confession de la foi de l'église catholique et apostolique d'Orient... augmentée de deux discours de notre saint père Jean Damascène sur la vénération de saintes images*. Venice, 1763 [in Russian; first edition in 1696].

Photii patriarchae Constantinopolitani epistulae et Amphilochia: Vol. IV. *Amphilochiorum pars prima*, Leendert Gerrit Westerink (ed.) (1986). Leipzig: Teubner.

Suidae lexicon. Ada Adler (ed.) (1928–1930). Leipzig: B.G. Teubner.

Textus Byzantini ad iconomachiam pertinentes. Hermann Hannephof (ed.) (1969). Leiden: Brill.

Secondary Sources

Akinian, P.N. (1947), "Simeon von Plinžahank (1188–1255) und seine übersetzungen aus dem Georgischen ins Armenische. II. Johannes von Damaskus in der armenische Literatur". *Handes amsorya*, 61: 193–219.

Antoniotti, Louise-Marie (1965), "La volonté divine antécédent et conséquent selon saint Jean Damascène et saint Thomas d'Aquin". *Revue Thomiste*, 65, 1: 52–77.

Arambatzis, Chrestos (2010), *Η ερμηνεία της πατερικής γραμματείας του 14ο και του 15ο αιώνα. Η αυθεντία και το κύρος του αγίου Ιωάννη Δαμασκηνού.* [The 14th and 15th century Interpretation of Patristic Literature. The Authority and Status of John Damascene]. Thessaloniki.

Arfeuil, Jean-Pierre. (1974), "Le dessein sauveur de Dieu. La doctrine de la prédestination selon saint Thomas d'Aquin". *Revue Thomiste*, 74, 4: 591–641.

Buytaert, Eligius, M. (1950), "St John Damascene, Peter Lombard and Gerhoh of Reichersberg". *Franciscan Studies*, 10: 323–343.

Callari, L. (1941), "Contributo allo studio della versione di Burgundio Pisano del 'De Orthodoxa Fide' di Giovanni Damasceno". *Reale Instituto Veneto di Scienze, Lettere ed Art*, "Atti", t. c, Parte II: Classe di Scienze morali e Letterarie. Venice: C. Ferrari; 197–246.

Geerard, M. and Noret, J. (eds) (2003), *Clavis Patrum Graecorum. A Cyrillo Alexandrino ad Iohannem Damascenum.* Corpus Christianorum Series Graeca. Turnhout: Brepols.

De Ghellinck, Joseph (1948), "L'entrée de Jean de Damas dans le monde littéraire occidental". In *Le mouvement théologique du XIIe siècle. Sa préparation lointaine avant le autour de Pierre Lombard et ses rapports avec les initiatives des canonistes. Études, recherches et documents*, 2nd edn. Museum Lessianum, Section historique No. 10. Bruges: De Tempel; 374–415.

Grégoire, José (1969), "La relation éternelle de l'Esprit au Fils d'après les écrits de Jean de Damas". *Revue d'Histoire Ecclésiastique*, 64, 3–4: 713–755.

Griffith, Sidney H. (2006), "The Church of Jerusalem and the 'Melkites': the making of an 'Arab Orthodox' Christian identity in the world of Islam (750–1050 CE)". In *Christians and Christianity in the Holy Land, from the Origins to the Latin Kingdoms*, Ora Limor and Guy G. Stroumsa (eds). Turnhout: Brepols.

Holl, Karl (1897), *Die Sacra Parallela des Johannes Damascenus.* Texte und Untersuchungen zur Geschichte der alt-christlichen Literatur, 16. Leipzig: J.C. Hinrichs.

Holland, Meridel (1983), "Robert Grosseteste's translations of John of Damascus". *Bodleian Library Record*, 11, 3: 138–154.

Khidašeli, V. (1977), "Le courant dogmatique dans la philosophie géorgienne des XIe–XIIe ss". *Essais d' histoire de la pensée philosophique géorgienne*, 5: 3–31.

Kopreeva, Tatjana N. (1983), "Neizvestnye otryvki iz Bogoslovija Ioanna Damaskina v prevode Ioanna Ekzarcha Bulgarskogo v spiske xv veka". *Paleobulgarica*, 7, 4: 93–100.

Matsoukas, Nikos (1969), "Φιλοσοφία και δογματική διδασκαλία του αγίου Ιωάννου Δαμασκηνού [Philosophy and the Dogmatic Teaching of St John Damascene]". *Επιστημονική Επετηρίς Θεολογικής Σχολής Θεσσαλονίκης*, 14: 253–300.

Lottin, Odon (1949), 'La psychologie de l'acte humain chez Saint Jean Damascène et les théologiens du XIIIe siècle occidental". *Psychologie et morale aux XIIe et XIIIe siècles.* Gembloux: J. Duculot.

Louth, Andrew (2002), *St John Damascene: Tradition and Originality in Byzantine Theology*. Oxford: Oxford University Press.

Lupton, Joseph H. (1884), *St John of Damascus*. The Fathers for English Readers. London: SPCK.

Parry, Ken (1996), *Depicting the Word: Byzantine Iconophile Thought of the Eighth and Ninth Centuries*. Leiden: Brill.

Pintea, Dumitru (1980), "Învăţătura Sfîntului Ioan Damaschin despre Maica Domnului". *Ortodoxia*, 32: 501–520.

Podskalsky, G. (1970), "Untersuchungen zu einigen Zentralbegriffen der patristischen Personspekulation in der vom Exarchen Johannes geschaffenen slavischen Erstübersetzung der Ἔκθεσις ἀκριβὴς τῆς Ὀρθοδόξου Πίστεως des Johannes von Damaskus". *Die Welt der Slaven*, 15, 2: 147–167.

Rapava, Maia (1976), *Ioane Damaskeli. Dialekhtika*. Tbilisi: Micnieraba.

Sahas, D.J. (1972), *John of Damascus on Islam. The 'Heresy of the Ismaelites'*. Leiden: Brill.

Schoof, T.M. (1974), "Jésus, instrument de Dieu pour notre salut. Sondage de la méthode théologique de Thomas d'Aquin". *Tijdschrift voor Theologie*, 14, 3: 217–244.

Siasos, Lambros (1989), *Πατερικὴ κριτικὴ τῆς φιλοσοφικῆς μεθόδου*. [Patristic Critique of Philosophical Method]. Thessaloniki: Pournaras.

Siclari, Alberto (1980), "La *Dialectica* di Giovani di Damasco e la *Summa logica* di Guglielmo di Occam". *Sprache und Erkenntnis in Mittelalter 1. Miscellanea Mediaevalia*, 13/1: 476–487.

Weiher, Eckehard (1969), *Johannes von Damaskus. Die Dialektik in Kirchenslavischer Uebersetzung*. Monumenta Slavicae Dialecti Veteris, Fontes et Dissertationes. Wiesbaden: Harrasowitz.

Wilkinson, John, Hill, Joyce, and Ryan, W.F. (1988), *Jerusalem Pilgrimage 1099–1185*. London: Hakluyt Society.

Zambelli, Paola (1982), "Albert le Grand et l'astrologie". *Recherches de théologie ancienne et médiévale*, 49: 141–158.

CHAPTER 19

Gregory of Narek

Abraham Terian

Introduction

Gregory of Narek remains largely unknown in western scholarship on medieval spirituality – regrettably so, since he deserves to be anthologized among its best representatives. Born near Lake Van, in the then Armenian Kingdom of Vaspurakan, c. 945, he spent his entire life at the monastery of Narek in the District of Ŕshtunik' – three miles from the lake's southernmost shore, today's Yemişlik Köyü – where he died in 1003. Consequently, in Armenian he is called Narekats'i, after the place with which he is associated; similarly, his renowned *Book of Lamentation*, which will be discussed herein, is called *Narek* for short.

Gregory was the son of Khosrov, a scholar who, after his wife's death, when Gregory was a child, became Bishop of Vaspurakan's District of Andzewats'ik'. This was before 950 (Khach'atryan 1996: 21–32, 36); however, some place Gregory's birth in the year 951, misreading the year of Khosrov's defying the authority of the catholicos who consecrated him, 954, as that of consecration (cf. Cowe 1991: 11). Khosrov, then an aged widower, took his younger sons, John (Yovhannēs) and Gregory (Grigor), to be educated at the famed monastery, whose abbot Anania was a paternal cousin of his deceased wife. Khosrov's eldest son, Isaac (Sahak), remained with him as his amanuensis. Our knowledge about the family mostly derives from four colophons by Gregory himself, transmitted by subsequent scribes. The first was appended to a manuscript of his father's two liturgical works (*Exposition of the Daily Office* and *Commentary on the Divine Liturgy*, in *Matenagirk' Hayots'* (MH) 10: 35–227; Cowe 1991), copied by Sahak and owned by Gregory (where Khosrov's title "Lord Bishop of Andzewats'ik'" is given with the date of completion, 950), and the others were appended to his own works (below, nos. 1, 3, and 7). Apart from information from these colophons and the "innerman" emerging from the prayers, we know little about Gregory's life – hagiographical

The Wiley Blackwell Companion to Patristics, First Edition. Edited by Ken Parry.
© 2015 John Wiley & Sons Ltd. Published 2019 by John Wiley & Sons Ltd.

embellishments notwithstanding. Some sparse, supplementary information may be gathered from his standard monastic education and the writings of his kin, especially the abbot Anania. His first eulogizer, Nersēs of Lambron (1153–1198; Bishop of Tarsus from 1175), simply repeats the colophonic information in a colophon of his own, in a manuscript of the prayers copied for him in 1173 (Matenadaran no. 1568). Nersēs shows profound appreciation for Gregory's prayers – apparently recovered during the pontificate of Nersēs's great uncle, Catholicos Nersēs IV of Klay (in office 1166–1173), known as "the Gracious" for his passionate ecclesiastical writings and pioneering ecumenical endeavors. No medieval Armenian writer was more influenced by Gregory than Catholicos Nersēs, who probably was the first to have our author's prayers, odes, and litanies anthologized in liturgical books.

Short History of Scholarship

The gripping appeal of Gregory's *Book of Lamentation* brought about its partial publication in the relatively early years of Armenian printing, thanks to the efforts of Oskan Erewants'i, in Marseilles, in 1673. His works reemerged in Constantinople in the eighteenth century, as a result of Patriarch Yakob Nalian's keen interest in the prayer book, which he had published locally in 1701. The publication of the entire corpus followed, by the Venetian Mekhitharists in 1827 and again in 1840. The text of Gregory's works, in part or in whole, was variously published and translated thereafter. By 1875 there were no less than 50 printings of the book. His mystic poetry gave new impetus to secular Armenian poetry during the nationalism awakened in nineteenth-century Constantinople, earning Gregory such accolades as "the foremost Armenian author of all times," "the most sacred name in Armenian letters," and so on.

In the Soviet era the corpus of his writings was viewed as exclusively poetry rather than essentially prayer, and the author was seen as an anti-clerical proto-communist. This was sufficient to justify the publication of a critical text of the book, the first such edition, sponsored by the National Academy of Sciences of the Armenian SSR (Khach'atryan and Ghazinyan 1985). Two good western translations followed, one into French (Mahé 2000; rev. ed. 2007) and another into English (Samuelian 2001). To commemorate the millennial of Gregory's death, the Armenian Catholicosate of Cilicia (headquartered in Antelias, Lebanon) published his collected works, utilizing the 1985 critical edition of the prayer book (albeit without the *apparatus criticus*) and the best available editions of the author's other works, with significant emendations (Aznaworian 2003). The 1985 critical edition, along with a more definitive text of the author's other works – thanks to newly collated manuscripts at the Matenadaran in Erevan – appeared in vols 12 (2008) and 10 (2009) in the ongoing series *Matenagirk' Hayots'* (*MH*; "Armenian Classical Authors"), began in 2003 under the patronage of the Lisbon-based Gulbenkian Foundation and the Armenian Catholicosate of Cilicia. The series may in time be dubbed as *Patrologia Armena* simply for bringing together conveniently the scattered sources for the study of the Armenian Fathers – a grossly neglected area in patristics (all references to ancient Armenian sources in this chapter are to the series *MH*). Subsequent to the publication of vol. 12, I have translated for an impending publication all the author's poetic works apart from the prayer book: his odes, litanies, and encomia, under the title *The Festal Works of Gregory of Narek* (in preparation).

Moreover, English and French readers are fortunate to have recent translations of Gregory's *Commentary on the Song of Songs* (Ervine 2007; Pétrossian 2010); and French readers, of his *Encomium on the Holy Virgin* (Dasnabédian 1995). A partial and gradually expanded Russian translation of the prayer book (Grebnev 1977) inspired Alfred Schnittke's "Concerto for Mixed Chorus," with various recordings of its performance since 1985. A complete Russian translation followed (Darbinyan-Melik'yan and Khanlaryan 1988). There are several translations of the *Book of Lamentation* into modern Western and Eastern Armenian – even two translations into Arabic and two separate, unpublished translations in Turkish (cited in Khach'atryan and Ghazinyan 1985: 228). Similarly, there are Western and Eastern Armenian translations of Gregory's *Odes* and *Exhortation*, and a Western Armenian translation of the *Encomia*.

Next to the popularity of Gregory's prayers, his odes have attracted considerable attention for their poetic excellence. Most of them appear in various translations, but not all (for a complete Czech translation, see the forthcoming work of Haig Utidjian). Together, they are ranked among the greatest and most popular works in Armenian poetry. Thus, a critical edition of the odes and the litanies, as that of the prayers, was published in the Armenian SSR (K'yoshkeryan 1981). Apart from text-critical studies, most Soviet–Armenian scholarship devoted to these odes, litanies, and prayers is flawed for want of theological input.

A flurry of publications appeared in 2003, when Armenians everywhere commemorated the millennial of Gregory's death. While most of these are irrelevant for students of patristics, special mention must be made of the published papers from two international conferences devoted to our author. These papers, assigned to specialists by the organizers, sum up fairly the better state of "Narekian" scholarship today (Mahé and Zekiyan 2006; Mahé *et al.* 2009–2010).

Overview of Monastic Education at Narek

By the tenth century Armenia had recovered from the ill effects of the Arab invasion. Relative peace, coupled with mercantile prosperity, had enabled the rise of new monasteries along the trade routes that traversed the land. And as everywhere else in the tenth century, monasteries were the centers of learning in Armenia, and that for privileged sons destined for the religious life. The basic curriculum in the monastic schools consisted of the three liberal arts of classical antiquity, known as the *trivium*: grammar, rhetoric, and logic. This was augmented by the study of Scripture; patristics, including hagiography; and theology, including some philosophy, bridged by the writings of Philo of Alexandria. Such education was considerably rich, given the availability of theological and literary works in Armenian, as hundreds of translated works and others of native origin bear witness in thousands of surviving manuscripts – despite the turbulent history of the Armenian people. Singing was inseparable from liturgy, learned through participation in the daily services. Biblical interpretation, associative as it was at the elementary level – that is, based on connecting terms and concepts in Scripture with an eye for "fulfillment" in the New Testament – was almost entirely allegorical at the advanced level. Every versed *vardapet*, as the ecclesiastic doctor or teacher in the Armenian Church is called, thrived on allegorization.

Gregory was one of them; and like few others in this period, he was called by the Hebrew equivalent of the title, *rabbi* (*Prayer* 72.4). Moreover, children of the elite could also receive secular education in the monasteries, with the addition of the *quadrivium*: mathematics, geometry, music, and astronomy – thus completing the seven liberal arts. Lifelong monastic commitment offered opportunities for higher learning beyond these foundations. In his *Discourse*, Gregory states: "I was dropped in the womb of the church; and being nursed with milk from her spiritual breasts, I was honored as a priest in her great house, and was privileged to partake of her old and new treasures, albeit unworthily" (*MH* 10: 1041). Monastic libraries were repositories of "old and new treasures," as further indicated by the plenitude of surviving Armenian manuscripts. The monastic complex included a scriptorium where all students were trained in calligraphy, and nearly all accomplished scribes were monks.

Gregory had the added benefit of tutelage by his learned kin. The literary tradition at the disposal of the founder and abbot, Anania of Narek, whom Gregory's brother John succeeded as abbot, must have been considerable. The monastic community at Narek was probably one of several reestablished communities that had fled maltreatment in Byzantine Cappadocia during the Byzantine–Abbasid conflicts of 934–944 and the ensuing Byzantine expansionism (Thierry 1980: 1–2; 1989: 82). This led to ever-increasing imperial demands for confession of Chalcedonian "Orthodoxy" in the territories that came under Byzantine control, and the number of Armenian-Chalcedonians was constantly on the rise in the eastern provinces of the empire. Consequently, there was a proliferation of relocated and new monasteries in the eastern part of Armenia (Maksoudian 1990–1991; Mahé 2000: 8–33; Pogossian 2012). The historian Asoghik (d. c. 1015) lists Narek among them, as a place "with multi-talented, highly accomplished singers and literary scholars" (*History*, 3.7, in *MH* 15: 750–752). The available learning was evidently accumulated over centuries prior to the monastery's possible relocation – rather than founding – only a generation earlier. In this sense one could speak more justifiably of the reestablished "School of Narek," a designation used in recent scholarship that looks merely into the literary output of the few known figures associated with the monastery (T'amrazyan 1999). A case for the relocation at Narek could also be argued on the basis of the considerable Greek influence on those few (Yarnley 1976).

Our author had at his disposal a wealth of biblical commentaries translated from Greek and Syriac, and others of native Armenian authorship. Of the latter commentaries, special mention must be made of two by Bishop Step'anos of Siwnik' (d. 735): *On the First Vision of Ezekiel* and *On the Four Gospels* (*MH* 6: 130–155); and an unusual *scholium* by Bishop Grigoris of Arsharunik' (d. c. 730): *Commentary on the Lections*, a Christological interpretation based on the structure of the *Lectionary*, in 34 chapters (*MH* 6: 31–91). Equally massive was the homiletic literature available to Gregory, including several homiliaries by native writers. The earliest of these, from the fifth century, are by Eghishē Vardapet (*MH* 1: 960–1052; 6: 999–1005; Thomson 2000) and Mambrē Vertsanogh (*MH* 1: 1095–1136). No less significant are the homilies and panegyrics by Catholicos Zak'aria of Dzag (in office 854–876) on the life of Christ and on the Virgin (*MH* 9: 26–356). Equally important, in the panegyrical tradition, are the encomia on the Holy Cross and the Theotokos by Bishop Petros of Siwnik' (d. 557), Dawit' of Nergin (d. c. 660), and T'ēodoros K'ṙt'enawor (d. c. 675).

Thanks to early translations, there was considerable interconnectedness of the various literatures of the Christian East. These permeated Armenia early in the fifth century with the invention of the Armenian letters and the rigorous translational activity that followed. Gregory, like his spiritual ancestors, is heir to the vast heritage of the Early Church, encompassing both Greek and Syriac patristic writings predating Chalcedon, which had been nurtured in the Armenian Church for the better part of the first millennium. Foremost of these are the works of Irenaeus, the Cappadocian Fathers, Chrysostom, and Ephraim of Nisibis. An understudied aspect of this inherited faith is the ascetic legacy of Evagrius of Pontus (d. 399), especially his notion of the eight evil patterns of thought and his views about unceasing, pure prayer with tears – the simplest and purest of all prayer that is contemplation. The Evagrian influence on Gregory was substantial, as seen in his repeated prayers with tears in the prayer book, and in this admonition: "Confess your thoughts to God, the Benefactor, as if thoughts were actions" (*Prayer* 45.1; cf. *Order and Rules of Prayer* 48, in *MH* 10: 1084). Of post-Chalcedonian works, those of Pseudo-Dionysius the Areopagite, composed in Syria at the turn of the sixth century and translated into Armenian by Step'annos of Siwnik' (d. 735), had considerable influence on the Armenian Church (Thomson 1987; La Porta 2007), as also on other churches in the East and the West. (The effects of the Dionysian works on historical developments in tenth-century Armenia, and more so on the monastery of Narek, will be discussed later.) To this inherited faith Gregory added his personal imprint. He is a marvelously responsive writer with that rare ability to expound the deeper issues of life, with both a theologian's precision and a poet's lyricism.

Given the wide diversity of mystical experiences and mystical theologies, it is difficult to trace the immediate influences on Gregory beyond those of the spiritual milieu of his monastic community. However, attempts have recently been made to identify Neoplatonic tendencies in his works, thought to have been influenced by Plotinian and Dionysian writings (T'amrazyan 2004). Gregory's familiarity with the latter corpus is to be expected – even though no clear terminological indications of a direct Dionysian influence are found in his works (La Porta 2009–2010). His thought patterns are quite complex and often find expression in composite neologisms. In a meritorious study of our author's use of words, Mirzoyan (2010: 163–211) lists these neologisms alphabetically; they cover 30 two-column pages. Mirzoyan goes on to provide a list of words that occur only in the works of Gregory and his father Khosrov, and another list of words that occur only in the works of Gregory and his mentor Anania.

Gregory's indebtedness to Anania is profound (see *Prayer* 28.6; cf. *Eulogy*, in *MH* 10: 1103–1105). The range of Anania's surviving works is impressive (*MH* 10: 309–657, inclusive of the introductions by T'amrazyan and Bozoyan), thanks to documentary research undertaken at the Matenadaran that has brought to light newly discovered works and has reclaimed his authorship of extrapolated texts once attributed to Anania of Sanahin (d. c. 1070). Collectively, his extant works have a curricular character, revealing much of the content of his teaching (T'amrazyan 1986).

They consist of: hortatory discourses on the priesthood, humility, transience (in verse), and careful administration of the sacraments; treatises on penitence with tears (in prosaic verse), moralia, and arithmology or number-mysticism; polemical diatribes on the Dyophysites and others; a panegyric in praise of the universal church, which a later subtitle appropriates for Ējmiatsin; and a brief denunciation of the T'ondrakeans, on whom more will be said later. The abbot's writings reflect the more immediate and lasting influence on Gregory, whose theological education is amply displayed in his early works and amplified with deeper mysticism in his later writings.

Narek in the Midst of Controversy

The tenth century was a turbulent period in the history of the Armenian Church. The catholicosal see, which was moved from Vagharshapat (Ējmiatsin) to Dwin in 484 and to Aght'amar in 927 or 931, was transferred to the village of Argina, near Ani, in 947, not long after the accession of Anania of Mokk' to the see (in office 943–965). To consolidate his authority in the northern region and to reassert the waning significance of his office, the catholicos clashed with the Bishop of Siwnik', Yakob, who had cemented ties with the geographically closer catholicosate of the Caucasian Albanians, the Aghuank', an affiliate of the Armenian Church since its Gregorid beginnings. Also, early in his rule, Anania of Mokk' confronted the schismatic Catholicos Sahak of Caucasian Albania over the latter's conciliatory interpretation of the Council of Chalcedon (*Ep.* i, in *MH* 10: 258–260). This made the Armenian catholicos less tolerant toward Byzantinophiles within his jurisdiction – contrary to the spirit of the Council of Shirakawan (862), which had adopted a nonconfrontational stance toward the Byzantines, even allowing intermarriage between Dyophysites and Miaphysites (Maksoudian 1988–1989). Anania of Mokk' opposed such marriages (*Ep.* i, in *MH* 10: 256); he even required the rebaptism of Dyophysites within his jurisdiction (Asoghik, *History*, 3.7, in *MH* 15: 754). He referred to the proliferation of Dyophysitism as a spreading cancer (*Ep.* i, in *MH* 10: 259). The extent of his intolerance toward the Byzantines and their perceived sympathizers in Armenia is seen in his criticism of Khosrov, Gregory's father, for Greek influence on his pronunciation of certain Armenian words.

  This surfaces in the first of two letters (ii–iii) issued by the catholicos against Khosrov after the latter's death in c. 960 and titled *The Reason for Anathematizing Khosrov the Bishop of Andzewats'ik'*. In it he gives two substantive reasons for the anathematization: (1) for considering all crosses, blessed or not, as equally sacred; and (2) for considering all bishops, including the catholicos, as of equal ecclesiastical rank (*MH* 10: 275–276; cf. Cowe 1991: 10–13). The issue of parity of bishops was instigated by the Bishop of Siwnik', Yakob, and has a history of its own in the rivalry between the two hierarchies. Khosrov, despite having received consecration at the hand of Anania of Mokk', sided with Yakob of Siwnik', who challenged Anania's lording way over the bishops. While Yakob and Khosrov had argued – possibly in some lost works – for the equality of the catholicosate and the episcopate on the basis of the traditional hierarchy of deacons, priests, and bishops, in two other letters (i, iv) Anania of Mokk' dwells on the Dionysian triads of these three and their parallel celestial hierarchy of angels in three triads; and he dares the opposition bishops to compare themselves with any of the bishops of the Apostolic Era – or with St Gregory the Illuminator, founder of the hierarchy of the Armenian Church (*MH* 10: 281–291; cf. *Ep.* iii, in *MH* 10: 277–280).

The sentiments against Catholicos Anania coincide, albeit for different reasons, with those of the anti-hierarchical, anti-church-establishment T'ondrakeans – a heretical movement variously identified since the tenth century with every known heresy as of Docetism. Most of what is said about them by the ancients is comparable to Nersessian's (1987: 5) observation about the earlier sects, that "many of the Armenian sources regarding the sects are ambiguous in that they do not relate to any specific sect." Notwithstanding the ambiguities even in the more reliable sources on the T'ondrakeans cited by him (55–66), and the fact that all were written by their adversaries long after the rise of the movement, the T'ondrakeans emerge not as Paulicians (contra Garsoïan (1967: 96), based on the connection she makes on the authority of Grigor Magistros (d. 1059), on whom see later) but as Aphthartodocedic-Eutychian extremists. They gave the eucharistic flesh and blood of Jesus little or no sacramental import and saw no relevance in certain other rituals, having limited their definition of church to the community of believers – rejecting the significance of church buildings and thus disparaging the very seat of hierarchical authority. Consequently, they were identified as enemies of the Church who rejected the orthodox sacraments and practices, and were persecuted on both sides of the Byzantine–Armenian border, eventually retreating from the eastern provinces of the empire to the easternmost regions of Armenia.

The demonized T'ondrakeans were most likely Monothelite Eutychians, having received their name from a radical understanding of *Theandrikos* in the writings of Pseudo-Dionysius (*Ep.* iv), as the reception history of the latter indicates. Especially significant are the glosses attributed to Maximus the Confessor (d. 662) to bring Pseudo-Dionysius into conformity with Chalcedonian Orthodoxy (Pelikan 1987: 15–17; Luibhéid and Rorem 1987: 265 n. 8). Their appellation, *T'ondrakets'i* in Armenian (mere transliteration of the Greek word, q.v. *Theandrikos* in Lampe (1961: 615)), must have been in vogue prior to the Armenian translation of Pseudo-Dionysius in the eighth century, where this theologically significant word is rendered *Astuatsayrakan* (q.v. in Thomson (1997: 38); the same Dionysian passage is cited by Anania of Narek in his counter to the Dyophysites, *The Basis of Faith* (*Hawatarmat*, in *MH* 10: 546), and added to *The Seal of Faith*, initially a seventh-century compilation of dogma (*Knik' hawatoy*, in *MH* 4: 230)). After all, Monothelitism appeared in the western provinces of Armenia (the Byzantine east) early in the seventh century as a logical offshoot of Eutychian Monophysitism and had a substantial appeal for a considerable period (cf. Dorfmann-Lazarev 2013: 364–365). For their Christological position the Eutychians were repeatedly denounced by Dyophysites and Miaphysites alike, and were persecuted especially after being radicalized in Armenia by Smbat of Zarehawan early in the ninth century (Magistros, *Ep.* iv–v (lxvii–lxviii), in *MH* 16: 192–207). As they were driven eastward, they must have congregated southwest of Manzikert, in a locality that conceivably derived its name, T'ondrak (today's Tendürek), from the faith identity of the newcomers into the District of Apahunik'. The proper name, unattested in earlier sources, survives in two other districts: Tarōn in the west and Kogovit in the east. After all, it would be strange for a heretical movement to derive its name from a toponym.

Moreover, Dionysian spirituality provided ideas and formulas that generated several beliefs besides conditioning others within the bounds of orthodoxy that were anticipated by the Cappadocian Fathers. Not the least of these is the doctrine of *theosis* or deification, which was but a logical *telos* in Christian mysticism: from likeness to God to participation and communion or union with the Divine (Kharlamov 2009: 4–6, 25–34, 58–61, 135–158, 225–234). Judging from the mystical theology of Gregory's prayer book, as we shall see below, the predominantly Byzantine doctrine must have been cherished at Narek. This may have been a factor in bringing the monastery further under scrutiny by the staunchly anti-Chalcedonian and overly suspicious Armenian hierarchy of the time.

With suspicions of heresy besetting his monastic establishment, Anania of Narek was probably compelled to write a treatise against the T'ondrakeans, the arch-heretics of his time. Such a treatise is mentioned in the works of three contemporaries: (1) twice in Gregory's admonition to the brotherhood of Kchaw (*MH* 12: 1087–1089), which will be discussed further; (2) in the above-mentioned *History* by Asoghik (3.7, in *MH* 15: 753); and (3) in a letter by the savant Gregory Magistros (d. 1059), who was heavily involved in persecuting the T'ondrakeans at the time (*Ep.* iv (lxvii), in *MH* 16: 196). The treatise is mentioned also in an encyclical by the above-mentioned Catholicos Nersēs of Klay, a great-grandson of Magistros (1871: 269), who knew of remnants of the T'ondrakeans in northern Mesopotamia; but only Magistros states that this treatise was written upon the request of Catholicos Anania of Mokk'. This work, however, no longer exists except for an excerpt utilized by the prolific writer and *vardapet* John of Erzĕnka (d. 1293) (*MH* 10: 436–438). Simply an ecclesiological fragment elaborating on the meaning of church, the excerpt has no mention of the T'ondrakeans or of anything inimical to the church.

Apparently the treatise was not enough to dispel suspicions, and the abbot was pressured to the very end, as revealed in a deathbed denunciation of the T'ondrakeans with a litany of anathemas attributed to him and most likely addressed to Catholicos Khach'ik of R̄shtunik' (in office 972–992), a nephew of Anania of Mokk' (*MH* 10: 649–657). There is no reason to doubt the authenticity of this coerced document sent "to the one who is 'just' unjustly and 'familiar' with the unfamiliar, an estranged relative (or, sibling), and who – being lord (or, master, used epithetically for bishops and other hierarchs) from birth to old age – does not recognize a servant's good deeds or faithful service." Moreover, in closing, the abbot reminds of his earlier, now lost, treatise against the T'ondrakeans. It was upon Catholicos Khach'ik''s request that Anania had also written his polemical response to the Dyophysites, as his contribution to the Armenian Church's counter to the Byzantines (*Hawatarmat*, in *MH* 10: 480–598). The latter work is mentioned by Ukhtanēs, who was a classmate of Gregory of Narek and later Bishop of Sebastia (970–985), and who wrote a history from biblical times to the schism because of Chalcedon upon the request of the abbot Anania for the same endeavor urged by the catholicos (*History*, in *MH* 15: 446–608). He calls the abbot Anania his "spiritual father" and himself "an unworthy disciple" (*MH* 15: 446). Of the tenth-century historians, only Asoghik mentions the T'ondrakeans, and that only in passing, as he refers to the appearance of Smbad "of the T'ondrakeans" (Arm. *T'ondrakats'*, not a toponym) when Catholicos Yovhannēs of Ova was in office (832/833–854/855); and again when listing the great *vardapets* of his time, including "the great philosopher Anania, who is a monk at Narek. To him belongs a treatise against the sect of the T'ondrakeans [*T'ondrakats'*] and other heretics"; but he says nothing more about them (*History* 3.3, 7, in *MH* 15: 742, 753).

Gregory of Narek's cautionary *Letter* to the brotherhood of Kchaw, a neighboring monastery in the Van region, is addressed to the abbot whose community has come under the influence of the "accursed T'ondrakeans" (*MH* 12: 1087–1089). The document – in which he draws repeated attention to the treatise by his abbot Anania – constitutes a summary of generally perceived tenets of the movement in his day. He begins with an apologetic disclaimer for "any semblance of polemics" in what he writes. He lists the sectarians' 14 tenets, albeit some repetitious (Nersessian 1987: 57–58). The short denunciation, with the comprehensive list at its core, could well be the reason for the survival of Gregory's works and of his saintly status in the Armenian Church. Whether or not he cherished anti-hierarchical sentiments, his father's encounter with Catholicos Anania of Mokk' to the point of being anathematized coupled with the mystical theology pursued at Narek and the poisoned atmosphere of the times were probable causes for his being thrown in the company of suspects. A statement of loyalty was exacted from those thus suspected, by having them denounce the T'ondrakeans in one form or another. Gregory's framing his denunciation as a letter of concern for monastic brothers has to be seen as part of his creative genius.

Undoubtedly, the anti-T'ondrakean documents originating from Narek were coerced. A written denunciation of the T'ondrakeans, whose name in the tenth century was equated with anti-hierarchical or anti-establishment movements, was tantamount to an oath of loyalty not only to the Church but also to its hierarchy, even submission to an obstinate hierarch.

Gregory's Works

Gregory's renown rests primarily on the excellence of his *Book of Lamentation*, in Armenian *Matean Voghbergut'ean*, a codex of predominantly penitential prayers from the closing years of his life and reflecting the height of his spiritual and literary attainment. By contrast, his earlier works are less known. With the exception of the odes, they do not always reflect the quality of his later achievement; nonetheless, they are literary gems that deserve scholarly attention. They are quite important works for the study of medieval Armenian lyric poetry and of the liturgical development of the time. Unlike his mournful, penitential prayers, a celebratory mood permeates these works. As his colophons indicate, two of his encomia, "On the Holy Cross" and "On the Holy Virgin," along with the *History of the Cross of Aparank'*, were commissioned works, as was his earlier *Commentary on the Song of Songs*. He must have attained recognition for his literary ability early in life to be asked to produce these compositions – to certain of which he refers in his prayers.

The expanded cataloguing of ancient manuscripts at the Matenadaran in recent years has led to forgotten works of Gregory of Narek; and the accompanying textual studies have helped settle hitherto unresolved questions regarding the authorship of long-known others in favor of our author. Of course, the rediscovered works require authorial substantiation, and this is remarkably well done in the introductions to these works now with the others in the *MH* series, in vols 10 and 12 (the latter devoted to our author in its entirety). Both T'amrazyan and Mirzoyan follow a sound method of authentication by focusing on Gregory's distinct language with its peculiar vocabulary.

Several of Gregory's long-known works have been mentioned in the preceding pages aimed at contextualizing them historically and, earlier, to acquaint the reader with the current state of scholarship. Here, then, is a list of Gregory's established works, as found in the *MH* series, where all his works are readily accessible for the first time. The titles are followed with page numbers in this new *textus receptus*. Helpful introductions by the respective editors of the mostly diplomatic texts precede the page numbers given here. Of particular importance nowadays are T'amrazyan's introductions in vol. 10, where he argues convincingly for the authorship of the four less-known works. These I have listed after those in vol. 12.

1. *Book of Lamentation* (Arm. *Matean oghbergut'ean*, as in *Prayer* 2.2; 9.1; 53:2; 70.3; 71:5; 88.2); in *MH* 12: 49–605. This is Gregory's *magnum opus* and the last of his works, written when looking death in the eye. It consists of 95 prayers, each comprised of several sections. According to his colophon, it was assembled over a period of 3 years, from fragments to completion in 1002, with the help of his older brother John, then abbot of Narek, who was with him "in the same pathway, seeing the same mystic vision."

2. *Odes and Litanies* (Arm. *Tagher ew Gandzer*; or, collectively, *Gandztetr*); in *MH* 12: 623–745. A collection of 30 hymnic odes and 11 litanies composed – along with the *Encomia* – as festal works, for Dominical and other feasts. In *Prayer* 34.10 the author alludes to his writings in this genre.

3. *Commentary on the Songs of Songs* (Arm. *Meknut'iwn Ergots' Ergoyn Soghomoni*); in *MH* 12: 760–882. The author's colophon at the end (pp. 882–883), dated AD 977, tells that he wrote it upon the request of Prince Gurgēn Artsruni (co-reigned as King of Vaspurakan with his brothers, 977–1003).

4. *Commentary on Job: "Who is This...?"* (Arm. *Meknut'iwn "Ov ē Da"i*); in *MH* 12: 885–910. On chapters 38 and 39, the first of God's two discourses comprising the epilogue of Job, beginning with the words "Who is this...?" (38:2).

5. *The Story of the Holy Cross of Aparank'* (Arm. *'Patmut'iwn Aparanits' S. Khach'in*); in *MH* 12: 913–929, on how a relic of the true Cross was brought to the monastery of Aparank' in the District of Mokk' (Gk. Moxoēnē; Syr. Bēth Moksāyē), in the Khizan region near Lake Van. The account concludes with anticipation of the next two encomia. The colophon at the end of the *Encomium on the Blessed Virgin* indicates that all three works were written for the bishop of the district, Step'anos.

6. *Encomium on the Holy Cross* (Arm. *Nerbogh i Surb Khach'n*), in two recensions: A in *MH* 12: 930–941, B in *MH* 12: 942–952. The long-known recension B preserves a preferred text. The encomium is written as a sequel to *The Story of the Holy Cross of Aparank'*.

7. *Encomium on the Blessed Virgin* (Arm. *Nerbogh i Surb Koysn*), in two recensions: A in *MH* 12: 953–963, B in 965–974. The author refers to this encomium in *Prayer* 80.1. The colophon found at the end, in both recensions (A in *MH* 12: 963–964, B in 974–975), names Step'anos Bishop of Mokk' as the receiver of the work (see above, no. 5).

8. *Encomium on the Holy Apostles* (Arm. *Nerbogh i Surb Afak'ealsn*); in *MH* 12: 976–989. The subtitle has: "An encomium recited in praise of the full circle of the twelve apostles, who are first in honor among the prominent heads, and to the seventy-two holy disciples of Christ." The author refers to this encomium in Prayer 82.1.

9. *Encomium on Saint James of Nisibis* (Arm. *Nerbogh i Surbn Yakob Mtsbnay*); in *MH* 12: 990–1005. St James (Jacob of Nusaybin), a signatory at the Council of Nicaea in 325, was the patron saint of the region where Gregory lived.

10. *Exhortation to Orthodox Faith and Pure and Virtuous Life* (Arm. *Ban khratu vasn ughigh hawatoyn ew mak'ur varuts' afak'inut'ean*); in *MH* 12: 1022–1084). A hortatory and admonitory text, written for a certain Vardan, a relative and official in the secretariat (possibly of the royal court of the Vaspurakan Artsrunis).

11. *Letter to the Admirable and Prominent Congregation of Kchaw* (Arm. *T'ught' i hoyakap ew yakanawor ukhtn Kchaway*); in *MH* 12: 1087–1089. Sent to the abbot of a neighboring monastic community to caution about the heretical T'ontrakeans.

12. *Discourse.* "Look within Yourself: Perhaps There Is Something Errant in Your Heart" (Arm. *Chaf. "Hayeats' yandzn k'o, guts'ē linits'i ban tsatsuk i srti k'o anawrēn"*); in *MH* 10: 1040–1072.

13. *Order and Rules of Prayer* (Arm. *Karg ew kanon aghawt'its'*); in *MH* 10: 1081–1094. Written upon the request of an anonymous monk, the treatise carries echoes from Khosrov's *Exposition of the Daily Office*.

14. *Eulogy for Vardapets and Wise Priests* (Arm. *Vardapetats' ew imastun k'ahanayits' vakhchani ban*); in *MH* 10: 1103–1105. Written to mourn the passing of an unnamed monastic teacher, probably the abbot Anania of Narek, and used by others to eulogize later *vardapets* and priests – as the redacted title suggests.

15. *Commentary by the Holy Teachers of the Church on "The Lord's Prayer"* (Arm. *Meknut'iwn srbots' vardapetats' ekeghets'oy arareal i "Hayr mer, or yerkins"n*); in *MH* 10: 1106–1110. A sentence-by-sentence commentary on Matt 6: 9–13, with some repeated lemmata indicating a chain of quotations, from anonymous Fathers.

Gregory's Mystic Theology

The remarks in this sketch of Gregory's mystic theology are limited to his prayer book, a book "mixed" with the Spirit (3.5). Its 95 prayers are often perceived as carrying the reader through the church: from the narthex to the nave and on to the altar, where the mystic union is symbolically realized. Just as often, this tripartite division is arbitrarily applied to the book, which does not permit such a structure. However, the author's mystic theology is much more intricate, based as it is on sacramental theology with its locus in the church.

Gregory presents his prayers, "a new book of psalms," not only as a lasting spiritual help to posterity (3.2, 3, 5; 26.4; 54.5; 66.1; 83.1; 90.6; 93.6) but as his best offering to God (2.2; 10:2; 34.10; 55.2; 70:3; 88.2, 3): a token of reciprocity for God's gifts that begin with birth "in the image of God." This kinship with the Divine image, damaged by sin and restored through redemption (19.1; 20.7; 40.3; 46.2–3; 67.1; 87.3), is the starting point of his mystic theology that at its apex allows him to claim to have seen God (5.2, 3; 27.6, 9; 82.5). The vision of God is realized in encountering the unapproachable Light, one of the most recurring words in his prayers. Early in his introduction of this theme, he prays: "At the start of these prayers with sobbing, let your kind will strengthen me even here so that I, a waverer, might not be found unfit to enjoy the edification by your light when the heavens open" (2.2; cf. 18.4, 7; 20.7; 27.2; 28.6; 32.6; 93.2, 19). Not that God is defined as light – this is only a metaphor for God (82.1; 95.1) whose image could not be drawn (92.5). God is the unknowable One (*passim*); even Christ, reachable as he is (89), remains incomprehensible (90.5). Yet, one could partake of the Divine, indeed participate in the life of the Divine and thus be united with God through the efficacy of the sacraments of the Eucharist and baptism (33 and 93; cf. 14.3; 49.1).

When carried to its fullness, the theology of baptism and the Eucharist could lead to belief in deification. Gregory expresses this conviction – not just the concept – with reference to the Eucharist in 52.3: "And what is overwhelming for me to say in sequence here, in remembrance of your great beneficence, is to become divine by the grace of election and to join you, O Creator, by partaking of your lordly body, and to be united with your luminous life, which is the fulfillment of the blessed promise." And again, with reference to baptism in 93:20: "Through this anointing we are bound again with hope to the ineffable mystery of your cross, O Christ; by being baptized into your death, O living One, we share in your eternal life, even you yourself, O God, being enabled to the utmost, eternally, fully, inseparably" (cf. 93.2, 6, 9, 11, 13, 24). It is this sacramental union with God, no less than the affinity with the Divine image, that enables the merging of the soul with the divine Spirit (78.4; 85.2; 90.5; 92.11). He considers the soul's every movement as a reminder of God (31.3).

The word "light" appears more than 40 times in *Prayer* 93, on the Holy Myron or sacred oil used for chrismation, ever conditioning the belief that through the sacraments one can really be united with God (93.2, 6, 9, 11, 13, 24). Chrismation is tantamount to being sealed with Christ by God, a confirmation of the hope to be with the Lord always. Gregory prays: "Give me the sweetness of hope, even though I do not deserve to have any portion of the offered light. Help me loosen the knot of this hidden mystery" (93.9). And again: "And we understand from this as a fitting interpretation, that the consummation of this mystic calling is realized in us, who have the foremost honor of being called Christians" (93.13). The church, as an edifice of light, "heavenly mother of light," indeed heaven on earth where light is dispensed, is the ideal locus for the mystic ascent to God's light. In *Prayer* 75, where he spells out his ecclesiology and where the word "light" is used 22 times, he exclaims at the outset: "Flying on the wings of light, behold, I have arrived in heaven."

In one of his most mystical prayers addressed to the Holy Spirit, in which he describes himself as one who has received "visions of light" and other "splendid visions" (33.3) and being "clothed with God, inside and out" (33.4), Gregory divulges a prayer he offered habitually before celebrating the Eucharist (33.6–7). He repeated this prayer as often as necessary, until its earnest hope or wish was realized: "I shall go on repeating the same sequence of words until the certainty that comes with the contemplation of light is wondrously revealed, heralding, proclaiming anew the good news of ever more peace" (33.7). This prayer has found a rightful place at the beginning of the Divine Liturgy of the Armenian Church, to be prayed by the celebrant (for more on this prayer, see Russell (1996–1997)).

One of Gregory's most intimate prayers is addressed to Mary for her intercession. He pleads: "Weave me, join me – a sinner who has sighed bitterly – into the happy and incensed company of those who have looked up to you, the plant of life with the blessed Fruit" (80.1). "Glorify your Son, by performing upon me the divine miracle of mercy and pardon, hand-maid and Mother of God" (80.2). The way he describes his closeness to her is possibly unparalleled in sacred literature devoted to the Theotokos. At one point he places himself in her lap, as he prays: "Please, let a drop of your virgin milk drop on me" (80.3). His intimacy extends to the Trinity: "O living Word: receive and present me, a debtor to all, atoned and cleansed, to your co-equal Spirit; that having been reconciled again through you, he may return to me; that through you the mighty One – by his own will – may present me to the Father. Thus, with him and through him, I may always be bound with grace to you – as closely as my breath, to be inseparably united with you" (24.4).

For Gregory, "Faith, that blessed and favored word, which lasts forever untarnished and unbounded, honored together with love and hope, brings the rewards of truly clear vision, perfect wisdom, intimacy with God and familiarity with the Most High" (10.4). Yet, for him, faith does not preclude doubt. "How much of the light of living hope can I mix with the darkness of doubt?" (68.4). His keen understanding of faith as emanating from doubt is a recurring theme in the prayers, even from the very first (1.2). Like faith and doubt, the duality of the mystic's role – as one who seeks and is sought – is often blurred. Gregory was good at playing this hide-and-seek game with God. Yet, aware of the mystery of his own reality vis-à-vis the superior mystery of God, he surrenders again and again. "It is important to confess and cast the veil from my face to one who seeks to know me" (19.3).

Gregory is rightly reckoned with those who have experienced the infinite and word-defying Mystery that is God. He articulates a theologically informed and mystically contemplated faith, especially in his prayers. His writings emanate from his ancestral faith; conversely, he has strongly influenced and enriched that faith while expressing or communicating it.

Bibliography

Primary Sources

Armenian Classical Authors. *Matenagirk' Hayots'* (abbr. *MH*), Zaven Yegavian (general editor) (2003–). Vols 1 ff. Antelias: Armenian Catholicosate of Cilicia.

Dionysius the Areopagite. *The Armenian Version of the Works Attributed to Dionysius the Areopagite*, Robert W. Thomson (ed./transl.) (1987). CSCO 488–489/

Scriptores Armeniaci 17–18. Louvain: Peeters.

Dionysius the Areopagite. *Pseudo-Dionysius: The Complete Works*, Colm Luibhéid and Paul Rorem (transl.) (1987). The Classics of Western Spirituality. New York: Paulist Press.

Ełishē. *A Homily on the Passion of Christ Attributed to Ełishē. Translated from the Classical Armenian with Introduction and Notes*, Robert W. Thomson (transl.) (2000). Eastern Christian Texts in Translation 5. Louvain: Peeters.

Gregory of Narek. *The Blessing of Blessings: Gregory of Narek's Commentary on the Song of Songs*, Roberta R. Ervine (transl. from the Armenian) (2007). Cistercian Studies 215. Kalamazoo, MI: Cistercian Publications.

Gregory of Narek. *Grégoire de Narek: Commentaire sur le Cantique des Cantiques. Introduction, traduction et notes*, Lévon Pétrossian (transl.) (2010). OCA 285. Rome: Pontificio Istituto Orientale, 2010.

Gregory of Narek. *Grégoire de Narek. Tragédie. Matean ołbergut'ean. Le Livre de Lamentation. Introduction, traduction et notes*, Annie Mahé and Jean-Pierre Mahé (transl.) (2000). CSCO 584/Subsidia 106. Louvain: Peeters.

Gregory of Narek. *Grigor Narekats'i: Matean oghbergut'ean* [Book of Lamentation], P.M. Khach'atryan and A.A. Ghazinyan (eds) (1985). Erevan: Armenian Academy of Sciences.

Gregory of Narek. *Grigor Narekats'i: Tagher ev Gandzer* [Odes and Litanies], Armine K'yoshkeryan (ed.) (1981). Erevan: Armenian Academy of Sciences.

Gregory of Narek. *Kniga skorbi: poèma/Grigor Narekatsi*, Naum Grebnev (transl.) (1977), Preface by Levon Mkrtch'yan. Erevan: Sovetakan Grogh. (Reprint, Erevan: Narek, 1995).

Gregory of Narek. *Kniga skorbnikh pesnopeniǐ/ Grigor Narekatsi*, M.O. Darbinyan-Melik'yan and L.A. Khanlaryan (eds) (1988). Pamiatniki pis'mennosti Vostoka 77. Moscow: "Nauka" Glav. red. vostochnoǐ lit-ry.

Gregory of Narek. *Le Panégyrique de la Sainte Mère de Dieu de Grigor Narekac'i: Introduction, traduction, commentaire*, Tamar Dasnabédian (transl.) (1995). Antélias, Liban: Catholicossat Arménien de Cilicie.

Gregory of Narek. *Paroles à Dieu de Grégoire de Narek. Introduction, traduction et notes*, Annie Mahé and Jean-Pierre Mahé (transl.) (2007). Louvain: Peeters.

Gregory of Narek. *S. Grigor Narekats'i. Matean oghbergut'ean ew ayl erkasirut'iwnk* [St Gregory of Narek: Book of Lamentation and Other Works], Zareh Aznaworian (ed.) (2003). Antelias: Armenian Catholicosate of Cilicia.

Gregory of Narek. *St. Grigor Narekats'i. Speaking with God from the Depths of the Heart: The Armenian Prayer Book of St. Gregory of Narek*. Thomas J. Samuelian (English translation and Introduction) (2001). Erevan: Vem Press.

Khosrov of Andzewats'ik'. *Commentary on the Divine Liturgy by Xosrov Anjewac'i*, S. Peter Cowe (translated with an Introduction) (1991). Armenian Church Classics. New York: St Vartan Press.

Nersēs of Klay (Shnorhali) (1871). *Ĕndhanrakan T'ught'k'* [Encyclicals]. Jerusalem: St James Press.

Secondary Sources

Dorfmann-Lazarev, Igor (2013), "Travels and studies of Stephen of Siwnik' (c.685–735): redefining Armenian orthodoxy under Islamic rule". In *Heresy and the Making of European Culture: Medieval and Modern Perspectives*, Andrew P. Roach and James R. Simpson (eds). Farnham: Ashgate; 355–381.

Garsoïan, Nina G. (1967), *The Paulician Heresy: A Study of the Origin and Development of Paulicianism in Armenia and the Eastern Provinces of the Byzantine Empire*. The Hague: Mouton.

Khach'atryan, Poghos (1996), *Grigor Narekats'in ev hay mijnadarě* [*Gregory of Narek and the Armenian Middle Ages*]. Ējmiatsin: Mother See Press.

Kharlamov, Vladimir (2009), *The Beauty of the Unity and the Harmony of the Whole: The Concept of Theosis in the Theology of Pseudo-Dionysius the Areopagite*. Eugene, OR: Wipf & Stock.

La Porta, Sergio. (2007), "The reception and influence of the corpus of works attributed to Dionysius the Areopagite in the medieval Armenian spiritual tradition". *ARC, The Journal of the Faculty of Religious Studies, McGill University*, 35: 211–226.

La Porta, Sergio (2009–2010), "Two visions of mysticism: the Corpus Dionysiacum and the Book of Lamentation." In Jean-Pierre Mahé *et al.* (2009–2010: 243–257).

Lampe, G.W.H. (1961), *A Patristic Greek Lexicon*. Oxford: Clarendon.

Mahé, Jean-Pierre and Zekiyan, Boghos Levon (eds) (2006), *Saint Grégoire de Narek, Théologien et Mystique*. OCA 275. Rome: Pontificio Istituto Orientale.

Mahé, Jean-Pierre, Rouhana, Paul, and Zekiyan, Boghos Levon (eds) (2009–2010), *Saint Grégoire de Narek et la liturgie de l'Église. Colloque international organisé par le Patriarcat Arménien Catholique à l'Université Saint-Esprit de Kaslik (USEK), Liban. Actes publiés.* Revue Théologique de Kaslik 3–4. Kaslik: Faculté Pontificale de Théologie/Université Saint-Esprit.

Maksoudian, Krikor. (1988–1989), "The Chalcedonian issue and the early Bagradits: the Council of Širakawan". *Revue des études arméniennes*, 21: 333–344.

Maksoudian, Krikor. (1990–1991), "A note on the monasteries founded during the reign of King Abas I Bagratuni". *Revue des études arméniennes*, 22: 203–215.

Mirzoyan, Hrach'ik Gh. (2010), *Narekats'iagitakan hetazotut'yunner* [*Studies on Narekats'i and Related Subjects*]. Erevan: Erevan State University.

Pelikan, Jaroslav (1987) "The odyssey of Dionysian spirituality". In *Pseudo-Dionysius: The Complete Works*, Colm Luibhéid and Paul Rorem (transl.). The Classics of Western Spirituality. New York: Paulist Press; 11–24.

Pogossian, Zaroui (2012), "The foundation of the Monastery of Sevan: a case study on monasteries, economy and political power in IX–X century Armenia". In *Le Valli dei Monaci: Atti del III Convegno Internazionale di Studio "De Re Monastica", Roma-Subiaco, 17–19 maggio, 2010*, Vol. 1, Letizia Ermini Pani (ed.). Spoleto: Centro Italiano di Studi sull'Alto Medioevo; 181–215.

Russell, James R. (1996–1997), "Armenian spirituality: liturgical mysticism and Chapter 33 of the Book of Lamentation of St. Grigor Narekac'i". *Revue des études arméniennes*, 26: 427–439.

T'amrazyan, Hrach'ya H. (1986), *Anania Narekats'i, Kyank'ě ev matenagrut'yuně* [*Anania of Narek: His Life and Works*]. Erevan: Armenian Academy of Sciences.

T'amrazyan, Hrach'ya H. (1999), *Narekyan dprots'ě* [*The School of Narek*]. Erevan: Hayastan.

T'amrazyan, Hrach'ya H. (2004), *Grigor Narekats'in ev Norplatonakanut'yuně* [*Gregory of Narek and Neoplatonism*]. Erevan: Nairi.

Thierry, Jean-Michel (1980), *Le couvent arménien d'Hoṙomos*. Matériaux pour l'archéologie arménienne 2. Louvain: Peeters.

Thierry, Jean-Michel (1989), *Monument arméniens du Vaspurakan*. Bibliothèque archéologique et historique 129. Paris: Libr. orientaliste Paul Geuthner.

Thomson, Robert W. (1997), *Indices to the Armenian Version of Pseudo-Dionysius the Areopagite: Greek–Armenian and Armenian–Greek*. Dutch Studies in Armenian Language and Literature 5. Amsterdam: Rodopi.

Yarnley, C.J. (1976), "The Armenian Philhellenes: a study of the spread of Byzantine religious and cultural ideas among the Armenians in the X–XIth centuries A.D." *Eastern Churches Review*, 8/1: 45–53.

CHAPTER 20
Gregory Palamas

Marcus Plested

Introduction

The foremost theologian of the late Byzantine era, S Gregory Palamas (c. 1296–1357) stands as a peculiarly intriguing instance of patristic reception and transmission. A self-consciously patristic writer, anxious above all else to demonstrate his continuity with the teaching of the Fathers, Palamas nonetheless pioneered a fresh and distinctive articulation of that tradition oriented around the distinction between the divine essence and the divine activity, operation, or energy. This is a distinction that many of his contemporaries found novel and, consequently, incompatible with the patristic witness. Such opposition notwithstanding, it was Palamas' interpretation and representation of patristic tradition that triumphed at a series of Constantinopolitan councils in 1341, 1347, 1351, and 1368, thereby decisively shaping the way in which the Fathers were to be read and interpreted in the Eastern Orthodox Church for centuries to come. And while Palamas' impact and legacy, not unlike that of Aquinas in the West, has been subject to peaks and troughs, it would not be an exaggeration to characterize modern Eastern Orthodox theology (and by extension modern Eastern Orthodox patristic studies) as broadly, if by no means exclusively, Palamite in character.

Palamas' own educational background and spiritual formation provided him with a rich repository of philosophical and theological material from which to draw. Well-born and a precociously gifted student of Aristotle in his youth, Palamas eschewed the glittering prizes of a secular career in favor of the monastic life. His was not, however, to be a life of either seclusion or stability. Despite brief spells at the Athonite monasteries of the Great Lavra and Esphigmenou, together with several more prolonged periods in various semi-eremitic communities, Palamas was to spend the greater part of his monastic career engaged in heated and very public theological controversy at the heart of the Empire in the midst of a tumultuous civil war. His writings, produced for the most part

The Wiley Blackwell Companion to Patristics, First Edition. Edited by Ken Parry.
© 2015 John Wiley & Sons Ltd. Published 2019 by John Wiley & Sons Ltd.

within the context of this controversy, bear witness to a solid grounding in classical philosophy together with a profound immersion in the theological and spiritual teaching of the Christian east. Looming most large among his patristic sources are Dionysius the Areopagite, the Cappadocian Fathers, St Cyril of Alexandria, St Maximus the Confessor, Macarius-Symeon (pseudo-Macarius), and Evagrius of Pontus. Palamas also displays a cautious sympathy with St Augustine (Flogaus 1996; Demetracopoulos 1997). Macarius-Symeon was of particular importance as an authority on the vision of the divine light, a theme absolutely central to Gregory's more recent ascetic sources and teachers within the Hesychast tradition, most notably St Gregory of Sinai, St Theoleptos of Philadelphia, and St Nikephoros the Hesychast.

Palamas and His Opponents

Palamas' entry into the theological fray is marked by his *Apodictic Treatises* of 1335, pressing the case for the possibility of apodictic or demonstrative argumentation within the sphere of theology contrary to the relativizing position on the *Filioque* espoused by Barlaam the Calabrian (c. 1290–1348) in his anti-Latin disputations of 1333–1334. The dispute with Barlaam widened to include a defense of the bodily postures adopted by the Hesychast monks in prayer coupled with a robust assertion of the possibility of authentic religious experience, as witnessed most especially in the vision of God as light – understood to be the same uncreated light that shone from Christ at the Transfiguration. Only in its later stages, witnessed in the third *Triad in Defence of the Holy Hesychasts* (1340), does the debate begin to turn around the distinction between the imparticipable divine essence and the participable divine operations, activities, or energies. This distinction, intended as a means of maintaining divine transcendence while simultaneously affirming the reality of God's self-revelation in and to the world, was from the outset presented as being in strict conformity with the teachings of the Fathers and Councils, whether this be the dynamic of union and distinction of Dionysius, the Cappadocian references to the (knowable) energies and (unknowable) essence of God, or the teachings of Maximus the Confessor and the Sixth Ecumenical Council on the relation between nature and energy. Barlaam was no great patristic scholar and had little answer to this claim of continuity. In any event, he became an irrelevance after the council of 1341 and the first formal conciliar adoption of the essence–energies distinction, departing Byzantium in high dudgeon.

A more serious opposition to Palamas' assertion of patristic fidelity emerged in the shape of Gregory Akindynos, a Hesychast monk with powerful connections (Nadal Cañellas 2006). Akindynos bases himself squarely on the patristic witness, relentlessly taxing Palamas as an innovator and betrayer of the united witness of the Fathers, all of whom are seen to declare and declaim the unity and simplicity of God. Athanasius, the Cappadocian Fathers, Cyril of Alexandria, and Dionysius the Areopagite are his chief resources in his attempt to paint Palamas as the worst sort of heretic – a polytheist – one who has created a multitude of divinities through an absurd sundering and mutilation of the divinity. Akindynos' charge of innovation was a powerful one and did much to diminish and undermine Palamas' position in the delicate years of the regency of John V, prior to the ascendency of the pro-Palamite emperor John VI Kantakuzene (1347–1354) and the attendant Palamite councils of 1347 and 1351. The council of 1351 is by far the most theologically expansive and detailed of the Palamite councils and is the source of the Palamite chapters contained within the Synodikon of Orthodoxy recited in principle throughout the Orthodox world on the Sunday of Orthodoxy, the first Sunday of Great Lent. Akindynos died shortly after the council of 1347 and was succeeded as leader of the anti-Palamite party by Nikephoros Gregoras, a learned monk and prolific scholar. Gregoras kept up the charge of patristic infidelity and wanton innovation against Palamas throughout the 1350s, adding for good measure a charge of incipient Platonism. But for all the efforts of such able opponents, Palamite theology was never to be seriously threatened again.

This all but unassailable position was confirmed by the Constantinopolitan council of 1368, summoned to respond to the rather belated attempt on the part of another learned monk, Prochoros Kydones, to call into question both Palamite theology and, significantly, the liturgical *cultus* of Palamas (d. 1357) (Plested 2012: 73–84). Prochoros reiterates the charge of innovation and patristic infidelity while also gleaning certain objections to Palamism from his reading and translation of Thomas Aquinas. Prochoros was condemned in no uncertain terms as a poor student of the Fathers and a crypto-Arian (and *not* for his Thomist leanings). The council of 1368 asserted in stark terms the strict conformity of Palamite teaching with the united witness of scripture and tradition, sealing that assertion with the formal recognition of Palamas as a Saint and Father of the Church (Rigo 2004: 127). The presiding patriarch, Philotheos Kokkinos (who had already written extensively against Gregoras), went on to compose the liturgical service in Gregory's honor, hailing him as "light of orthodoxy" and "invincible champion of theologians." The service was appointed to be celebrated not only on the day of his repose (November 14) but also on the second Sunday of Great Lent as a second "Triumph of Orthodoxy" (the first being the commemoration on the first Sunday of the restoration of the icons in 843). The condemnation of Prochoros served to generate a number of extensive theological defenses of Palamite theology, most notably by the works on the light of Thabor composed by Theophanes of Nicaea and the former Emperor John Kantakuzene (by then a monk after his deposition in 1354).

A concerted campaign was launched by successive Palamite patriarchs of Constantinople to ensure the acceptance of Palamite theology across the Orthodox world, a task largely completed by the end of the fourteenth century. One of the very few voices publicly opposing the Palamite "innovation" after 1368 was Prochoros' elder brother Demetrios, a statesman of great power and unusual longevity protected by his close association with the Emperors John V and Manuel II. Demetrios, a Roman Catholic convert, had long kept his reservations about Palamas under wraps but found such discretion impossible to maintain after his brother's condemnation, attacking the "new dogmas" of Palamas as an intolerable assault on the divine simplicity warranted neither by Scripture, nor by patristic tradition (Gregory of Nazianzus being his chief witness), nor by reason (Candal 1962).

Latin reactions to Palamite theology were not immediately enthusiastic. The papal legate Paul of Smyrna was present in 1355 at one of the dialogues between Palamas and Gregoras and appears to have reported back unfavorably to Rome on this new development in Orthodox theology, notwithstanding Palamas' constant insistence on the strictly traditional character of his teaching and the conciliatory efforts of John Kantakuzene (Voordeckers and Tinnefeld 1987). But the hesitations of the legate do not appear to have impacted the official stance of the Church of Rome, which has consistently remained reluctant to make a stumbling block of the essence–energies distinction. Certainly, Rome felt no imperative to press the question at the reunion council of Ferrara–Florence (1438–1439), despite initially suggesting it as a possible area for clarification. The Byzantines, for their part, were forbidden from discussing the question by Emperor John VIII. Writers opposed to the Florentine union continued, however, to emphasize the essence–energies distinction as a fundamental difference between Greek east and Latin west. Most prominent among these are the successive leaders of the anti-unionist party down to and beyond the Fall of Constantinople in 1453, St Mark of Ephesus and George (later Patriarch Gennadios) Scholarios. Scholarios numbers the failure to acknowledge the distinction with the *Filioque* and the papal claims to primacy as among the few regrettable recent aberrations of the Church of Rome embraced perforce by Thomas Aquinas, whom he otherwise regards as "the most excellent expositor and interpreter of Christian theology" (Petit *et al.* 1928–1936: vol. 5, 1–2).

Scholarios was also to find resources elsewhere within medieval Latin scholasticism for a nuancing of Palamite theology, notably in terms of the category of formal distinction associated with Duns Scotus. Several other Byzantine Palamites (such as John Kantakuzene and Theophanes of Nicaea) had also drawn on Latin theology in their expositions and defense of Palamite theology, speaking, for instance, of the distinction as "conceptual" as opposed to "real." Such nuancing (which continued into the Ottoman period) has been read as a watering down of Palamite theology (Jugie 1932) or even as a conscious departure from Palamas (Demetracopoulos 2011). Perhaps more compelling is the intriguing suggestion that the Byzantine Palamites were feeling their way towards an expression of a more than notional intra-divine distinction that in no way compromised the divine simplicity and which went operated beyond the parameters of a simple choice between *distinctio rationis* and *distinctio realis*. In this analysis, the Byzantine *diakrisis kat'epinoian* corresponds precisely to neither of these options but rather more closely to the Latin *distinctio rationis cum fundamento in re* (Levy 2012). Be that as it may, it is at least doubtful that Palamas' notion of a "real" distinction corresponds precisely with the *distinctio realis* of Latin scholasticism. Any deviation from the language of real distinction in Byzantine theologians better versed in Latin scholasticism than Palamas (as in Scholarios' use of the Scotist category of formal distinction) need not, therefore, be regarded as a betrayal but rather as a nuance of Palamite teaching.

The Early Modern Period

The efforts of Scholarios helped assure the prominence of the theology of St Gregory Palamas in the Eastern Orthodox Church of the immediate post-Byzantine period, as manifest in the Council of Constantinople of 1484. This council formally renounced the Florentine union and appointed chrismation for the reception of converts from Roman Catholicism. In the service of reception produced for this purpose the Council includes by implication the Palamite councils in its reference to the councils "fully confessed by the Holy Church of the Greeks" to which converts must profess adherence. Among the few theologians of note in this period is Manuel of Corinth (c. 1460–c. 1551), an epigone of Scholarios who helped perpetuate his master's legacy, including treating the essence–energies distinction as one of the cardinal points of difference between east and west (and, incidentally, commending Aristotle, pagan though he was, for perceiving the distinction) (*Patrologia Orientalis* 17: 498). The essence–energies distinction crops up in the famous correspondence between Patriarch Jeremiah II and the Lutheran divines, with the patriarch reproducing in his second letter (1579) one of St Mark of Ephesus' syllogisms in defense of the distinction (Karmires 1953: 443). By contrast, George Kalivas (d. after 1527), another anti-Latin writer of this period, fails to mention the distinction in all his extensive polemic against the Latins or even in his treatise on the Transfiguration (Podskalsky 1988: 88).

As we move into the sixteenth century, the essence–energies distinction appears to fade from view as a central theological concern. There is little trace of it in Maximos Margounios (1549–1602), while Gabriel Severos (1540–1616) affirms it without suggesting that it constitutes one of the chief dividing issues between Greeks and Latins (these being, after the model of the Council of Florence, the procession of the Holy Spirit, papal primacy, the use of azymes, purgatorial fire, and the blessedness of the saints). Meletios Pegas (1549–1601), Patriarch of Alexandria from 1590 until his death, omits any mention of it in all his voluminous *oeuvre* comprising much anti-Latin material and his widely circulating catechetical work, Ὀρθόδοξος διδασκαλία (1596). Meletios's nephew Cyril Lukaris (1570/1572–1638), Patriarch of Constantinople (with several interruptions) from 1620 until his violent death in 1638, followed his uncle in strenuously opposing the Catholic expansionism manifested in the union of Brest–Litovsk (1696). Lukaris finds no place for Palamas in his theological purview, which is hardly surprising given his sympathies with Calvin evidenced in his *Confession* and his general sense of the value of Protestant theology in the battle against Roman Catholicism. Palamas is also absent from the summaries of Eastern Orthodox teaching produced by two other authors of the period willing to take some inspiration from Protestantism: the *Dogmatic Letter* (1640) of Theophilos Korydaleus and the *Confession* of Metrophanes Kritopoulos (1624/1625).

But Lukaris' flirtation with Protestantism produced far more antipathy than sympathy. Indeed, it generated a huge wave of reaction in Eastern Orthodox circles, bringing with it in some quarters a renewed emphasis on the theology of St Gregory Palamas. George Koressios (after 1566–c. 1660), a polymath who served as "Theologian of the Great Church," stresses the failure to recognize the essence–energies distinction as among the most lamentable *lacunae* of Latin theology (Plested 2012: 151–154). Sebastos Kyminetes (1630–1702) follows suit in his *On the Difference between Essence and Energies, against the Latins*. The Palamite distinction is, however, absent from the limpid and systematic *Synopsis of Sacred Theology* produced by the learned Athonite monk Nicholas Koursoulas (c. 1602–1652). It is also, and more significantly, absent from the classic canonized *Confessions* of the seventeenth century, those of Peter Mogila, Metropolitan of Kiev, and Dositheos Notaras, Patriarch of Jerusalem. These were adopted by, respectively, the general councils of Jassy (Iaşi) (1642) and Jerusalem

(1672) with Jerusalem reiterating Jassy's adoption of Mogila's *Confession*. The absence of Palamas from the *Confession* of Dositheos is especially puzzling given that Dositheos was an avowed and ardent Palamite who published a great deal of overtly Palamite theology in his compendious anti-Latin miscellanies: the *Tome of Reconciliation* (1694), the *Tome of Love* (1698), and the *Tome of Joy* (1705). The absence of the theme from the *Confession* may plausibly be explained by its character as a bulwark and safeguard against Protestantizing tendencies within the Eastern Orthodox Church. Protestants have never been in much danger of embracing Palamism.

As we move into the eighteenth century, the pattern of Palamite reception remains patchy but with some overall increase in spread and intensity. The confession of faith of the Council of Constantinople (1727), issued in response to continuing Catholic pressure in the Orthodox heartlands, strenuously affirms the uncreated nature of the divine illumination as manifest on Thabor and the distinction between the uncreated divine operation or energy and the unapproachable divine essence. On the other hand, Eustratios Argenti (c. 1687–c. 1758), the most able and erudite polemicist of the time, makes no mention of it in all his extensive writings against Roman Catholic positions, although it must be admitted that he focuses on ecclesiological and liturgical matters, saying relatively little even about the supremely vexed question of the *Filioque* (Ware 1964). Other prominent theologians of the eighteenth century do, however, embrace the essence–energies distinction. Vincent Damodos (1700–1752) affirms the distinction on the basis of patristic testimony, albeit without mentioning the name of St Gregory Palamas (Podskalsky 1988: 415). He follows some of the later Byzantine Palamite theologians (cf. *supra*) in nuancing the distinction as "conceptual" as opposed to "real." Damodos was a talented and creative theologian and philosopher, strictly traditional in his theology but willing to engage seriously with Enlightenment ideas. His legacy bore spectacular fruit in the life and work of his sometime student Eugenios Boulgaris (1716–1806), an extraordinary figure and tower of learning who graced for a time both the Prussian and Russian courts. Boulgaris was a zealous champion of Palamas and of Palamite theology and may be given some credit for helping spark the Hesychast renaissance of the late eighteenth century.

Chief among the disciples of Boulgaris is St Athanasios of Paros (1721–1813). Athanasios produced an improved version of Boulgaris' *Theological Compendium* (Θεολογικόν) in the shape of his *Epitome or Summary of the Divine Dogmas of the Faith* (1806). Athanasios' treatment of the essence–energies distinction follows Boulgaris very closely, including a discussion of the various merits of Thomist and Scotist takes on the question. Athanasios will often strengthen what Boulgaris has to say about the errors of Aquinas on this issue and goes so far as to single out Aquinas and Bonaventure as "great enemies of our Church" for their opposition to the essence–energies distinction. He is also famed as a leading figure in the *Kollyvades* movement, a powerful movement dedicated to liturgical renewal and, more generally, to a process of Orthodox *ressourcement* with particular emphasis on the Hesychast tradition. Much of this effort was vested in the gathering and publishing of patristic and Byzantine works, especially those bearing on the experience of God and the prayer of the heart. Athanasios planned a complete edition of the works of St Gregory Palamas but was unable to bring the task to fruition. He handed this daunting undertaking over to his own disciple, St Nikodemos the Hagiorite (1749–1809), whose own project was stymied by the declaration of the Austrian authorities (then in control of Venice, the chief publishing center for Orthodox materials stemming from the Ottoman Empire) that Palamas' works constituted subversive material (Citterio 2002: 924). Nikodemos had more success in his collaboration with Makarios (Notaras) of Corinth (1731–1805), a collaboration that produced, *inter alia*, the *Philokalia* (1782). This great anthology of patristic and ascetic texts from the fourth to fifteenth centuries reproduces a solid chunk of Palamas' oeuvre, including the *One Hundred and Fifty Chapters* and the *Tome of the Holy Mountain*, texts that expound his theological teaching in precise and unambiguous terms. The *Philokalia* in its Slavonic form, the *Dobrotolubiye* (1793), produced by St Paissy Velichkovsky, was to spark a remarkable Hesychast renaissance in Russian and the Slav lands. That said, Paissy does not include Palamas (or Maximus for that matter) in his selection. Indeed, even the Russian version of the *Dobrotolubiye* published by St Theophan the Recluse (1877–1889), despite restoring some of Palamas' works, omits precisely the two works mentioned above as most theologically explicit.

The Modern Period

Russian tradition had, in fact, long lagged behind the Greek in terms of its explicit profession of Palamite theology. There is barely any trace of the essence–energies distinction in any of the theological manuals or catechisms of the eighteenth or nineteenth century. Indeed, liturgical commemoration was almost the only place one might readily find the legacy of Palamas in Russia throughout that period. A certain retrieval of Palamas is evident among the Russian Slavophiles, most notably Ivan Kireevsky (1806–1856), who valued Palamas above all as a mystical theologian. Palamas was published in the nineteenth century, in Migne's *Patrologia graeca* in 1865 and in Russian translation in 1895. But it is only in the early twentieth century that we begin to see a serious theological reappropriation of Palamas within Russian Orthodox circles, and that largely among the Russian sophiologists. Here, the pioneering figure is Fr Pavel Florensky (1882–1937), who digs deeply into Palamas principally in order to understand the nature of the mystic's experience of God. A still more substantial appropriation of Palamas is evident in the work of Fr Sergius Bulgakov (1871–1944). Bulgakov characterizes his vision of the divine wisdom as an outworking of the patristic tradition, and in particular of the Palamite essence–energies distinction. While acknowledging that Palamas' articulation of God and God's self-revelation fell somewhat short of a fully articulated sophiology, he is adamant that it exhibits a fundamental concordance in its "inner sense" (Bulgakov 1987: 181 (2009: 156)).

Bulgakov passed on some of his enthusiasm for Palamas to Fr Georges Florovsky (1893–1979), whom he appointed to teach patristics at the Institut St-Serge in Paris. Florovsky came to regard Bulgakov's sophiological enterprise as perilous in the extreme and put forward a notion of a "neo-patristic synthesis" as a deliberate counter to what he regarded as an illegitimate outworking of patristic tradition. Palamas is presented as a key component of this neo-patristic synthesis, standing at the apex of a long tradition of Christian Hellenism. In practice, however, Florovsky has relatively little to say about

Palamas and focuses rather more on St Athanasius and the Cappadocian Fathers (and to some extent St Augustine) as the lynchpins of his proposed (but never fully accomplished) neo-patristic synthesis. A more thoroughgoing neo-patristic appropriation of Palamas is evident in the work of Vladimir Lossky (1903–1958). In his classic *Essai sur la théologie mystique de l'Église d'Orient*, Lossky (1944) presents Eastern Orthodox theology in strictly Dionysian and Palamite terms, arguing that mystical experience of the transcendent tri-personal God (understood in terms of the essence–energies distinction) constitutes the defining genius of the Eastern Orthodox Church vis-à-vis the overly rational, impersonal, insufficiently apophatic, and abstract theology of the Latin West, of which Augustine and Aquinas are the chief exemplars.

Lossky's vision of Palamas found an immensely able expositor in Fr John Meyendorff (1926–1992), author of the classic *Introduction à l'étude de Grégoire Palamas* (1959) and editor of the *Triads in Defence of the Holy Hesycahsts* (1973). Meyendorff is undoubtedly the foremost apostle of neo-Palamism in the twentieth century. Meyendorff argues forcefully for the strict continuity of Palamas with the patristic tradition within which he lays particular emphasis on the Cappadocian Fathers and Macarius-Symeon (pseudo-Macarius). For Meyendorff there is a gulf fixed between Latin and Greek theology, between Augustine and Aquinas on the one hand and the Cappadocian Fathers and Palamas on the other hand:

> Indeed, as all scholars today would agree the real difference between the Latin – Augustinian – view of the Trinity, as a single Essence, with personal characters understood as 'relations', and the Greek scheme, inherited from the Cappadocian Fathers, which considered the single divine Essence as totally transcendent, and the Persons, or *hypostaseis* – each with unique and unchangeable characteristics – as revealing in themselves the Tri-personal divine life, was the real issue behind the debates on the *Filioque*.

And what is more:

> The Orthodox side, however – from Blemmydes, to Gregory of Cyprus and to Palamas – was gradually transcending a purely defensive stand, by discovering that the real problem of the *Filioque* lies not in the formula itself, but in the definition of God as *actus purus* as finalized in the *De ente et essentia* of Thomas Aquinas, vis-à-vis the more personalistic trinitarian vision inherited by the Byzantines from the Cappadocian Fathers (Meyendorff 1986: 678).

In this schema, Augustine's "essentialism" reaches its apogee in Aquinas just as the "personalism" of the Cappadocian Fathers receives its perfect expression in Palamas. In fairness to Meyendorff, we may note that "all scholars" is amended to "most" in later versions of this paper. Other notable scholars of the Russian Orthodox diaspora to contribute to the extraordinary Palamite renaissance of the twentieth century include Archbishop Basil Krivocheine and Archimandrite Cyprian Kern.

It must also be acknowledged that the recovery–discovery of Palamas also impacted the Russian Orthodox Church behind the Iron Curtain. Alexei Losev (1893–1988), a close associate of Florensky, applied Palamite theology to modern philosophical debates about the nature of language, valuing it as a useful safeguard against what he perceived as the proto-Kantianism of Barlaam and his ilk. The great polymath Sergei Avernitsev (1937–2004) was an avowed devotee of Palamas and composed the entry on the saint for the *Great Soviet Encyclopedia*. More recently, Sergei Horujy has emerged as a prominent and prolific advocate of neo-Palamism in Russia, interpreting the whole edifice of Eastern Orthodox spirituality and theology in unambiguously Palamite and Hesychast terms.

It is not only the Russians who have rediscovered Palamas in the twentieth century. Gregorios Papamichael, a professor of the University of Athens, produced the pioneering *Ὁ Ἅγιος Γρηγόριος ὁ Παλαμᾶς* in 1911, a book stemming out of his studies in St Petersburg. This was at a time when the great manuals of Greek Orthodox theology paid little attention to Palamas. Zikos Rhosis' *Σύστημα Δογματικῆς τῆς Ὀρθοδόξου Καθολικῆς Ἐκκλησίας* (1903) does acknowledge the essence–energies distinction, whereas the more influential *Δογματική τῆς Ὀρθοδόξου Ἀνατολικῆς Ἐκκλησίας* (1907) of Christos Androutsos does not. The distinction does reach the last great manual of Greek Orthodox theology, Panayiotis Trembelas' *Δογματική τῆς Ὀρθοδόξου Καθολικῆς Ἐκκλησίας* (1959–1961), albeit without receiving any great prominence. A great stimulus to the retrieval of Palamas was provided by Panagiotes Chrestou's publication of the collected works of Palamas: *Γρηγορίου τοῦ Παλαμᾶ συγγράμματα* (1962–1992). The Palamite revival in modern Greece is associated with figures such as Demetrios Koutroubis, Fr John Romanides, Christos Yannaras, Panayiotis Nellas, and George Mantzarides. For all of these writers, Palamas represents the pinnacle and summation of Orthodox theology and stands in strict conformity with Greek patristic tradition. For some of these, especially Romanides and Yannaras, Palamas is construed in strictly anti-Latin and anti-western terms. Palamas is also affirmed and admired by perhaps the outstanding Orthodox theologian and ecumenist of our time, Metropolitan John Zizioulas, although in practice Palamas does not play a pivotal role within his theological achievement. Palamite theology does, by contrast, figure prominently in the work of Fr Nicholas Loudovikos, a theologian and philosopher who has parted company with Zizioulas on a number of issues but retains something of his sometime teacher's relatively irenic attitude vis-à-vis the west.

A remarkable retrieval of Palamas is also evident in modern Romania, sparked by Fr Dumitru Stăniloae (1903–1993), certainly one of the foremost theologians of the twentieth century. Stăniloae's earliest published work bears on Palamas: *Învăţăura Sfântului Grigorie Palama* (1938). Stăniloae had translated Androutsos in his younger days but made sure to include Palamite theology in his own dogmatic synthesis, *Teologia Dogmatică Ortodoxă* (1978). This work is arguably the closest thing to a "neo-patristic synthesis" yet achieved. Stăniloae also included a great deal of additional material from St Gregory Palamas in his much-expanded Romanian version of the *Philokalia* (*Filokalia*, 1946–1992). The Serbian Orthodox Church has been similarly marked by a neo-Palamite revival, as amply witnessed in figures such as Archimandrite Justin Popović and Bishop Atanasije Jevtić. An honorable mention is also due to Metropolitan Kallistos Ware, the pre-eminent expositor of Eastern Orthodox Christianity in the English-speaking world and without doubt an enthusiastic admirer and compelling propagator of the theology of St Gregory Palamas.

Palamas in Western Perspective

The twentieth century has, in short, witnessed a remarkable retrieval of Palamas in the Eastern Orthodox world. While hardly forgotten in the preceding centuries, the twentieth century saw Palamas attain a centrality and normative status within Orthodoxy only paralleled in the last century of the Byzantine Empire (1351–1453). But while the late Byzantine prominence of Palamas was conditioned largely by an intra-Byzantine debate on the nature of religious experience, the modern retrieval of Palamas has been shaped in large measure within the context of dialogue with the Catholic and Protestant west. The Christian west, as we have hinted, has never been much taken by Palamas. In this sense, the rather sniffy attitude of the papal legate Paul of Smyrna in the fourteenth century has rather set the tone. Palamas has tended to be dismissed (for example, in the *Opus de theologicis dogmatibus* of the Jesuit theologian Denys Petau (Petavius)) or, more commonly, ignored in the west. In this respect, it may be pertinent to note that throughout the late Byzantine and early modern period the Orthodox East was vastly better informed about contemporary Latin theology than vice versa.

Something, however, seems to change in the early twentieth century, with a raft of erudite but scathing criticisms of Palamas, most notably Fr Martin Jugie's excoriating articles on Palamas and Palamism in the *Dictionnaire de théologie catholique* (Jugie 1932). Jugie regards Palamism as "un dogme à peu près mort" in the Greco-Russian Church, hanging on only by virtue of its residual place in the liturgical cycle (Jugie 1932: 1810). Jugie was to give further substance to his claims in Volume 2 of his *Theologia dogmatica christianorum orientalium ab ecclesia dissidentium* (Jugie 1933) and in his *Le schisme byzantin* (Jugie 1941). There may have been a little wish-fulfillment in his pronouncement of the death of Palamism, a doctrine he found abhorrent. While based on immense knowledge and research, Jugie certainly exaggerates the extent to which those who did follow Palamas in the centuries after his death watered down the teachings of their master (in what he calls a "palamisme mitigé" (Jugie 193: 1795)). Jugie was, nonetheless, allied in his disapprobation of Palamism by figures such as Simon Vailhé, Adrian Fortescue, and Sébastien Guichardan. The retrieval of Palamas by figures such as John Meyendorff was pursued in conscious opposition to such scathing attacks.

Western scholars of the post-war period have been scarcely more sympathetic to Palamas, although they have usually been a little more courteous. Rowan Williams (1977) exposed some of the philosophical weaknesses of Palamism in an article that generated an elegant defense by Kallistos Ware (1977). Dorothea Wendebourg (1980) treats Palamas as a functional modalist quite incapable of doing justice to the distinction of persons. She even characterizes the triumph of Palamism as the "defeat of Trinitarian theology." Catherine LaCugna (1991) finds the real distinction between the imparticipable essence and participable energies in God philosophically incoherent and positively dangerous, going so far as to assert that it "breaks the back of orthodox Trinitarian theology." She finds particularly worrying the affirmation that the multiple energies of God are the single operation of the Trinity, concluding that this erases the particular characteristics of the person and breaks the properly inseparable connection between economic and immanent Trinity. Robert Jenson (1997) has also pursued a similar line of attack. While admiring Palamas' teaching on deification, the essence–energies distinction is presented as nothing less than a "disaster." John Milbank (2013) has also declared the distinction philosophically and theologically inadmissible. As yet, few Orthodox writers have attempted to defend Palamas against such trenchant critiques. Here, honorable mention is due to David Bradshaw (2004; 2013) and Theodor Tollefsen (2012), both of whom affirm the Palamite distinction as consistent not only with patristic tradition but also with Aristotelian philosophy, properly understood.

Conclusion

In conclusion, it may be maintained that the theology of St Gregory Palamas remains very much at the center of Eastern Orthodox self-understanding on a global level. Palamite theology is certainly not an optional extra for the Orthodox Church today, being irrevocably entrenched and entwined in her conciliar, liturgical, and ascetic traditions. That said, it is instructive to note the extent to which positive affirmation of Palamite doctrines has tended to wax and wane over time. While never entirely neglected and serving as a perennial point of Orthodox–Catholic difference in the fifteenth to nineteenth centuries, it is only in the twentieth century that Palamite theology regained the prominent place it had in the last century of the Byzantine Empire – and that, as we have noted, for somewhat different reasons. This contemporary retrieval has served as a salutary reminder of the centrality and indispensability of mystical experience and the reality of *theosis*. It has, however, also led to some exaggeration of the place of Palamas in the Orthodox firmament, coupled with a regrettable tendency to construe Palamas in contradistinction to a construct of western theology. We may cautiously hope that the twenty-first century will see Palamas take up a less conspicuous but more embedded place within Eastern Orthodox theology, no longer vaunted as the apex of a tradition construed in contradistinction to the west but treasured by East and west alike as a supremely eloquent witness to the reality of deification and the simultaneity of divine transcendence and immanence.

Bibliography

Primary Sources

Demetrios Kydones, *De personarum proprietatibus in Trinitate ad Constantinum Asanem*, Manuel Candal (1962), "Demetrio Cidonio y el problema trinitario palamitico". *Orientalia christiana periodica*, 28: 75–120.

Gregory Palamas, Γρηγορίου τοῦ Παλαμᾶ συγγράμματα, five vols. Panagiotes Chrestou et al. (1962–1992). Thessalonica.

Gregory Palamas, *Triads in Defence of the Holy Hesycahsts*, John Meyendorff (1973). Spicilegium Sacrum Lovaniense. Études et documents 30. Louvain: Peeters.

Gregory Palamas, *The One Hundred and Fifty Chapters*, Robert Sinkewicz (1988). Studies and Texts 83. Toronto: Pontifical Institute of Mediaeval Studies.

Gregory Palamas. 'Il *Tomo Sinodale* del 1368' in *Gregorio Palamas e oltre: studi e documenti sulle controversie teologiche del XIV secolo bizantino*. Antonio Rigo (2004). Orientalia Venetiana, 16. Florence: Leo S. Olschki; 55–134.

John VI Kantakuzene, *Refutationes duae prochori cydonii et disputatio cum Paulo Patriarcha*

Latino epistulis septem tradita, Edmond Voordeckers and Franz Tinnefeld (1987). Corpus Christianorum Series Graeca 16. Turnhout: Brepols.

George Scholarios, *Oeuvres complètes*, eight vols, Louis Petit, Xenophon Sidéridés, and

Martin Jugie (1928–1936). Paris: Maison de la Bonne Presse.

Karmires, John (1953), Τὰ δογματικὰ καὶ συμβολικὰ μνημεῖα τῆς Ὀρθοδόξου Καθολικῆς Ἐκκλησίας, vol. 2. Athens.

Secondary Sources

Bradshaw, David (2004), *Aristotle East and West*. Cambridge: Cambridge University Press.

Bradshaw, David (2013), "The concept of the divine energies". In *Divine Essence and Divine Energies*, C. Athanasopoulos and C. Schneider (eds). Cambridge: James Clarke; 27–49.

Bulgakov, Sergius (1987), *Le buisson ardent*, Constantin Andronikof (transl.). Lausanne: Editions L'Age d'Homme. (English translation: Allen, Thomas (transl.) (2009), *The Burning Bush*. Grand Rapids, MI: Eerdmans.)

Citterio, Elia (2002), "Nicodemo Agiorita". In *La théologie byzantine et sa tradition*, vol. 2, G. Conticello and V. Conticello (eds). Turnhout: Brepols; 905–978.

Demetracopoulos, John (2011), "Palamas transformed. Palamite interpretations of the distinction between God's 'essence' and 'energies' in Late Byzantium". In *Greeks, Latins, and Intellectual History 1204–1500*, M. Hinterberger and C. Schabel (eds). Recherches de Théologie et Philosophie Médiévales – Bibliotheca 11. Louvain: Peeters; 263–272.

Demetracopoulos, John (1997), Αὐγουστῖνος καὶ Γρηγόριος τοῦ Παλαμᾶ. Τὰ προβλήματα τῶν Ἀριστοτελικῶν κατηγοριῶν καὶ τῆς Τριαδικῆς ψυχοθεολογίας. Athens: Parousia.

Flogaus, Reinhard (1996), "Der heimliche Blick nach Westen: zur Rezeption von Augustins De trinitate durch Gregorios Palamas". *JÖB*, 46: 275–297.

Jenson, Robert (1997), *Systematic Theology*, vol. 1. New York: Oxford University Press.

Jugie, Martin (1932), "Palamas, Grégoire" and "Palamite, controverse". In *Dictionnaire de théologie catholique*, tome XI/2, A. Vacant,

E. Mangenot, and E. Amman (eds); Paris: Letouzey et Ané; 1735–1818.

Jugie, Martin (1933), *Theologia dogmatica christianorum orientalium ab ecclesia dissidentium*, vol. 2. Paris: Letouzey & Ané.

Jugie, Martin (1941), *Le schisme byzantin*. Paris: Lethielleux.

LaCugna, Catherine (1991), *God for Us: The Trinity and Christian Life*. San Francisco, CA: HarperCollins.

Levy, Antione (2012), "Lost in translation? *Diakrisis kat'epinoian* as a main issue in the discussions between fourteenth-century Palamites and Thomists". *The Thomist*, 76: 431–471.

Lossky, Vladimir (1944), *Essai sur la théologie mystique de l'Église d'Orient*. Paris: Éditions du Cerf.

Meyendorff, John (1959), *Introduction à l'étude de Grégoire Palamas*. Paris: Éditions du Seuil.

Meyendorff, John (1986), "The Mediterranean world in the thirteenth century, theology: east and west". In *The 17th International Byzantine Congress: Major Papers*. New Rochelle, NY: Caratzas; 669–682. (Revised versions in: Chrysostomides, J. (ed.) (1988), *Kathēgētria* (Festschrift Joan Hussey). Camberley: Ashgate; and the collected volume Meyendorff, John (1996), *Rome, Constantinople, Moscow: Historical and Theological Studies*. New York: St Vladimir's Seminary Press; 73–86.)

Milbank, John (2013), "Christianity and Platonism in East and West." In *Divine Essence and Divine Energies*, C. Athanasopoulos and C. Schneider (eds); Cambridge: James Clarke; 158–209.

Nadal Cañellas, Juan (2006), *La résistance d'Akindynos à Grégoire Palamas: enquête historique, avec traduction et commentaire de quatre traités édités récemment.* Spicilegium Sacrum Lovaniense. Études et documents 51. Louvain: Peeters.

Plested, Marcus (2012), *Orthodox Readings of Aquinas.* Oxford: Oxford University Press.

Podskalsky, Gerhard (1988), *Griechische Theologie in der Zeit der Türkenherrschaft: die Orthodoxie im Spannungsfeld der nachreformatorischen Konfessionen des Westens (1453–1821).* Munich: Beck.

Stiernon, Daniel (1972), "Bulletin sur le palamisme". *Revue des études byzantines,* 30: 231–341.

Tollefsen, Torstein Theodor (2012), *Activity and Participation in Late Antique and Early Christian Thought.* Oxford: Oxford University Press.

Ware, Kallistos (1964), *Eustratios Argenti: A Study of the Greek Church under Turkish Rule.* Oxford: Clarendon Press.

Ware, Kallistos (1977), "The debate about Palamism". *Eastern Churches Review,* 9: 45–63.

Wendebourg, Dorothea (1980), *Geist oder Energie. Zur Frage der innergöttlichen Verankerung des christlichen Lebens in der byzantinischen Theologie.* Munich: Kaiser.

Williams, Rowan (1977), "The philosophical structures of Palamism". *Eastern Churches Review,* 9: 27–44.

Part IV
Studies in Reception History II: Collective Fathers

CHAPTER 21

The Cappadocian Fathers

H. Ashley Hall

Introduction

This chapter examines the general contours defining the reception of the Cappadocian Fathers. Given the scope of their influence throughout the subsequent Christian tradition, it is necessary to be selective in this examination. Therefore, we will pay particular attention to the following: the modern critical resources that help the scholar trace the Cappadocian text reception, to outlining the popular perception of the Cappadocians through various early histories (which shaped their reception for later generations), and then to examining the significant stages in the reception of each Cappadocian up to the present, with particular attention to the availability of and interest in the material by or attributed to the three theologians. In the process, the particular reception of the Cappadocian Fathers will be set against the backdrop of the broader and more general trends of patristic reception; namely, the periods in which their works sparked more interest from subsequent readers and why this was so, their reception in the manuscript tradition compared with the arrival of printed codices, and the problem of spurious or misattributed works (both of which are a particular concern regarding Gregory of Nyssa). Given their well-deserved reputation for theology that is both orthodox and dynamic, as well as for being theologians of exemplary learning, the reception of the Cappadocian Fathers is particularly illustrative of the larger concerns in the particular discipline to which this book is dedicated.

The Wiley Blackwell Companion to Patristics, First Edition. Edited by Ken Parry.
© 2015 John Wiley & Sons Ltd. Published 2019 by John Wiley & Sons Ltd.

Defining "The Cappadocians"

Identifying the Cappadocians is not as straightforward as it may first appear. The first task is to acknowledge that the "the Cappadocians" is a construct that is not only relatively new, it has also been variously understood. This study will use the now standard designation of St Basil of Caesarea ("the Great"), St Gregory of Nazianzus ("the Theologian"), and St Gregory of Nyssa. This is not to say that the appreciation of their brilliance or understanding of their relation to each other was unknown. Indeed, the early ecclesiastical histories and the testimony of great theologians (e.g., Jerome) made clear the acclaim of the three theologians. And yet, the grouping of the Cappadocians as "the great three" is not consonant with the larger span of the tradition. Within the Greek and Byzantine tradition (since the eleventh century), when anyone thought of a grouping of three great theologians they almost certainly thought first of the three great hierarchs: Basil, Gregory Nazianzen, and John Chrysostom. As a general rule, up until the modern period, the term "the Cappadocian Fathers" was never used. If people gestured toward something like a "Cappadocian theology," they certainly associated Basil and Gregory Nazianzen as comrades in arms against Arianism. This "partnership" was established quite early, the seeds of which were planted as early as Gregory's funeral oration for Basil (*Oration* 43).

More variable, however, has been whether to add one or more to the pair. Within the tradition, Gregory of Nyssa stands something of a distance, though his family ties to Basil were well known and his own reputation as a theologian was firmly established (e.g., Gregory had been named by the Emperor Theodosius to oversee the implementation of the decrees of the Council of Constantinople throughout Pontus). Moreover, various scholars have been inclined to add other theologians (either in addition to or to the exclusion of Gregory of Nyssa). For example, among patristic scholars in the sixteenth century, Philip Melanchthon (1497–1560) connected Basil and Gregory Nazianzen to Gregory of Neocaesarea (or Thaumaturgos/the Wonderworker) in an effort to demonstrate the apostolic legacy of the Nicene faith against the anti-Trinitarianism of Miguel Servetus (1509/1511–1553) and Johann Campanus (c. 1500–1575). Alternatively, Erasmus of Rotterdam (1466–1536), in an effort to restore the legacy of Origen of Alexandria, emphasized the indebtedness Basil and Gregory Nazianzen owed to the great exegete (though he did not "group" the three as "Cappadocians"). The particulars of the alternative constellation of names properly associated with the title "The Cappadocians" need not detain us nor detract from the now accepted consensus. It is worth noting, however, that a search for the currently employed phrases "the Cappadocians," "Cappadocian theology," or "the Cappadocian solution" in the Latin or Greek tradition would be, on the surface, both misleading and proffer divergent results.

Modern Scholarly Tools

Tracing the reception of the Fathers in general and the Cappadocians in particular has become easier in the last century of scholarship. Nonetheless, our sketch of past material is and will remain imperfect; new manuscripts are being discovered, and centuries of war and decay mean that some items have long disappeared from the historical record. The following bibliography will be of assistance to both the novice who desires a general scope of what is available and the established scholar looking for the reception of a particular text. The Migne *Series Graeca* (MPG) contains the works of Basil (vols 29–32), Gregory Nazianzen (vols 35–38), and Gregory of Nyssa (vols 44–46). The *Corpus Christianorum Series Graeca* (CCSG), documenting subsequent scholarship since Migne, has a subseries each dedicated to Basil (*Bibliotheca Basiliana Universalis*, BBU, five vols) and to Gregory Nazianzen (*Corpus Nazianzenum*, CCCN, 24 vols, in process). Likewise, Brill has published the research begun by Werner Jaeger into the works of Gregory of Nyssa (*Gregorii Nysseni Opera*, GNO, 10 vols, in process). Especially helpful is the *Clavis Patrum Graecorum: Supplementum* (CPG) in the CCSG series, which provides references to critical editions, studies, and modern translations of Cappadocian material. Likewise, the *Sources Chrétiennes* (SC) has offered modern French translations of many Cappadocian works. Aside from the reception history of a text recorded in the introduction of critical editions, scholars interested in reception history will find the yeoman's work of identifying and tracing the span of Cappadocian texts and editions detailed in the *Catalogus Translationum et Commentariorum* begun by Paul Oskar Kristeller; volumes 2, 3, and 5 contain detailed accounts regarding the works of Gregory Nazianzen and Gregory of Nyssa. A specialized but nonetheless helpful record of Cappadocian reception during the transalpine Renaissance is the *Verzeichnis der im deutschen Sprachbereich erschienenen Drucke des 16. Jahrhunderts* (VD16), which records every known publication within the German-speaking territories during the sixteenth century. And so, the challenge for the modern scholar is not getting access to Cappadocian material. Rather, the challenge is in summarizing the broad but variated reception of these three great Cappadocians, who made many lasting contributions not only to theology but also to philology, rhetoric, and poetry.

Tracing the Legacy of the Cappadocians through the Church Histories

There was never a lack of appreciation for Basil of Caesarea and Gregory Nazianzen. In no small part, this is due to the efforts of the early ecclesiastical histories. What follows in this section is a highly concise narrative of what is found within the more significant histories as a way of highlighting the popular legacy of these theologians.

Oration 43 of Gregory Nazianzen

The foundation of subsequent material about the Cappadocians, especially Basil, was built on Gregory Nazianzen's *Oration* 43, which endured as a popular text (PG 36: 493–605; SC 384). It has been esteemed for its eloquence and mastery of classical form in service to Christian purposes. The information Gregory Nazianzen provided on Basil would be incorporated into later works. Gregory begins the eulogy by explaining his delay in the composition of the work (1, 2); then offers an account of Basil's ancestors (3); proof of their piety (4–8); his parents (9, 10); physical description (10); praise of

Basil's learning in Cappadocia and Constantinople (11–14) and then continued in Athens (14–24); his life as a priest and the corruption he encountered (25–27); his struggles against them (28–36); his election as bishop (37, 38); his struggles to defend the pure faith against his fellow bishops and the emperor (38–59); a description of his moral qualities and his works (60–69); a comparison with biblical figures, especially John the Baptist (70–77); his death and burial (78–80); concluding praise of Basil for his piety (81); address to Basil and solemn prayer (82). It was Gregory Nazianzen's dramatic account in the oration of Basil's confrontation with the Emperor Valens and his prefect that was the most repeated; it became, in fact, iconic. As with the telling of any good story, Gregory heightens the mood by sharpening his characters. The treachery of the emperor is revealed in no uncertain terms and endures as the dramatic device to highlight Basil's orthodoxy, courage, and humility.

Eusebius of Caesarea, *Historia Ecclesiastica* and Rufinus' Latin Translation

Owing to the date of its composition (Between 303 and 312), Eusebius' *Church History* does not include the Cappadocians (CPG 20, 45–906). Around 403, Rufinus translated Eusebius's *History* and added two books of his own, bringing the chronicle up to 398 (the death of Theodosius I) (PL 21, 461–560). In Book 2, chapter 9, Rufinus describes Basil and Gregory together, often contrasting their talents: "thus it was that a different grace was active in each of them to achieve one work of perfection" (Amidon 1997: 72). Rufinus records both that Basil came from a noble family and that he studied in Athens, where he excelled in rhetoric. Upon returning home he dedicated himself to the work of the Church, living a monastic life for 13 years, before being called to "instruct the people." He taught them "to assemble, to build monasteries, to give time to psalms, hymns, and prayers, taking care of the poor and furnish them with proper housing and necessities of life, to establish the way of life of virgins, and to make the life of modesty and charity desirable to almost everyone." Finally, Rufinus states that he has translated Basil's monastic *Rule* (the shorter *Asceticon*) and eight sermons.

St Jerome, *De Viris Illustribus*

St Jerome composed the first and most "basic source for the history of ancient Christian literature," in his *On Illustrious Men* (PL 22, 631). Composed c. 392, Jerome begins his chronicle of notable writers with St Simon Peter and concludes with himself. All three Cappadocians are described by Jerome, though Gregory Nazianzen takes the lion's share of interest among the three. This is likely due to the extended personal contact between Jerome to Gregory in Constantinople. There are only brief and relatively flat descriptions of Basil and Gregory of Nyssa, despite their acknowledged significance. Jerome commends three of Basil's works to the reader: *In Hexaemeron*, *De spiritu sancto*, and *Contra Eunomium*. Gregory of Nyssa is noted primarily for how Gregory Nazianzen read aloud passages of the former's *Contra Eunomium* at the Council of Constantinople.

Socrates, *Historia Ecclesiastica*

Socrates began his ecclesiastical history in 305 (where Eusebius's ends) and brought his ecclesiastical history up to 439. This history mentions all three Cappadocians, but, like Rufinus, the focus is upon the efforts of Basil and Gregory Nazianzen. Socrates first mentions Basil and Gregory in chapter 23, concerning those who devoted themselves to the monastic life. A full introduction to both men occurs in chapter 26, in which Socrates highlights the most important aspects of their lives and works. He mentions that both men so excelled in virtue and eloquence that one would be hard pressed to choose one over the other. He notes that they studied in Athens, mastering the art of rhetoric from the preeminent practitioners of the art. Rejecting a successful public career, Basil and Gregory retired to a monastic retreat, during which they commented on Origen's works, which, the author notes, were being misused by the Arians. Returning to active life, Basil became a deacon (and later a bishop), during which time he was tireless in his instruction of the people against the raging of the Arians. Likewise, Gregory Nazianzen took over the pastoral work of his father's diocese, visiting Constantinople often, bringing comfort to the oppressed orthodox community there. Towards the end of the chapter, Socrates mentions Gregory of Nyssa as the brother of Basil, who "emulated [Basil's] eloquence in teaching, and completed after his death Basil's treatise on the [*Hexaemeron*], which had been left unfinished ... and many of [Nyssa's] orations are still extent" (Schaff and Wace 1995: 110–111).

Sozomen, *Historia Ecclesiastica*

Sozomen composed his ecclesiastical history sometime soon after 439. His history, in nine books, covers the period from 324 to 422. Gregory of Nyssa is only mentioned once (see chapter 9 of the text). Like Socrates (upon whom his account is based), Sozomen often discusses Basil and Gregory Nazianzen as a pair. The two are first mentioned in chapter 18, which comments on Julian's edict to exclude Christians from teaching in the schools. Apollinaris of Laodicea, Basil, and Gregory Nazianzen are portrayed as defenders of the union between literature and theology. In chapter 17, Sozomen repeats in his account the friendship between Basil and Nazianzen, their education in Athens and Antioch, their adoption of the monastic life and study of Origen, and from the works of Origen they were able to defeat the Arians. He adds a curious tidbit: that Basil and Gregory decided in which region they would preach by lot.

Chapters 4, 5, and 7 offer a brief account of Gregory Nazianzen's efforts to encourage the Nicene community at Constantinople, his election as bishop of that city, the subsequent leadership of the council there, and his abdication. Sozomen offers a flat account of those who opposed Gregory and his forced abdication. He emphasizes that Gregory's resignation from the episcopal throne was a matter of his choice and reflected his humility. In chapters 15 and 16, Sozomen also provides much information on the conflict between Emperor Valens and the orthodox, the leadership of which seems to have been given over to Basil due to his prominent role in the story.

Theodoret of Cyrrhus *and* Cassiodorus

Theodoret composed his own church history, which appeared posthumously c. 449. He refers to Gregory Nazianzen and Gregory of Nyssa only in passing (see chapter 27). There is one account of Basil, which focuses on the encounters between the bishop and Emperor Valens. As in Sozomen, the illness of the emperor's son is directly linked to his oppression of Basil, and Theodoret even inserts an allusion to the plagues of Egypt. Theodoret's account on Basil is noteworthy for two reasons. First, when he tells the reader of Valens's visit to the Epiphany services, Theodoret says that the emperor and the bishop had been reconciled. Theodoret adds that Basil fell out of the emperor's favor a second time, and the emperor resolved to exile him. However, when the document was brought to the emperor for him to sign, his pen broke. This happened a second and then a third time. This event filled the emperor with fear and he resolved to leave Basil in peace.

So far, we have seen how the histories discussed here were dependent upon one another to varying degrees, and how all of them intended to pick up where Eusebius left off. After 540, Cassiodorus and his assistant Ephiphanius edited a compilation of these Greek histories into a single Latin translation, called the *Historia tripartita*. The corresponding accounts are woven into one continuous narrative. This collection of translated Greek histories would become the standard source of church history in the Latin Church throughout the Middle Ages. In fact, many of the individual histories that make up Cassiodorus's *Historia* would not be rediscovered in the West as independent sources in their original languages until the 1520s, as a result of the work of Beatus Rhenanus. One final western source of information about the Cappadocians that should be noted here is The *Golden Legend* of Jacobus de Voragine. He mentions Gregory of Nazianzen and Gregory of Nyssa, but only provides an account of Basil, who is as much of a miracle worker as he is a theologian.

As the reader will observe, Basil and Gregory Nazianzen are the two Cappadocians most highlighted, nearly to the exclusion of Gregory of Nyssa. This reality would have a profound consequence for the relative ignorance of the latter's work until the early seventeenth century. Even then, as the next section will describe, the effort toward proper attribution for Gregory of Nyssa's work (long credited to his brother and Gregory Nazianzen) was just beginning.

As mentioned earlier, the attempt to record the general reception of the Cappadocian Fathers is peppered with difficulties. Greater clarity is achieved if the reader wishes to discern the reception of particular texts, since critical editions are available; but that task is beyond the scope of this chapter. A more accessible grasp of the reception can be had by examining the printed editions since the sixteenth century, but that too presents obvious limitations. Another aspect of reception is the reality of *spuria* (works by less-orthodox authors masquerading as Cappadocian or misattributions, such as certain homilies by Gregory of Nyssa attributed to Basil). How previous theologians approached the text and the value they placed upon it is not always the same as our own. For instance, some in the sixteenth century doubted the authenticity of Basil's *De Spiritu sancto* and great importance was given to Gregory of Nyssa's *De natura hominis* – which we now know was written by Nemesius of Emesa. The form in which subsequent theologians had access to earlier writers can also tell an important story: Was the complete work available or was the author using quotations preselected through florilegia? Moreover, in what language(s) were the texts available? If a translation, what is the quality? There are other considerations, but all of these are significant factors in determining the reception of Cappadocian material and realities for which to account when making claims about the influence of the Cappadocians on later theologians and scholars, especially in religious controversies. With these parameters in mind, it is possible to offer the following general description of Cappadocian sources.

The Reception of Cappadocian Material: A Select Examination

Basil of Caesarea

A highly detailed study of the reception of Basil's work is available from Paul J. Fedwick, the sheer size of which is a testament to Basil's legacy and influence. Moreover, many of Basil's principle works are available in critical editions (CPG §2835–3008). Basil's fame was firmly established in his own time, and there was never a lack of interest in or availability of his writings. The historical sources mentioned in the previous section (especially two of the earliest, *Oration* 43 and *De viris illustribus*) all highlight Basil, perpetuating his fame as a pillar of orthodoxy.

Mirroring his influence in life, there is a strong Greek manuscript tradition of Basil's major and minor works. For instance, within a decade of his death, Basil's *Homiliae in hexaemeron* exerted a foundational influence over Ambrose's own commentary on Genesis. Likewise, there is an equally strong manuscript tradition of translations of Basil's works in various languages (Armenian, Syrian, Arabic, Coptic, and Georgian). The earliest Latin translators of Basil were Rufinus, who translated the *Asceticon paruum*, eight homilies on the psalms and various topics, and two treatises on fasting (c. 397–98); and Eustathius (c. 400), who translated the *Hexaemeron* (CPG §2876; CSEL 86; §2836, 2845–2847, 2850, 2855–2856, and 2859). The Franciscan friar and founder of the Fraticelli, Angelo da Clareno (1247–1337), while serving as a missionary to Armenia, introduced several ascetical works of Basil to Latin audiences to undergird his own attacks on clerical wealth and power (CPG §2875, 2880–2887, 2889, 2891, 2895, 2897, §2896, *De baptismo libri duo*; and §2900, *Epistulae* 2, 22, 23, 150, and 173). Basil's homilies on various topics (especially of the Psalms and moral topics, such as fasting, envy, or humility) are often grouped together in the manuscript tradition, while the homilies on creation form their own textual tradition (Pauli 1998: 97).

The sixteenth century produced the first effort to collect all of Basil's works into a single edition. These include the 1515 (Rome) edition by Raffaelo Maffei, the 1528 (Hagenau) Greek edition by Vincent Obsopoeus, the 1532 (Basel) Greek edition by Erasmus, the 1540 (Basel) Latin edition by Wolfgang Musculus, and the 1551 (Basel) Greek edition by Janus Cornarius. The Maffei edition (Rome, 1515) was a single volume (173 pages) of various works in Latin translation, including: Gregory Nazianzen's *Oration* 43; 17 of Basil's sermons on the Psalms (two of which are spurious); 20 "moral homilies"; a composite of *De Baptismo*, sections 1–2; and 10 "ascetica" (all spurious). The sermons on the Psalms are most likely the Latin translation of Rufinus, *Homiliae super psalmos* (CPG §2836). The ascetic works are the *Asceticon magnum sive Questiones* (CPG §2875), the *Asceticon parvum* (CPG §2876), the *Regulae morales* (CPG §2877), *Sermo* 15, *De vita monastica* (CPG §2893), and the *Constitutiones asceticae* (CPG §2895). Paul Fedwick provides information on these texts (Fedwick 1993–2004: 2/2, 202–205). In 1520, a Latin edition was published in Paris (of which Ulrich Zwingli owned a copy). The Obsopoeus edition (Hagenau, 1528) is dedicated to famed Nuremberg Humanist Willibald Pirkheimer (Fedwick 1993–2004: 2/2, 205–207). This work contains a collection of 118 letters in Greek – 61 from Basil and 57 from Gregory Nazianzen – and concludes with a biography of Basil taken from the Suida. Though the preface claims to offer previously unpublished material, five of the letters had been published in 1499. The stated source for his edition was a collection of manuscripts once owned by King Corvinus of Hungary (1458–1490). The Erasmus edition (Basel, 1532) is dedicated to Jocopo Sadoleto, bishop of Carpentras and a respected Latinist. This Greek edition of 674 pages contains the six sermons of the *Hexaemeron* (PG 32, 209–494; CPG §2835); an assortment of homilies, some on the Psalms (some spurious); Book 1 of *De Spiritu Sancto* (PG 32, 108–173; CPG §2839); and reprints of the letters of Basil and Gregory Nazianzen first published in the Obsopoeus edition of 1528, with only "slight variations in some of the titles" (Fedwick 1993–2004: 2/2, 208–217; 2/2, 849). The Musculus edition (Basel, 1540) is a two-volume work in Latin. It contains some works by Gregory Nazianzen (including *Oration* 43 and 80 letters), along with Basil's sermons on the *Hexaemeron*, several letters and homilies, including a reprint of the Maffei edition from 1515 (Fedwick 1993–2004: 2/2, 221–225; 2/2, 855; Way 1971: 115). Finally, the Cornarius edition (Basel, 1551) was an attempt to provide all the known works of Basil in Greek within one volume (a Latin translation became available the next year) (Fedwick, 1993–2004: 2/2, 236–239; 2/2, 859). Cornarius reprinted the Erasmus edition of 1532 (which itself reproduced the Obsopoeus edition of 1528) along with a reprint of a 1535 edition produced in England by Reginald Pole (Fedwick, 1993–2004: 2/2, 217–221). An excellent summary study of the influence of Basil's works in the age of Calvinist Orthodoxy is offered by Irena Backus (2001: 841–865).

Given the diversity of works to cover and broad translation tradition, this chapter will (guided in part by Jerome's own recommendation to his readers) frame the reception of Basil around six works: *Adversus Eunomium, Homiliae in hexaemeron, Asceticon paruum, Ad Adolescentes, De humilitate,* and *De spiritu sancto.*

Adversus Eunomium

Adversus Eunomium was a well-regarded work of Basil, though not exactly well known. That is, Basil's contributions to a complex theological problem were well known but the work does not seem to have been in much demand through the tradition. This is perhaps due to the fact that, as a dogmatic work on a topic that was soon settled and accepted as orthodox, there was not much interest in (or need) to study the work. Yet, the *Adversus Eunomium* suddenly becomes the topic of heated debate and fervent study during the Council of Florence (1439), especially concerning the contested issue of the *Filioque.* The Latins highly favored the work, as they saw it as the crucial justification (from a Greek author) of the procession of the Holy Spirit from the Father and the Son (Stinger 2001: 488–489). As theologians turned to their manuscripts, there were variant readings of key passages, which led to mutual accusations of tampering and deliberate misreading. The controversy prompted Bishop Bessarion of Nicaea (1403–1472; later, a Cardinal and émigré to Rome) to study the matter further from older manuscripts available to him in Constantinople, leading him to become convinced that the Latin position was correct. In 1442, Bessarion commissioned fellow émigré George Trebizond to create a Latin translation of the text (which he translated and published alongside Basil's *De Spirito sancto*) (Stinger 2001: 489; Backus 1990a).

Homiliae in Hexaemeron

As mentioned earlier, Basil's later sermons on the *Hexaemeron* (nine homilies given c. 378) were well received and directly influential on other authors (even helping to create a specific genre of exegesis on creation). The homilies have a strong tradition in the Greek and Latin manuscripts. The work is also prominent in the *catenae* (though no references to Basil appear in the *glossa ordinaria*) (CPG §2835; Matter 2001: 83–111). Book III of John Scotus Eriugena's *Periphyseon* quotes extensively from the *Hexaemeron* in praise of Basil's literal exegesis (Otten 2001: 42). The last major theological opus of Robert Grosseteste (c. 1175–1253) was a work of the same name. Basil's work played a key role, in that the Cappadocian is quoted (in long passages) second only to St Augustine (Lewis 2001: 206). Grosseteste's source, however, was the Latin translation by Eustathius. In the fifteenth century, the *Hexaemeron* appeared in two Latin translations, one commissioned by Pope Pius II from Lampugnino Birago and the second from the pen of John Argyropoulos, his only foray into patristic translations (Stinger 1998: 230).

Asceticon Paruum

The ascetical works of Basil form a long and complex tradition. Basil's thoughts on the matter were certainly key, as his own ascetic example and advice were exemplary. Yet, properly speaking, Basil's ascetical works do not constitute a "rule," at least as commonly understood in western monasticism. Moreover, not all of the recipients of Basil's ascetic advice were monks; some were men and women wanting to incorporate ascetic ideals into their daily life based on examples from the Gospels. It was for this reason, in fact, that Philip Melanchthon used Basil as a means to criticize and provide a counter-example to the monasticism of the late medieval period (Hall 2014: 166). Likewise, Melanchthon also argued that Basil's ascetical works (which in the sixteenth century included the *Constitutiones asceticae*) were riddled with spurious inclusions, and subsequent scholarship has shown him to have been correct. Despite the vast influence of Basil's ascetical works, the original Greek *Asceticon paruum* (c. 360–370) did not survive; it is known only through Rufinus' Latin translation and a later Syrian translation. The *Asceticon magnum* (after 373) is composed of longer commentaries and revised versions of the previous *Asceticon paruum* (CPG §2875–2895; BBU, vol. III, *Ascetica*). The subsequent manuscript tradition collected these works into a corpus of Basil's ascetic literature, along with a prologue, several letters, and commentaries (Pauli 1998: 96; Silvas 2005).

Ad Adolescentes

Ad adolescentes (variously titled in the tradition as *De poetarum, oratorum, historico-rumque ac philosophorum legendis libris*) was composed toward the end of Basil's career (Schucan 1973). St John of Damascus commends the work to his readers (Deferrari 1926: 371, 374–375), and Symeon the Metaphrast includes quotations of the work in his menologion (PG 32, 120–1376). The manuscript traditions often included this work within collections of Basil's homilies (Pauli 1998: 97). The letter would have a profound effect in western Europe during the Renaissance. Leonardo Bruni offered a significant Latin translation (Venice, 1470), and 19 editions followed. From 1501 to 1521, the work was printed 26 times in the German territories (VD 16, B652–677). In two early works concerning the reform of higher education, Philip Melanchthon echoes Basil's program. In 1519, the first printed Greek edition was produced by Spanish Humanist Hernán Núñez of Alcalá. So important was this work to the Humanist vision of education, in 1537 (Basel) an edition of Basil's *Instituenda studiorum ratione ad nepotes suos* was printed with reflections on pedagogy from Erasmus and Melanchthon. The Society of Jesus likewise included it as part of its *Ratio studiorum*. Calvinist Hugo Grotius produced a Greek edition in 1623. In 1819, C.A.F. Frémon made a significant contribution when he compared and corrected previous editions; it was Frémon's work that would be copied into the Migne.

De Humilitate

The homily *De humilitate* is not significant throughout most of the tradition. It is, however, noteworthy in the life of Philip Melanchthon. The homily was published in Erasmus' 1532 collection of Basil's works. Basil frames his homily around the first chapter of Paul's First Letter to the Corinthians (1 Cor 1: 26–30). Basil remarks that no one should consider herself to be righteous except in so far as she has been made righteous through the grace and merits of Jesus Christ alone. Melanchthon, whose method for reading the Church Fathers was to collect "true testimonies," found in this brief homily a clear affirmation of the gospel (which, in his context, was summarized by the Evangelical Lutheran doctrine of justification by grace through faith alone). References to this homily punctuate Melanchthon's later letters, orations, and treatises, and it is featured in the last portrait made of Melanchthon in his own life time (Hall 2014: 13–14, 100–102).

De Spiritu Sancto

De spiritu sancto was written c. 374–375 against the Pneumatomachians. Arguably, Basil's defense of the full divinity of the Holy Spirit (through a theological argument based on a careful examination of grammar), despite his "economy of words," was accepted in the revisions made by the Council of Constantinople (381) to the Nicene Creed. The treatise is very important in the history of doctrine but does not seem have had an enduring legacy, in part perhaps because its goal was achieved so conclusively fairly soon after its composition. The most interesting aspect of its reception was a minor skirmish in the sixteenth century when Erasmus doubted its authenticity (and argued so in his 1532 edition); he found the grammar and syntax too awkward and unworthy of such a great author. Also interesting is that arguments about Basil's authorship of the treatise had nothing to do with the reference to "unwritten verities." The early polemics of the Reformation did not find this phrase fodder for conflict in the way that seventeenth- and eighteenth-century confessional polemicists would.

Gregory of Nazianzen

Like Basil, the works of Gregory Nazianzen have a long and deep testimony in reception history (CPG §3010–3128). In fact, one could make a convincing argument that Gregory's legacy as an author was stronger than that of Basil's. In history, Gregory was able to step out of the shadow of Basil that trailed him in life. In addition to being named "the Theologian," Gregory was also hailed as the "Christian Demosthenes." Gregory was studied not only for his theological insight but also for his mastery of Attic Greek, making his works among the most copied and studied in the Christian tradition (especially among the Byzantines and post-medieval western Europeans). Agnes Clare Way (1971; 1976) offers a detailed genealogy of Gregory's reception, of which I offer an outline here. Likewise, far greater detail can also be found in the CCSG.

Like Basil, Gregory's works never suffered from neglect. Several manuscripts of his work exist in many translations, including Coptic, Syriac, Ethiopian, Armenian, Slavonic, and Arabic (Way 1971: 47). Starting from the sixth century, a tradition of commentaries on his works emerges explaining the grammar and vocabulary, as well as historical and literary allusions in his orations. Also at this time, a very popular biography of Gregory was written, the *Vita Sancti Gregorii Theologi* (Gregorius Presbyter 2001). Nearly every subsequent century produced such a commentary: Maximus the Confessor, Cosmos of Jerusalem, Basilius Minimus, Michael Psellus, Elias of Crete, and Joannes Zonaras all contributed to Gregory's reception (Way 1971: 46–47). As we saw in the previous section, Jerome burnished Gregory's reputation as a pillar of orthodoxy for western audiences. The first Latin translation of Gregory's work (namely, nine orations) was provided by Rufinus, of which over 150 manuscript copies exist today. More works of Gregory were made available in Latin when John Scotus Eriugena translated Maximus Confessor's *In Ambigua Sancti Gregorii*, which included nineteen orations, two poems, and one letter (Way 1971: 47). The fifteenth-century revival of Greek letters in western Europe (the result of Byzantine theologians seeking shelter after 1453) also produced new translations.

The greatest boon to Gregory's reception occurred in the sixteenth century; the VD16 lists 63 printed works of Gregory. Of the 63, 50 are in Latin, 9 in Greek, and 4 in German (Hall, 2014: 251). Up until that time, the interest in Gregory was widely dispersed but there was no effort to create a unified collection (i.e., an *opera omnia*). In 1504, 66 of Gregory's poems appeared from the Aldine Press (Manutius, Venice) as part of a series of Christian poetry (*Poeta Christiani*, vol. 3). Way (1971: 65–68) provides a list of the poems included. Likewise, since Gregory's fame was so closely bound to that of Basil's, Gregory's works often appear in early editions dedicated to the writings of Basil. The single-volume 1515 edition of Basil's works (Maffei, Rome) contained a translation of Gregory's *Oration* 43.

Editions singularly dedicated to Gregory soon followed. The first attempt appears to date from 1508, when 10 works by Gregory were published by Johannes Adelphus (using translations from Rufinus) in Strasbourg (VD16 G3032; Hall 2014: 251). In 1516, the Aldine Press published *Orationes lectissimae XVI*, which contained the *Five Theological Orations* (i.e., *Orations 27–31*; CPG §3010, SC 250). In 1519, Peter Mosellanus, the great philologist at the University of Leipzig, produced another popular translation of the *Theological Orations*. In 1536, the Aldine Press produced nine more orations. In 1528, Vincent Obsopoeus published *Basilii Magni et Gregorii Nazianzeni epistolae graeca*, which included 118 letters (from the manuscript collection of King Corvinus of Hungary), 57 of which came from Gregory (VD16 B688; Fedwick, 1993–2004: 2/2, 206, n. 15). The Erasmus edition of Basil's works (1532) reprinted these letters. Melanchthon made his own translations of some minor works of Gregory; he also created workbooks of the *Theological Orations* (in Latin and in Greek) to demonstrate proper grammatical form and theological content for his students (Hall 2014: 82–84). Likewise, Johannes Oecolampadius produced several translations of Gregory's poems and orations (Hall 2014: 250–251 n. 95). According to Way (and in contrast to the earlier tradition), the most popular translations in the sixteenth century were primarily didactic in nature; these included the *Apologeticus*, the *Five Theological Orations*, *Oratio de Pace prima*, *De pauperum amore*, *In Theophania*, and *In Pentecosten*. The most popular poems were *Exhortatio ad Virginem* and the *Monasticha* (Way 1971: 49).

The first Greek edition and attempt at an *opera omnia* appeared in 1550 (Hervagius, Basel); it contained nearly all of the orations, many poems, and 80 letters (Way 1971: 47). That same year, a single-volume Latin translation was issued by Wolfgang Musculus, which gathered material of Gregory's that he had published earlier (1540) with Basil's works, the 30 orations translated by Willibald Pirkheimer (published in 1531), with five new translations. These included *Christus patiens*, *Orations 1 & 2*, *In Ezechielem*, and *In Ecclesiasten* (Way, 1971: 48). The most complete *opera omnia* of the period was produced in 1569 (and revised in 1583) by the abbot Jacques de Billy de Prunay (Backus 1993). A second collection was made available in 1571 (using some of the work of de Billy) by Joannes Levvenklaius. It was Jacques de Billy's efforts that formed the basis of Migne's edition (MPG 35–38). Alongside Greek editions and Latin translations, vernacular editions also began to appear in the sixteenth century and continued unabated (Way 1971: 49–51). The first apparent attempt to create a critical collection of Gregory's work was made in 1914 by the Krakow Academy of Science, but this was never completed. To date, the *Sources Chrétiennes* has produced 10 volumes of Gregory's works, beginning in 1974. The *Corpus Christianorum: Corpus Nazianzenum* began in 1988 and has, to date, produced 24 volumes, searchable through their webpage.

Gregory of Nyssa

In the 1940s, Werner Jaeger exclaimed that Gregory was unknown, despite the large body of works he left behind. Interestingly, Jaeger's lament was preceded by a nearly identical one in the title page of Melchior Neuss' 1537 edition of Gregory's *Apologia de hexaemeron*. Both laments are a slight exaggeration, since Gregory was indeed well known and some of his works found an enduring audience; though there are exceptions, such as the *Libri Carolini* (c. 790 but not widely distributed until published in 1549), which cavalierly states that it will ignore the authority of Gregory because his works are not known to the authors (CPG §3135–3236; Otten 2001: 4). As with Basil and Gregory Nazianzen, the Renaissance provided greater access to Gregory's writings. Nonetheless, as a general statement, Jaeger's lament does underline the fact that Gregory was not as highly regarded as Basil and Gregory Nazianzen and the renewed interest in the Cappadocians was not equally distributed. Moreover, the two significant documents associated with Gregory of Nyssa labored under false attribution until the late nineteenth century. Gregory's *De differentia essentiae et hypostasis* (his first work to be printed) was for a long time attributed to his brother, Basil (Silvas 2007: 247–260). Conversely, a work long associated with Gregory, *De natura hominis*, was actually written by Nemesius of Emesa. Still another important work (*De vita Moyses*) did not garner the necessary critical study and improved translation until the twentieth century. Adding to the relative obscurity of Gregory is that two of the theologians who helped perpetuate his legacy – Evagrius and John of Damascus – copied out long sections of Gregory's work without clear attribution or citation. Thus, many theologians were indeed reading Gregory but without knowing it. It is possible that this ambiguity served Gregory well. His embrace of Origen (especially regarding *apokatastasis*) and Neo-Platonism caused "considerable embarrassment" to subsequent editors (Meredith 1999: 139). Therefore, it is possible that authors found it easier to use (and thus promote) Gregory's legacy while not drawing attention to their particular source.

Nonetheless, what was embarrassing for some was inspiring for others. Indeed, it was Gregory's ascetic and mystical theology that was most enduring, especially in the Byzantine, Syrian, and Arabic traditions, as witnessed by the volume of extant work in those languages. Gregory's longest dogmatic work, *Contra Eunomium*, was well received in the tradition due to the efforts of Maximus the Confessor and John of Damascus, yet its influence waned over time as the Arian, Apollinarist, and Sabellianist controversies receded (CPG §3135; GNO 1–2; SC 521, 524, and 551). His most popular work was exegetical, *De opificio hominis* (not to be confused with *De natura hominis* by Nemesius) (CPG §3154; GNO *Epistula Canonica*; SC 6). Though Gregory's reception history is still being developed, scholars have traced his influence through three prominent theologians: Ps-Denis the Areopagite (late fifth/early sixth century), Maximus the Confessor (580–662), and Gregory Palamas (1296–1359). Werner Jaeger posits that Evagrius Ponticus (346–399) was the most likely mediator between Gregory and the Syrian tradition (Wicher 1984: 16).

Maximus the Confessor is an essential link between Gregory's age and the subsequent tradition. It was Maximus who copied out large sections of Gregory's works and commented upon Gregory's insights (Wicher 1984: 18). It was Maximus, likely sensitive to the anti-Origenism of his day, who wrote an *Apology* for Gregory, distinguishing Gregory's perspective from that of the beleaguered reputation of the Alexandrian. Likewise, John of Damascus (675–749) found guidance in Gregory's works. The third section (entitled *fons scientiae*) of the Damascene's *De fide orthodoxa* contains long citations of Gregory's works, though not always with clear references to the source (Wicher 1984: 18). Others contributed to Gregory's reception history: Photius (c. 810–893) reflected on the content and style of the *Contra Eunomium*, and the commentary on the Song of Songs by Michael Psellus (c. 1017–1078) includes references from Gregory's work. Likewise, other Byzantine authors of the eleventh and twelfth centuries also quoted extensively from Gregory (Wicher 1984: 19–20). In the Latin Church, Gregory's works were introduced by Denis Exiguus (c. 470–c. 544), who offered the first Latin translation of *De opificio hominis*. His translation would remain the standard circulated copy until a new translation became available in 1567 (Wicher 1984: 23).

Various passages from Gregory's other works were included in florilegia and quoted by theologians. Isidore of Seville (c. 560–636) offered quotations from Gregory, though he often confused and conflated Gregory of Nyssa and Gregory Nazianzen. The Carolingian renaissance of the ninth century introduced Gregory to a wider audience, especially through two Celtic scholars, Dungal of Bobbio (fl. 811–828) and John Scotus Eriugena (c. 815–c. 877). Eriugena quoted large sections (using his own translation) of *De opificio hominis* in his *De divisione naturae*. This work would also introduce Gregory into the thought and writing of William of St Thierry (c. 1075–1148). Eriugena's other works also reveal a relatively broad reception of Gregory's writings. The biggest influx of material to the Latin Church came with the translation of John of Damascus' *De fide orthodoxa* in the twelfth century. It was Burgundio of Pisa (d. 1193) who translated the entirety of *De natura hominis*, for which he (not having any reason to doubt the attribution) continued to identify Gregory as the author. Burgundio's translation was very popular. Albert Magnus, Thomas Aquinas, and other scholastics would cite the work, a problem only perpetuated for scholars of the Renaissance who used Johannes Cano's revised translation of the same.

Through the late fifteenth and sixteenth centuries, Gregory benefited from the introduction of Greek patristic sources in the Latin Church via the Byzantine émigrés. Though the previously mentioned misattributions were not corrected, there was an increased interest in the works of Gregory and more of his works became available to an eager audience. In 1446, George Trebizond offered a loose translation (at times, more of an interpretation) of *De vita Moysis*. Gregory's *Epistola II, De iis qui adeunt Hierosolyma* became the focus of a minor polemical skirmish between Protestant and Roman Catholic theologians in the latter half of the sixteenth century. The letter (in which Gregory is critical of pilgrimages to holy places) was cited by the authors of the *Madgeburg Centuries* in their effort to demonstrate that the Lutheran Reformers could claim the authority of much of the theology and practice of the early Church. The subsequent debate over the content of the letter, now carried out primarily between Reformed and Roman Catholic theologians, raged for decades. Likewise, a similar controversy erupted over Gregory's Eucharistic theology (Wicher 1984: 29–31). Though the interpretation of Gregory was often polemical, interest in Gregory transcended the confessional divide.

The first printed Greek edition of one of Gregory's works was *De opificio hominis* (Venice, 1536). The first Latin edition of something approaching a "collection" of Gregory's work appeared in 1537 (Cologne). The first major Latin collection appeared in 1550 (Verona). Seven treatises in Greek appeared in 1587 (Augsburg). The first Greek edition with Latin translation and notation appeared in 1596, the work of two Jesuit scholars, Fronton du Duc and Jacob Gretser. Subsequent Greek editions appeared in 1698 (by Lorenzo Alessandro Zaccagni, Rome) and in 1731 (Giambattista Caraccioli, Pisa). The first vernacular editions of Gregory's works became available in the 1560s (in French, German, and Italian). The editions of Zaccagni and Caraccioli were reprinted, along with *spuria*, in Andreas Galand's *Bibliotheca veterum Patrum* (1765–1781). In 1833, Angelo Mai published two previously unedited works in Latin translation (a subsequent edition in 1847 provided the Greek text). J.P. Migne's editions (vols 44–46) were the first effort to incorporate all of Gregory's authentic works into a single volume, though it was largely based on the flawed 1638 edition (Paris) of Aegidius Morellus (Wicher 1984: 32). This was the textual situation in the early twentieth century in which Ulrich von Wilamowitz-Moellendorff of Berlin (whose efforts were continued and expanded by Werner Jaeger and Giorgio Pasquali) and the editors of *Sources Chrétiennes* began their work. To date, 10 volumes of Gregory's works are available in the *Gregorii Nysseni Opera* editions and they are searchable on the Brill website.

Conclusion

The reception history of the Cappadocians is rich and diverse, a reality that certainly reflects the caliber of devotion, discernment, and didactic qualities of the three great theologians. Alongside St Augustine, St John Chrysostom, and St Thomas Aquinas, their influence is both substantial and enduring. There was never a period in which their reputation was unappreciated or texts were not sought out. When the Cappadocians experienced a "renaissance" (such as in the sixteenth and twentieth centuries), it was the result of their well-respected works becoming more available to an already eager audience or seen as a means of shedding new light on subsequent concerns. Since the close of the fourth century, subsequent theologians in the Christians tradition have known (or known that they should know) the works of the Cappadocians. However, as we have demonstrated, not every Cappadocian Father received the same acclaim, and not every work received the same attention and interest in the span of the tradition; some became objects of less interest (such as Basil's *Adversus Eunomium*), others garnered more over time (such as Gregory of Nyssa's *De vita Moysis*), while the brilliance of others never waned (such as Gregory Nazianzen's orations and poetry). The scholar interested in the history of ideas and the development of Christian thought will see in the reception of the Cappadocians their acclaim as touchstones and "pillars of orthodoxy." The twentieth and twenty-first centuries have made the texts from the Cappadocians more widely distributed in a variety of languages than ever before (though, as we have documented, this desire to disseminate and translate their works was never absent). The record of the Cappadocian reception is a testimony to their enduring power to delight, challenge, and edify future generations who would worship the divine mystery that is the Triune God.

Bibliography

Primary Sources

Amidon, Philip R. (1997), *The Church History of Rufinus of Aquileia: Books 10 and 11.* New York: Oxford University Press.

Deferrari, Roy (1926), *St. Basil and His Letters*, vol. 4. Harvard: Loeb Classics.

Gregorius Presbyter (2001), *Vita Sancti Gregorii Theologi*, X. Lequeux (ed.). Corpus Christianorum Series Graeca 44. Turnhout: Brepols.

Jaeger, Werner, Langerbeck, Hermann, Hörner, Hadwig, Mühlenberg, Ekkehard, and Drobner, Hubertus R. (eds) (1952–present), *Gregorii Nysseni Opera*. Leiden: Brill.

Migne, J.-P. (ed.) (1857–1866) *Patrologiae cursus completus: Series Graeca*. Paris: Migne.

Schaff, P. and Wace, H. (1995). *Socrates, Sozomen: Church Histories*. Nicene and Post Nicene Fathers 2. Peabody, MA: Hendrickson (reprint).

Silvas, Anna (2007), *Gregory of Nyssa, The Letters: Introduction, Translation, and Commentary*. Supplement to *Vigilae Christianae*, vol. 83. Leiden: Brill.

Silvas, Anna (2005), *The Asketikon of St. Basil the Great*. Oxford: Oxford University Press.

Silvas, Anna (2014), *Basil of Caesarea, Questions of the Brothers: Syriac Text and English Translation*. Texts and Studies in Eastern Christianity, 3. Leiden: Brill.

Secondary Sources

Backus, Irena (2001), "Calvinist orthodoxy: patristic scholarship", in *The Reception of the Church Fathers in the West*, vol. 2, Irena Backus (ed.). Leiden: Brill.

Backus, Irena (1993), *La patristique et les guerres de religion en France Étude de l'activité littéraire de Jacques de Billy (1535–1581) O.S.B.* Turnhout: Brepols.

Backus, Irena (1990a), "Some fifteenth- and sixteenth-century Latin translations of the Greek Fathers, c. 1440–1565: Basil of Caesarea by Trapezuntius, Argyropulos, Cornarus, and Strigel; Justin Martyr by Perionius, Gelenius, and Lange". *Studia Patristica*, 18: 305–321.

Backus, Irena (1990b), *Lectures humanistes de Basile de Césarée: Traductions latines (1439–1618)*. Paris: Brepols.

Bezzel, Irmgard (ed.) (1983–present), *Verzeichnis der im deutschen Sprachbereich erschienenen Drucke des 16. Jahrhunderts: VD16*. Stuttgart: Hiersemann.

Fedwick, Paul Jonathan (1993–2004), *Bibliotheca Basiliana Universalis: A Study of the Manuscript Tradition of the Works of Basil of Caesarea*, five vols. Turnhout: Brepols.

Geerard, M. and Noret, J. (1998), *Clavis Patrum Graecorum Supplementum*. Turnhout: Brepols.

Haelewyck, Jean-Claude (ed.) (1988–present), *Corpus Christianorum: Corpus Nazianzenum*, 24 vols. Turnhout: Brepols.

Hall, H. Ashley (2014), *Philip Melanchthon and the Cappadocians: A Reception of Greek Patristic Sources in the Sixteenth Century*. Göttingen: Vandenhoeck & Ruprecht.

Lewis, Neil (2001), "Robert Grosseteste and the Church Fathers". In *Reception of the Church Fathers*, vol. 1, Irena Backus (ed.). Leiden: Brill.

Matter, E. Anne (2001), "The Church Fathers and the *Glossa Ordinaria*". In *The Reception of the Church Fathers in the West*, vol. 1, Irena Backus (ed.). Leiden: Brill.

Meredith, Anthony (1999), *Gregory of Nyssa*. London: Routledge.

Otten, Willemien (2001), "The texture of tradition". In *Reception of the Church Fathers*, vol. 1, Irena Backus (ed.). Leiden: Brill.

Pauli, OSB, Judith, (1998), "Basil of Caesarea". In *Dictionary of Early Christian Literature*, Siegmar Döpp and Wilhelm Geerlings (eds). New York: Herder and Herder.

Schucan, Luzi (1973), *Das Nachleben von Basilius Magnus "ad adolescentes": Ein Beitrag zur Geschichte des christlichen Humanismus*. Geneva: Droz.

Stinger, Charles L. (2001), "Italian Renaissance learning". In *Reception of the Church Fathers*, vol. 2, Irena Backus (ed.). Leiden: Brill.

Stinger, Charles L. (1998), *The Renaissance in Rome*. Bloomfield, IN: Indiana University Press.

Way, Agnes Clare (1976), *Catalogus Translationem et Commentariorum: Medieval and Renaissance Latin Translations and Commentaries, Annotated Lists and Guides*, vol. 3, F. Edward Cranz (ed.). Washington, DC: Catholic University of America.

Way, Agnes Clare (1971), *Catalogus Translationem et Commentariorum: Medieval and Renaissance Latin Translations and Commentaries, Annotated Lists and Guides*, vol. 2, Paul Oskar Kristeller (ed.). Washington, DC: Catholic University of America.

Wicher, Helen Brown (1984), "Gregorius Nyssenus". In *Catalogus Translationum et Commentariorum: Medieval and Renaissance Latin Translations and Commentaries*, vol. 5, F. Edward Cranz (ed.). Washington, DC: Catholic University of America.

CHAPTER 22

The Desert Fathers and Mothers

John Chryssavgis

Introduction

One of the fascinating puzzles confronting scholars dealing with the fourth and fifth centuries concerns the origin, development, and reception of *The Sayings of the Desert Fathers*. How and where were the *Apophthegmata* recorded? More importantly and interestingly, how were these *Sayings* ultimately collected and published? Finally, how and where were they received through the centuries? The *Sayings* constitute one of the most complex problems in patristic literature (Guy 1962: 7).

The modern revival of interest in the lifestyle of the Egyptian Fathers and Mothers is deeply indebted to the early desert literature and the desert dwellers themselves. Their *Sayings* – whether in the alphabetical and anonymous collections or in their systematic collections – are preserved in various collections in all languages of the Christian tradition, including Greek, Latin, Syriac, Armenian, Sahidic, Bohairic, and Ethiopian, together with similar texts and lives in their Coptic, Georgian, and Arabic versions. According to Samuel Rubenson:

> Even if we limit ourselves to the printed collections of sayings, we are still dealing with about 2500 different sayings, preserved in seven major and five minor collections. Of these sayings the great majority are found in several collections; some 600 are even found in almost all the major collections, while only some hundred are attested in no more than one collection. There is no doubt that the collections for most of their material all derive from a common origin (Rubenson 1990: 146).

Rubenson is supervising an extensive and comprehensive research project at Lund University, whose purpose is to analyze the *Apophthegmata Patrum* in relation to classical educational material and literary models by means of diverse perspectives and methods in an effort to appreciate the emergence of Christian culture and modes of education as well as the relationship between Antiquity and Christianity. While this ambitious, albeit vital, program will focus on the Gaza tradition, a critical study of the reception of desert literature would also need to explore later manuscript collections, such as the tenth-century *Pavlos Evergetinos*. Clearly, most monasteries possessed their own *Gerontikon* or *Paterikon*; Guy (1984: 221) refers to these as "collections of the sabaitical type."

Indeed, to adapt the words of Adolf von Harnack: "If I may be permitted to use strong language, I should not hesitate to say that no book has had a more stultifying effect on Egypt, Western Asia, and Europe than" the *Apophthegmata Patrum* (Waddell 1936: 7). This chapter provides a brief historical and literary excursion into "the encroaching desert" (Goehring 1999: ch. 5) in order to place the *Apophthegmata* in their cultural and spiritual context.

From Egypt to Palestine

During the late fourth and through the fifth centuries, some of the key representatives of Egyptian monasticism began to disperse, for a variety of reasons, to the neighboring regions of Palestine and Sinai. Such an event may have been the result of the close of the foundational and formative era of the first generation of monastics that took flight into the desert of Egypt. Alternatively, it may have been caused by the persecution of the more intellectual representatives of the contemplative life in the region, especially those influenced and shaped by Evagrius of Pontus (345–399). Perhaps, however, it was also the consequence of a general trend and growing movement of migration throughout the seminal lands of monasticism. Monks now began to travel eastward. Nevertheless, they did not travel alone; at any rate, they did not have the feeling of innovating, at least in the way that Antony's biographer and Pachomius' biographical accounts appear to imply about these men. By this time, monasticism was well established in the Roman Empire, while some of the key texts were already available. Nor were these migrating monastics alone in two other ways: first, they often traveled with their disciples; and, second, they brought with them an entire tradition of "stories" and "sayings" that shaped their understanding of the ascetic way.

Already in the biography of Hilarion, written by Jerome in around 390, there is an endeavor to forge a connection between Hilarion of Palestine and Antony of Egypt. Hilarion, it seems, spent several months in the circle of Antony and his friends. This possibly occurred during the time of Antony's first emergence from the desert (around 304–305). It was Antony who inspired Hilarion to return to Palestine where his parents had died, and to give away his inheritance – albeit at the tender age of just 15 – in order to live a life based on that of Antony.

It appears that Egypt constituted a kind of model for those who aspired to a life of seclusion and silence in other, neighboring monastic regions. If Jerome is correct – for he is mostly a good storyteller – then Hilarion marks the beginning of a long and significant connection between the ways and words of the Egyptian elders and the rules and writings of their Palestinian successors. Therefore, both Epiphanius and Jerome brought back to Palestine a way of life that they clearly learned in Egypt.

The *Sayings* also actually record several bonds between the desert of Egypt and the desert of Sinai. Following the death of Antony (d. 356), Abba Sisoes left Scetis and traveled eastward, choosing, however, to settle no farther east than Antony's inner mountain. There he remained for 72 years. This would bring us to around the year 429. From there, Sisoes would not have very far to go to Clysma, very close in fact to the opening of the Sinaite desert. Clysma was situated at the very tip of the Red Sea, on the side of the Suez Gulf; Sisoes would sometimes even meet at that crossroad with elders from the Sinaite region. For example, he had occasion to meet a certain Ammoun of Raithou (not Ammoun of Nitria), who came to seek the advice of Sisoes, as recorded in his *Sayings* 17, 21, 26, 28, and 50. A road existed, certainly from the age of Egeria, from Pelusium through Clysma to Pharan. From there, a paved path led to the holy mountain of Sinai itself. Indeed, the monks of Raithou would frequent Clysma for commercial exchange and social contact, especially as they were by far the most isolated of the Sinaite inhabitants (Dahari 2000: 113–146). There is a *Saying* about Abba Joseph of Pelusium, who stayed for a while on Sinai (Cronius 5); another *Saying* describes Abba "Nikon, who lived on Mt. Sinai." (Nikon 1). Yet another *Saying* refers to Abba Megethios (Megethios 2), "who lived on the river bank at Sinai"; and Abba Xoios the Theban "who one day visited the mountain of Sinai" (Netras 1).

Another personality from this period, Porphyry, spent some 5 years in Scetis of Egypt, returning in 377 to inhabit a cell in the valley of the Jordan and, later, to become bishop of Gaza in Palestine (395–420). Indeed, *The Sayings of the Desert Fathers* include the names of other Palestinian monks, whether by origin or by adoption: Gelasius, Epiphanius, Theodore of Eleftheropolis, Hilarion, Cassian, Phocas, and Philagrios. It is fairly certain that the *Apophthegmata* were put into written form in the circles of such monks, as well as in the circle of disciples of Poemen, probably in Gaza in about 480.

The connection, however, between the desert of Egypt, the dunes of Gaza, and the mountain of Sinai becomes particularly noticeable when Abba Silvanus settled with his disciples in Gerara in the early fifth century. We have at our disposal 26 sayings, in the alphabetical collection alone, from this group of monks.

We can identify the names of four of Silvanus' disciples: Zaccharias, Mark, Netras, and Zenon. Zaccharias was perhaps the first and closest of the disciples, and also succeeded Silvanus in 414. But it is said that, "the old man loved Mark because of his obedience." He is the one who heard his elder calling him and left unfinished the letter "omega," which he was writing at the time. He was a copyist, and therefore well educated:

> It was said of Abba Silvanus that at Scetis he had a disciple called Mark, whose obedience was great. He was a scribe... Once Silvanus knocked on the door of Mark's cell and said: "Mark." Hearing the old man's voice, Mark jumped up immediately and the old man sent him off to do some work... Then he went into Mark's cell and picked up his book and noticed that he had begun to write the letter 'omega,' but when he had heard the old man, he had responded without finishing to write the letter (Mark 1; see also Silvanus 1–2).

This small group was quite probably both refined and cultivated. From the *Sayings* attributed to them, we already know that they had one copyist among them. In addition to this, however, Zaccharias was learned in Hebrew, and Netras was qualified to be ordained bishop of Pharan, in the Sinai Peninsula. We also know that they liked to entertain visitors, and – at least in Sinai – they tended to a garden. In addition, the alphabetical collection tells us that Mark's mother was wealthy. These may be among the reasons that they left Egypt during the first Origenist crisis. After a brief sojourn at Sinai, they moved to Palestine, beside the river that flowed in the area of Gerara (Silvanus, in Guy (1984: 47)). The fifth saying of Mark in the *Apophthegmata* records his wish not to accompany the group to Palestine but to remain in Sinai, where he died:

> It was said of Abba Silvanus, that when he wished to go away to Syria, his disciple Mark said to him: "Father, I do not want to leave this place [of Sinai], nor to let you go away, abba. Stay here for three days." And on the third day, Mark died.

Another well-known monk and monastic author in this region was Abba Isaiah of Scetis. A later emigrant from Egypt, Isaiah had spent many years in a monastery, but had also resided in the desert of Scetis. He moved to Palestine, fleeing fame, between 431 and 451. He first settled near Eleftheropolis, moving finally to Beit Daltha near Gaza, some four miles from Thavatha. There he stayed for several decades, serving for his contemporaries and visitors as a living example of the old Scetiote ascetic life, until his death in 488 or 489. A small number of the alphabetical *Sayings* are attributed to this Isaiah; although these are not directly linked to his Greek writings, they are found in the Coptic fragments (Guillaumont 1956). By contrast, a much larger number of the systematic *Sayings* are easily attributed to Isaiah of Scetis.

This is not the last that we hear of these places. For, Gaza and its environs are indelibly marked by the presence of two remarkable elders in the next century: Barsanuphius and John; and by the products of their teaching: their *Letters: Questions and Answers*, as well as by their disciples, especially Dorotheus. Indeed, the city of Thavatha is mentioned on the Madeba Map, a mosaic map from a church in Madeba (modern Jordan) dating from the latter part of Justinian's era (Glucker 1987: 18–20), and thus almost coinciding with the latter part of the lives of Barsanuphius and John.

We do not know exactly when Barsanuphius, himself an Egyptian monk, entered the region of Thavatha and chose to be enclosed as a recluse in a nearby cell. From this position, he offered counsel to a number of ascetics who were gradually attracted around the Old Man as he developed a reputation for discernment and compassion. One of these monks, Abba Seridos, who also attended to Barsanuphius, was appointed abbot of a monastic community, probably established in order to organize the increasing number of monks that looked to Barsanuphius as their elder. Seridos was the only person permitted to communicate with Barsanuphius, acting as a mediator for those who wished to submit questions in writing and to receive a response through the same avenue.

Sometime between 525 and 527, another hermit, named John, came to live beside Barsanuphius, who surrendered his own cell to him, while he moved to a new cell nearby. Barsanuphius became known as "the holy Old Man" or "the Great Old Man," a Coptic term familiar among Egyptian circles, and ascribed also by Palladius to Antony "the Great." John is simply called "the Other Old Man." The two shared the same way of life and supported one another's ministry.

There are around 850 letters that survive from these two Old Men, a treasure house of information from a variety of people about life at the time. Monks in communities, hermits in isolation, spouses in families, professionals in society: all asking questions, submitted in writing to the wise elder, and receiving a response through their scribes. The responses of the elders are spontaneous and balanced, wise and witty, reminiscent of their predecessors in the desert of Egypt.

The lifestyles of the ascetics living in Egypt and later in Palestine – or, indeed, their ascetic ways of dying unto themselves and the world – were not the only aspects that were imitated and copied during this period. In particular, it was the *Apophthegmata Patrum* that permeated throughout the Christian world and were preserved by the disciples of these same sages, and the disciples of their disciples. Thence, they were transferred into the whole of the ancient world and translated into all languages of early Christendom. One of the most likely places that these *Sayings* were recollected and then collected was in Palestine, partly due to its geographical proximity to Egypt, but also due to the steady progression of Egyptian monks to the southern parts of Judaea. This diffusion of the *Apophthegmata* on the one hand and the emigration of the Fathers and Mothers on the other hand is surely not unrelated. Already, Fr Lucien Regnault has demonstrated how *The Sayings of the Desert Fathers*, in both their alphabetical and anonymous or systematic collections, are found in seminal texts of the time. Such texts include the *Life of Saint Melanie the Younger*, attributed to her confidant and chaplain Gerontius and dating to the middle of the fifth century; the *Life of Saint Euthymius*, written by Cyril of Scythopolis in the latter half of the sixth century; and the *Reflections* of Zosimas, who founded a community in the first half of the sixth century. In particular, Regnault highlights the role of the monasteries of Seridos and of Dorotheus in the Gaza region, and the *Correspondence* of Barsanuphius and John as well as the *Works* of their disciple Dorotheus, all of which offer the richest documentation in this regard (Regnault 1981: 320–330).

Melanie's *Life* refers to one of the sayings of the *Apophthegmata*; Euthymius' *Life* contains three such sayings; while Zosimas' treatise makes numerous citations of these sayings, implying perhaps that the latter borrowed these from existing written texts. Euthymius and Zosimas also reveal having heard various sayings of the *Apophthegmata* from others, which attests to the fact that these were widely known and, possibly, even accessible more or less everywhere in monastic circles of lower Palestine by the middle of the sixth century. Indeed, Zosimas' reference to "the sayings of the holy elders" (Avgoustinos 1913: 17) is perhaps the earliest such characterization of the sayings with this specific title.

The *Reflections* of Abba Zosimas appear for the first time in English translation below. We are told by the author that:

> The blessed Zosimas always loved to read these *Sayings* all the time; they were almost like the air that he breathed (*Reflections* XII, b).

Like *The Sayings of the Desert Fathers* themselves, these "reflections" were spoken and not written down by Zosimas. In content and style, they very much resemble the *Ascetic Discourses* of Abba Isaiah of Scetis. Zosimas flourished between 475 and 525, from the period just after the fourth Ecumenical Council (in 451) until around the time of the great Gaza elders, Barsanuphius, John, and Dorotheus. He is mentioned several times by Dorotheus of Gaza, who knew him personally and visited him as his younger contemporary and compatriot. Dorotheus may in fact be the compiler of the *Reflections* of Abba Zosimas.

In particular, Fr Lucien Regnault highlights the role of the monasteries of Seridos and of Dorotheus in the Gaza region, together with the *Correspondence* of Barsanuphius and John as well as the *Works* of their disciple, Dorotheus, all of which offer the richest documentation in this regard.

The *Letters* of Barsanuphius and John, again dating to the first half of the sixth century, frequently quote or evoke the *Sayings*. In fact, there are at least 80 direct references to the *Apophthegmata* themselves, while numerous phrases recommend them as a basis for spiritual practice and progress, sometimes by name (16 times) but mostly by implication (34 times). There are at least 55 references to *The Sayings of the Desert Fathers* in the writings of Dorotheus alone. In his *Teachings* I, 13 (PG: 1633C), he also seems to be the first writer to designate the *Apophthegmata* as the "*Gerontikon*" (or the *Book of Elders*). Might, therefore, this Dorotheus also be one of those responsible for the collection of the *Sayings* themselves? Certainly Dorotheus (*Teachings* 24) is the only ancient witness to the single saying attributed to Basil in the alphabetical collection of *The Sayings of the Desert Fathers* (Regnault 1981: 328), while both Barsanuphius and Dorotheus refer to the *Rules* of Saint Basil.

During the fourth and the early fifth centuries, the golden age during which *The Sayings of the Desert Fathers* flourished, the words of the elders were preserved both in the heart and by word of mouth. They were precisely that: sayings; and these circulated both in Egypt and in Palestine as a result of the fluid movement between the two "seminal" lands, but especially as a result of the eastward influx of monks from Egypt to Palestine, whether forcefully or freely. It seems that later generations of ascetic leaders and authors sensed the importance of transmitting, even translating, their Egyptian roots for future generations in both East and West. Thus, Evagrius (*Praktikos* 106–112) and John Cassian (*Institutes* V, 24–41) included several sayings from the *Apophthegmata* in their influential writings. Abba Isaiah of Scetis inserted numerous of these sayings, both recognizable and original, in his *Ascetic Discourses*, possibly regarding himself as responsible for preserving and promoting the words of the elders that he knew and lived with in Egypt. The abundant references to the *Sayings* in the *Letters* of Barsanuphius and John further attest to their concern that the ways and words of the ancient elders be pondered and practiced.

Indeed, the *Letters* of Barsanuphius and John, and especially the ones addressed by, and to, Dorotheus of Gaza (*Letters* 252–338), reveal yet another element that gradually disappeared from *The Sayings of the Desert Fathers*, as these began to be collated and edited: the original transmission of the wisdom of the Egyptian desert preserved the spontaneity of the profound advice and impressive actions of the Desert Fathers and Mothers. However, during the stage of transition from an oral culture to a written text, the *Sayings* became a little more static and began to lose sight of the personal element that sparked these words; more particularly and significantly, the process and struggle that shaped these words were also concealed. What was recorded was the intense drop of wisdom, without the stages that led to the final product. What is missing is the ongoing process – all of the contentions, hesitations, and limitations of the spiritual aspirant. *The Sayings of the Desert Fathers*, for instance, often present the spiritual reality in *the way that it should be, rather than in the way that it is* – with all the denials, the doubts, and the temptations. Yet, in Barsanuphius and John, we witness each of the painful stages unfolding in slow motion before our very eyes, like a film consisting of many gradually changing pictures. Here is one example of this progressive development of a thought and response.

Question 293. Question from the same brother to the same Old Man: If a brother does something that is not very significant, yet I am afflicted by this act on account of my own will, what should I do? Should I keep silent and not give rest to my heart, or should I speak to him with love and not remain troubled? And if the matter afflicts others, and not me, should I speak for the sake of the others? Or would this appear as if I have just taken on a cause?

Response by John. If it is a matter that is not sinful but insignificant, and you speak simply in order to give rest to your heart, then it is to your defeat. For, you were not able to endure it as a result of your weakness. Just blame yourself and be silent. However, if the matter afflicts others, tell your abbot; and whether he speaks or tells you to speak, you will be carefree.

Question 294. Question from the same person to the same Old Man: If I speak to the abbot for the sake of the others, I suspect that the brother will be troubled; so what should I do? And if he afflicts both the others and me, should I speak for the sake of the others, or should I keep silent in order not to satisfy myself? If I suspect that he will not be grieved, should I also speak for myself, or should I force myself against this?

Response by John. As far as the turmoil of the brother is concerned, if you speak to the abbot, then you have nothing to worry about. When it is necessary to speak for the sake of others, and you are worried about it, then speak for them. As for yourself, only force yourself not to speak.

Question 295. Question from the same to the same: But my thought tells me that if my brother is troubled against me, he will become my enemy, thinking that I slandered him to the abbot.

Response by John. This thought of yours is wicked; for, it wants to prevent you from correcting your brother. Therefore, do not prevent yourself from speaking, but do so according to God. For indeed, the sick that are being healed will even speak against their doctors; yet the latter do not care, knowing that the same shall thank them afterward.

Question 296. Question from the same to the same Old Man: If I look at my thought and notice that it is not for the brother's benefit that I wish to speak to the abbot, but with the purpose of slandering him, should I speak or keep silent?

Response by John. Advise your thought to speak according to God and not for the sake of slander. And if your thought is conquered by criticism, even so speak to your abbot and confess to him your criticism, so that both of you may be healed – the one who was at fault and the one who was critical.

Question 297. Question from the same to the same: If my thought does not allow me to confess to the abbot that I am speaking to him with the purpose of slandering the brother, what should I do? Should I speak or not?

Response. Do not say anything to him, and the Lord will take care of the matter. For, it is not necessary for you to speak when this harms your soul. God will take care of the brother's correction as He wills.

There is a further reason why the collector and editor of the *Apophthegmata* may be from the circle of monks in Seridos' community. A schematic comparison between the Egyptian and Palestinian elders may be helpful in this regard. Isaiah, Zosimas, Barsanuphius, and Dorotheus all seem to *display certain characteristics in common with and in contrast to the desert dwellers.* For instance, each of these four prominent figures is balanced and un-polemical in their nature and in their counsel, much like the disposition of the Egyptian monastics whose sayings are preserved in the collections. In general, they do not reveal the confessional rifts that affected so much of Christendom during this period. They are far less militant than other representatives of both the Chalcedonian and non-Chalcedonian circles. Other contemporary ascetics, such as Sabas, while compassionate and nonjudgmental in their outlook, are nevertheless deliberately and defensively concerned with confessional doctrine. It is no wonder, then, that an icon of the Great Old Man graces the altar-cloth fresco in the Great Church of Wisdom in Constantinople, beside those of Antony of Egypt and Ephraim the Syrian.

Yet, the Gaza elders also differ from their Egyptian counterparts inasmuch as they are on the whole more educated and widely read. This feature may not be entirely unknown among the Desert Fathers and Mothers, but it is rather exceptional. Barsanuphius' responses to questions about Origenist tendencies among certain representatives of the monastic tradition (in *Letters* 600–607), together with John's explanations of the Great Old Man's words, reveal an elder who appreciates fine intellectual distinctions without at the same time being absorbed by these to the detriment of his life of prayer. Thus, in another set of 13 questions (between *Letters* 151 and 167), being responses to a certain Euthymius whose mind is almost obsessed with allegorical interpretations and details, Barsanuphius recommends humility and silence.

At some point in time, then, between the work of Abba Isaiah of Scetis and the correspondence of the two Old Men of Gaza, there appears to have occurred a shift in the appreciation of the *Sayings*. Abba Isaiah senses that he is a *part of the tradition of the Desert Fathers*, that he has transplanted this tradition from the chosen land to an adopted land, and that he is obliged to keep that memory alive in his new homeland. Abba Barsanuphius and his disciples, particularly the gifted Dorotheus, sense that they are a *part of a new tradition,* closely linked to the past and yet at the same time clearly looking to a different experience and a different environment. The attitude of Abba Isaiah and Abba Zosimas is backward looking to the golden age of Egypt. Barsanuphius and Dorotheus are forward looking to the diverse monastic population that they are serving and the different monastic culture that they are confronted with. In fact, their presence in the region of Gaza, that intersection and cross-section of peoples and pilgrims, may well be the reason why the alphabetical collection of *The Sayings of the Desert Fathers* bring together so many pieces from the worlds of Egypt, Sinai, Palestine, Asia Minor, Syria, and as far east as Persia. The region also numbered Arabs, Greeks, Latins, Armenians, Georgians, and others. Moreover, the monks of this region were deeply influenced by Barsanuphius' openness toward foreigners imposed by a dynamic of positive interaction. Indeed, Barsanuphius was quite clear about the role of his contemporaries; it was, as he determines in *Letter* 569, to pray for the salvation of the whole world, orthodox and non-orthodox, pious and pagan:

> There are three men, perfect in God, who have exceeded the measure of humanity and received the authority to loose and bind, to forgive and hold sins. These stand before the shattered world, keeping the whole world from complete and sudden annihilation. Through their prayers, God combines His chastisement with His mercy. And it has been told to them, that God's wrath will last a little longer. Therefore, pray with them. For the prayers of these three are joined at the entrance to the spiritual altar of the Father of lights. They share in each other's joy and gladness in heaven. And when they turn once again toward the earth, they share in each other's mourning and weeping for the evils that occur and attract His wrath. These three are John in Rome and Elias in Corinth, and another in the region of Jerusalem. I believe that they will achieve His great mercy. Yes, they will indeed achieve it. Amen.

Undoubtedly, Barsanuphius possessed the discerning boldness before God, as well as the humanity to claim within his heart that he was the third of these ascetics.

In brief, Abba Isaiah and Abba Zosimas lamented over the loss of the past, while Barsanuphius and Dorotheus learned ways of relating to the present and looking to the future. The song of Isaiah and Zosimas declared with sorrow: "By the rivers of Babylon, there we sat down and there we wept, when we remembered Zion" (Psalm 137.1); the challenge of Barsanuphius and Dorotheus discerned: "How could we sing the Lord's song in a foreign land?" (Psalm 137.4) They understood that the tradition of the *Apophthegmata* demanded more than just repetition; it required unpacking and appropriation in a new way.

The Desert Mothers

The desert, of course, defied gender distinction and discrimination; anyone could enter the desert. And the sayings of the desert Mothers were also collected – whether in the sayings of the abbas (or *paterika*, which survive) or the ammas (or *miterika*, which are not extant). For instance, the alphabetical collection preserves the *apophthegmata* of three desert Mothers: Sarah, Syncletica, and Theodora. Women were welcomed as desert dwellers and even as spiritual directors. Moving into the desert implied a radical break with social constraint and involved a bold step into the realm of freedom: freedom from subjection, freedom from possession, and freedom from exploitation.

Of course, the world of the desert literature was still controlled by the men: it was they that did the collecting, the preserving, and the editing. However, almost tongue in cheek, Amma Sarah was unafraid to mingle with the men and remind them that they had not yet surrendered their worldly attachments and gender roles, remarking: "It is I who am a man; and you are like women!" (*Saying* 9) In the desert, the women reminded the men that their goal was to overcome conventional forms; their focus was the heavenly kingdom, where "there is no longer male or female, for all are one ... heirs according to the promise" (Gal. 3.28–29).

Conclusion

In their foundational and formative years, the *Apophthegmata Patrum* were received by word of mouth, from elder to disciple, from cell to cell, and from generation to generation. What began as a verbal tradition, conveying the charisma and allure of the wise and saintly *geron* – whether *abba* or *amma* – was gradually recorded in writing, becoming a written tradition that conveyed the virtues and ways, the wit and wisdom of former generations. What began as an inspirational feature increasingly became an instructional facet and even institutional factor for the monastics that followed – whether living as hermits or in communities. Ultimately, the transmission of the extensive literature known to us as the Sayings of the Elders aimed at the transformation of their disciples and readers, who sought to imitate the Lives of the Saints. The reception of the early *Apophthegmata Patrum* was essentially to become the foundation for the formation of the later readers (Rapp 2010: 130).

Yet, even as scholars continue – in the words of the Jesuit scholar and Bollandist precursor, Heribert Rosweyde (1569–1629) – "pumicing again [and again] the sheepskins of the old fathers" (Waddell 1936: 7), it becomes apparent to me that the reason for transcribing and documenting these informative and influential *Sayings* is less any political motivation than a realistic recognition and rationalization of the signs of the times. Whether alphabetical or anonymous, systematic or thematic, the recording and reception of the *Sayings* as a written tradition and literary form is ultimately a way – beyond variables and variations, as well as beyond consistency and conformity – not only of preserving the words of the elders for future generations, but primarily of promoting the virtues of these elders for purposes of instruction and imitation.

Bibliography

Primary Sources

Apophthegmata Patrum
Ward, Benedicta (ed.) (1975), *The Sayings of the Desert Fathers*. The Alphabetical Collection. London: Mowbrays.

Ward, Benedicta (ed./transl.) (2003), *The Desert Fathers: Sayings of the Early Christian Monks*. Penguin Classics (rev.).

Ward, Benedicta (transl.) (1986), *The Wisdom of the Desert Fathers: Systematic Sayings from the Anonymous Series of the Apophthegmata Patrum*. Oxford: SLG Press.

Barsanuphius and John

Neyt, F. and de Angelis, P. (1997), *Barsanuphe et Jean de Gaza, Correspondance*, vol. I, i. In *Sources Chrétiennes* 426, Paris. For a complete English translation of Barsanuphius and John, see John Chryssavgis (2006–2007), *The Correspondence of Barsanuphius and John, with translation, introduction, notes and complete indices*, two volumes. Washington, DC: Catholic University Press.

Cassian

Stewart, Columba (1998), *Cassian the Monk*. New York: Oxford University Press.

Evagrius

Bamberger, John Eudes (ed.) (2006), *Evagrius Ponticus: The Praktikos. Chapters on Prayer*. Kalamazoo, MI: Cistercian Publications.

Isaiah of Scetis

Chryssavgis, J. and Penkett, P.R. (2002), *Abba Isaiah of Scetis: Ascetic Discourses*. Kalamazoo, MI: Cistercian Publications.

Sozomen

Historia Ecclesiastica VI, 32, 8 in J. Bidez and G.C. Hansen (eds) (1960), *Die Griechischen Christlichen Schriftsteller der Ersten Jahrhunderte*, 50. Berlin: Akademie.

Secondary Sources

Avgoustinos (ed.) (1913), *Reflections of Abba Zosimas*, Jerusalem. For an English translation of The Reflections of Abba Zosimas, see J. Chryssavgis (2008), *In the Heart of the Desert: The Spirituality of the Desert Fathers and Mothers*, 2nd edition. Bloomington, IN: World Wisdom Books; 111–158.

Avi-Yonah, M. (1954), *The Madeba Mosaic Map*, Jerusalem.

Chitty, Derwas (1977), *The Desert A City: An Introduction to the Study of Egyptian and Palestinian Monasticism under the Christian Empire*. Crestwood, NY: St. Vladimir's Seminary Press (Oxford: Blackwell, 1966).

Dahari, U. (2000), *Monastic Settlements in South Sinai in the Byzantine Period: The Archaeological Remains*. Jerusalem: Israel Antiquities Authority.

Devreesse, R. (1954), *Introduction à l'étude des manuscrits grecs*. Paris: Klincksieck.

Driver, Steven (2002), *John Cassian and the Reading of Egyptian Monastic Culture*. New York: Routledge.

Glucker, C.A.M. (1987), *The City of Gaza in the Roman and Byzantine Periods*. BAR International Series 325., Oxford: BAR.

Goehring, James E. (1999), *Ascetics, Society, and the Desert: Studies in Early Egyptian Monasticism*. Harrisburg, PA: Trinity Press International.

Guillaumont, A. (1956), *L'ascéticon copte de l'abbé Isaïe. Fragments sahidiques édités et traduits*. Cairo: Publications de l'Institut français d'Archéologie orientale.

Guy, Jean-Claude (1962), *Recherches sur le tradition grecque des Apophthegmata Patrum*. Subsidia Hagiographica 36. Brussels: Société des Bollandistes.

Guy, Jean-Claude (1984), *Recherches sur le tradition grecque des Apophthegmata Patrum*, 2nd ed. Brussels: Société des Bollandistes.

Harmless, William (2004), *Desert Christians: An Introduction to the Literature of Early Monasticism*. Oxford University Press.

Rapp, Claudia (2010), "The origins of hagiography and the literature of early monasticism: purpose and genre between tradition and innovation". In *Unclassical Traditions, Volume 1: Alternatives to the Classical Past in Late Antiquity*, Christopher Kelly, Richard Flower, and Michael Stuart Williams (eds). Cambridge University Press.

Regnault, L. (1981), "Les *Apophtegmes des Pères* en Palestine aux IVe et Ve siècles". *Irénikon*, 54.

Rubenson, Samuel (1990), *The Letters of Antony: Origenist Theology, Monastic Tradition and the Making of a Saint*. Lund University Press.

Swan, Laura (2001), *The Forgotten Desert Mothers: Sayings, Lives and Stories of Early Christian Women*. Paulist Press.

Van Dijk, Mathilde (2006), "Disciples of the desert: Windesheim biographers and the imitation of the Desert Fathers". In *The Encroaching Desert: Egyptian Hagiography and the Medieval West*, Jitsa Dijkstra and Mathilde van Dijk (eds). Leiden: Brill; 257–280.

Van Parys, Michel (1988), "Abba Silvain et ses disciples". *Irénikon*, 61.

Waddell, Helen (1936), *The Desert Fathers*. London: Constable (rev. 1977).

Ward, Benedicta (1987), *Harlots of the Desert: A Study of Repentance in Early Monastic Sources*. Cistercian Publications.

CHAPTER 23

The Iconophile Fathers

Vladimir Baranov

Introduction

In the Eastern Orthodox Churches the Iconophile Fathers are celebrated for their struggle in defense of sacred images in the eighth and ninth centuries. This struggle was manifested both in their persecution on the part of the Iconoclastic authorities and in their writings. With the exceptions of John of Damascus and Theodore Abū Qurrah, their lives and writings were primarily associated with Constantinople as a center of the imperial Iconoclastic policies.

Generally, scholars have been interested in the Iconophile Fathers as thinkers who developed the Byzantine theology of image, which was destined to become a part of Orthodox identity to this day. However, the best way to assess the dynamics of the authority and reception of the Iconophile Fathers in the later tradition of the Orthodox Church is to turn to their representations in church decoration at various periods.

Images of the Iconophile Fathers

Despite his fame as the first defender of images and confessor, Patriarch Germanos appears in apses only on the periphery of the Byzantine world: in Cappadocian churches of the tenth-eleventh century (Teteriatnikov 1996: 88), and in two early twelfth-century Novgorod churches (St Sophia Cathedral and St Nicholas Cathedral). In middle and late Byzantine art, Germanos is represented rarely (St Nicholas tis Stigis near Kakopetria in Cyprus, Old St Clement in Ochrid, and Pantanassa in Mistra). In the calendar cycles, Germanos is depicted together with Epiphanios of Cyprus, whose memory is celebrated on the same day (Dormition Church at Gračanica; Holy Apostles in the Patriarchate of Peć).

The Wiley Blackwell Companion to Patristics, First Edition. Edited by Ken Parry.
© 2015 John Wiley & Sons Ltd. Published 2019 by John Wiley & Sons Ltd.

The same pattern occurs with Patriarch Nikephoros, who in the ninth century appeared in several polemical illuminations of the militantly anti-Iconoclastic marginal Psalters, and in a mosaic in the rooms above the southwest ramp and vestibule of Hagia Sophia, but after that he is depicted only rarely, mostly in the fresco calendar cycles, including those in the church of the Holy Ascension in the Visoki Dečani and in the monastery church of the Theotokos at Gračanica, and on one occasion appearing in the former context of his fame as an Iconophile champion next to representations of other Iconophile patriarchs, Germanos and Methodios (Church of the Hodegitria in the Patriarchate of Peć).

Yet even in the case of those Iconophile saints whose images were more numerous, such as John of Damascus, it seems that the creators of the iconographic programs did not appeal to a single established status of St John as an Iconophile saint. He was rather acknowledged as a "Marian" homilist and hymnographer, and was often depicted together with other Byzantine liturgical poets, such as Cosmas of Maiuma (Timios Stavros at Pelendri on Cyprus; at Gračanica), or Joseph and Theodore Graptos (St Panteleimon in Nerezi (Patterson-Ševčenko 2002); in the squinches of the parecclesion in Kariye Camii at Constantinople; St George at Staro-Nagoričino). In the exonarthex in Kariye Camii the medallions with John of Damascus and Cosmas of Maiuma flank the image of the Blachernitissa Theotokos, while in St George in Pološko and in the church of Christ the Savior in Verrhoia, the representations of these two adopted brothers with scrolls frame the composition of the Dormition of the Theotokos.

At the Georgian monastery of the Cross in Jerusalem, John of Damascus' role as a poet is reinforced in his paired standing representation with Maximos the Confessor (apparently reflecting the Palestinian origin of both Fathers), and by the kneeling small figure of the famous Georgian poet Shota Rustaveli, who lived in the monastery in the twelfth century and who addresses John of Damascus on the fresco. Sometimes John of Damascus appears among the ascetic monks; for example, in the narthex of the church of Archangel Michael at Lesnovo, in St Niketas near Skopje, in the church of Sts Joachim and Anna (Kraljeva) at Studenica, in the Visoki Dečani church, in the church of Archangels Michael and Gabriel at Kastoria, and on an icon-tablet of Novgorod where he is accompanied by St John of the Ladder and St Arsenios.

The only Father whose images seem to be steadily connected with the Iconophile connotation, in addition to his authority as a hymnographer, seems to be Theodore the Stoudite, who often accompanies the image of the Iconophile martyr Stephen the Younger (Matka church of St Andrew at Skopje; the church of St Niketas the Goth at Čučer; the parecclesion of St Nicholas in the monastery church of the Theotokos at Gračanica). However, the relative popularity of his images in monumental art may be to a large degree due to the popularity of the Stoudite *Typikon* in the Orthodox world.

Texts of the Iconophile Fathers

The images show that the Iconophile Fathers paradoxically appear in church art mostly in their "non-iconophile" roles. Indeed, their iconophile writings are very relevant to our modern media- and image-based culture, whereas for the Byzantines the polemical writings of the Iconophile Fathers seem mostly to have been relevant until the point when their purpose was fulfilled; that is, until Iconoclasm was defeated. After that, the writings against Iconoclasm were used only sporadically and for other purposes, while in the later tradition those writings not directly concerned with Iconoclasm were mostly used. And yet the essence and the intent of the writings of the Iconophile Fathers – that is, the dogma of icon veneration – was preserved in the daily practice of the Church.

Some writings by the Iconophile Fathers continued to live on independently, such as the *Short History* of Patriarch Nikephoros, or his *Apologeticus atque Antirrhetici*, excerpted and used in a completely different setting in the Hesychast Controversy. The compendium *Expositio fidei* (CPG 8043) by John of Damascus, including a chapter on icons (IV, 16) had immense influence in various linguistic and religious environments, both in the East and in the West. At the same time, some Iconophile writings went into oblivion in Byzantine use. The *Homily on the Icons and the Cross against the Heretics* (CPG 8033), attributed to Patriarch Germanos, survived only in Georgian (van Esbroeck 1999: 19–55) and Slavonic translations (Baranov 2006), incidentally having a marked influence among a few known iconophile texts in these regions (on the Old Russian use of the text, see Kriza (2006: 381–382)). The text of the Νουθεσία γέροντος περὶ τῶν ἁγίων εἰκόνων ("The Admonition of the Old Man on the Holy Icons"; Melioranskij 1901: v–xxxix) was published on the basis of a single discovered manuscript; it shows a marked contrast in popularity to the closely related *Adversus Constantinum Cabalinum* (CPG 8114), which is a reworking of the Νουθεσία γέροντος using the *Apologies in Defense of Images* by John of Damascus (CPG 8045; for the list of parallels, see Melioranskij (1901: 2–15, 18–20)). The *Refutation* of the Iconoclastic Council of 815 by Patriarch Nikephoros was edited only in 1997 from two surviving manuscripts (Featherstone 1997). Seven short treatises on the making of images by the same Patriarch Nikephoros survived only in three manuscripts and were edited very recently (Declerck 2004), as well as the anonymous refutation of the fragments by the last Iconoclastic Patriarch John the Grammarian (single manuscript, the first part is edited in Evdokimova (2011)).

It is not always easy to trace the later fate of the texts owing to their plasticity, both during the Iconoclastic Controversy and later texts were cut and reused for various purposes, attributed to other authors, and the boundaries between the genres were easily trespassed. In addition to the reworking of the Νουθεσία γέροντος, a good example of how the various writings were reutilized is the *Life of Stephen the Younger* by Stephen the Deacon. For describing the martyrdom of an Iconophile saint under the Emperor Constantine V the author uses not only other hagiographical writings, such as *Homilies on Patapios and Therapon* by Andrew of Crete or the *Life of Euthymios* by Cyril of Scythopolis, but also the *Acts of the Seventh Ecumenical Council*, the Iconophile polemical tract *Adversus Constantinum Cabalinum*, and some liturgical texts (Auzépy 1999: 103–168).

In the post-Iconoclastic epoch the importance and usefulness of the polemical writings from the second stage of the struggle against Iconoclasm, with their scholastic and philosophical leaning, must have superseded the importance of the earlier writings in defense of images, including even the *Apologies in Defense of Images* by John of Damascus which survived in a relatively modest number of manuscripts. As opposed to the earlier writings, which were either represented by popular polemical tracts (*Adversus Constantinum Cabalinum* and the related *Adversus Iconoclastas* (CPG 8121) by John of Jerusalem, the *Homily on the Cross and Icons against the Heretics* (attributed to Patriarch Germanos)) or, conversely, such systematic Christology-based treatises as the *Apologies* of John of Damascus, the "scholastic" writings of the second Iconoclasm dealing with general principles of the epistemology of the image could be easily excerpted and used as brief and clear philosophical statements at a later time.

The final victory over Iconoclasm in 843 not only gave a powerful impetus to the flourishing of Iconophile hagiography. The normative Iconophile Orthodoxy viewed its roots not only and not so much in the theological arguments of Iconophile champions, but in the antiquity of icon veneration as well as in miracles linked to icons and saints, which were also challenged during the Iconoclastic age. The *Life of Patriarch Tarasios* by Ignatios the Deacon mentions twice (chapters 49 and 55) the encomiastic efforts of the patriarch aimed at glorifying the martyrs. Although none of these works have survived, the writings of the patriarch testify to the revival of interest in hagiography already in the interval between the two Iconoclastic periods (Euthymiades 2011: 95). The florilegia in defense of images mostly constituting the miracles from the icons were a powerful instrument that had a life of their own long after their initial purpose was fulfilled (see the *stemma* of the possible relationship between the Iconophile florilegia in Alexakis (1996: Appendix VI, 360)). The florilegium attached to *The Letter of the Three Patriarchs* may serve as a good example of the later life of Iconophile texts. The collection of icon miracles from *The Letter* was included in the *Epistula ad Theophilum imperatorem* of pseudo-John of Damascus (CPG 8115) and later arranged into a coherent metaphrastic story. In the tenth century the collection was enriched with some other miracles, and from the eleventh century began its life both as an independent collection of edifying miracle stories and a depository of miracles used in various homilies (Harvalia-Crook 2003).

The post-Iconoclastic hagiographical revival was paralleled by the hymnographic revival which had started even earlier with the works of John of Damascus and Cosmas of Maiuma and was continued by Theodore the Stoudite and his brother Joseph of Thessalonica (Wolfram 2003), culminating in Joseph the Hymnographer, who engaged in an ambitious hymnographic project to compose a canon for every saint for every day of the church year, eventually writing over 450 canons (Patterson-Ševčenko 1998). The earliest *Menaia* compiled by Joseph, Theophanes, and George of Nicomedia date back to the ninth century; they built on and replaced the earlier *Tropologia*, taking over some structural details, genres, and individual liturgical pieces, composed by such authors of the eighth century as Andrew of Crete, Patriarch Germanos, John of Damascus, and Cosmas of Maiuma. Already at the early stage of development at the border of the ninth–tenth centuries, the *Menaia* include a great number of saints who lived in the Iconoclastic period (Nikiforova 2010: 110). The later hymnographic tradition sometimes appealed to the authority of the earlier Iconophile Fathers. Thus, the *Canon on the Image of Christ not made-by-hands* (Aug. 16, second plagal (sixth) Tome) from the printed *Menaion* with the acrostic Σῆς ἐκσφράγισμα Σῶτερ ὄψεως σέβω is ascribed to Patriarch Germanos, although the historical and stylistic features of the *Canon* do not support Germanos' authorship.

The Patriarch Photios

When Photios found himself on the patriarchal throne, he was destined to face the challenges much like Patriarch Methodios, whose entire tenure (843–847) went under the sign of dealing with the former Iconoclast clergy and the Stoudite opposition (Dvornik 1948: 13–16; Darrouzès 1987). The issue of image veneration was one of the important vectors of Patriarch Photios' policies, both internally and externally. Externally, both patriarchates of Photios (858–867 and 877–886) were marked by the fierce controversy with the West concerning the *Filioque* issue and the jurisdiction over the territories of Moravia and Bulgaria, which were the arena of competing Christianizing efforts on the part of Rome through the Eastern Frankish missionaries, and Byzantium (Dvornik 1948; Simeonova 1998: 223–247). The theme of icon veneration as a distinct aspect of Byzantine Orthodoxy is prominent in his Photios' educational letter to Prince Boris of Bulgaria, where the passage dedicated to the Seventh Ecumenical Council is comparable in size to the summaries of all previous Ecumenical Councils taken together (Laourdas and Westerink 1983: 1–39; on the contents and reception of the letter, see Simeonova (1998: 112–156)).

The practical aspect of the missionary activities must have also been associated with the message of icon veneration, instrumental in converting the Slavs to the kind of Christianity for which both the doctrine and the practice of icon veneration, with the names of Iconophile Fathers attached to it, was already an integral and unchallengeable part. Quite tellingly, the Byzantines sources (Theophanes Continuatus and the *Chronicle* of Pseudo-Symeon), although somewhat differing in the circumstances of the conversion of Boris-Michael, describe it as the direct result of his seeing the representation of the Great Judgment (Dujčev 1961), incidentally with the iconography described in detail and recommended for edification in the *Adversus Constantinum Cabalinum* (PG 95, 324D–325A).

One of the internal problems that Photios had to face was some Iconoclastic sympathies in Byzantium, which must have remained an issue until the end of the ninth century. Photios' Council of 861 and the Ignatian Council of 869–870 found it necessary to condemn Iconoclasm once again. Photios insisted on the universal recognition of Nicaea II as the Seventh Ecumenical Council, since the Roman Church had not counted it among the Ecumenical Councils, and such recognition was achieved at the Photian Council of 879–880. In his letter to the asecretis Nicolas, Photios' disciple Arethas of Caesaria at the very end of the ninth century mentions some simple-minded people who were led into confusion by the Iconoclastic argumentation (Westerink 1968: 75–81).

Photios' entire patriarchate was aggravated by the inner split of the Byzantine Church, formally united under the auspices of the victorious Iconodulia. Being the protégé of the head of the imperial government Caesar Bardas, Photios was supposed to replace the figure of Patriarch Ignatios (847–858 and 867–877) who entered into a bitter conflict with the Caesar. Photios was nominated to the position of patriarch from the secular rank of *protasekretis* and was speedily consecrated, causing canonically grounded protests of the zealots. Photios was the heir of Methodios' moderate policy towards the former Iconoclasts, and had to face opposition from the rigorist party of the

Ignatians and the Stoudites, who, in their unbending attitude, appealed to the spiritual heritage and authority of such Iconophile champions as Theodore the Stoudite and Naukratios. Photios could build up his spiritual authority on the basis of his different but equally noble Iconophile lineage.

Through his uncle on his mother's side, Photios was a relative of Empress Theodora. Photios' father was Sergios the Confessor, a nephew of Patriarch Tarasios, who presided at the Seventh Ecumenical Council. Sergios is commemorated on May 13 in the *Synaxarium* and the *Menologium*, and was likely the author of the *Ecclesiastical History* from the cod. 67 of Photios' *Bibliotheca*, which might have possibly survived in part as the chronicle known under the title of *Scriptor incertus* (Treadgold 2002: 6). Sergios lost his wealth and rank for his Iconodulic views and died in exile with his wife under the Iconoclastic Emperor Theophilos. Photios and his brother Tarasios, the addressee of the *Bibliotheca*, were named after Iconophile saints (on the early biography of Photios, see Mango (1977: 135–139) and Treadgold (2002)).

Yet the motives of self-representation alone can hardly explain the recurrent allusions to Iconoclasm and icon veneration appearing in Photios' writings (as it is claimed in Mango (1977)). The *Amphilochia* contain eight other discussions of problems connected with icon veneration; these treatises are the reworkings of Photios' letters written to private persons, which casts doubts on the claim of Mango that Photios' references to Iconoclasm were primarily the means of personal propaganda. The *Homilies* also contain some explicit references to Iconoclasm (see the references in Dvornik (1953: 86, 88–92, 93–95) and the *Index* in Mango (1958: 322)). Moreover, without explicitly referring to the Iconoclasts, in the *Amphilochia* 231 (Westerink 1987: 14–15) Photios presents and refutes Christology, strikingly close to that of the Byzantine Iconoclasts as exemplified by the *Horos* of 754, fragments of the Iconoclastic Patriarch John the Grammarian, and the refutation of Theodore the Stoudite (Baranov 2013).

At the same time, recurrently referring to Iconoclasm and its dangers, Photios barely uses the writings of the previous Iconophile Fathers. The *Bibliotheca* mentions only the Acts of the Seventh Ecumenical Council (cod. 20), the *Breviarium* of Patriarch Nikephoros (cod. 66), the *Ecclesiastical History* of Sergios the Confessor (cod. 67), and *De Vera et Legitima Retributione* of Patriarch Germanos (CPG 8022, not surviving, cod. 233) (Treadgold 1980). Treadgold explained the absence of major theological polemics in the synopsis by an early date of compiling the *Bibliotheca* (845) when these works could still have been out of circulation, being suppressed under Iconoclasm which had recently ended (Treadgold 2002: 10). However, according to the apparatus, provided by the editors of the later *Letters and Amphilochia* (Westerink 1988: 12–24), of all the Iconophile writings Photios only once uses the *Epistula* of Pope Hadrian II to Tarasios, twice the *Epistula ad Theophilum imperatorem* of pseudo-John of Damascus, and once the third *Apology in Defense of Images* by John of Damascus. Photios does not refer to Theodore the Stoudite and uses Nikephoros only in one *Letter* and once in the *Amphilochia* for canonical matters. This fact is surprising and requires at least a hypothetical explanation.

According to the suggestion of Afinogenov, Photios, in spite of his great respect for Patriarch Nikephoros and the praise of his *Short History*, simply could not get hold of Nikephoros' writings, which were in the possession of the Stoudites at the time. They obtained the private library and archive of Patriarch Nikephoros, which was inherited by Patriarch Methodios, through Patriarch Ignatios, who, after Methodios' death, decided to relocate the archive to the Stoudios monastery and not to the library of the Patriarchate in order to control the anti-Stoudite sentiments contained in the writings of Methodios (Afinogenov 2006). Photios' use of Theodore the Stoudite's writings must have also been restricted due to his inability to use the library of the Stoudios monastery because of his breach with the Stoudites.

The *Synodikon of Orthodoxy*

Despite a relative lack of references to the writings of the Iconophile Fathers at the time of Photios, the memory of the Iconophile Fathers ended up being codified in the calendar of the Orthodox Church. Commemoration days of the Iconophile saints were introduced, as well as a feast day of the Restoration of Icons on the First Sunday of Great Lent, which involved a special rite with reading the eternal memory to the Orthodox Fathers and anathemas to the Iconoclasts. The earliest version of the *Synodikon of Orthodoxy* is marked by the literary style of Patriarch Methodios (Afinogenov 2004: 147); its Georgian translation reflects the early stage of the text (van Esbroeck and Karadeniz 1987). The names recited in it during the rite were mostly concerned with the second Iconoclasm, with the Emperors Leo III and Constantine V, but no mention of the Patriarchs Germanos and Tarasios was made. The Feast of Orthodoxy reenacted the memory of Iconoclasm throughout the whole liturgical year and in the eleventh and fourteenth centuries was supplemented by the anathemas to other heretics (Gouillard 1967).

The regular Feast of Orthodoxy is first mentioned in the *Kletorologion* of Philotheos, which dates to 899, and is firmly established in the imperial *Book of Ceremonies* of the mid-tenth century (on the performance of the rite, see Barber (2007: 2–19) and Flusin (2010)). According to the *Synaxarion* of the Theotokos Evergetis monastery in Constantinople (mid-twelfth century), the reading of the *Synodikon* was preceded by the reading of two texts of the miracles coming from icons of Christ from Beirut and from the Antiphonetes icon, two texts with the historical accounts of the Restoration of icons under Empress Theodora, and two theoretical texts on icons: one of the *Epistles* of Pope Gregory II to Leo III, and a reading from the *Parva Cathechesis* by Theodore the Stoudite (see the references in Barber (2007: 5–13)). There is some evidence that in the middle of the eleventh century in the heat of the struggle with the pope and the Church of Rome, Patriarch Michael Kerularios (1043–1058) excluded the name of Theodore the Stoudite from the *Synodikon* since Theodore many times in his writings appealed to the authority of Rome. However, Michael Kerularios was forced to restore the name of Theodore after the Stoudites appealed to the emperor with their complaint (Bekker 1838–1839: II, 555, note).

The Image of Edessa

The transfer of the Image of Christ not made-by-hands – the icon *par excellence* miraculously made by Christ Himself – from Edessa to Constantinople in 944 became the statement of Byzantine Iconodulia and the final stage of eradication of any memory of

Iconoclasm. Although eventually the Edessa image found its place in the Pharos church together with the rest of the imperial collection of relics, its immediate location upon arrival in Constantinople might have been the Chalke Gate at the entrance to the Great Palace in a small church which may have been built by Romanos Lekapenos especially for housing the Edessa Image (Engberg 2004). The day of the triumphal celebration of the arrival of the Edessa image in Constantinople (Aug. 16) was chosen to oust a relic of the Iconoclastic past – the memory of the deliverance of the capital from the Arabs by the general who became the Iconoclastic Emperor Leo III, commemorated on the same day.

The event naturally gave rise to a whole series of writings in various genres. It is not surprising that in these writings we may find some echoes of the image debate of two centuries before. Of numerous Iconophile authors mentioning the Edessa Image in support of the antiquity and divine inspiration of icon production, established by Christ Himself, the *Narratio de Imagine Edessena*, chapter 18 lists the authors of the *Letter of the Three Patriarchs* as credible witnesses to its history (Guscin 2009: 39). Chapter 35 of the *Narration* explains the rite of veneration and the procession with the enthroned image of Christ not made-by-hands on the first Sunday of Great Lent – the day of commemorating the restoration of icon veneration or the Sunday of Orthodoxy – using the language of the *Mystagogy* of Patriarch Germanos (CPG 8023) and substituting such symbolic representations of Christ in the liturgical exegesis as the Gospels and the Eucharistic Gifts with the Edessa Image – the iconic symbol of Christ, acting as the head of the liturgical procession (Gerstel 1999: 74; Guscin 2009: 66–67).

In the Christological exegesis of the process of transferring Christ's face to the cloth, the Sermon of Gregorius Referendarius mentions twice a characteristic detail that, theoretically, was not required for explaining the miraculous origin of the image: Christ wiped his sweat and thus transferred his image to the cloth (Guscin 2009: 77.6, 86.2, cf. 153), which in some way parallels the very process of "transferring" the image to the prepared board by means of colors in the process of icon painting. For this detail the author of the sermon must have used the *Epistula as Theophilum imparatorem*, containing the same specific detail ("divine sweat," Gauer 1994: 84.24), missing from the identical passage of the *Letter of the Three Patriarchs*.

The Eleventh Century

In spite of its major achievements in ecclesiastical art, the eleventh century marks a departure from the theology of the image of the Iconophile Fathers among Byzantine intellectuals. Michael Psellos is the earliest example of this process. In many passages Psellos describes icons and miracles coming from them, calling himself "a most fastidious viewer of icons" (Cutler and Browning 1992: 27; for the passages and the analysis, see Barber (2007: 61–98)). However, the icon for Psellos is not a sacred object representing and revealing the divine image of God-made-flesh, but an object calling forth to transcend and overcome its materiality. Building upon the antique theories of vision, Psellos perceives an icon as a medium, allowing the viewer to see the image of Christ or the Theotokos not in itself but through itself.

This line of reasoning was further developed by Psellos' disciple John Italos. The charges against Italos at his trial include the accusation of an Iconoclastic act of throwing stones at an icon of Christ (Gouillard 1985: 155, lines 376–377), but we should keep in mind that Iconoclasm as the last great heresy of the past was often evoked at the moments in later doctrinal controversies, when the adversaries were compared to Iconoclasts, and the allies to the Iconodulic Fathers as the exemplary champions of Orthodoxy. Although the charges of Iconoclasm were not included in the anathemas against Italos, which became a part of the *Synodikon of Orthodoxy*, the materials of the case reveal Italos' Platonizing understanding of image theology (see the summary in Barber (2007: 117–123)).

In the same Platonic vein as Psellos, Italos calls for worshipping the immaterial image of Christ transcending its iconic representations as material "shadows" which only obliquely reveal the divinity, evoking the shadows from Plato's Cave (Schukin, 2008; for the verbal parallels between Psellos and Italos, see Barber (2007: 126–127)). Italos' interest in the philosophical meaning of image is manifested in a short treatise, *On Images* (Joannou 1956: 151; trans. Barber 2007: 124–125), where Italos provides the description of various types and functions of images. In fact, this short treatise is the summary of the classification of images from the *Apologies* of John of Damascus, yet completely denuded of any Christological connotations underlying Damascene's justification of image veneration.

The accusations of Iconoclasm were revived in connection with the seizure of precious religious objects, including liturgical vessels with images, by the Emperor Alexios Komnenos in 1081–1082 for replenishment of the impoverished treasury. Leo, the Metropolitan of Chalcedon and one of the judges at the trial of Italos, made dogmatic objections to the emperor's order, accusing those who destroyed the sacred representations for whatever purpose, of impiety. Dogmatic disputes lasted for several years and resulted in the condemnation of Leo at the Council of Constantinople in 1086. This did not stop the controversy; at another Council of Constantinople in 1094 Leo repented of his errors and was restored to his former position. Both Leo of Chalcedon and his chief adversary Eustratios of Nicaea, the student of Italos, argued about icon veneration using the conceptual framework elaborated during the Iconoclastic controversy; the theological arguments of the dispute differed concerning the role of the "character" – the intrinsic image of God, reproduced in the icon – and "matter" bearing the representation (Lourié 2006).

Leo argued that the iconic matter (εἰκονικὴ ὕλη), upon which the image of Christ was imprinted, deserved veneration as revealing his image (χαρακτήρ), inseparable from his divine hypostasis which had to be worshipped. In support of his position, in the *Letter* to Nicholas of Adrianople, Leo of Chalcedon (Lauriotes 1900: 414A–416A, 445A–447A, 455B–456B) referred to Theodore the Stoudite, the *Definition* of the Seventh Ecumenical Council, the *Synodikon of Orthodoxy*, and the *Troparion* from the Canon to the Edessa Image (Grumel 1950: 136).

This controversy forced the authorities to step in, and Isaak Sebastokrator commissioned a florilegium of excerpts from the Iconophile Fathers on veneration of icons to rebut the opinion of Leo of Chalcedon. The florilegium has not survived and is known only from its description and indirect evidence; it included passages from Theodore the Stoudite, Patriarch Nikephoros, Patriarch Germanos, and the Seventh Ecumenical Council (for more detail on the contents, see Barber (2007: 143–147)). The Synod of 1084, where

Isaak played a leading role, condemned Leo's position. The case of Leo was ultimately resolved in a synod of 1094/1095 summoned by Alexios I, where Leo was formally reconciled with the Church. In support of the traditional doctrine on worship of Christ and the Holy Trinity and the veneration of icons, the Synod cited the letter of Theodore the Stoudite to Athanasios from Isaak's florilegium. The case of Leo was concluded by reading the final passage from the *Synodikon of Orthodoxy*. Following the debate, c. 1111, the court theologian Euthymios Zigabenos wrote a review of the main heresies entitled *Panoplia Dogmatica* at the request of Alexios I. The treatise included a chapter on Iconoclasm, closely following an earlier collection *Against the Iconoclasts* which contained 24 fragments with definitions related to images, excerpted from the writings of John of Damascus, Patriarch Nikephoros, and Theodore the Stoudite (Hergenroether 1869; Thümmel 1991: 134–144). The collection, compiled between the death of Patriarch Nikephoros in 828 and the composition of the *Panoplia Dogmatica*, proved to be quite topical for various periods of Byzantine intellectual history and survived both as a part of various dogmatic collections (in addition to the *Panoplia*, the *Thesaurus Orthodoxae Fidei* by Nicetas Choniates from the early thirteenth century, containing the names of Nikephoros, Photios, and Theodore the Stoudite in the title, and the *Syntagma alphabeticum* by Matthew Blastares of 1335 with the omission of the name of Nikephoros in the title and three passages belonging to Nikephoros) and as an independent treatise. The attribution of the treatise to Photios is unlikely, since, as we will have mentioned above, the anti-Iconoclastic writings of Theodore the Stoudite and Nikephoros were hardly available to Photios.

In addition to the Synod's appeal to the Iconophile Fathers, Leo's position provoked another response that gives us a glimpse into the intellectual climate of Byzantium at the time. Eustratios, the Metropolitan of Nicaea, focused his attack on Leo's position concerning depictability of the natures in Christ, distinguishing between that which is according to nature and that which is produced according to art, much in the spirit of the Byzantine Iconoclasts. Eustratios came to the conclusion that icons were only of limited value as representations of some accidents available to the senses but not of the essence of the depicted. Arguing for the old and canonical formula that only God deserved worship, Eustratios denied the worship to the Logos in the icon, since in his opinion image was distinct from divinity, even in the case of the Incarnated Logos (for the summary of the argument, see Barber (2007: 101–112)). In defense of the relative veneration of icons, Eustratios, in fact, operated with Iconoclastic Christological arguments on the impossibility of depicting both the divine and human nature that was assumed by Christ, assigning the icons as having only an "intellectual" relation to the prototype as opposed to the "ontological" relation, established by the Iconophile Fathers.

This controversy reveals the measure of oblivion concerning the Iconophile doctrine among the ecclesiastical intellectuals of late eleventh-century Byzantium. Paradoxically, in his zeal to defend religious images, Leo of Chalcedon distorted the doctrine on the relationship between the enmattered image and its prototype, which the Iconophile Fathers fought for during the Iconoclastic Controversy. The opponent of Leo, Eustratios could not bring icon veneration back to the Fathers either. In his attempts to disprove the "extreme" Iconodulia of Leo, he operated in a different, this time philosophical, paradigm, in effect trying to push religious imagery too far into the shade as mere material symbols.

The Fourteenth and Fifteenth Centuries

Accusations of Iconoclasm were revived during the Hesychast Controversy in the fourteenth century (Featherstone 1983). Nikephoros Gregoras was the first to rediscover the writings of Patriarch Nikephoros and introduce them into the debate around 1347. The writings of Nikephoros were known to Gregoras under the name of another Iconophile champion, Theodore Graptos. Gregoras learned of Theodore Graptos from the earlier version of the *Life of Michael the Synkellos*, which he reworked in the 1320s. Supporting his claim by quotes from "Theodore Graptos," whom Gregoras considered the main figure of struggle against Iconoclasm, he accused the Palamites of Iconoclasm within his broader charges of Messalianism and Bogomilism in his *First* (Beyer 1976: 153, 309) and *Second Antirrhetici* (unpublished, Ms. Laurent. gr. LVI. 14: f. 1–161), and in the *Historia Rhomaike* (Bekker and Schopen 1829–1855: vol. 2, 943). The Palamites first challenged the authority of "Theodore Graptos," but eventually accepted the authority of the writings and started to use them against the anti-Palamites, in turn accusing them of Iconoclasm. In total, nine authors cited *Apologeticus atque Antirrhetici* (PG 100, 205–832) and *Contra Eusebium* (Pitra 1852: 371–503) of Patriarch Nikephoros during the Hesychast Controversy, including four Palamites – Joseph Kalothetes, Philotheos Kokkinos, John VI Kantakouzenos, and Gregory Palamas himself – and five anti-Palamites – Isaak Argyros, Theodore Dexios, John Cyparissiota, and Manuel Kalekas in addition to Gregoras (see the survey in Lukhovitskij (2013: 210–213)).

The appeal to the authority of Theodore Graptos and his writings continued into the fifteenth century; in 1445, Gennadios Scholarios wrote a treatise, entitled "...πρὸς κῦρ Ἰωάννην τὸν Βασιλικὸν ἐρωτήσαντα περὶ τῆς τοῦ μακαρίου Θεοδώρου τοῦ Γραπτοῦ ῥήσεως, ἀφῆς οἱ ματαιόφρονες Ἀκινδυνισταὶ θορυβοῦσιν" ("To Lord Ioannes Basilikos who asked about the saying of the Blessed Theodore Graptos, about which the vain-thinking followers of Akindynos shout") (Petit *et al.* 1928–1936: III, 204–228), aimed at explaining the phrase of Nikephoros on the inextricable connection between the substance and energy, which Nikephoros wrote to refute the Iconoclastic charge of circumscription of the divinity in the icon of Christ, and which anti-Palamites, both in the fourteenth and in the fifteenth centuries, found useful for challenging the Palamite doctrine of the uncreated energies, distinct from the divine substance. Ironically, the figure of Patriarch Nikephoros is absent from the famous late-fourteenth-century icon of the Triumph of Orthodoxy from the British Museum, which visually reenacted the memory of ninth-century Iconoclasm amidst the Hesychast Controversy (Kotoula 2006).

Conclusion

This review of the reception of the Iconophile Fathers shows both an ongoing interest in them and the degree of oblivion in relation to their actual writings. In the memory of the Orthodox world, Byzantine Iconoclasm became renowned as the last major heresy of Byzantium. Byzantine Orthodoxy to a large extent identified itself as the

Church that overcame Iconoclasm. Over the ensuing centuries the accusation of being an iconoclast was often repeated, yet there was no real understanding of the essence of the position of the iconoclasts, and of the iconophile response, upholding the use of icons – Iconoclasm became a reference point but was not discussed in depth. In the Byzantine tradition, the memory of the Iconophile Fathers as the victors in the struggle over Iconoclasm was codified in hagiography and liturgical celebrations, whereas the reflection upon the theology of sacred images was mostly left to the past. It has been mainly in the modern period that a renewed interest in Byzantine iconophile thought has developed (Parry 1996).

Bibliography

Primary Sources

Baranov V.A. (2006), "Unedited Slavonic translation of the 'Apology on the Cross and on the Holy Icons' attributed to Patriarch Germanus of Constantinople (CPG 8033)". In *Scrinium 2*, A.V. Mouraviev and V.M. Lourie (eds). St. Petersbourg: Byzantinorossica; 7–40.

Bekker, I. (ed.) (1838–1839), *Georgius Cedrenus*, two vols. Corpus Scriptorum Historiae Byzantinae 8–9. Bonn.

Bekker, E. and Schopen, L. (eds) (1829–1855), *Nicephori Gregorae Byzantina historia*, three vols. Bonn: Weber (repr. Cambridge: University Press, 2012).

Beyer, H.-V. (ed.) (1976), *Nikephoros Gregoras. Antirrhetica I*. Wiener Byzantinische Studien 12. Vienna: Verlag der Österreichischen Akademie der Wissenschaften.

Declerck, J. (2004), "Les sept opuscules *Sur la fabrication des images* attribués à Nicéphore de Constantinople". In *Philomathestatos. Studies in Greek and Byzantine Texts Presented to Jacques Noret for his Sixty-Fifth Birthday*, B. Janssens, B. Roosen, and P. Van Deun (eds). Orientalia Lovaniensia Analecta 137. Leuven: Peeters; 105–164.

Evdokimova, A. (2011), "The first antirrhetic answering the main points in illegal speeches by John Heresiarchus, Lekanaruspex and ex-Parhedros of Byzantium against Christ's Image, or rather against the True Incarnation of God's Son. The first edition of the manuscript Escorial Y-II-7". *Scrinium*, 7: 200–205.

Featherstone, J.M. (ed.) (1997), *Nicephori Patriarchae Constantinoploitani Refutatio et eversio definitionis synodalis anni 815*. CCSG 33. Turnhout/Leuven: Brepols/University Press.

Gauer, H. (ed.) (1994), *Texte zum byzantinische Bilderstreit: der Synodalbrief der Drei Patriarchen des Ostens von 836 und seine Vewandlung in sieben Jahrhunderten*. Studien und Texte zur Byzantinistik 1. Frankfurt: Peter Lang.

Gouillard, J. (1967), "Le *Synodikon de l'Orthodoxie*. Édition et commentaire". *Travaux et mémoires*, 2: 1–316.

Gouillard, J. (1985), "Le procès officiel de Jean l'Italien, les actes et leurs sous-entendus". *Travaux et Mémoires*, 9: 133–174.

Grumel, V. (1950), "Léon de Chalcédoine et le canon de la Fête du saint Mandilion". *Analecta Bollandiana*, 68: 135–152.

Guscin, M. (2009), *The Image of Edessa*. The Medieval Mediterranean 82. Leiden: Brill.

Harvalia-Crook, E. (2003), "A witness to the later tradition of the florilegium in *The Letter of the Three Patriarchs* (BHG 1386): an anonymous collection of icon stories (Hierosolymitanus S. Sabas gr. 105)". In *Porphyrogenita: Essays on the History and Literature of Byzantium and the Latin East in Honour of Julian*

Chrysostomides, J. Chrysostomides and C. Dendrinos (eds). Aldershot: Ashgate; 341–367.

Hergenroether J. (ed.) (1869), *Monumenta graeca ad Photium eiusque historiam pertinentia. Ratisbona*; 53–62.

Joannou, P. (ed.) (1956), *Ioannes Italos Quaestiones quodlibetales ('Ἀπορίαι καί λύσεις)*. Ettal: Buch-Kunstverlag.

Laourdas, B. and Westerink, L.G. (eds) (1983), *Photii Epistulae et Amphilochia*, vol. 1. Leipzig: Teubner.

Lauriotes, A. (1900) "'Ἱστορικὸν ζήτημα ἐκκλησιαστικὸν ἐπὶ τῆς βασιλείας' Ἀλεξίου Κομνήνου, Ἐκκλησιαστικὴ". *Ἀλήθεια*, 20: 352–358, 362–365, 403–407, 411–416, 445 447, 455–456.

Melioranskij, B.M. (1901) *Georgij Kiprianin i Ioann Ierusalimljanin, dva maloizvestnuch bortsa za pravoslavie v VIII veke* [*George of Cyprus and John of Jerusalem – Two Little Known Champions of Orthodoxy in the Eighth Century*]. St. Petersburg.

Petit, L., Siderides, X.A., and Jugie, M. (eds) (1928–1936), *Oeuvres complètes de Georges (Gennadios) Scholarios*, eight vols. Paris: Maison de la Bonne Presse.

Pitra, J.B. *Spicilegium Solemniense*. Vol. 1. Paris, 1852 (repr. Graz: Akademische Druk, 1962).

Thümmel, H.-G. (1991), "Eine Schrift über das Wesen der Ikone 'Gegen die Bilder stürmer'". In *Bilderlehre und Bilderstreit*. Würzburg: Augustinus-Verlag; 127–144.

Van Esbroeck, M. (1999), "Un discours inédits de saint Germain de Constantinople sur la Croix et les Icônes". *OCP*, 65: 19–55.

Van Esbroeck, M. and Karadeniz, N. (1987), "Das Synodikon vom Jahre 843 in georgischer Übersetzung". *Annuarium Historiae Conciliorum*, 19: 300–313.

Westerink L.G. (ed.) (1968), *Arethae Scripta Minora*, vol. 1. Leipzig: Teubner.

Westerink L.G. (ed.) (1987–1988), *Photii Patriarchae Constantinopolitani Epistulae et Amphilochia*, vol. 6. Fasc. 1–2. Leipzig: Teubner; (Fasc. 1, 1987; Fasc. 2, 1988).

Secondary Sources

Afinogenov D. E. (2004) "*Povest' o proshchenii imperatora Feofila*" *i Torzhestvo pravoslaviya.* ["Narration on forgiveness of the Emperor Theophilos" and the Restoration of Icons]. Moscow: Indrik.

Afinogenov, D.E. (2006), "Did the patriarchal archive end up in the Monastery of Studios? Ninth century vicissitudes of some important document collections". In *Monastères, images, pouvoirs et société à Byzance*, M. Kaplan (ed.). Byzantina Sorbonensia, 23. Paris: Publications de la Sorbonne; 125–133.

Alexakis, A. (1996), *Codex Parisinus Graecus 1115 and Its Archetype*. Dumbarton Oaks Studies 34. Washington, DC: Dumbarton Oaks Research Library and Collection.

Auzépy M.-F. (1999), *L'Hagiographie et l'Iconoclasme Byzantin: Le cas de la Vie d'Étienne le Jeune*. Birmingham Byzantine and Ottoman Monographs. Brookfield, VT: Ashgate Publishing Company.

Baranov V.A. (2013), "*Amphilochia* 231 of Patriarch Photius as a possible source on the Christology of the Byzantine Iconoclasts". In *Studia Patristica* 68. Papers presented at the Sixteenth International Conference on Patristic Studies held in Oxford 2011, M. Vinzent (ed.). Leuven: Peeters; 371–379.

Barber, Ch. (2007), *Contesting the Logic of Painting. Art and Understanding in Eleventh-Century Byzantium*. Visualising the Middle Ages 2. Leiden: Brill.

Cutler, A. and Browning, R. (1992) "In the margins of Byzantium? Some icons in Michael Psellos". *Byzantine and Modern Greek Studies*, 16: 21–32.

Darrouzès, J. (1987), "Le patriarche Méthode contre les Iconoclastes et les Stoudites". *Revue des études byzantines*, 45: 15–57.

Dujčev, I. (1961), "Légendes byzantines sur la conversion des Bulgares". *Sborník prací filosofského fakultetu*. Brnênského Üniversitem, t. X.

ïada hist. 8 (1962): 7–17 (repr. Idem. *Medioevo bizantino-slavo*. Vol. 3. *Altri saggi di storia politica e letteraria*. Storia e letteratura. Raccolta di Studi e Testi 119. Rome: Edizioni di Storia e letteratura, 63–76).

Dvornik, F. (1953) "The Patriarch Photius and Iconoclasm". *Dumbraton Oaks Papers*, 7: 67–97.

Dvornik, F. (1948), *The Photian Schism History and Legend*. Cambridge: Cambridge University Press (repr. 1970).

Engberg S. (2004), "Romanos Lekapenos and the Mandilion of Edessa". In *Byzance et les reliques du Christ*, J. Durand, and B. Flusin (eds). Paris: Association des Amis du Centre d'Histoire et Civilisation de France; 121–142.

Euthymiades S. (2011), "Hagiography between the 'Dark Age' to the age of Symeon Metaphrastes (eighth–tenth centuries)". In *The Ashgate Research Companion to Byzantine Hagiography*. Vol. 1. *Periods and Places*, S. Euthymiades (ed.). Farnham: Ashgate; 95–142.

Featherstone, J.M. (1983), "An Iconoclastic episode in the Hesychast Controversy". *Jahrbuch der österreichischen Byzantinistik*, 33: 179–198.

Flusin, B. (2010), "Le triomphe des images et la nouvelle définition de l'Orthodoxie. À propos d'un chapitre du *De cerimoniis* (I. 37)". In *Orthodoxy and Heresy in Byzantium*, A. Rigo and P. Ermilov (eds). Quaderni di Nea Rōmī 4. Rome: Università degli Studi di Roma "Tor Vergata"; 3–20.

Gerstel, Sh. (1999), *Beholding the Sacred Mysteries: Programs of the Byzantine Sanctuary*. Monographs on the Fine Arts, 70. Seattle, WA: College Art Association, University of Washington Press.

Kotoula, D. (2006), "The British Museum Triumph of Orthodoxy icon". In *Byzantine Orthodoxies*, A. Louth and A. Casiday (eds). Publications for the Society for the Promotion of Byzantine Studies 12. Aldershot: Ashgate; 121–128.

Kriza, A. (2006), "Vizantijskie istochniki drevnerusskogo bogoslobiya ikony – chet'i teksty Torzhestva Pravoslaviya" [Byzantine sources of the Old Russian theology of icon – reading texts of the Sunday of Orthodoxy]. *Studia Slavica Hungarica*, 51/3–4: 373–386.

Lourié, B. (2006), "Une dispute sans justes: Léon de Chalcédoine, Eustrate de Nicée et la troisième querelle sur les images sacrées". *Studia Patristica*, vol. 42, F. Young, M. Edwards, and P. Parvis (eds). Leuven: Peeters; 321–339.

Lukhovitskij, L. (2013), "Historical memory of Byzantine Iconoclasm in the fourteenth century: the case of Nikephoros Gregoras and Philotheos Kokkinos". In *Aesthetics and Theurgy in Byzantium*, S. Mariev and W.-M. Stock (eds). Byzantinisches Archiv 25. Berlin: de Gruyter; 205–234.

Mango, C. (1977), "The liquidation of Iconoclasm and the patriarch Photios". In *Iconoclasm: Papers Given at the Ninth Spring Symposium of Byzantine Studies, University of Birmingham, March 1975*, A. Bryer and J. Herrin (eds). Birmingham: Centre for Byzantine Studies, University of Birmingham; 133–140.

Mango, C. (trans., intro, and comm.) (1958) *The Homilies of Photius, Patriarch of Constantinople*. Dumbarton Oaks Studies 3. Cambridge, MA: Harvard University Press.

Nikiforova, A. Yu. (2010), "Rozhdenie Minei: Grecheskie Minei IX–XII vv" [The birth of the Menaion: Greek Menaia of the ninth–twelfth centuries]. *Vestnik Pravoskavnogo Svyato-Tikhonovskogo gumanitarnogo universiteta III: Filologiya*, 4 (22): 103–122 (with English summary).

Parry, K. (1996), *Depicting the Word: Byzantine Iconophile Thought of the Eighth and Ninth Centuries*. Leiden: Brill.

Patterson-Ševčenko, N. (1998), "Canon and calendar, the role of a ninth century hymnographer in shaping the celebration of the saints". In *Byzantium in the Ninth Century: Dead or Alive?*, L. Brubaker (ed.). Ashgate; 101–114.

Patterson-Ševčenko, N. (2002) "The five hymnographers at Nerezi". *Palaeoslavica*, 10/2: 55–68.

Schukin, T. (2008), "Iconoclastic fragment of the *Apologetic Note* by John Italos". *Scrinium* 4, V.A. Baranov and B. Lourié (eds). St. Petersburg: Axioma; 249–259.

Simeonova, L. (1998), *Diplomacy of the Letter and the Cross: Photios, Bulgaria and the Papacy, 860s–880s.* Amsterdam: A.M. Hakkert.

Teteriatnikov, N. (1996), *The Liturgical Planning of Byzantine Churches in Cappadocia.* Orientalia Christiana Analecta 252. Rome: Pontificio Instituto Orientale.

Treadgold, W. (1980), *The Nature of the Bibliotheca of Photius.* Dumbarton Oaks Studies 18. Washington, DC: Dumbarton Oaks Center for Byzantine Studies.

Treadgold, W. (2002), "Photius before his patriarchate". *Journal of Ecclesiastical History*, 53.1: 1–17.

Wolfram, G. (2003), "Der Beitrag des Theodoros Studites zur byzantinischen Hymnographie". *Jahrbuch der Österreichischen Byzantinistik*, 53: 117–125.

Part V
Studies in the Fathers

CHAPTER 24
Scripture and the Fathers

Paul Blowers

Introduction

Only a wide-ranging analysis can do justice to the multidimensional role of Holy Scripture in the collective work of the Church Fathers. It is inadequate, for example, to think that if we reconstruct the science of patristic biblical interpretation we have finished the task. Scripture was not, in the early Christian era, an isolatable object of scholarly examination, as if interpreters could achieve real critical distance from these texts. Rather, Scripture was already the presupposition of Christian identity, collective memory, and self-definition. It authorized and warranted Christian convictions about the origins and destiny of the world and about the unique work of Jesus Christ for the world's salvation. In late antiquity, the churches could not look back on a time when Christianity was not in conversation with inherited sacred texts and attending to the adoption of new "apostolic" Scripture complementing and perfecting the ancient revelation. Before we turn to interpretation as such, therefore, we must consider issues of the identification, stabilization, and authorization of scriptural sources in early Christian tradition.

Scripture and the Rule of Faith

Prior to the fourth century, the Christian Bible was a fluid reality. We cannot overemphasize the distinction between the circulation of Jewish and Christian *Scripture*, into the second century, and the gradual emergence of a Christian biblical *canon* from the second to the fourth centuries, though the latter hardly had a universally definitive closure. Nor should we underestimate the fact that the so-called "Hebrew Bible" – the authoritative textual tradition of which dates well beyond the early Common Era – was

The Wiley Blackwell Companion to Patristics, First Edition. Edited by Ken Parry.
© 2015 John Wiley & Sons Ltd. Published 2019 by John Wiley & Sons Ltd.

not the foundational Scripture for earliest Christianity. It was the "Septuagint," which names an array of Greek translation traditions to which the early churches recurred; see Law (2013: 1–32). Reverence for the Septuagint was routine in early Greeks interpreters like Origen, but it endured in the time of Augustine, who, though a Westerner, censured Jerome for translating the Vulgate Old Testament from the Hebrew rather than the Septuagint (*Ep.* 71.4–5, CSEL 34: 352–353), especially when the Old Latin translations had been based on the latter.

Most important for our purposes, the earliest churches were using scriptural texts for teaching, preaching, and liturgy before they had collectively authorized them or framed them within a definitive canon of Old and New Testaments; see Barton (1997: 24–34). Frances Young (1997: 49–75, 257–264) speaks of primitive Christianity accumulating its own repertoire of "classic" Scriptures. While the Jewish scriptural inheritance included the Torah and clusters of Prophets, Psalms, and Wisdom writings that consistently proved normative and formative in Christian communities, the New Testament is more complicated. The writings of the Apostle Paul, for example, were ostensibly the first full Christian-authored texts to be made widely available, but Paul's own apostolic authority itself was contested in some circles well into the second century. Justin Martyr doubtless knows Paul and clearly appropriates some of his ideas in the *Dialogue with Trypho the Jew* (e.g., *Dial.* 23.4–5), but without ever mentioning Paul's name, since no authority could ever eclipse Jesus's own, and since the harmony of Synoptic Gospel traditions was for Justin, and for his student Tatian, the bottom line (Pervo 2010: 195–198). Paul's legacy, moreover, was open to reinvention by Gnostics and Marcionites as well as by orthodox writers like Irenaeus.

In these circumstances, it is not surprising that certain pre-Nicene Fathers forced the issue of scriptural authority by appealing to an identifiable and universal "canon of truth" or "rule of faith" that epitomized both the apostolic teaching tradition and the integrity of received Scripture. In its variant renditions in writers like Irenaeus (*Adv. haer.* 1.10.1; 1.22.1; 3.4.2; *Epideixis* 3, 6), Tertullian (*De praescr. haer.* 13.1–6; *De virg. vel.* 1; *Adv. Prax.* 2.1–20), and Origen (*De princ.* 1, Pref. 1–8; *Comm. Jo.* 32.16; *Comm. Matt.*, ser. 33), the rule of faith reads more like a teaching syllabus or even a sermon outline than a creed, setting forth the anchors supporting the coherence of the faith: the one God who is Creator of all things; Jesus Christ, the incarnate Son and Savior; the Holy Spirit who spoke through the prophets and sanctifies the faithful, and so on.

The early rule of faith has been variously described as embodying the authority of church tradition to expound scriptural revelation; as a doctrinal principle latent or implicit in Scripture and serving as the criterion of its interpretation; as an emerging strategy of rational argument from, by, and for the integrity of the Christian faith; and as a rhetorical, narrative, or dramatic principle exhibiting the primary "plot" tying together Old and New Testaments and playing out still in the church's foreground (Blowers 1997). These need not be mutually exclusive but rather complementary descriptions of how the rule was deployed and promulgated by its patristic exponents. The modern historical critic might balk at those exponents' claims to the pure originality and irreformability of the rule (cf. Irenaeus, *Adv. haer.* 1.10.–3, SC 264: 158–166; Tertullian, *De virg. vel.* 1, CSEL 76: 79; *De praescr. haer.* 13.6, SC 46: 106–107), but the fact stands that they considered it a secure standard for authorizing and interpreting sacred Scripture. Particularly in Irenaeus and Tertullian, the rule is so deeply embedded in Scripture that it functions as a proxy of the scriptural canon itself (Armstrong 2010).

The official closing of a Christian biblical canon was a long and complicated process that entailed episcopal judgments (e.g., Cyril of Jerusalem, *Cat.* 4.35, PG 33: 497C–500B; Athanasius, *Ep. festalis* 39, NPNF 4: 551–552; Gregory Nazianzen, *Carm. theol.* 1.1.12, PG 37: 472–474; Augustine, *De doct. chr.* 2.8.13–14; Green 1995: 68–70), the sway of learned scholars and theologians (e.g., Jerome, *Ep.* 107.12, CSEL 55: 302–303), and the decisions of regional councils (Carthage, Laodicea, etc.). And yet settling the canon did not abruptly resolve persisting hermeneutical issues such as the relation between ancient "prophecy" and its (continuing) Christocentric fulfillment (see Skarsaune (1987)), the bridging of "Old" and "New" Testaments (see Barton (1997: 63–105)), or the dialectical tension between the "letter" and the "spirit" of Scripture as a whole. The scriptural canon had grown up, as it were, with the churches' reading strategies and processes of interpretation. Patchworks of scriptural *testimonia* had interlinked prophetic and apostolic texts and, by extension, helped assure that whole writings, not just excerpts, would acquire authority. What became canonical was Scripture that gradually proved effective for demonstrating the unique status of Jesus Christ.

Such demonstration, meanwhile, was in the minds of patristic interpreters an unceasing task since, as Origen insisted (*Princ.* 4.3.14) and others generally concurred, Scripture is inexhaustible in its richness, the font of the endlessly "fuller meaning" (*sensus plenior*) of the Christian mystery. Whatever the status of the canon at any given point, this excavation of Scripture's riches had to continue for the sake of Christian identity and self-definition.

Patristic Theology of Scripture and Its Interpretation

One does not find in the Fathers an assortment of "theories" of the inspiration of Scripture such as were spelled out much later in Protestant dogmatics; but without question, patristic interpreters cultivated a theology of scriptural revelation that profoundly shaped their exegetical protocols and procedures. Generally for the Fathers, both the divine accommodation to human language in Scripture and the church's discernment of God's revelation within the earthen vessels of these material texts (Origen, *De princ.* 4.1.7) constituted a single grand "economy" (*oikonomia*), a single arrangement under which God, as the primary author of revelation, providentially and strategically crafted its written form in order to instruct humanity toward salvation (Farkasfalvy 1968).

Irenaeus of Lyons and Origen are seminal here. Answering the dual challenges of Marcionism and Gnosticism, Irenaeus set out in his treatise *Against Heresies* much more than a patchwork of *testimonia* to the orthodox faith. He investigated and amplified the overarching dramatic plot or rhetorical argument (*hypothesis*) running throughout prophetic and apostolic Scripture (*Adv. haer.* 3.16.6; 3.24.1; 4.1.1; 5.2.2). It was the Gnostics, he claimed, who interpreted Scripture piecemeal and thus distorted it (*Adv. haer.* 1.8.1; 1.9.4, SC 264: 112–116, 150; cf. Tertullian, *De praescr. haer.* 39.5–7, SC 46: 143–145). Scripture has its mysteries and hidden depths to be sure, but it is rendered plausible according to the rule of faith in the continuing work of drawing out its *sensus plenior* (*Adv. haer.* 1.10.3, 2.28.3).

More important for Irenaeus, the whole *hypothesis* of Scripture centered on the person and work of Jesus Christ as the "recapitulation" of the triune God's purposes in creation and redemption (*Adv. haer.* 1.10.1; 3.16.6–9). Thus, it is not simply a case, as in some of the Apologists like Justin, of Christ having fulfilled ancient prophecies. Nor is the *hypothesis* of Scripture a purely chronological sequence of creation, the fall, redemption, the time of the church, and the final consummation, with Christ as a climactic "middle" of the story. The Creator's project from before the foundations of the world was to reveal himself in Jesus Christ, so that all God's economies, or dispensations, were intrinsically Christocentric. It was only to the crucified Lord, the "Lamb who was slain," that the Creator originally opened the "book" containing the secrets of "heaven and earth" (*Adv. haer.* 4.20.2, SC 100: 628–630). Christ – and so too the rule of faith – grounded the unity and harmony of Scripture and granted the church interpretive clarity:

> If, therefore, according to the rule which I have stated, we leave some questions in the hands of God, we shall both preserve our faith uninjured, and shall continue without danger; and all Scripture, which has been given to us by God, shall be found by us perfectly consistent; and the parables shall harmonize with those passages which are perfectly plain; and those statements the meaning of which is clear, shall serve to explain the parables; and through the many diversified utterances [of Scripture] there shall be heard one harmonious melody in us, praising in hymns that God who created all things (*Adv. haer.* 2.28.3, ANF 1: 400).

In *On First Principles* Book IV, a climax rather than an appendix to the treatise as a whole, Origen is less interested in producing a handbook of rules for interpreting Scripture than in demonstrating, on the basis of the cosmology and eschatology elicited in Books I–III, the providential shape of the whole economy of revelation (Daley 1998). The Logos is universal Pedagogue, since he is the preexistent exemplar for all rational creatures (*logika*), whom he instructs not only through his historical incarnation, but also through his continuing communication in the *scriptural* Word, which leads them to perfection. Inspiration of Scripture includes the Holy Spirit's work in crafting the material text, in which case nothing in it is accidental or meaningless; but this fully coordinates with the providential strategy of the Logos to mediate and modulate the sacred text to creatures according to their capacity and merit (*Contra Celsum* 4.71; *De princ.* 4.3.14; 4.4.2). At the level of exegesis and interpretation, the dialectics of "letter" and "spirit" (cf. 2 Cor. 3:6) is for Origen grounded in a more fundamental distinction between the material text and its broader intentionality, or *skopos*. Annihilation of the literal meaning (*gramma*; *historia*) of the text was not an option. The literal sense, even if sometimes involving apparent absurdities or outright impossibilities – things which Origen labels purposive "obstacles" (*skandala*; *De princ.* 4.2.7–4.3.15) – was nevertheless redeemed in the overall "providential" objective (de Lubac 2007: 118–128). Only the most naïve reader would draw from holy war traditions in the Old Testament a simple lesson on how to destroy one's enemies in God's name. The detailed accounts of wars in Joshua and Judges must intrinsically have served an ulterior, nobler purpose.

Origen's achievement was to develop a theology of revelation into which he integrated a sophisticated theology of interpretation. At the heart of both was the conviction that the divine Logos was himself living and active in the sacred text. Real communion with God, not just the extraction of spiritual wisdom from the text, was the goal. Nowhere in Origen's exegetical works is this more explicit than in his *Commentary on the Song of Songs*, which he dubbed a mystical "drama" of the Logos (Bridegroom) eluding but alluring the soul (Bride) in order to enflame the soul's deep desire for things divine (*Comm. in Cant.* Prol. 1). The Song was thus also a magnificent allegory of the rigorous quest of biblical interpreters to pursue the "concealed" and polymorphous Logos in Scripture (*Comm. in Cant.* 1.2). Accordingly, Origen imposed on the interpreter a strong ascetical discipline and a protocol of exegetical virtues governing the science of interpretation (Martens 2012: 89–106, 161–191). If the trained interpreter was not morally and spiritually worthy to discern the Word, how could the simple reader have any hope of doing so?

Interpretive Models and Practices in the Fathers

Needless to say, the varying contexts of biblical interpretation in the early church are crucial for understanding the developing models and methods of patristic exegesis. In the age of the Apostolic Fathers and the Apologists, an age of severe vulnerability for the churches at multiple levels, biblical hermeneutics mirrored the root challenge of adopting and authorizing scriptural texts in order to lend definition to Christianity vis-à-vis Judaism, pagan religious culture, and the heterodoxies on Christianity's horizon. Interpretation needed to furnish the churches with their own sacred past. The strongly supersessionist *Epistle of Barnabas* looked to wrest the Septuagint from the Jews and establish it – albeit selectively – as Christian Scripture (*Ep. Barn.* 4.6–8). Justin Martyr believed that the apostles themselves handed on the ancient prophecies to the Gentiles (*1 Apol.* 49.5), thus sanctioning his own exegesis as just such an "apostolic" ministry of confirming to the nations (notably the Empire) the fulfillment of prophecies in the work of Christ and in the whole reality of Christianity. Though working from antecedent collections of prophetic *testimonia* (Skarsaune 1987: 141–242; Heine 2007: 97–141), Justin believed, much like Origen later on, that the Logos himself directed the whole scheme of prophecy and fulfillment:

> ...when you hear the utterances of the prophets spoken as it were personally, you must not suppose that they are spoken by the inspired themselves, but by the Divine Word who moves them. For sometimes he declares things that are to come to pass, in the manner of one who foretells the future; sometimes he speaks as from the person of God the Lord and Father of all; sometimes as from the person of Christ; sometimes as from the person of the people answering the Lord or his Father, just as you can see even in your own writers, one man being the writer of the whole, but introducing the persons who converse. And this the Jews who possessed the books of the prophets did not understand, and therefore did not recognise Christ even when he came... (*1 Apol.* 36; ANF 1: 175).

The "proof from prophecy" did not abruptly end with the second- or third-century Apologists. The scholar-bishop Eusebius of Caesarea reinvigorated it in the early fourth century. In his *Prophetic Extracts* and *Commentary on Luke*, composed while the Diocletianic persecution was still raging, Eusebius provided a fresh array of Old Testament *testimonia* and Gospel fulfillments to reassure Christians of Christ's messianic identity and victory. This work supported his broader apologies, the *Demonstration of the Gospel* and the *Preparation for the Gospel*, all in a triumphalistic campaign to show how biblical prophecies, having their climactic outcome in Christ, nonetheless continued to be fulfilled in the church's foreground and in the emerging regime of Constantine, a new "Moses" (*Vita Const.* 1.12; *Hist. Eccl.* 9.9.5–8) and the viceroy of Christ on earth. Another transitional figure of the early fourth century, Lactantius, presupposed the validity of prophetic proof-texting while also finding adumbrations of Christian truth in the pagan poets and philosophers (*Div. inst.* 1.2.1–1.6.17; 4.5.3–10; 4.14.1–17). The proof from prophecy was assimilated as a mainstay in later patristic hermeneutics, but with the end of persecution and the new privileged status of Christianity in the Roman Empire, biblical interpretation changed with the times. In exegesis and preaching, attention largely turned from apologetics to drawing out the full doctrinal, moral, and religious implications of Scripture for Christians of widely different backgrounds, social location, and depth of integration into the church.

Patristic biblical exegesis truly burgeoned and diversified in the fourth and fifth centuries. Already Origen had pioneered a model of scholarly commentary on Scripture (Neuschäfer 1987; Martens 2012: 41–106). His tools proved enduring: close philological, literary, and rhetorical analysis of the biblical text; attention to variant recensions; elucidation of Scripture with Scripture, and so on. Eusebius, Didymus the Blind, and Jerome produced learned commentaries, each with his own distinctive agenda but strongly dependent on Origen's spadework. Eusebius's *Commentary on Isaiah* (Ziegler 1975; Armstrong 2013), written after Constantine's ascendency, is at one level an expansion on the proof from prophecy exhibited in his earlier works, demonstrating the *historia* through which the church moved "from its pre-Incarnational existence to its fulfillment in the *eschaton*" in ways the Hebrew prophets foresaw (Hollerich 1999: 26–33, 67–102). For instance, in his *Commentary* on Isaiah 60:3–4 ("...and nations shall come to your light, and kings to the brightness of your rising"), Eusebius discerns a prophecy fulfilled in Constantine's own baptismal illumination and rising, a true light to the nations (Armstrong 2013: xxiii–xxv, 290–291). By contrast, Didymus the Blind, fourth-century scholar and pedagogue, produced *Commentaries* on Genesis, Job, Ecclesiastes, the Psalms, and Zechariah intended principally to perpetuate Origen's legacy for a new generation of Alexandrian Christians by interpreting Scripture as the inexhaustible source of Christian *philosophia* and training in virtue (Layton 2004).

Jerome, the most diligent early Western disciple of Origen's biblical scholarship, and a prolific translator of Origen's exegetical and homiletic works into Latin, mimicked the master's careful attention to philological and grammatical analysis. He also allowed the disciplined use of "spiritual" or allegorical interpretation where Scripture invited it. But in the end, Jerome's disenchantment with Origen's speculative theology induced him to desist from honoring the legacy of the great Alexandrian. Thus, one can see a distinct difference between Jerome's *Commentary on Ephesians*, which closely follows Origen's own (Heine 2002), and his later *Commentary on Matthew*, where he departs sharply from some of Origen's exegeses. This alienation drove a wedge between Jerome and those monastics, like Rufinus of Aquileia (another Latin translator of Origen), who remained passionately devoted to Origen's achievement.

In fact, Origen's legacy was much vaster than learned commentaries. He was post-humously a highly controversial figure in desert monasticism in the East, where some of the sages explicitly disputed his speculative interpretations (Abba Lot 1, in Ward [1975: 121]; Barsanuphius and John, *Ep.* 600). But his model of "spiritual" exegesis, characterized by allegorical readings that enabled the "transposition" (*metalêpsis*) of scriptural narratives into archetypal scripts for aspiring souls, found an enduring place in the teaching of the desert abbas. In order to become a "son of Abraham" spiritually, Origen claimed, "every person must, by interpreting the whole Abrahamic history allegorically, perform all of Abraham's deeds spiritually" (*Comm. Jo.* 20.10; Preuschen 1903: 337). Allegory in the desert was often modest by comparison, as in this dictum from Abba Poemen in Egypt:

> A brother asked Abba Poemen, "What should I do?" The old man said to him, "When Abraham entered the promised land he bought a sepulchre for himself and by means of this tomb, he inherited the land." The brother said to him, "What is the tomb?" The old man said, "The place of tears and compunction." (Abba Poemen 50, Ward 1975: 173)

And yet Origen's allegorically supported profiling of virtuous biblical saints like Abraham was compelling in the context of the largely oral culture of the desert where monks had meager access to texts of Scripture and depended on hearing the Word in liturgy or from their elders who could render the distant texts immediately relevant to their ascetical struggles (Burton-Christie 1993; Driscoll 2005: 123–141).

Meanwhile, Origenian hermeneutics had strong monastic champions in Evagrius Ponticus, Nilus of Sinai, and John Cassian. Evagrius, for example, made full use of Origen's famed tripartite disciplines of "ethics, physics, and contemplation" (respectively modeled in Proverbs, Ecclesiastes, and Song of Songs, *Comm. in Cant. Prol.* 3.1, 6, SC 375: 128, 132), though Evagrius chose the rubrics of "practical, natural, and theological" philosophy (e.g., *Praktikos* 1, SC 171: 499; *Schol. in Prov.* 247, SC 340: 342). Nilus of Sinai reiterated Origen's mimetic exegesis and the principle of becoming biblical characters *spiritually* by re-embodying their virtues (*Ep.* 2.223, PG 79: 316B–317A). John Cassian picked up on Origen's doctrine of the multiple senses of Scripture (*Collationes* 14.8, CSEL 13.2: 404–407) and helped assure a place for Origenian allegory in Western monastic tradition.

Not all of Origen's disciples in late antiquity, however, were monks. The Cappadocian Fathers, scholar-bishops all, and non-monastics who still passionately promoted the ascetical life, used Origen extensively in excavating the multilayered richness of scriptural revelation (McGuckin 2005). Basil of Caesarea and Gregory of Nazianzus edited an anthology, the *Philokalia* of Origen, which, among other things, showcased the sophistication of his approach to the Bible (SC 302). In his *Homilies on the Hexaemeron*, Basil expressed reservations about overly speculative allegory (e.g., *Hom.* 3.9), but ultimately could justify spiritual interpretation in view of revelation's deep mysteries and his audiences' religious needs (Lim 1990).

Of the Cappadocians, Gregory of Nyssa was by far most prolific in appropriating Origen's interpretive model. Much like Origen, he sanctioned spiritual interpretation – be it "tropological" (moral), "allegorical," or "anagogical." "We shall not quarrel about the name as long as a firm grasp is kept on thoughts that edify" (Prol. *Hom. in Cant.*, Norris 2012: 2–5). Such was necessary both to obviate absurdities or offenses in Scripture and to do justice to its transcending and transformative meaning (Heine 1984). In addition, Gregory strongly emphasized the principle, rooted in Origen, of tracking the *akolouthia*, or "sequence" in biblical texts, the orderly progression of a narrative or the precise organization of material in a book (like the Psalms) that might signal, on the spiritual level, vectors guiding souls in their journey toward God (Daniélou 1956). Also with Origen, Gregory believed that biblical writings have a transcendent orientation, a larger divine objective or *skopos*, the sight of which the interpreter must not lose in dealing with textual intricacies.

In the West, besides Jerome, Ambrose of Milan proved in the late fourth century to be one of the greatest devotees of the Alexandrian–Origenian hermeneutical legacy. He showed no qualms with allegorical interpretation, especially since much of his exposition of Scripture came in pastoral, catechetical, and mystagogical works (Wood 2011). For Ambrose, Scripture was in essence the rhetoric of spiritual formation. In his *De officiis*, or treatise *On the Duties of the Clergy*, Ambrose profiled biblical characters as exemplars of the four cardinal virtues to encourage moral and ascetical discipline among priests, while in his treatises on the patriarchs, he turned Abraham, Isaac, Jacob, and Joseph into reanimated symbols of the Christian soul.

This brings us to Ambrose's most famous baptizand, Augustine, who, as a bishop in North Africa, far eclipsed him in hermeneutical influence. Even if we cannot situate Augustine in the trajectory of Origen's Western legatees, his work paralleled Origen's on many points. Differences notwithstanding, Books I–III of Augustine's *On Christian Doctrine*, like Book IV of Origen's *On First Principles*, situate hermeneutical considerations within a larger schema of the journey of souls toward God, or, in Augustine's words, toward the "enjoyment" (*fructus*) of the Trinity (*De doct. chr.* 1.4.4–1.10.10, Green 1995: 14–22). Augustine, like Origen, viewed Scripture as a complex constellation of symbols or "signs" (*signa*) of variant clarity and ambiguity ordered for the training of the diligent (*De doct. chr.* II–III, Green 1995: 56–194).

Augustine's exegetical corpus is vast if we include his sermons, but as Manlio Simonetti accurately observes, the gamut of his interpretive paradigm appears representatively in his various commentaries on Genesis 1–3 (Simonetti 1994: 104–105; Hill 2002). Augustine's early apologetic interest in countering Manichaean exegesis of the biblical cosmogony by using allegory gave way, in his final foray, the *Commentary on the Literal Meaning of Genesis*, to a more holistic model. Focusing on the creation story as real history, a history with semantic complexity and thickness, "literal" exegesis became an all-out investigation of the deeper theological scope of the text, in which there was room for "scientific" and allegorical interpretation alike (Norris 2003). Here, indeed, was an enormous contribution to the later history of exegesis, as medieval theological commentators like Thomas Aquinas, even the Protestant Reformers, appropriated the principle of "literal" meaning as the carefully intuited divine intentionality of biblical texts.

Returning to the East, much attention has rightly been given to the so-called "Antiochene school" of biblical interpretation, which historians have often distinguished as a grand protest to the Alexandrian–Origenian tradition. Setting them against each other is valid to the extent that certain of Antioch's representatives – Eustasthius, Diodore of Tarsus, and Theodore of Mopsuestia – strongly criticized the allegorizing whims of their Alexandrian-inspired counterparts (Young 1997: 161–185). When Theodore, for example, treats Paul's famous "allegory" of Sarah and Hagar (Gal. 4:22–31), he immediately references "people who have great zeal for overturning the meaning of the divine scriptures, and by breaking up everything placed there fabricate from themselves certain foolish fictions and give their folly the name of allegory" (*Comm. in Epp. Pauli*, Greer 2010: 112, 113). Doubtless, Theodore was aware that Origen (*De princ.* 4.2.6) and his sympathizers had validated allegorical interpretation on Paul's own example.

The Antiochenes have thus often been characterized as the guardians of the "literal" or "historical" sense in Christian antiquity. But this, and their aversion to allegory, have been overplayed, as has the scholarly polarization of Alexandrian and Antiochene hermeneutical strategies. For one thing, *historia* as an exegetical term in Greek patristic usage is complex. The Antiochenes, devout in grammatical and rhetorical approaches to Scripture (Schäublein 1974), were concerned less with revelation's "factual record" (in a modern sense) than in narrative consistency such as funded moral and spiritual instruction (Young 1997: 161–185). As Diodore stated, referencing Paul's Hagar–Sarah "allegory" (Gal. 4:24), "Scripture does not repudiate in any way the underlying prior history but 'theorizes,' that is, it develops a higher vision (*theôria*) of other but similar events in addition, without abrogating history" (*Pref. to Comm. on Ps. 118*, Froelich 1984: 88). Though there were, to be sure, differences between Origenian allegory and this kind of *theôria*, there was also convergence insofar as the goal was to discern a larger economy or intelligibility governing Scripture as a whole, lest it be locked exclusively into its mundane contexts. Antiochenes too, then, revered "spiritual" meaning.

Scripture and Christian Piety in the Fathers

A striking contrast between patristic and modern historical–critical interpretation is the Fathers' fairly universal assumption that Scripture, in its deep structure, is not a register of ancient religious cultures but a divine economy of salvation and moral transformation. Its utility (*ôpheleia*) to this end is pervasive (e.g., Origen, *Hom. in Num.* 27.1–2). Moral and "spiritual" interpretation, in turn, served in one sense to open up horizons and insights from within even the most obscure and troubling of biblical texts (e.g., Maximus the Confessor's *Quaestiones ad Thalassium* and *Quaestiones et dubia*).

The Fathers evidence a broad array of contexts in which, and media through which, the Bible shaped moral and religious life. Early on, the *Didache* portrays the novice Christian as standing on the threshold of two choices: the Way of Life and the Way of

Death, the former placing one in a relation of immediate discipleship under the scriptural commandments of Christ and the Decalogue (Holmes 2007: 344–368). Tertullian focused on the *simplicity* and *perspicuity* of Scripture as a rule of life. "What we are ourselves," he writes, "that also the Scriptures are (and have been) from the beginning," which is why heretics' misconstrual of Scripture reflected outwardly in their cunning ways (*De praescr. haer.* 38, ANF 3: 261). Not surprisingly, in turn, certain of Tertullian's moral writings, such as his treatise *On the Shows*, are works of casuistry, directly addressing Scripture's clear or inferred command to ethical issues faced by Christians.

Even more basic and pervasive in patristic literature, however, was the framing and forming of Christian moral virtues through imitation (*mimesis*) of exemplars whose lives were dramatized in a rich variety of biblical narratives. A classic of this type is Gregory of Nyssa's *Life of Moses*, a work that, in separate but complementary sections, unfolds the *historia* of Moses's spiritual progress and the *theoria* of its deeper mystical meaning, especially as disclosed in the Sinai Theophany (Ferguson and Malherbe 1978). Meanwhile, Christian preaching teemed with these moral *exempla*. John Chrysostom, the most prolific homilist of late antiquity, filled his sermons with all manner of heroic figures from Scripture, none more compelling than the Apostle Paul, the biblical and extra-biblical epithets of whom John deployed as miniature profiles of Paul's imitable virtues (Mitchell 2002). Also crucial were the rich narratives and characterizations developed in martyrological and hagiographical literature, the latter of which burgeoned from the fourth century on. Some martyrological works deployed the basic image of Jesus himself as "martyr" (Rev. 1:5; 3:14), but expanded on scriptural profiles (Stephen, Paul, etc.) and apocalyptic imagery in order to encourage fidelity and endurance among current believers (Deléani-Nigoul 1984; Saxer 1997). Hagiographical works became increasingly sophisticated in developing intertextual linkages between biblical saints, historic saints, and those now called to holy living in the present. Works such as the *Life of Daniel the Stylite* (Baynes and Dawes 1977: 7–84) and the *Life of Simeon the Holy Fool* (Krueger 1996), for example, drew resonances from the life of Jesus to craft the more recent vita of the monastic saint as a model of evangelical asceticism in contemporary times.

Monasticism in the long run provided enduring models for developing spiritual disciplines from and with Scripture. John Cassian, among others, set the standard for the *lectio divina*, a meditative and contemplative mode of reading the Bible (*Coll.* 10.11; 14.8, 11, CSEL 13: 303–306, 404–407, 411–413), deeply indebted to Origenian hermeneutics, that became a mainstay in Western monastic tradition leading into the Middle Ages (Robertson 2011: 81–103).

The intersection between this kind of spiritual reading of Scripture, scholarly commentary on Scripture, and the broader religious and liturgical life of the early churches is particularly evidenced in the use and interpretation of the Psalms (Daley 2003; Waltke and Houston 2010). The Psalms were not only the original hymnal of early churches and monasteries, they had long been treated as rich in Christocentric prophecy (cf. Heb. 1:5, 5:5; Acts 2:34; Heb. 1:13) and were ultimately the subject of more patristic commentary than any other biblical writing because they seemed to comprehend so many aspects of Christian faith and experience. Athanasius urged the reading of the Psalter as therapy for the soul (*To Marcellinus*), and John Cassian recommended that the

Christian so internalize the Psalms that he or she would become their virtual author (*Coll.* 10.11, CSEL 13: 305). Augustine's extensive *Explanations of the Psalms* combined both spiritual reading and theological exposition into a "homiletic commentary" that conveyed the "whole Christ" (*totus Christus*) – that is, Christ as the Psalter's definitive centerpiece (and sometimes speaker) – in solidarity with his body the church, which found its true voice in the language of the Psalms (Cameron 1999).

Discernment of the inner poetics of the Bible as transformative for Christian piety was a special strength of the Syriac Fathers, some of whom developed scriptural interpretation itself as a form of poetics. The *Odes of Solomon*, perhaps as early as the second century, never directly cite Scripture but instead work through allusion, and extract evocative biblical images that can be amplified and expanded. *Ode* 11, for example, draws upon abundant biblical images of living water, the folly of sin cast off like an old garment and replaced by the Lord's garment, new creation and Paradise, all in eulogizing the mystery of baptism (Charlesworth 1977: 49–59). Much later, Ephrem the Syrian made imaginative connections between the waters of creation (Gen. 1:2), the waters of the Virgin's womb, the Jordan's waters in which Jesus was baptized, and the waters in which Christian baptizands were now being sanctified (*Hymnus de ecclesia* 36.1, 3–6, CSCO 198: 90–92; *Hymnus de epiphania* 12.1, CSCO 187: 173). Other, later Syriac writers, like Narsai and Jacob of Serugh, emulated Ephrem's pattern in their sermons on spiritual and sacramental themes. Still later, the prolific Byzantine hymnist Romanos the Melodist (sixth century), himself of Syrian provenance, took scriptural narratives, including the Gospel accounts of Jesus' life, and crafted miniature dramatic scripts in his *Kontakia*, or sermonic hymns. Romanos introduced dialogues between biblical *dramatis personae* to enhance the suspense or pathos of the story, and so also implicate the audience into its plot, sometimes through a kontakion's choral refrains (Lash 1995).

Scripture and Theological Controversy in the Patristic Age

We can only briefly touch at last on the enormous domain of the role of Scripture in the doctrinal controversies of the patristic age. The early "proof from prophecy" was less a mode of theological interpretation per se than a function of apologetics. It aimed more at verifying than expounding Christian truth-claims. But the Fathers' use of Scripture to warrant, demonstrate, and explicate Christian doctrine also commenced quite early, often in polemical debates with perceived heterodoxies. Important and enduring strategies included: (1) attending to the precise grammar and syntax of scriptural texts as signals to right doctrine; (2) developing constellations of texts that supported or qualified each other in constructing orthodoxy; (3) articulating a *theologically* "literal" understanding of disputed texts; and (4) deferring to appropriately intuited "spiritual" meanings.

The first strategy could range from simple proof-texting to elaborate analyses of scriptural discourse. Tertullian exemplifies the former when, controverting the Christian Platonist Hermogenes over matter's co-eternity with God, he quotes the precise wording of oracles in Isaiah 40:23 ("I am the *first!*") and 44:24 ("I stretched out the heavens *alone*") (*Adv. Herm.* 6.1–2, SC 439: 94–96). The latter is boldly attested in the tension between the Eastern Fathers' reading of the Greek in Romans 5:12 – according to which all sinned *because* (*eph' hôi*) Adam sinned – and Augustine's reading of the very different prepositional phrase in the Old Latin (*in quo omnes pecca verunt*), supporting his notion of the ontological implication of all humanity in Adam's own sin (e.g., *De nuptiis et concupiscentia* 2.42, 45, CSEL 42: 296, 298–299). The consequences for theological anthropology East and West proved enormous. On a quite different track, Gregory of Nyssa countered Arian opponents like Eunomius by delving more philosophically into the very nature of scriptural discourse as constrained, like all language, by *diastêma*, the radical ontological fault-line between uncreated and created reality that precluded human intelligence from circumscribing the pure mystery of the Trinity (Douglass 2005).

The second strategy frequently appeared in the extended Trinitarian and Christological controversies. Arians and pro-Nicenes alike used it. Proverbs 8:22 ("The Lord created me the beginning of his works..."), read prosopologically as the Logos's (Wisdom's) own dictum, cut to the heart of the controversy. Arians interlinked Proverbs 8:22 with other texts to demonstrate that the Logos/Son was a created being: Colossians 1:15, calling the Son "firstborn of creation"; John 14:28, where Jesus asserts, "The Father is greater than I"; and so on. Pro-Nicenes, however, applied Athanasius's strategy (*Or. contra Arianos* 2.44–82) of relating these and other allegedly subordinationist texts solely to Christ's created human nature. They also integrated texts to qualify Proverbs 8:22, such as Philippians 2:6–11 and Hebrews 1:1–2:10, affirming how the Son intrinsically enjoyed equality and preexistence with the Father, as well as texts espousing Christ's unique role in creation as the one through whom all things were originally made (John 1:3, 10; 1 Cor. 8:6; Rom. 11:36; Col. 1:16–17; Heb. 1:2; 2:10).

We find the third strategy quite explicitly in Augustine's *Commentary on the Literal Meaning of Genesis* (Hill 2002), wherein the bishop of Hippo, as noted earlier, challenged erroneous (viz. Manichaean) readings of the creation story and undertook to coordinate various exegetical angles of approach in order to unfold the fuller meaning of the Hexaemeron for the church. Others among the Fathers, such as Cyril of Alexandria in his theological exegesis of the Gospel of John (*Comm. Jo.*, PG 73: 9A–1056A; 74: 9A–756C), similarly aspired to this kind of exegetical "montage," interweaving literal and nonliteral senses for the sake of an integrative, "theologically literal" interpretation.

Finally, the strategy of appealing to higher "spiritual" or mystical meaning often appeared not only as a response to naïve literalism (a charge often leveled against theological heterodoxies), but also to counter competing allegorical interpretations. A prime example here is Origen's exegesis of the Song of Songs as an allegory of Christ's intimacy with the soul or church, in which, besides instructing Christians, Origen was opposing contemporary rabbinic interpretation of the Song as an ode of the love binding Yahweh and the people of Israel (Kimelman 1980). Already in antiquity, but later also in medieval exegesis, "allegory" signaled both doctrinal and mystical senses of the scriptural text, thus serving both dogmatics and spiritual devotion, two things between which the Fathers generally sought to maintain a very close relation.

Bibliography

Primary Sources

ANF = *The Ante-Nicene Fathers: Translations of the Writings of the Fathers Down to A.D. 325*. Edinburgh/Buffalo, NY: T&T Clark/Christian Literature Company, 1867–1897 (cited by volume).

Armstrong, J. (transl.) (2013), *Eusebius of Caesarea: Commentary on Isaiah*. Downers Grove, IL: IVP Academic.

Baynes, N. and Dawes, E. (transl.) (1977), *Three Byzantine Saints: Contemporary Biographies*. Crestwood, NY: St Vladimir's Seminary Press.

Charlesworth, J. (ed./transl.) (1977), *The Odes of Solomon: The Syriac Texts*. Missoula, MT: Scholars Press.

CSCO = Corpus Scriptorum Christianorum Orientalium. Leuven: Peeters, 1903– (cited by volume).

CSEL = Corpus Scriptorum Ecclesiasticorum Latinorum. Vienna: Austrian Academy of Sciences, 1866– (cited by volume).

Ferguson, E. and Malherbe, A. (eds/transl.) (1978), *Gregory of Nyssa: Life of Moses*. New York: Paulist Press.

Froelich, K. (ed./transl.) (1984), *Biblical Interpretation in the Early Church*. Philadelphia: Fortress Press.

Green, R.P.H. (ed./transl.) (1995), *Augustine: De doctrina christiana*. Oxford: Oxford University Press.

Greer, R. (transl.) (2010), *Theodore of Mopsuestia: Commentary on the Minor Epistles of Paul* (with adjoining Latin text ed. H.B. Swete, 1880–1882). Atlanta: SBL.

Heine, R. (ed./trans.) (2002), *The Commentaries of Origen and Jerome on St. Paul's Epistle to the Ephesians*. Oxford: Oxford University Press.

Hill, E. (transl.) (2002). *Augustine: On Genesis*. Works of St. Augustine 1.13. Hyde Park, NY: New City Press.

Holmes, M. (ed./transl.) (2007), *The Apostolic Fathers: Greek Texts and English Translations*, third edition. Grand Rapids, MI: Baker Academic.

Lash, E. (ed./transl.) (1995). *Romanos the Melodist: On the Life of Christ: Kontakia*. San Francisco, CA: HarperCollins.

Norris, R. (ed./trans.) (2012), *Gregory of Nyssa: Homilies on the Song of Songs*. Atlanta: SBL.

NPNF = *A Select Library of the Nicene and Post-Nicene Fathers of the Christian Church*, Series 2. Edinburgh: T&T Clark; Buffalo, NY: Christian Literature Company, 1886–1900 (cited by volume).

PG = *Patrologia Graeca*. Paris: J-P. Migne, 1857–1866 (cited by volume).

Preuschen, E. (ed.) (1903), *Origenes: Der Johanneskommentar.* Griechischen christlichen Schriftsteller – Origenes Werke 4. Leipzig: J.C. Hinrich.

SC = Sources Chrétiennes. Paris: Éditions du Cerf, 1944– (cited by volume).

Ward, B. (ed./transl.) (1975), *The Sayings of the Desert Fathers: The Alphabetical Collection*. Kalamazoo, MI: Cistercian Publications.

Ziegler, J. (ed.) (1975). *Eusebius: Der Jesajakommentar.* Griechischen christlichen Schriftsteller – Eusebius Werke 9. Berlin: Akademie-Verlag.

Secondary Sources

Armstrong, J. (2010), "From the κανὼν τῆς ἀλήθειας to the κανὼν τῶν γραφῶν: the rule of faith and the New Testament canon". In *Tradition and the Rule of Faith in the Early Church: Essays in Honor of Joseph T. Lienhard, S.J.*, R. Rombs and A. Hwang (eds). Washington, DC: Catholic University of America Press; 30–47.

Barton, J. (1997), *Holy Writings, Sacred Text: The Canon in Early Christianity*. Louisville, KY: Westminster John Knox Press.

Blowers, P. (1997), "The *Regula Fidei* and the narrative character of early Christian faith". *Pro Ecclesia*, 6: 199–228.

Burton-Christie, D. (1993), *The Word in the Desert: Scripture and the Quest for Holiness in Early Christian Monasticism*. New York: Oxford University Press.

Cameron, M. (1999), "*Enarrationes in Psalmos*". In *Augustine through the Ages: An Encyclopedia*, A. Fitzgerald (ed.). Grand Rapids, MI: Eerdmans; 290–296.

Daley, B. (1998), "Origen's *De Principiis*: a guide to the principles of Christian scriptural interpretation". In *Nova et Vetera: Patristic Studies in Honor of Thomas Patrick Halton*, J. Petruccione (ed.). Washington, DC: Catholic University of America Press; 3–21.

Daley, B. (2003), "Finding the right key: the aims and strategies of early Christian interpretation of the psalms". In *The Psalms in Community: Jewish and Christian Textual, Liturgical, and Artistic Traditions*, H. Attridge and M. Fassler (eds). Leiden: Brill; 189–205.

Daniélou, J. (1956), "*Akolouthia* chez Grégoire de Nysse". *Revue des sciences religieuses*, 27: 219–249.

Deléani-Nigoul, S. (1984), "L'utilisation des modèles bibliques du martyre par les écrivains du IIIe siècle". In *Le monde latin antique et la Bible*, J. Fontaine and C. Petri, (eds). Paris: Beauchesne; 315–338.

De Lubac, H. (2007), *History and Spirit: The Understanding of Scripture according to Origen*, A. Nash (transl.). San Francisco, CA: Ignatius Press.

Douglass, S. (2005), *Theology of the Gap: Cappadocian Language Theory and the Trinitarian Controversy*. New York: Peter Lang.

Driscoll, J. (2005), *Steps to Spiritual Perfection: Studies on Spiritual Progress in Evagrius Ponticus*. New York: Newman Press.

Farkasfalvy, D. (1968), "Theology of scripture in St. Irenaeus". *Revue Bénédictine*, 78: 319–333.

Heine, R. (1984), "Gregory of Nyssa's apology for allegory". *VigiliaeChristianae*, 38: 360–370.

Heine, R. (2007), *Reading the Old Testament with the Ancient Church: Exploring the Formation of Early Christian Thought*. Grand Rapids, MI: Baker Academic.

Hollerich, M. (1999), *Eusebius of Caesarea's Commentary on Isaiah: Christian Exegesis in the Age of Constantine*. Oxford: Oxford University Press.

Kimelman, Reuven (1980), "Rabbi Yoḥanan and Origen on the Song of Songs: a third-century Jewish–Christian disputation". *Harvard Theological Review*, 73: 567–595.

Krueger, D. (1996), *Symeon the Holy Fool: Leontius' Life and the Late Antique City*. Berkeley, CA: University of California Press.

Layton, R. (2004), *Didymus the Blind and His Circle in Late-Antique Alexandria: Virtue and Narrative in Biblical Scholarship*. Urbana, IL: University of Illinois Press.

Lim, R. (1990), "The politics of interpretation in Basil of Caesarea's *Hexaemeron*". *Vigiliae Christianae*, 44: 351–370.

Law, T.M. (2013), *When God Spoke Greek: The Septuagint and the Making of the Christian Bible*. New York: Oxford University Press.

Martens, P. (2012), *Origen and Scripture: The Contours of the Exegetical Life*. Oxford: Oxford University Press.

McGuckin, J. (2005), "Patterns of Biblical exegesis in the Cappadocian Fathers: Basil the Great, Gregory the Theologian, and Gregory of Nyssa". In *Orthodox and Wesleyan Scriptural Understanding and Practice*, S.T. Kimbrough (ed.). Crestwood, NY: St Vladimir's Seminary Press; 37–54.

Mitchell, M. (2002), *The Heavenly Trumpet: John Chrysostom and the Art of Pauline Interpretation*. Louisville, KY: Westminster John Knox Press.

Neuschäfer, B. (1987), *Origenes als Philologe*, two vols. Basel: Friedrich Reinhard.

Norris, R. (2003), "Augustine and the close of the ancient period of interpretation". In *A History of Biblical Interpretation 1: The Ancient Period*, A. Hauser and D. Watson (eds). Grand Rapids, MI: Eerdmans; 380–408.

Pervo, R. (2010), *The Making of Paul: Constructions of the Apostle in Early Christianity*. Minneapolis, MN: Fortress Press.

Robertson, D. (2011), *Lectio Divina: The Medieval Experience of Reading*. Collegeville, MN: Liturgical Press.

Saxer, V. (1997), "The influence of the Bible in early Christian martyrology". In *The Bible in Greek Christian Antiquity*, P. Blowers (ed./transl.). Notre Dame, IN: University of Notre Dame Press; 342–374.

Schäublein, C. (1974), *Untersuchungenzu Methode und Herkunft der antiochischen Exegese*. Cologne: Peter Hanstein.

Simonetti, M. (1994), *Biblical Interpretation in the Early Church*, J. Hughes (transl.). Edinburgh: T&T Clark.

Skarsaune, O. (1987), *The Proof from Prophecy: A Study in Justin Martyr's Proof-Text Tradition: Text-Type, Provenance, Theological Profile*. Leiden: Brill.

Waltke, B. and Houston, J. (2010), *The Psalms as Christian Worship: A Historical Commentary*. Grand Rapids, MI: Eerdmans.

Wood, C. (2011), "Anamnesis and allegory in Ambrose's *De sacramentis* and *De mysteriis*". *Letter and Spirit*, 7: 51–66.

Young, F. (1997), *Biblical Exegesis and the Formation of Christian Culture*. Cambridge: Cambridge University Press.

CHAPTER 25

Hagiography of the Greek Fathers

Stephanos Efthymiadis

Introduction

Hagiography, a modern term, which since the eighteenth century has denoted both
the corpus of literary texts devoted to holy men and women as well as the study of
these texts from a literary and historical perspective, has taken some time to become
a distinctive literary genre. Through their panegyrics on the martyrs and their biographies of contemporary holy figures, the fourth-century Fathers of the Church
actively contributed to establishing Christianity's literary identity, exploiting its
potential, and enhancing its appeal and prestige (Efthymiadis 2014: 3–8). Moreover,
their writings in praise of Christian saints were included in Byzantine hagiographical
collections (starting with the *Menologia* of the ninth century) and became standard
works of reference for future generations of hagiographers, especially those who
clung to a sophisticated prose style or those who found in them a suitable script for
portraying their own subjects. Yet read in the context of the literary and social climate
of the late Roman age in which they were written and pronounced, these works would
hardly qualify as pioneering examples of a new literary genre. Rather, they were
simply understood as being part of or building on other extant genres of Greek and
Latin rhetoric, namely the Roman biography, the epideictic panegyric and, to a lesser
extent, romance literature.

In fact, in this period the Fathers themselves were unaware of their status as pioneers
and where their efforts would finally lead. Athanasios of Alexandria, for instance,
would have hardly imagined his pioneering *Life of Antony* as the inspiration and matrix
for the entire body of subsequent ascetic literature or shaping the hagiographical narrative for centuries to come. Yet it was no doubt he who laid one of the critical foundation
stones of an edifice which, in the course of time, gained generic autonomy, even if by

The Wiley Blackwell Companion to Patristics, First Edition. Edited by Ken Parry.
© 2015 John Wiley & Sons Ltd. Published 2019 by John Wiley & Sons Ltd.

and large this was the result of the critical mass of its texts and the significant service hagiography did to the cause of the so-called "cult of saints" or of the cult of sainthood in general. In addition to Athanasios' particular contribution, it is also the Church Fathers, as representatives of Christian rhetoric, who deserve the credit for the development of another hagiographical sub-genre, one which acquired a new dynamic with the urban expansion of Christianity. Their enkomia of the holy martyrs would constitute a long chapter in the history of Christian rhetoric (Delehaye 1966: 133–169) and greatly contributed to the standardization of the themes and forms of expression of hagiographical panegyric. As a distinctive sub-genre, this form enjoyed literary popularity in most periods of the Byzantine millennium.

Interpreted in its broadest possible definition – as the mass of writings about the acts of the martyrs and other kinds of holy men and women – hagiography mattered to the Church Fathers, because it nurtured the cult of saints and the cause of the ideal life in Christ in general. The cult of saints, as witnessed in a specific place and with regard to precise historical circumstances, provided the Church Fathers with the necessary excuse to take up the eulogy of the heroes of the Christian faith. For those Fathers who in their lifetime acted as public figures, extolling the martyrs of Early Christianity and highlighting the saintly paradigm of contemporary holy men and women went hand in hand with their preaching and pastoral activity and, more often than not, with their engagement in religious or doctrinal polemic. All in all, the importance that the Fathers placed on the holy is also mirrored in the not insignificant part that hagiography played for most of them in their literary output. What is more, one way or another, their works celebrating the Christian saints were thematically and doctrinally affiliated with their exegetical and religio-political writings.

Athanasios and the *Vita Antonii*

A preoccupation with anti-pagan and anti-heretical polemic is certainly discernible in the *Life of Antony* (*BHG* 142). Athanasios of Alexandria (c. 295–373) integrated his polemic against monastic sympathy for the Arian movement and tendency to remain aloof from doctrinal conflict (Brakke 1995: 135–138, and ch. 4) into a text that was in formal terms an extended *Letter* and a response to a request from some monks in the West for information about the life of Antony as an ascetic (Bartelink 1994: 124–128). Not contenting himself with a dry report on the impressive feats of an Egyptian ascetic dwelling in isolation in the desert, he infused his narrative with what might be called a large dose of "theological edification." Moreover, though he allotted considerable space to his protagonist's struggle against the demons, from the point at which Antony attained spiritual perfection (Bartelink 1994: ch. 14 ff.), he portrayed him as a charismatic preacher who could both edify an audience and repel the attacks of pagan philosophers and apologists of heresy alike (Hägg 2011; 2012: 383–387). Portraying the Egyptian ascetic in such a fashion somewhat contradicted the author's introductory statement that, as a child, Antony had not shown any enthusiasm for letters and learning. Yet Athanasios' narrative is built upon the successive stages in his hero's spiritual career and ascension, and culminates in Antony's final words of counsel (once again denouncing the Arian heresy) and his physical description as a man who remained untouched by a life of torment (Bartelink 1994: chs 91–93).

Athanasios' preoccupation with the vicissitudes and questions that plagued contemporary Christianity is also manifested in the emphasis he places on voluntary martyrdom. Though he lived in the remote desert, Antony is presented first as willing to pursue a martyr's fate in Maximinus II's persecution (308–313) and then as emulating the Christian martyrs by virtue of his ascetic example (Bartelink 1994: chs 46 and 47). In fact, for Athanasios, Antony's struggle in the desert was a new kind of martyrdom, based upon personal mortification and everyday sacrifice (Gemeinhardt 2012). By making such statements in his narrative, Athanasios to some extent justifies his choosing to record the feats of a different kind of Christian hero, the solitary ascetic who, once the age of persecution was ended, followed a different path of holiness from the Early Christian martyr. In a sense, he was in a latent dialogue with the other contemporary apologists of Christianity, whose homiletic activity was solely devoted to those who bore witness to the Christian faith by suffering martyrdom at the hands of some pagan tyrant. We cannot tell if Athanasios, too, had served the cause of the martyrs by writing their *Passions*. As a matter of fact, a number of *Passions* have come down to us under Athanasios' name, yet hardly any of them can be ascribed to him with any certainty.

Written in c. 360 – that is, shortly after the death of the saint in 356 – the *Life of Antony* was extraordinarily widely circulated in the East and West. Translations into other languages were quick to follow, with two Latin versions being attested before 373. This success is also reflected in the comments of other contemporary Fathers. In his *Laudation of Athanasios* (*BHG* 186 – Or. 21), Gregory of Nazianzos characterized the *Life* as "a rule of monastic life in the form of a narrative" (Mossay 1980: 118), and a few years later the same text was recommended by John Chrysostom for his congregation to read (*Homily on St Matthew*, VIII.7, *PG* 57: 88–89).

The Cappadocians

Neither Gregory of Nazianzos nor John Chrysostom went down the same route as their somewhat older contemporary, Athanasios. Overall, the model of the ascetic life outside the civilized world was never a crucial element in their teaching. Moreover, the priorities of their flocks in the urban locations of Cappadocia, Constantinople, and Antioch, their sees of pastoral and preaching activity, were quite different from those of the Egyptian Christians. Naturally enough, their "hagiographic" activity primarily revolved around the praise of early Christian martyrs and the eulogy of contemporary holy men and women tightly linked with the secular life, whether in an indefatigable engagement with anti-heretical polemic or a pious way of life in the circumscribed circumstances of the "new Christian" family (Van Dam 2003). Gregory's contribution to the first category of texts is limited to his brief sermon (*BHG* 457 – Or. 24) on St Kyprianos, reconstructed as a hybrid figure combining Kyprianos of Carthage, bishop and martyr in the third century, and the legendary Faust-like magician Kyprianos of Antioch (Delehaye 1921). The sermon, not devoid of anti-Arian hints, was delivered at the church of St Anastasia in Constantinople on October 2 or 3, 379, and showcases Gregory's skill in rhetorical amplification and extemporization (McGuckin 2001: 251–253). His devotion to the martyrs is further manifested in his *Panegyrical Oration on the Maccabees* (*BHG* 1007), in which he has the opportunity to bridge, on the one hand, Jewish and Christian martyrdom and, on the other hand, to espouse the two faiths' shared opposition to paganism, currently being reinstated as the official religion of the Roman Empire by the Emperor Julian. According to his introductory words, the Maccabees, being pure of soul, knew the Word before the Incarnation, and, though they lived long before the time of Christ, they were just as commendable as the Christian martyrs (Ziadé 2007: 136–175). In fact, this oration, probably first delivered in Nazianzos in 362 (that is, in Julian's reign) and then reworked in Constantinople, encapsulates much of Gregory's defense of the cult of the martyrs and recapitulates his polemic against those who criticized it. In a different context, the same idea is developed in his *Oration 11*, a composite piece pronounced on a *panegyris* of Cappadocian martyrs (Calvet-Sebasti 1995: 336–346).

Nonetheless, a second cluster of texts pertaining to his contemporaries is a much better representation of his literary output. The above-mentioned *Laudation of Athanasios* was composed in Constantinople when Gregory was living in the city (379–381) and was delivered on the occasion of an official commemoration of the saintly Church Father. The orator gives a survey of the various phases of Athanasios' unwavering commitment to the cause of the true doctrine and the evil figures he clashed with. On the other hand, in the most extensive and most sophisticated of his prose works, the *Funeral Oration for St Basil* (*BHG* 245 – Or. 43), a masterful piece of Christian rhetoric that finds echoes in almost every piece of high-brow Byzantine literature, the priorities were different. Gregory's dear friend, teacher, and fellow student in Athens is portrayed as the blessed offspring of a noble family with a long history of piety and who took great care with his education, of which the obvious culmination was his period of studies in Athens. The orator's attention then turns to Basil's sacerdotal engagement with Christianity and his episcopal career, followed by an account of his virtues and praise of his valuable written legacy. This oration would have little in common with any form of hagiography were it not for the long *synkrisis*, comparing Basil with various biblical figures, the highly emotionally charged account of his death, and above all the fact that Gregory refers to him in the peroration as a saint. Gregory must have pronounced a shorter and arguably less elaborate version sometime after Basil's demise in 379, perhaps on January 1, 381 or 382, at the latest. At that time, Gregory was still touched by the taint of his resignation from the patriarchal throne and flight from Constantinople.

Some years earlier, between 368/369 and 374, he had composed his other *Funeral Orations* commemorating the loss of close members of his family: his brother Caesarios (*BHG* 286), who suffered an untimely death, his sister Gorgonia (*BHG* 704), and his father Gregory the Elder (*BHG* 730v). In these orations the Nazianzen can hardly hide his autobiographical and autohagiographical intentions, which extended to the literary reconstruction and idealization of his own family (Hägg 2005). Of the three Orations the hagiographical portrayal seems to have been best suited to Gorgonia, a married woman whose qualities are said to transcend her gender and transport her into the realm of sanctity. It may be legitimately argued that, leaving aside the *Passions* of female martyrs, this text represents the beginnings of female hagiography (Burrus 2005).

However, a clearer example emerges in the slightly later and more elaborate work, the *Life of Makrina*, written by another Cappadocian, Gregory of Nyssa.

As a saintly figure, Makrina exemplifies the pious and moderate asceticism practiced in the confines of the household, what her biographer once calls "the school of virtue" (Woods Callahan 1986: 410), and not in the wilds of the desert. The idea of achieving virtue within the domestic sphere is central to this elaborate piece of Christian rhetoric, the work (as mentioned above) of Makrina's and St Basil of Caeasarea's brother, Gregory of Nyssa. He proposes a model of sanctity which sharply contrasts with that of Athanasios of Alexandria and his *vita Antonii*. Moreover, it is couched in the form of a long letter, though, in terms of generic categorization, it is essentially a "philosophical biography." Like his namesake from Nazianzos, Gregory of Nyssa is obsessed with the lives and deaths of members of his family, brings out sentimental scenes from their shared home life, and repeatedly underscores his sister's readiness for martyrdom and self-sacrifice. Makrina's last moments on her deathbed and the ensuing mourning are reported in such detail (Woods Callahan 1986: 396–414) as to persuasively convey the picture of a woman committed to Christian virtue and worthy to be venerated as a saint.

In addition to Makrina, Gregory commemorated his brother St Basil in a highly encomiastic discourse that precedes, by a year or two, the elegant *Funeral Oration* of the Nazianzen. St Basil is exalted here as the perfect man of God, who deserved to be compared with and was the successor in virtue to some of the holiest figures in the Bible, such as Abraham, Moses, Elijah, and above all St Paul. Moreover, by virtue of his staunch opposition to Valens, the pro-Arian emperor, the Nyssen equated his brother with St John the Baptist and his opposition to Herod. By and large, Gregory is not sketching a family likeness here, nor is he evoking any personal memories, but rather he seeks to emphasize what an exceptional person his brother was.

While in Constantinople in 385, Gregory reserved a laudatory discourse for another, even more eminent woman, the Empress Placilla, wife of Theodosios I. In addition to the orthodoxy of her faith, she excelled in works of charity, especially ministering to the poor and lepers. Elaborating on funerary themes in the first half of his *Funeral Oration* (*BHG* 1548 – *CPG* 3182), Gregory treats her as a saint, highlighting her humility, self-abnegation, and willingness to do good (PG 46, cols 877–892).

Gregory of Nyssa's far from negligible hagiographical output comprises another important text, the *Life and Miracles of St Gregory the Wonderworker (Thaumaturgos)* (*BHG* 715). This Gregory was Origen's pupil, who was credited with the evangelization of Pontos in the third century, while serving the town of Neokaisareia as bishop from c. 240 to c. 270. Pronounced as a panegyric within a century of the saint's death, the account reproduces what had been handed down through the Church and local oral tradition, namely details of his missionary work and performance of miracles, healing ones or otherwise. Being quite unfamiliar with the writings of his namesake, the author strove to embellish and promote his historical role, projecting his own and his contemporaries' views in an artfully structured composition (Van Dam 1982; Mitchell 1999). A word must also be said about his works glorifying the cult of the martyrs: one *Enkomion* of Stephen the First-Martyr, one on the Holy Apostles (wrongly considered a second about Stephen), one on Theodore the Recruit, and three on the Forty Martyrs of Sebasteia. They were delivered on the occasion of corresponding celebrations in towns that he visited as an itinerant pilgrim in the period between his return from exile in 377 and 383 (Daniélou 1955; Maraval 1999: 195–197; Mühlenberg 2012). Interestingly, in his third *Homily on the Forty Martyrs*, he indulges in a digression about a family matter, saying that his mother, Emmelia, had built a sanctuary dedicated to them on the family estate near the small town of Ibora in Pontos (Lendle 1990: 166–168). In his *Enkomion* of Theodore (*BHG* 1760), delivered in Euchaita, again in Pontos, he gave a rhetorical description of the *Martyrion*; that is, the church where the saint's relics were deposited and venerated (Cavarnos 1990: 62–64; Leemans 2010). It is precisely the fact that all these texts were delivered *viva voce* before a Christian congregation that accounts for their straightforward prose style, being less elaborate than that of his endeavors on Makrina and Gregory the Wonderworker.

Gregory of Nyssa's compositions bear witness to a remarkable expansion of the cult of the Forty Martyrs of Sebasteia, the saintly heroes of the first collective Christian *Passio*, which drew its inspiration partly from the biblical story of the *Maccabees*. However, the most famous encomiast of these martyr-soldiers, who froze to death in a lake near Sebasteia, was not Gregory but his brother St Basil. In his eponymous Homily (*BHG* 1205), preached in the martyrs' shrine in Sebasteia in 373, the Cappadocian Father extols the unanimity of their brave resistance to the tyrant and invites his audience to imitate them in an equally bold confession of the Christian faith. His main source for this oration, which is both rhetorical and documentary, must have been an anonymous *Passio* (*BHG* 1201) together with the so-called *Testament of the Martyrs* (*BHG* 1203), which records their desire to be buried together (Karlin-Hayter 1991).

Unlike the other Cappadocians, who turned their attention to contemporary holy figures too, Basil seems not to have had any interest in celebrating saints other than the martyrs of his diocese in Caesarea. His overall interest in their cult is highlighted in various ways in his correspondence, but is poorly reflected in the production of *enkomia*. In fact, from his prolific literary output we can single out only three genuine homilies, delivered between 372 and 376, that relate to locally venerated martyrs, such as Gordios (*BHG* 703), Julitta (*BHG* 972), and Mamas (*BHG* 1020). Basil was fully conscious that, by eulogizing them in public, he could directly strengthen the faith of the lay members of his flock and provide Caesarea with a Christian history, in recollecting the age of persecution as a living memory (Rousseau 1994: 182–189; Métivier 2005: 305–322; Limberis 2011: 41–52). In none of these rather short pieces does the orator pay much attention to the details of the martyr's story, stressing instead in each instance to a particular narrative theme such as, for instance, St Gordios' retreat from the city, St Julitta's renunciation of mundane vainglory, or St Mamas' retreat from the world as a shepherd.

John Chrysostom

As in other matters too, things were different with Basil's younger contemporary, John Chrysostom (c. 346–407). As the originator of the Christian panegyric, he devoted his rhetorical skills and energies to honoring a large number of martyrs in the two cities where he acted as public orator and preacher: Antioch and Constantinople. His preaching activity officially started with his ordination in the Syrian metropolis in 386 and was transferred to the Eastern Roman imperial capital during the period when he was Patriarch of Constantinople (398–404). Each city made its own contribution to the history of Christianity, but, whether sooner (in the case of Antioch) or later (in Constantinople), the cult of the martyrs and their relics would eventually become an integral part of liturgical life there. Naturally enough, given its early role in the cult of the martyrs and the fact that John spent longer there as a presbyter than he did as a patriarch in Constantinople, it was arguably in Antioch that the overwhelming majority of his homilies with hagiographical content were written. Although there has been much research into the distribution of John's genuine works between the two cities and the question is still, at least to some extent, open to debate (Mayer 2005), we may assign to his period in Antioch, the city-cradle of numerous cults of indigenous or imported martyrs (Delehaye 1933: 116–206) the homilies on Sts Babylas, Julian, Ignatios (the first martyr and Bishop of Antioch), Eustathios (another Bishop of Antioch), the Antiochene virgins Pelagia, Domnina, Bernike, and Prosdoke (the last three in a single text), Romanos (an honorary Antiochene), Lucian (first an ascetic, then a presbyter of Antioch), Drosis, Barlaam, Philogonios, and Meletios (the last two former bishops of Antioch involved in the disputes about the ecumenical council of Nicaea), and the soldiers Juventinus and Maximinus (martyred under the Emperor Julian). We must also add a number of homilies on martyrs in general (some of which must have been pronounced in Constantinople) and on Egyptian martyrs (*BHG* 1192) in particular. As a matter of fact, since the new imperial capital could only boast a very few martyrs of its own, the translation of relics from other places and their deposition in its churches had to make up for this deficiency. Accordingly, John delivered a *Homily on St Phocas* (*BHG* 1537), whose relics reached the capital in January 400, as he did later on the occasion of the arrival of the relics of three unnamed martyrs (*BHG* 1191p), providing a vivid description of the celebration (Kelly 1995: 139–141). His Homilies on the Maccabees (*BHG* 1008–1010a) must also be tentatively assigned to his period in Constantinople.

We should not seek in Chrysostom the orderly, well-structured *enkomia* modeled upon the rhetorical conventions of the panegyric as a genre. These were much more revered and elaborated on by the Cappadocian Fathers. The key aspect of his homilies on saints is a rather loose and extemporaneous rhetorical discourse, which allows him to indulge in incidental attacks on pagans and heretics and in moralistic comments, all narrative features that permeate John Chrysostom's *œuvre*.

Not without cause, the text that has reaped the lion's share of scholarly attention is the long Homily on St Babylas, bishop and martyr of Antioch under Emperor Decius (*BHG* 207). It must date from 378–379, namely prior to St John's ordination as presbyter, and can be divided into the rhetorical elaboration of the *Passion* proper and an account of the "recent" translation of the saint's relics to Daphne, a suburb of Antioch associated with the cult of pagan deities. The author took this text as his cue for an attack on paganism and its most prominent supporters, the philosophers and the Emperor Julian. After making a long defamatory attack on the latter, he goes on to give an account of the fire that burned down parts of the temple of Apollo (Schatkin 1990: chs 76–91 and 92–117).

Cyril of Alexandria and Severos of Antioch

The keen interest shown by the fourth-century Fathers in promoting the cult of saints, both martyrs and non-martyrs, in the post-Constantinian era found only a faint response from the theologians who took up the defense of the true faith (however they defined it) in subsequent centuries. True, the new social and literary landscapes were less and less reminiscent of the period that followed the cessation of persecution, when opposition to paganism and doctrinal dissidence were at their height. Apparently, even when the atmosphere was equally polemical, political, or ecclesiastical, engagement was less conducive to the writing of hagiography. In that respect, Cyril of Alexandria (c. 378–444), a prolific writer and a Church Father deeply entrenched in the struggle against pagans and Christian "heretics," is a case in point. Soon after his elevation to the episcopacy in 412, he espoused the cause of the emerging cult of Sts Cyrus and John, who would ultimately take over the healing function of the pagan deity Isis. However, only some faint traces of this activity have survived in the form of some short homilies (*BHG* 472–474), which altogether add up to a meagre dossier on the introduction of this cult. Interestingly, this paucity of information on the origins of the cult was already attested in the *Laudation* and the *Miracles* of the two saints composed by Sophronios of Jerusalem two centuries later.

Another prolific theologian and a Church Father who became the leading figure of anti-Chalcedonian Christians, Severos of Antioch (456–538) has a much better record. Of his 125 so-called *Cathedral Homilies*, all dating from his patriarchate (512–518) and preached in various shrines, mostly extant today in Syriac translation, a fair few are dedicated to the praise of Antiochene martyrs (Allen and Hayward 2004: 49–52). To some extent, Severos' choices in this matter chime with those of John Chrysostom and reflect their common endeavor to assess (or reassess) the heroic Christian past of that city. The list is eclectic and comprises, on the one hand, martyr saints whose cult was local to or particularly revered in Antioch – for example, Thekla, Ignatios, Barlaam/ Barlaha, Romanos (*Homilies* 1, 35, 80), Drosis (*Homilies* 100 and 114), Julian, Babylas, and Sergios and Bacchos – and, on the other hand, saints common to all Christians, such as Stephen, Antony, the Forty Martyrs of Sebasteia, Basil of Caesarea, and Gregory of Nazianzos (the last two in a single text).

Severos' reliance on Chrysostom is far from evident, and most of his sources must be traced back to *Passions* or other written documents that cannot easily be identified. But something else in his *œuvre* that deserves attention are the *Homilies* devoted to otherwise unattested saints; for example, the martyr and former recluse Dometios (*Homily* 51) and Leontios of Tripolis (Homilies 27 and 50) (Allen 2009; 2010). As an orator preaching about martyrs and other saints, Severos rarely betrays his doctrinal orientation. Yet he often admonishes his audience not to associate with the enemies of what represented for him the true faith, and he addresses moral issues which harked back to his glorious predecessor's *œuvre*; for instance, the condemnation of the games and the hippodrome.

John of Damascus

With the end of late antiquity in the seventh century, the figure of the bishop–preacher who, on the occasion of festal celebrations, paid his pastoral tribute to martyrs and other saints, disappeared for some time, at least until the end of the eighth century. Along with other genres of Byzantine literature, hagiography suffered a serious decline and, when it resurfaced, it bore the signs of a critical transformation (Efthymiadis 2014: 10, 260–261). During the eighth century, the most important center of Greek culture, albeit in a religious setting, lay outside the Byzantine orbit in Arab-held Palestine. It was to this outpost and the monastic domain of the Lavra of St Sabas that we owe the revitalization of theology, homiletics, and hagiography. Among the *opera minora* of John of Damascus, the theologian–defender of the veneration of icons and the most preeminent writer in this milieu, we must reckon a small number of hagiographical works. Leaving aside the *Laudation of St Anastasia* (*BHG* 83b), which must be spurious, these concern (in alphabetical order): St Artemios (*BHG* 170), St Barbara (*BHG* 217), and St John Chrysostom (*BHG* 879) (Kazhdan 1999: 28–29; 84–87).

It is hard to determine what prompted the selection of these particular saints and what particular circumstances dictated these texts' compositions. Quite a short text, the *Enkomion of John Chrysostom* is unambitious, and though it shows no sign of having been delivered orally, given its brevity, it might very well have been. In essence, it provides a sketchy account of the stormy life of the Antiochene filled out with rhetorical flourishes. As regards the *Hypomnema on St Artemios* and the *Enkomion of St Barbara*, addresses to a "sacred festival and community of people assembled by God" and similar allusions inserted in the narrative (Kotter 1988: 201 203, 257) suggest that these texts were to be read out before a congregation on the feast day of the relevant saint. In reconstructing the *Passio* of Artemios, a military saint martyred in the reign of Julian, the author declares he has drawn heavily on the fifth-century *Ecclesiastical History* of the Arian Philostorgios (of which it preserves extracts) and some other texts. The name "John the Monk," which appears in the title in the majority of the manuscripts, can plausibly be identified with John Damascene, though a small part of the manuscript tradition ascribes it to a certain John of Rhodes. Many features in this text deserve attention: the method of compilation by excerpting from other writings (a literary process typical of the theologian John), the historical character of the text, the dialogical contest of Emperor Julian with the martyr, the citation of verses of Euripides, put in the mouth of the Apostate.

Conversely, the extensive *Enkomion of St Barbara* is an exquisite piece of rhetoric betraying a learned author who skillfully elaborated on the *Passions* of this woman martyr that he had at his disposal. After a long exordium, the account makes much of the martyr's disagreements with her cruel pagan father. Yet this does not unfold in dialogue but rather in a third-person account filled with many rhetorical addresses. Interestingly, the first section of the concluding ovation of the martyr is couched in the form of repeated salutations (*chaire*, "hail"), a formula also found in the homilies of another contemporary Palestinian, Andrew of Crete, and seen in its most developed form in the Akathistos Hymn.

Theodore of Stoudios

The revival of Byzantine letters toward the end of the eighth century saw several intellectuals showing an interest in celebrating the saints. The only significant theologian, however, whose written legacy comprises works of hagiography is the iconophile monastic Theodore of Stoudios, abbot of the eponymous monastery (759–826). The majority of his surviving *Enkomia* date from the period between the two Iconoclasms (730–787 and 815–843). As with the rest of his many-sided literary activity, his hagiography, which is split between the celebration of contemporary and earlier saints, did not only aim to edify his monastic audience but in many cases was also concerned with influencing the educated elite of the capital.

To begin with, the Funeral Laudations of his mother Theoktiste (*BHG* 2422) and his uncle, Plato, Abbot of Sakkoudion (*BHG* 1553), must have been delivered between 797 and 802 and in 814 respectively. Theodore's attempts to honor and venerate his relatives coincided with a general need for contemporary hagiography (that is, the creation of new heroes) and his personal aspirations to endorse the "canonization" of his family members. In a sense, this was an endeavor that harked back to the age of the Cappadocians and their efforts to promote a kind of family cult and implicitly sketch their auto-hagiographical portrait (Efthymiadis and Featherstone 2007: 13–25).

Two of his other *Enkomia* were, to all appearances, linked with works of art. First, the *Panegyric on the Beheading of St John the Baptist* (*BHG* 864) can be associated with the iconography of the Stoudite church in Constantinople, as it contains a detailed description of a series of icons portraying the different stages of the Forerunner's martyrdom. We should connect this panegyric with the restoration and repainting of the famous basilica of Stoudios once the Stoudite community had moved from Asia Minor to Constantinople. The *Enkomion of St John the Evangelist* (*BHG* 929) refers to the inauguration of another Stoudite church. In the peroration, Theodore implores the saint to receive those who had generously built his beautiful church (*PG* 99, 778C). According to the oldest preserved *Life of Theodore* (vita B), one such church was built by Theodore at his uncle Plato's request, when Theodore was still a simple monk. The future abbot of Stoudios not only adorned the walls of the church with frescoes but also covered the floor with "a sparkling golden mosaic" (*PG* 99, 244B–C).

These and his other works on early Christian saints associate Theodore's hagiographical activity with the so-called metaphrastic tendency that marked Byzantine hagiography in the ninth and tenth centuries. As a practice, *metaphrasis* involved the reworking and stylistic reshaping of older texts, mostly *Passions*, creating new, rhetorically polished accounts. The *Enkomion of St Arsenios* (*BHG* 169) is the result of an elaboration on and a synthesis of isolated biographical episodes pertaining to this Late Antique holy ascetic. In his prologue, Theodore presents an apologia for having reworked this material which he had done his best to make coherent, into a "seamless narration" (*PG* 99, 849C). Similar indications of reworking can be traced in his *Laudation of the Apostle Bartholomew* (*BHG* 230). However, his most elaborate piece was chronologically his last, the *Panegyric on St Theophanes the Confessor* (*BHG* 1732b), the compiler of the World Chronicle covering the period from 284 to 814 AD. In it the author celebrates the translation of the saint's relics to the monastery of Megas Agros and honors his holy, well-born abbot with a sophisticated account, enshrining episodes from the persecution his hero suffered in the Second Iconoclasm.

Gregory Palamas

The rhetorical praise of saints was also a homiletic preoccupation for the last of the Church Fathers of the Byzantine era. According to his biographer Patriarch Philotheos Kokkinos (Tsamis 1985: 468), Gregory's *Enkomion of Peter of Athos* (*BHG* 1506) was his earliest work, written at the age of 36 (that is, in 1333) during a sojourn on the Holy Mountain. St Peter was the first known hermit to live on Mount Athos before its development as a coenobitic center. His biography, created from disparate narrative elements, most probably in the eleventh century, was adopted by Gregory as a good platform for promoting the ideology of Hesychasm (Rigo 1995). Internal evidence suggests that this was a work for oral delivery, destined for a congregation beyond Athos.

Next, but still in this Athonite period, which ended in 1337, we must place his *Homily on St John the Baptist* (*BHG* 846), addressed to a monastic audience and filled with exhortations to renounce the world physically and spiritually, thereby emulating the paradigm of ascetic life. His other homilies on saints pertain to holy figures from the New Testament and must have been pronounced before a lay audience, in all likelihood while Gregory was Archbishop of Thessaloniki (1347–1359). Not surprisingly, these homilies have all the characteristics of a catechetical discourse which, after reviewing scenes from the Gospels or the Acts of the Apostles, concludes with words of spiritual counsel. Thus, the *Homily on St John the Evangelist* (*BHG* 932n) ends with the admonition to care for your neighbor; the *Homily on St Mary Magdalene* (*BHG* 1162e) invites the flock to practice Christian virtues; and the *Homily on Sts Peter and Paul* (*BHG* 1501) dwells on the doctrine of repentance. Finally, in his *Homily on St Demetrios* (*BHG* 548), the patron saint of his city, Archbishop Gregory warns his fellow citizens against those who menace the true faith in various ways.

In all these speeches, which are not particularly long, the Hesychast Father abstained from adopting a sophisticated prose style, thereby acknowledging the priority he gave to comprehensibility over demonstrating an orator's rhetorical skills. In fact, whether their subjects of praise were the traditional saints of Christianity or, less often, their own contemporaries, all the Fathers served the cause of hagiography in accordance with their public ministry and in light of their ecclesiastical and political authority. In the course of the fourth century, the golden age of Christianity, the praise of saints took different forms of discourse in tandem with the models of sainthood suggested. These forms and models never ceased to fascinate those who were to undertake similar tasks thereafter, be they Church Fathers or simple hagiographers. As pious and edifying exempla, saints of all kinds were the ideal vehicle for advancing claims about ancestral liturgical practices, for encouraging the sentimental attachment of the Christian flock to the cult of saints, and, especially when these saints were contemporary holy figures, for exemplifying and reassessing the ideal Christian life.

Bibliography

Abbreviations

BHG   François Halkin, *Bibliotheca hagiographica Graeca*, I–III, Subsidia Hagiographica 8a (Brussels: Subsidia Hagiographica: Société des Bollandistes, 1957).

CPG   *Clavis Patrum Graecorum*, ed. Maurice Geerard, vols II–IV (Turnhout: Brepols, 1974–1980).

Primary Sources

Athanasios of Alexandria, *Life of Antony* (*BHG* 140) with French tr.: *Athanase d'Alexandrie, Vie d'Antoine*, ed. Gerhard J.M. Bartelink, Sources Chrétiennes 400. Paris: Éditions du Cerf, 1994 (2004, 2nd edn); English tr.: Tim Vivian and Apostolos N. Athanassakis, *Athanasius of Alexandria, The Life of Antony: The Coptic Life and The Greek Life*, Cistercian Studies Series 202. Kalamazoo, MI: Cistercian Publications, 2003; and (abbreviated) David Brakke, "Athanasius of Alexandria, Life of St. Antony of Egypt", in *Medieval Hagiography: An Anthology*, ed. Thomas Head. New York: Routledge, 2001, 1–30.

Basil of Caesarea, *Homily on the Forty Martyrs of Sebasteia* (*BHG* 1205, *CPG* 2863): PG 31, 508–525; *Homily on St Gordius* (*BHG* 703, *CPG* 2862), PG 31, 489–507; *Homily on St Mamas* (*BHG* 1020, *CPG* 2868): PG 31, 589–600; *Homily on St Julitta* (*BHG* 972, *CPG* 2849): PG 31, 237–261.

Cyril of Alexandria, *Homily 18 – Fragments on the Translation of the Relics of Sts Cyrus and John* (*CPG* 5262 – *BHG* 472–474): PG 77, 1100–1105.

Gregory of Nazianzos, *Funeral Oration to St Athanasios* (*BHG* 186 – Oration 21): ed. and French tr., Justin Mossay, *Grégoire de Nazianze. Discours 20–23*, Sources Chrétiennes 270. Paris, 1980, 110–192.

Funeral Oration to St Basil (*BHG* 245 – Oration 43): ed. and French tr., Jean Bernardi, *Grégoire de Nazianze, Discours 42–43*, Sources Chrétiennes 384, Paris: Éditions du Cerf, 1992; English tr., Leo McCauley *et alii*, *Funeral Orations by Saint Gregory Nazianzen and Saint Ambrose*, The Fathers of the Church 22. Washington, DC, 1953, 27–99.

Funeral Orations to Caesarios (*BHG* 286– Oration 7) and to *Gorgonia* (*BHG* 704–Oration 8): ed. and French tr., Marie-Ange Calvet-Sebasti, *Grégoire de Nazianze, Discours 6–12*, Sources Chrétiennes 405 (Paris 1995); English tr., Leo P. McCauley *et alii, Funeral Orations by Saint Gregory Nazianzen and Saint Ambrose*. Washington, DC: The Catholic University of America Press, 1953, 5–25, 101–118.

Homily on St Kyprianos (*BHG* 457 – Oration 22): ed. and French tr., Justin Mossay, *Grégoire de Nazianze, Discours 24–26*, Sources Chrétiennes 284. Paris: Éditions du Cerf, 1981, 40–84.

Gregory of Nyssa, *Life of Gregory the Wonderworker (Thaumaturgus)* (*BHG* 715 – *CPG* 3184): ed. Günther Heil, in *Gregorii Nysseni Sermones. Pars II*. Leiden: Brill, 1990, 1–57; English tr., Michael Slusser, *Saint Gregory Thaumaturgus: Life and Works*, Washington, DC: The Catholic University of America Press, 1998, 41–87.

Letter on the life of Makrina (*BHG* 1012): ed. Virginia Woods Callahan, 'Vita S. Macrinae', in *Gregorii Nysseni opera ascetica* (*GNO* 8/1), ed. Werner Jaeger, John P. Cavarnos, Virginia Woods Callahan, Leiden: Brill, 1986, 370–414; older ed. Paul Maraval, *Grégoire de Nysse. Vie de sainte Macrine*, Sources Chrétiennes 178, Paris: Éditions du Cerf, 1971, 136–266; English tr., Anna M. Silvas, *Macrina the Younger, Philosopher of God*, Medieval Women: Texts and Contexts 22, Turnhout: Brepols, 2008, 109–148; *Funeral Oration to Placilla*

(*BHG* 1548 – *CPG* 3182): ed. Andreas Spira, *Gregorii Nysseni: Sermons, Pars Prior*, vol. IX. Leiden: Brill, 1967, 475–490; *Life of Theodore the Recruit* (*BHG* 1760– *CPG* 3183): ed. John P. Cavarnos, *Gregorii Nysseni Sermones. Pars II*. Leiden: Brill, 1990, 61–71; *Oration on St Stephen the First-Martyr* I and II (*BHG* 1654, 1657 – *CPG* 3186, 3187): ed. Otto Lendle, *ibid.*, 75–94, 97–105; *Oration on St Basil his Brother* (*BHG* 264 – *CPG* 3185): ed. Otto Lendle, *ibid.*, 109–134; *Oration on the Forty Martyrs of Sebasteia* Ia, Ib, and II (*BHG* 1206, 1207, 1208 – *CPG* 3188, 3189): ed. Otto Lendle, *ibid.*, 137–142, 145–156, 159–169.

Gregory Palamas, Gregorios Palamas, Συγγράμματα. Τόμος Ε΄. Κεφάλαια ἑκατὸν πεντήκοντα, Ἀσκητικὰ Συγγράμματα, Εὐχαί. Ed. Panagiotes K. Chrestou, Thessaloniki 1992, 161–191; other Homilies on saints in ed. Panagiotes Chrestou, Γρηγορίου τοῦ Παλαμᾶ, Ἅπαντα τὰ ἔργα, vols. X and XI, Thessalonike 1985; English tr., Christopher Veniamin, *St Gregory Palamas, The Homilies*, Waymart, PA: Mount Thabor Publishing, 2009.

John Chrysostom, *Discours sur Babylas*, edited by Margaret A. Schatkin, with the collaboration of Cécile Blanc and Bernard Grillet, Sources chrétiennes 362. Paris: Éditions du Cerf, 1990; *Homily in St Matthew*, VIII.7, *CPG* 4424, *PG* 57, cols 88–89. Other homilies of hagiographical interest (*CPG* 4344–4365), in *Patrologia Graeca*, vols 50, 58, and 63.

John of Damascus, *Hypomnema to St Artemios* (*CPG* 8082 – *BHG* 170): ed. Bonifatius Kotter, *Die Schriften des Johannes von Damaskos*, vol. 5, Patristische Texte und Studien 28. Berlin: De Gruyter, 1988, 202–245; *Laudation of St Barbara* (*CPG* 8065 – *BHG* 217), *ibid.*, 256–278; *Laudation of St Anastasia* (*BHG* 83b), *ibid.*, 289–303; *Enkomion of St John Chrysostom* (*CPG* 8064 – *BHG* 879), *ibid.*, 359–370.

Severos of Antioch, *Cathedral Homilies* – *CPG* 7035: *Patrologia Orientalis* (various vols).

Theodore of Stoudios, *Enkomion to Plato* (*BHG* 1553): *PG* 99, 804–850; *Funerary Catechism for his Mother* (*BHG* 2422): Stephanos Efthymiadis (ed.) and Jeffrey M. Featherstone (English tr.), "Establishing a holy lineage: Theodore the Stoudite's funerary catechism for his mother (*BHG* 2422)", in *Theatron. Rhetorische Kultur in Spätantike und Mittelalter/ Rhetorical Culture in Late Antiquity and the Middle Ages*, ed. Michael Grünbart, Millennium Studies. Berlin: De Gruyter 2007, 13–51 (=S. Efthymiadis, *Hagiography in Byzantium: Literature, Social History and Cult*, Variorum Reprints. Farnham: Ashgate Variorum, 2011, XI); *Enkomion of Arsenios* (*BHG* 169): ed. Theodoros Nissen, "Das Enkomion des Theodoros Studites auf den heiligen Arsenios", *Byzantinisch-neugriechische Jahrbücher* 1 (1920), 246–262; older edition: *PG* 99, 849–881. *Panegyric of Theophanes the Confessor* (*BHG* 1792b): ed. and French tr., Stephanos Efthymiadis, "Le panégyrique de S. Théophane le Confesseur par S. Théodore Stoudite (BHG 1792b). Édition critique du texte intégral", *AB* 111 (1993), 259–90; and *AB* 112 (1994), 104; *Laudation of the Apostle Bartholomew* (*BHG* 230), ed. Ula Westerbergh, *Anastasius Bibliothecarius Sermo Theodori Studitae de S. Bartholomaeo*, Studia Latina Stockholmensia 9 (1963), 41–48.

Secondary Sources

Allen, Pauline (2009), "Welcoming foreign saints to the Church of Antioch", *Journal of the Australian Early Medieval Association* 5, 9–20.

Allen, Pauline and Hayward, C.T.R (2004), *Severus of Antioch*, The Early Church Fathers. London: Routledge.

Allen, Pauline (2010) "Loquacious locals. Two indigenous martyrs in the homilies of Severus of Antioch", in *Martyrdom and Persecution in Late Antique Christianity. Festschrift Boudewijn Dehandschutter*, ed. Johan Leemans, Bibliotheca Ephemeridum

Theologicarum Lovanensium CCXLI. Leuven: Uitgeverij Peeters, 1–14.

Brakke, David (1995), *Athanasius and the Politics of Asceticism*. Oxford: Oxford University Press (revised paperback ed.: *Athanasius and Asceticism*. Baltimore, MD: Johns Hopkins University Press, 1998).

Burrus, Virginia (2005) "Life after death: the martyrdom of Gorgonia and the birth of female hagiography", in *Gregory of Nazianzus: Images and Reflections*, eds Jøstein Bortnes and Tomas Hägg. Copenhagen: Museum Tusculanum Press, 153–170.

Daniélou, Jean (1955) "La chronologie des sermons de Grégoire de Nysse", *Revue des Sciences Religieuses* 29, 346–372.

Delehaye, Hippolyte (1921) "Cyprien d'Antioche et Cyprien de Carthage", *Analecta Bollandiana* 39, 314–332.

Delehaye, Hippolyte (1933), *Les origines du culte des martyrs*, Subsidia Hagiographica 20. Brussels: Société des Bollandistes.

Delehaye, Hippolyte (1966) *Les Passions des martyrs et les genres littéraires*, Subsidia Hagiographica 13b. Brussels: Société des Bollandistes.

Efthymiadis, Stephanos (ed.) (2014) *The Ashgate Research Companion to Byzantine Hagiography*, Volume II: *Genres and Contexts*. Farnham: Ashgate.

Gemeinhardt, Peter (2012) "*Vita Antonii* oder *Passio Antonii*? Biographisches Genre und martyrologische Topik in der ersten Asketenvita", in *Christian Martyrdom in Late Antiquity (300–450 AD). History and Discourse, Tradition and Religious Identity*, eds. Peter Gemeinhard and Johan Leemans. Arbeiten zur Kirchengeschichte 116. Berlin: De Gruyter, 79–114.

Hägg, Tomas (2005) "Playing with expectations: Gregory's Funeral orations on his brother, sister and father", in *Gregory of Nazianzus: Images and Reflections*, eds Jøstein Bortnes and Tomas Hägg. Copenhagen: Museum Tusculanum Press, 133–151.

Hägg, Tomas (2011) "The *Life of St Antony* between biography and hagiography", in *The Ashgate Research Companion to Byzantine Hagiography*, Volume 1: *Periods and Places*, ed. Stephanos Efthymiadis, Farnham: Ashgate, 17–34.

Hägg, Tomas (2012) *The Art of Biography*. Cambridge: Cambridge University Press.

Karlin-Hayter, Patricia (1991) "Passio of the XL martyrs of Sebaste. The Greek tradition: the earliest accounts", *Analecta Bollandiana* 109, 249–305.

Kazhdan, Alexander, P. (in collaboration with L.F. Sherry and C. Angelidi) (1999), *A History of Byzantine Literature (650–850)*. Athens: National Hellenic Research Foundation-Institute for Byzantine Research, Research series 2.

Kelly, John, N.D. (1995) *Golden Mouth. The Story of John Chrysostom. Ascetic, Preacher, Bishop*. Ithaca, NY: Cornell University Press.

Leemans, Johan (2010) "Hagiography and historical–critical analysis: the earliest layer of the Dossier of Theodore the Recruit (BHG 1760 and 1761)", in *Martyrdom and Persecution in Late Antique Christianity. Festschrift Boudewijn Dehandschutter*, ed. Johan Leemans. Leuven: Uitgeverij Peeters, 135–160.

Limberis, Vasiliki M. (2011) *Architects of Piety: The Cappadocian Fathers and the Cult of the Martyrs*. Oxford: Oxford University Press.

Maraval, Pierre (1999) "Les premiers développements du culte des XL martyrs de Sébastée dans l'Orient byzantine et en Orient", *Vetera Christianorum* 36, 193–215.

Mayer, Wendy (2005) *The Homilies of St John Chrysostom. Provenance. Reshaping the Foundations*. Orientalia Christiana Analecta 273. Rome: Pontificium Institutum Orientalium Studiorum.

McGuckin, John A. (2001) *Saint Gregory of Nazianzus. An Intellectual Biography*. Crestwood, NY: St Vladimir's Seminar Press.

Métivier, Sophie (2005) *La Cappadoce (IVe–VIe siècle). Une histoire provinciale de l'Empire romain d'Orient*, Byzantina Sorbonensia 22, Paris: Publications de la Sorbonne.

Mitchell, Stephen (1999) "The life and lives of Gregory Thaumaturgus", in *Portraits of Spiritual Authority: Religious Power in Early Christianity, Byzantium and the Christian Orient*, ed. Jan W. Drijvers and John W. Watt. Leiden: Brill, 99–138.

Mühlenberg, Ekkehard (2012) "Gregor von Nyssa über die Vierzig und den ersten Märtyrer (Stephanus)", in *Christian ersten Martyrdom in Late Antiquity (300–450 AD). History and Discourse, Tradition and Religious Identity*, ed. Peter Gemeinhardt and Johan Leemans. Arbeiten zur Kirchengeschichte 116. Berlin: De Gruyter, 115–132.

Rigo, Antonio (1995) "La Vita di Pietro l'Athonita (*BHG* 1506) scritta da Gregorio Palama", *Rivista di Studi Bizantini e Neoellenici* n.s. 32, 177–190.

Rousseau, Philip (1994) *Basil of Caesarea, The Transformation of the Classical Heritage XXVI.* Berkeley, CA: University of California Press.

Tsames, D.G. (1985), Φιλοθέου Κωνσταντινουπόλεως τοῦ Κοκκίνου. Ἁγιολογικὰ ἔργα. Α´ Θεσσαλονικεῖς ἅγιοι. Thessalonike: Centre of Byzantine Research.

Van Dam, Raymond (1982) "Hagiography and history: the life of Gregory Thaumaturgus", *Classical Antiquity* 1, 272–308.

Van Dam, Raymond (2003) *Families and Friends in Late Roman Cappadocia*, Philadelphia, PA: University of Pennsylvania Press.

Ziadé, Raphaëlle (2007) *Les martyrs Maccabées: de l'histoire juive au culte chrétien. Les homélies de Grégoire de Nazianze et de Jean Chrysostome*, Supplements to Vigiliae Christianae 80. Leiden: Brill.

CHAPTER 26
Liturgies and the Fathers

Hugh Wybrew

Introduction

Worship was central to the life of the Christian Church from the beginning. At its heart was the celebration of what the New Testament calls the Lord's Supper or the breaking of bread, and which very soon came to be called the Eucharist. While rites of initiation are generally not ascribed to any particular theologian or bishop, eucharistic liturgies, and in particular eucharistic prayers, often bear the name of a distinguished teacher or chief pastor particularly venerated in the church that used them. In some cases the ascription clearly does not reflect the actual authorship of the person named. In others there is a strong likelihood that it does.

In the first eight centuries there is much more material relating to the Eastern liturgical traditions than to the Western. It is now generally accepted that there was no uniformity in worship in the earliest centuries (Bradshaw and Johnson 2012). Each local church had its own tradition. By the fourth century, with the developing organization of the Church, those centers which later emerged as patriarchates developed distinctive liturgical traditions that gradually displaced others within their respective spheres of influence. To Rome, Alexandria, and Antioch were added from the fourth century Constantinople and Jerusalem. Edessa and Nisibis were home to important theological schools of Syriac Christianity. By the eighth century Rome in the West and Constantinople in the East were becoming dominant ecclesiastical and liturgical influences in their respective spheres.

The Wiley Blackwell Companion to Patristics, First Edition. Edited by Ken Parry.
© 2015 John Wiley & Sons Ltd. Published 2019 by John Wiley & Sons Ltd.

Liturgical Texts

The followers of Jesus Christ formed a sect within Judaism. Their worship developed within the traditions of Jewish worship. Like Jesus himself, the first disciples went to the temple in Jerusalem. They attended synagogue on the Sabbath and observed Jewish practices in their homes. The earliest surviving text relating to worship is the Didache, now generally dated to about 60. It includes instructions for baptizing and prayers of thanksgiving to be said before and after a meal, which may or may not have been a Eucharist in the technical sense. There is also a gathering on the Lord's Day for the breaking of bread and thanksgiving, which is called a sacrifice. The Didache is unique, if the accepted dating is roughly accurate, as the only witness to early Christian worship from the apostolic period other than New Testament references (Whitaker 2003; Bradshaw and Johnson 2012).

There are other texts that claim apostolic origin, but are certainly later. They include the Apostolic Tradition of Hippolytus (early third–late fourth century), the Didascalia Apostolorum (third century), and Apostolic Constitutions (late fourth century). These compilations form a group known as church orders, which give instructions for the conduct of the Christian communities in which they were written and for their liturgical worship. The later church orders draw on the earlier, while adding new material of their own.

The First Three Centuries

There are references to worship in the writings of the Apostolic Fathers and the Ante-Nicene Fathers (Jasper and Cuming 1987; Whitaker 2003). Justin Martyr, in his First Apology (c. 150) and Dialogue with Trypho, gives the earliest detailed description of rites of initiation and the Eucharist, from which the contents of a eucharistic prayer in Rome may with some accuracy be deduced. The Apostolic Tradition of Hippolytus also describes initiation rites and includes the text of a eucharistic prayer used by a newly consecrated bishop. The work can only be reconstructed from later manuscripts, and it probably includes material dating from the early third to the late fourth centuries. Both Hippolytus and Justin say that the eucharistic prayer was in principle extempore. It seems that Christian worship, like contemporary Jewish worship, made little if any use of fixed texts, even if there was a tradition of what the prayers used in worship should include.

Texts from the first three centuries forming part of the so-called Apocryphal New Testament, such as the Acts of John and of Thomas, also give information about initiation and the Eucharist. Although they come from communities usually thought to be influenced in varying degrees by Gnostic ideas, their initiation rites seem to have been similar to those of more orthodox communities, even if details may be conditioned by their own specific beliefs. They conclude with the celebration of the Eucharist (Whitaker 2003).

Other pseudepigraphal texts come from churches more in the mainstream of Christian tradition. They bear the name of a Christian evangelist or teacher connected with the church from which they derive. A eucharistic liturgy of the Church of the East bears the name of Addai, traditionally a disciple of the apostle Thomas, and Mari his disciple (Brightman 1896). There is no evidence for the use of the liturgy before the seventh century, but the oldest stratum of the eucharistic prayer is generally held to date from the third century and to derive from Edessa, a theological center of East Syriac Christianity where the influence of Judaism remained strong. A notable feature of this prayer is the absence of an institution narrative. Closely related with it is the Third Anaphora of St Peter, used in the Maronite Church in Lebanon, whose liturgical tradition stems from the West Syriac tradition centered on Antioch (Jasper and Cuming 1987). Both are probably descended from a common Syriac ancestor.

Developments from the Fourth Century

The latter half of the fourth century saw the appearance of fixed liturgical texts for both initiation and the Eucharist. It also saw the beginning of the formation of liturgical families, centered on the churches of the great cities of the Roman Empire: Rome, Alexandria, Antioch, Constantinople, and Jerusalem.

Alexandria and Egypt

The Sacramentary of Sarapion of Thmuis (c. 350) represents a local Egyptian tradition in the Nile Delta. It includes prayers for use in initiation (Whitaker 2003) and the celebration of the Eucharist (Jasper and Cuming, 1987), as well as at other services. They differ in several respects from the Alexandrian tradition, whose anaphora, ascribed to St Mark, the traditional first evangelist of the city, became the eucharistic prayer used throughout Egypt. The final form of the Liturgy of St Mark, used in the Coptic Orthodox Church, dates from the thirteenth century (Brightman 1896), but from earlier fragments it is possible to form a good idea of what its eucharistic prayer may have been like about 400 (Jasper and Cuming 1987). A eucharistic prayer in Coptic named after Cyril of Alexandria is an earlier form of the anaphora of St Mark, and dates from after 431. A characteristic of the Egyptian tradition, found in all prayers from the fourth century onwards, is that the intercessions are included in the section before the Sanctus.

A eucharistic prayer bearing the name of St Basil is one of the earliest still in use in the Coptic Orthodox Church. Of West Syriac type; it may have represented the tradition of Cappadocia, and so attracted Basil's name. It could have been brought to Egypt by Basil himself, who spent some time in Alexandria in 357, though it would be unusual for an anaphora to bear the name of a layman (Jasper and Cuming 1987).

Antioch, West Syria, and Constantinople

The liturgical tradition of Antioch is closely linked with that of Jerusalem, and became that of Constantinople. Its influence spread over the whole of Syria. The earliest witness to the rites of initiation and the Eucharist in Jerusalem are Cyril of Jerusalem's

Mystagogical Catecheses (see later). Toward the end of Cyril's episcopate the nun Egeria was in Jerusalem on pilgrimage, and her journal describes in detail the services of Holy Week, including the final preparation of candidates for baptism. The eucharistic rite of Jerusalem, dated to around 400 and named after St James, is related to Cyril's rite. It was later adopted in Antioch, and was widely used in West Syria for several centuries. Its apostolic origin was accepted as authentic until relatively recent times. A Syriac version is still used in the Syriac Orthodox Church, whose eucharistic liturgy includes some 80 anaphoras. Another late-fourth-century witness to the Antiochene tradition is the Apostolic Constitutions, compiled c. 375. It contains a description of the rites of initiation and the earliest complete eucharistic liturgy; sometimes known as the Clementine rite, this church order's full title is the Constitution of the Apostles through Clement (Jasper and Cuming 1987).

The first textual witness to the liturgies of initiation and the Eucharist in Constantinople is the Codex Barberini (c. 790) (Parenti and Velkovska 1995). No name is attached to the rite of initiation, but names are attached to the two eucharistic prayers. One is a developed form of the Egyptian anaphora of St Basil. Recent scholarship has inclined to think Basil himself may well have been responsible for its final recension, which would then date from the late fourth century. West Syrian in structure, it reflects Basil's theological thought, and includes a number of scriptural quotes, a characteristic of late fourth century eastern eucharistic prayers. It is one of the two eucharistic prayers still in use in the Eastern Orthodox Church. Syrian and Armenian versions of Byzantine Basil represent an earlier form of the text than the final Greek.

The other anaphora in the Codex Barberini is ascribed to St John Chrysostom. Recent scholarly study has concluded that the present form of this prayer is probably the work of John himself, perhaps when he was a presbyter in Antioch. It is closely related to the Syriac Anaphora of the Twelve Apostles, both perhaps deriving from a common original. They are broadly the same as far as the institution narrative, after which the Twelve Apostles seems to follow closely the anaphora of St James, while its intercessions apparently derive from Egyptian Basil.

At the time the Codex Barberini was written, the anaphora normally used in Constantinople was that of St Basil. By about 1000 the anaphora of St John Chrysostom had replaced it, the anaphora of St Basil being used on only 10 days of the year. The two prayers are closely related, not least in their second halves, and especially in the intercessions, which come in their West Syrian position after the anamnesis and epiclesis.

East Syria

The Church of the East uses two eucharistic liturgies in addition to that of Addai and Mari. In the sixth century, Leontius of Byzantium ascribed a liturgy to Theodore of Mopsuestia, one of that church's venerated teachers. It is, says Leontius, full of "blasphemies": one phrase in it reflects Antiochene Christology. In the thirteenth century, Abdisho (Ebedjesu) ascribes a "prolix liturgy" to Nestorius. Quite probably the eucharistic prayers ascribed to Nestorius and Theodore go back in substantially their present form to the formative period of the Church of the East in the early fifth century.

They seem to be related to the anaphora of Addai and Mari as well as to those of Basil and Chrysostom, and to the Liturgical Homilies of Narsai (see later). Theodore and Nestorius could have had a hand in their shaping. A characteristic of these three East Syriac eucharistic prayers is the position of the epiclesis after the intercessions and before the final doxology.

Rome and the West

If the "Clementine" Liturgy is the first complete text of a eucharistic rite in the East, the first citation of the central portion of a eucharistic prayer in the West is found in the De Sacramentis and the De Mysteriis of Ambrose, bishop of Milan 374–397 (Yarnold 1981). These two closely related texts describe the rites of initiation and the Eucharist. Ambrose claims to follow the Roman church in all things, although he acknowledges that the foot-washing in the Milanese initiation rite had no parallel in Rome. Found in some other Western rites, Ambrose justifies its use it by insisting that Rome is not the sole repository of wisdom.

Fifth-century evidence for Roman rites is scanty. Pope Innocent's letter to Bishop Decentius of Gubbio mentions aspects of baptismal and eucharistic practice; and the letter of John the Deacon to Senarius written c. 500 answers the latter's questions about Roman baptismal practice. The earliest textual witness to the Roman rite is the so-called Leonine Sacramentary (Mohlberg et al. 1966). Not strictly a sacramentary, it is a collection of libelli, originally separate sheets with the variable prayers used at the Eucharist on different occasions. The only surviving manuscript dates from the seventh century, and while some of the prayers may be Leo's own compositions as pope (440–461), it includes Roman material of the fifth and sixth centuries. The first known Roman sacramentary is ascribed to Pope Gelasius (492–496) (Mohlberg et al. 1968). The earliest manuscript, probably written near Paris, dates from the mid-eighth century and contains Gallican as well as Roman material. Perhaps a seventh-century compilation, it includes rites of initiation and the first complete text of the Roman Canon of the Mass in almost its final form. The relationship of the latter to the eucharistic prayer from which Ambrose quotes is problematic. Though later in date than Ambrose's prayer, it includes sections reflecting second- or third-century eucharistic theology. Other sections are known to have been added after Gelasius' time.

This Frankish Gelasian Sacramentary circulated widely in Gaul in the later eighth century. It reflects the Roman presbyteral rite, and has no more connection to Pope Gelasius than has the Leonine to Pope Leo. The Gregorian Sacramentary, roughly contemporary with the Gelasian, and so later than the time of Gregory himself, reflects papal usage. The Ordo Romanus Primus, compiled probably about 700, describes in detail the ceremonial of a papal mass in Rome (Jasper and Cuming 1987).

No name has ever been attached to the old Roman Canon. It differs from Eastern anaphoras in that the first part of the prayer is not fixed, as in the East, but consists of a Preface that varies according to the liturgical feast or season, while after the Sanctus and Benedictus the prayer is made up of distinct sections, some of which are also variable. The Roman rite seems to have been similar to that used in North Africa, while outside Rome's immediate circle of influence, in northern Italy, Gaul, and Spain, a family of rites developed with similarities to both the Roman rite and some Eastern liturgical traditions. Gallican and Mozarabic (Spanish) eucharistic prayers include more variable material than the Roman Canon (Jasper and Cuming 1987).

Liturgical Catecheses

Much of our information about liturgical worship in both East and West comes from late-fourth-century catechetical lectures given to those who had just been baptized or were about to be (Yarnold 1981). Reference has already been made to Ambrose of Milan's lectures, the principal evidence for rites of initiation and the Eucharist in northern Italy. Regarding the Eucharist, Ambrose exhorts the newly baptized not to be like the Greeks, who only receive communion once a year. The decline in lay communion seems to have begun towards the end of the fourth century, and to have spread gradually throughout the East and into the West. By the later Middle Ages few lay Christians anywhere received communion more than once a year, if that.

Roughly contemporary with Ambrose are the Mystagogical Catecheses of Cyril of Jerusalem. Delivered during Easter Week to the newly baptized, they explain the rites and their meaning, supplying valuable information about liturgical practices in the Holy City. Their date is uncertain. Cyril was bishop of Jerusalem c. 349–386. Most manuscripts ascribe the lectures to his successor John, some to both bishops. The concluding rites of initiation took place at the Easter Vigil, beginning on the evening of Holy Saturday and ending with the Eucharist early on Easter morning. Some features of the rite seem to be modeled on the rites of initiation of the mystery cults. The eucharistic prayer described by Cyril is both curious and significant. A brief preface on the theme of creation leads to the Sanctus, followed by an invocation of the Holy Spirit to change the bread and wine into the body and blood of Christ. Intercessions for the living and the departed are then offered in the presence of Christ's propitiatory sacrifice, which guarantees that they will be heard. Cyril seems to have been the first to speak of awe and fear in the presence of the sacrament, and to teach that the eucharistic sacrifice is completed with the consecration of the eucharistic gifts rather than with their reception.

Cyril's invocation of the Holy Spirit reflects the developed theology of the Third Person of the Trinity enunciated at the Council of Constantinople of 381. A similar epiclesis is found in the liturgy of the eighth book of the Apostolic Constitutions. Combined with an earlier invocation of the Holy Spirit on the worshippers for the fruits of communion, the epiclesis became a fixed characteristic of Eastern anaphoras, together with the inclusion of comprehensive intercessions within the eucharistic prayer. The anaphora of James, derived in part from the Jerusalem anaphora to which Cyril bears witness, includes such an epiclesis (Jasper and Cuming 1987). Unlike Cyril's prayer, James' anaphora includes material between the Sanctus and Epiclesis that includes thanksgiving for redemption leading into an institution narrative and an anamnesis.

John Chrysostom delivered his Catechetical Lectures in Antioch, enabling us to follow baptismal and eucharistic rites there in detail, and to compare them with other local West Syrian rites. The early Antiochene rites of initiation appear to have had no anointing (or laying-on of hands) after the triple immersion in water, which was followed immediately by eucharistic communion. Not far from Antioch, Theodore, like John a native of Antioch and a fellow student of his, delivered his baptismal catecheses sometime after 392 when he became bishop of Mopsuestia. The rites he explains belong to the West Syrian family, and the anaphora on which he comments is the same in structure as Chrysostom's. But one aspect of his commentary is significant, for he is the first witness to the tradition, which subsequently flourished in the Christian East, of interpreting the eucharistic rite as symbolic of events in the life of Christ. The entry of the bread and wine represent Christ going to his passion, their deposition on the altar his burial, while his resurrection is symbolized by the consecration of the eucharistic elements. Although later Theodore came to be suspected of "Nestorian" tendencies, he became one of the acknowledged teachers of the Church of the East, together with his teacher Diodore of Tarsus. His catecheses, delivered originally in Greek, survive only in Syriac translation.

Liturgical Homilies and Commentaries

Late-fourth-century mystagogical catecheses belong to a time when the majority of candidates for baptism were still adults. In principle at least, they were baptized at the Easter Vigil in the course of awe-inspiring rites. But in the course of the fifth century adult baptism became less common, as most of the population became Christian. With infant baptism increasingly the norm, catechetical lectures disappeared. Their place was to some extent filled by homilies and commentaries on baptism and the Eucharist, designed for the edification of church members rather than the instruction of the newly baptized (Bornert 1966). Among the earliest to have survived are the Liturgical Homilies of Narsai (Connolly 1909).

East Syrian

Narsai was one of the great teachers and poets of the East Syrian tradition whose life spanned the fifth century. He was one of the founders of the new School at Nisibis after the expulsion of the followers of Ibas from Edessa after his death in 457. The center of Antiochene theology now moved eastwards beyond the persecuting reach of the East Roman Empire. The move marks the beginning of the formation of the distinct Church of the East, to be called "Nestorian" by the official Church of the Roman Empire. Its ecclesiastical center came to be Seleucia–Ctesiphon in Persian Mesopotamia. In one of his homilies Narsai celebrates the three revered teachers of this church: Diodore, Theodore, and Nestorius. Two others explain the meaning of baptism and the Eucharist. Like most of his homilies, they are written in narrative verse in couplets.

The baptismal rite on which Narsai comments is clearly in the early Syrian tradition, to which a number of texts bear witness, among them the third-century Didascalia Apostolorum (Whitaker 2003). Its chief characteristic, by comparison with other rites, is that there is no anointing after the baptismal bath, which is followed immediately by participation in the Eucharist. By contrast, more is made of the pre-baptismal anointing. Only in the seventh century does a post-baptismal anointing appear in the Church of the East, in the rite ascribed to the Patriarch Ishoyabh III (647–658). He had traveled in the West and seems to have known Greek, and to have been favorably impressed by Greek practices. Narsai's eucharistic prayer seems closely related to the anaphora of Addai and Mari, and to the anaphoras of Nestorius and Theodore. He speaks constantly of the "adorable" and "dread" "mysteries," using freely, in relation to the eucharistic offering, the language of awe and fear associated with Cyril of Jerusalem. In particular, all should be in fear when the adorable mysteries are accomplished by the descent of the Spirit. Narsai is an early witness to the clericalization of the Eucharist, which is offered by the priest "with great fear and trembling" while the congregation looks on, and to the clerical practice of saying the eucharistic prayer in a low voice inaudible to the people. The clergy in Constantinople had adopted this custom by 565, when Justinian issued a law ordering the clergy to say it and other prayers in a loud voice. About a century later the practice had reached Rome. Like Theodore of Mopsuestia, on whose catechetical homilies he drew, Narsai understands the rite as symbolizing key moments in the life of Christ.

West Syrian

West Syrian liturgical commentators write within a tradition of liturgical interpretation that stems from a short commentary on baptism and the Eucharist of unknown authorship, written sometime in the fifth century and influenced by the Antiochene tradition (Varghese 2004).

In general, West Syrian liturgical commentators are similar in approach and style to Greek writers. Jacob of Sarug (c. 451–521) was one of the first to compose liturgical homilies in Syriac. Known as "The Flute of the Spirit," he was a leading Miaphysite poet and theologian. More than 700 verse homilies, or memre, are ascribed to him. Written in 12-syllable lines, they include three on baptism, four on the Eucharist, and others on feasts of the Lord. Unlike Narsai, Jacob does not comment on rites and liturgical details. A baptismal rite and a liturgy are ascribed to him. George, bishop of the Arab Tribes (d. 724), wrote two important liturgical commentaries, a 12-syllable metrical "Memra on the Consecration of Myron" and an "Exposition of the Mysteries of the Church," George apparently based the latter on the fifth-century treatise, but drew extensively on the Ecclesiastical Hierarchy of Dionysius the Pseudo-Areopagite and the Alexandrian tradition. Jacob of Edessa (c. 633–708), too, was influenced in his approach by the fifth-century commentary. He was responsible for ordering the Syrian Orthodox liturgy, and wrote a "Discourse on the Myron" and a "Commentary on the Eucharist (qurobo)" addressed to George the Stylite. In the latter, Jacob draws on the Pseudo-Areopagite and makes use of the allegorical method of interpretation as well as the typological. His account of baptism describes the rite attributed to Severus of which Jacob made a revision. In the ninth century, Moses Bar Kepha's commentaries on Baptism, the Eucharist, and the Consecration of the Myron draw on these earlier writers.

The treatise "On the Ecclesiastical Hierarchy," of unknown authorship but attributed to Dionysius the Areopagite, was probably written c. 500 in northern Syria (Liubheid 1987). The author claims to be an Athenian convert of St Paul's. He may have been sympathetic to the Miaphysites. He certainly drew on the Alexandrian theological tradition and on neoplatonist philosophy. He sees the goal of human life as deification, a goal that can be achieved because of the union of human nature with God in Jesus Christ. Christians can enter into this union themselves by rising from material realities to the spiritual realities to which they point through contemplation. Those who have been purified and illumined can see the Eucharist for what it truly is, the sacrament of union with God.

Dionysius describes the rites of initiation and of the eucharistic synaxis. The synaxis is so called because it gathers believers into a unity among themselves, an essential condition for being drawn into communion with the One. In this sense it is the essential completion of all the other sacraments. Its unifying effect is symbolized at the very beginning when the bishop leaves the sanctuary to cense the congregation and then returns to his place. In so doing he symbolizes God, who in His love for humankind comes into the material world in order to raise human beings to the spiritual contemplation of the One. The readings and psalmody prepare the worshipper for the celebration of the mysteries by drawing together in contemplation of God's works those who are being prepared for divinization. Those not yet purified or illumined or sufficiently stable in contemplation, the catechumens, penitents, and those possessed by demons are now dismissed, for they are incapable of admission to the mysteries.

The holy bread and cup of blessing are then presented, and the kiss of peace exchanged. Uniting worshippers among themselves, the kiss enables them to be united with the One. The bishop and clergy wash their hands in preparation for the most holy sacrifice, an action that signifies the need to be as free as possible from anything unworthy of the sacrifice. Its performance in the presence of the gifts signifies that only Christ can purify them completely in preparation for union with God. The bishop, himself already united with the One, celebrates the mysteries and distributes the sacrament of union to the communicants, who share in the life, and union with God, of the Word who united human nature with himself and so divinized it.

The Byzantine Orthodox Tradition

Although the authenticity of the Dionysian corpus was questioned in the East, on the grounds that it was not cited by later Fathers and, therefore, could not be first century, it was nonetheless accepted into the patristic tradition. As a consequence, these writings carried considerable authority and were influential in the Eastern Church and later in the Western. Maximus the Confessor, among others, made use of them in his Mystagogy, written somewhere between 628 and 630 (Berthold 1985). An opponent of the monenergist and monothelete heresies propagated by the Emperor Heraclius and Patriarch

Sergius of Constantinople, he suffered persecution and exile. His is the first Byzantine liturgical commentary to have survived, and is generally assumed to be based on the eucharistic rite of the Great Church of Christ, which still preserved its early simplicity of structure, although already with the addition of some secondary elements. Written in all probability for monks, it interprets the rite as a means of mystical ascent to union with God. Maximus drew on Origen and Evagrius, and twice refers to "The Ecclesiastical Hierarchy" of Dionysius. His intention is to lead his readers to knowledge of the mystery of God. Though hidden, it is revealed in creation, in scripture, and in the symbolism of the Liturgy (as the Eucharist came to be called in the Eastern Orthodox tradition), and can be apprehended though contemplation, which pierces through the rite's symbolism to grasp the reality it represents. For Maximus, symbols, images, and figures – terms he seems to use more or less synonymously – contain the reality of which they are the sign.

The Mystagogy gives a twofold explanation of the Eucharist. First, it represents the whole history of God's saving plan from the incarnation to the second coming of Christ. Participation in the mysteries both points to and in part realizes the divinization of humankind through grace in the world to come. But as well as this general significance, the Liturgy has a special meaning, for it symbolizes the mystical ascent of the soul to God. Just as the different elements of the rite symbolize different stages in the history of salvation, so they also signify the stages by which the soul flees from error and the confusion of material things and attains to union with the one God.

Understandably, Maximus urges all Christians to attend church regularly and never to miss the holy synaxis, as he calls the Eucharist. For it is there in particular that the grace of the Holy Spirit is invisibly present to transform and change worshippers, whether or not they are able to feel this. For him the church building itself is a kind of sacrament, and the first part of the Mystagogy explains its symbolic significance. With a special appeal for monastics, the Mystagogy was widely read, judging by the number of surviving manuscripts. The first Byzantine work of its kind, it helped to establish a tradition, and to popularize a way of understanding and living the Liturgy that became integral to the Eastern Orthodox tradition.

That tradition was further developed in the early eighth century by Germanos, Patriarch of Constantinople 715–733. His "Ecclesiastical History and Mystical Contemplation" is one of the chief sources of information about the Liturgy in the eighth and ninth centuries, which had developed significantly since the seventh (Meyendorf 1984). This was an important period for the development of Byzantine worship, for it witnessed the controversy over the veneration of icons and their ultimate vindication. The Liturgy itself came to be understood as a kind of icon, and the "Ecclesiastical History" laid the foundation for subsequent liturgical interpretation.

The full title of Germanos' treatise is significant. The latter part links the work with the approach of Maximus the Confessor and Dionysius the Pseudo-Areopagite, for whom the Liturgy was primarily symbolic of eternal realities. But following a tradition going back to Theodore of Mopsuestia, Germanos gives greater prominence to the Liturgy as a contemplation of the events of salvation history. He brings together the Alexandrian and Antiochene traditions, and this is evident in his interpretation of the church building and clerical vesture, as well as of the rite itself. The three antiphons, added to the beginning of the rite since the seventh century, signify the prophecies that foretold the coming of Christ, the gospel his coming in the incarnation. The entry of the gifts at the Great Entrance signifies Christ's going to his passion, and their placing on the altar his burial. The resurrection is proclaimed in the opening dialogue of the eucharistic prayer and the removal of the veil from the gifts. From then on the celebration of the mysteries is the realization of the redemption Christians have already received by grace. The church's worship on earth is united with that of the angels in heaven, and the celebration of the Liturgy is an anticipation of the future Kingdom.

The Western Tradition

In the West, the "De Ecclesiasticis Officiis" of Isidore of Seville (c. 560–636) is the earliest surviving treatise on the liturgy (Knoeble 2008). It describes the Mozarabic liturgy in Spain. Its first part describes the Eucharist, the Divine Office, the major feasts in the church calendar, and various ecclesiastical practices. The second part describes the different ministries exercised in the church, and the rites of initiation. The work is of great importance for the study of the worship of the church in Spain in the seventh century and of the contribution Isidore himself made to it. A theologian as well as a liturgical scholar, he greatly influenced the development of catholic doctrine and practice in the Spanish church. His works are descriptions of liturgical services rather than commentaries on their mystical or symbolic significance.

Amalarius of Metz (c. 780–850/851) spent 2 years in Constantinople as the papal representative. He became familiar with the Byzantine tradition of liturgical interpretation, which through him made its way into the Western tradition. His "Eclogae de officio missae" is a description of the Roman episcopal Mass, and gives a mystical interpretation of the different parts of the service. In the "De Ecclesiasticis Officiis," Amalarius explains the formularies and ceremonies of the Eucharist, the daily Office, and other services, and deals with the liturgical seasons from Septuagesima to Pentecost, especially with Holy Week. He was responsible for compiling an Antiphonary, which he attempted to introduce in the Diocese of Lyons during his episcopate there, and on which he seems to have commented in his "De Ordine Antiphonarii."

Amalarius lived at a time when Roman and Gallican liturgical customs were coming together to form the composite rite that eventually replaced the Roman rite in Rome itself and throughout most of Western Christianity. His writings give valuable information about the state of the liturgy at the beginning of the ninth century, and he was influential in shaping what became the Roman rite in the Middle Ages.

Liturgical Hymnography

Some of the earliest Christian hymns are thought to be embedded in the New Testament. Of later compositions, the earliest to have survived is the "Bridle of colts untamed," a hymn to Christ preserved by Clement of Alexandria. Another early hymn is the "Phos hilarion," "O gladsome light," which came to be a fixed part of Vespers in the Byzantine Orthodox tradition. In the fourth century the use of hymns became more general. A text of the "Gloria in excelsis" appears in the Apostolic Constitutions c. 375, and found its way into Byzantine Orthros (Matins) and Compline, as well as into the Roman Mass. In Constantinople in the fourth century both Arians and Nicenes composed hymns as party slogans in doctrinal controversies. Latin hymns appear later than their Greek and Syriac equivalents (Walsh with Husch 2012). When they appear in the fourth century, they tend to be composed for use at specific times of day and at liturgical seasons, although Ambrose made use of them in his conflict with the Arians in Milan. The "Te Deum" is the best-known Latin hymn, written in rhythmic prose rather than verse.

In the fifth century some came to think that only scriptural hymns should be used in worship. In 563 the Council of Braga forbade the singing of non-biblical poetical compositions in church, a decision reversed by the Council of Toledo in 633 AD. In the East, single-stanza troparia like the "Monogenes" and "Cherubicon" appeared in services from the fifth century. Such short troparia were later joined by kontakia of 18–30 stanzas, and from the seventh century were combined in what were known as canons. Other poetic compositions called Akathistos hymns became very popular in the East.

Hymns came to form a much more important part of the liturgy of the hours in the East than in the West. Eastern hymnography, too, was richer in doctrinal content than Western. The hymnographic tradition of the East reflected the dogmatic teaching of the Ecumenical Councils to a far greater extent than did Western liturgical hymnody (Wellesz 1961; Topping 1997).

Eastern Hymnography

Ephrem the Syrian (c. 306–373), known as the "Harp of the Spirit," is the outstanding hymnographer of the Christian East (McVey 1989; Brock 1990). An orthodox Nicene Christian deacon, he was a prolific author of homilies in verse and of hymns. Written in Syriac, they celebrate the Christian mysteries, and greatly influenced subsequent Syriac and Greek hymnography. Over 500 of his hymns survive, arranged after his death into cycles. The most famous are those on Faith, on Paradise, on the Descent of Christ into Hell, in part of a sequence on Nisibis.

Among those influenced by Ephrem was Romanos the Melodist, born in Syria probably in the last quarter of the fifth century At some point he moved to Constantinople, where he apparently spent the rest of his life until his death somewhere between 555 and 565. Perhaps the most famous liturgical poet in the East Roman Empire, he is famous for a series of some 80 surviving kontakia, or chanted verse sermons (Lash 1996). They are made up of brief stanzas called ikoi, each ending with the same refrain. The initial verses of some of his kontakia remain in use in Eastern Orthodox worship. The Akathistos hymn to the Mother of God is attributed to him.

Andrew of Crete (c. 660–740) was also a Syrian, born in Damascus. A theologian, he defended icons during the Iconoclastic controversy. He composed many hymns, notably canons, a form he is said to have invented. A canon is based on the nine biblical canticles, used at Orthros or Matins in the Eastern Orthodox Church. At first sung by themselves, in the seventh century troparia began to be inserted between the verses of the canticles, not unlike antiphons in the West. In time the canticles dropped out of normal use, except for the Magnificat. Canons now consist normally of eight odes, with a short refrain between the troparia that make up each ode. Andrew's penitential "Great Canon," made up of 250 strophes, is used in Great Lent.

Cosmas the Melodist was contemporary with Andrew (c. 675–c. 751). Born in Damascus, he was adopted by John of Damascus' father. Early in the eighth century he became a monk at the Lavra of St Sabbas near Jerusalem. Cosmas wrote liturgical hymns in Greek, and was noted in particular for composing canons for the major festivals. Fourteen of them were incorporated into Eastern Orthodox liturgical books. He also wrote idiomela, shorter poems on religious subjects. The content of his hymns is largely biblical and doctrinal.

John of Damascus (c. 655–c. 750), like his father, became a high official in the court of the Caliph of Damascus. With Cosmas he became a monk of St Sabbas. Like Andrew of Crete, he defended the making and veneration of icons. His most important work is the "Fount of Knowledge," a synthesis of patristic thought of whose three parts that "On the Orthodox Faith" is the most significant. Some of John's religious poems entered the liturgical tradition, among them his best-known work the Easter Canon used at Matins.

Western Hymnography

Hilary of Poitiers (c. 315–367/368) is the earliest known western hymn writer. He was the leading Latin theologian of his time, called the "Athanasius of the West" because of his defense of Nicene Trinitarian orthodoxy. He was perhaps influenced by Greek hymnography during his exile. Ambrose of Milan (c. 339–397) became well known as a hymn writer, although only three extant hymns can be ascribed to him with certainty. He set a precedent for the style of Latin hymnography, simple, direct, and devotional. His influence caused hymns to become an integral part of Western public worship, though they were admitted to the daily office of the conservative Roman Church only in the twelfth century.

Aurelius Clemens Prudentius (348–c. 413) was a wealthy Spanish lawyer and provincial governor. Toward the end of his life he became an ascetic. His Christian poems from this last period were influenced by Ambrose. The 12 hymns of his "Cathemerinon" included hymns for the hours of the day, for festivals, and for the dead. Others were didactic or polemical. Some found a place in the Roman daily office. They were often lengthy compositions, not intended for liturgical use, and came to be so used only in shortened form. Sedulius (floruit fifth century), of whom little is known, wrote a biblical epic called the Carmen Paschale and an Abecedarian Hymn to Christ, parts of which were used liturgically. Magnus Felix Ennodius (473–521), who became bishop of Paviain in 514, wrote a dozen hymns in Ambrosian style. Venantius Fortunatus (c. 530–c. 609), appointed bishop of Poitiers c. 600, sometimes known as "the last of the Roman poets," was a poet and hymn writer at the Merovingian court. Among other Latin hymn writers were Bede the Venerable (672/673–735) and Theodulph of Orleans (d. 821).

Conclusion

The worship of the earliest Christian communities was rooted in the traditions of Jewish synagogue and domestic worship. In the fourth century, Jewish temple worship and contemporary mystery cults had some influence on the way Christian worship was presented. From the beginning, Christian liturgical worship had doctrinal implications. The Latin tag *lex orandi lex credendi* points both to the influence of practice on belief and to that of doctrine on liturgical worship. The association of the great theologians of the first eight centuries with baptismal and eucharistic liturgies is generally tangential. Christian teachers in both East and West inherited the liturgical traditions of their local church. There is no evidence that bishops composed complete baptismal or eucharistic rites, although their theological convictions did modify the content of inherited prayers. In only a few cases is there reasonable certainty that the final recension of a eucharistic prayer can be attributed to a particular episcopal theologian. But doctrinal developments, particularly in the fourth and fifth centuries, were clearly reflected in liturgical texts. This is particularly true of eucharistic prayers and hymnography, especially in the liturgical traditions of Eastern Orthodoxy, whose liturgical texts embody the dogmatic language of the ecumenical councils to a greater extent than those of the Latin West. East Syrian texts reflect the Christological tradition of the Antiochene school. If the *lex orandi* of the early church shaped its *lex credendi*, the *lex credendi* of the patristic period profoundly influenced the church's *lex orandi*.

Bibliography

Primary Sources

Ephrem the Syrian, Hymns. Introduction and translation by Kathleen McVey (1989). Paulist Press.

Ephrem the Syrian, Hymns on Paradise. Introduction and translation by Sebastian Brock (1990). New York: St Vladimir's Seminary Press.

Germanus of Constantinople, On the Divine Liturgy. Introduction and translation by Paul Meyendorf (1984). New York: St Vladimir's Seminary Press.

Isidore of Seville, De Ecclesiasticis Officiis. Introduction and translation by Thomas L. Knoeble (2008). The Newman Press.

Maximus the Confessor, Selected Writings. Introduction and translation by George C Berthold (1985). Paulist Press.

Mohlberg, Leo Cunibert, Eizenhöfer, Leo, and Siffrin, Petrus (eds) (1966), *Sacramentarium Veronense (Sacramentarium Leonianum).* Rome: Casa Editrice Herder.

Mohlberg, Leo Cunibert, Eizenhöfer, Leo, and Siffrin, Petrus (eds) (1968), *Liber Sacramentorum Romanae Ecclesiae (Sacramentarium Gelasianum).* Rome: Casa Editrice Herder.

Narsai, *The Liturgical Homilies of Narsai,* Introduction and translation by Dom R.H. Connolly 1909). Cambridge: Cambridge University Press.

Parenti, S. and Velkovska, Elena (eds) (1995), *L'Eucologio Barberini Gr. 336.* Rome: C.L.V. Edizioni Liturgiche.

Pseudo-Dionysius, The Complete Works, Introduction and translation by Colm Liubheid (1987). London: SPCK.

Romanos the Melodist, *On the Life of Christ: Kontakia. Chanted Sermons by the Great Sixth-Century Poet and Singer.* Introduction and translation by Archimandrite Ephrem Lash (1996). San Francisco, CA: HarperCollins.

Secondary Sources

Bornert, R. (1966), *Les Commentaires Byzantins de la Divine Liturgie*. Paris: Institut français d'Études byzantines.

Bradshaw, Paul and Johnson, Maxwell (2012), *The Eucharistic Liturgies: Their Evolution and Interpretation*. SPCK.

Brightman, F.E. (1896), *Liturgies Eastern and Western. Vol 1, Eastern Liturgies*. Oxford: Clarendon Press.

Jasper, R.C.D and Cuming, G.J. (1987), *Prayers of the Eucharist, Early and Reformed*. Pueblo.

Topping, Eva Catafygiotu (1997), *Sacred Songs: Studies in Byzantine Hymnography*. Minneapolis, MN: Light and Life Publishing Company.

Varghese, Baby (2004), *West Syrian Liturgical Theology*. Ashgate.

Walsh, Peter G. with Husch, Christopher (ed./transl.) (2012), *One Hundred Latin Hymns: Ambrose to Aquinus*. Harvard University Press.

Wellesz, Egon (1961), *A History of Byzantine Music and Hymnography*. Oxford: Clarendon Press.

Whitaker, E.C. (2003), *Documents of the Baptismal Liturgy*, 3rd edn, Maxwell E. Johnson (ed.). SPCK/Alcuin Club.

Yarnold, E. (1981), *The Awe-Inspiring Rites of Initiation*. St Paul Publications.

CHAPTER 27

Fathers and the Church Councils

Richard Price

The Council Fathers

Who were "the Fathers"? The term is to be found in a few texts of the first three centuries to refer to Christian teachers of the past with whom the writer felt in continuity,
but these passages are few and far between (Graumann 2002: 18–22). Use of the term
became frequent, however, during the controversy of the mid-fourth century over the
authority of the Council of Nicaea (325) and its creed; the bishops of Nicaea were now
referred to as "Fathers." This usage was adopted not only by their admirers but also by
their critics (as in the Creed of Sirmium, in Athanasius, *De synodis* 8.7). This aroused
Athanasius' indignation: "How can they give the name of 'Fathers' to their predecessors, when they now impeach their judgement?" (*De synodis* 13.2). For Athanasius
himself the term connoted honor and authority. His pro-Nicene allies and successors
inherited this usage: the "Fathers" were the bishops of Nicaea and all recognized
Christian writers who defended, or had anticipated, the Nicene faith.

In the letter from the Council of Constantinople of 381 (later called the Second
Ecumenical Council) to the emperor Theodosius I, the bishops summarized their work
as follows: "We pronounced some concise definitions, ratifying the faith of the Fathers
at Nicaea and anathematizing the heresies which have sprung up in opposition to it"
(Alberigo 2006: 39). The same council, in its letter to Pope Damasus, referred to the
bishops at Nicaea as the "318 Fathers" (Alberigo 2006: 61), with reference to a biblical
prototype, the 318 helpers of Abraham (Gen 14:14). The "holy Fathers of Nicaea" or
the "318 holy Fathers" were from now on standard expressions whenever Nicaea or its
creed was mentioned. At the same time, a broader use of the expressions "Fathers" or
"holy Fathers" continued, with reference to the bishops who wrote in defense of the
Nicene faith or simply handed it down in their dioceses.

The Wiley Blackwell Companion to Patristics, First Edition. Edited by Ken Parry.
© 2015 John Wiley & Sons Ltd. Published 2019 by John Wiley & Sons Ltd.

The ecumenical councils that followed Nicaea could also claim to be attended by "holy Fathers." When used before or during a council, the phrase was merely conventional; but when used subsequently of the bishops who had attended a council recognized as authoritative, it expressed respect. In the long controversy that followed Chalcedon, its keenest adherents extended their claim of inerrancy beyond the conciliar decrees to the bishops who had taken part. As Deacon Ferrandus, as spokesman for the African Church, wrote to the emperor Justinian:

> Regarding the ancient Fathers who are known to have attended the Council of Chalcedon, it is not fitting for their deliberations to be defamed, their judgement revised, and their verdict altered... Whatever we know to have been uttered, transacted, decreed and confirmed there was worked by the ineffable and secret power of the Holy Spirit (Price 2009a: I, 113–115).

Here, ecumenical councils are treated as comparable to Scripture, and the Fathers who attended them as comparable to the biblical writers.

We still need to ask: who, among so many Fathers, received particular veneration? Which of the great Fathers of the Church actually attended an ecumenical council? Athanasius attended the Council of Nicaea, but only in the junior capacity of a deacon, assisting his bishop, Alexander of Alexandria. Gregory Nazianzen chaired the First Council of Constantinople (381), unhappily. Theodoret of Cyrrhus was the only intellectual luminary who attended the Council of Chalcedon in 451, but his sympathy with Nestorius put a question mark against his orthodoxy, and he was never ranked as one of the "Fathers" of the Church. Finally, no major Father attended Constantinople II or III or the Second Council of Nicaea (787). But there is one great example of a major Church Father dominating a council, and that is Cyril of Alexandria at the First Council of Ephesus (431).

The Great Fathers at the Councils

Although it is misleading to say that Cyril "chaired" the Council of Ephesus, since the chairmanship was shared with other metropolitan bishops (Price 2009b: 242–245), he may certainly be said to have been the dominant influence among the bishops who made up the majority council. Famously, at no stage did all the bishops meet together. Cyril of Alexandria and his supporters called a meeting of the council and conducted a first session (on June 22, 431) before John of Antioch and his party arrived; a third of the bishops who were already at Ephesus issued a public protest and refused to attend. The work of the first session was the condemnation of Nestorius of Constantinople for heresy. What is important for our topic is the authority attached at this session to the writings of Cyril himself.

The debate started with a reading of the Nicene Creed, and then of Cyril's Second Letter to Nestorius, in which the Nicene Creed forms a foundation for the refutation of Nestorianism. There followed an *interrogatio* (consultation of the bishops in turn) in which all the bishops present, one by one, declared that these two texts were in agreement. The individual responses, repetitive though they are, reward attention (*ACO* I.1.2, 13–31; Graumann 2002: 371–382). It soon emerges that the bishops accorded the same respect to the letter as to the creed: they laud both as perfect expressions of the orthodox faith, the latter having the advantage of "expounding more fully what is there [in the creed] said in summary," as one of the bishops put it. As the *interrogatio* proceeds, it becomes clear that what the bishops are concerned to express is not simply a favorable judgment on Cyril's letter, but their own adhesion to the doctrine expressed in creed and letter alike, as if they themselves, rather than Cyril, were being judged. Take the response of Domninus of Opus in Greece:

> We recognize what has been defined by the most holy archbishop Cyril and now rightly put on a par with the holy council at Nicaea of the 318 Fathers, and we rightly acknowledge that it is to be fully upheld together with them. I believe in the Father and Son and the Holy Spirit, and I vow to remain in it till the end of my life and to die in it.

The bishop is vowing lifelong fidelity to the faith defined in the letter and the creed, two texts he places "on a par." The creed and the letter are said by several speakers to inspire faith "through the grace of the Holy Trinity"; and some of them assert that the letter, no less than the creed, had been inspired by the Holy Spirit.

If Ephesus was dominated by Cyril and his teaching, a similar role was played, surreptitiously and without public acknowledgement, by Maximus the Confessor at the Lateran Synod of 649, to which Maximus himself attributed ecumenical authority. The purpose of the synod was to condemn the Eastern churches (notably the patriarchate of Constantinople) for the support it gave to the doctrine of one will and one operation in Christ. It was Maximus who had persuaded the papacy that this was a grievous heresy offensive to God; the course of the council followed his judgment (tendentious though it was) of the issues and how to respond to them. A peculiarity of the synod is that in its published acts, a series of speeches, of great theological sophistication, are placed in the mouths of the council's chairmen – Pope Martin and two Italian metropolitans. It is agreed in current scholarship that the speeches were composed originally in Greek by Greek monks under the leadership of Maximus the Confessor. Not surprisingly, they are expressive of his own highly sophisticated understanding of the theological issue at stake. Maximus himself is named only once in the Acts – as one of the signatories to a petition from Greek monks in Rome, who make a request that the Acts of the synod be translated into Greek (*ACO*² I, 55). It was precisely these monks (in all probability) who at this very time were compiling the Acts and composing the speeches they contain, and all in the Greek language; but they needed to maintain the pretense that the Acts were the authentic record of a council conducted in Latin.

Citation of the Fathers at Councils

These are two cases of the unusual situation where the proceedings of a council were dominated by a living Church Father – though there is, of course, a great difference between the status enjoyed by Cyril of Alexandria, even in his own lifetime, and the standing of Maximus the Confessor, whose "patristic" authority not only was accorded posthumously, but in the full sense of the term is a creation of the patristic revival of modern times. "Councils" and "Fathers" were more commonly connected, as we saw above, through the use of the term "Fathers" to refer to all the bishops who attended a major council. At the same time, of course, the term was used in a broader use, to refer to champions and expositors of the Nicene faith, whether or not they ever attended a major council; and to the teaching of this larger body the councils came to attach more and more weight. The appeal to their teaching at councils commonly took the form of the reading out of florilegia consisting of excerpts from their writings arranged thematically. What this implies about how the Fathers were read will be discussed in the final section of this chapter. Our immediate topic is a factual preliminary: the use at councils of patristic florilegia as prime evidence for the truths of Christian doctrine.

This took time to develop. The florilegium at the end of Basil of Caesarea's *De Spiritu sancto* (ch. 29) is not a real example, since Basil cites his predecessors not as authorities on questions of dogma but as witnesses to liturgical practice; and as late as the 380s Gregory Nyssa responded to a claim by Eunomius to have "the saints" on his side by insisting on the unique authority of the biblical writers (*Contra Eunomium* III 1.7–21). It was only *after* the fourth century, and the completion of the work of the champions of Nicene orthodoxy (Athanasius and the Cappadocian Fathers), that there was a patristic tradition, reliable and weighty, to appeal to.

We may witness the development of the patristic florilegium in texts produced by Cyril of Alexandria. The first florilegium we have from his pen is the one in his address (shortly before the Council of Ephesus) to two of the sisters of Theodosius II, Arcadia and Marina. There, indeed, we find three pages (in Schwartz's edition) of patristic citations. However, later in the same document we find no fewer than 48 pages of citations from the New Testament (*ACO* I.1.5, 65–118). The appeal to the Fathers is still in second place. But at the council itself a breakthrough occurred. The Acts of the session of June 22 contain a florilegium of excerpts from orthodox Fathers, condemnatory of Nestorius *avant la lettre* (*ACO* I.1.2, 39–45). The role played by this florilegium in the debates of June 22 is unclear, but the same florilegium reappears in the Acts of the session of July 22. Here, it follows the Nicene Creed immediately, after a brief introduction that runs as follows:

> Because certain people pretend to profess and accept it [the creed], but in fact misinterpret the force of the ideas according to their own opinions and distort the truth, being sons of error and children of perdition, it has become absolutely necessary to set out passages from the holy and orthodox Fathers that can show convincingly in what way they understood the creed and had the confidence to proclaim it, so that, evidently, all who hold the correct and irreproachable faith may also understand, interpret and proclaim it accordingly (*ACO* I.1.7, 89).

Here, finally, the appeal to the Fathers moves to center stage. Taking together the Acts of June 22 and those of July 22, we may conclude that the First Council of Ephesus achieved its main work, the condemnation of Nestorius, not by theological argumentation but by establishing the criterion of orthodoxy, namely the Nicene Creed as interpreted by the Fathers of the Church. The Fathers cited in the florilegium (slightly expanded in the version of July 22) extend chronologically from St Cyprian to Atticus of Constantinople, who died a few years previously. But we have seen that at the decisive session of June 22 it was Cyril of Alexandria himself who was hailed as the supreme expositor of the Nicene faith.

He retained this status at the Council of Chalcedon (451). At the second session of the council the following documents were read out: the Nicene Creed, the creed attributed to the Council of Constantinople of 381 (now accorded ecumenical status), Cyril's Second Letter to Nestorius, his *Laetentur caeli* letter to John of Antioch, and the Tome of Pope Leo. It was these same documents that were singled out as authoritative in the council's Definition of the Faith. Did this mean that the living Pope Leo, present at the council through his representatives, was now elevated to the same status as the recently deceased Cyril (d. 444)? The answer is given in the Definition of the Faith that the council approved a few days later:

> The council has accepted as in keeping [with the creeds of Nicaea and Constantinople] the conciliar letters of the blessed Cyril, then shepherd of the church of Alexandria, to Nestorius and to those of the Orient, for the refutation of the madness of Nestorius and for the instruction of those who with pious zeal seek the meaning of the saving creed. To these letters it has attached appropriately, for the confirmation of the true doctrines, the letter written by the president of the great and senior Rome, the most blessed and holy Archbishop Leo, to Archbishop Flavian, [now] among the saints, for the confutation of the perversity of Eutyches, since it agrees with the confession of the great Peter and is a universal pillar against those with false beliefs (*ACO* II.1, 325; Price and Gaddis 2005: II, 203).

It is important to note the distinction made between Cyril's letters, as providing an authoritative interpretation of the Creed, and Leo's Tome, as "confuting the perversity of Eutyches." We may therefore say that Chalcedon accorded to Cyril the same respect that he had enjoyed at Ephesus. Tragically, of course, many of his followers, in the aftermath of the council and in the centuries that followed, felt that the Chalcedonian Definition, with its insistence on "two natures" in Christ after the union, had betrayed his teaching. But that was certainly not the intention of the council itself.

What do we find when we proceed to the Fifth Council – Constantinople II (553)? The main issue at the council was whether to issue a formal condemnation of what were known as the "Three Chapters" – the person and works of Theodore of Mopsuestia and certain writings by Theodoret and Ibas of Edessa. Early in the proceedings the chairman (the patriarch of Constantinople) set out the procedure which the council was to follow: it was to test the Three Chapters against the chief documents of the orthodox faith (*ACO* IV.1, 36–37). He first cited the decrees of the preceding four councils, and then continued:

> In addition we follow in everything the holy Fathers and teachers of the Church, Athanasius, Hilary, Basil, Gregory the Theologian and Gregory of Nyssa, Ambrose, Augustine, Theophilus, John of Constantinople, Cyril, Leo and Proclus, and we accept

everything they expounded on the orthodox faith and in condemnation of heretics. We also accept the other holy and orthodox Fathers who preached the orthodox faith in the holy Church of God irreproachably till the end (Price 2009a: I, 224).

It is significant that the names listed are confined to the golden age of the Church Fathers, from the mid-fourth to the mid-fifth centuries. These were the Fathers who were the classic expounders of Nicene orthodoxy. Cyril's name receives no particular emphasis, but yet again it is clear from the proceedings of the council that his name had special authority. The writings by Theodoret and Ibas condemned in 553 were attacks on Cyril, and were condemned for this reason. Theodore's standing was tested at the council by the reading (and inclusion in the Acts) of two documentary collections. The first was a florilegium of heretical extracts from his writings; the second was an anthology of "what the holy Fathers said about him and what is contained in imperial laws and historical writings" (*ACO* IV.1, 73). This was less a florilegium of extracts than a presentation of carefully selected documents (some in their entirety) to prove specific points. Here, pride of place was taken yet again by the letters and controversial writings of Cyril of Alexandria, for in the late 430s Cyril had conducted a campaign against Theodore's memory (Price 2009a: I, 271–279). It was a great embarrassment that, under pressure from the emperor Theodosius II, Cyril had written to John of Antioch, closing this campaign and conceding that it was improper "to revile the dead, even if they are laymen, and all the more if they departed from this life in the episcopacy" (*ACO* IV.1, 106). It was argued in 553 that the numerous other letters in which Cyril had worked for the condemnation of Theodore proved that this aberrant letter was a forgery. The dependence on historical texts could raise historical problems, which had to be solved – by scholarship of a sort. But it was perfectly true that Cyril had abandoned his campaign against Theodore only under compulsion. But what is significant for us is that here again Cyril featured as the great authority in matters of Christology, while the role played by other Fathers was a secondary one.

Seventh-Century Florilegia

For the use at major councils of florilegia of extracts from a wide range of Fathers we have to move on to the seventh century, to the Acts of Constantinople III (680–681) and its precursor, the Lateran Synod of 649, both concerned to condemn the heresy of one operation and will in Christ (monoenergism and monotheletism) and to define his two operations and wills (dyoenergism and dyotheletism) as the only doctrine compatible with the previous councils and the "approved Fathers" (to cite a favorite phrase). The fifth, final, and longest session of the Lateran Synod was dominated by the reading of a series of specially composed florilegia. The total number of excerpts they included was 165; deducting the 42 taken from heretics, we find 123 excerpts from the Fathers. Of these, eight are from supposedly pre-Nicene writers, but in fact all these passages are pseudepigraphal and post-Nicene (including two from Dionysius the Areopagite); meanwhile, only three are from sixth-century writers, and none from the seventh century. This means that the vast majority (112 in number) were taken from the great Fathers from the mid-fourth to the mid-fifth centuries, with Cyril of Alexandria again having pride of place. This heavy emphasis on the golden age of the Fathers from Athanasius to Cyril is typical of late antique patristic florilegia.

The eastern churches ignored the Lateran Synod, and disunion between the Latin West and the Greek East resulted, leading at times to a formal breach of communion. But in the late 670s Emperor Constantine IV decided that the Church had to be reunited and summoned a new ecumenical council, the Third Council of Constantinople (680–681), as a way of forcing the eastern bishops to accept the Roman teaching on wills and operations in Christ. At this council, after an appeal to the previous councils had been found inconclusive, the debate concentrated on the presentation and criticism of rival florilegia. A substantial florilegium was presented by Patriarch Macarius of Antioch, as the leader of the monotheletes, which was countered by a dyothelete florilegium produced by the Roman delegates. The monothelete one is not included in the Acts as such, but excerpts cited from it (in an attempt at refutation) and a comparable and contemporary florilegium preserved in Syriac (London, British Library, Add. 14535) give us a reasonable idea of its contents. It is clear that both sides appealed not only to the same Fathers but often to the same passages. For the Fathers who had spoken of "operation" or "will" in Christ had not been concerned to count them, and the same passage was often open to both a monothelete and a dyothelete reading.

How then could the debate advance? The dyotheletes attempted to trump their opponents in two ways. First, they read out seven passages from Macarius' florilegium in turn, each one together with an adjoining passage (in the same work) that Macarius had "suppressed," to prove that Macarius' appeal to the Fathers had depended on taking passages out of context. Macarius explained his omissions by making the admission (as the Acts word it) that "The passages that I excerpted I excerpted for my own purposes" (*ACO*[2] II.1, 238). A statement that citations have to be selective is made to sound like a confession of guilt, and at the close of the examination the council Fathers denounced Macarius for having compounded his theological errors by deliberately misrepresenting and distorting the teaching of the Fathers.

Let us take one example – a citation by Macarius from the pseudo-Athanasian *De incarnatione et contra Arianos* (*ACO*[2] II.1, 268–270). Against Arian claims that subordinationist language used of Christ in the New Testament implies his inferiority to the Father, the writer interprets each case as relating not to Christ's Godhead but to his manhood, and to his manhood in an extended sense (PG 26. 1020A–1024A). So he interprets 1 Cor 15:28 on the Son being "subjected" to the Father as relating not to Christ himself but to the time "when all of us are subjected to the Son and found to be his members." Likewise, he interprets Acts 2:36, on God making Jesus at his resurrection "both Lord and Christ" as referring not to the person of Christ but to "his manhood, that is, the whole Church." He concludes his analysis with the "two wills, one human, which is of the flesh, and the other divine" of which Christ spoke at Gethsemane ("Let not my will but yours be done," Lk 22:42), and says that this is to be understood "in the same way" as the contrast between the "thoughts of God" and "those of men" that was exhibited by St Peter when he reacted to disbelief to Christ's prediction of his passion (Mt 16:22–23). Our Acts give the passage that immediately follows and which

Macarius had "suppressed": "For coming in the likeness of men, he deprecated the passion as man, but being God and being impassible in his divine essence, he eagerly accepted the passion and death." This makes plain that the "deprecation of the passion" was indeed Christ's; it may appear that in shifting the reference from Christ himself to us men, with our fear of God, as Macarius appears to have done, he was guilty of a grave distortion. But interpreting the human will that recoiled from the passion as *our* will, which Christ adopted in solidarity, had a long patristic tradition behind it. One cannot say that the council of 680–681 succeeded in its attempt to demonstrate that the monotheletes had distorted the teaching of the Fathers.

The other way in which the council of 680–681 tried to discredit the monothelete florilegia was by claiming that its own dyothelete florilegium was uniquely authentic. Marcel Richard (1951) has pointed out that one consequence of the reliance on florilegia was that florilegia begot yet new florilegia, the original texts were neglected, and false attributions abounded. To obviate this danger (at least in appearance), the dyothelete florilegium presented by the Roman legates was read out twice, first at the seventh session and then again at the tenth, when each passage was checked by the patriarchal notaries and librarians against a complete text of the work in question. In every case the Acts of the session record a comparison of the excerpt cited with a "papyrus volume" or "parchment volume" in the patriarchal library of Constantinople, and in every case the two were found to correspond. Was this really the case? At one point a passage was read out that was a commentary on Mt 26:40, allegedly from John Chrysostom's *Homilies on Matthew*. It was duly "compared to a papyrus volume equally in the library of this sacred patriarchate, and found to correspond" (*ACO²* II.1, 298); but in fact the passage is not to be found in this work or indeed in any extant work by a Greek Father. And credulity is strained when the reading proceeds to excerpts from monophysites and monotheletes, whose collected works are unlikely to have reposed in the patriarchal library. But of course, in the context of this session the passage cited and the authentic text simply *had* to correspond; the whole procedure was a ritual rather than a piece of scholarship. Everyone at the session will have been aware of this; one cannot talk of deception when no one was deceived.

Florilegia at the Seventh Council

The seventh and last of the great councils recognized in both East and West was the Second Council of Nicaea (787), directed against iconoclasm. Here again the primary mode of argument was the appeal to the tradition of the Fathers, and here again this tradition was presented in the form of extracts collected in florilegia.

At the fourth and fifth sessions of the council we witness not the mere reading of florilegia prepared beforehand but (if we are to believe the Acts) the actual process of the composition of one. Patriarch Tarasius of Constantinople, as the chairman, invited the presentation of passages from the Fathers. The response, from bishops and clerics who must have been primed in advance, was immediate and plentiful. The patriarchal secretaries started the ball rolling, but the bishops soon joined in the game, not only citing passages that could have been taken from preexistent florilegia (though none are mentioned), but also producing (to all appearances) volumes of complete works from which they were able to cite new and appropriate evidence. This transformation of a conciliar session into a seminar of research students who had done thorough homework strains credulity, and a more careful examination of the record reveals something different. If the bishops had come to the council with volumes from their own libraries, we would expect them to boast of the fact. But of the many codices they, or monks, produced for reading at these sessions only three are said to have come from libraries other than the patriarchal library of Constantinople, and only one of these from a library outside Constantinople. The natural inference is that all the other volumes came from the patriarchal library and had been supplied by the patriarchal staff. Why then were these volumes produced by bishops or monks and not by the patriarchal staff itself? What was the purpose of this curious arrangement? It must have been intended to disguise the fact that the whole proceedings were being run by a small clique around the patriarch of Constantinople, and to present the iconophile case as reflecting the learning of the Byzantine church as a whole. In addition, it represented an attempt to overcome a problem that arose from the dependance on patristic florilegia — the reduction of the role of the bishops to that of silent auditors, and the reduction of the Acts to a series of pre-prepared documents. The lively fiction of these sessions, in which a florilegium is composed before our eyes, gave the bishops a creative role and restored significance to the actual conciliar sessions.

Another point of significance is a change in the criterion of what made a citation authoritative. By the end of the fourth century the "Nicene Fathers" had extended beyond those present at the council of 325 to all Christian writers who upheld the Nicene faith; at the council of 553 we found a standard list of prime patristic authorities, dating from the mid-fourth to the mid-fifth century; at the seventh-century councils the same list still held, but was supplemented with passages from later bishops and theologians, even emperors, which had authority less because of who was writing than because of their fidelity to the tradition. Now in the eighth century the net had to be extended still further. The Fathers of the golden age had referred to images, if at all, only incidentally; the strongly worded passages were all by critics of images, such as Eusebius of Caesarea and Epiphanius of Salamis. In consequence, the council of 787 had to draw on popular sources that earlier councils would not have regarded as authoritative – such as lives of saints and collections of miracle stories, generally by authors either insignificant or anonymous. This was not a surrender to popular piety, but a decision to promote it. From now on the "orthodox tradition" was as firmly rooted in the devotional practices of the whole Christian people as in an intellectual continuity that was constantly in danger from foreign invasion, oppression, and impoverishment.

Councils and the Patristic Tradition

We have seen how at the ecumenical councils the appeal to the Church Fathers came to take the form of the presentation of lengthy florilegia of suitable extracts from their writings. What does this tell us of the respect paid to them?

The most important point to be made is that the appeal to the Fathers was not in *support* of rational argumentation – a demonstration of the truth through analysis and deduction – but in *place* of it. The Acts of the First Council of Ephesus do not analyze and refute the teaching of Nestorius, but simply demonstrate that it was contrary to the consensus of the Fathers, by juxtaposing selected texts or assertions of Nestorius to those of orthodox teachers. The same is true of the later councils. Even the Acts of the Lateran Synod of 649, which include lengthy theological lucubration, do so not in order to prove that the Fathers were right (which was taken for granted), but in order to strengthen the claim that the teaching of the council was in accord with the Fathers.

But if inerrancy was attributed to the patristic tradition as a whole, this could not apply to every statement to be found in a Church Father. The sheer number of citations in the florilegia used at councils is itself indicative: it betrays an awareness that the Fathers were not always infallible, or always expressing the common faith of the Church. A distinction had to be acknowledged between the official teaching of the Church, most clearly expressed in creeds and councils, and the personal opinions (we would say the *theologoumena*) of particular Fathers, or the utterances of Fathers on particular occasions to meet specific needs (Bolotov 2006: 337–349). This point was made by Patriarch Sergius of Constantinople when he wrote to Pope Honorius in 634 to explain why he did not approve of a formal assertion of either monoenergism or dyoenergism:

> We judged it necessary instead to follow in everything the well-tried statements, synodically defined, of the holy Fathers, and not those made occasionally by some Fathers, whose aim in this matter was not to expound their teaching on the matter clearly and unquestionably, so as to erect it into a dogmatic canon and rule (*ACO²* II.2, 544).

Honorius replied in similar vein:

> Even if perchance some people, speaking indistinctly, have taught certain things, condescending to form the ideas and conceptions of those who are still immature, it is not proper to make into doctrines of the Church things which each individual, teeming in his own thoughts, proposes as a personal opinion (*ACO²* II.2, 554).

It was useful to make this point, when one's opponents produced a patristic citation or two that told in their favor; but if overstated, it ran the danger of undermining the appeal to patristic authority. For the appeal to the Fathers implied a belief in a consistent and consonant tradition – that the Fathers down the centuries were in agreement with each other. This appeal went together with a presumption that novelty was always a sign of error. In all, the patristic appeal imposed a view of the tradition that excluded a recognition of change, even of development, and where individual Fathers were appealed to not for anything distinctive or original in their works but for their witness to the common tradition.

This mode of reading the Fathers was soon standard throughout Christendom, and continues in the Orthodox Church today. In contrast, western study of the Fathers since at least the nineteenth century tends to concentrate on the distinctive and original contribution of each. In consequence, a coherent history of patristic theology has come to depend on the notion of development – that ideas that originated in one writer could later become part of the Church's common heritage. From this standpoint, the Orthodox insistence on a uniform and virtually changeless tradition looks uncritical and unscholarly. But a concentration on the new and original ideas in each Father – with a consequent neglect of their less original writings and a marginalization of those Fathers who were not original thinkers (such as John Chrysostom and John of Damascus) – is equally selective and tendentious.

Most seriously of all, our stress on originality distances us from the mentality of the very writers we are trying to understand. Notions of "development" of doctrine are particularly disastrous when applied to the work of the great councils, which would have been horrified at any suggestion that they were making "advances" in theology, when in fact their only aim was to defend the faith of earlier generations against what they saw as heretical innovation (or the revival of heresies already condemned). Theologians writing in their studies were not subject to the same restrictions, but even when they were consciously tackling problems that had received inadequate attention from their predecessors their aim was to uphold, clarify, and articulate the "correct" and "orthodox" faith, defined in terms that were conservative and traditionalist. The study of the Fathers must not lose sight of the context in which they operated.

This is not the way in which we study the Fathers today, or indeed any body of writing. It derived from the tradition of appealing to proof texts in Scripture. Appeal was not made to the teaching of St Paul, or any of the biblical writers, as different and distinct, since as inspired writers they were not writing as individuals, each with his own theological insights, but as mouthpieces of the Holy Spirit. Instead, appeal was made to selected passages of Scripture, and often individual verses, as divine oracles; all of these, when speaking of the same subject, possessed necessarily the same meaning, for Truth is one. The Fathers, of course, were not thought of as inspired writers in the same literal sense; but their authority depended on their status not as theologians, each with his own mind and his own ideas, but as witnesses to the common faith. A collection, therefore, of extracts from a number of Fathers, discoursing on the same topic, was agreed to be trustworthy evidence of the traditional teaching of the Church. The extracts confirmed each other. It was not necessary to interpret them individually, or to examine the contexts from which they were taken. Modern criticism of florilegia, as imposing an artificial uniformity on the patristic tradition, misses the point.

Finally, essential for our understanding of this procedure is the way in which "approved Fathers" were cited at councils in opposition to "condemned heretics." Just as florilegia of orthodox passages were produced, so were florilegia of excerpts from the heretics. The acts of the sessions of June 22 and July 22 at Ephesus contain not only a florilegium of excerpts from orthodox Fathers but also a florilegium of heretical excerpts from the sermons of Nestorius. Likewise, the orthodox florilegium presented by the Roman legates at Constantinople III concludes with an additional 19 passages from acknowledged heretics, and the orthodox florilegia read out at the Lateran Synod of 649 were followed by two heretical florilegia, made up of 42 excerpts. The two cases are, of course different: the passages from Nestorius were intended to justify his condemnation, while the passages in the seventh-century florilegia are taken from acknowledged heretics of the past, with the purpose of proving that the contemporary monotheletes were their disciples. But in both cases the appeal to the Fathers was made in the context of a dualist conception of theological debate – orthodoxy versus heresy, truth against falsehood. Such dualism went back to the genesis of Christian theology – to the anti-Gnostic teachers of the second century, such as Irenaeus, who presented his own teaching as going back to Saints Peter and Paul and that of his opponents as deriving from Simon Magus, "the father of all heretics" (*Adversus haereses* III, pref. and ch. 3).

In the course of the Trinitarian and Christological controversies of the late antique period, it became possible to present orthodoxy as opposed not to a single heresy or family of heresies but to pairs of heresies, both of which had departed from the road of the truth, though in opposite directions. So Trinitarian orthodoxy was contrasted both to Sabellianism (which confounded the Persons) and to Arianism (which denied the common nature); and Christological orthodoxy was contrasted both to Nestorianism (which divided Christ into two persons) and Monophysitism (which fused his Godhead and manhood into a single nature). A clear expression of this idea occurs in Boethius:

> There comes into being in him a double nature and a double substance, because he is God-man and one person, since the same is man and God. This is the middle path between two heresies, just as the virtues also hold a middle place. For every virtue is situated in an honourable position midway between extremes (*Contra Eutychen et Nestorium* VII, 72–78).

"Orthodoxy" (in accordance with the Greek word ὀρθός, from which it derives) was both the *straight* path and the *correct* one. The work of the Fathers had been to describe this road, which itself, as changeless truth, was preexistent and God given. The work of the councils was to take these descriptions, which of necessity were in harmony with each other, and on their basis to produce a map of the one road ("the way" that was Christ, Jn 14:6). The basic plan had been set out in the Nicene Creed, and later councils added in further details, "not as though they were inserting something omitted by their predecessors" but to clarify their teaching in the face of later heresies (to echo the words with which the Chalcedonian Definition defined the work of the First Council of Constantinople, *ACO* II.1, 325). In this way a particular conception of the work of the councils produced a particular understanding of what the Fathers had achieved and of how they were to be read.

Bibliography

Primary Sources

ACO (*Acta Conciliorum Oecumenicorum*) I, *Concilium Universale Ephesinum*, Eduard Schwartz (ed.) (1922–1929), five vols. Berlin: Walter de Gruyter.

ACO II, *Concilium Universale Chalcedonense*, E. Schwartz (ed.) (1932–1938), six vols. Berlin: Walter de Gruyter.

ACO IV.1, *Concilium Universale Constantinopolitanum sub Iustiniano habitum*, Johannes Straub (ed.) (1971). Berlin: Walter de Gruyter.

ACO² (*ACO* Series II) I, *Concilium Lateranense a. 649 celebratum*, Rudolf Riedinger (ed.) (1984). Berlin: Walter de Gruyter.

ACO² II, *Concilium Universale Constantinopolitanum Tertium*, Rudolf Riedinger (ed.) (1990–1992), two parts. Berlin: Walter de Gruyter.

ACO² III, *Concilium Universale Nicaenum Secundum*, Erich Lamberz (ed.) (2008–), three parts. Berlin: Walter de Gruyter.

Ambrose, *De fide*, Otto Faller (ed.) (1962), CSEL 78. Vienna: Hoelder–Pichler–Tempsky.

Athanasius, *De synodis*. In *Werke* II.1, *Die Apologien*, Hans-Georg Opitz (ed.) (1940–1941). Berlin: Walter de Gruyter; 231–278.

Basil of Caesarea, *De Spiritu sancto*, Benoît Pruche (ed.) (1968), Sources Chrétiennes 17 bis. Paris: Éditions du Cerf.

Boethius, *Contra Eutychen et Nestorium*. In Boethius (1973), *The Theological Tractates and the Consolation of Philosophy*, H.F. Stewart, E.K. Rand, and S.J. Tester (transl.). Cambridge, MA: Harvard University Press.

Gregory of Nyssa, *Contra Eunomium*. In *Opera* II, Werner Jaeger (ed.) (1960). Leiden: Brill.

Irenaeus, *Adversus haereses (Contre les hérésies)* III, Adelin Rousseau (ed.) (1974), Sources Chrétiennes, 210–211. Paris: Éditions du Cerf.

Ps.-Athanasius, *De incarnatione et contra Arianos*, PG 26: 984–1028.

Secondary Sources

Alberigo, Giuseppe (ed.) (2006), *Conciliorum Oecumenicorum Generaliumque Decreta*, vol. 1, *The Oecumenical Councils from Nicaea I to Nicaea II (315–787)*. Turnhout: Brepols.

Alexakis, Alexander (1996), *Codex Parisinus Graecus 1115 and its Archetype*. Washington, DC: Dumbarton Oaks.

Bolotov, V.V. (2006), "K voprosu o Filioque". In *K voprosu o filosofii Erigeny*, A.I. Brilliantov (ed.). St Petersburg: Olega Abyshko; 335–381.

Galtier, Pierre (1951), "Saint Cyrille d'Alexandrie et Saint Léon le Grand à Chalcédoine". In *Das Konzil von Chalkedon: Geschichte und Gegenwart, I*, Aloys Grillmeier and Heinrich Bacht (eds). Würzburg: Echter; 345–387.

Graumann, Thomas (2002), *Die Kirche der Väter*. Tübingen: Mohr Siebeck.

Graumann, Thomas (2009), "The conduct of theology and the "Fathers" of the Church". In *A Companion to Late Antiquity*, Philip Rousseau (ed.). Oxford: Wiley–Blackwell.

Graumann, Thomas (2010), "Protokollierung, Aktenerstellung, und Dokumentation am Beispiel des Konzils von Ephesus (431)". *AHC*, 42: 7–34.

Graumann, Thomas (2011), "Orthodoxy, authority and the (re-) construction of the past in church councils". In *Invention, Rewriting, Usurpation: Discursive Fights over Religious Traditions in Antiquity*, Jörg Ulrich, Anders-Christian Jacobsen, and David Brakke (eds). Frankfurt am Main: Peter Lang; 219–237.

Price, Richard (2009a), *The Acts of the Council of Constantinople of 553*, two vols. Liverpool: Liverpool University Press.

Price, Richard (2009b), "Presidency and procedure at the early ecumenical councils". *AHC*, 41: 241–274.

Price, Richard, and Cubitt, Catherine (2014), *The Acts of the Lateran Synod of 649*. Liverpool: Liverpool University Press.

Price, Richard, and Gaddis, Michael (2005) *The Acts of the Council of Chalcedon*, three vols. Liverpool: Liverpool University Press.

Price, Richard, and Jankowiak, Marek (forth-
coming), *The Acts of the Third Council of
Constantinople (680–1)*, two vols. Liverpool:
Liverpool University Press.

Richard, Marcel (1951), "Les florilèges
diphysites du Ve et du VIe siècle." In *Das
Konzil von Chalkedon: Geschichte und
Gegenwart*, I, Aloys Grillmeier and

Heinrich Bacht (eds). Würzburg: Echter;
721–748.

Riedinger, Rudolf (1998), *Kleine Schriften zu
den Konzilakten des 7. Jahrhunderts.* Turnhout:
Brepols.

Uthemann, Karl-Heinz (2001), "Zur Rezeption
des Tomus Leonis in und nach Chalkedon".
StPat, 34: 572–604.

CHAPTER 28

The Fathers and Scholasticism

James R. Ginther

Introduction

It would be difficult to conceive of any text or idea from medieval theology that would
not include some imprint of a Father of the early church. It is now an expectation that
nearly every doctrinal assertion and each theological argument born in the Middle
Ages can be traced back to a patristic epigram or whole text. Over 40 years ago, the late
Jaroslav Pelikan, playing on a famous dictum of Alfred North Whitehead, suggested
that the whole of medieval theology could be considered as a "series of footnotes to
Augustine" (Pelikan 1971: 330). This does not make medieval theology derivative and
unoriginal, but rather emphasizes its heavy dependence upon patristic texts.

The overwhelming presence of patristics in medieval theology might make modern
readers conclude that this was a natural and even inevitable occurrence. It is tempting
to think of the medieval reading of patristic sources as a passive consuming as they
were readily available for such use. But it is in fact difficult to draw this conclusion once
the historical details are examined. Between the fading Carolingian renaissance of the
eighth and ninth centuries and the tumultuous eleventh century, access to patristic
texts was limited. The *Confessions* of Augustine, for example, disappeared almost
entirely from the Anglo-Saxon world for some 200 years. It was not until the end of the
eleventh century that new English copies of this seminal text were produced and began
to be distributed widely (Webber 1996). This was hardly an isolated instance. The list
of extant witnesses to Cassiodorius' *Expositio Psalmorum* show that almost one-third
of them were produced in the twelfth century alone (Halporn 1981). The same can be
said of his *De anima*, another text that would gain popularity in scholastic thought
(Halporn 1959).

The Wiley Blackwell Companion to Patristics, First Edition. Edited by Ken Parry.
© 2015 John Wiley & Sons Ltd. Published 2019 by John Wiley & Sons Ltd.

The Fathers and Medieval Canon Law

Indeed, it is necessary to point out that the theologians of the schools were not invoking a heretofore unknown set of resources; rather, they were regaining texts that early medieval theologians had cultivated centuries earlier. The catalyst for this second bite at the patristic apple was not theological education in the first instance, but instead a much broader concern: the shape of Christian society. The reform movements of the eleventh century, long known as the "Gregorian" reform, certainly entailed careful reflection upon the papacy and its role in ecclesial leadership, but its scope also included the analyses on concomitant political authorities, moral practices, social structures, legal theories, and even from time to time reflection on the rapid economic growth that had begun to reshape European society in the second millennium (Cushing 2005). All these topics were framed within the concept of Christian society to such a degree that one could use the concept of "Christendom" to describe Europe with greater confidence by the end of the eleventh century (Nirenberg 2009).

The desire to further establish a Christian society was fostered by a return to the roots of Christianity. The emerged in two related ways. There was first a growing interest in the behaviors and practices of the early church which fell under the rubric of *ecclesia primitiva*. Papal reformers and legal scholars were particularly interested in connecting the changes emerging in the eleventh–twelfth centuries to the normative practices of early Christianity. Much of this was idealized and often ahistorical, but the *ecclesia primitiva* was an important heuristic and rhetorical device of the reformers (Olsen 1969; 1985). The second was a broader social movement. Confronted with an ecclesial leadership that had gained since 1050 both substantial influence over social practices and concentrated wealth, many Christians in the late eleventh and early twelfth centuries began to question whether the Church had lost its way. Bishops seemed more concerned with maintaining political power and protecting property than the care of souls. The solution was to consider the life of the apostles as the true model of Christian practice. This meant that authentic Christianity was defined as simple poverty that freed the individual to proclaim the gospel and focus on devotion to God and love of neighbor (McDonnell 1955; Bolton 1983; Tavard 1987). The *vita apostolic* challenged ecclesial authorities to reconsider their priorities, a challenge that sometimes led to social unrest and eventually to a response that often included charges of disobedience and heresy.

Both concepts were related textually, as the writings of the early Church Fathers supplied the details and arguments. It was the work of canon lawyers who began to take a fresh look at the patristic sources and use them in an innovative manner. The significant attribute of canon law from the eleventh century onwards was that collections were now organized systematically and not chronologically or by textual types (conciliar canons, papal letters, etc.). These collections, beginning most markedly with Burchard of Worms (d. 1025), had an argument to make about the nature of ecclesial authority and Christian behavior (Austin 2004). This is not to say that earlier collections lacked a framework or any ideological agenda. The ninth-century Pseudo-Isidorian decretals, for example, compiled (and regularly forged) canons that emphasized the importance of papal authority, but its organization sometimes diminished the import of this issue (Berman 1983: 93). Canon law collections prior to 1000 were generally compiled to act as resources to guide bishops in their adjudication of Christians under their care. Beginning in the eleventh century, the new collections had a more overt goal: to make arguments about – and so provide the legal evidence for – how a prelate ought to execute his office and sit in judgment of his diocese. The primary result was a more universal conception of how the Church should regulate itself.

This new goal resulted in an increased use of the Fathers. The more complex that canon law collections became the more they drew upon patristic sources. The *Decretum* of Burchard drew 14% of its content (247 of 1783 textual units) from patristic writings. At the end of the eleventh century, Yves of Chartres' *Collectio tripartita* increased the amount of patristic sources to 20% (755 of 3760 units). Three decades or so later, Gratian's massive *Decretum* drew one-third of its sources from the Fathers – around 1200 of its 4000 units (Werckmeister 1997: 61–66).

Gratian's *Decretum* is a watershed moment in canon law (Landau 2008). The first 20 distinctions of his collection present a complex theory of law that would generate substantial discussion for the next four centuries (Thompson 1993). Moreover, his systematic treatment and arrangement of legal topics became the norm for canon law up to the twentieth century, and so for the rest of the Middle Ages there are no new canon law collections. Later popes updated the collection with additional books, but Gratian's work remained at the core of the study and practice of canon law. With so much theoretical material to consider, and all the relevant sources in one textual locus, canonists soon lost interest in integrating patristic sources in their commentaries (Werckmeister 1997: 76–77). Scholars have also treated Gratian as a watershed in another way, namely the beginning of the separation of law and theology. However, this is inaccurate. While canon law and theology both began to develop their own methodologies and subject matter, there remained a large amount on intersecting between the two disciplines. This was particularly true of sacramental and pastoral theology, where theologians had to reflect on the practical implications of the theological arguments (de Ghellinck 1948: 465–472).

Reading the Fathers

The practical reason why scholastic theologians consulted Gratian was that his ordering of legal topics acted as an index to the writings of the Fathers. This was not the only means of gaining access to this massive corpus, however. While scholastic theologians gave privilege to four Latin Fathers – Augustine, Ambrose, Gregory the Great, and Jerome – these were not the only patristic sources available to them. In reading the Fathers for theological purposes, there were two major issues: gaining access to the content of those writings as quickly and efficiently as possible, and developing a methodology for dealing with inconsistencies within that tradition.

Gaining Access

The breadth of scholarship that the Fathers provided could itself be an obstacle to their use in theological argument, and this was especially true of the theology of the schools. In past centuries, when most of theological scholarship was fostered in the monastery,

THE FATHERS AND SCHOLASTICISM   417

a scholar had the luxury of extensive time to read widely (and above all slowly) the patristic texts in the monastery's library. A commentary on Scripture could be the fruit of years and even decades of careful reading, so that the relevant patristic texts almost dissolved into the monk's own writing (Leclercq 1984). The emergence of education centers in the late eleventh century outside the monastery gate had no such luxury of time. Students remained in the classroom for only a few years and so there was a greater urgency to expose them to as many theological resources as possible in a shorter period of time. Masters were also required to become proficient in the liberal arts as well as theology. From 1200 onwards, that demand included integrating some newly translated texts, texts that were difficult to understand. And, since these schools were situated in urban centers and had the express purpose of teaching future priests and prelates, the theologians of the schools increasingly were consulted on many nonacademic matters (Southern 1995). The serenity of the cloistered desk where a scholar could read and meditate in silence was not always available to the scholastic theologian. The pressure of time, however, did not mean that theologians wanted to cut corners. Instead, it drove them to consider more efficient means of using their textual resources.

The solution was found in three textual technologies, although the first was hardly a scholastic invention. One way to move through the patristic corpus was using a *florilegium*. This was like an anthology, although it was more often composed of excerpts rather than complete texts (Rigg 1996; Dionisotti 1997). Patristic florilegia litter the manuscripts written from the twelfth century to the end of the Middle Ages. Sometimes they comprise extensive excerpts, while others are a collection of a few lines from various works. Their purpose was always the same: to bring together patristic sources about a specific topic or a constellation of topics. The modern reader might object to florilegia on the grounds that the text can easily be distorted if an excerpt is taken out of context and its meaning attached to a set of texts that are organized around an external subject matter. That could certainly be the case, although it must be remembered that the florilegium was a search technology and not necessarily a hermeneutical tool. Florilegia also presupposed familiarity with the entire text in question, but this did not prevent lazier readers from relying too much on excerpts in order to understand and use a Church Father in their arguments. Ultimately, florilegia became indispensable for preachers who wished to draw upon patristic sources for either an argument or an example to illustrate a theological point. The most effective compiler for patristic florilegia was Thomas of Ireland (d. c. 1338). His *Manipulus florum* is an exhaustive collection of some 6000 sayings of the Fathers and classical and medieval authors. It is organized under 266 alphabetically ordered topics related to preaching and theological discourse. Its popularity continued well into the modern period (Rouse and Rouse 1979; Nighman 2005).

The second way of gaining access is rarely described as a textual technology, but rather as a literary form: the *Ordinary Gloss* (*Glossa ordinaria*). This text was basically a commentary on the whole Bible, in which patristic citations were attached to a biblical lemma. The technological aspect concerns the on-page presentation. While it took a few decades in the twelfth century to perfect, the basic approach was to present the biblical text in the center of the page and in a larger font (and with explanatory notes written interlineally), with the patristic sources written around it (de Hamel 1984; Smith 2009: 91–139).

This format remained stable in all subsequent manuscript copies of the Gloss, and early modern printers mimicked this *mise-en-page* when they printed it. The idea of glossing a text was in use well before the eleventh century, which is why so many scholars prior to 1920 identified the ninth-century scholar Walafrid Strabo as the originator (Gibson 1992: 5–6). The current scholarly consensus is that the Ordinary Gloss emerged initially from the School of Laon and eventually underwent major revisions and additions until it reached some textual stability in the middle of the twelfth century. Under the care of Hugh St-Cher, OP (d. 1264), a group of thirteenth-century Dominicans attempted to update the Gloss, but their revisions never gained much attention outside of Paris. A more successful, but limited in scope, revision was the *Golden Chain* (*Catena aurea*) of Thomas Aquinas. In 1263, while Thomas was teaching at the Dominican *studium* in Orvieto, Italy, Pope Urban IV requested him to create a gloss on the Gospels. Thomas completed the project in 5 years. Not only did he draw from the Gloss, he also incorporated additional patristic sources, including some that were translated from the Greek for this very project. The *Catena* enjoyed wide success in the Middle Ages and beyond, including its first English translation by John Henry Newman (Torrell 1996: 1.136–151). The only major competitor to the Gloss was the *Postillae* of Nicholas of Lyra (c. 1270–1349), who provided literal commentary on the entirety of Scripture. Lyra's project differed significantly from the Gloss, but his works were often integrated with the Gloss in early modern printings (Nicholas of Lyra 1588).

The sources included in the Gloss span the gamut of Latin patristic texts. It cites from the works of Augustine, Jerome, Origen (courtesy of the translation by Rufinus), Gregory the Great (and his compiler, Paterius), Cassiodorus, and Ambrose. The Gloss did much to enhance the authoritative status of the Venerable Bede (d. 735), the Carolingian theologians Paschasius Radbertus (d. 865), Hrabanus Maurus (d. 856), and Haimo (d. 878) and Remigius (d. 908) – both of the city of Auxerre. There were also a number of biblical books where the majority of comments originate with one of two twelfth-century theologians, Anselm of Laon and Gilbert Universalis of Auxerre (Matter 1997; Andrée 2011).

There could be no more effective indexing system for gaining access to the Fathers. All students and masters in theology, from the dawn of the cathedral schools in the eleventh century to the university that emerged in the thirteenth century, knew the sacred page from beginning to end. All their activity, from hearing lectures, to disputing, to even writing commentaries on the *Sentences* of Peter Lombard, was directed to reading and expounding the Bible (Ginther 2005). The Gloss thus served two purposes. First, it provided a universal resource for reading the biblical text. Some scholars have suggested that the Gloss was created as a means to provide some stability to the allegorical interpretation of Scripture (Evans 1984: 37–47). While that view has not attained much consensus, it is significant to note that most of the glosses themselves betray a greater interest in the spiritual senses of Scripture. The second purpose was that as a theologian reflected on a specific topic and consulted the relevant texts of the Bible he would gain immediate access to a patristic authority – provided the gloss had originated with such a source.

The only drawback of the Gloss as an index was that it was one-dimensional. The biblical text may act as the topical index to the Fathers, but in modern search parlance it only returned one result (sometimes two or three). The Gloss provided no means to interconnect two Fathers on a single topic. One person did seek to develop a system that would act as a larger index to patristic sources. In the mid-thirteenth century, Robert Grosseteste (c. 1170–1253) developed a complex indexing system with some unique attributes. Grosseteste was a polymath, who began in natural philosophy and then moved to theological studies late in life at Oxford (Ginther 2004; Southern 1986). Grosseteste read widely and had a propensity to annotate books. That propensity perhaps led him to devise a schema that would allow him to cross-reference all the sources he had digested. This turned into the *Tabula*, a topical index that survives in one manuscript.

Topical indices and systematic concordances, the third textual technology that provided access to the Fathers, had been in use for centuries by the time Grosseteste compiled his. Indeed, it is worth nothing that Grosseteste's *Tabula* was somewhat of a throwback, as most scholastics had begun to use the relatively new idea of an alphabetic concordance (Rouse and Rouse 1982). Grosseteste organized the entire index system under nine *distinctiones*, or headings, with each of these having many subheadings. And for each of these subheadings Grosseteste listed the relevant biblical passages followed by the appropriate patristic sources. In the margins, Grosseteste would on occasion note a non-Christian source (and oddly where he places all his citations of Boethius!). Then, Grosseteste devised an image, a phraseogram, that would somehow represent the topic. These were drawn next to the heading. The real purpose of these 440 phraseograms was their placement in the margins of Grossetsete's own books. The reader – for example, of Gregory's *Moralia in Iob* – would be able to go to the index and discover biblical texts and patristic sources that spoke to the same topic that had been annotated in the margin (Rosemann 1995). Clearly, Grosseteste put a substantial amount of thought into this system, but it would appear it collapsed under the weight of its own complexity. No other copy of the index has survived; and to date, only books that we know Grosseteste used or owned have the phraseograms in the margins. There is another index that originates in Paris in the latter half of the thirteenth century, but its notation system is different and the index is less complete than Grosseteste's.

A more successful indexing system was developed by the Dominican Robert Kilwardby (c. 1215–1279). Kilwardby wanted to ensure that as his students worked their way through the *Sentences* of Peter Lombard (now a textbook in teaching theology) they would be able to understand the patristic heritage that underlay this textbook. Kilwardby was particularly interested in providing easy access to the Augustinian corpus, but he also paid attention to the other Latin Fathers that inhabited Lombard's text. His *Index of the Original Works of the Fathers* (*Tabula super originalia patrum*) provided three tools. First, he composed a summary (*intentio*) of each section of a patristic work. Then, he provided a full alphabetical, systematic index of the main topics of the work. Finally, he composed an alphabetical concordance of selected words (Callus 1948). Kilwardby then used this same approach for a schematic summary of the *Sentences*, which was very popular in the early fourteenth century (Rosemann 2007: 85–90).

All these excerpted texts and indices might lead the modern student to conclude that scholastic theologians were not holistic readers. This is hardly the case. The scholastic period enjoyed a major increase in the number of manuscript copies of the works. This began with monastic communities, which were particularly adept at copying and sharing sources. One well-researched network is the Anglo-Norman monasteries. Brought together after the Norman Conquest in 1066, these English and French Benedictine houses began to share their libraries so that additional copies could be made of their holdings. Lanfranc of Bec (d. 1089) and Anselm of Canterbury (d. 1109) both ensured these monastic houses became well stocked, a strategy that also allowed them to fill the libraries they used with texts they had wanted. A reconstructed list of the library contents at Bec, for example, in the early twelfth century shows 71 patristic works (including Bede), and the list includes Greek Fathers who had been translated into Latin: Didymus, Eusebius of Caesarea, Gregory Nazianzen, Gregory Nyssa, John Chrysostom, Origen, and Theodore of Mopsuestia (Caspar 2004: 206–209). As the universities began to establish themselves in medieval Europe, book producers began to pop up in places like Oxford and Paris, where they did a brisk trade in creating cheap copies of the Bible, the *Sentences*, and pastristic texts for students and masters alike. Even Franciscans, whose own Rule forbade the ownership of books save for Books for Mass and Office, amassed copies of the Fathers for their convent libraries (Humphreys 1990).

There were times in which the excerpted text came into conflict with the full text. Perhaps the most celebrated is the trial of Gilbert of Poitiers (d. 1154) that took place after the Council of Rheims in 1148. Gilbert was a well-respected theologian who was well trained in both the liberal arts and theology. He studied at Poitiers, Chartres, and Laon. At Laon, he spent a number of years under the personal tutelage of Anselm of Laon. One of his major texts was a commentary on the Psalms, a text that would play a significant role in the development of the Gloss and that has often been called the Middle Gloss (*glossa mediatura*). Gilbert returned to Chartres to take up a teaching post and then transferred to Paris. All this impressive education formed Gilbert into a brilliant theologian who also had outstanding capabilities in logic and rhetoric. He found himself attracted to Boethius, and soon Gilbert produced a commentary on his "sacred works" (*opuscula sacra*) (Haring 1966a).

The commentary raised a number of eyebrows, including those of Bernard of Clairveaux (d. 1153). More than two decades earlier, Bernard had pursued Peter Abelard for his theology of the Trinity and had him condemned for it. Now it seemed that another had taken Abelard's place and was once again teaching a similar Trinitarian heresy. In 1147, Bernard convinced Pope Eugenius III to hold a trial in Paris where Gilbert would be held accountable. Bernard's retinue, however, failed to prepare adequately and could not present any documentation about the supposed teachings of Gilbert. Pope Eugenius dismissed the case, but Bernard won a reprieve when the pope agreed to hear the case again the following year at Rheims. After the Council of Rheims concluded, Pope Eugenius hastily convened a second trial to hear the case. Bernard and his supporters were better prepared, but inadequate documentation remained a problem. They did indeed come this time with a summary of Gilbert's teaching. And, they also came with a florilegium of patristic sources that demonstrated how Gilbert was out of step with the Catholic tradition. Their list of citations took up a single sheet of paper.

Gilbert brought his entire library. He had no florilegium, but rather entire books (*libros integros*) of the Fathers. And then he went on to quote extensively from those books to demonstrate his orthodoxy. With the trial dragging on due to all these long quotations – and the tide appeared to be turning in Gilbert's favor – his accusers asked for an adjournment. They promptly emptied the cathedral library of all its patristic volumes and pored over them that night. They returned the next day armed with their own set of complete books to counter Gilbert, Church Father by Church Father. The damage, however, had been done (Haring 1966b). The implications about Gilbert as heretic aside, this event points to the importance of whole texts in the theological discourse in the schools.

Harmonizing the Fathers

Regardless of whether a scholastic theologian read a text in part or in whole, he would eventually run into a major difficulty: sometimes the Fathers were in conflict with one another. In modern scholarship, such a concern seems almost trite and irrelevant. The lack of uniformity amongst the many historical sources of the Christian faith does not automatically bring into question the veracity of that faith. For a medieval scholastic theologian, however, inconsistencies – and even outright contradiction – potentially undermined, in the best case, their methodology, and in the worst case the very nature of the theological enterprise. The Fathers of the Church were the saints and doctors (*sanctiet doctores*) of the Christian faith. Some theologians even went so far as to claim that the Fathers wrote under the Holy Spirit's inspiration (Piazzoni 1982: 917). Even if a theologian did not furnish the Fathers with such high authority, the persistent question remained: when there was a contradiction, which Father was to be believed?

Peter Abelard is probably best known to modern scholars for documenting this problem in a work entitled *Sic et Non* (Boyer and MacKeon 1977). This work, revised at least twice during his period of theological study, was an arrangement of excerpts from the Fathers organized by theological topics of Abelard's choosing. Abelard simply cited a Father for an opposing position on that topic. The work never gained much notoriety, probably because its purpose was never properly discerned. It would appear that Abelard was attempting to create a "casebook" text, drawing from a common way to teach law in his century. A casebook would provide a set of resources that were contradictory, and this would allow the student the opportunity to exercise his legal theory and practice his adjudication skills. There is good evidence that Abelard in fact drew from canon law collections for the enumeration of his topics and the patristic sources cited (Marenbon 1997: 61–62). Abelard himself seems to have used his collection in his own later writings (Marenbon 2001: xxiii–xxiv), but it attracted no later commentary or annotation. In some respects, *Sic et Non* suffered from the same problem as his other major theological texts: it laid out a large and tantalizing project, but its execution was incomplete and, thus, unsatisfactory (Colish 1994: 47–51).

Abelard at best resolved any contradictions on a case-by-case basis. He was not alone in pursuing an ad hoc solution to the disharmony of patristic authority. In general, scholastic theologians adopted three ways to resolve any conflict between the Fathers. The first (and these are not presented in any particular order) was to point to errors in translation. A conflict in reading scripture amongst the Fathers could be explained by the fact that there were different renderings of the sacred page circulating in the early Church. The phrase *alia translation* (another translation) in a text was a marker that the scholastic theologian had encountered an unfamiliar or uncommon biblical reading in a patristic text. These could also be used to argue that the linguistic variation was at the cause of a contradiction in the Fathers. This did not mean that this was an actual historical assertion, but rather an easy way to resolve the conflict (Principe 1976: 112–114).

Second, a patristic contradiction could be resolved by pointing to specific historical circumstances. This could function in two different ways. First, the claim could be made that the opposing Fathers simply misunderstood one another. Robert Grossetsete resolved a conflict between Jerome and Augustine concerning the role of the Law in the first generation of Christians. This was not an invented conflict: Augustine and Jerome had addressed the problem directly in their letters. In his *De cessation legalium* (*On the Cessation of the Law*), Grosseteste faced the conflict head on and carefully described the position of each. He noted that this kind of discord should not worry the reader. Sometimes good music included dissonance that added to its beauty. Moreover, such conflict demands careful reflection on the matter, and that can only benefit a Christian's understanding of the Faith. Despite those sentiments, for Grosseteste this was simply a case of Jerome misunderstanding Augustine's position. Furthermore, even though Augustine pressed his case to the detriment of Jerome's, Grosseteste concludes that, in the end, Augustine would find agreement with Jerome since Jerome was responding to an inaccurate understanding of Augustine's position (Dales and King 1986: 164–186). The other means of employing a historical method was to point out that circumstances had changed. This was used primarily when it appeared that a patristic position contradicted contemporary ideas and practices, or when a Church Father appeared to be saying something heterodox (Principe 1976: 114–115). In these cases, scholastic theologians adopted a "development of doctrine" model, noting that at times terminology had to become more precise in response to heretical movements, or that ecclesial practice had changed to some degree (Colish 1994: 46–47).

The final method for bringing harmony to the patristic universe could be called the "one or none" solution. In some circumstances, scholastic theologians had no compunction in striking out on their own choosing to ignore any difference of theological opinion in the tradition. More commonly, however, a scholastic theologian would latch onto a specific Church Father and advance the argument using that Father as an interpretive lens for all other patristic sources. This generally describes the *Four Books of the Sentences* of Peter Lombard. The success of Lombard's textbook is due to two important features. First, as Abelard had tried to with his *Sic et Non*, Lombard produced an effective collection of casebook studies; that is, a set of textual touchstones that a master could use to guide his students through the theological labyrinth of the western, catholic tradition (Silano 2007: xxvi–xxx). The difference between the two Peters is that Lombard was comprehensive in his treatment and so attained the status of an actual textbook. The second feature is that Lombard does not simply list the sources relevant to the topic at hand, but rather makes an argument with these sources. For the most part, his is an Augustinian vision, and so not surprisingly Augustine is the most cited of all the Fathers. For example, in book 1, distinction 2,

Lombard raises the basic Trinitarian question of how to understand unity and plurality when speaking of the Godhead. Augustine drives the argument here, and the subsequent citations of Ambrose and Hilary of Poitiers are used not as counterpoints, but as a means to clarify and advance Peter's reading of Augustine's *De trinitate* (Silano 2007: 11–18).

The Fathers and Paradigm Shifts

As noted in the Introduction, the Middle Ages was an Augustinian world, where the former bishop of Hippo's religious epistemology and theological teachings held a strong sway over a thousand years of theological work. Even as new sources, such as Aristotle, challenged the "Augustinian synthesis," none ever succeeded in replacing Augustine's worldview. All scholastic theologians were to some degree Augustinians, although some were more devoted to maintaining his theology than others (Marrone 2001; Saak 2002). So dominant was this one corpus of works that it can be easy to overlook two other Church Fathers, who in the end had a subtle but profound influence on scholastic theology.

The first was John of Damascus. Although he lived after the "patristic" period, to the Western medieval world he was as much a Church Father as the Venerable Bede. Thanks to an Italian jurist, Burgundio of Pisa, John's works were translated into Latin around 1148. These writings, known collectively as *De fide orthodoxa*, were initially given the title of *Sententiae*, and that first title speaks to its influence. Marcia Colish contends that the twelfth century witnessed the invention of systematic theology. It began in Laon, stretched out to Chartres and Paris and then finally to other urban centers in England and the Continent. Moreover, it was Peter Lombard who fully grasped what a systematic approach to theologizing could provide for scholars, priests, and prelates (Colish 1994: 33–90). John's influence here has often been muted, in light of the theological heritage of the twelfth century that Peter so carefully engaged. Peter was certainly reacting to his predecessors, but his *Book of Sentences* is a result of a careful reading of John of Damascus – even he does not admit to its presence until book 3. The way he structured his work, the questions he raised, and the solutions he provided bear the indelible mark of the Damascene (De Ghellinck 1948: 335–346, 368–415).

The second Greek Father had an even more profound influence, an influence that modern scholarship is still trying to assess adequately: Pseudo-Dionysius the Areopagite. Until the sixteenth century, theologians identified this author as the disciple of Paul mentioned in Acts 17. None of them ever came close to realizing that he came from sixth-century Syria and he was more likely a disciple of Proclus. His initial entry into the medieval west in the ninth century resulted in only limited interest. It was not until the twelfth century that the Dionysian corpus began to make its mark. The ninth-century translation was literal and very wooden, and so of little help to its Latin audience; eventually, two later translations began to circulate. Even then, the corpus itself was difficult to understand, but eventually it gained more and more readers. In the first half of the thirteenth century, several scholars at the University of Paris produced an official text of the corpus, replete with summaries and other study aids. Two decades later, Robert Grosseteste produced a superior translation of the entire corpus (Dondaine 1953; McEvoy 2003).

The impact of Pseudo-Dionysius was multivalent. He bolstered discussions of the scope and limits of theological language and gave validation to using mundane and carnal language in talk of the divine. His central thesis was that God is ultimately unknowable by the human mind, unless that knowledge is mediated. All creation was formed to empower that mediation, formed into hierarchies, which spoke to the relational character of all creation. Pseudo-Dionysius not only found a powerful connection with the existing neo-Platonic concepts that pulsed through all of medieval theology, it also encouraged connections between reason and experience. The Dionysian corpus allowed scholastic theologians to forge strong links between their speculative work and the affective activity of mystics. Nearly every major theologian from the thirteenth to the fifteenth century fell under the spell of the Areopagite (Rorem 1993; Coakley and Stang 2009). Of all the aspects of the influence of the Church Fathers in medieval theology, this one area is still in the beginning stages of its scholarship. There is much textual and editorial work that must be completed before modern scholar can fully appreciate the impact of this one corpus. The initial findings do indicate that the term "paradigm shift" is well in order.

Conclusion

On April 26, 1326, a young Francesco Petrarch climbed Mt Ventoux in Provence, France. He recounted in a later letter that he was deeply affected by the natural beauty he could survey from its apex. The most profound moment, however, occurred when he took out his pocket-sized copy of Augustine's *Confessions*. The book fell open, Petrarch recounts, to a passage that reminded him that humanity takes time to wonder about nature but rarely time to think about itself. Many scholars consider what he did in response to that moment of reading a Church Father the beginnings of the Italian Renaissance (Hainsworth 2010: 220–224). It signifies at least the two essential features of the Renaissance: the importance of classical texts and the centrality of human experience in knowledge. Furthermore, the Church Fathers enjoyed continued attention, especially as Renaissance ideals spread to northern Europe in the fifteenth and sixteenth centuries, since they were considered part of the classical world Renaissance thinkers wished to recover. Moreover, the patristic corpus grew in size as more Greek Fathers were rendered into Latin and new textual research began to separate spurious texts from authentic ones, as in the case of Erasmus distinguishing between Ambrose and "Ambrosiaster" (Souter 1927: 44–49). Jerome was soon viewed as the ideal Christian scholar for his linguistic skill and dexterity.

Beyond that, however, the Renaissance introduced no significant change in the role of the Church Fathers in theological scholarship. Theologians continued to read the Fathers as carefully as their medieval predecessors. They discovered their texts in the same ways and struggled with the same challenge of finding harmony amongst patristic discord. The post-medieval world had accepted the medieval assumption that all good theological discourse was founded upon the Fathers of the Church.

Bibliography

Primary Sources

Gilbert of Poitiers (1966), *The Commentaries on Boethius*, N. Haring (ed.). Toronto: Pontifical Institute of Mediaeval Studies.

Gratian (1993), *The Treatise on Laws (Decretum DD. 1–20)*, A. Thompson (transl.). Washington, DC: Catholic University of America Press.

Hugh of St-Victor (1982), *Sententiae de divinitate*. A.M. Piazzoni (ed.), "Ugo di San Vittore auctor delle Sententiae de divinitate". *Studi Medievali*, 23: 912–955.

Nicholas of Lyra (1588), *Biblia sacra cum glossis, interlineari et ordinaria, Nicolai Lyrae Postilla*. Venice: n.p.

Peter Abelard (2001), *Collationes*, J. Marenbon (ed./transl.). Oxford: Clarendon Press.

Peter Abelard (1977), *Sic et Non*, B.B. Boyer and R. MacKeon (eds). Chicago, IL: University of Chicago Press.

Peter Lombard (2007), *The Sentences, Book I: The Mystery of the Trinity*, G. Silano (transl.). Toronto: Pontifical Institute of Mediaeval Studies.

Petrarch, Francesco (2010), *The Essential Petrarch*, P. Hainsworth (ed./transl.). Indianapolis, IN: Hackett Publishing.

Robert Grosseteste (1986), *De cessation legalium*, R.C. Dales and E.B. King (eds). Auctores Britannici Medii Aevi, 7. London: British Academy.

Secondary Sources

Andrée, Alexander (2011), "Anselm of Laon unveiled: the *Glosae svper Iohannem* and the origins of the *Glossa ordinaria* on the Bible". *Mediaeval Studies*, 73: 217–260.

Austin, Greta (2004), "Jurisprudence in the service of pastoral care: the *Decretum* of Burchard of Worms". *Speculum*, 79: 929–959.

Berman, Harold J. (1983), *Law and Revolution: The Formation of the Western Legal Tradition*. Cambridge, MA: Harvard University Press.

Bolton, Brenda (1983), *The Medieval Reformation*. New York: Holmes Meier.

Callus, Daniel A. (1948), "The 'Tabula super originalia patrum' of Robert Kilwardby, OP". In *Studia mediaevalia in honorem Reverendi Patris Raymundi Joseph Martin*. Bruges: De Tempel; 243–270.

Caspar, Giles E.M. (2004), *Anselm of Canterbury and his Theological Inheritance*. Aldershot: Ashgate Press.

Coakley, Sarah and Stang, Charles M. (eds) (2009), *Re-thinking Dionysius the Areopagite*. Chichester: Wiley–Blackwell.

Colish, Marcia (1994), *Peter Lombard*, two vols. Leiden: Brill.

Cushing, Kathleen (2005), *Reform and the Papacy in the Eleventh Century: Spirituality and Social Change*. Manchester: Manchester University Press.

Dionisotti, A.C. (1997), "On fragments in classical scholarship". In *Collecting Fragments/ Fragmentesammeln, Aporemata: Kritische Studienzur Philologiegeschichte*, G.W. Most (ed.). Göttingen: Vandenhoeck & Ruprecht; 1–33.

Dondaine, H.F. (1953), *Le corpus dionysien de l'Université de Paris au XIII siècle*. Rome: Edizioni di Storia e letteratura.

De Ghellinck, Joseph (1948), *Le movement théologique du XIIe siècle*. Bruges: De Tempel.

Evans, G.R. (1984), *The Language and Logic of the Bible: The Earlier Middle Ages*. Cambridge: Cambridge University Press.

Gibson, Margaret (1992), "The place of the *Glossa ordinaria* in medieval exegesis". In *Ad Literam: Authoritative Texts and Their Medieval Readers*, M.D. Jordan and K. Emery, Jr (eds). Notre Dame, IN: University of Notre Dame Press; 5–27.

De Hamel, Christopher (1984), *Glossed Books of the Bible and the Origins of the Paris Book Trade*. Dover, NH: D.S. Brewer.

Ginther, James R. (2004), *Master of the Sacred Page: A Study of the Theology of Robert Grosseteste*. Aldershot: Ashgate Press.

Ginther, James R. (2005), "There is a text in this classroom: the Bible and theology in the medieval university". In *Essays in Medieval Philosophy and Theology in Memory of Walter H. Principe, CSB: Fortresses and Launching Pads*, J.R. Ginther and C.N. Still (eds). Aldershot: Ashgate Press; 31–51.

Halporn, James W. (1959), "The manuscripts of Cassiodorius' *De anima*". *Traditio*, 15: 385–387.

Halporn, James W. (1981), "The mansucripts of Cassiodorius' *Expositio Psalmorum*". *Traditio*, 37: 388–398.

Haring, Nicolaus (1966b), "Notes on the Council and the Consistory of Rheims (1148)". *Mediaeval Studies*, 38: 38–59.

Humphreys, K.W. (1990, *The Friars' Libraries*. Corpus of British Medieval Library Catalogues, 1. London: British Library.

Landau, Peter (2008), "Gratian and the *Decretium Gratiani*". In *The History of Medieval Canon Law in the Classical Period, 1140–1234: From Gratian to the Decretals of Pope Gregory IX*, W. Hartmann and K. Pennington (eds). Washington, DC: Catholic University of America Press; 22–54.

Leclercq, Jean (1984), "*Otium monasticum* as a context for artistic creativity". In *Monasticism and the Arts*, T. Gregor and J. Dally (eds). Syracuse, NY: Syracuse University Press.

Matter, E. Ann (1997), "The Church Fathers and the *Glossa Ordinaria*". In *The Reception of the Church Fathers in the West, from the Carolingians to the Maurists*, I. Backus (ed.), two vols. Leiden: Brill; 1.83–1.111.

Marenbon, John (1997), *The Philosophy of Peter Abelard*. Cambridge: Cambridge University Press.

Marrone, Steven (2001), *The Light of Thy Countenance: Science and Knowledge of God in the Thirteenth Century*. Leiden: Brill.

McDonnell, Ernest W. (1955), "The *vita apostolica*: diversity or dissent". *Church History*, 24: 15–31.

McEvoy, James J. (2003), *Mystical Theology: the Glosses by Thomas Gallus and the Commentary of Robert Grosseteste on De mystica theologia*. Paris: Peeters.

Nighman, Chris L. (2005), "Commonplaces on preaching among commonplaces for preaching? The topic *Predicatio* in Thomas of Ireland's *Manipulus florum*". *Medieval Sermon Studies*, 49: 37–57.

Nirenberg, David (2009), "Christendom and Islam". In *The Cambridge History of Christianity, 4: Christianity in Western Europe c. 1100–1500*, M. Rubin and W. Simons (eds). Cambridge: Cambridge University Press; 149–169.

Olsen, Glenn (1969), "The idea of the *ecclesia primitiva* in the writings of the twelfth-century canonists". *Traditio*, 25: 61–86.

Olsen, Glenn (1985), "Reference to the *ecclesia primitiva* in the *Decretum* of Burchard of Worms". In *Proceedings of the Sixth International Congress of Medieval Canon Law*, K. Pennington (ed.). Monumenta Iuris Canonici, Series C: Subsidia 7. Vatican City: Biblioteca apostolica vaticana; 289–307.

Pelikan, Jaroslav (1971), *The Christian Tradition, 1: The Emergence of the Catholic Tradition (100–600)*. Chicago, IL: University of Chicago Press.

Principe, Walter H. (1976), "Thomas Aquinas' principles for interpretation of patristic texts". *Studies in Medieval Culture*, 8–9: 111–121.

Rigg (1996), "Anthologies and Florilegia", in *Medieval Latin: An Introduction and Bibliographical Guide*. Ed. F.A.C Mantello and A.G. Rigg, 708–712. Washington DC: Catholic University of America Press.

Rorem, Paul (1993), *Pseudo-Dionysius: A Commentary on the Texts and an Introduction to their Influence*. Oxford: Oxford University Press.

Rosemann, Philip (1995), "Robert Grosseteste's *Tabula*". In *Robert Grosseteste: New Perspectives on His Thought and Scholarship*, J. McEvoy (ed.). Instrumenta Patristica, 26. Steenbrugge: Kluwer; 321–335.

Rosemann, Philip (2007), *The Story of a Great Medieval Book: Peter Lombard's Sentences. Rethinking the Middle Ages, 2*. Toronto: Broadview Press.

Rouse, Richard and Rouse, Mary (1979), *Preachers, Florilegia and Sermons: Studies on the Manipulus Florum of Thomas of Ireland*. Studies and Texts, 47. Toronto: Pontifical Institute of Mediaeval Studies.

Rouse, Richard and Rouse, Mary (1982), "*Statim invenire*: schools, preachers and new attitudes to the page". In *Renaissance and Renewal in the Twelfth Century*, R.L Benson and G. Constable (eds). Cambridge MA: Harvard University Press; 201–225.

Saak, Eric L. (2002), *High Way to Heaven: The Augustinian Platform Between Reform and Reformation, 1292–1524*. Leiden: Brill.

Smith, Lesley (2009), *The Glossa Ordinaria: the Making of a Medieval Biblical Commentary*. Leiden: Brill.

Southern (1986), *Robert Grosseteste: the Growth of an English Mind in Medieval Europe*. Oxford: Clarendon Press.

Southern, Richard W. (1995), *Scholastic Humanism and the Unification of Europe*, two vols. Oxford: Blackwell.

Souter, Andrew (1927), *The Earliest Commentaries on the Epistles of St Paul: A Study*. Oxford: Clarendon Press.

Tavard, George H. (1987), "Apostolic life and church reform". In *Christian Spirituality: High Middle Ages and Reformation*, J. Raitt, B. McGinn, and J. Meyendorff (eds). London: Routledge; 1–11.

Torrell, Jean-Pierre (1996), *Saint Thomas Aquinas*, R. Royal (transl.), two vols. Washington, DC: Catholic University of America Press.

Webber, Teresa (1996), "The diffusion of Augustine's *Confessions* in England during the eleventh and twelfth centuries". In *The Cloister and the World. Essays in Medieval History in Honour of Barbara Harvey*, J. Blair and B. Golding (eds). Oxford: Clarendon Press; 29–45.

Werckmeister, Jean (1997), "The reception of the Church Fathers in canon law". In *The Reception of the Church Fathers in the West, from the Carolingians to the Maurists*, I. Backus (ed.), two vols. Leiden: Brill; 1.51–1.81.

CHAPTER 29

The Fathers and the Reformation

Irena Backus

Introduction

The growing emphasis on returning to ancient pagan sources in the Renaissance entailed a return to early Christian sources as a corollary. These were found of vital importance in resolving problems of the cultural identity of Christianity and of differences of doctrine in the climate of religious unrest fostered first by the Great Schism and the Conciliarist movement, and somewhat later by the series of events that followed Luther's break with Rome. Moreover, humanists who worked mainly outside the university context favored the method known as imitative readings of early authors which enabled them to absorb the given author's doctrine, ethical values, and his rhetoric. This approach necessitated the availability of a complete text. The emphasis here was not so much on early Church doctrine and its authority irrespective of context as on a particular author's teaching and eloquence as conveyed by the sum total of his writings. North of the Alps, the patristic Renaissance took place somewhat later. Prior to Erasmus and his accomplishments, it was mediated, at least partly, through the religious renewal movement known as the *Devotio moderna*. This movement, started in 1384, set up communities of pious laymen and women (Brothers and Sisters of the Common Life) and also foundations for the Augustinian Canons of the Windesheim Congregation. It was active mainly in the Netherlands. The lives of its members were to mirror the life of Christ and the apostles in contrast with that of the decadent monastic orders. Among their chief concerns was education and patristic piety. Through their activity of copying translating and excerpting from patristic manuscripts, they propagated the writings not just of Augustine, but also of Gregory the Great, Cassian, John Chrysostom, Origen, Hilary of Poitiers, Eusebius of Emesa, Cyprian, Pseudo-Dionysius, and so on. They studied the fathers first and foremost as models of piety (Staubach in Backus 1997: vol. 1, 405–440)

The Wiley Blackwell Companion to Patristics, First Edition. Edited by Ken Parry.
© 2015 John Wiley & Sons Ltd. Published 2019 by John Wiley & Sons Ltd.

In universities, Christian texts continued to be seen as means of providing true propositions about faith, which could be extracted from their context and gathered into collections of sentences. However, the two methods often combined, which meant, among other things, that collections of patristic sayings in the fourteenth and fifteenth centuries were more accurate and better founded textually (Saak in Backus 1997: vol. 1, 367–384) as new manuscripts of complete works were discovered. The best example here are the florilegia such as the *Milleloquium Sancti Augustini* (1345) by Bartholomew of Urbino (produced outside university circles but much used within them), which consisted of about 15 000 passages drawn not from other florilegia but from Augustine's original works. This interest was not limited to Augustine; other Fathers, such Pseudo-Dionysius, Ambrose, and more recent authorities, such as Anselm, were subjected to a similar treatment, albeit less intensively. Whereas non-university humanist circles of the period favor the diffusion of complete texts of the Fathers, universities tend to remain attached to the sentential approach. For the first time, however, theologians become aware that each individual *sententia* is a quotation from a longer text. The university circles were also slow to recognize the importance of the Greek Fathers, Pseudo-Dionysius (whose authenticity was not challenged in universities until much later) constituting the most notable exception. At the same time, a new interest for Augustine's theology was manifesting itself among the Augustinian friars such as Gregory of Rimini, who espoused the doctrine of predestination as being due exclusively to God's grace without any preceding merit. Some modern historians have argued that this tendency among the Augustinian friars, an order to which Martin Luther belonged until 1524 (Saak in Backus 1997: vol. 1, 367–384), was in fact a foreshadowing of the Reformation. Other historians have argued that this is a reductive view and that the Reformation should also be seen as an inheritor of the Renaissance south of the Alps (Weis in Hillerbrand 1996: vol. 2, 264). Be that as it may, the religious and intellectual tradition in the western world was undergoing profound changes in the fourteenth and fifteenth centuries. This very complex situation brought about nearly three centuries of unprecedented development both in the number of patristic works made available and in the diversity of treatments and uses they were put to.

The Greek Fathers

Lorenzo Valla (1407–1457) is generally considered as the pioneer in the application of humanist methods to theology. Rejecting scholastic philosophy, he explicitly advocated a return to the Greek and Latin fathers, such as Basil, Gregory of Nazianzus, Ambrose, and Jerome, as they alone preserved the true method by not confusing theology and philosophy. Valla also challenged the authenticity of the Dionysian corpus, a view that did not find extensive support in the fifteenth and sixteenth centuries. While Valla favored a philological approach to theology, other, earlier humanists favored a rhetorical approach. This was based on their optimistic view of man as created in God's image, which, after being obscured by the original sin, was renewed through redemption. The best example of this approach was Pier Paolo Vergerio (c. 1370–1444), who contributed to establishing Jerome as the ideal of classical learning and moral virtue dedicated to Christian scholarship and eloquence. He was also the first to identify the apostles and early martyrs with public leaders of pagan antiquity who promoted political peace, and to consider early Christianity as a model of civic virtue (McManamon 1985). The most lively center of patristic learning in the late fourteenth and early fifteenth centuries was Florence, where Coluccio Salutati promoted both Greek (it was he who brought over the famous Greek teacher, Manuel Chrysoloras) and Latin studies. Salutati's own collection comprised manuscripts of most of the Latin Fathers, including notably Lactantius, Jerome, Augustine, and Ambrose, together with such Greek Fathers as he knew (Chrysostom in particular) who represented, in his view, the height of literary, moral, civic, and theological achievement. That they did was very largely due to the fact that they had themselves received a classical education. It was Salutati who asked Leonardo Bruni to translate Basil's *Ad iuuenes* in 1403 as part of his defense of a humanist education program. The work to this day is extant in over 300 manuscripts and over 100 editions, c. 1470–c. 1560 (Gianni in Cortesi and Leonardi 2000: 45–47). However, the first humanist to devote himself actively to patristic studies, treating them as his chief concern and not just as a by-product of the pagan classics, was Ambroggio Traversari (1386–1439), a Camaldolese monk (Stinger 1977). As well as transcribing and making emendations to manuscripts of several Latin Fathers, such as Tertullian (fallen into oblivion until then), Lactantius, Ambrose, and Jerome, whom he particularly respected, he was the first Western scholar since Burgundio of Pisa (c. 1110–1193) to translate several Greek patristic texts into Latin. Traversari's earliest translations of Basil, Chrysostom, and Climachus' *Scala paradisi* were all to do with encouragement to monastic life. By the mid-1420s he was also translating Athanasius' *Contra gentes* and *De incarnatione verbi*. Among his other translations we might mention the Sermons of Ephrem, Chrysostom's Homilies on 1 and 2 Timothy and Titus, as well as parts of Basil's *Contra Eunomium* for the Council of Florence (1439). He is best known, however, for his Latin version of Pseudo-Dionysius, which found a much wider public at the time.

The Council of Florence did much to foster and further the study of Greek Fathers. In its wake, George of Trebizond (1396–c. 1474), a Cretan émigré turned papal scribe, translated Basil's *Contra Eunomium* I–V and *De Spiritu sancto* (1442). Both versions were to be revised by him in 1467/1468. They were initially carried out at the request of Bessarion, who had attended the Council as a pro-union bishop of Nicaea. The "Western" version of *Contra Eunomium*, which had interpolated several passages on the double procession of the Holy Spirit, played a crucial role in the *Filioque* discussions with the Greek delegation (Backus 1990: 97–114). In 1440, Bessarion was made cardinal by Eugenius IV and continued to foster an interest in Greek patristics from Rome. Trebizond, who was to become a prominent member of Bessarion's circle, was also responsible for Latin translations of Cyril of Alexandria's *Thesaurus* (excerpts of which had also been used in the conciliar debates), Chrysostom's Homilies on Matthew 26–88, and Eusebius' *Praeparatio euangelica*. Of the Italian humanists sponsored by Bessarion, Cristoforo Persona (d. 1485) translated the Pauline commentaries of Theophylactus, which he attributed to Athanasius, a large number of Chrysostom's moral sermons, and Origen's *Contra Celsum*. Major patristic achievements dating from the pontificate of Sixtus IV after Bessarion's death include Johannes Argyropulos' translation of Basil's *Hexaemeron* (Backus 1990: 83–94) and Lilio Tifernate's translation of Philo's Old

Testament commentaries. All these works, with the exception of Trebizond's translation of Basil's *De Spiritu sancto*, which fell into oblivion as a result of an incidental omission, were subsequently printed and reprinted until well into the sixteenth century. A later prominent representative of Italian humanist translators of the fathers is Raffaele Maffei (1451–1522), who translated some of Chrysostom's works and many treatises of the Cappadocians, including a collection of Basil's sermons and letters later printed with the Trebizond and Argyropulos versions.

Apart from the usefulness of some Greek Fathers in the double procession debates and the exploitation of Chrysostom's homilies on Matthew 16 and John 21 in support of Peter's primacy, patristic literature throughout this period provides humanists with a useful counter-authority to scholasticism. It also provides a valuable source of the doctrine of man's preeminence over other creatures. First and foremost, however, all humanists valued the Fathers as expositors of the Biblical text, which they regarded as the sole normative expression of Christianity, regardless of their individual views on the primacy of Peter, and so on. At the same time, Fathers were increasingly cited in debates over the nature of the true Church during the conciliar period, with authors like John Wyclif and Marsiglio of Padua making extensive use of Augustine and Jerome in their attacks on the doctrine of Peter's primacy (Backus 2003: 6–38). Canonists of the period, while still relying on the *Decree of Gratian* and the *Sentences* of Peter Lombard, make increasing use of the acts of the early Councils (which they knew only indirectly) and of Eusebius' *Historia ecclesiastica* in Jerome's version.

In the first quarter of the sixteenth century the most eminent editors of patristic texts, such as Erasmus, Jacques Lefèvre d'Étaples, or Beatus Rhenanus, function outside of university circles. Erasmus is the most famous of them. During his lifetime he produced editions of Jerome (1516), Cyprian (1520), Arnobius the Younger, whom he mistook for Arnobius the Elder (1522), Hilary (1523), John Chrysostom (1525), Irenaeus (1526), Athanasius (1527), Ambrose (1527), Augustine (1529), Gregory of Nazianzus (1531), Basil (1532), and Origen (1536). Of those, his editions of Jerome, Ambrose, Augustine, Cyprian, and Hilary contain the complete works as available at the time. His edition of Augustine was intended as an improvement upon the 1505 Basel edition. Erasmus' preface does not refer to any classically Augustinian doctrines, such as the issue of grace and free will which so preoccupied most theologians of his era and before him. His only significant Greek edition is that of Basil's *De Spiritu sancto* (1532). Erasmus' interest in the fathers was partly doctrinal, partly linguistic and rhetorical, and partly devotional. He also aimed to produce the most accurate possible text (den Boeft in Backus 1997: vol. 2, 537–572). We might note that his preference goes to the western Fathers and that, like the Italian humanists of previous generations, he combines an interest in patristics with an interest in pagan antiquity.

Among other outstanding examples of this type of humanist learning we might mention Beatus Rhenanus (1485–1547), who edited several pagan authors as well as producing first editions of Tertullian (1521), the *Ecclesiastical History* of Eusebius–Rufinus, and the *Historia tripartita* (1523). Jacques Lefèvre d'Étaples (c. 1450–1536), more inclusive than Erasmus in his attitude to the writings of the early Church, is best known for first editions of the interpolated version of Ignatius' *Epistles* (1498), Hermas' *Shepherd* (1513), and Rufinus' version of the Pseudo-Clementine *Recognitions* (1504).

As the century progresses we see that an increasing number of patristic editions emanate from university circles regardless of whether they are Catholic or Protestant. Some
examples here are the Protestant Theodore Beza's (d. 1605) Greek–Latin edition of
Pseudo-Athanasius' *Dialogi de Trinitate* and Basil's *Contra Eunomium* (Geneva, 1570),
François du Jon's edition of Tertullian (1590), and the Catholic Wolfgang Lazius' edition
of the Pseudo-Abdias version of the Lives of the Apostles (1551) and Gentien Hervet's
edition of Clement of Alexandria (1551).

Latin Versions

While there was an increasing tendency in the course of the century to publish Greek
Fathers in Greek–Latin editions, the Latin version remained the norm. Many of the
translations or editions of both Greek and Latin Fathers that appeared in the sixteenth
century are a conscious effort to improve upon earlier efforts. The best example here are
the attempts of the Bern reformer Wolfgang Musculus and of the French Carthusian
Geoffroi Tilmann to improve upon George of Trebizond's, Argyropulos', and Maffei's
versions of Basil (published respectively in Basel 1540 and in Paris 1547). Musculus'
edition came out in the same year as the completely new Latin translation by the
German physician Janus Cornarius (d. 1558), which proved more popular with both
Catholics and Protestants than either Musculus' or Tilmann's revisions of the earlier
versions. The same Cornarius was responsible for the first Greek edition of Basil's
complete works (Basel, 1551) and for the first Latin translation of the *Panarion* of
Epiphanius of Salamis (Basel, 1543) (Backus 1990: 35–77).

Although increasing concern with textual accuracy, which is observed in the course of
the century, seems to stand at odds with the prevailing tendency to publish only the Latin
translations of the Greek Fathers, this is in fact far from being the case. Quite often, the
absence of a Greek text, which is more frequently encountered in Roman Catholic editions,
is due simply to lack of competent printers. Jacques de Billy (1535–1581), the French
Benedictine responsible for the first edition of the works of Gregory of Nazianzus (1569),
complained about this quite openly. Indeed, although he was able to obtain copies of several Greek manuscripts from the Vatican, not just of Gregory but also of Isidore of
Pelusium (1585) and of Johannes of Damascus' *Sacra Parallela* (as part of his *Opera
omnia*, 1577), de Billy only ever published Latin versions of these Fathers. At the same
time, however, the Vatican, which acted as provider of manuscripts, wanted biblical quotations from Fathers such as Gregory to be translated by the Vulgate. This suggests a
preference for the Latin version of Christianity in the post-Tridentine Roman Catholic
establishment (Backus 1993: 87–127). There were no such injunctions in the Protestant
camp. Protestant printers, especially those in Basel and Geneva, were often also those
who had Greek fonts. Indeed, partly due to this and partly due to the tradition established
by Erasmus and Froben, Basel became in the sixteenth century the center of Greek and
Latin patristic production. Only those editions which had an openly anti-Reformation
purpose expressed in prefaces, marginal notes, or indexes tended to appear in Rome or
Paris (Petitmengin 1966). By the mid-sixteenth century, however, all patristic editions,
whatever their confessional slant and language, were marked by a concern to achieve the

greatest possible degree of textual accuracy. This humanist heritage was common to both Catholics and Protestants and was given added momentum by the reforms subsequent to the Council of Trent. This was the most important legacy of Renaissance humanism.

The Role of Religious Orders

Particularly interesting is the role of the religious orders of the Jesuits and Benedictines in the propagation of patristic literature in the sixteenth–eighteenth centuries. The Jesuits produced some very famous patristic scholars, but they never devoted themselves to the production of patristic writings exclusively in the way that the Benedictine Congregation of St Maur was to do in slightly later years. However, the Fathers were crucial to the Jesuit theology. The spirituality of the Greek Fathers was especially congenial to them as some of it mirrored the spirituality of their founder Ignatius Loyola. For this reason ascetic writings of the Desert Fathers were of particular appeal. While with some notable exceptions – such as the editions of Fronton du Duc (1558–1624), Jacques Sirmond (1559–1651), and Jacob Gretser (1562–1625) – the Jesuit contribution to patristic learning as such was less significant, their contributions to the realm of hagiography with Jean Bolland's (1624–1665) foundation of the *Acta sanctorum* and the Society of Bollandists which gave hagiography an academic standing are especially noteworthy (Bertrand in Backus 1997: vol. 2, 889–950). They also contributed to the publication of works of Church history as witnessed by the publications of Francisco Torres (1509–1584).

The French congregation of St Maur is the last stage in the reform of the Benedictine Order in France before the French Revolution. The reforms began in the fifteenth century spurred on by humanism and reached their peak after the Council of Trent. Between 1660 and 1715 the Maurists undertook the editions of most of the Church Fathers. Some of their editions are considered as authoritative to this day, and most were taken up by Jacques-Paul Migne (1800–1875) into his *Patrologia Latina* (221 vols, 1844–1864) and *Patrologia graeca* (162 vols, 1857–1866). The Maurist program of the editions of the Fathers was part and parcel of the order's spiritual reform. The congregation was not an academy or a research center. The Fathers were valued first and foremost as Doctors who teach contempt of the world, mortification of the senses, horror of fleshly pleasures, and who provide an example of how to live in Christ. Among the works they edited, monastic rules figure prominently together with ascetic works. Their most famous edition is perhaps that of St Augustine, 1679–1700. Their other editions include the works of Ambrose (1686–1690), Hilary (1693), Jerome (1693–1706), Athanasius (1698), Chrysostom (1718), Justin Martyr (1742), and Gregory of Nazianzus (1778). Some of their editions appeared in the vernacular (Hurel in Backus 1997: vol. 2, 1009–1038).

Luther and Calvin

Martin Luther was marked more by the late medieval Augustinism than by humanism. However, once he became convinced that the biblical message emphasized faith at the expense of good works, he became interested in establishing a sharp distinction between the authority of the Bible, which he considered as absolute, and that of the Fathers, which he thought limited and relative; that is, subject to correction in the light of Scriptural evidence. He states this notably in *Von den Konziliis und Kirchen* (1539), where he lists the chief Fathers together with their contributions to Christian doctrine. This slightly cautious attitude did not stop other reformers, such as Johannes Oecolampadius of Basel, relying on Fathers such as Irenaeus to defend their doctrine of the symbolic presence in the Eucharist against Roman Catholic attacks. Indeed, Irenaeus was used in controversies even before the appearance of Erasmus' edition of his *Adversus haereses* in 1526. A bitter struggle over Irenaeus, which began early on in the century, carried on right up until the 1590s. The Fathers were also useful to reformers in their internal quarrels, such as the eucharistic dispute of 1525–1536 between Zwinglians and Lutherans, in which both sides appealed to Cyril's, Chrysostom's, and Augustine's exegesis of the Gospel of John. Recent editions, especially those of Erasmus, provided an invaluable store of textual and historical evidence, which was frequently open to conflicting theological interpretations. Both Protestants and Catholics used these editions. Whereas Luther tried to divide sharply the Fathers' authority from that of the Bible, Ulrich Zwingli and Martin Bucer adopted the "implicit normativity" approach. They tended to interpret the Bible through institutional and individual writings of the early Church, which they interpreted in turn through the Bible. This approach made for a closer coexistence of biblical and patristic authority in their works. However, they were just as aware of the Fathers' limitations as Luther and did not hesitate to criticize their doctrine or their exegetical method when they deemed it necessary; that is, when it diverged too far from their own beliefs. As regards exegesis, while sharing the humanist penchant for the Fathers as prime expositors of Scripture (more so than Catholic theologians of the period), they were nonetheless extremely critical of their tendency to resort to allegory. Origen in particular was unpopular because of this.

John Calvin, aware of both the supremacy of Scripture and of its silence on certain points, used the Fathers where he thought that Scripture could not provide all the necessary evidence. His recourse to the Cappadocians and to Cyril of Alexandria to support the Nicene doctrine of the Trinity, to Augustine to support his doctrine of predestination, and to a variety of patristic sources to support the Geneva model of Church government are examples of this.

Confessional Identities

Once the boundaries between confessions became better defined, the main purpose for Protestants and Catholics alike was to use the doctrines of the early Church to help construct a confessional identity. This wish of both parties to give themselves a past also explains the appearance of new confessionally oriented *Histories* of the early Church: the *Centuries of Magdeburg* (1554–1574) for all the Churches issued from the Reformation and the *Ecclesiastical Annals* of Caesar Baronius (1588–1603) for the Catholics. Both were based on recent patristic editions and on unpublished material; each took historical scholarship to then unprecedented heights (Backus 2003: 358–382). The main drive of both Protestant and Catholic scholars to produce patristic editions, which were free from what they deemed to be heterodox glosses and "corruptions," also dates from the Tridentine and post-Tridentine period. The editions of Irenaeus provide a good example here. The Erasmus edition of *Contra haereses* is given a Protestant identity in 1570 by Nicolas Des Gallars, who adds the Greek fragments of Epiphanius and anti-Roman glosses. A few years later (1575) François Feu-ardent, o.f.m., publishes the complete text for the first time, giving it an openly anti-Protestant orientation. As philosophy declined, ecclesiastical writers whose thought was marked by Greek philosophy tended to be misunderstood. A good example here is Clement of Alexandria, whose works, available from 1550 onwards, were valued above all as a source of Greek culture (see later). Clement was not drawn into confessional debates in the same way as the other ante-Nicene Fathers, and it was not until the late seventeenth century that his thought began to interest theologians such as François Fénélon (1651–1715), the French spiritual writer, author of works on the existence of God and similar.

The later sixteenth and seventeenth centuries also witnessed the publication of a number of guides to patristic editions and literature. On the Protestant side, theologians such as Andreas Hyperius (*Methodus*, 1567), Abraham Scultetus (*Syntagma*, 1598–1613), and André Rivet (*Criticus sacer*, c. 1612) produced digests intended to ensure that pastors gave a Protestant interpretation of the Fathers. Roman Catholic guides, such Sixtus of Siena's *Bibliotheca sancta*, Possevino's *Apparatus sacer*, or Bellarmine's *De scriptoribus ecclesiasticis* (1613), which was intended as the contemporary equivalent of Jerome's *De viris illustribus*, fulfilled a similar function in the Catholic camp (Backus 2003: 196–236).

All in all, it can be said that there are marked similarities of approach to patristic studies between Catholic and Calvinist post-Tridentine scholars. What distinguishes them is their attitude to the *consensus patrum*. For Catholics, the idea of the Fathers of the first seven centuries constituting a unified body of doctrine, which supports the teaching of the Roman Church, is fundamental. Calvinists tend to privilege particular Fathers to support particular doctrines and do not see the body of doctrine of the first seven centuries as homogeneous, although in their view it does on the whole support their own doctrines. Significantly, in the post-Tridentine period the most eminent patristic scholars are either Calvinist or Catholic. What characterizes the Lutheran Church of the period is its interest in the history of the Church as an institution in progressive decline since the apostolic period up until its revival by Luther's Reformation. This theological conviction naturally led to the unearthing and publication of Christian apocryphal material as proof of the comparative purity of the Early Church. Significantly, it is Michael Neander's editions of Luther's Greek Catechism of 1564 and 1567 which include pieces such as the *Protogospel of James* and Prochorus' Acts of John. This tradition is carried over into the large collection of *Orthodoxographa* of Johann Jakob Grynaeus, published in 1569 before the author's conversion from Lutheranism to Calvinism. All these texts were published in Basel. Interest in Christian apocryphal literature, particularly texts such as the Pseudo-Abdias version of the Lives of the Apostles, published in three different versions in 1531, 1551, and 1552 and reprinted several times, was also present among some Roman Catholic scholars. However, their publication was not so much meant to encourage an interest in history as to foster piety in the form of saint worship, and so on. Other Roman Catholic scholars, such as Bellarmine, were united with their Calvinist counterparts in firmly refuting the authenticity and value of all Christian apocryphal literature, not only Pseudo-Abdias, but also Prochorus' Acts of the Apostle John and others.

Old Heresies in New Guises

The definition of a religious identity inevitably entailed defining what one was *not*, and this meant attaching new importance to the definition of heresy. This, in turn, meant that Catholic theologians, especially after the end of the Council of Trent (1563) as confessional positions hardened, felt impelled to refute as heresies all systems of beliefs other than their own. Several of these theologians produced lists or catalogues of heresies very often identifying "heresies" of their own era with those of the early Church on the principle attributed to Saint Jerome that "to point to the origin of a heresy is to refute it." The logic behind this was simple: early heresies were systems of belief that had been refuted and condemned by the Church. If they could be assimilated to more recent doctrinal movements that sprung up before or during the Reformation period, these could be viewed as condemned from the outset. This strategy is evidenced by the French Jesuit Gabriel du Préaux or Prateolus (1511–1588) (Backus 2003: 385–390) in his extremely popular *Alphabetical Catalogue of lives, sects and doctrines of all heretics* first published in Cologne in 1569. The *Catalogue* is especially interesting as du Prèaux in his preface, addressed to Charles de Humières, bishop of Bayonne, draws a comparison between heresy and political rebellion on the one hand and heresy and philosophical systems on the other hand. He can, therefore, establish parallels between heretical sects (as he calls the Protestant Churches) and different schools of ancient Greek philosophy.

His entry on Cynics and Waldensians is a very good example of this. The Cynics were an ancient Greek school of philosophy who believed that the object of humans was to live a life of virtue in agreement with nature. This meant rejecting all conventional desires for wealth, power, health, and fame, and by living a simple life free from all possessions. As reasoning creatures, people could gain happiness by rigorous training and by living in a way that was natural for humans. They believed that the world belonged equally to everyone, and that suffering was caused by false judgments of what was valuable.

Now the Waldensians, so named after their founder Pierre de Valdes, were a Christian sect of twelfth-century origin combining various movements all condemned by medieval Church councils. They practiced itinerant preaching and voluntary poverty, believed that the vernacular Bible should be made available to all Christians, and opposed capital punishment. The Waldensians quickly became interested in the Reformation and took advice from leading reformers as early as 1530. In the period between 1555 and 1565, the French and German Waldensians in particular formed themselves into Protestant communities and the French Waldensians adopted Calvin's teaching as well as a Calvinist confession of faith and church ordinance. Du Préaux's entry on the Cynics identifies them with Waldensians and "other heresies of this sort":

> The Cynics were a philosophical school and followers of Antisthenes who was the first to
> introduce this type of philosophy. The name *Cynics* derives either from Cynosarges

(or: Kunosarges), the gymnasium where Antisthenes taught or from their canine-like severity of their discourse with which they attacked people's lifestyles or else from the unhesitating way in which they had sexual relations in the open air like dogs. Diogenes Laertius talks about this in his *Lives* of the philosophers referring to Crates and Hipparchia (Hicks 1923: vol. 2, 100–101).

Waldensians and similar heretics some centuries back were not ashamed to imitate these carnal and bestial philosophers as they asserted that anyone was allowed to couple with women shamelessly like dogs. In accordance with St Peter's prophecy (1 Peter 4, 3–4), their licentiousness was copied by many others who also spurned the governing powers and blasphemed against authority (Du Préaux 1605: 138).

Du Préaux's real purpose here was not to put together a real catalogue in any sense of the word or to give an accurate account of either the Cynics or the Waldensians. His entry is based on unreliable and hostile sources so as to constitute a classic piece of Counter-Reformation polemics.

The Case of Clement of Alexandria

However, there are some notable exceptions to the confessional, polemical, and theological use of the Fathers, as is shown by Clement of Alexandria's reception in the Renaissance and the Reformation. Having no medieval heritage, Clement, in contrast with Greek Fathers such as Basil of Caesarea, was rediscovered only very late on in the Renaissance. His doctrine was to prove difficult to integrate into theological debates and controversies of the period. The figure of the Gnostic in particular was highly ambivalent and could be interpreted to mean either the good Christian in the accepted sense of the term or one of the pure on earth, endowed with a secret knowledge of God. As for the rest of his teaching, Catholic and Protestant theologians alike tended to pick out this or that aspect of it according to their specific preoccupations. The first edition of his works came out during the Tridentine period of the Reformation when confessional positions were hardening. However, in contrast with other ante-Nicene Fathers, such as Irenaeus, Tertullian, or Cyprian – whom both Catholics and Protestants tried to reclaim as "their own" – the theological reception of Clement was diffident.

It is fully in keeping with his rather clandestine reputation that Clement was one of the very rare Greek Fathers who was published in Greek before he was published in Latin. He thus stands in sharp contrast with the Cappadocians, such as Basil of Caesarea or Gregory of Nazianzus, and in even sharper contrast with Chrysostom, who was not printed in Greek until Henry Savile's edition of 1610–1613. The first Latin edition of Clement's works came out a year after the *editio princeps*, in 1551, in Florence. The translator was Gentien Hervet, the well-known post-Tridentine Roman Catholic controversialist and translator of Aristotle and several Greek Fathers. By the time he produced the translation, Hervet had left the service of Cardinal Pole and joined that of the Cardinal Marcello Cervini, who, as is well known, was a member of the Roman curia. Cervini was favorable to learning and extremely keen to implement the Tridentine decrees, especially those to do with eliminating corruption among the higher clergy.

While Hervet was naturally a supporter of the Tridentine decrees, he was also, in common with all Roman Catholic translators and editors active in that period, concerned with purifying the Fathers for the use of the Church and with showing that their writings foreshadowed the Roman Catholic hierarchy as against the ideas of the Reformation. Clement obviously proved resistant to this treatment because Hervet's preface is redolent above all of the latter's reformism and of his humanist concern with making ancient authors available for the greater public good. Clement's use in confessional struggles or his theological significance is adverted to only briefly. In fact, as we shall see, Clement proves something of a theological embarrassment because of his concept of Gnosis and the Gnostic, his most distinct contribution to Christian thought. To Hervet, he is Cervini's spiritual ancestor: a monument to ancient learning and to clerical mores. Hervet also sees Clement as useful to the educated public and to the clergy. Hervet cannot focus on the central issue of the Gnostic as one endowed with special knowledge because this would contradict the very aim of the Counter-Reformation, which is to have as wide an appeal as possible. The best solution to the problem is to gloss over the question of the Gnostic in the translation and to present Clement as the most erudite, and therefore one of the most useful, of early Christian authors. However, Hervet obviously feels that, unlike the other ante-Nicene authors, Clement requires guarantors in the post-Nicene church before he can become respectable.

Although he finds no explicit theological guarantors, Hervet comes up with some recommendations of Clement's usefulness to lay and clerical readers. Referring in passing to the testimonies of Eusebius, Theodoret, Jerome, and others, he focuses on Cyril of Alexandria, who commends Clement as "a man who was eloquent and most learned and who investigated the depths of Greek writings with care and enthusiasm such as can be rivalled by very few of those who wrote before him" (Hervet 1551: fol. A2 r). Indeed, according to Hervet, he will provide an inexhaustible source of knowledge to those interested in Greek histories. He will also interest those who like Greek poetry, as he cites several poets whose works have perished. Those who want to know about pagan rituals and sacrifices will find him as accurate as to leave no doubt about Christianity being the only possible religion. Those who are interested in philosophy will find that he knows all the philosophical schools and they will be able to take it on his authority that Christian philosophy is truly inspired and promulgated by God, whatever the skeptics may say. In a word, Clement can be put to a variety of intellectual and cultural uses, all of them lay. Discouraged by the embarrassing notion of the Gnostic, Hervet makes only a very brief mention of Clement's theological and ecclesiastical usefulness: the Alexandrian, according to him, explains and refutes all the heresies of the Early Church which have resurfaced, including Lutheranism. He also has a great deal to say about ethical norms, so that those who try to institute a reform of the clergy will pray that the Holy Spirit who inspired Clement, a simple priest, to such heights of virtue would similarly inspire sixteenth-century Catholic bishops (Hervet 1551: fol. A2 v).

Despite the popularity of Hervet's editions, both Protestant and Catholic authors were reluctant to make use of him in their theological writings. He was cited sparingly, if at all. However, from the 1550s up until the early seventeenth century we see some interest in assessing Clement among both Roman Catholic and Protestant theologians.

This results in him either being forced into a position of an *auctoritas*, in which he is inevitably found wanting, or simply being used as a source of citations and *exempla* from antiquity, more suitable for lay than for theological use.

In Bellarmine's *Controversies of the Christian faith* (*Controuersiae Christianae fidei*) "the teacher of Origen," as he calls Clement, is not an authority like any other. The cardinal obviously finds him to be important as an ante-Nicene Father, but uses him sparingly and does not hesitate to draw the reader's attention to what he considers Clement's doctrinal aberrations. This does not stop him, however, from making an attempt to get Clement involved in characteristic Reformation controversies. The best examples of this are his chapters on the papacy, on the mediatorship of Christ, and on Christ's descent into hell. In the section *On the Roman pontiff* (*De Romano pontifice*) he takes on the Protestant challenge to Peter's primacy (Bellarmine 1610: vol. 1, 747–749). His opponents cite the fact that ancient authors do not agree on the date of Peter's arrival in Rome or on the identity of his successor. To show the falsity of this argument, Bellarmine contends that Christ's death on the cross is also an article of Christian faith, and yet many ancient authors disagree about its date. He cites several examples of this disagreement, including Clement and Lactantius among those who think wrongly that Christ died at the age of 30, an opinion not to be followed, any more than that of Irenaeus who had the Savior crucified at the age of 48 (Bellarmine 1610: vol. 1: 748). In this instance Clement is made to fit into an extraneous rhetorical framework. Bellarmine uses him to check a point of his own doctrine, not to identify with his teaching.

Elsewhere, Bellarmine singles out Clement. While arguing for the reality of Christ's descent into hell, the cardinal disputes that his descent actually made converts, and that some who were damned repented and so were saved, especially pagans. Clement's opinion, which is naturally contrary to this received Roman Catholic view, is dismissed as "improbable" (Bellarmine 1610: vol. 1, 573).

With Bellarmine's ecclesiastical use of Clement in his controversies against "protestant heretics" – be they Calvinists, Lutherans, or Antitrinitarians – we are very far away from the main issues in Clement's writings. We are equally far removed from Hervet's lay portrayal. Bellarmine has done his best to clericalize the Alexandrian father.

Some 30 years later the Calvinist self-taught theologian Philippe de Mornay, seignur du Plessis Marly, makes fairly extensive use of Clement in his *Truth of the Christian religion against Atheists, Epicureans, Pagans and Jews*. Although sometimes viewed as the first Protestant Apologist, we should remember that du Plessis was first and foremost a layman, and that he was writing in the vernacular primarily for the lay public. The author of *De la vérité* could access Clement only via Hervet's first edition with the latter's preface advocating a lay use, which is no doubt why he referred to it as extensively as he did. He seems to have been the first author to rely on Clement to show that Christianity is not just the only true religion but also the true philosophy. Moreover, he is the only sixteenth-century author to pick up on Clement's dual view of the Logos as universal reason and the Saving Mediator who stands between man and God. However, du Plessis' particularity lies in his adaptation of the Alexandrian to a lay context. On the whole, he sees Clement as a worthy precursor and a highly reliable source of information, to be placed on the same footing as Athenagoras or Justin Martyr. He therefore uses the *Stromata* and other works as a treasure trove of references and snippets of information which he transposes into a different context. Arguing, for example, that God is universal reason, du Plessis disparages all attempts made by human reason to reach God. To support his argument, he cites Xenophanes after Clement's *Stromata*. The quotation he selects is one where Xenophanes says that if animals tried to depict God they would portray him as one of them, being incapable of comprehending anything beyond themselves. Human reason, he implies, is equally constrained. On the other hand, du Plessis shows no interest in Clement's role in the early consensus of the Church, his views on marriage, or indeed his concept of the Gnostic.

Conclusion

Between the fourteenth and the eighteenth centuries patristic literature became an intrinsic part of Christian civilization. It left the narrow confines of theological debate. The fathers provided the model of Biblical interpretation, spirituality, style, eloquence, and religious polemics. They were taken seriously as witnesses to a particular textual reading, and as historians of both pagan and Christian civilizations. Gradually, their works began to be translated into the vernacular.

Bibliography

Primary Sources

Bellarmine, Robert (1610), *De controuersiis Christianae fidei aduersus huius temporis haereticos liber primus ... edition vltima Controuersiarum ab ipso authore auctaet recognita [...]*. Lyon: Pillehote.

Diogenes Laertius (1923), *Lives and Opinions of Eminent Philosophers*, R.D. Hicks (ed.), two vols. London: Heinemann.

Du Plessis Mornay, Philippe (1590), *De la vérité de la religion chrétienne contre les athées, épicuriens, païens et juifs*. Geneva: Jacob Stoer.

Du Préaux, Gabriel (1605 [1569]), *Elenchus haereticorum omnium qui ab orbe condito ad nostra usque tempora veterumque et recentium auctorum monimentis prodidi sunt vitas, sectas et dogmata complectens alphabetico ordine digestus*. Cologne: Arnold Quentel.

Hervet, Gentien (1551), *Clementis Alexandrini omnia quae quidem extant opera nunc primum e tenbris eruta latinitateque donata, Gentiano Herueto Aurelio interprete, Laurentius Torentinus ducalis typographus excudebat*. Florence: n.p.

Secondary Sources

Backus, Irena (1990), *Lectures humanistes de Basile de Césarée. Traductions latines (1439–1618)*. Paris: Etudes augustiniennes.

Backus, Irena (1993), *La patristique et les guerres de religion en France. Étude de l'activité littéraire de Jacques de Billy (1535–81) O. S. B., d'après le MS Sens 167 et les sources imprimées*. Paris: Études augustiniennes.

Backus, Irena (ed.) (1997), *Reception of the Church Fathers in the West. From the Carolingians to the Maurists*, two vols. Leiden: Brill.

Backus, Irena (2003), *Historical Method and Confessional Identity in the Era of the Reformation, 1378–1615*. Leiden: Brill.

Backus, Irena (2010), "Lay and theological reception of Clement of Alexandria in the

Reformation. From Gentien Hervet to Fénélon". In *Between Lay Piety and Academic Theology*, Ulrike Hascher-Burger, August den Hollander, and Wim Janse (eds). Leiden: Brill; 353–372.

Bury, Emmanuel and Meunier, Bernard (eds) (1993), *Les Pères de l'Église au 17ᵉ siècle*. Paris: Cerf.

Cortesi, Maria Rosa (2002), *Atti del convegno 'I Padri sotto iltorchio'. Le edizioni dell'antichità cristiana nei secoli 15–16.* Tavarnuzze: Sismel.

Cortesi, Maria Rosa and Leonardi, Claudio (eds) (2000), *Tradizioni patristiche nell'Umanesimo. Atti del convegno Istituto Nazionale di studisul Rinascimento.* Biblioteca Medicea Laurenziana, Firenze 6–8 febbraio 1997. Tavarnuzze: Sismel.

Grane, Leif, Schindler, Alfred, and Wriedt, Markus (eds) (1993), *Auctoritas patrum: zur Rezeption der Kirchenväterim 15. und 16. Jahrhundert.* Contributions on the Reception of the Church Fathers in the 15th and 16th Century. Mainz: Steiner.

Grane, Leif, Schindler, Alfred, and Wriedt, Markus (eds) (1998), *Auctoritas patrum II: neue Beiträge zur Rezeption der Kirchenväterim 15. und 16. Jahrhundert.* Contributions on the Reception of the Church Fathers in the 15th and 16th Century. Mainz: Steiner.

Hillerbrand, Hans (ed.) (1996), *The Oxford Encyclopedia of the Reformation.* Oxford: Oxford University Press.

McManamon, S.J.J. (1982), "Innovation in early modern rhetoric. The oratory of Pier Paolo Vergerio the Elder". *Rinascimento*, 22: 3–32.

McManamon, S.J.J. (1985), "Pier Paolo Vergerio the Elder and the beginnings of the humanist cult of Jerome". *The Catholic Historical Review*, 7: 353–371.

Petitmengin, P. (1966), "À propos des éditions patristiques de la Contre- Réforme". *Recherches Augustiniennes*, 4: 199–251.

Stinger, Charles L. (1977), *Humanism and the Church Fathers: Ambrogio Traversari (1386–1439) and Christian Antiquity in the Italian Renaissance.* Albany: State University of New York Press.

CHAPTER 30
The Fathers in Arabic

Alexander Treiger

Introduction

The Middle East is the birthplace of Christianity and the homeland of the majority of those we call the Church Fathers. Despite formidable challenges and tragic historical events (including those unfolding today), the Middle East has retained a significant Christian presence. Enter an Arabic-speaking Orthodox parish – whether in the Middle East or in the diaspora – and you will hear the priest's or deacon's exclamation "al-Hikma, fal-nastaqim!" – the Arabic equivalent of the Greek "Σοφία, ὀρθή!" ("Wisdom, attend!"). Said at the "little entrance" during vespers or the divine liturgy, this exclamation immediately brings home the fact that Arabic-speaking Christians of the Middle East – descendants of the earliest Christian communities established by the apostles – have faithfully preserved, in Arabic, the Eastern Christian liturgical heritage.

As liturgy is inseparable from theology, the same holds true for the patristic tradition. Arabic-speaking Christians have been translating the Church Fathers continuously from the eighth century to the present. Thousands of manuscripts – many of which are more than a millennium old – with over a thousand Arabic translations of the Church Fathers are extant in Middle Eastern, European, Russian, and American libraries. Sadly, these Arabic translations have not been adequately studied, and only a fraction of them (less than 1%) have been edited. Additionally, Arabic is only rarely given the recognition it deserves as an essential language for the history of the Church; hence the relative neglect of the Arabic translations of the Church Fathers – even in comparison with other "Oriental" versions: Syriac, Georgian, Armenian, Coptic, and Ethiopic – in most manuals of patristics. It is no exaggeration to say that the study of the Fathers in Arabic is still in its infancy.

To get an orientation as to what was translated, one needs to consult Georg Graf's monumental *Geschichte der christlichen arabischen Literatur* (Graf 1944–1953),

The Wiley Blackwell Companion to Patristics, First Edition. Edited by Ken Parry.
© 2015 John Wiley & Sons Ltd. Published 2019 by John Wiley & Sons Ltd.

particularly the first volume, devoted to translations. Crucial updates are available in Joseph Nasrallah's *Histoire du mouvement littéraire dans l'Église melchite* (Nasrallah 1979–1996), though its use is hampered by a lack of indexes. Other, more focused studies – particularly those of Joseph-Marie Sauget (1998: 9–14, 147–282) and Samir Khalil Samir (1986; 1992; and numerous others) – have analyzed Arabic translations of specific patristic authors or texts and/or the contents of individual manuscripts. Useful references to "versiones arabicae" can also be found in the *Clavis Patrum Graecorum* (Geerard and Noret 1974–2003). For Gregory of Nazianzus we are fortunate to have a fully searchable online database of Arabic manuscripts of his works, detailing their content (http://pot-pourri.fltr.ucl.ac.be/manuscrits/nazianze_arabe/default.cfm). The compilers of this database – Jacques Grand'Henry and Laurence Tuerlinckx of the Université catholique de Louvain (Belgium) – have also published critical editions of Arabic versions of several of Gregory of Nazianzus' *Orations*, with annotated French translations (Grand'Henry 2013 and references therein). Gregory of Nazianzus remains the only Church Father the Arabic translations of whose works have been semi-systematically edited.

It is important to realize that even all these studies together provide very incomplete information as to what Arabic translations of patristic sources are actually available. Working through Arab Christian manuscripts with patristic content, digital copies of which can be ordered from the libraries holding them, or, in the case of many Middle Eastern collections, from the Hill Museum & Manuscript Library in Collegeville, Minnesota (http://www.hmml.org), one will easily discover previously uncatalogued or inadequately catalogued translations. Many areas still remain unexplored, and significant discoveries await serious researchers.

In what follows, I shall offer an overview of the field, focusing on the history of the Arabic translations of the Church Fathers, their reception by Arab Christian and Muslim authors, and two additional issues of interest: Arabic translations of *lost* Greek patristic texts and Arabic translations of the Latin Fathers.

A Brief History of the Arabic Translations of the Church Fathers

Arabic-speaking Christianity is older than Islam, as several Arab tribes had been Christianized in the fourth, fifth, and sixth centuries (Hainthaler 2007). Apart from a number of poems (transmitted orally) and a handful of inscriptions, they left behind no literary production, and so it is only after the Muslim conquest of the Middle East in the seventh century that Middle Eastern Christians gradually adopted Arabic as their *written* and (to varying degrees) their liturgical language. As knowledge of their ancestral languages – Greek, Aramaic/Syriac, and Coptic – was decreasing, Middle Eastern Christians launched a massive attempt to translate their patristic heritage into Arabic.

While Christians of all denominations were involved in translating the Church Fathers, the Arabic-speaking Orthodox Christians of the Middle East – called "Roman" (i.e., Byzantine) Orthodox (*al-Rum al-Urthudhuks*) or, formerly, "Melkites" (*Malakiyyun*) (Noble and Treiger 2014) – produced the majority of these translations (Treiger 2015). The earliest centers of Melkite translation activity were the monasteries of Palestine, particularly the great lavra of Mar Saba east of Bethlehem. In the eighth and ninth centuries, Mar Saba was a cutting-edge multilingual translation center, where translations were carried out between no fewer than four languages: Greek, Syriac, Arabic, and Georgian. Around 800 at Mar Saba, two monks Abramios and Patrikios, translated works of Isaac of Nineveh (his so-called "First Collection") from the original Syriac into Greek; this Greek translation soon became an international bestseller (Brock 1999–2000). Within 50 years, other Sabaite monks (whose names, unfortunately, we do not know) translated Isaac from Syriac virtually simultaneously into Arabic and Georgian (Pataridze 2011).

Other Church Fathers, translated from Greek and Syriac into Arabic in Palestine, include John Chrysostom, Aphrahat, "Ephraem Graecus," Cyril of Jerusalem, Evagrius (under the name of Nilus of Ancyra), Diadochus of Photike, Mark the Monk, John of Apamea, Jacob of Sarug, Barsanuphius of Gaza, Cyril of Scythopolis, John Climacus, John Moschus (under the name of Sophronius of Jerusalem), Pseudo-Athanasius (*Quaestiones ad Antiochum ducem*) [CPG 2257], Anastasius of Sinai, and Leontius of Damascus. Fragmentary translations of select works of Basil of Caesarea, Gregory of Nazianzus, and John of Damascus were also made during this period (Treiger 2014). Translation activity included also biblical (Griffith 2013: 97–154) and liturgical texts (Leeming 2003) – a process that continued and, in the case of liturgical translations, even intensified in later centuries. Significantly, this Palestinian translation activity was taking place simultaneously with the better known 'Abbasid Graeco-Arabic translation movement in Baghdad, which involved production of hundreds of Arabic translations of Greek philosophical and scientific works and in which Christian translators were, of course, also prominently involved (Gutas 1998; Griffith 2008: 106–128). It is an interesting and hitherto unresolved question whether there was any cross-pollination between the two translation activities (cf. Treiger 2015: 203).

After the Byzantine reconquest of northern Syria in the mid-tenth century, Antioch became the most important center of Graeco-Arabic translation activity. It was there that Arabic translations of an entire library of patristic texts were produced. Antonios, the abbot of the monastery of St Symeon the Stylite the Younger on the Black Mountain near Antioch in the second half of the tenth century, translated into Arabic John of Damascus' *Dialectica*, the *Exposition of the Orthodox Faith*, and six shorter treatises, John Climacus' *Book of the Ladder* (a second Arabic translation of this work!) (Treiger 2015: 209–218), as well as his near-contemporary Paul of Monemvasia's *Beneficial Tales*. Ibrahim ibn Yuhanna (d. c. 1030), who held the Byzantine honorific title of "protospatharios," translated into Arabic Gregory of Nazianzus' *Orations*, 52 homilies of "Ephraem Graecus," Gregory of Nyssa's *Encomium to St. Ephrem* [CPG 3193], Dionysius the Areopagite's *On Good and Evil* (=*Divine Names*, chapter 4, §18–35), and Basil of Caesarea's second homily on the Great Lent [CPG 2846]. Ibrahim ibn Yuhanna is also the author of an important hagiographical work: the life of the patriarch of Antioch Christopher (martyred in 967).

By far the most prolific Antiochene translator was the Orthodox deacon 'Abdallah ibn al-Fadl (mid-eleventh century). He translated into Arabic works of John Chrysostom, Basil of Caesarea, Gregory of Nyssa, Maximus the Confessor, Pseudo-Caesarius, John of Damascus, Andrew of Crete, Isaac of Nineveh (from the Sabaitic Greek version), and Pseudo-Maximus' sacro-profane florilegium *Loci communes* (Daiber 2012). In addition, his Arabic translation of the Psalms became the most influential in the Christian Arab world; it even features in the inscriptions of the famous "Aleppo-Zimmer" (a room from a seventeenth-century Arab Christian house in Aleppo), currently at the Pergamon museum in Berlin (Ott 1996: 193–200). 'Abdallah ibn al-Fadl's own theological and philosophical works, based on a wide variety of Greek and Arabic sources, both Muslim and Christian, can be said to represent a meeting point of two "Hellenisms": the Hellenism of Byzantium and the Hellenism of the Caliphate (Noble and Treiger 2011; 2014: 171–187; Treiger 2011–2013).

Contemporaneously with this burgeoning translation activity in Antioch, Arabic translations of the Church Fathers were also produced in other cities and regions. In 1009, in Damascus, the Melkite translator Ibn Sahqun translated into Arabic the entire Dionysian corpus (Treiger 2005; 2007; Bonmariage and Moureau 2011). His translation includes an interesting "appendix" (found also in many Greek manuscripts of Pseudo-Dionysius), with citations from Polycrates of Ephesus' *Epistle to Victor* [CPG 1338], Clement of Alexandria's *Can a Rich Man Be Saved* [CPG 1379], and Philo's *De vita contemplativa*, all of them culled from Eusebius' *Ecclesiastical History* (Parker and Treiger 2012).

Of the important translation centers, Egypt deserves close attention, though it is still insufficiently understood. It is clear that both Egyptian Melkites and Copts were involved in translating the Church Fathers into Arabic. Among the Melkites, one can mention the tenth-century bishop of Old Cairo Theophilos (Tawfil ibn Tawfil), a native of Damascus, who translated from Greek into Arabic John Chrysostom's ninth homily on penitence [CPG 4333.9] as well as the Gospels. In 1335, another Melkite translator from Cairo, Qustantin ibn Abi l-Ma'ali (who later became a monk at Sinai with the name Antonios) produced an Arabic translation of the *Typikon of Mar Saba*.

Among the Copts, one can mention Jarih (or perhaps Jurayj=George?) ibn Yuhannis al-Rarawi, a monk at the monastery of St Macarius in Wadi al-Natrun (Scetis), who in 964 produced an Arabic translation of Basil of Caesarea's *Hexaemeron* and Gregory of Nyssa's *De opificio hominis*. This translation, possibly made from an intermediary Syriac version rather than directly from Greek, is preserved in a unicum manuscript in Vienna and has not been studied (Fedwick 1981: 486). It is clear, however, that it is different from 'Abdallah ibn al-Fadl's direct Graeco-Arabic translation of the same two works, produced in Antioch in the eleventh century. (It is to be noted that a *third* Arabic translation of Basil of Caesarea's *Hexaemeron*, of unknown provenance, and distinct from the other two, also exists; it is preserved in two eighteenth/nineteenth-century manuscripts at the Orthodox patriarchate in Damascus. It may well be that it is, in fact, a *revision* of 'Abdallah ibn al-Fadl's version, as it often happens that later translations are not completely independent, but are revisions of older ones.)

Some patristic texts were translated from Coptic into Arabic in Egypt. These include the *Letters* of St Antony, translated from Sahidic Coptic at the monastery of St Antonios in Egypt in 1271 (Rubenson 1995: 20–21, 29–34), some homilies of, and attributed to, Shenute of Atripe (Graf 1944–1953: vol. I, 461–464; Ghica 2001; Swanson 2005; 2008), and the eighth-century *Apocalypse of Pseudo-Athanasius* [CPG 2195], translated, it would seem, twice: by Sulayman ibn Tashbish at the monastery of St Macarius in Wadi al-Natrun (Scetis) and by Murqus, bishop of Sakha (c. 1200) (Graf 1944–1953: vol. I, 277–279; Witte 2009). The same Murqus of Sakha also translated into Arabic

Severus of Nastarawah's ninth-century Coptic *Homily on the Life of St. Mark* (Graf 1944–1953: vol. I, 265–267).

The Copts were prominent in the production of anthologies, adaptations, abridgements, and "editions" of patristic texts in Arabic (cf. Sidarus 2013). Thus, the Copto-Arabic author Severus ibn al-Muqaffaʿ (d. after 987) produced an important patristic anthology in Arabic, *The Book of Precious Pearls* (Maiberger 1972; Davis 2008: 205–209). This anthology focuses on Christology – a major bone of contention between the various Christian communities in the Caliphate. Another, anonymous patristic florilegium, *Confession of the Fathers*, also mainly Christological in content, was compiled about a century later (c. 1078), mostly from texts translated from Coptic intermediaries into Arabic (Youssef 2003; Davis 2008: 208–209).

The Copto-Arabic theologian al-Safi ibn al-ʿAssal (d. before 1260) prepared a number of adaptations and abridgements of earlier (Melkite) Arabic translations of Greek patristic literature, mostly ethical and ascetic, such as John Chrysostom's homilies on the Gospel of Matthew and on the Gospel of John, John Climacus' *Book of the Ladder*, Isaac of Nineveh's works (based on ʿAbdallah ibn al-Fadl's Graeco-Arabic translation), and some others. These adaptations enjoyed a wide circulation in Egypt (Graf 1944–1953: vol. II, 396–397; cf. Samir 1978a: 193–194; Davis 2008: 253).

The Copts also produced several medieval Arabic "editions" of key patristic ascetic texts, both Greek and Syriac, such as works of Evagrius, the *Macarian Homilies*, John of Dalyatha, and Isaac of Nineveh. To take the case of Evagrius first, while his treatise *On Prayer* [CPG 2452] was originally translated into Arabic in one of the Melkite monasteries of Palestine (under the name of Nilus of Ancyra), a second translation (under the name of Evagrius himself) was prepared in Egyptian circles. This second translation is preserved as part of an Arabic Egyptian collection of Evagrian treatises, containing 13 items and extant in at least six manuscripts, the oldest of which dates to the late thirteenth century (Samir 1992; Géhin 2006).

The *Macarian Homilies* also exist in Arabic in two different versions. An integral Arabic translation of the Macarian "Collection IV" was produced in the eleventh century and is extant in two manuscripts; it is ascribed to Macarius and is clearly of Melkite Antiochene origin (though the translator is unknown). The second Arabic version, ascribed to Symeon the Stylite, is of unknown provenance, but was probably edited in Egypt; it is preserved in a number of manuscripts, mostly of Egyptian origin. Significantly, it includes 14 hitherto unidentified texts, not found in the Greek tradition (Strothmann 1975; Samir 1978b).

In the case of the Arabic translation of the eighth-century East-Syriac mystic John of Dalyatha, we are fortunate to know the names of the translators: hieromonk Ibrahim and deacon Yuhanna (Nakad 1980). They must have lived before 1182, the date of the earliest Arabic manuscript (now at the monastery of St Antonios in Egypt). Given their knowledge of Syriac and the likely Egyptian provenance of the translation, perhaps the translators were monks of the famous "monastery of the Syrians" (Dayr al-Suryan) in Wadi al-Natrun (Scetis) or of the monastery of St Paul the Anchorite in Egypt's Eastern Desert.

The case of Isaac of Nineveh is particularly complicated. As mentioned above, his works (the so-called "First Collection") were first translated from Syriac into Arabic in the first half of the ninth century in Palestine. In the mid-eleventh century, the Antiochene translator 'Abdallah ibn al-Fadl prepared a second translation of the same First Collection, this time from Greek. Finally, an "edition" of Arabic translations of Isaac in four "books" was prepared in Egypt. The third book of this edition incorporates 'Abdallah ibn al-Fadl's Graeco-Arabic translation, while the other three books contain independent Arabic translations of Isaac's texts, not only from the First Collection, but also from Isaac's Second and Third Collections, as well as a number of hitherto unidentified texts (Chialà 2002: 334–338).

It should also be noted that there is yet another Arabic adaptation of Isaac. In the early tenth century, the Arabic-writing "Nestorian" physician Hanun ibn Yuhanna ibn al-Salt authored *Three Letters, Extracted from Works of St. Isaac of Nineveh on Asceticism and Monasticism*. This is a very interesting compilation, which integrates some authentically Isaacian material with unidentified ascetic traditions of East Syriac and even Muslim origin. In fact, the abundance of Islamic turns of phrase and frequent, if often covert, allusions to the Qur'an and Hadith (Islamic oral tradition) make it likely that this work was commissioned by a Muslim ascetic (whom Ibn al-Salt characterizes as a "stranger," indicating that he was unfamiliar with the Syriac language) and was written for a Muslim audience.

After an apparent hiatus of a few centuries, translation activity intensified in the early modern period (seventeenth and eighteenth centuries), with the Melkites again playing a central role. Though most translations focused on contemporary or near-contemporary Greek material (while Melkite Catholics were similarly engaged in translating contemporary or near-contemporary Latin, Italian, and French works of Catholic theology), patristic works also received attention. Thus, for instance, the patriarch of Antioch Athanasius III Dabbas (r. 1685–1694 and 1720–1724) translated from Greek 34 homilies of John Chrysostom (Graf 1944–1953: vol. III, 129–131; Nasrallah 1979–1996: vol. IV.1, 138), while the eighteenth-century translator Mas'ad Nashu' prepared new Arabic versions of select works of Athanasius of Alexandria and of John Chrysostom's Commentaries on the Acts of the Apostles and Paul's Epistles (Graf 1944–1953: vol. III, 141–142; Nasrallah 1979–1996: vol. IV.2, 221–223). This process continued in the modern period (the nineteenth century to the present), when some patristic works appeared in new translations, produced not only from Greek but also from a variety of modern vernaculars, particularly French, Italian, German, English, and Russian; new Arabic translations of patristic works from the original Greek – such as the Melkite Catholic archimandrite Adrianos Shakkur's Arabic translation of John of Damascus' *Exposition of the Orthodox Faith*, first published in 1984 – have also appeared in print.

Arab Christian and Islamic Reception(s) of the Arabic Translations of the Church Fathers

Arab Christian Reception

There is no question that Arabophone Christianity is deeply rooted in the patristic tradition. Many Arabic-writing Christian theologians – notably the early ninth-century Arab Orthodox (Melkite) theologian Theodore Abu Qurra (Lamoreaux 2005) – can be meaningfully described as intellectual heirs to the Church Fathers, even as they were writing in a completely new context of Muslim-governed societies (with interludes of Byzantine, Crusader, and Mongol rule) and were therefore chiefly concerned with responding to the intellectual and social challenge of Islam (Noble and Treiger 2014).

There are, unfortunately, very few studies of how exactly Arabic-writing Christian authors used patristic sources. A systematic examination of this question – across the various Christian denominations – would be extremely worthwhile, but it cannot be undertaken here. I shall therefore limit myself to one, relatively well researched tradi-tion: Copto-Arabic Christianity. In his insightful study of Copto-Arabic Christology, Stephen Davis has shown that it is profoundly indebted to "Alexandrian patristic views of the Incarnation and human participation of the divine" and "may be understood as a dynamic record of cultural reception in which successive generations have reclaimed and recontextualized the theology of the Alexandrian church fathers" (Davis 2008: 1). As is to be expected, in the field of Christology, Copto-Arabic authors, such as Severus ibn al-Muqaffaʻ, the author of the aforementioned patristic anthology *The Book of Precious Pearls*, relied heavily on the Alexandrian Fathers – Athanasius and Cyril of Alexandria – as well as on Severus of Antioch. It is somewhat more surprising, however, that, as Davis shows, in other, non-Christological domains Severus ibn al-Muqaffaʻ "virtually ignored" the Alexandrians, giving preference to other patristic authorities, such as "Basil of Caesarea, Gregory of Nazianzus, Epiphanius, and John Chrysostom" (Davis 2008: 207–208).

This correlates well with the patristic citation patterns exhibited by another impor-tant Copto-Arabic theologian, Ibn al-Rahib (d. c. 1290). Owing to Adel Sidarus' source-critical study of Ibn al-Rahib's still unpublished theological encyclopedia *Book of Proof* (*Kitab al-Burhan*), we are in a position to evaluate his use of patristic authorities (Sidarus 2010: 132–142). As Sidarus indicates, it is not the Greek or Coptic authors of the Church of Alexandria, but rather the Cappadocian Fathers, particularly Gregory of Nazianzus, that are most frequently cited in Ibn al-Rahib's *Book of Proof*. A similar phenomenon is observable in some other Copto-Arabic authors of the thirteenth and fourteenth cen-turies – the so-called "golden age" of Copto-Arabic literature (Sidarus 2010: 132, n 12). This is due to the fact that for their access to most aspects of the patristic tradition (with the exception of Christological prooftexts) Copto-Arabic authors largely depended on Arabic translations produced by Melkites in Palestine and Antioch, and Melkite transla-tors were more interested in the Cappadocians (and in other authors, such as John Chrysostom, "Ephrem Graecus," Isaac of Nineveh, Anastasius of Sinai, and John of Damascus) than in the Alexandrian theologians.

In fact, some of Ibn-Rahib's patristic quotations demonstrably go back to Melkite Arabic translations. Thus, on one occasion, Ibn al-Rahib reproduces chapter 86 from John of Damascus' *Exposition of the Orthodox Faith*. This chapter was translated into Arabic in Palestine in the ninth or early tenth century (certainly prior to Antonios' late-tenth-century translation of the entire work) (Treiger 2014: 85–86, 109; 2015: 210–216). In 1230, during his visit to Damascus, the Copto-Arabic author al-Asʻad ibn al-ʻAssal copied this chapter from a (presumably Melkite) Damascene manuscript; he then brought his copy to Egypt. Ibn al-Rahib simply reproduced this chapter from al-Asʻad ibn al-ʻAssal's copy (Samir 1978a).

It is evident that the way in which Copto-Arabic theologians – and Arabic-writing Christians in general – appropriated the patristic heritage was shaped by their own sensitivities and concerns. Thus, when Severus ibn al-Muqaffa' cites Gregory of Nyssa's statement about Christ's extreme "self-emptying" (kenosis) to the degree that He even paid tribute to Caesar, the word "tribute" is deliberately translated as jizya, the name of the poll tax that Christians (as well as other non-Muslims) had to pay to the Muslim authorities under Islamic law. Severus ibn al-Muqaffa''s Copto-Arabic readers were thus made to understand that by paying the jizya and complying with other restrictions imposed on them by their Muslim overlords they could see themselves as imitating Christ (Davis 2008: 229–230).

The translators themselves frequently modified the translated texts, in part because certain patristic concepts were foreign to their worldview. A good example of this is the Arabic translation of Dionysius the Areopagite. The translator, the Melkite Ibn Sahqun (early eleventh century), a native of Homs active in Damascus, apparently felt uncomfortable about the Dionysian concept of "union" (henosis) with the supra-essential Deity and therefore replaced it with a more innocuous phrase, "contemplation of the [divine] oneness" (Treiger 2007: 377). The patristic notion of "deification" (theosis) was similarly toned down in Ibrahim ibn Yuhanna's translation of Gregory of Nazianzus' Orations (Tokay 2011: 240–241, 247). Relatedly, the Arab Orthodox (Melkite) translator and theologian 'Abdallah ibn al-Fadl from Antioch (mid-eleventh century) interpreted the patristic dictum "God became man, and [sic] man became God" (cited in the name of Gregory of Nazianzus) as referring not to theosis, but to the union of the divine and human in Christ, which took place uniquely in Christ alone (Noble and Treiger 2011: 412). This restrictive "Christological" interpretation, precluding the possibility of human beings' deification, is prominent also in the medieval Copto-Arabic tradition (Davis 2008: 257–258, 315–316). Incidentally, the question of the possibility of theosis has been hotly debated in the Coptic Church in modern times. While deification is central to the thought of the prominent Coptic monastic theologian Matta al-Miskin ("Matthew the Poor," 1919–2006), the late Coptic Pope Shenouda III (r. 1971–2012) branded this idea a heresy and even denied that the Fathers could have taught it (Davis 2008: 272–278).

Islamic Reception

It is quite rare that Islamic sources display awareness of the patristic tradition. Nonetheless, it is to be noted that the tenth-century Muslim historian al-Mas'udi, who was very much au courant of contemporary Middle Eastern Christianity, mentions "the book of Dionysius the Areopagite on the [Christian] mysteries," the tenth-century Muslim bibliographer Ibn al-Nadim cites Theodore of Mopsuestia's commentary on Genesis (Samir 1977), while the twelfth-century Muslim heresiographer al-Shahrastani makes reference to Isaac of Nineveh, citing his view that the punishment in hell will be temporary rather than eternal. Additionally, Muslim gnomological collections – for example, Ibn Hindu's Spiritual Sayings and Greek Aphorisms (early eleventh century), Mubashshir ibn Fatik's The Choicest Maxims and the Best

Sayings (eleventh century), and al-Shahrazuri's *The Promenade of Spirits and the Garden of Joys* (thirteenth century) – preserve citations from Basil of Caesarea and Gregory of Nazianzus (Strohmaier 1977: 142).

Some patristic texts were translated or adapted into Arabic as part of, or in connection with, the Baghdad translation movement and were subsequently (and often unawares) used by Muslim scholars. Thus, an Arabic translation of Nemesius of Emesa's *De natura hominis* (misattributed to Gregory of Nyssa) was used by the ninth-century Muslim philosopher al-Kindi (Haji-Athanasiou 1982; Samir 1986); Pseudo-Gregory Thaumaturgus' *Disputatio de anima ad Tatianum* [CPG 1773] was adapted into Arabic and circulated under the name of Avicenna (Gätje 1971); the doxographical section of Hippolytus of Rome's *Refutatio omnium haeresium* [CPG 1899] was adapted into Arabic under the title *The Book of Ammonius on the Opinions of the Philosophers* (the so-called "Doxography of Pseudo-Ammonius"; Rudolph 1989); while an Arabic compilation, based on Diodore of Tarsus' lost work on providence (on which, see Weis (1968)) and Theodoret of Cyrrhus' *De providentia* [CPG 6211], circulated in the Muslim tradition under the name of the ninth-century Arab Christian "Nestorian" writer Jibril ibn Nuh and his more famous contemporary, the Muslim author al-Jahiz (Gibb 1948).

A particular case that deserves attention is the influence of the sixth-century Egyptian Christian philosopher and theologian John Philoponus. Many of Philoponus' works, including his *Against Proclus on the Eternity of the World* [CPG 7266], *Against Aristotle on the Eternity of the World*, and *On the Contingence of the World* [CPG 7274], were translated or adapted into Arabic. (The last-mentioned work is, in fact, extant only in an Arabic summary.) His ideas exercised a considerable influence on Islamic philosophy and theology, though some were met with criticism by Muslim Aristotelians; thus, the tenth-century Muslim philosopher al-Farabi authored a refutation of Philoponus' critique of Aristotle (Chase 2012).

Of course, it is possible that the Church Fathers influenced Islamic philosophy and theology not only via the Arabic translations of their works, but also indirectly, through the mediation of Arabic-speaking Christian scholars familiar with patristic texts in the original languages. Thus, it has been suggested that the ninth-century Arab Christian translator of Plotinus' *Enneads*, 'Abd al-Masih ibn Na'ima al-Himsi (who may have been a Melkite or a Maronite), was familiar with the Dionysian corpus either in Greek or in Syriac, and that Dionysian ideas therefore had an indirect impact on his Arabic adaptation of Plotinus, the so-called *Theology of Aristotle* (Adamson 2002: 106–109, 162–165). Similarly, in one of his Persian letters, the eleventh/twelfth-century Muslim theologian al-Ghazali expresses ideas strikingly similar to patristic, particularly Origenist, speculations on paradise as the spiritual "place" of contemplation of God; he even indicates that these ideas were popular among philosophers and Christians. It is quite possible that al-Ghazali was familiar with these ideas through oral transmission. This subject of a possible patristic influence on Islamic philosophical and theological ideas is still insufficiently researched and deserves a careful and sustained examination – for a starting point, see Gardet (1947), Seale (1964), and Wolfson (1976).

Two Issues of Interest

Arabic Translations of Lost Greek Patristic Texts

Arabic translations of Greek patristic texts become especially important when they provide access to authors and works no longer available in the Greek originals. A particularly striking case of an Arabic translation preserving an otherwise lost text is the *Noetic Paradise*. Originally written in Greek, probably in Palestine, in the eighth or ninth century, this patristic masterpiece is available only in a (presumably eleventh-century) Arabic translation. The title of the treatise refers to the angelic realm from which the human mind (*nous*) was expelled after the Fall, just as the human body was expelled from the bodily paradise. The text describes the ways in which one ought to "till" the earth of one's heart, cultivating the virtues and combating the vices, in order to have one's *nous* purified and readmitted to the noetic paradise (Noble and Treiger 2014: 188–200; a complete English translation is in preparation).

Other examples of patristic texts lost in Greek and preserved in Arabic (or in Arabic together with other "Oriental" versions) include: 14 unidentified texts preserved in the aforementioned Egyptian "edition" of the *Macarian Homilies* (Strothmann 1975; Samir 1978b); a text of "Ephraem Graecus" on Satan and death, preserved also in Georgian (Morozov 2009); (Pseudo?) John of Damascus' *Expositio et declaratio fidei* [CPG 8078]; and Strategius' account of the Persian conquest of Jerusalem in 614 [CPG 7846], preserved also in Georgian (Garitte 1973–1974). Arabic translations may also help reconstruct the history of transmission and even lost Greek adaptations of existing patristic texts (van Esbroeck 1989).

Arabic Translations of the Latin Fathers

Arabic translations of the Latin Fathers are quite rare (at least until the seventeenth century) and have not been sufficiently investigated. Some of John Cassian's works were translated very early on, from an intermediate Greek version. (This Greek version is now conveniently available in Tzamalikos (2012), though, controversially, Tzamalikos has argued that John Cassian never existed and that this Greek version is the original, authored by a little known sixth-century monk, "Cassian the Sabaite," and then adapted into Latin.) The earliest Arabic translation of a work by John Cassian (or this "Cassian the Sabaite") is that of *On the Holy Fathers Living at Scetis* (Tzamalikos 2012: 168–246); it is extant in a Vatican Arabic manuscript dating to 885, and so must be earlier than that.

Another relatively early translation is the late-tenth-century Antiochene translator Antonios' Arabic version of Pope Gregory the Great's *Book of Dialogues*, also produced from an intermediary Greek version (Nasrallah 1979–1996: vol. III.1, 285).

Other translations of the Latin Fathers do not appear until the early modern times. We know of eighteenth- and nineteenth-century translations of Augustine's works (Graf 1944–1953: vol. III, 218, 220, 495 and vol. IV, 256) and of rather crude seventeenth-century Arabic versions of sections of Thomas Aquinas' *Summa theologica* and

Summa contra gentiles (Graf 1944–1953: vol. IV, 256). The Coptic Catholic author Raphael Tuki (or al-Tukhi) (d. 1787), who taught Coptic and Church rite at the Collegio Urbano de Propaganda Fide in Rome, translated into Arabic the Old Testament (from the Latin Vulgata), Augustine's sermons, select works of Pope Leo the Great, and even several works of Gregory of Nyssa – for example, his *Commentary on the Song of Songs* and *Homilies on the Beatitudes* (from an intermediary Latin version) (Graf 1944–1953: vol. IV, 161–162). Many Arabic-writing Catholic authors (e.g., the seventeenth-century Maronite scholar Ishaq al-Shidrawi and the eighteenth-century Syrian Catholic patriarch Ishaq ibn Jubayr) in their works written in Arabic routinely refer to Latin Church Fathers and medieval Latin authorities (Graf 1944–1953: vol. III, 349 and vol. IV, 49).

Avenues for Future Research

As this survey of the Arabic translations of the Church Fathers will have demonstrated, the field needs considerably more attention. A fully searchable computer database of Arabic patristic translations needs to be created, which will allow scholars to conduct philological analyses of these translations and comparisons between them and Islamic, Christian, and Jewish theological works in Arabic. In cases where the Greek or Syriac originals of the Arabic translations of the Church Fathers are lost, complete critical editions need to be prepared, and the texts need to be translated into English or other European languages to make them accessible, for the first time, to scholars of Eastern Christianity and patristics.

Another important task is investigating the ways in which Arabic patristic translations were read, interpreted, and used by Arabic-speaking Christians as well as by Muslims and (possibly) Jews in the pre-modern period. This kind of research has the potential to transform, perhaps even to revolutionize, our understanding of the links between the Greek and Syriac patristic tradition and Arab Christian, Islamic, and Jewish thought.

Bibliography

Adamson, Peter (2002), *The Arabic Plotinus: A Philosophical Study of the* Theology *of* Aristotle. London: Duckworth.

Bonmariage, Cécile, and Moureau, Sébastien (2011), "Corpus Dionysiacum Arabicum: Étude, édition critique et traduction des *Noms Divins* IV, §1–9". *Le Muséon*, 124.1–2: 181–227; 124.3–4: 419–459.

Brock, Sebastian (1999–2000), "From Qatar to Tokyo, by way of Mar Saba: the translations of Isaac of Beth Qatraye (Isaac the Syrian)". *ARAM*, 11–12: 475–484.

Chase, Michael (2012), "Philoponus' cosmology in the Arabic tradition". *Recherches*

de théologie et philosophie médiévales, 79.2: 271–306.

Chialà, Sabino (2002), *Dall'ascesi eremitica alla misericordia infinita: Ricerche su Isacco di Ninive e la sua fortuna.* Florence: Leo S. Olschki.

Daiber, Hans (2012), "Graeco-Arabica Christiana: the Christian scholar 'Abd Allāh ibn al-Fadl (11th c. A.D.) as transmitter of Greek works". In *Islamic Philosophy, Science, Culture, and Religion: Studies in Honor of Dimitri Gutas*, David C. Reisman and Felicitas Opwis (eds). Leiden: Brill; 3–9.

Davis, Stephen J. (2008), *Coptic Christology in Practice: Incarnation and Divine Participation* in Late Antique and Medieval Egypt. Oxford: Oxford University Press.

Fedwick, Paul J. (1981), "The translations of the works of Basil before 1400". In Basil of Caesarea: Christian, Humanist, Ascetic. A Sixteen-Hundredth Anniversary Symposium, vol. 2, Paul J. Fedwick (ed.). Toronto: Pontifical Institute of Mediaeval Studies; 439–512.

Gardet, Louis (1947), "Rencontre de la théologie musulmane et de la pensée patristique". In Revue Thomiste, 55: 45–112 [reprinted with modifications in Gardet, Louis, and Anawati, Georges (1948), Introduction à la théologie musulmane: essai de théologie comparée. Paris: J. Vrin; 191–237].

Garitte, Gérard (1973–1974), Expugnationis Hierosolymae A.D. 614 recensiones arabicae, four vols. Louvain: Secrétariat du corpus SCO.

Gätje, Helmut (1971), Studien zur Überlieferung der aristotelischen Psychologie im Islam. Heidelberg: Universitätsverlag Winter.

Geerard, Maurice, and Noret, Jacques (1974–2003), Clavis Patrum Graecorum [=CPG], seven vols. Turnhout: Brepols.

Géhin, Paul (2006), "La tradition arabe d'Évagre le Pontique". Collectanea Christiana Orientalia, 3: 83–104.

Ghica, Victor (2001), "Sermon arabe pour le troisième dimanche du Carême, attribué à Chenouté (cod. Par. ar. 4761)". Annales islamologiques, 35: 143–161.

Gibb, Hamilton A.R. (1948), "The argument from design: A Muʿtazilite treatise attributed to al-Jāḥiẓ". In Ignace Goldziher Memorial Volume, vol. 1, Samuel Löwinger and Joseph Somogyi (eds). Budapest: Globus; 150–162.

Graf, Georg (1944–1953), Geschichte der christlichen arabischen Literatur, five vols. Vatican: Biblioteca Apostolica Vaticana.

Grand'Henry, Jacques (ed.) (2013), Sancti Gregorii Nazianzeni Opera: Versio arabica antiqua IV: Orationes XI, XLI (arab. 8, 12). Turnhout: Brepols.

Griffith, Sidney H. (2008), The Church in the Shadow of the Mosque: Christians and Muslims in the World of Islam. Princeton, NJ: Princeton University Press.

Griffith, Sidney H. (2013), The Bible in Arabic: The Scriptures of the "People of the Book" in the Language of Islam. Princeton, NJ: Princeton University Press.

Gutas, Dimitri. (1998), Greek Thought, Arabic Culture: The Graeco-Arabic Translation Movement in Baghdad and Early Abbasid Society (2nd–4th/8th–10th centuries). London: Routledge.

Hainthaler, Theresia (2007), Christliche Araber vor dem Islam: Verbreitung und konfessionelle Zugehörigkeit: Eine Hinführung. Leuven: Peeters.

Haji-Athanasiou, Metri (1982), "Le traité de Némésius d'Emèse de Natura Hominis dans la tradition arabe". Thèse de Doctorat d'État en Philosophie, Université de Paris I Panthéon–Sorbonne.

Lamoreaux, John C. (transl.) (2005) Theodore Abu Qurrah. Provo, UT: Brigham Young University Press.

Leeming, Kate (2003), "The adoption of Arabic as a liturgical language by the Palestinian Melkites". ARAM, 15: 239–246.

Maiberger, Paul (1972), "Das Buch der kostbaren Perle" von Severus ibn al-Muqaffaʿ: Einleitung und arabischer Text (Kapitel 1–5). Wiesbaden: Franz Steiner (Maiberger's edition of the rest of the text is still unpublished).

Morozov, Dmitry A. (2009), "Zateriannye teksty Efrema Sirina" ["Lost texts of Ephrem the Syrian"]. Simvol, 55: 377–388.

Nakad, Michel (1980), "La version arabe des lettres de Jean de Dalyatha: introduction, traduction, notes, comparaison avec le texte syriaque", two vols. Thèse pour le Doctorat de 3e Cycle (Philosophie), Université de Paris IV–Sorbonne.

Nasrallah, Joseph (1979–1996), Histoire du mouvement littéraire dans l'église melchite du Ve au XXe siècle, three vols in six parts (vol. II.2 Rachid Haddad (ed.)). Louvain/Damascus: Peeters/Institut français de Damas.

Noble, Samuel, and Treiger, Alexander (2011), "Christian Arabic theology in Byzantine Antioch: ʿAbdallāh ibn al-Fadl al-Antākī and his *Discourse on the Holy Trinity*". *Le Muséon*, 124.3–4: 371–417.

Noble, Samuel, and Treiger, Alexander (2014), *The Orthodox Church in the Arab World (700–1700): An Anthology of Sources*. DeKalb, IL: Northern Illinois University Press.

Ott, Claudia (1996), "Die Inschriften des Aleppozimmers im Berliner Pergamonmuseum". *Le Muséon*, 109.1–2: 185–226.

Parker, Emily, and Treiger, Alexander (2012), "Philo's odyssey into the medieval Jewish world: neglected evidence from Arab Christian literature". *Dionysius*, 30: 117–146.

Pataridze, Tamara (2011), "Les *Discours Ascétiques* d'Isaac de Ninive: étude de la tradition géorgienne et de ses rapports avec les autres versions". *Le Muséon*, 124.1–2: 27–58.

Rubenson, Samuel (1995), *The Letters of St. Antony: Monasticism and the Making of a Saint*. Minneapolis, MN: Fortress Press.

Rudolph, Ulrich (1989), *Die* Doxographie des Pseudo-Ammonios: *Ein Beitrag zur neuplatonischen Überlieferung im Islam*. Stuttgart: F. Steiner.

Samir, Samir Khalil (1977), "Théodore de Mopsueste dans le 'Fihrist' d'Ibn an-Nadīm". *Le Muséon*, 90: 355–363.

Samir, Samir Khalil (1978a), "Al-As'ad Ibn al-'Assāl copiste de Jean Damascène à Damas en 1230". *Orientalia Christiana Periodica*, 44: 190–194.

Samir, Samir Khalil (1978b), Review of Strothmann (1975). *Orientalia Christiana Periodica*, 44: 494–498.

Samir, Samir Khalil (1986), "Les versions arabes de Némésius de Ḥomṣ". In *L'eredità classica nelle lingue orientali*, Massimiliano Pavan and Umberto Cozzoli (eds). Rome: Istituto della Enciclopedia Italiana; 99–151.

Samir, Samir Khalil (1992), "Évagre le Pontique dans la tradition arabo-copte". In *Actes du IVe Congrès Copte, Louvain-la-Neuve, 5–10 septembre 1988*, vol. 2, Marguerite Rassart-Debergh and Julien Ries (eds). Louvain-la-Neuve: Université catholique de Louvain; 125–153.

Sauget, Joseph-Marie (1998), *Littératures et manuscrits des chrétientés syriaques et arabes*. Vatican: Biblioteca Apostolica Vaticana.

Seale, Morris S. (1964), *Muslim Theology: A Study of Origins with Reference to the Church Fathers*. London: Luzac.

Sidarus, Adel Y. (2010), "Les sources d'une somme philosophico-théologique copte arabe (*Kitâb al-Burhân* d'Abû Šâkir ibn al-Râhib, XIIIe siècle)". *Miscellanea Bibliothecae Apostolicae Vaticanae*, 17: 127–163.

Sidarus, Adel Y. (2013), "From Coptic to Arabic in the Christian literature of Egypt (7th–11th centuries)". *Coptica*, 12: 35–56.

Strohmaier, Gotthard (1977), "Patristische Überlieferung im Arabischen". In: *Das Korpus der griechischen christlichen Schriftsteller: Historie, Gegenwart, Zukunft*, Johannes Irmscher and Kurt Treu (eds). Berlin: Akademie-Verlag; 139–145 [reprinted in Strohmaier, Gotthard (1996), *Von Demokrit bis Dante: Die Bewahrung antiken Erbes in der arabischen Kultur*. Hildesheim: Olms; 167–173].

Strothmann, Werner (1975), *Makarios/Symeon: Das arabische Sondergut*. Wiesbaden: Otto Harrassowitz.

Swanson, Mark N. (2005), "St. Shenute in seventeenth-century dress in Paris B.N. ar. 4761". *Coptica*, 4: 27–42.

Swanson, Mark N. (2008), "Searching for Shenoute: a Copto-Arabic homilary in Paris, B.N. arabe 4796". In *Christianity and Monasticism in Upper Egypt: Akhmim and Sohag*, Gawdat Gabra and Hany N. Takla (eds). Cairo: American University in Cairo Press; 143–153.

Tokay, Elif (2011), "Continuity and transformation in the Arabic translation of Gregory Nazianzen's *Oration on Baptism (Oration 40)*". In *Origenes und sein Erbe in Orient und Okzident*, Alfons Fürst (ed.). Münster: Aschendorff Verlag; 227–253.

Treiger, Alexander (2005), "New evidence on the Arabic versions of the *Corpus Dionysiacum*". *Le Muséon*, 118.3–4: 219–240.

Treiger, Alexander (2007), "The Arabic version of Pseudo-Dionysius the Areopagite's *Mystical Theology*, Chapter 1: Introduction, Critical Edition, and Translation". *Le Muséon*, 120.3–4: 365–393.

Treiger, Alexander (2011–2013), "'Abdallāh ibn al-Faḍl al-Anṭākī". In: *Christian–Muslim Relations: A Bibliographical History*, David Thomas and Alex Mallett (eds). Leiden: Brill; vol. 3, 89–113; vol. 5, 748–749.

Treiger, Alexander (2014), "Syro-Arabic translations in Abbasid Palestine: the case of John of Apamea's *Letter on Stillness* (Sinai ar. 549)". *Parole de l'Orient*, 39: 79–131.

Treiger, Alexander (2015), "Christian Graeco-Arabica: prolegomena to a history of the Arabic translations of the Greek Church Fathers." *Intellectual History of the Islamicate World*, 3: 188–227.

Tzamalikos, Panayiotis (2012), *A Newly Discovered Greek Father: Cassian the Sabaite Eclipsed by John Cassian of Marseilles*. Leiden: Brill.

Van Esbroeck, Michel (1989), "Incidence des versions arabes chrétiennes pour la restitution des textes perdus". In *Traductions et traducteurs au Moyen Âge, Actes du Colloque international du CNRS (Paris, 26–28 mai 1986)*, Geneviève Contamine (ed.). Paris: Éditions du CNRS.

Weis, Heinz-Gerhard (1968), "Diodor von Tarsus, Περὶ προνοίας". In *Paul de Lagarde und die syrische Kirchengeschichte*. Göttingen: Lagarde-Haus.

Witte, Bernd (2009), "The Apocalypse of Pseudo-Anastasius". In *Christian–Muslim Relations: A Bibliographical History*, vol. 1, David Thomas and Barbara Roggema (eds). Leiden: Brill; 274–280.

Wolfson, Harry A. (1976), *The Philosophy of the Kalām*. Cambridge, MA: Harvard University Press.

Youssef, Youhanna Nessim (2003), "The quotations of Severus of Antioch in the *Book of the Confessions of the Fathers*". *Ancient Near Eastern Studies*, 40: 173–224.

CHAPTER 31

The Greek of the Fathers

Klaas Bentein

> I propose ... to view the Early Christian Greek literature ... not as one entity, but as several of them – several Christian Greek literatures, as it were (Sevčenko 1980:62–63).

Introduction

How does one describe "the Greek of the Fathers"? The writings of the Church Fathers encompass many thousands of pages, and their language can be approached from a variety of angles. Moreover, patristic, and by extension Early Christian Greek, literature certainly does not form a homogeneous entity, as Sevčenko (1980) emphasizes by proposing the existence of different Christian "literatures," each with different themes, audiences, linguistic profiles, and so on.

A distinction that is commonly made, and that may be helpful in this regard, is that between "genre," "style," and "register," genre referring to culturally recognized categories (e.g., *oratory*, *historiography*, *tragedy*), "style" to the individual's use of language (e.g., *humorous*, *quirky*, *disjointed*), and "register" to contextually determined configurations of language (e.g., *written* versus *oral*). Of these three concepts – each of which has a "form" and a "content" side – register seems to be the most adequate for our present purposes: it provides a framework that is sufficiently general to describe the language of a large group of authors, yet allows us to capture some important linguistic differences between their writings (compare Browning (1978: 103) with regard to "the language of Byzantine literature").

According to Michael Halliday, who has dedicated most of his scholarly career to the relationship between language and context, three main "vectors of context" should be recognized (e.g., see Halliday (1978)). These are called *field* (which concerns the nature

The Wiley Blackwell Companion to Patristics, First Edition. Edited by Ken Parry.
© 2015 John Wiley & Sons Ltd. Published 2019 by John Wiley & Sons Ltd.

of the social activity; e.g., science), *tenor* (which concerns the interactants and their social relation; e.g., the social status of the author), and *mode* (which concerns the ways in which interactants come in contact; e.g., oral communication). On the basis of each of these three vectors different types of registers can be determined, for example, "philosophical," "scientific," "political" (*field*), "low," "middle," "high" (*tenor*), and "written," "oral" (*mode*). Registers related to mode seem to be the least interesting for our present purposes, since only written texts have been preserved. Registers related to field are more interesting, since "religious" (Christian) could be considered a register, which on the formal side would be mainly reflected in lexical choice (e.g., see Mohrmann (1957)). Most interesting, however, are registers related to the "tenor" variable, since they allow us to differentiate the writings of the Fathers with regard to a greater number of linguistic features, and relate their linguistic choices to contextual factors such as the author and his audience. As noted by Høgel (2002: 24–25), "field" may influence this third type of register on an abstract level: the "high" register is connected with grand themes, as it is taken to confirm the grandness of the subject (as with homilies and laudations; the same can often be seen in prologues).

The Ancients themselves seem to have been well aware of these different linguistic strata, as they refer to them on various occasions (e.g., see Sevčenko (1981: 295–297)). In recent years, Greek linguists have described a number of specific (tenor-related) registers, especially with regard to post-classical and Byzantine Greek. Porter (1989: 152–153), for example, proposes to distinguish between four registers, called "vulgar" (e.g., private letters), "non-literary" (e.g., Epictetus), "literary" (e.g., Flavius Iosephus), and "Atticistic" (e.g., Plutarch). However, it remains unclear exactly which contextual and/or linguistic features underlie these registers, a strand of research that is still at an early stage. On the linguistic side, Horrocks (2007) has recently proposed a list of register-markers (for three registers: "basic/non-literary," "official and scientific/technical," and "literary"), which can be situated in the domains of textual coherence, complementation, verb morphology, and so on; in other words, in linguistic areas where from a historic point of view drastic changes are known to have taken place. Another difficulty is that the proposed registers overlap to a certain extent, as a result of which scholars have proposed the notion of a register-*scale* or *continuum* (e.g., see Wahlgren (2010: 527)). In the present outline, too, no strict distinction between registers will be upheld.

In the "The Language of the Fathers and the Development of Christianity" section, I give an outline of the linguistic choices made by the Fathers, as well as the contextual factors that played a role in this choice. A distinction is made between four main periods, which, following Drobner (2007), can be referred to as "Apostolic and Post-apostolic Literature," "Literature of the Period of Persecution," "Literature of the Ascending Imperial Church," and "Literature of the Transition from Late Antiquity to the Early Middle Ages." Evidently, only a general outline can be offered here. Space does not allow addressing a number of more specific issues that are relevant to the present discussion, such as (i) register variation between different works of one and the same author, or within one and the same work, (ii) the differences between authors adopting a similar register, and (iii) the effects of ongoing diachronic change on the outlook of our registers. In the final section some sample texts are discussed.

The Language of the Fathers and the Development of Christianity

Apostolic and Post-apostolic Literature

While Jesus addressed the Galilean peasants in Aramaic, the New Testament is written in Greek. As Judge (2008: 4) notes, this can be related to the fact that Christianity flourished at an early stage in the great cosmopolitan cities of the eastern Mediterranean: the writers of the New Testament were Jews of Palestinian associations, their readers the Greek-speaking members of Hellenistic communities. When Adolf Deissmann (e.g., see Deissmann 1908) observed the linguistic similarities between the language of the New Testament and the newly discovered papyri and ostraca (attesting to the language of "simple and unlearned men") in terms of vocabulary and morpho-syntax, he concluded that (a) New Testament Greek should not be considered a special linguistic species (often called "New Testament Greek" or "Biblical Greek") and (b) the social context of Christianity should be situated in the lower parts of society:

> The social structure of Primitive Christianity points emphatically to the lower, occasionally to the middle class. Primitive Christianity stands in but slight relationship to the upper class at the beginning (Deissmann 1908: 6).

In the course of the twentieth century, both conclusions have been much discussed (for the Greek of the New Testament, see Janse (2007) for example). On the basis of a social study of the New Testament, Judge (2008: chs 1 and 5), among others, has argued that Christianity should not be viewed as an exclusively "popular" movement, restricted to the poor and underprivileged, but that it also consisted of people of substance. A new consensus now seems to have emerged, whereby primitive Christianity is no longer seen as a movement of the proletarian lower class:

> Das hellenistische Urchristentum ist weder eine proletarische Bewegung unterer Schichten gewesen, noch eine Angelegenheit gehobener Schichten. Charakteristisch für seine soziale Struktur ist vielmehr, dass es verschiedene Schichten umfasste – und damit verschiedene Interessen, Gewohnheiten, Selbstverständlichkeiten (Theissen 1974: 268).

Conceptually, Christianity must have appeared particularly attractive to a number of societal classes (e.g., see Theissen 1974: 264; Vogt 1975), such as slaves (because of the principle of equality between men), women (because of the high esteem for women and virgins), and more in general people who were religious and accepted the idea of a single God but did not want to go through the different Jewish rituals. Other societal classes, on the other hand, must have been particularly detracted (e.g., see Gagé 1964; Vogt 1975), including aristocrats/senators (who had everything to lose), soldiers (who needed to be able to take another man's life), and peasants (who were more difficult to reach, and had their own local gods).

The writings of the so-called "Apostolic" Fathers, too, are written in lower-register Greek. Browning (1983: 49) even goes so far as to note that "the Apostolic fathers ... wrote

as they spoke." In Ignatius' letters, for example, we find various lower-register characteristics, such as a reduced set of connective particles (mainly γάρ, οὖν, and δέ),
unclassical words and Latin loanwords (e.g., ἐξεμπλάριον), the improper use of prep-
ositions (e.g., ἐν to denote agent or instrument), the progressive periphrasis (εἰμί with
the present participle), the rather unfrequent use of the optative (which is mainly
reserved for wishes), and so on. Similar features can be found in Hermas' *Shepherd*
[→**Fragment 1**], the *Didachè*, and to a lesser extent Clement of Rome's letters. Various
socio-cultural factors seem to have been relevant for this linguistic choice (cf. Browning
1978: 107; Horrocks 2010: 152–153): (a) that the members of the Christian
community did not belong to the educated elite; rather, they may have felt a certain
contempt for the pagan grammarians and rhetoricians; (b) that the Septuagint and
the New Testament, which enjoyed prestige as literary models, were themselves written in a lower-register; (c) that their writings were primarily intended for in-group
communication, with an audience that would better receive the message in a language (register) they understood.

Literature of the Period of Persecution (Mid-Second to Early Fourth Centuries)

After the initial stage of Christianity, there came about a process of geographical
expansion (primarily Syria, Asia Minor, Greece, and Italy, next to Gaul, Britain, and
Spain). This process was very much aided by three preceding ages of Hellenization,
which had resulted in the establishment of Greek as a *koinè* or *lingua franca*. Socially,
too, Christians started to address the higher strata of society, with a missionary zeal
that was otherwise unknown in antiquity. In their "outreach communication"
(Wahlgren 2010: 530), however, Christian authors had to make a compromise with
regard to their language use: as Norden (1974[1909]: 513) notes, if second-century
writers had addressed a highly educated pagan public using the language of the
Apostolic Fathers, their writings would either not have been read, or rejected as "fish-
ermen's" writings (and in fact, as Norden (1974[1909]: 517) notes, to this public the
Christian writings of the earliest period must have appeared "stilistische Monstra").
This can be situated within the context of "Atticism," a phenomenon that had reached
its peak by the second century CE in the higher cycles of society, and whereby writing
well (that is, similarly to the great Classical writers) became the measure of everything:
"gut oder Schlecht schreiben galt als das Distinktiv von Griechen und Barbaren"
(Norden 1974[1909]: 517). As such, the higher register was adopted by several
Fathers, although it should be noted that its classicism differs from that of the fourth-
century authors, being less diffused and of a somewhat different nature (cf. Fabricius
1967: 195–197; Klock 1987: 115).

The above-mentioned process of evangelization soon led the Church to take a
defensive position, not only against the state (which was normally tolerant of
foreign cults and religions, as long as no exclusive adherence was demanded), but
also against philosophical and other ideological attacks (including the fact that the
Christians' claim for religious superiority was based on writings that were written

in the language of the socially lower classes – compare Origen's *Contra Celsum*, 1.27 for the "vulgarity" of Christianity: οἴεται εἶναι ἰδιωτικήν, διὰ τὸ ἰδιωτικὸν καὶ οὐδαμῶς ἐν λόγοις δυνατὸν ἰδιωτῶν μόνων κρατήσασαν "he [Celsus] believes that [the Christian doctrine] is vulgar, and on account of its vulgarity and its want of reasoning power, obtained a hold only over the ignorant"). For this reason, several of the authors of what Drobner (2007) calls "the period of persecution" are commonly referred to as "apologists" and their works as "apologies": they speak to the pagan majority in self-defense, typically adopting a didactic form of speech (cf. Jaeger 1961: 26–27). In this context, Wifstrand (1962: 63) mentions Tatian, Melito of Sardis, and the letter to Diognetus as "the earliest examples of rhetoric in Christianity." He characterizes their language as elevated, but primarily because of the presence of figures of speech such as antithesis, chiasmus, apostrophe, and so on (which could be considered "stylistic" rather than "registerial"), rather than it being truly Atticizing. Tatian, for example, uses both higher and lower-register features in his *Address to the Greeks*: on the one hand we encounter the optative, particles such as γοῦν, δήπου, and τοιγαροῦν, the verbal adjective in -τέος, perfect forms (including the future perfect) and quotes from classical authors, and on the other hand there are short uncomplicated sentences with little subordination, ὅστις for ὅς, thematic for athematic forms (e.g., ἱστάνω for ἵστημι), and post-classical vocabulary. Justin Martyr, however, seems to have employed a less elevated language: "Justin, du point de vue de la civilisation grecque, est à peine plus qu'à demi cultivé" (Wifstrand 1962: 27). Justin also employed a rather uncommon genre; that is, the dialogue.

As a result of these cultural comprises, the question of the relationship between faith and παιδεία became more and more prominent. As Klock (1987: 61–62) writes:

> Damit wuchs auch die Gefahr der Überfremdung, die dazu hätte führen können, dass das Christentum von seiner kulturell noch überlegenen Umwelt aufgesogen wurde. Sein unantiker Exklusivitätsanspruch hat dies verhindert, doch die Frage, ob der innerste Kern der Glaubensbotschaft durch die Aneignung profaner Bildung berührt werde, war nicht befriedigend gelöst und trat um so schärfer hervor.

A program to bring these two strands together was first developed in second- and third-century Alexandria, with Clement of Alexandria and Origen. The language use of these two Fathers is strikingly different, which, as Browning (1978: 107) notes, can be connected to a difference in audience/purpose. Clement of Alexandria, who is still close to the apologists, uses a highly rhetorical and classicizing language (cf. Wifstrand 1962: 64), addressing himself to an educated pagan public [→**Fragment 2**]. Origen, on the other hand, who is mainly engaged with doctrinal polemic within the Christian church, writes in what Browning calls "technical Koine" (a register also used by medical and mathematical writers). For this purpose, Origen employs traditional forms of Greek scholarship, such as the scientific treatise, critical edition, commentary, and so on (cf. Jaeger 1961: 57).

Literature of the Ascending Imperial Church (Early Fourth Century to circa 430)

The fourth century, as is well known, is the great age of Christianity: after the difficult times from Decius to Diocletian, 'l'église entra soudain dans le plein soleil de la faveur impériale', as Wifstrand (1962: 65) writes. The turning point in the history of the Church was Constantine's conversion and his establishment of religious tolerance. At the end of the century, after a brief revival of pagan religion under Julian the Apostate, Christianity became the public religion of the Roman state under Theodosius, at which point Christians (especially the bishops) entered in a new relation to political power. This must have given a further boost to the spreading of Christianity to the higher social strata, although it should be noted that (a) the spread of Christianity was already fairly substantial in the third century and (b) people from the higher social classes were not won over immediately because there was religious tolerance. As Jaeger (1961: 70) writes:

> For a large part of this class of people [the social elite, KB], the resistance to Christianity was not in the first place an internal religious problem or a positive faith, but a cultural issue. The tradition of their classical education had become for them a religion and had considerable power.

At the forefront of a move towards a Christian "neoclassicism" (Jaeger 1961: 74–75), which had its origins in the great Alexandrians (see earlier), we find "the Cappadocian Fathers," as Basil of Caesarea [→**Fragment 3**], Gregory of Nazianzus, and Gregory of Nyssa are often referred to, together with John Chrysostom. The register chosen by these highly educated men from the higher social classes was, unsurprisingly, the higher one, which, the Atticistic movement had determined, consisted in an imitation of the Classics: in their works we find linguistic features such as the optative, the full range of particles, the dual, the synthetic perfect and future, -ττ- for -σσ- and ξ- for σ-, many references to the classics, and so on (e.g., see Lee (2010) with regard to Basil of Caesarea). At the lexical level, however, words and expressions from the Septuagint and the New Testament were integrated "like technical terms or quotations from a foreign tongue" (Browning 1983: 49–50, cf. Fabricius 1967: 194; Horrocks 2010: 155), and in this respect the Atticism of the fourth-century Fathers must be considered different from the severe Atticism propagated by a figure such as Libanius.

Qualitatively, the works of the Fathers of this third period can compete with the best of pagan literature, and the fourth century is therefore often referred to as "the golden age of patristic literature." With Jaeger (1961: 79–80) we can say that "it was the ambition of these men to create a real Christian literature, able to offer worthwhile products in every literary genre," which is reflected by the fact that Jerome attempted to catalogue Christian authors with their works. Poetry also came to be written, the dominant figure in the field being Gregory of Nazianzus. Gregory's poetry is learned poetry, intended for a select audience. It is composed in classical genres (e.g., didactic poetry, hymn, elegy, epigram) and (quantitative) meters (e.g., dactylic hexameter, iambic trimeter, elegiac distich), containing allusions to earlier poetry, as well as many rare forms and words/expressions.

Literature of the Transition from Late Antiquity to the Early Middle Ages

The choice of the Church Fathers to write in high-register Greek had great importance, since "[their] prestige as models to be imitated was immense throughout the Byzantine period" (Browning 1978: 105). Having become Christian "classics" themselves, they had a huge impact on posterity and its attitude towards the "old" classics and their language. Examples of later Fathers writing in high-register language include Theodoret of Cyrrhus in the field of historiography, Maximus the Confessor in the field of theology, and John of Damascus in the field of homiletics. As Adrados (2005: 199) writes, with Justinian closing the academy in Athens (529 CE), "the Christians ... were given the formidable task of continuing the Attic level of Greek prose and rescuing Ancient Greek literature from obscurity."

Christian prose works written in a lower register can be found within two main genres, both of which were addressed at a broader public; that is, chronicles and saints' biographies (though it should be noted that examples of high-register hagiography are not entirely absent; cf. Høgel 2002: 26–27). Examples of such works written by Fathers of the Church are infrequent, which can be explained by the fact that they often had a high education, and targeted a somewhat different audience. Two early examples, which strictly speaking belong to the previous period discussed, would be Athanasius' *Life of Anthony* [→**Fragment 4**] and Eusebius' *Chronicle*. The latter is only preserved in fragments, whose prose style Treadgold (2007: 26) considers "unpretentious," noting that it was more a technical treatise than a literary work. On this *Chronicle* Eusebius later based his pioneering *Church History*, which is a "more polished and more careful work" (Treagold 2007: 33). Although it is often stressed that the work has little literary elegance, from a purely linguistic point of view it contains various higher-register features, such as the optative, a large set of particles, perfect forms, as well as some poetic words.

In poetry, a genre with a more popular character is that of hymnography (Grosdidier de Matons (1977: 286), in fact, makes a comparison between the language of hymnography and hagiography). While this is a genre that has a long prehistory, being attested already in Archaic times, it develops its own forms during the Patristic age. Three periods are commonly distinguished: an early period (fourth–fifth centuries – associated with the literary form of the "troparion" and the "sticheron"), a middle period (fifth–seventh centuries – associated with the literary form of the "contacion"), and a late period (seventh–ninth centuries – associated with the literary form of the "canon"). The middle period is typically considered the apex, its most well-known and most important representative being Roman the Melodist [→**Fragment 5**]. Well-known representatives of the later period are Andrew of Crete and John of Damasc. Roman the Melodist's hymns were meant to be sung (the stanzas by a cantor and the refrain by a choir) for a large audience, and therefore needed to be comprehensible. They present a number of lower-register features, including the use of simple and accessible vocabulary (rather than archaisms), parataxis, the replacement of second by first aorist forms, the use of periphrastic forms (including εἰμί with the aorist participle), and the absence of the infinitive and optative (see further Grosdidier de Matons (1977: 285–327)). It is also worth noting that an accentual rather than a quantitative meter is used (the latter had

become a real difficulty, since quantitative distinctions had been lost due to the ongoing
sound changes). As such, these poems show little continuity with the language of traditional Greek poetry as represented by Gregory of Nazianzus.

Sample Texts

Hermas: Shepherd (ed. Joly)

Our first fragment was written by Hermas, a freed slave and small-businessman. The
Shepherd is addressed to a Roman audience, and enjoyed great popularity in antiquity.
Through the entire work the main character, Hermas, sees celestial figures who reveal him
truths in the form of mandates, visions, and parables. Formally, the work is an apocalypse,
which is a rather uncommon genre among the Apostolic literature; letters, as the ones
written by Ignatius and Clement, constitute the more traditional format. In the following
passage (from the first vision), Hermas encounters his former mistress, Rhode:

> Ὁ θρέψας με **πέπρακέν** με Ῥόδῃ τινὶ **εἰς** Ῥώμην· μετὰ πολλὰ ἔτη ταύτην ἀνεγνωρισάμην
> καὶ ἠρξάμην αὐτὴν ἀγαπᾶν ὡς ἀδελφήν. μετὰ χρόνον τινὰ λουομένην **εἰς** τὸν ποταμὸν τὸν
> Τίβεριν εἶδον καὶ ἐπέδωκα αὐτῇ τὴν χεῖρα καὶ ἐξήγαγον αὐτὴν ἐκ τοῦ ποταμοῦ. ταύτης οὖν
> ἰδὼν τὸ κάλλος διελογιζόμην ἐν τῇ καρδίᾳ μου λέγων· Μακάριος **ἤμην** εἰ τοιαύτην γυναῖκα
> 5 **εἶχον** καὶ τῷ κάλλει καὶ τῷ τρόπῳ. μόνον τοῦτο ἐβουλευσάμην, ἕτερον δὲ οὐδέν. μετὰ
> χρόνον τινὰ **πορευομένου μου** εἰς Κούμας καὶ δοξάζοντος τὰς κτίσεις τοῦ θεοῦ, ὡς μεγάλαι
> καὶ ἐκπρεπεῖς καὶ δυναταί εἰσιν, περιπατῶν **ἀφύπνωσα**. καὶ πνεῦμά **με** ἔλαβεν καὶ ἀπήνεγκέν
> **με** δι᾽ ἀνοδίας τινός, δι᾽ ἧς ἄνθρωπος οὐκ ἐδύνατο ὁδεῦσαι· ἦν δὲ ὁ τόπος κρημνώδης καὶ
> ἀπερρηγὼς **ἀπὸ** τῶν ὑδάτων. διαβὰς οὖν τὸν ποταμὸν ἐκεῖνον ἦλθον εἰς τὰ ὁμαλά, καὶ **τιθῶ**
> 10 τὰ γόνατα καὶ ἠρξάμην προσεύχεσθαι τῷ κυρίῳ καὶ ἐξομολογεῖσθαί μου τὰς ἁμαρτίας.
> προσευχομένου δέ μου ἠνοίγη ὁ οὐρανός, καὶ **βλέπω** τὴν γυναῖκα ἐκείνην ἣν ἐπεθύμησα
> ἀσπαζομένην με ἐκ τοῦ οὐρανοῦ, λέγουσαν· Ἑρμᾶ, χαῖρε. βλέψας δὲ εἰς αὐτὴν λέγω αὐτῇ·
> Κυρία, τί σὺ ὧδε ποιεῖς; ἡ δὲ **ἀπεκρίθη** μοι· Ἀνελήμφθην ἵνα σου τὰς ἁμαρτίας ἐλέγξω πρὸς
> τὸν κύριον. λέγω αὐτῇ· Νῦν σύ μου ἔλεγχος εἶ; Οὔ, φησίν, ἀλλὰ ἄκουσον τὰ ῥήματα ἅ σοι
> 15 **μέλλω λέγειν**.

(Herm. 1.1.1–6)

He who had brought me up sold me to one Rhode in Rome. Many years after this I recognized her, and I began to love her as a sister. Some time after, I saw her bathe in the river
Tiber; and I gave her my hand, and drew her out of the river. The sight of her beauty made
me think with myself, 'I should be a happy man if I could but get a wife as handsome and
good as she is.' This was the only thought that passed through me: this and nothing more.
A short time after this, as I was walking on my road to the villages, and magnifying the
creatures of God, and thinking how magnificent, and beautiful, and powerful they are, I fell
asleep. And the Spirit carried me away, and took me through a pathless place, through
which a man could not travel, for it was situated in the midst of rocks; it was rugged and
impassible on account of water. Having passed over this river, I came to a plain. I then bent
down on my knees, and began to pray to the Lord and to confess my sins. And as I prayed,
the heavens were opened, and I see the woman whom I had desired saluting me from the

sky, and saying, 'Hail, Hermas!' And looking up to her, I said, 'Lady, what are you doing here?' And she answered me, 'I have been taken up here to accuse you of your sins before the Lord.' 'Lady,' said I, 'are you to be the subject of my accusation?' 'No,' said she; 'but hear the words which I am going to speak to you' (tr. Roberts-Donaldson, slightly modified)

We can note the presence of lower-register features such as (a) the perfect with a perfective (aoristic) value (l. 1); (b) εἰς with a locative value (ll. 1, 2) and ἀπό with a causative one (l. 9); (c) ἤμην for ἦν (l. 4); (d) the use of the bare imperfect (ἤμην) to denote hypothetical consequentiality (l. 4); (e) the incorrect use of the genitive absolute (l. 6); (f) post-classical ἀφυπνόω "I fall asleep" (l. 7); (g) the repetition of the enclitic pronoun με (ll. 7–8); (h) τιθῶ for τίθημι (l. 9); (i) βλέπω for ὁράω (l. 11); (j) ἀπεκρίθη for ἀπεκρινάμην (l. 13); (k) periphrastic μέλλω (l. 15) as an immediative future (English "I am going to"). Noteworthy from a more general point of view are the short paratactic sentences, the fact that connective particles are not used consistently (and are mainly limited to οὖν and δέ), and the predominantly VSO (verb–subject–object) word order (cf. Horrocks 2010: 277–281).

Clement of Alexandria: Protreptic (ed. Marcovich)

The "protreptic" was a common literary genre in Antiquity; in it, the author encourages his audience to the study of a subject, typically philosophy. Aristotle, Epicurus, and Cicero, for example, are known to have written such "hortatory addresses." Clement's purpose is to convince his cultivated audience of the superiority of Christianity, criticizing the pagan cults and myths:

Ἀλλ' ἐκ πατέρων, **φατέ, παραδεδομένον** ἡμῖν ἔθος ἀνατρέπειν οὐκ εὔλογον. Καὶ τί δὴ οὐχὶ τῇ πρώτῃ τροφῇ, τῷ γάλακτι, χρώμεθα, ᾧ **δήπουθεν** συνείθισαν ἡμᾶς ἐκ γενετῆς αἱ τίτθαι; Τί δὲ αὐξάνομεν ἢ μειοῦμεν τὴν πατρῴαν οὐσίαν, καὶ οὐχὶ τὴν ἴσην, ὡς **παρειλήφαμεν,** διαφυλάττομεν; Τί δὲ οὐκέτι τοῖς κόλποις τοῖς πατρῴοις ἐναποβλύζομεν, ἤ καὶ τά ἄλλα, ἃ

5   νηπιάζοντες ὑπὸ μητράσιν **τε** ἐκτρεφόμενοι γέλωτα ὤφλομεν, ἐπιτελοῦμεν ἔτι, ἀλλὰ σφᾶς αὐτούς, καὶ εἰ μὴ παιδαγωγῶν ἐτύχομεν ἀγαθῶν, ἐπανωρθώσαμεν; Εἶτα ἐπὶ <**μὲν**> τῶν πάτων αἱ παρεκβάσεις καίτοι ἐπιζήμιοι καὶ ἐπισφαλεῖς οὖσαι, ὅμως γλυκεῖαί πως προσπίπτουσιν, ἐπὶ **δὲ** τοῦ βίου οὐχὶ τὸ ἔθος καταλιπόντες τὸ πονηρὸν καὶ ἐμπαθὲς καὶ ἄθεον, κἄν οἱ πατέρες χαλεπαίνωσιν, ἐπὶ τὴν ἀλήθειαν **ἐκκλινοῦμεν** καὶ τὸν ὄντως ὄντα πατέρα **ἐπιζητήσομεν,** οἷον

10 δηλητήριον φάρμακον τὴν συνήθειαν ἀπωσάμενοι; Τοῦτ' αὐτὸ γάρ **τοι** τὸ κάλλιστον τῶν ἐγχειρουμένων ἐστίν, ὑποδεῖξαι ὑμῖν ὡς ἀπὸ μανίας καὶ τοῦ τρισαθλίου τούτου ἔθους ἐμισήθη ἡ θεοσέβεια· οὐ γάρ ἄν ἐμισήθη ποτὲ ἡ ἀπηγορεύθη ἀγαθὸν τοσοῦτον, οὖ μεῖζον οὐδὲν ἐκ θεοῦ **δεδώρηταί** πω τῇ τῶν ἀνθρώπων γενέσει, εἰ μὴ συναρπαζόμενοι τῷ ἔθει, εἶτα **μέντοι** ἀποβύσαντες τὰ **ὦτα** ἡμῖν, οἷον ἵπποι σκληραύχενες ἀφηνιάζοντες, **τοὺς χαλινοὺς**

15 **ἐνδακόντες,** ἀποφεύγετε τοὺς λόγους, ἀποσείσασθαι **μὲν** τοὺς ἡνιόχους ὑμῶν τοῦ βίου ἡμᾶς ἐπιποθοῦντες, ἐπὶ **δὲ** τοὺς κρημνοὺς τῆς ἀπωλείας ὑπὸ τῆς ἀνοίας φερόμενοι, ἐναγῆ τὸν ἅγιον ὑπολαμβάνετε τοῦ θεοῦ λόγον. Ἕπεται **τοιγαροῦν** ὑμῖν κατὰ τὸν Σοφοκλέα τὰ ἐπίχειρα τῆς ἐκλογῆς, **νοῦς φροῦδος, ὦτ' ἀχρεῖα, φροντίδες κεναί.**

(Clem., *Prot.* 10.89.1–3, 10.90.1)

But you say it is not creditable to subvert the customs handed down to us from our fathers. And why, then, do we not still use our first nourishment, milk, to which our nurses accustomed us from the time of our birth? Why do we increase or diminish our patrimony, and not keep it exactly the same as we got it? Why do we not still vomit on our parents' breasts, or still do the things for which, when infants, and nursed by our mothers, we were laughed at, but have corrected ourselves, even if we did not fall in with good instructors? Then, if excesses in the indulgence of the passions, though pernicious and dangerous, yet are accompanied with pleasure, why do we not in the conduct of life abandon that usage which is evil, and provocative of passion, and godless, even should our fathers feel hurt, and betake ourselves to the truth, and seek Him who is truly our Father, rejecting custom as a deleterious drug? For of all that I have undertaken to do, the task I now attempt is the noblest, viz., to demonstrate to you how inimical this insane and most wretched custom is to godliness. For a boon so great, the greatest ever given by God to the human race, would never have been hated and rejected, had not you been carried away by custom, and then shut your ears against us; and just as unmanageable horses throw off the reins, and take the bit between their teeth, you rush away from the arguments addressed to you, in your eager desire to shake yourselves clear of us, who seek to guide the chariot of your life, and, impelled by your folly, dash towards the precipices of destruction, and regard the holy word of God as an accursed thing. The reward of your choice, therefore, as described by Sophocles, follows: "The mind a blank, useless ears, vain thoughts." (tr. Roberts-Donaldson)

We can note the presence of higher-register linguistic features such as: (a) the use of enclitic φατε rather than λέγετε (l. 1), (b) the particles δή, δήπουθεν, μέν ... δέ μέντοι, τε, τοι, τοιγαροῦν (ll. 1, 2, 5, 6, 8, 10, 13, 15, 16, 17); (c) the synthetic perfect (ll. 1, 3, 13); (d) the synthetic future (l. 9); (e) οὖς rather than ὠτίον (l. 14); (f) the Platonic image/expression τοὺς χαλινοὺς ἐνδακόντες (Pl., *Phdr.* 254d) (ll. 14–15); (g) the quote from Sophocles (l. 18) (Soph., *Fragm.* 949.2). Noteworthy from a more general point of view are the long, complex sentences, and the frequent employment of the participle (in all its uses).

Basil the Great: To young men (ed. Boulenger)

In his famous and much-discussed essay *To young men*, Basil the Great treats the relationship between Christian and pagan-antique *paideia*. The treatise is formally addressed to his nephews (age 15/16?) (perhaps with a wider Christian audience in mind), who were confronted with the classics on a daily basis in their education. Basil notes that classical texts are morally valuable for Christians when (a) they incite to virtue or (b) illustrate how virtue can be realized. Such texts have a preparatory or "propaedeutic" value: they provide a preliminary training before one is ready to approach the Holy Scriptures. Basil's treatise has some affinity with Clement's *Protreptic*, since the nephews are admonished to seek an anticipation of the truth in the pagan authors.

Ἀλλά ταῦτα **μέν** που κἂν τοῖς ἡμετέροις λόγοις τελειότερον **μαθησόμεθα·** ὅσον δὲ σκια-
γραφίαν τινά τῆς ἀρετῆς, **τό γε νῦν εἶναι,** ἐκ τῶν ἔξωθεν παιδευμάτων περιγραψώμεθα. Τοῖς
γάρ ἐπιμελῶς ἐξ ἑκάστου τὴν ὠφέλειαν ἀθροίζουσιν, ὥσπερ τοῖς μεγάλοις τῶν ποταμῶν,
πολλαὶ γίνεσθαι πολλαχόθεν αἱ προσθῆκαι **πεφύκασι.** Τὸ γάρ καὶ **σμικρὸν ἐπὶ σμικρῷ**
5   κατατίθεσθαι, οὐ μᾶλλον εἰς ἀργυρίου προσθήκην ἢ καὶ εἰς **ἠντιναοῦν** ἐπιστήμην, ὀρθῶς
ἔχειν ἡγεῖσθαι τῷ ποιητῇ προσῆκεν.΄Ο **μὲν** οὖν Βίας τῷ υἱεῖ, πρὸς Αἰγυπτίους ἀπαίροντι, καὶ
πυνθανομένῳ τί ἂν ποιῶν αὐτῷ μάλιστα **κεχαρισμένα πράττοι·** «Ἐφόδιον, ἔφη, πρὸς γῆρας
κτησάμενος», τὴν ἀρετὴν **δὴ** τὸ ἐφόδιον λέγων, μικροῖς ὅροις αὐτὴν περιγράφων, ὅς γε
ἀνθρωπίνῳ βίῳ τὴν ἀπ' αὐτῆς ὠφέλειαν ὥριζετο. ἐγὼ **δὲ** κἂν τὸ Τιθωνοῦ τις γῆρας, κἂν τὸ
10   Ἀργανθωνίου λέγῃ, κἂν τὸ τοῦ μακροβιωγῆρας, κἂν τὸ Ἀργανθωνίου λέγῃ, κἂν τὸ τοῦ
μακροβιωτάτου παρ' ἡμῖν Μαθουσάλα, ὃς χίλια ἔτη τριάκοντα δεόντων βιῶναι λέγεται, κἂν
σύμπαντα τὸν ἀφ' οὗ **γεγόνασιν** ἄνθρωποι χρόνον ἀναμετρῇ, ὡς ἐπὶ παίδων διανοίας
γελάσομαι, εἰς τὸν μακρὸν ἀποσκοπῶν καὶ **ἀγήρω** αἰῶνα, οὗ πέρας οὐδὲν ἔστι τῇ ἐπινοίᾳ
λαβεῖν, οὐ μᾶλλόν γε ἢ τελευτὴν ὑποθέσθαι τῆς ἀθανάτου ψυχῆς. Πρὸς **ὅνπερ** κτᾶσθαι
15   **παραινέσαιμ'** ἂν τά ἐφόδια, πάντα λίθον, κατὰ τὴν παροιμίαν, κινοῦντας, ὅθεν ἂν μέλλῃ
τις ὑμῖν ἐπ' αὐτὸν ὠφέλεια **γενήσεσθαι.** Μηδ' ὅτι χαλεπά ταῦτα καὶ πόνου δεόμενα, διά
τοῦτ' ἀποκνήσωμεν. ἀλλ' ἀναμνησθέντας τοῦ παραινέσαντος, ὅτι δέοι βίον **μὲν** ἄριστον
αὐτὸν ἕκαστον προαιρεῖσθαι, ἡδὺν **δὲ** προσδοκᾶν τῇ συνηθείᾳ **γενήσεσθαι,** ἐγχειρεῖν τοῖς
βελτίστοις. Αἰσχρὸν γάρ τὸν παρόντα καιρὸν προεμένους ὕστερόν ποτ' ἀνακαλεῖσθαι τὸ
παρελθόν, ὅτε οὐδὲν ἔσται πλέον ἀνιωμένοις.

(Bas., *Leg. Lib. Gent.* 10)

To be sure, we shall become more intimately acquainted with these precepts in the
sacred writings, but it is incumbent upon us, for the present, to trace, as it were, the sil-
houette of virtue in the pagan authors. For those who carefully gather the useful from
each book are wont, like mighty rivers, to gain accessions on every hand. For the precept
of the poet which bids us add little to little must be taken as applying not so much to the
accumulation of riches, as of the various branches of learning. In line with this Bias said
to his son, who, as he was about to set out for Egypt, was inquiring what course he could
pursue to give his father the greatest satisfaction: "Store up means for the journey of old
age." By *means* he meant virtue, but he placed too great restrictions upon it, since he
limited its usefulness to the earthly life. For if any one mentions the old age of Tithonus,
or of Arganthonius, or of that Methuselah who is said to have lacked but thirty years of
being a millenarian, or even if he reckons the entire period since the creation, I will laugh
as at the fancies of a child, since I look forward to that long, undying age, of the extent of
which there is no limit for the mind of man to grasp, any more than there is of the life
immortal. For the journey of this life eternal I would advise you to husband resources,
leaving no stone unturned, as the proverb has it, whence you might derive any aid. From
this task we shall not shrink because it is hard and laborious, but, remembering the precept that every man ought to choose the better life, and expecting that association will
render it pleasant, we shall busy ourselves with those things that are best. For it is shame-
ful to squander the present, and later to call back the past in anguish, when no more time
is given. (tr. Padelford)

We can note the presence of higher-register linguistic features such as: (a) the
synthetic future (ll. 1, 13, 16, 18); (b) the absolute infinitive (l. 2); (c) particles such as

γε, δή, μέν ... δέ and -περ (ll. 1, 2, 6, 8, 9, 14, 17, 18); (d) the synthetic perfect (ll. 4, 7, 12); (e) the form ἡντιναοῦν (l. 5); (f) the optative (ll. 7, 15, 17); (g) the reference to Hesiod (*Op.* 361) (l. 4); (h) adjectives in -ως, following the "Attic" declension (l. 13). Noteworthy from a more general point of view are the long, complex sentences.

Athanasius: Life of Anthony (ed. Bartelink)

Athanasius' most important ascetic work, probably written during a priod of exile in the desert, is the *Life of Anthony*, which became the hagiographical model *par excellence*. It was designed, as stated in the preface, for circulation among monks overseas, to inform them about Anthony's life. As Sevčenko (1980:62) notes, the *Life* shows little respect for and understanding of classical culture: the main figure, the hermit Anthony, is an illiterate Copt, who does not speak Greek, and converses with the 'Hellenic' philosophers through an interpreter.

Οὕτω μὲν οὖν ἑαυτὸν ἄγων ἠγαπᾶτο **παρά** πάντων ὁ Ἀντώνιος. Αὐτὸς δὲ τοῖς σπουδαίοις πρὸς οὓς ἀπήρχετο, γνησίως ὑπετάσσετο καὶ καθ' ἑαυτὸν ἑκάστου τὸ πλεονέκτημα τῆς σπουδῆς καὶ τῆς ἀσκήσεως κατεμάνθανεν. **Καὶ** τοῦ μὲν τὸ χαρίεν, τοῦ δὲ τὸ πρὸς τάς εὐχάς σύντονον ἐθεώρει· καὶ ἄλλου μὲν τὸ ἀόργητον, ἄλλου δὲ τὸ φιλάνθρωπον κατενόει· **καὶ** τῷ μὲν

5   **ἀγρυπνοῦντι**, τῷ δὲ φιλολογοῦντι προσεῖχεν· **καὶ** τὸν μὲν **ἐν** καρτερίᾳ, τὸν δὲ **ἐν** νηστείαις καὶ **χαμευνίαις** ἐθαύμαζεν· καὶ το ῦ μὲν τὴν πραότητα, τοῦ δὲ τὴν **μακροθυμίαν** παρετηρεῖτο· πάντων δὲ ὁμοῦ τὴν εἰς τὸν Χριστὸν εὐσέβειαν καὶ τὴν πρὸς ἀλλήλους ἀγάπην ἐσημειοῦτο. **Καὶ** οὕτω πεπληρωμένος **ὑπέστρεφεν εἰς** τὸν ἴδιον τοῦ **ἀσκητηρίου** τόπον· λοιπὸν αὐτὸς τά παρ' ἑκάστου συνάγων εἰς ἑαυτὸν ἐσπούδαζεν ἐν ἑαυτῷ τά πάντα δεικνύναι. **Καὶ** γάρ

10   ἐσπούδαζεν ἐν ἑαυτῷ τά πάντα δεικνύναι. **Καὶ** γάρ πρὸς τοὺς καθ' ἡλικίαν ἴσους οὐκ ἦν φιλόνεικος ἢ μόνον ἵνα μὴ δεύτερος ἐκείνων ἐν τοῖς βελτίοσι φαίνηται. **Καὶ** τοῦτο ἔπραττεν ὥστε μηδένα λυπεῖν, ἀλλά κἀκείνους ἐπ' αὐτῷ χαίρειν. Πάντες μὲν οὖν οἱ ἀπὸ τῆς κώμης καὶ οἱ φιλόκαλοι, πρὸς οὓς εἶχε τὴν συνήθειαν, οὕτως αὐτὸν ὁρῶντες, ἐκάλουν θεοφιλῆ **καὶ** οἱ μὲν ὡς υἱόν, οἱ δὲ ὡς ἀδελφὸν ἠσπάζοντο.

(Ath., *V. Anton.* 1.4.1–4)

Thus conducting himself, Antony was beloved by all. He subjected himself in sincerity to the good men whom he visited, and learned thoroughly where each surpassed him in zeal and discipline. He observed the graciousness of one; the unceasing prayer of another; he took knowledge of another's freedom from anger and another's loving-kindness; he gave heed to one as he watched, to another as he studied; one he admired for his endurance, another for his fasting and sleeping on the ground; the meekness of one and the long-suffering of another he watched with care, while he took note of the piety towards Christ and the mutual love which animated all. Thus filled, he returned to his own place of discipline, and henceforth would strive to unite the qualities of each, and was eager to show in himself the virtues of all. With others of the same age he had no rivalry; save this only, that he should not be second to them in higher things. And this he did so as to hurt the feelings of nobody, but made them rejoice over him. So all they of that village and the good men in whose intimacy he was, when they saw that he was a man of this sort, used to call him God-beloved. And some welcomed him as a son, others as a brother. (tr. Ellershaw)

We can note the presence of lower-register linguistic features such as (a) παρά as an agent expression (l. 1); (b) post-classical ἀγρυπνέω (with the meaning of "I am watchful"), χαμευνία, μακροθυμία, ὑποστρέφω (with the meaning of "I return"), ἀσκητήριον (ll. 5, 6, 8); (c) the construction of ἐθαύμαζεν with ἐν rather than the accusative or genitive case (l. 5). Particularly noteworthy from a more general point of view are the short paratactic sentences, and the very frequent use of connective καί.

Roman the Melodist: Hymn on the Nativity (ed. Grosdidier de Matons)

Roman the Melodist's hymns are often considered one of the highlights of Byzantine literature. While hymnography as a genre goes back to Archaic times, Roman's liturgical hymns (so-called "contacia") represent an innovation, which he perfected. The following is a fragment from his *Hymn on the nativity*, Roman's best-known work, in which Mary and the *Magi* address each other (the insertion of direct speech being a typical characteristic of Roman's work):

```
      Οἱ δὲ μάγοι εὐθὺς    ὥρμησαν εἰς τὸν θάλαμον,
        καὶ ἰδόντες Χριστὸν    ἔφριξαν, ὅτι εἴδοσαν
        τὴν τούτου μητέρα,    τὸν ταύτης μνηστῆρα,
        καὶ φόβῳ εἶπον  «Οὗτος υἱός ἐστιν ἀγενεαλόγητος;
5       Καὶ πῶς, παρθένε,    τὸν μνηστευσάμενον
        βλέπομεν ἀκμὴν ἔνδον τοῦ οἴκου σου;
        Οὐκ ἔσχε μῶμον    ἡ κύησις σου·
        μὴ ἡ κατοίκησις ψεχθῇ    συνόντος σοι τοῦ ἰωσὴφ·
        πλῆθος ἔχεις φθονούντων    ἐρευνώντων ποῦ ἐτέχθη
10      παιδίον νέον,  ὁ πρὸ αἰώνων Θεός.

      — Ὑπομνήσω ὑμᾶς,   μάγοις Μαρία ἔφησε,
        τίνος χάριν κρατῶ    τὸν Ἰωσὴφ ἐν οἴκῳ μου·
        εἰς ἔλεγχον πάντων    τῶν καταλαλούντων·
15      αὐτὸς γὰρ λέξει ἅπερ ἀκήκοε    περὶ τοῦ παιδίου μου·
        ὑπνῶν γὰρ εἶδεν    ἄγγελον ἅγιον
        λέγοντα αὐτῷ    πόθεν συνέλαβον·
        πυρίνη θέα    τὸν ἀκανθώδη
        ἐπληροφόρησε νυκτὸς    περὶ τῶν λυπούντων αὐτόν·
20      δι' αὐτὸ σύνεστί μοι    Ἰωσὴφ δηλῶν ὡς ἔστι
        παιδίον νέον    ὁ πρὸ αἰώνων Θεός.

      Ῥητορεύει σαφῶς    ἅπαντα ἅπερ ἤκουσεν·
        ἀπαγγέλλει τρανῶς    ὅσα αὐτὸς ἑώρακεν
25      ἐν τοῖς οὐρανίοις    καὶ τοῖς ἐπιγείοις·
        τὰ τῶν ποιμένων,    πῶς συνανύμνησαν πηλίνοις οἱ πύρινοι·
```

ὑμῶν τῶν μάγων,   ὅτι προέδραμεν
ἄστρον φωταυγοῦν   καὶ ὁδηγοῦν ὑμᾶς·
διὸ ἀφέντες   τὰ προρρηθέντα,
30   ἐκδιηγήσασθε ἡμῖν τὰ νῦν γενόμενα ὑμῖν,
πόθεν **ἥκατε**, πῶς δὲ   συνήκατε ὅτι ὤφθη
παιδίον νέον,   ὁ πρὸ αἰώνων Θεός.»

(Rom., Mel. 10.10–12)

The magi at once hastened into the room / and, seeing Christ, they trembled as they saw / his mother and her betrothed. / And in fear they said, "This is a son without ancestry. / And how is it, O Virgin, that at this moment we see / your betrothed within your house? / Was your conceiving blameless? / Will people not find fault at Joseph's living with you? / You have a multitude of jealous people enquiring where there has been born / A little Child, God before the ages". "I will tell you", Mary said to the magi, / "why I keep Joseph in my house: / to refute all those who slander me. / He will tell what he has heard about my Child. / For in his sleep he saw a holy angel / who told him how I had conceived. / In the night a fiery vision told / the creature of thorn about the things which grieved him. / That is why Joseph is with me, to show that there is / A little Child, God before the ages." / "He proclaims nearly all he has heard. / He declares openly all that he has seen / in heaven and on earth: / the story of the shepherds, how beings of fire sang praises with ones of clay, / that of you, magi, how a star hastened before you, / lighting your way and guiding you. / And so, leaving aside all that you said before, / now recount to us what has befallen you. / Where have you come from, how did you understand that there had appeared / A little Child, God before the ages?" (tr. Lash)

We can note the presence of lower-register linguistic features such as: (a) the aorist form εἴδοσαν (for εἶδον) (l. 2); (b) post-classical usages such as μνηστήρ "fiancé," πῶς "how come, why," βλέπω "I see," κρατῶ "I have, hold," καταλαλέω "I slander," συνανυμνέω "I celebrate in song together with" (ll. 3, 5, 6, 13, 14, 26); (c) ἔνδον as a preposition (l. 6); (d) the use of the causative particle διό (l. 29); (e) the perfect form ἥκατε (l. 31). Noteworthy from a more general point of view is the use of very short, paratactic sentences, and the reduced set of particles.

Conclusion

As this short overview may have shown, the 'Greek of the Fathers' was quite varied. One promising way of addressing this linguistic variation is, I have argued, by means of the concept 'register'. Whereas initially the writings of the Church Fathers can be situated towards the lower end of the register-continuum, soon the higher register was adopted, so that a dialogue could be initiated with the higher, pagan strata in society. Once Christianity became the state religion, the higher register continued to form the standard, with the exception of some genres.

Bibliography

Adrados, F.R. (2005), *A History of the Greek Language*. Leiden: Brill.

Browning, R. (1978), "The language of Byzantine literature". In *The 'Past' in Medieval and Modern Greek Culture*, S. Vryonis (ed.). Malibu, CA: Undena Publications; 103–133.

Browning, R. (1983), *Medieval and Modern Greek*, 2nd edn. Cambridge: Cambridge University Press.

Deissmann, A. (1908), *New Light on the New Testament*. Edinburgh: T&T Clark.

Drobner, H.R. (2007), *The Fathers of the Church*. Peabody, MA: Hendrickson.

Fabricius, C. (1967), "Der sprachliche Klassizismus der griechischen Kirchenväter: Ein philologisches und geistesgeschichtliches Problem". *JAC*, 10: 187–199.

Gagé, J. (1964), *Les classes sociales dans l'Empire romain*. Paris: Payot.

Grosdidier de Matons, J. (1977), *Romanos le Mélode et les origines de la poésie religieuse à Byzance*. Paris: Editions Beauchesne.

Halliday, M. (1978), *Language as Social Semiotic*. London: Hodder Arnold.

Høgel, C. (2002), *Symeon Metaphrastes: Rewriting and Canonisation*. Copenhagen: Museum Tusculanum Press.

Horrocks, G. (2007), "Syntax: from Classical Greek to the Koine". In *A History of Ancient Greek*, A.P. Christidis (ed.). Cambridge: Cambridge University Press; 618–631.

Horrocks, G. (2010), *Greek: A History of the Language and its Speakers*, 2nd edn. Oxford: Wiley–Blackwell.

Jaeger, W. (1961), *Early Christianity and Greek Paideia*. Cambridge, MA: Harvard University Press.

Janse, M. (2007), "The Greek of the New Testament". In *A History of Ancient Greek*, A.-F. Christidis (ed.). Cambridge: Cambridge University Press; 646–653.

Judge, E.A. (2008), *Social Distinctives of the Christians in the First Century*. Peabody, MA: Hendrickson.

Klock, C. (1987), *Untersuchungen zu Stil und Rhythmus bei Gregor von Nyssa*. Frankfurt am Main: Athenäum Verlag.

Lee, J.A.L. (2010), "Why didn't St Basil write in New Testament Greek?". *Phronema*, 25: 3–20.

Mohrmann, C. (1957), "Linguistic problems in the early Christian church". *VC*, 11, 11–36.

Norden, E. (1974[1909]), *Die antike Kunstprosa vom VI. Jahrhundert V. Chr. bis in die Zeit der Renaissance*, 7th edn. Leipzig: Teubner.

Porter, S.E. (1989), *Verbal Aspect in the Greek of the New Testament*. New York: Lang.

Sevčenko, I. (1980), "A shadow outline of virtue: the Classical heritage of Greek Christian literature". In *The Age of Spirituality. A Symposium*, K. Weitzmann (ed.). New York: Metropolitan Museum of Art; 53–73.

Sevčenko, I. (1981), "Levels of style in Byzantine prose". *JÖB*, 31: 289–312.

Theissen, G. (1974), "Soziale Schichtung in der korinthischen Gemeinde. Ein Beitrag zur Soziologie des hellenistischen Urchristentums". *ZNW*, 65: 232–272.

Treadgold, W.T. (2007), *The Early Byzantine Historians*. New York: Palgrave Macmillan.

Vogt, J. (1975), "Der Vorwurf der sozialen Niedrigkeit des frühen Christentums". *Gymnasium*, 82: 401–411.

Wahlgren, S. (2010), "Byzantine literature and the Classical past". In *A Companion to the Ancient Greek Language*, E.J. Bakker (ed.). Oxford: Wiley–Blackwell; 527–538.

Wifstrand, A. (1962), *L'église ancienne et la culture grecque*. Paris: Éditions du Cerf.

CHAPTER 32

The Latin of the Fathers

Carolinne White

Introduction

In Jerome's Letter 49, in the course of a lengthy attempt at self-defense after the publication of his tirade against marriage in the work attacking Jovinianus, he lists a number of Latin writers –Tertullian, Cyprian, Minucius Felix, Marius Victorinus, Lactantius, Hilary, and Ambrose. This list reveals those Christian Latin authors regarded as authoritative at the end of the fourth century; indeed, if we supplement this list with a few writers whose authority came to be accepted in the following centuries, namely Jerome himself, Augustine, Gregory the Great, Isidore of Seville, and Bede, we have an overview of the most influential writers who, during the period 200–720, can collectively be termed "the Latin Fathers." These writers formed a chain through time, as it were, with each link conscious of those that came before it, whether admiring or critical, and with each link inspiring and influencing the thought and writing of those that came after it, well beyond the date 720.

As well as their commitment to, and broad vision of, their Christian faith, these writers have in common a high degree of learning – in classical literature, in Holy Scripture, and, as time went on, in their predecessors' works on matters of Christian doctrine, spirituality, and lifestyle. Their education – and for the earlier writers this took place within the traditional non-Christian education system – would have included the study of grammar and rhetoric, with emphasis on the imitation of classical literary models; they might also study Greek, philosophy, law, or other subjects of the quadrivium. This is not to say that all wrote uniformly in imitation of classical models; they were also exposed to other styles and registers of writing in Latin, as well as being aware of linguistic varieties resulting from the inevitable difference between spoken and written Latin and from regional differences. As imperial government gradually gave way to ecclesiastical dominance in the western Roman Empire, education, too, became

The Wiley Blackwell Companion to Patristics, First Edition. Edited by Ken Parry.
© 2015 John Wiley & Sons Ltd. Published 2019 by John Wiley & Sons Ltd.

increasingly the responsibility of the Church: at the end of our period Bede provides an example of one whose learning in the classical liberal arts, as well as in Scripture and the writings of his predecessors, was gained exclusively within the monastery, stocked with books from Rome by his teacher, the abbot of Monkwearmouth–Jarrow, Benedict Biscop. So, despite the changes as Christianity went from being a persecuted religion at the beginning of the period, to the official religion and then the predominant cultural force, we can see a strong element of continuity in the influences on these writers, which remained a varying combination of Scripture, earlier Christian writers, and non-Christian culture.

However, it seems that Christians only began to use Latin as a written language for their works on religious matters at a relatively late date, some 150 years after the death of Christ, for Greek was the first language of the early Church – the language of its Bible, both in the Old Testament (in the much venerated version of the Septuagint translation from the Hebrew, made in the third century BC) and as the original language of the New Testament (which itself incorporated a handful of Latin terms into its Greek). The liturgy, too, was performed in Greek, in the west as well as the east, until the papacy of Damasus (366–384), when Latin gained the ascendancy. Even the first works of Christian apology and anti-heretical polemics in the west were composed in Greek, works such as Clement of Rome's First Letter to the Corinthians, written in the last years of the first century, the *Adversus Haereses*, composed around 180 by Irenaeus, a native of Smyrna who became bishop of Lyons, and the works of Hippolytus of Rome in the early third century. However, already by the end of the second century the first two of these works existed in Latin translations – indeed, Irenaeus' work has survived complete solely in a Latin translation. The predominance of Greek as the language of the early Church is not surprising if one bears in mind not only that the use of the Bible in Greek would have given that language authority in the Church but also that Greek and Latin bilingualism was widespread in many parts of the Roman Empire at this period, among the educated as well as more generally in large cities and trading centers.

The Latin of the Bible

Nevertheless, as Christianity put down roots in Rome and other areas of the Western Empire where Latin was the principal language, a need was felt for a Latin translation of the Bible. Various versions of these early Biblical translations survive, marked by regional variants and different choices of synonyms. To these versions, as evidenced in a multiplicity of fragments in extant manuscripts and as citations in early Christian literature, is now given the general, and rather misleadingly simple, name of *Vetus Latina* (Old Latin). However, the textual history is complex, and much work remains to be done, primarily at the *Vetus Latina Institut* in Germany, before a full account of these Christian texts is available.

Despite the importance of these texts, and their linguistic influence, it seems unlikely that any official Latin version of the whole Bible existed at this early period when the Church was still growing at a local level rather than as a centralized institution; it may be that there were simply local versions of the most commonly used books of the Bible, such as the Psalms and Gospels. Sometimes, it seems, an ad hoc translation, orally or in writing, was made of a verse or passage without resort to a preexistent translation (Frisius 2011: 21).

It is possible that the earliest translations of the Bible into Latin were made in North Africa. Evidence of this is provided by the account of the interrogation by the Roman authorities of the 12 Latin-speaking Christian men and women collectively known as the Scillitan martyrs, executed in Carthage in 180. This account, usually said to be the first surviving work of a specifically Christian nature composed in Latin, mentions a (presumably Latin) copy of some of St Paul's Epistles in their possession.

A few years later an account of the events leading up to the martyrdom in 203 of Perpetua and Felicitas contains a handful of quotes from the Old and New Testaments, indicating familiarity with a Latin Bible.

More evidence as to the use of the early Latin Bible text becomes available once the theological and polemical writings of the Church Fathers begin to appear – of whom Tertullian, writing in about 200, is acknowledged to be the first. Tertullian demonstrates a broad acquaintance with both the Old and New Testaments, but in citing from the Bible his citations of any passage are not always uniform; this suggests that he translated some passages himself, an indication that there remained a degree of freedom of translation. For example, in his work *De praescriptione haereticorum*, he translates the Greek word *aperantos* from 1 Tim. 1: 4 variously as *interminabilis* and *indeterminatus*, choosing not to employ the synonym *interminatus* that occurs in Cicero and Apuleius but which was later used in the Vulgate.

Fifty years later, by the time Cyprian, also at Carthage, is writing prolifically, and Novatian is producing his work on the Trinity in Rome, the Biblical citations are more uniform, likely evidence of the existence of an official text. However, despite the greater uniformity apparent from the mid-third century, even as late as the end of the fourth century Augustine refers (*de Doctrina Christiana* II 11.34) to "the infinite variety of Latin translators" of the Bible.

Before considering the language of the Latin Fathers it is important to outline the characteristics of the language and style of these early Latin versions, both the *Vetus Latina* and of Jerome's revised versions, given that this text formed the linguistic, stylistic, and theological basis of so much Latin literature, permeating the Latin language at all levels right through the Middle Ages.

An example of the Latin of the New Testament is given in a passage from St Mark's Gospel (1: 9–13, with the English translation of the Revised Standard Version):

> *et factum est in diebus illis venit Iesus a Nazareth Galilaeae et baptizatus est in Iordane a Johanne et statim ascendens de aqua vidit apertos caelos et Spiritum tamquam columbam descendentem et manentem in ipso et vox facta est de caelis "tu es Filius meus dilectus, in te conplacui" et statim Spiritus expulit eum in desertum et erat in deserto quadraginta diebus et quadraginta noctibus et temptabatur a Satana eratque cum bestiis et angeli ministrabant illi*
>
> (In those days Jesus came from Nazareth of Galilee and was baptized by John in the Jordan. And when he came up out of the water, immediately he saw the heavens opened and the Spirit descending upon him like a dove; and a voice came from heaven, "Thou art

my beloved Son; with thee I am well pleased." The Spirit immediately drove him out into the wilderness. And he was in the wilderness forty days, tempted by Satan; and he was with the wild beasts; and the angels ministered to him.)

A marked characteristic of the Latin syntax of the Bible is that it tends to follow the Greek and (in the Old Testament) the Hebrew closely so as to remain faithful to the message of the text. Augustine states (*de Doctrina Christiana* II 15.53) that, of the various Latin versions, he considers the one he calls the *Itala* (by which he probably means a version familiar in Italy) to be the best when read alongside the original Greek because it is closer to the original and its meaning therefore clearer. On the other hand, without the original, a literal translation might seem incomprehensible: in the same work (III 1–2) Augustine advises the reader of Scripture to arm himself with a knowledge of languages, a good all-round education, a reliable text derived from a comparison of different manuscripts, and to attempt to understand ambiguous passages either by trying different ways of punctuating and articulating them, or by applying a figurative interpretation, to see if either of these methods offers an understanding in harmony with the fundamentals of Christian doctrine. Jerome gives a different reason for retaining a literal translation: he claims in Letter 57 that when translating Scripture he does so more literally than when translating nonscriptural texts because the word order of the original has a mystery that needs to be preserved. This literalness was evident even in the choice of words, with the translators retaining Hebrew words (such as *alleluia* and *amen*) and Greek ones in Latin form (such as *ecclesia, apostolus, baptismus, eucharistia, pascha, evangelium, angelus,* and *baptizare*), which were to become everyday words in Christian Latin.

On the level of semantics, ordinary words such as *dominus, oratio, vita, mors,* and *caro*, frequently took on a new significance or semantic range in the new theological context.

Or to look at the Latin of the Bible from a different point of view, one might characterize it, as Lactantius did in the early fourth century (*Divine Institutes* V 1), as being aimed at the understanding of ordinary people. Indeed, Jerome explicitly says in Letter 49, when working on his revised translation, that the Latin of the Bible should speak "*universo hominum generi*" (to the whole human race) and not just to a few educated people who find Cicero's eloquence more attractive.

But while one might argue for the benefits of a literal translation, of a plain style and everyday language (for these need not be ungrammatical), it has to be admitted that the Latin of the Bible repelled many – at least those who had had a classical education, who are the ones whose opinions on the matter have come down to us. Arnobius (*Adversus Gentes* I 58–59) admits that critics may be right in charging the Latin of the Bible with being *trivialis et sordidus* (vulgar and lacking refinement), but this does not affect the truth of what is being communicated, he claims, any more than the fact that certain fruits are prickly on the outside prevents them being delicious to eat. Jerome (*Letter* 22. 30) and Augustine (*Confessions* III 5. 9) also confess that they initially found this Latin rebarbative, as containing what they were trained to regard as solecisms and barbarisms. It may have been the case, as Tertullian says in his work *De Testimonio Animae* (4), that no one comes to the Bible unless he is a Christian, but being a Christian was no guarantee that one would find it an easy read.

But even Jerome and Augustine, with their high standards, had to come to terms with it: as Augustine puts it *"plerumque loquendi consuetudo vulgaris utilior est significandis rebus quam integritas litterata"* (the colloquial manner of speaking is often more effective than the propriety of literary language when it comes to signifying things; *De Doctrina Christiana* III 3. 15). In the same work (II 13. 45) he goes further when he pours scorn on the linguistic and stylistic straitjacket imposed by the concept of barbarisms and solecisms, putting the question *"quid est ergo integritas locutionis nisi alienae consuetudinis conservatio, loquentium veterum auctoritate firmatae?"* (What, then is correctness of speech but the maintenance of the practice of others, as established by the authority of ancient speakers?) And when Jerome was asked by Pope Damasus in 383 to produce a revised version of the Latin Bible, he did not simply sit down with a copy of the complete text and turn it into Ciceronian Latin, as is clear from Jerome's preface to his version of the Gospels. Nor did he translate it afresh from beginning to end. Instead, he carefully revised the existing Latin translations with reference to different versions of the Greek Septuagint and, where relevant, to the original Hebrew (though he did make enough changes for Augustine to feel the need to take him to task, in his Letter 71, for changing the text in a way that would be unpopular among his conservative congregations).

A comparison of the early Latin version of a well-known passage from the book of Genesis with Jerome's revision of the same text illustrates how the text of the Bible might change:

Vetus Latina
In principio fecit Deus caelum et terram. Terra autem erat invisibilis et incomposita. Et tenebrae errant super abyssum et Spiritus Dei superferebatur super aquas et dixit Deus fiat lux et facta est lux et vidit Deus lucem quia bona est et divisit Deus inter lucem et tenebras et vocavit Deus lucem diem et tenebras vocavit noctem et facta est vespera et factum est mane dies unus

Jerome's version
In principio creavit Deus caelum et terram, terra autem erat inanis et vacua et tenebrae super faciem abyssi et spiritus Dei ferebatur super aquas dixitque Deus fiat lux et facta est lux et vidit Deus lucem quod esset bona et divisit lucem ac tenebras appellavitque lucem diem et tenebras noctem factumque est vespere et mane dies unus

The *Vetus Latina* version here is closer to the Greek of the Septuagint version of the Old Testament, with *invisibilis* for the Greek *aoratos*, *incomposita* for *akataskeuastos*, and *superferebatur* as a calque on *epefereto*. Most of the changes introduced by Jerome here are stylistic, as for example the change from "et" to enclitic "-que." Throughout the Bible the amount of variation between the *Vetus Latina* and Jerome's version varies depending on linguistic and stylistic elements; occasionally the differences are nonexistent, as in the opening of St John's Gospel, where Jerome was perhaps conscious of the importance of retaining the mystery of the word order.

However, Jerome's versions were not immediately accepted by his contemporaries: many medieval writers, such as Gregory the Great and Bede, allude to various versions of the Bible, including the *Vetus Latina*, and it was not until the Council of Trent in the sixteenth century that Jerome's version was accorded the title *Vulgata*, referring to its widespread acceptance, in place of the *Vetus Latina*, which had been known as the *vetus editio* or, indeed, rather confusingly, as the *editio vulgata* by Jerome and his successors.

With reference to the attitude of the patristic writers to the Latin Bible it is important to remember that these writers, however well educated, were aware that despite the plain language the Latin text was frequently, for a variety of reasons, opaque and in need of elucidation. This fact was to generate a large proportion of all Latin patristic writing, in the form of commentaries and other works as various as Augustine's *De Doctrina Christiana* and Jerome's *Nomina Hebraica*, ancillary to the understanding of the biblical text that lay at the heart of Christian life.

Pre-patristic Latin Writings

From the biblical texts providing the subject of, and the language for, so much patristic literature, we turn to look briefly at the Latin used in specifically Christian writings in the period around the time of the first Latin patristic writer, Tertullian. Evidence derives from two works describing events already mentioned, composed originally in Latin: the short *Acts of the Scillitan Martyrs* and the *Passion of Perpetua and Felicitas*. Other works in Latin from this period are the translations from Greek of Clement of Rome's *First Letter* and of the work on heresies by Irenaeus of Lyon. These are the forerunners of a line of influential Latin translations of Greek works such as that of Athanasius' *Life of Antony* by Evagrius of Antioch in the fourth century.

Clement's *First Letter* is a literary work impregnated with the Greek of the Septuagint. Its very literal translation, possibly dating from the second century, reveals a Latin similar to that of parts of the *Vetus Latina*. The following excerpt (section 42, with English translation based on Greek original) shows that such words as *evangelizare*, *resurrectio*, and *baptizare* have clearly become part of the Christian Latin lexis, though the translator uses *minister* for the Greek word *diakonos* rather than the Latin form *diaconus*, first appearing in Tertullian. Sometimes he appears to confuse different senses of a Greek word, as when he translates *kata* as *secundum* (i.e., "according to") rather than with a word meaning "throughout," which is the correct sense of *kata* here:

> Apostoli nostri euuangelizati sunt ab Jhesu Xristo Domino nostro. Jhesus Xristus a Deo missus, apostoli a Xristo. Facta sunt ergo utraque ordine ex voluntate Dei. Mandata igitur accipientes et impleti per resurrectionem Domini Jhesu Xristi, et fideles facti verbo Dei, cum plenitudine Spiritus sancti exierunt euuangelizare regnum Dei incipere venire. Secundum municipia ergo et civitates predicantes, et eos qui obaudiebant voluntati Dei baptizantes preponebant primitiva eorum, probantes spiritu, in episcopos et ministros, qui incipiebant credere. Et hoc non novum: ex multis enim temporibus scriptum erat pro episcopis et ministris. Sic enim dicit scriptura, "praeponam episcopos eorum in justitia et ministros eorum in fide." (Isaiah 60.17)

> (The apostles received the gospel for us from the Lord Jesus Christ; Jesus Christ was sent from God. Christ therefore is from God and the apostles are from Christ. Both accordingly came in proper order by the will of God. Receiving their orders, therefore and being filled

with confidence because of the Resurrection of the Lord Jesus Christ, and confirmed in the word of God, with all assurance of the Holy Spirit, they went forth preaching the Gospel of the Kingdom of God that was about to come. Preaching, accordingly, throughout the country and the cities, they appointed their first-fruits, after testing them by the spirit, to be bishops and deacons of those who should believe. And this they did without innovation since many years ago things had been written concerning bishops and deacons. Thus Scripture says in one place: "I will establish their bishops in justice and their deacons in faith.")

The *Acts of the Scillitan Martyrs* provides evidence of spoken Latin in an official situation at the end of the second century, namely the interrogation of the Christians by the proconsul who states, regarding his own religion, "*juramus per genium domni nostri imperatoris et pro salute ejus supplicamus, quod et vos quoque facere debetis*" ("we swear by the genius of our lord emperor and we pray for his welfare and you ought to do this too"), to which the Christian replies uncompromisingly, "*ego imperium huius seculi non cognosco; sed magis illi Deo servio, quem nemo hominum vidit nec videre oculis potest. Furtum non feci sed siquid emero teloneum reddo, quia cognosco domnum meum, regem regum et imperatorem omnium gentium*" ("I do not recognize the rule of this world; rather I serve that God whom no man has seen and whom he cannot see with his eyes. I have committed no crime and whatever I buy I pay tax on because I recognize my Lord, the king of kings and the ruler of all peoples"). It is notable how he transfers the terms used of the supreme secular ruler to the Christian God.

The *Passion of Perpetua and Felicitas* is a more complex text, combining colloquial first-person narrative and dialogue from Perpetua and one of her fellow prisoners, as well as accounts of dreams, all set within a more literary narrative framework.. The subject and much of the lexis are distinctively Christian, including *martyr, catechumenus, diabolus,* and *angelus,* and yet on the whole the Latin is less reminiscent of the Bible than of a work like the first-century *Cena Trimalchionis* of Petronius. A Greek translation, possibly made by the same author, allows one to see the unusual use of certain words, such as *refrigerare* (a word used by Christians in literal and figurative senses) meaning (in section 3) "to be gladdened," in the phrase *refrigeravi absentia eius,* used with the ablative where the Greek uses the genitive absolute.

Christian Latin: A Distinct Language?

The question of how far the Latin exemplified in these passages reflects the everyday speech of Christians, and how far it was influenced by the biblical language, is difficult to resolve with any certainty. One influential way of portraying the Latin of the early Christians was presented by the Dutch scholar Jos Schrijnen in the 1930s and developed by his colleague Christine Mohrmann. Basing their original theory on a study of the earliest Christian Latin texts and inscriptions, together they posited that Christian Latin was a *Sondersprache,* a distinct language of a distinct social group, living within the Roman Empire but distinguished by their different worldview and beliefs, by their liturgical practices, their reading of the Bible, and the fact that until the early fourth century they were a persecuted minority. However, Tertullian, in his *Apology* (42), stresses the fact that Christians are just like everyone else when he says to the pagan officials to whom the work is addressed,

> navigamus et nos vobiscum et militamus, et rusticamur et mercamur, proinde miscemus artes, operas nostras publicamus usui vestro. Sed si caerimonias tuas non frequento, attamen et illa die homo sum.
>
> (We are sailors and serve in the army along with you, we also practice farming and trade; in addition we share the same skills and we allow you to benefit from the products of our labor. If I do not attend your rituals, even on that day I am still a human being.)

There is nothing here that points to a significant difference of language between Christians and non-Christians (Burton 2008: 149). It is nevertheless true – even if one does not accept Schrijnen and Mohrmann's controversial theory that Christian Latin was distinct with regard to vocabulary, semantics, morphology, syntax and even meter, nor their distinction between "direct" and "indirect," between "integral" and "partial" Christianisms – that Latin did adopt new words and meanings to apply to Christian concepts, particularly for terms of church organization (such as *episcopus*, *presbyter*, and *diaconus*), for the sacraments (such as *baptisma* and *eucharistia*), and terms for those who disrupt the Church (such as *hereticus*, *schisma*, and *apostata*). If we view this not so much as a distinct language setting Christians apart, but as a set of technical terms that passed into the language and might be understood, if not used, by non-Christians, might we draw a parallel with the language developing to cope with the IT revolution of our own time – with neologisms like "to google" and the semantic extension of existing words like text, web, browse, surf, file, folder, and twitter? This revolution has had a global effect on people's lifestyle and worldview, though how these social and technological changes will be affected by longer term developments is probably as unpredictable to us as the future of Latin and Christianity was to the early patristic writers.

Alongside such words entering the lexis early, there were other terms associated with Christian theology and church organization that only appeared as Christianity developed, terms whose earliest use is often attested in patristic writings. For example, terms such as *trinitas* (a new word formed by analogy with the preexistent *unitas*) and *persona* (a preexisting word that becomes almost a technical term for the persons of the Trinity) first appear in Tertullian. Other words are used by Tertullian but not by later writers, and yet others only emerge after Tertullian.

Patristic Latin

Before examining excerpts from the Latin Fathers, it is to be noted that in approaching these writings it is necessary to take into account not only the Latin texts of the Bible and the linguistic building blocks used by the early Christians to express their faith and doctrine, but also their rhetorical skills, learned as part of their non-Christian education. Admittedly there is an ambiguity here no less than in their attitude to biblical Latin, in that sometimes they express the view that God's truth, in its pure and simple state, does not need the decoration provided by rhetoric to be attractive and effective, as Lactantius points out in *Divine Institutes* III 1 (indeed, rhetoric is associated with deceptiveness), while at other times they argue that Christian truth deserves to be communicated as effectively as possible. If authorization is needed for the use of rhetoric, Augustine provides it by stating that rhetoric can be used both for truth and falsehood, and indeed that rhetoric covers not only the theory and practice of Cicero, but also the Latin of the Bible (*De Doctrina Christiana* IV 6. 28). These writers, despite their modest claims to the contrary, are aware that they themselves are *docti* (educated) and have at their disposal the rhetorical tools to tailor what they wish to communicate to any particular audience so that, in the words of Augustine, they may be listened to with understanding, with pleasure, and with obedience (*De Doctrina Christiana* IV 15. 87). Rhetorical skill involves judging the subject matter and the audience, and choosing the right register: Jerome discusses different "*genera dicendi*" in his Letter 49 and Augustine, following Cicero, distinguishes three different styles for different subjects (*De Doctrina Christiana* IV 17. 96), giving examples of each from Scripture and from the works of Cyprian and Ambrose.

The following passages are selected to provide examples of some of the different styles and genres used in patristic writings, in order to show various ways in which the Bible was used, as well as demonstrating that not all patristic texts are dense with Christian terms. For a comparison with the Latin of non-patristic Christian texts of this period, the reader may consult such texts as the fourth-century *Peregrinatio Etheriae* or the sixth-century *Rule of St Benedict*.

Tertullian

In the *Apology* written in 197, Tertullian addresses the provincial governors of the Roman Empire with a vivid picture of contemporary Roman life as well as providing a statement of Christian belief and practice. To the reader it seems as if he is listening in to one side of a courtroom drama: the forensic style is full of biting aphorisms – for example, "*non nisi grande aliquid bonum a Nerone damnatum*" ("nothing except what was sublimely good was condemned by Nero") – and wordplay. Tertullian avoids the use of Christian terms and biblical references, even in dealing with Christian doctrine, presumably because he is addressing a pagan audience. This chapter forms the climax of the work.

Apology, chapter 50

Sed hoc agite, boni praesides, meliores multo apud populum, si illis Christianos immolaveritis. Cruciate, torquete, damnate, atterite nos: probatio est enim innocentiae nostrae iniquitas vestra. Ideo nos haec pati Deus patitur. Nam et proxime, ad lenonem damnando Christianam potius quam ad leonem, confessi estis labem pudicitiae apud nos atrociorem omni poena et omni morte reputari. Nec quicquam tamen proficit exquisitior quaeque crudelitas vestra: illecebra est magis sectae. Plures efficimur, quotiens metimur a vobis; semen est sanguis Christianorum. Multi apud vos ad tolerantiam doloris et mortis hortantur, ut Cicero in Tusculanis, ut Seneca in Fortuitis, ut Diogenes, ut Pyrrhon, ut Callinicus. Nec tamen tantos inveniunt verba discipulos, quantos Christiani factis docendo. Illa ipsa obstinatio, quam exprobratis, magistra est. quis enim non contemplatione ejus concutitur ad requirendum, quid intus in re sit? Quis non, ubi requisivit, accedit, ubi accessit, pati exoptat, ut totam Dei gratiam redimat, ut omnem veniam ab eo compensatione sanguinis sui expediat? Omnia enim huic operi delicta donantur. Inde est, quod ibidem sententiis vestris gratias agimus; ut est aemulatio divinae rei et humanae, cum damnamur a vobis, a Deo absolvimur.

(But carry on like this, you excellent governors; you will be much more popular with the people if you sacrifice the Christians to them! Crucify, torture, condemn, crush us! For your wickedness proves our innocence. This is why God suffers us to suffer these things. Recently, by condemning a Christian woman to be handed over to a pimp rather than to a lion, you admitted that we consider a stain on our virtue more terrible than any punishment or any death. All your acts of cruelty do not profit you in the least, rather they attract people to our sect. We spring up in greater numbers whenever we are cut down by you: the blood of Christians acts as a seed. Many of you have encouraged people to endure pain and death, as Cicero did in the *Tusculan Disputations*, as Seneca did in his book *On Chances*, and as Diogenes, as Pyrrhon, as Callinicus did. Yet their words have not gained as many disciples as Christians have in teaching by example. This very stubbornness which you reproach us for acts as a teacher. For who is not inspired by witnessing it to inquire what the motive for this stubbornness can be? Who, when he has inquired about it, does not adopt it himself? Who, when he has adopted it, does not choose to suffer so as to acquire the whole grace of God, so that by the payment of his blood, he may obtain forgiveness from God? For by this act all sins are forgiven. That is why we give thanks when you sentence us; since there exists a rivalry between divine and human things which means that when we are condemned by you, we are acquitted by God.)

Ambrose

Ambrose provides an example of an early Christian hymn, probably written in the 380s. It is composed in eight verses of four lines of iambic dimeters, a form so immediately popular that it became the standard for Latin hymns in the Middle Ages. In this hymn for Advent and Christmas he balances images and language from both Old and New Testament, new Christian terms and traditional linguistic usage to convey the theological significance of Christ's birth. The English hymn "Come, thou redeemer of the earth" is a translation of the second and following verses.

Intende qui regis Israel,	(Hear us, O King of Israel,
Super Cherubim qui sedes,	Above the Cherubim enthroned;
Appare Ephrem coram, excita	Shine forth upon Ephraim,
Potentiam tuam et veni.	Arouse your power and come.
Veni, redemptor gentium,	Come redeemer of the peoples,
Ostende partum Virginis,	Show to us the Virgin birth,
Miretur omne saeculum:	That the entire world may marvel
Talis decet partus Deum.	At such a birth, worthy of God.
Non ex virili semine,	But by the Spirit's mystic breath
Sed mystico spiramine,	Not from a man's seed
Verbum Dei factum est caro	The Word of God was made flesh
Fructusque ventris floruit.	And the fruit of her womb blossomed.
Alvus tumescit Virginis,	While the Virgin's stomach swells

Claustrum pudoris permanet,	The gates of chastity are closed,
Vexilla virtutum micant,	The banner of her virtues shines:
Versatur in templo Deus.	She is the temple where God resides.
Procedat e thalamo suo,	Let him come forth from his room
Pudoris aula regia,	Which is chastity's royal hall,
Geminae gigas substantiae,	A hero of a twofold nature,
Alacris ut currat viam.	He is keen to run his course.
Egressus eius a patre,	From the Father he goes out,
Regressus eius ad patrem	To the Father he returns,
Excursus usque ad inferos,	Down to hell he first descends,
Recursus ad sedem Dei.	Then to the seat of God ascends.
Aequalis aeterno Patri,	Equal to the eternal Father,
Carnis tropaeo cingere,	Gird on the trophy of the flesh,
Infirma nostri corporis,	Strengthening with enduring power
Virtute firmans perpeti.	Our bodily infirmity.
Praesepe jam fulget tuum	Already your manger shines out,
Lumenque nox spirat novum,	The darkness emits a new light:
Quod nulla nox interpolet	May this light no night destroy,
Fideque jugi luceat.	May it shine out with constant faith.)

Jerome

At the end of his *Letter* 117 Jerome excuses himself for having written but a brief note: he explains that he has not had time to weave his discourse from the flowers of Scripture as he usually does. A good example of his more usual practice is taken from the final chapter of his famous *Letter* 22 to the young girl Eustochium, in which he inspires her to a life of virginity.

Letter 22.41

Egredere quaeso paulisper de carcere, et praesentis laboris ante oculos tuos tibi pinge mercedem, quam nec oculus vidit, nec auris audivit, nec in cor hominis ascendit. (1 Cor. 2: 9). *Qualis erit illa dies, cum tibi Maria, mater Domini, choris occurret comitata virgineis? cum post Rubrum Mare, submerso cum suo exercitu Pharaone, tympanum tenens Maria soror Aaron in sua manu, praecinet responsuris: "Cantemus Domino; gloriose enim honorificatus est: equum et ascensorem projecit in mare"* (Exod. 15: 1). *Tunc Thecla in tuos laeta volabit amplexus. Tunc et ipse sponsus occurret, et dicet: "Surge, veni proxima mea, speciosa mea, columba mea, quia ecce hyems transivit, pluvia abiit sibi"* (Song of Songs 2: 10–11). *Tunc et angeli mirabuntur, et dicent: "Quae est ista prospiciens quasi diluculum, speciosa ut luna, electa ut sol"* (Song of Songs 6: 9)? *...Quotiescumque te vana saeculi delectaverit ambitio: quoties in mundo aliquid videris gloriosum, ad paradisum mente transgredere: esse incipe quod futura es, et audies sponso tuo: "Pone me sicut umbraculum in corde tuo; sicut signaculum in brachio tuo"* (Song of Songs 8: 6), *et corpore pariter ac mente munita clamabis, et dices: "Aquae multae non potuerunt extinguere caritatem, et flumina non operient eam"* (Song of Songs 8: 7).

(Come out for a while from your prison, please, and picture before your eyes the reward for your present hardships, a reward "which eye has not seen, nor ear heard, neither has it entered into the heart of man." What will that day be like, when Mary, the mother of the Lord, will come to meet you, accompanied by groups of virgins; when, after the Red Sea and after Pharaoh with his army has drowned beneath its waves, Miriam, the sister of Aaron, with a timbrel in her hand, will chant to the answering crowds, "Let us sing to the Lord, for he had triumphed gloriously: the horse and his rider he has thrown into the sea." Then Thecla will fly rejoicing into your arms. Then shall your Bridegroom himself come to meet you and say, "Rise up, my love, my fair one, my dove, and come, for the winter is past and the rain is over and gone." Then the angels will gaze in wonder and say, "Who is this girl who looks forth as the morning, fair as the moon, clear as the sun?"...Whenever the empty attractions of this world delight you, whenever you see something magnificent in this world, transport yourself in thought to paradise. Begin to be what you will be, and you will hear your Bridegroom say, "Set me as a seal in your heart and as a seal on your arm". And then, strengthened in mind and body, you will cry out, "Many waters cannot quench love, neither can the floods drown it.")

Augustine

Letter 91 to Nectarius, written in about 409, shows Augustine discussing pagan and Christian views but without the use of overt Christian technical language:

Intuere paululum ipsos de Republica libros, unde illum affectum amantissimi civis ebibisti, quod nullus sit patriae consulendi modus aut finis bonis. Intuere, obsecro te, et cerne quantis ibi laudibus frugalitas et continentia predicetur, et erga conjugale vinculum fides, castique honesti ac probi mores, quibus cum prepollet civitas, vere florere dicenda est. Hi autem mores in ecclesiis toto orbe crescentibus, tanquam in sanctis auditoriis populorum docentur atque discuntur, et maxime pietas qua verus et verax colatur Deus, qui haec omnia, quibus animus humanus divinae societati ad inhabitandam aeternam coelestemque civitatem instruitur et aptatur, non solum jubet aggredienda, verum etiam donat implenda.

(Consider for a little those books, On the Republic, from which you imbibed that sentiment of a most loyal citizen, that there is no limit either in measure or in time to the claims which their country has on the care and service of right-hearted men. Consider them, I beg you, and observe how great are the praises there bestowed on frugality, self-control, conjugal fidelity, and those chaste, honorable and upright manners, the prevalence of which in any city entitles it to be spoken of as flourishing. Now the churches which are multiplying throughout the world are, as it were, sacred seminaries of public instruction, in which this sound morality is inculcated and learned, and in which, above all, men are taught the worship due to the true and faithful God who not only commands men to attempt, but also gives grace to perform, all those things by which the soul of man is furnished and fitted for fellowship with God, and for dwelling in the eternal and heavenly kingdom.)

In his *Sermon* 379 (of which the following passage is the opening section), Augustine addresses his congregation on the feast of John the Baptist, bringing out the significance of this saint in the context of Christian theology with reference to the biblical narrative and by means of an epigrammatic, balanced, and direct style:

Beatus Joannes, fratres charissimi, cujus hodie nativitatem celebramus, tam magnus exstitit inter homines, ut Dominus noster Jesus Christus tale ei testimonium perhiberet, dicens: Inter natos mulierum non surrexit major Joanne Baptista (Matt. 11: 11). *Audivimus, cum Evangelium legeretur, quam mirabiliter fuerit ex desperatione conceptus, et quanto Spiritus sancti testimonio procreatus. Pater ejus eo quod non credidit, obmutuit. Annuntiatus ergo per Angelum, et non creditus, patris vocem abstulit, natus linguam resolvit* (Luke 1: 20, 64). *Accipe ergo in hujus rei mysterio magnum sacramentum. Ante Dominum Jesum Christum Joannes praemissus est, missi sunt Prophetae per superiora saecula, nec defuerunt qui Christum praedicarent. Tantus enim judex venturus erat, ut multi deberent praeire praecones. Ab ipso prorsus exordio generis humani non cessavit se Christus prophetare, et venturum praenuntiare. Novissime missus est Joannes homo, sed quo homine nullus exstitit major. Venturus erat Dominus Jesus, non homo tantum, sed et Deus: utique et Deus et homo; Deus semper, ad tempus homo; Deus ante tempora, homo in fine temporum; Deus ante saecula, homo in fine saeculi. Deus qui hominem fecit, propter hominem dignatus est homo fieri, quem fecit. Venturo ergo Domino Jesu Christo, qui plus est quam homo, ne putaretur tantum esse homo, testimonium debuit illi perhibere magnus homo.*

(The blessed John, whose birthday is being celebrated today, stood out as so great a man among men, that the Lord Christ bore this kind of witness to him, saying, 'Among those born of woman none has arisen greater than John the Baptist. We heard, when the holy Gospel was read, how wonderfully he was conceived when there was no hope of such a thing, with what a testimonial from the Holy Spirit he was begotten; his father, because he did not believe, was struck dumb; so when John was announced by the angel and not believed, he deprived his father of speech, and when he was born he loosened his father's tongue. So then, receive now from me the inner significance and meaning in this great and mysterious affair. John was sent before the Lord Christ. Prophets had also been sent beforehand through previous ages; there was no lack of them to proclaim Christ. In fact, from the very origin of the human race, Christ did not cease to prophesy himself and foretell his own coming. Last of all was born John, a human being, but one than whom none greater had ever existed. However, the Lord Jesus was going to come, not only a human being but also God; both God and human of course – God always, human at a point in time; God before the ages, human at the end of the age. God who made man, thought fit for the sake of man to become what he had made. So when the Lord Jesus Christ was about to come, who is more than man, in case he should be thought to be only a man, it was right that a great man should bear him testimony.)

Bede

Bede is perhaps best known for his *Ecclesiastical History of the English People*, but his biblical commentaries and educational works show him writing in different styles. In his commentaries he frequently quotes from Jerome, Augustine, Ambrose, and Gregory the Great, and also strives to imitate Jerome's style (Sharpe 2005: 350). This feature is one indication that Bede was writing in the later period of the patristic writers. In his educational works on grammar, natural phenomena, and calendars he is more dependent on predecessors, such as Pliny and Isidore, though in the following Bede is in less dependent mode. He indicates in passing his Christian allegiance when referring to Christmas with the phrase "*ubi nunc natalem Domini celebramus,*" but also reveals that this link in the patristic chain is writing in the context of the English culture of the early eighth century.

The Reckoning of Time (*De temporum ratione*): chapter 15

Antiqui autem Anglorum populi (neque enim mihi congruum videtur aliarum gentium annalem observantiam dicere et meae reticere) iuxta cursum lunae suos menses computavere. Unde et a luna Hebraeorum et Graecorum more nomen accipiunt: siquidem apud eos luna mona, mensis appellatur monath. Primusque eorum mensis, quem Latini Ianuarium vocant, dicitur Giuli; deinde Februarius, Solmonath; Martius, Hredmonath; Aprilis, Eosturmonath; Maius, Thirmilchi; Iunius, Lida; Iulius, similiter Lida; Augustus, Weodmonath; September, Halegmonath; October, Winterfilleth; November, Blodmonath; December, Giuli, eodem quo Ianuarius nomine vocatur. Incipiebant autem annum ab octavo kalendarum Ianuariarum die, ubi nunc natalem Domini cele-bramus. Et ipsam noctem nunc nobis sacrosanctam, tunc gentili vocabulo Modranect, id est matrum noctem, appellabant, ob causam, ut suspicamur, ceremoniarum quas in ea pervigiles agebant.

(The English peoples of old (for I do not think it appropriate to mention the reckoning of the year of other peoples and not mention that of my own) calculated their months according to the moon's course. And so, in the same way as the Jews and Greeks, they also took their word for 'month' from the moon: for in their language the moon is "mona," and the word for month is "monath." Their first month, which the Romans call January, is called Giuli; next February, called Solmonath; March, Hredmonath; April, Eosturmonath; May, Thirmilchi; June, Litha; July is also called Litha; August, Weodmonath; September, Halegmonath; October, Winterfilleth; November, Blodmonath; December has the same name as January, Giuli. They started the year from the eighth day of the Kalends of January [25 December], which is when we now celebrate our Lord's birthday. And the very night that we now regard as holy, they called Modranecht, in their own language, in other words, the night of mothers, because, we suspect, of the all-night ceremonies they used to perform then.)

Conclusion

While bearing in mind that the language used by each writer was influenced by his per-sonality, education, situation, and audience, one may suggest that patristic Latin is dis-tinguished by the fact that it demonstrates the author's familiarity with Scripture, with his patristic predecessors, and with classical culture, as well as a constant attention to the possibility of a spiritual, nonliteral interpretation: as Bede says in his commentary on Genesis, "*cuncta sacri eloquii series mysticis est plena figuris*" ("the whole sequence of sacred utterance is full of figurative meanings"). Yet it should be noted that patristic writers often convey their message, their vision of God and humankind, in a language that would be perfectly intelligible, and even interesting and relevant, to a non-Christian audience. The Latin of the Fathers is of interest because of the way it struggles not only to come to terms with the language of the Bible, importing and developing specifically Christian terms, but also to adapt classical culture to a Christian context. While con-stantly wary of the possibly detrimental effects of aspects of classical culture, the patristic writers are able to select and reinterpret what they considered valuable, while growing in confidence with regard to the increasingly impressive and comprehensive Christian culture that they were helping to create. Much work remains to be done, with the help of new technology, to elucidate the language of this culture which forms an essential part of the history of Latin.

Bibliography

Primary Sources

Acts of the Scillitan Martyrs, J.A. Robinson (ed.) (1891), The Passion of S. Perpetua. Cambridge: Cambridge University Press; 112–116.

Ambrose, Hymns. In A.S. Walpole (1922), Early Latin Hymns. Cambridge: Cambridge University Press. English translation of Intende qui regis Israel by C. White (2000), Early Christian Latin Poets. London: Routledge.

Arnobius, Adversus Gentes, J.-P. Migne (ed.) (1844). PL 5, 718–1288. Paris.

Augustine, Confessions. CCSL 27 (1981). English translation by H. Chadwick (2008), Oxford: Oxford University Press.

Augustine, De Doctrina Christiana. Latin text with English translation by R.P.H. Green (1995). Oxford: Clarendon Press.

Augustine, Letters, A. Goldbacher (ed.) (1895–1923). CSEL 34, 44, 57, 58. Vienna. English translation of Letter 91 in Fathers of the Church series, vol. 18 (1953). Washington, DC: Catholic University of America Press.

Augustine, Sermons, J.-P. Migne (ed.) (1865). PL 38–39. Paris. English translation of Sermon 379 by Edmund Hill (1995) in The Works of St. Augustine III/10: Sermons 341–400. New York: New City Press.

Bede, De Temporum Ratione, C.W. Jones (ed.) (1943) in Opera de temporibus. Cambridge, MA: The Mediaeval Academy of America; 175–291. English translation by Faith Wallis (1999), The Reckoning of Time. Liverpool: Liverpool University Press.

Clement of Rome's First Letter to the Corinthians., C. Schaefer (ed.) (1941), S. Clementis Romani Epistula ad Corinthios quae vocatur prima, graece et latine. Florilegium Patristicum 44. Bonn. English translation in Fathers of the Church series, vol. 1 (1962). Washington, DC: Catholic University of America Press.

Irenaeus, Adversus Haereses. Latin text and French translation edited by A. Rousseau (1965–1982) in Sources Chrétiennes. Paris.

Jerome, Letters, I. Hilberg (ed.) (1996), CSEL 54–56. Vienna. Adkin, Neil (2003), Jerome on Virginity: A Commentary on the Libellus de virginitate servanda (Letter 22). Leeds: Francis Cairns. Translated by F.A. Wright (1975). Loeb Classical Library. London: Heinemann.

Lactantius, The Divine Institutes, J.-P. Migne (ed.) (1844). PL 6, 111–822. Paris. English translation in Fathers of the Church series, vol. 49 (1954). Washington, D: Catholic University of America Press.

Tertullian, Apologeticum, CCSL I (1954), 85–171. English translation in Fathers of the Church series, vol. 10 (1950). Washington, DC: Catholic University of America Press.

Tertullian, De Testimonio Animae, CCSL I (1954), 175–183. English translation in Fathers of the Church series, vol. 10 (1950). Washington, DC: Catholic University of America Press.

Tertullian, De Praescriptione Haereticorum, CCSL I (1954), 187–224.

The Passion of St. Perpetua, J.A. Robinson (ed.) (1891), The Passion of S. Perpetua. Cambridge: Cambridge University Press; 60–94. English translation by C. White (2010) in The Lives of Roman Christian Women. Penguin Classics: Harmondsworth.

Vetus Latina (1952–). Beuron: Vetus Latina Institut.

Vulgate (1975). Biblia Sacra juxta vulgatam versionem, two vols. Stuttgart: Württembergische Bibelanstalt.

Secondary Sources

Bardy, G. (1948), La question des langues dans l'église des chrétiens. Paris: Beauchesne.

Blaise, A. (1954), Dictionnaire latin-francais des auteurs chrétiens. Turnhout: Brepols.

Burton, P.H. (2000), *The Old Latin Gospels: A Study of the Texts and Language*, esp. "Old Latin as a linguistic document" (pp. 149–191) and "Jerome's translation technique" (pp. 192–199). Oxford: Oxford University Press.

Burton, P.H. (2007), *Language in the Confessions of Augustine*. Oxford: Oxford University Press.

Burton, P.H. (2008), "On revisiting the Christian Latin Sondersprache hypothesis". In *Textual Variation: Theological and Social Tendencies*, H.A.G. Houghton and D.C. Parker (eds). Piscataway, NJ: Gorgias Press; 149–171.

Burton, P.H. (2011), "Christian Latin". In *A Companion to the Latin Language*, J. Clackson (ed.). Oxford: Wiley–Blackwell; 485–501.

Clackson, J. and Horrocks, G. (2007), *The Blackwell History of the Latin Language*. Oxford: Blackwell.

Elliott, J.K. (1995), "The translation of the New Testament into Latin: the Old Latin and the Vulgate". In *Aufstieg und Niedergang der römischen Welt*, II.26.1, H. Temporini and W. Haase (eds). Berlin: Walter de Gruyter; 198–245.

Frisius, Mark A. (2011), *Tertullian's Use of the Pastoral Epistles, Hebrews, James, 1 and 2 Peter, and Jude*. Studies in Biblical Literature 143. New York: Peter Lang.

Herzog, R. (ed.) (1993) *Restauration et renouveau: la littérature latine de 284 à 374 après J.-C.* Turnhout: Brepols.

Mohrmann, Christine (1958), "Theorie der Altchristlichen Sondersprache". In *Études sur le latin des chrétiens* I. Rome: Edizioni di storia e letteratura; 3–19.

Mohrmann, Christine (1958–1997), *Études sur le latin des chrétiens*, four vols. Rome: Edizioni di storia e letteratura.

Müller, Roman (2001), "Niveauhebung im Latein der Christen". In *Sprachbewusstsein und Sprachvariation im lateinischen Schrifttum der Antike*. Munich: C.H. Beck; 314–320.

Sanders, G. and van Uytfanghe, M. (eds) (1989), *Lingua Patrum: Bibliographie signalétique du latin des chrétiens*. Turnhout: Brepols.

Schrijnen, Jos (1934), "Le latin chrétien devenu langue commune". *Revue des Études Latines*, 12: 96–116.

Sharpe, Richard (2005), "The varieties of Bede's prose". In *Aspects of the Language of Latin Prose*, J.N. Adams, M. Lapidge, and T. Reinhardt (eds). London: Proceedings of the British Academy; 339–355.

CHAPTER 33

Reimagining Patristics: Critical Theory as a Lens

Kim Haines-Eitzen

Introduction

It has now been 10 years since the publication of Elizabeth Clark's (2004) *History, Theory, Text: Historians and the Linguistic Turn*, which made a critical intervention into debates often overheard in the hallways of conference hotels or in humanities departments following academic talks. Words and phrases like "undertheorized" or "too theoretical," "positivist" or "deconstructionist," or "postmodern" and "cultural relativist" are often bandied about as evaluative critiques as though everyone knows exactly what they mean. Such terms sometimes become a succinct way to dismiss arguments without really engaging with them. Some scholars of late antiquity have suggested that the application of "critical theory" to the study of patristic literature or history is a uniquely or predominantly North American phenomenon; others have argued that theory threatens the very basis of patristics as a field of study, for it calls into question basic assumptions about texts, interpretation, history, and, above all, the reliability of our sources. Such claims notwithstanding, one thing is certain: the application of theoretical insights from a variety of disciplines to the study of patristics has taken root in recent decades and continues to grow and flourish.

This goal of this chapter is not to trace the history of the use of "theory" in the study of patristics; previous scholars have prepared excellent syntheses (e.g., Brakke 2002). Nor do I wish to locate the "theoretical" impulse in one geographic location or another: even a cursory look at the recent monographs and articles appearing in the *Oxford Early Christian Studies* series, *Studia Patristica*, the *Journal of Early Christian Studies*, and the *Patristic Monograph Series* suggests that critical theory has begun to shape work in patristics in striking ways and that the influence cuts across geographical borders. Rather, my goal in this chapter is first to unpack what is meant by "theory" in these various scholarly debates; next I turn to the work of Elizabeth Clark and

The Wiley Blackwell Companion to Patristics, First Edition. Edited by Ken Parry.
© 2015 John Wiley & Sons Ltd. Published 2019 by John Wiley & Sons Ltd.

others to highlight some of the ways in which theory, especially poststructuralism, has been productively incorporated into the study of patristic literature; finally, I turn to some remaining key issues into which theory may provide insight and suggest new directions for an invigorated field of patristics. Throughout the chapter, my argument is not against the continued publication of critical editions, translations of a wide array of patristic texts, historical work on various church fathers, or the study of late ancient theological debates, ritual practices, monasticism, and so forth. My argument is rather simple: "theory" encourages us to be self-critical in our interpretive work, to attend to the ways our understanding of patristic literature is tied to our location, experience, and perspective, and to reflect on our methods and practice of reading, translation, interpretation, and critical understanding. "Theory" and "patristics," in their broadest senses, can be productively knit together to offer us new insights into the world of late antiquity.

What is Theory?

The place to begin is with what we mean by the term "theory." And, by extension, with what we mean exactly when we say someone's work is "too theoretical" or "undertheo-rized." As many "theorists" have noted, the term itself in modern scholarship is rather difficult to define, although this has not prevented numerous attempts to define it, many of them quite excellent (e.g., Culler 1997; Eagleton 1983; 2003). We usually assume that "we know it when we see it," but this is hardly helpful for a serious engagement with theory. In many instances, we say "theory" is driving the scholarship when we see reference to figures like Jacques Derrida, Michel Foucault, Roland Barthes, Jacques Lacan, Julia Kristeva, Stanley Fish, Judith Butler, and many others, but this is also an unhelpful way to define "theory." A name might be a signpost of *something*, but it is hard to know what exactly that *something* is. Some scholars, such as Jonathan Culler, have argued for a generic definition of "theory" – namely, a "miscellaneous genre" that "has come to designate works that succeed in challenging and reorienting thinking in fields other than those to which they apparently belong ... Works regarded as theory *have* effects beyond their original field" (Culler 1997: 3). Here is a key point about "theory": we can detect the use of "theory" when an author or speaker introduces a framework or linguistic signal – a phrase, word, or idea – that seems unrelated to the object of the paper or talk. This may be why some scholars argue that "theory" distorts history or claim that "theory 'gets in between' the critic and the work," a point to which I will return below (Eagleton 2003: 93).

Terry Eagleton's *After Theory* proposes an even wider definition of "theory": he argues for "theory" as "a reasonably systematic reflection on our guiding assumptions": "It is this critical self-reflection which we know as theory. Theory of this kind comes about when we are forced into a new self-consciousness about what we are doing" (Eagleton 2003: 2, 27). Eagleton's definition in combination with Culler's is worth pondering: theory as a critical self-consciousness that emerges when we utilize insights from fields different from our own (i.e., possibly far from patristics) provides a way to reimagine and invigorate the field of patristics in its widest sense, as "the heritage of the early church as forming a distinctive cultural reality" (Kannengiesser 2004: 3). It is theory that might challenge Kannengiesser's definition of "patristics," for theory – as I will argue – has helped us interrogate notions of "reality" and "culture" and even a uniform monolithic entity such as "the early church." On this point, Rey Chow's definition of poststructuralist theory, with which Clark begins her *History, Theory, Text*, is especially helpful: "the paradigm shift introduced by post-structuralism, whereby the study of language, literature, and cultural forms becomes irrevocably obliged to attend to the semiotic operations involved in the production of meanings, meanings that can no longer be assumed to be natural" (Clark 2004: x).

One of the most lucid discussions about recent developments in historiography and the role of theory in the study of late ancient Christianity is Peter Brown's (2008[1988]) "Introduction" to the Twentieth-Anniversary Edition of his path-breaking book, *The Body and Society*. Here, he outlines his intellectual genealogy upon the writing of the 1988 volume:

> I brought to the writing of *Body and Society* the momentum of my own previous researches, nurtured in a British tradition of social anthropology. If I had learned anything from the work of Edward Evans-Pritchard and Mary Douglas, it was that societies other than our own were opaque to us, unless we undertook the careful task of parsing the alien language with which they spoke about themselves (Brown 2008[1988]: xxvii).

For Brown, "parsing" means reading a text in its original language, translating, and interpreting in the broadest sense: "If we read the religious texts of late antiquity in the right manner, crucial words in their vocabulary might help us to enter hitherto unexplored corners of late antique society" (Brown 2008[1988]: xxviii). Brown moves then beyond social anthropology to the insights of poststructuralism and, in particular, to his encounter with Michel Foucault, whose "breathtaking capacity to defamiliarize" shaped in significant ways Brown's own treatment of late antique texts (Brown 2008[1988]: xxxv). It is precisely this element of "defamiliarization" that inheres in the application of theory, since theory enables us to see familiar texts – indeed, ones we may have read many times – with new insights and from new vantage points.

In teaching, I have found it helpful to explain "theory" by analogy – namely, by comparison to photography. When we take a photograph or see a photograph, we often assume that the image produced is an unmediated, unfiltered representation of an object. And yet the French literary theorist Roland Barthes insisted that:

> ...Photography's Referent is not the same as the referent of other systems of representation. I call "photographic referent" not the *optionally* real thing to which an image or a sign refers but the *necessarily* real thing which has been placed before the lens, without which there would be no photograph. Painting can feign reality without having seen it. Discourse combines signs which have referents, of course, but these referents can be and are most often "chimeras". Contrary to these imitations, in Photography I can never deny that *the thing has been there* (Barthes 1981: 76).

Since the advent of Photoshop, of course, one can easily dispute Barthes' final claim; however, his general point is an early effort at one of the central claims of poststructuralist theory – namely, that there remains a crucial distance between discursive constructions (the optionally real) and historical realities (the necessarily real). Moreover, Barthes was seeking to refocus attention not on the unmediated transparency of a photograph, but rather on the perception and reception of a photograph. Part of what Barthes was driving at has now been developed more fully by recent theorists of photography, who argue that "a photograph, like a painting, sculpture, or drawing, always reflects both on what is depicted and on itself" (Van Gelder and Westgeest 2011: 5). The point is rather simple and, I would argue, one that many scholars now accept even if they disdain "theory": patristic texts (as well as late ancient material remains) do not provide us with a transparent record of reality, but require our careful and critical interpretation and even deconstruction.

Theory is analogous to photography in another sense: I argue that theory is a lens used to focus on a particular object in the same way that a camera lens is attached to a camera body to focus and bring light (aperture) on a particular object. For patristics scholars, the object for a given study may be the gendered body, monasticism or monastic rules, the rhetoric of a particular church father, biblical interpretation, theological and Christological debates in the early church – the possibilities are endless. What is needed for any investigation of an object is a lens that provides an angle of view (i.e., perspective) and one that is appropriate to the particular object, one that will shed light on the object and bring it into focus, and one that provides a new framing of an object. Attaching a different lens is a way of seeing something new or seeing something from a new perspective. To capture the photographic shot of a bird on a distant tree would require a different lens from a close-up of the wings of a damselfly. As James Francis has suggested on visual representation in late antiquity:

> we need to look more broadly at the viewing process itself – that is, the variety of ways in which an image can communicate and the variety of modes in which it can be seen, keeping in mind that viewing itself is culturally constructed (Francis 2009: 288).

When applied to pre-modern texts more broadly, or patristic literature more specifically, the idea of theory as a lens helps us to frame the object in new ways: one might use, for example, a macro lens to take a close view of the interpretation of a single verse; or perhaps a wide-angle lens is important to get a sense of the sweep of ascetic impulses from antiquity to the Middle Ages. Theory can provide a range of lenses, and when it is applied well it is not with the aim to distort some sort of "objective" reality, but rather with the aim to focus our view, to help us understand and shape our perspective, and to make a familiar text seem unfamiliar so that we can arrive at new interpretations of ancient texts.

Amidst the rather dizzying array of theoretical approaches now appearing in scholarship on late ancient Christianity – including feminist theory, literary theory, thing theory, cultural theory, queer theory, network theory, psychoanalytic theory, postcolonial theory, affect theory, spatial theory, ritual theory – one in particular has changed quite radically our view of history and the work of the historian: poststructuralist theory. It is this development in historiography that Elizabeth Clark traced so well in her *History, Theory, Text* in 2004. I turn now to a brief summary of this book and the important implications that poststructuralism poses for the study of late antiquity and, specifically, patristic literature. What follows is a substantial revision and summary of a review article I published in 2005 (Haines-Eitzen 2005).

Elizabeth Clark's *History, Theory, Text* and the Legacy of Poststructuralism

The study of pre-modern texts – in particular, the writings of the church fathers – benefits from and contributes to a theoretically informed intellectual history. This claim lies at the center of Clark's *History, Theory, Text*, which traces nineteenth- and twentieth-century developments in historiography and critical theory with special attention to poststructuralist thought. As she has demonstrated so clearly throughout her work, especially in recent decades, Clark's ostensible aim is to illustrate the vital role that theory must play in historiography. In doing so, she aligns with other historians, such as Dominick LaCapra and Joan Wallach Scott, in arguing for a practice of history that is self-reflective, one that queries the assumptions of our sources and the distance between their discursive rhetoric and historical reality (i.e., utilizes deconstructionist analyses), and takes seriously our limitations in reconstructing "what actually happened" in the past. Far from a "lament" for the discipline of history, however, Clark (2004: 2) argues that "critical theory has provoked lively discussions elsewhere in the humanities and provides intellectual historians, including students of early Christianity, with new conversation partners."

Over the course of eight lucid and highly informed chapters, Clark proceeds to outline critical developments in historiography, beginning with the critique of Leopold von Ranke's notion of objectivity – history as a record of things as they "actually happened" – and she articulates important questions for historians today: Is "objectivity" possible in history writing? To what extent are the location, experience, and bias of the historian implicated in any project of history writing? Can or should we read ancient texts to reconstruct an objective past reality? Put differently, to what extent do texts reveal and/or reflect reality? If texts are not transparent records of what actually happened, then how should we read them? What is historiography if not the reconstruction of what happened in the past? Such questions emerged over the latter half of the twentieth century as the implications of Swiss structural linguist Ferdinand de Saussure's claims about the arbitrary connections between linguistic signs (i.e., words) and concepts (the signified) and sound images (the signifier). "Later theorists," Clark argues, on the basis of this de Saussurean notion of "the arbitrariness of the sign," "posited that the 'real' is known only in and through its discursive construction, established through an intralinguistic system of differences" (Clark 2004: 47).

Poststructuralism, Clark suggests, is crucial to a theoretically informed field of patristics: the deconstructionism of French philosopher Jacques Derrida and the "new intellectual history" as exemplified by Michel Foucault, Michel de Certeau, Roger Chartier, and Dominick LaCapra provide an important opportunity for the study of pre-modern texts, but they are not an excuse for "lazy scholarship" (Clark 2004: 157). "I claim," Clark writes, "that Christian writings from late antiquity should be read first and foremost as literary productions before they are read as sources of social data. Joining theoretical to social–scientific and theological–philological analyses will enrich the field" (Clark 2004: 159). Published academic work both prior and subsequent to Clark's book illustrates the significance of poststructuralist theory for our understanding of late ancient Christianity, and Clark notes some exemplary publications in her concluding chapter. For example, Averil Cameron's widely cited *Christianity and the Rhetoric of Empire* drew upon poststructuralist (especially Foucauldian) attention to discourse and representation "to show that a large part of Christainity's effectiveness in the Roman Empire lay in its capacity to create its own intellectual and imaginative universe, and to show how its own literary devices and techniques in turn related to changing contemporary circumstances" (Cameron 1991: 6).

Nowhere has the legacy of poststructuralism been applied more keenly than in studies of gender, asceticism, sexuality, desire, and the body, as I suggested earlier with respect to Brown's pioneering work. The bibliography, indeed, is too vast to enumerate comprehensively in this chapter. Poststructural theory has enabled scholars to understand the constructed nature of gender and sexuality, how power and politics are interwoven with such constructions, and how ideas about the human body and about masculinity and femininity mapped on to theological controversies; put differently, Foucault's work "invites" us "to consider the continuities and discontinuities, the paradoxical strangeness and familiarity of the late ancient world from the vantage point of the present" (Boyarin and Castelli 2001: 371). Already in 1995, David Brakke applied the work of Foucault to the study of Athanasian asceticism:

> Athanasius explicitly said that the purpose of his spiritual programme was to enable a person to "form oneself' (τυποῦν ἑαυτόν). This language of self-formation identifies Athanasius' ascetic regime as one of the programmes in antiquity that Michel Foucault has called 'technologies of the self'" (Brakke 1995: 143).

More recently, Brakke's work on demons has shown again how the work of Foucault – and post-colonial and psychoanalytic theories (outgrowths of poststructuralism) – continues to be important for understanding "how monastic authors presented the struggle between the monk and his demonic opponents and how these presentations served to create the new social identity of the Christian monk and his multiple roles" (Brakke 2006: 158).

A few additional examples will suffice to show the range of work influenced by poststructuralism and its extension into queer theory, affect theory, postcolonial theory, and cultural theory: the work of Elizabeth Castelli (1986; 1991; 2004), for example, on women, asceticism, and sexuality in early Christianity and more recently on martyrdom, has shown how bodies, especially the bodies of women and martyrs, were constructed and controlled to make broader claims about religious identity; Daniel Boyarin (1993; 2004) has attended to issues of sexuality and religious identity in light of poststructuralist thought; Virginia Burrus (2000; 2008) has treated masculinity and Trinitarian debates, the construction of heresy, and more recently on shame in late ancient Christianity with a thoroughgoing use of poststructuralist, psychoanalystic, and affect theory; Kate Cooper (1996) on asceticism and gender in the Apocryphal Acts demonstrated that the female characters were deployed in the service of male constructions of authority, power, and masculinity; Elizabeth Clark (1999: 27) has written extensively on asceticism and the interpretation of scripture "to explore the rhetoric of ascetic argumentation"; in my own recent work on women, writing, and representation in early Christianity (Haines-Eitzen 2012) and my early work on early Christian scribal practices I have sought to understand textual transmission and gender within complex textual communities and practices of reading and interpretation in early Christianity (Haines-Eitzen 2000; 2012). Patricia Cox Miller's recent book on the corporeal imagination in late antiquity notes the influence of Foucault and many other theorists and draws especially from "thing theory" and insights from theories of the image; she seeks "to show how the life of affect, while fully instantiated in corporeality, was endowed with a creative, cognitive function" (Cox Miller 2009: 17). Catherine Chin's (2008: 171) study of late ancient grammatical literature seeks to "consider Christianization as the creation of a narrative possibility," and her engagement with modern critical theory is exceptionally insightful. Georgia Frank's important work on late ancient pilgrimage was indebted to Cameron's use of Foucauldian discourse theory and approached "the *History of the Monks in Egypt* and the *Lausiac History* more as literary creations than as historical chronicles" (Frank 2005: 5). Claudia Rapp's (2005) book on bishops in late antiquity situated itself in critique of the sociological theories of Weber and in collaboration with the approach of Peter Brown. These are just a few of the many examples that could be brought to demonstrate that poststructuralism continues to shape pastristics.

As we have seen, a central problem for historians with poststructuralism is the gap that appears at times too wide to cross – namely, the distance between rhetoric and reality, between words and things. Andrew Jacobs has incorporated postcolonial theory – which recognizes power differentials in the construction of discourse – in part because of "its refusal to separate rhetoric from reality" and because it lends itself particularly well to a nuanced reading of patristic writings about Jews and Jewish identity (Jacobs 2004: 206). Moreover, Jacobs moves beyond highly rhetorical literary patristic texts to include material culture – namely the archaeological remains of late ancient Jerusalem, the ritualization of pilgrimage, and the emergence of the cult of relics. Most recently, Jacobs has productively applied postcolonial, psychoanalytic, and feminist theory in his treatment of the late ancient interpretation of Christ's circumcision to argue that "the diverse and often unexpected ways that this curious mark on the body of Christ pops up in ancient Christian discourse reveals a great deal about the making of Christian culture and identity" (Jacobs 2012: 12).

What Clark and others have called the "Linguistic turn" to signal the roots of poststructuralism in linguistics, others have more broadly called the "cultural turn." At first this may appear confusing, yet the use of "cultural turn" highlights the expansion and extension of poststructuralist thought into diverse areas; according to Dale Martin and Patricia Cox Miller:

"The cultural turn" in late ancient studies ... refers not to one particular theoretical or methodological innovation, but to a broad shift in textual and historical analyses of a newly defined field of study, analyses influenced, to be sure, by cultural anthropology and the social sciences, but more recently by a wide diversity of theories and methods borrowed from poststructuralism: various literary theories, discourse analysis, ideology critique, theories of the construction of the body and the self, feminist and gender studies, ritual studies. Indeed, the very diversity of new theoretical approaches is one of the remarkable characteristics of "the cultural turn" in recent late ancient studies (Martin and Cox Miller 2005: 9).

We might add to Martin's list by noting the work of Derek Krueger (2004), who incorporates performance theory into his understanding of authorship in late ancient Byzantium. Theories of the body have naturally extended also into theories of the senses: recent work on smell by Susan Harvey (2006) and my own current work on sound in the late ancient desert suggest that more can be done to explore the interplay of body, representation, and experience. In sum, poststructuralism has effected a wide array of studies that rethink how we treat our pre-modern texts, what meaning we attempt to derive from them, and the extent to which we can utilize these texts to reconstruct history.

Conclusions

Critical theory has shaped patristics in important and useful ways, as even a cursory and illustrative sampling demonstrates. This is indeed a lively time for patristics, with membership in our professional societies at what appears to be all-time highs. Patristics itself has undergone significant transformations institutionally, ideologically, and theoretically. Theory has had a role to play in this newly invigorated field, I would argue, because it has helped us ask new questions of old texts. Frederick Norris's North American Presidential Address in 1994 summed up the situation for patristics as follows:

> The strongest difference between the old [i.e., positivist; undertheorized] and the new [i.e., poststructuralist; theoretically-informed] patristics is not whether theology or history will provide the interpretive frame ... What is crucial is how we, who work hard on the close reading of texts, can use that study to teach ourselves how much the paradigms of our controlling communities form the conclusions we reach. What we need in our fields of inquiry are people who 'combine a methodological self-consciousness with an obvious delight in the careful reading of complex texts,' people who know that "objectivity is not in any pure form a possibility" but at the same time have no desire "to look at the past with the willful intention of seeing [in it their] own prejudices and concerns" ... we need not give up on the historical–critical task just because we recognize that we have a location within interpretive communities (Norris 1994: 451).

Apart from any territorial and disciplinary differences, Norris makes a central point: theoretical insights have encouraged – indeed, required – us to become increasingly attentive to the bias of our sources and more aware of our own positions and perspectives in the process of interpreting patristic literature.

In this sense, our notions of "theory" may learn something from the Greek *theoria* in its visual and spatial sense: a seeing, a viewing, a beholding, a spectacle, and, in context, a viewing that requires travel to a sanctuary or festival, to a site of seeing. Indeed, as Thomas Tweed has suggested, theory is like travel – it enables us to see a new landscapes, to behold new wonders, and to reflect on ourselves throughout the journey: "Theories are simultaneously proposals for a journey, representations of a journey, and the journey itself" (Tweed 2006: 9). We may continue to unearth new patristic sources and prepare new critical editions that provide us with new objects of study; it is our ability to travel to unfamiliar landscapes and, even more, to see anew familiar territories and texts that enables our field to thrive. Patristics long ago abandoned narrow and restrictive confines. What emerges now is a field with elastic and flexible contours. Theory has helped to shape a reimagined patristics and promises to provide new lenses from which to view the late ancient rich and dynamic spectacle of patristic literature.

The time has come, I think, for us to move beyond labels like "too theoretical" and "theory laden." Poststructuralism, as one of several modern literary movements, has been an extremely important development in historiography and, by extension, in patristics. As we continue to hone our practices of reading, it is crucial to employ the interpretive tools available to us, and those tools include now a wide array of theoretical insights. Patristics is at its best in careful reading of our sources with properly fitting lenses that enable us to notice and reflect on something new about that past and ourselves.

Bibliography

Barthes, Roland (1981), *Camera Lucida: Reflections on Photography*, Richard Howard (ed.). New York: Hill and Wang.

Boyarin, Daniel (1993), *Carnal Israel: Reading Sex in Talmudic Culture*. Berkeley, CA: University of California Press.

Boyarin, Daniel (2004), *Border Lines: The Partition of Judaeo-Christianity*. Philadelphia, PA: University of Pennsylvania Press.

Boyarin, Daniel and Castelli, Elizabeth (2001), "Foucault's *The History of Sexuality*: the fourth volume, or, a field left fallow for others to till". *Journal of the History of Sexuality*, 10: 357–374.

Brakke, David (1995), *Athanasius and the Politics of Asceticism*. Oxford: Clarendon.

Brakke, David (2002), "The early church in North America: late antiquity, theory, and the history of Christianity". *Church History*, 71: 473–491.

Brakke, David (2006), *Demons and the Making of the Monk: Spiritual Combat in Early Christianity*. Cambridge: Harvard University Press.

Brown, Peter (2008[1988]), *The Body and Society: Men, Women, and Sexual Renunciation in Early Christianity*. New York: Columbia University Press.

Burrus, Virginia (2000), *"Begotten, Not Made": Conceiving Manhood in Late Antiquity*. Stanford, CA: Stanford University Press.

Burrus, Virginia (2008), *Saving Shame: Martyrs, Saints, and Other Abject Subjects*. Philadelphia, PA: University of Pennsylvania Press.

Cameron, Averil (1991), *Christianity and the Rhetoric of Empire: The Development of Christian Discourse*. Berkeley, CA: University of California Press.

Castelli, Elizabeth (1986), "Virginity and its meaning for women's sexuality in early

Christianity". *Journal of Feminist Studies in Religion*, 2: 61–88.

Castelli, Elizabeth (1991), "'I will make Mary male': pieties of the body and gender transformation of Christian women in late antiquity". In *Body Guards: The Cultural Politics of Gender Ambiguity*, Julia Epstein and Kristina Straub (eds). New York: Routledge; 29–49.

Castelli, Elizabeth (2004), *Martyrdom and Memory: Early Christian Culture Making*. New York: Columbia University Press.

Chin, Catherine (2008), *Grammar and Christianity in the Late Roman World*. Philadelphia, PA: University of Pennsylvania Press.

Clark, Elizabeth A. (1999), *Reading Renunciation: Asceticism and Scripture in Early Christianity*. Princeton, NJ: Princeton University Press.

Clark, Elizabeth A. (2004), *History, Theory, Text: Historians and the Linguistic Turn*. Cambridge, MA: Harvard University Press.

Cooper, Kate (1996), *The Virgin and the Bride: Idealized Womanhood in Late Antiquity*. Cambridge, MA: Harvard University Press.

Cox Miller, Patricia (2009), *The Corporeal Imagination: Signifying the Holy in Late Ancient Christianity*. Philadelphia, PA: University of Pennsylvania Press.

Culler, Jonathan (1997), *Literary Theory: A Very Short Introduction*. Oxford: Oxford University Press.

Eagleton, Terry (1983), *Literary Theory: An Introduction*. Minneapolis, MN: University of Minnesota Press.

Eagleton, Terry (2003), *After Theory*. New York: Basic Books.

Francis, James A. (2009), "Visual and verbal representation: image, text, person, and power". In *A Companion to Late Antiquity*, Philip Rousseau (ed.). Chichester: Wiley–Blackwell; 285–305.

Frank, Georgia (2000), *The Memory of the Eyes: Pilgrims to Living Saints in Christian Late Antiquity*. Berkeley, CA: University of California Press.

Haines-Eitzen, Kim (2000), *Guardians of Letters: Literacy, Power, and the Transmitters of Early Christian Literature*. New York: Oxford University Press.

Haines-Eitzen, Kim (2005), "Reimagining patristics: theory's vital role in the study of premodern texts". *Church History*, 74: 816–820.

Haines-Eitzen, Kim (2012), *The Gendered Palimpsest: Women, Writing, and Representation in Early Christianity*. New York: Oxford University Press.

Harvey, Susan Ashbrook (2006), *Scenting Salvation: Ancient Christianity and the Olfactory Imagination*. Berkeley, CA: University of California Press.

Jacobs, Andrew S. (2004), *Remains of the Jews: The Holy Land and Christian Empire in Late Antiquity*. Stanford, CA: Stanford University Press.

Jacobs, Andrew S. (2012), *Christ Circumcised: A Study in Early Christian History and Difference*. Philadelphia, PA: University of Pennsylvania Press.

Kannengiesser, Charles (2004), *Handbook of Patristic Exegesis*, two volumes. Leiden: Brill.

Krueger, Derek (2004), *Writing and Holiness: The Practice of Authorship in the Early Christian East*. Philadelphia, PA: University of Pennsylvania Press.

Martin, Dale and Cox Miller, Patricia (eds) (2005), *The Cultural Turn in Late Ancient Studies: Gender, Asceticism, and Historiography*. Durham, NC; Duke University Press.

Norris, Frederick W. (1994), "Black marks on the communities' manuscripts". *Journal of Early Christian Studies*, 2: 443–466.

Rapp, Claudia (2005), *Holy Bishops in Late Antiquity: The Nature of Christian Leadership in an Age of Transition*. Berkeley, CA: University of California Press.

Tweed, Thomas A. (2006), *Crossing and Dwelling: A Theory of Religion*. Cambridge, MA: Harvard University Press.

Van Gelder, Hilde and Westgeest, Helen (2011), *Photography Theory in Historical Perspective*. Chichester: Wiley–Blackwell.

Index

Printed in the USA
CPSIA information can be obtained
at www.ICGtesting.com
LVHW081926191123
764380LV00022B/111